Meet the *Southern Living* Foods Staff

On these pages we show the Foods Staff (left to right in each photograph) at work as they compile, test, taste, and photograph the recipes that appear each month in *Southern Living*.

Susan Payne and Margaret Chason Agnew (seated in front), Associate Foods Editors

Jean Wickstrom Liles, Foods Editor

Above: B. Ellen Templeton and Deborah Lowery, Assistant Foods Editors

Right: Nancy Nevins, Test Kitchens Director; Kaye Adams (seated in front), Assistant Test Kitchens Director

Catherine Garrison, Karen Brechin, and Jodi Jackson (seated), Editorial Assistants

Charles Walton IV, Senior Foods Photographer; Beverly Morrow, Photo Stylist

Above: Peggy Smith and Jane Cairns, Test Kitchens Staff

Left: Diane Hogan and Patty Vann, Test Kitchens Staff

Southern Living®

1986 ANNUAL RECIPES

Oxmoor House®

Copyright 1986 by Oxmoor House, Inc.
Book Division of Southern Progress Corporation
P.O. Box 2463, Birmingham, Alabama 35201

Southern Living®, *Cooking Light*®, *Breakfasts & Brunches*®,
Summer Suppers®, *Holiday Dinners*®, and *Holiday Desserts*® are
federally registered trademarks of Southern Living, Inc.

Library of Congress Catalog Number: 79-88364
ISBN: 0-8487-0686-2
ISSN: 0272-2003

Manufactured in the United States of America
First Printing 1986

Southern Living® *1986 Annual Recipes*

Southern Living®
    Foods Editor: Jean Wickstrom Liles
    Associate Foods Editors: Margaret Chason Agnew,
      Susan Payne
    Assistant Foods Editors: Deborah G. Lowery,
      B. Ellen Templeton
    Editorial Assistants: Catherine Garrison, Karen Brechin,
      Jodi Jackson
    Test Kitchens Director: Nancy Nevins
    Assistant Test Kitchens Director: Kaye Adams
    Test Kitchens Staff: Diane Hogan, Jane Cairns, Peggy
      Smith, Patty Vann
    Photo Stylist: Beverly Morrow
    Senior Foods Photographer: Charles E. Walton IV.
      Additional photography by *Southern Living*
      photographers: Bob Lancaster, page 190; John
      O'Hagan, 287; Jim Bathie, ii bottom right, 11, 26, 27,
      48, 56, 82, 64, 144, 145, 203; Mary-Gray Hunter, 189;
      Sylvia Martin, 273, 306, 308, 333; Gary Clark, ii top
      left; Courtland Richards, ii top right, iii bottom right.
    Production: Clay Nordan, Wanda Butler

Oxmoor House, Inc.
    Senior Foods Editor: Katherine M. Eakin
    Senior Editor: Joan Denman
    Editor: Olivia Kindig Wells
    Editorial Assistants: Mary Ann Laurens,
      Karen Parris Smith
    Production Manager: Jerry Higdon
    Art Director: Bob Nance
    Designer: Carol Middleton
    Illustrator: David Morrison
    Production: Rick Litton, Theresa Beste

Cover: *Tradition and delicious flavor make special treats for the
holidays: (from front) Old-Fashioned Sugar Cookies, Christmas Eve
Punch, Chocolate Cake With Double Frosting, Ambrosia Cookies,
and Dark Praline Clusters. (Recipes, pages 313 and 314.)*

Page i: *Set out the food for fondue; then let guests make their own
choices. Recipes include (from front) Walnut-Fried Brie, Shrimp
Fondue, and Browned New Potatoes. Sauces in vegetable cups are
(clockwise from top) Classic Béarnaise Sauce, Horseradish Sour
Cream, and Herbed Green Sauce. (Recipes begin on page 244.)*

Page iv: *Roast Ducklings With Cherry Sauce (page 312) and Sweet
Potato Balls (page 312) team up for a holiday menu. In the
background our cover cake, Chocolate Cake With Double Frosting
(page 314), is sliced, showing three luscious layers of chocolate.*

Back cover: *A twist of the dough, a dash of cinnamon, and a
drizzle of glaze turn hot roll mix into Maple-Nut Coffee Twist
(page 290), a treat for any time of the year.*

Table of Contents

Main-Dish Salad (page 191)   *Chicken Enchilada Soup (page 22)*   *Melon Wedges with Berry Sauce (page 178)*

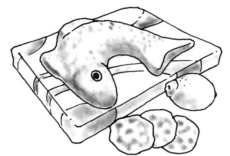

Our Year At Southern Living®

As *Southern Living* celebrated its 20th anniversary this year, we stopped to reflect on the changes that have taken place since 1966 in Southern kitchens. From extensive research and from your letters and telephone calls, we found there have been some dramatic changes in family life-styles and cooking habits since our first issue, February 1966. We've seen changes in *what* you cook, *how* you cook it, and even *who* cooks it.

It has been our aim for the past two decades to produce food stories and recipes that appeal to you. In staying attuned to your food needs and preferences, we discovered that many of you enjoy cooking, have an active life-style, and are interested in good nutrition.

Because time and convenience are big concerns, we know that you're interested in quick-and-easy recipes. You've asked for and have shared your favorite recipes using convenience products and short-cuts, with the end product often tasting as if hours had gone into its making. You've even streamlined many of your traditional Southern recipes by using a mix or frozen product.

You want to trim the cooking preparation time, and we've responded with recipes using quick-cooking methods, such as microwaving, stir-frying, and sautéeing.

Because many of you own a microwave oven, a wok, or a food processor, we offer recipes that help you better utilize these appliances in your meals.

Other time-saving factors we stress include organizing your kitchen and planning weekly menus in advance. We've encouraged you to analyze your kitchen and rearrange cabinets and drawers if necessary and to store small appliances, pans, and utensils close to where you use them. We've suggested that you make your grocery list from your weekly menus, and plan one major grocery trip a week. Even though fewer family members are gathering together at mealtime, many of them are involved today in shopping and meal planning as well as preparing meals.

We find that many of you continue to be concerned about good nutrition and cutting calories. You're interested in decreasing your sugar and sodium consumption and are cooking with less fat. Your favorable response to our monthly *Cooking Light* feature convinced us you wanted and needed more low-calorie recipes. Therefore, in February we devoted a special section to *Cooking Light*. Prepared by our registered dietitian, this section not only proves that low-calorie eating can be enjoyable but also shows you how to modify your favorite recipes for light cooking. Each recipe includes a detailed analysis of six nutrients along with the calorie count, taking the guesswork out of nutritious eating.

As we put the finishing touches on our *1986 Annual Recipes*, a salute goes to the competent staff of home economists who test, taste, and evaluate each recipe we publish. This dedicated group constantly searches for new food ideas to present to you. Because our life-styles and interests are similar to yours, we're also in need of quick-and-easy recipes, low-calorie dishes, and time-saving preparation methods. For that reason, it may not surprise you to know that "What's for dinner?" is the most frequently asked question in *our* homes, too.

Thanks to *you*, our readers, for sharing the favorite recipes that have already passed a taste test in your homes throughout the South. With pride, we claim that a generous amount of the "personal touch" goes into each recipe.

Our *1986 Annual Recipes* represents the best of *Southern Living* for the past year. We're proud that this cookbook continues the tradition started by *Southern Living* in 1966 to provide the South with delicious recipes and gracious entertaining ideas.

Jean Wickstrom Liles

January

Chili Warms Up The Menu

Although some authorities feel the origin of chili can be traced back to a much older civilization, Texans generally claim credit for inventing the fiery concoction as we know it. Whether or not the claim is valid, chili does owe much of its widespread popularity to the introduction of chili powder in the 1890's (by a Texan named William Gebhardt). It contained ground chiles, cumin, black pepper, oregano, and garlic—the same basic ingredients it does now. This early convenience product made it easy to produce a respectable-tasting version of chili anywhere, so the use of chili powder quickly transcended Southwestern boundaries.

That is not to say that there is widespread agreement on what constitutes an authentic chili. Even the basics are debated: chopped meat versus ground, beans or no beans, tomatoes and other vegetables or no vegetables at all. Add to this the fact that every renowned chili cook has a secret ingredient.

We'll leave the final decision on authenticity up to you. Instead, we offer a sampling of great chili recipes from readers in Texas, Alabama, Arkansas, and Mississippi. The range of ingredients runs the gamut, so you're sure to find one you like.

Cowboy Chili makes an ideal entrée for a cold winter evening. Dress up individual servings with toppings of cheese and onion.

QUICK-AND-EASY CHILI CON CARNE

1 pound coarsely ground beef
1 medium onion, chopped
1 (15-ounce) can red kidney beans, undrained
1 (14½-ounce) can whole tomatoes, undrained
1½ teaspoons chili powder
1 teaspoon dried whole oregano
¾ teaspoon salt
½ teaspoon cumin seed, crushed
Avocado slices (optional)
Chopped fresh cilantro (optional)

Cook ground beef and onion in a large skillet until browned, stirring to crumble meat. Drain.

Stir in beans, tomatoes, chili powder, oregano, salt, and cumin seed. Reduce heat, and simmer, uncovered, 15 minutes, stirring occasionally. Garnish each serving with avocado and cilantro, if desired. Yield: 4½ cups.

Jana Dominquez,
Navasota, Texas.

COWBOY CHILI

1 pound dried pinto beans
¾ cup chopped onion
¼ cup plus 2 tablespoons chili powder
8 cloves garlic, minced
¼ cup vegetable oil
3 pounds boneless chuck, cut into ½-inch cubes
1½ cups chopped onion
1 large green pepper, chopped
8 cloves garlic, minced
¼ cup plus 2 tablespoons chili powder
2 (14½-ounce) cans tamales, undrained (optional)
Additional chopped onion
Shredded Cheddar cheese

Sort and wash beans; place in a Dutch oven. Cover with water 2 inches above beans; cover and let beans soak overnight.

Drain beans; cover with water. Add ¾ cup chopped onion, ¼ cup plus 2 tablespoons chili powder, and 8 cloves garlic. Cover and simmer 1 hour or until beans are tender, adding more water if necessary.

Heat oil in a large Dutch oven. Add beef, 1½ cups chopped onion, chopped green pepper, and 8 cloves garlic; cook over medium heat until beef is browned. Add beans and ¼ cup plus 2 tablespoons chili powder to beef mixture; cover and simmer 1 hour.

Add tamales, if desired, and simmer 30 minutes. Sprinkle with onion and cheese. Yield: 2½ quarts.

Aladine Standish,
Houston, Texas.

CHILI CON CARNE

16 large dried red chiles
11 cups water
2 pounds round steak, cut into ½-inch cubes
3 tablespoons vegetable oil
2 cups water
1 large onion, chopped
2 cloves garlic, crushed
2 tablespoons chili powder
1 tablespoon ground cumin
1 teaspoon dried whole oregano
½ teaspoon salt
2 (16-ounce) cans ranch-style beans, undrained

Wash chiles, and place in a large Dutch oven; add 11 cups water. Cover and bring to a boil. Remove from heat, and let stand, covered, 45 minutes or until softened.

Drain chiles, reserving ½ cup soaking liquid. Wearing rubber gloves, pull off stems, slit chiles open, and rinse away seeds under running water. Place half the chiles and ¼ cup of soaking liquid in blender; process until pureed. Repeat with remaining chiles and remaining ¼ cup soaking liquid. Press pureed mixture through a sieve using the back of a spoon; then set puree aside.

Brown steak in hot oil in a large Dutch oven. Add 2 cups water, onion, garlic, chili powder, cumin, oregano, salt, and pureed mixture. Cover and simmer 1½ hours. Add beans, and heat thoroughly. Yield: 7 cups.

Varniece Warren,
Hermitage, Arkansas.

CHUNKY CHILI

2 teaspoons vegetable oil
2 pounds round steak, cut into ½-inch cubes
1 small onion, chopped
1 clove garlic, crushed
1 (10½-ounce) can beef broth
1 cup water
2 teaspoons sugar
2 teaspoons dried whole oregano
1 teaspoon ground cumin
2 dashes of paprika
2 bay leaves
2 dashes of hot sauce
1 (8-ounce) can tomato sauce
1 (4-ounce) can chopped green chiles, drained
2 tablespoons cornmeal

Heat oil in a large Dutch oven; add round steak, onion, and garlic, and cook until beef is browned. Add beef broth, water, sugar, oregano, cumin, paprika, bay leaves, and hot sauce; mix well. Cover and cook over low heat 1 hour, stirring occasionally.

Add tomato sauce, chiles, and cornmeal to beef mixture, mixing well; continue cooking an additional 30 minutes. Remove bay leaves. Yield: 4½ cups.

Jerry Collums,
Brandon, Mississippi.

VENISON CHILI

½ pound salt pork, cut into 4 pieces
2 pounds venison, coarsely ground
2 medium onions, chopped
1 (16-ounce) can tomatoes, undrained
1 cup water
¾ cup red wine
2 to 3 large green chiles, diced
1 clove garlic, minced
3 tablespoons chili powder
¾ teaspoon oregano
½ teaspoon cumin seeds, crushed

Cook salt pork in a Dutch oven over medium heat until brown. Add venison

and onion; cook, stirring frequently, until meat is browned. Stir in remaining ingredients. Reduce heat, and simmer, uncovered, 1 hour; stir occasionally. Remove salt pork before serving. Yield: 2 quarts.

David Lowery,
Birmingham, Alabama.

Be Creative With Tortillas

Most Americans can't buy fresh hot tortillas from a neighborhood tortillería like folks in Mexico can, but supermarkets in our country sell a lot of the versatile bread rounds.

To create a tasty appetizer, spread tortillas with refried beans, roll them jellyroll fashion, and fry them into crisp dippers for guacamole. For lunch, tortillas substitute for rye bread in the traditional ham-and-cheese sandwich. And don't be surprised to see chimichangas for dessert. Pineapple Dessert Chimichangas sport the familiar wrap, but show off a sweet new filling.

We've also included a recipe for our readers who have been curious about frying tortilla shells for Mexican salad.

All of these recipes call for either 6- or 8-inch flour tortillas. Both sizes are usually available at larger supermarkets; sometimes you'll find them fresh in the meat department and sometimes frozen.

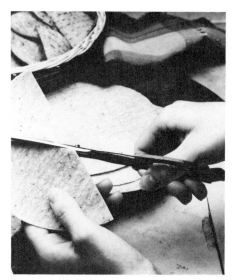

Cut corn tortillas into six triangles, and fry in hot oil to make your own tostados. Stale tortillas work best.

Layers of shredded chicken, cheese, and green onions between fried flour tortillas add up to Cheesy Chicken-Tortilla Stack. Wrap the Mexican treat in foil, and bake.

CHEESY CHICKEN-TORTILLA STACK

½ cup vegetable oil
6 (8-inch) flour tortillas
1 (8-ounce) carton commercial sour cream
½ teaspoon seasoned salt
½ teaspoon hot sauce
2½ cups shredded cooked chicken
2½ cups (10 ounces) shredded Monterey Jack cheese
1¼ cups (5 ounces) shredded Longhorn cheese
½ cup plus 2 tablespoons minced green onions
1½ tablespoons butter or margarine, melted
⅓ cup shredded lettuce
¼ cup chopped tomato

Heat oil to 375° in a 10-inch skillet. Fry tortillas, one at a time, in hot oil 3 to 5 seconds on each side or until tortillas hold their shape and begin to crisp. Drain tortillas well on paper towels; set aside.

Combine sour cream, seasoned salt, and hot sauce. Place 1 tortilla on a lightly greased baking sheet; spread about 1 tablespoon sour cream mixture over tortilla. Sprinkle with ½ cup shredded chicken, ½ cup Monterey Jack cheese, ¼ cup Longhorn cheese, and 2 tablespoons green onions. Repeat all layers 4 times. Top with remaining tortilla. Reserve remaining sour cream mixture. Brush top tortilla and sides of tortillas with melted butter.

Cover with foil; bake at 400° for 25 minutes. Immediately remove foil after baking; place tortilla stack on serving plate. Spread remaining sour cream mixture on top tortilla; sprinkle with shredded lettuce and chopped tomato. Cut into wedges, and serve immediately. Yield: 4 servings.

TEX-MEX HAM-AND-CHEESE SANDWICH

¾ cup (3 ounces) shredded Monterey Jack
  cheese
½ cup diced cooked ham
3 tablespoons chopped green chiles
½ cup shredded lettuce
4 (6-inch) flour tortillas
1 tablespoon butter or margarine, melted
2 tablespoons butter or margarine
Commercial taco sauce (optional)

Combine cheese, ham, chiles, and lettuce, tossing well. Brush one side of
each tortilla with melted butter. Place 2
tortillas, buttered side down, on work
surface. Spoon cheese mixture evenly
over the 2 tortillas, pressing with the
back of a spoon. Top with remaining
tortillas, buttered side up; press top tortillas gently.

Melt 2 tablespoons butter on a griddle or large skillet over medium-high
heat. Place tortilla sandwiches on griddle; grill until bottom is crisp and lightly
browned; carefully turn sandwiches to
grill other side. Serve with taco sauce, if
desired. Yield: 2 servings.

MEXICAN SALAD IN A SHELL

Vegetable oil
4 (8-inch) flour tortillas
1 pound ground beef
1 (1.25-ounce) package taco seasoning mix
2 cups shredded iceberg lettuce
¼ cup diced onion
1½ cups (6 ounces) shredded Longhorn
  cheese
1 medium tomato, chopped
Commercial taco sauce

To make the crunchy base for Mexican
Salad in a Shell, plunge a flour tortilla into
hot oil, and press down with tongs to form
the cup shape.

Heat 2 inches oil in a large saucepan
to 375°. Drop 1 tortilla into oil; immediately press down center of tortilla with
opened tongs, shaping tortilla like a
bowl. If bubbles form in tortilla, press
them flatly against side of saucepan with
tongs. Fry tortilla 30 seconds; turn tortilla cup over, and fry an additional 30
seconds, or until lightly browned. Drain
on paper towels. Repeat procedure with
remaining tortillas.

Brown ground beef in a large skillet,
and drain. Add taco seasoning mix, and
cook according to package directions.
Set mixture aside.

Place tortilla shells on individual serving plates. Arrange shredded lettuce
evenly in each tortilla shell; top with
ground beef mixture, diced onion,
shredded cheese, and chopped tomato.
Serve with taco sauce. Yield: 4 servings.

ROLLED TORTILLA DIPPERS

16 (6-inch) flour tortillas
1 cup refried beans
½ cup (2 ounces) shredded Cheddar
  cheese
Vegetable oil
Guacamole Dip

Work with 1 tortilla at a time, keeping remaining tortillas covered. Spread
1 tablespoon refried beans slightly off-
center of tortilla, leaving a 1-inch margin at both ends. Sprinkle 1½ teaspoons
cheese over beans. Roll up tortilla
tightly, jellyroll fashion, starting at end
closest to filling; secure with wooden
picks. Set aside.

Repeat entire procedure with all

For Rolled Tortilla Dippers, spread refried
beans on a tortilla, and sprinkle with
shredded Cheddar cheese. Then roll up the
tortilla jellyroll fashion.

remaining tortillas, keeping rolled tortillas covered. Cover and refrigerate
until ready to fry, up to 4 hours. (Tortillas may also be frozen in an airtight
container up to 2 months before frying.)

When ready to fry, heat 1 inch of oil
in a heavy skillet to 375°. Fry several
tortilla rolls at a time in hot oil until
golden brown. Drain on paper towels.
Remove wooden picks. Serve warm
with guacamole dip. Yield: 16 appetizer
servings.

Note: Corn tortillas can be substituted
for flour tortillas if they are fried before
filling to soften them. Fry each in ¼
inch hot oil about 5 seconds on each
side or until softened. Drain well on
paper towels; then fill and fry as
directed.

Guacamole Dip:

½ small onion
1 clove garlic, cut in half
1 medium avocado, peeled and chopped
½ small tomato, peeled and cut into
  chunks
1 tablespoon lemon juice
½ teaspoon salt
⅛ teaspoon hot sauce

Position knife blade in food processor
bowl. Add onion and garlic; process 30
seconds or until coarsely chopped. Add
remaining ingredients; process 1 minute
or until blended and only very small
chunks of vegetables remain, scraping
sides of bowl twice. Yield: 1¼ cups.

PINEAPPLE DESSERT CHIMICHANGAS

2 (15¼-ounce) cans pineapple tidbits
3 tablespoons butter or margarine
3 tablespoons all-purpose flour
½ cup sugar
¾ teaspoon grated lemon rind
1 teaspoon lemon juice
6 (8-inch) flour tortillas
Vegetable oil
Powdered sugar

Drain pineapple, reserving ¼ cup
juice; set aside.

Melt butter in a heavy saucepan over
low heat; add flour, stirring until
smooth. Cook 1 minute, stirring constantly. Gradually add reserved juice
and sugar; cook over medium heat, stirring constantly, until mixture is thickened and bubbly. Stir in pineapple,
lemon rind, and lemon juice. Set aside
to cool.

Wrap tortillas tightly in foil; bake at
350° for 15 minutes.

Work with 1 tortilla at a time, keeping the remaining tortillas covered. Spoon a rounded ⅓ cup pineapple mixture off-center of tortilla. Fold nearest edge over to cover filling. Fold in both sides, envelope fashion. Roll tortilla, and secure with wooden picks. Repeat with remaining tortillas, keeping rolled tortillas covered.

Fry chimichangas in 1 inch hot oil (375°) about 1 minute on each side or until golden brown. Drain on paper towels. Remove wooden picks, and dust with powdered sugar. Serve warm or cold. Yield: 6 servings.

KING-SIZE BUÑUELOS

⅓ cup sugar
1 tablespoon ground cinnamon
10 (6-inch) flour tortillas
Vegetable oil
Honey
Chopped pecans

Combine sugar and cinnamon, mixing well; set aside.

Fry tortillas, 1 or 2 at a time, in ¼ inch hot oil (375°) for 20 to 30 seconds on each side or until crisp and golden brown. Drain on paper towels.

While tortillas are still warm, sprinkle with sugar mixture. To serve, drizzle with honey, and sprinkle with chopped pecans. Yield: 10 buñuelos.

![COOKING LIGHT.]

Cut Calories, Not Calcium, With These Recipes

Adults as well as children need calcium. Osteoporosis, the loss of tissue that leaves bones porous and brittle, affects 15 to 20 million Americans. This serious condition is more prevalent among older white women, but men are also at risk. It develops gradually, but bones may begin to show loss of tissue in men and women by age 35. But for some women, this tissue loss may start as early as age 25.

Currently there is no reversal for osteoporosis, but it can be prevented and slowed or halted once bone loss starts

to occur. The key is an adequate calcium intake. The recommended calcium allowance for adults is 800 milligrams a day. Studies show, however, that the average American diet supplies only 450 to 550 milligrams a day.

People who diet frequently to lose weight run a greater risk of having osteoporosis. Every time you lose pounds, you also lose bone tissue, since few, if any, weight-reduction diets include adequate amounts of calcium.

An added incentive for eating plenty of calcium-rich foods is that a growing number of research studies now indicate that an adequate calcium intake throughout life may help protect against high blood pressure.

Most nutrition experts agree that the best way to get calcium is from food rather than supplements. Dairy products provide the most available source of the nutrient. But this doesn't have to present a dilemma for dieters who see dairy foods as having a high-fat, high-calorie content. Low-fat and skim dairy products are nutrition bargains not only because they are lower in fat and calories, but they also usually have a slight edge over whole-milk products when it comes to calcium content.

If you're not a milk drinker, don't despair. You can also get calcium from some nondairy sources, such as kale, collard greens, mustard greens, and salmon with edible bones. Our collection of calcium-rich recipes shows you how to make the most of dairy and nondairy sources in some delicious low-calorie dishes.

SALMON LOAF WITH CUCUMBER-DILL SAUCE

1 (16-ounce) can salmon with bones, drained and flaked
¾ cup fine dry breadcrumbs
⅔ cup skim evaporated milk
¼ cup diced onion
¼ cup diced green pepper
1 egg, beaten
1 tablespoon lemon juice
¼ teaspoon celery salt
¼ teaspoon pepper
Vegetable cooking spray
Cucumber-Dill Sauce

Combine salmon, breadcrumbs, milk, onion, green pepper, egg, lemon juice, celery salt, and pepper; mix well. Press mixture into an 8- x 5- x 3-inch loafpan coated with cooking spray; bake at 375° for 45 to 50 minutes or until done. Remove from oven; let stand 3 minutes.

Remove from pan. Serve with Cucumber-Dill Sauce. Yield: 6 servings (about 176 calories and 227 milligrams calcium per serving).

Cucumber-Dill Sauce:

¾ cup plain low-fat yogurt
½ cup unpeeled diced cucumber
¼ cup reduced-calorie mayonnaise
1 tablespoon minced fresh onion
1 teaspoon chopped fresh parsley
¼ teaspoon dried whole dillweed
⅛ teaspoon salt

Combine all ingredients; mix well. Cover sauce, and chill 30 minutes; stir before serving. Yield: 1½ cups (about 12 calories and 14 milligrams calcium per tablespoon).

OPEN-FACE TOFU-VEGGIE SANDWICHES

¼ cup coarsely chopped, peeled cucumber
1 tablespoon Italian reduced-calorie salad dressing
8 ounces tofu, drained and coarsely chopped
2 hard-cooked eggs, chopped
2 tablespoons sliced celery
1 tablespoon chopped green pepper
1 tablespoon chopped green onion
1 tablespoon chopped pimiento, drained
1 tablespoon plain low-fat yogurt
1 tablespoon reduced-calorie mayonnaise
1 tablespoon Italian reduced-calorie salad dressing
⅛ teaspoon salt
⅛ teaspoon pepper
2 whole wheat English muffins, halved
4 leaf lettuce leaves
3 tablespoons alfalfa sprouts

Combine cucumber and 1 tablespoon Italian dressing; set aside.

Combine tofu, eggs, celery, green pepper, green onion, pimiento, yogurt, mayonnaise, 1 tablespoon Italian salad dressing, salt, and pepper; toss well.

Top each muffin half with a lettuce leaf. Spoon tofu mixture onto lettuce; top with alfalfa sprouts and reserved cucumber mixture. Yield: 4 servings (about 179 calories and 117 milligrams calcium per serving).

DOUBLE-CHEESE POTATOES

3 cups thinly sliced unpeeled new potatoes
¼ cup diced onion
2 teaspoons reduced-calorie margarine, melted
1½ teaspoons all-purpose flour
¾ cup skim milk
½ cup part-skim ricotta cheese
⅓ cup (1½ ounces) shredded sharp Cheddar cheese
¼ teaspoon salt
¼ teaspoon pepper
½ teaspoon dry mustard
1 teaspoon caraway seeds
Vegetable cooking spray
Paprika
2 tablespoons chopped fresh parsley

Cook potatoes in boiling water to cover until partially tender; drain.

Sauté onion in margarine in a heavy saucepan until tender. Add flour, stirring until smooth. Cook 1 minute, stirring constantly. Gradually add milk; cook, stirring constantly, until mixture is thickened and bubbly. Remove from heat; add cheese, salt, pepper, mustard, and caraway seeds. Stir mixture until cheese melts.

Place half of potato slices in a 1½-quart casserole coated with cooking spray; top with half of sauce. Repeat layers; sprinkle with paprika and parsley. Cover and bake at 350° for 25 to 30 minutes. Yield: 6 servings (about 144 calories and 150 milligrams calcium per serving).

VEGETABLE-CHEESE POTATO TOPPER

1 (8-ounce) carton plain low-fat yogurt
½ cup part-skim ricotta cheese
1 tablespoon grated cucumber
1 tablespoon grated green pepper
1 tablespoon grated onion
¼ teaspoon salt
⅛ teaspoon white pepper

Combine all ingredients; mix well. Cover and chill 2 to 3 hours; spoon over baked potatoes. Yield: 1½ cups (about 13 calories and 32 milligrams calcium per tablespoon).

Mrs. John B. Wright,
Greenville, South Carolina.

Tip: Avoid purchasing green-tinted potatoes. The term used for this condition is "light burn," which causes a bitter flavor. To keep potatoes from turning green once you have bought them, store in a cool, dark, dry place.

BROCCOLI-SWISS SOUP

3½ cups skim milk
½ cup skim evaporated milk
1½ tablespoons cornstarch
¼ teaspoon pepper
2½ teaspoons chicken-flavored bouillon granules
Dash of hot sauce
¼ teaspoon dry mustard
1 cup (4 ounces) shredded Swiss cheese, divided
1 (10-ounce) package frozen chopped broccoli, thawed and drained
¼ teaspoon imitation butter flavoring
Chopped chives (optional)
Carrot curls (optional)

Combine skim milk, evaporated milk, cornstarch, pepper, bouillon granules, hot sauce, and mustard in a large saucepan; mix well. Cook over medium heat, stirring constantly, until smooth and thickened. Add ½ cup cheese; stir until cheese melts. Add broccoli and butter flavoring; cook until thoroughly heated. Ladle into 4 bowls; sprinkle with remaining ½ cup cheese. Garnish with chives and carrot, if desired. Yield: 4 cups (about 243 calories and 669 milligrams calcium per 1-cup serving).

LIGHT BAVARIAN DESSERT

1 tablespoon unflavored gelatin
¼ cup cold water
1¾ cups cold water
1 cup instant nonfat dry milk powder
1 cup low-fat cottage cheese
¼ cup sugar
1 teaspoon vanilla extract
¼ teaspoon almond extract
1 (11-ounce) can mandarin oranges in light syrup, drained
2 kiwifruit, peeled, sliced, and halved

Soften gelatin in ¼ cup cold water in a small saucepan for 5 minutes. Cook over low heat, stirring frequently, until gelatin dissolves. Set aside.

Combine 1¾ cups cold water, dry milk powder, cottage cheese, sugar, vanilla, and almond extract in container of an electric blender. Process until smooth; add gelatin mixture, and process 10 to 15 seconds. Pour mixture into a bowl; chill until consistency of unbeaten egg white.

Set aside several pieces of each fruit for garnish. Layer remaining fruit and gelatin mixture into six 8-ounce dessert dishes. Top with reserved fruit. Chill until firm. Yield: 6 servings (about 167 calories and 274 milligrams calcium per serving).

Mrs. R. A. Patrick,
Tallahassee, Florida.

PEACH COOLER

1 cup cultured low-fat buttermilk
2 (16-ounce) cans sliced peaches in light syrup, drained and coarsely chopped
¼ teaspoon almond extract
2½ cups vanilla ice milk

Combine buttermilk, peaches, and almond extract in container of electric blender; process until smooth. Add ice milk; blend 30 seconds or until smooth. Yield: 5 servings (about 180 calories and 152 milligrams calcium per 1-cup serving).

Edna M. Battey,
Steinhatchee, Florida.

Serve Black-Eyed Peas For Luck

Black-eyed peas are traditional on New Year's Day, but that doesn't mean you have to serve them the same old way. Here are some new ideas for preparing this "lucky" vegetable.

Keep in mind that black-eyed peas have a lot going for them even after January 1. They're relatively inexpensive whether you buy them fresh, dried, frozen, or canned. And because black-eyed peas are a good source of iron and phosphorous and also contain some protein, they're a nutritious choice that's available all year long.

BLACK-EYED PEA SKILLET DINNER

1 pound ground beef
1¼ cups chopped onion
1 cup chopped green pepper
2 (16-ounce) cans black-eyed peas, drained
1 (16-ounce) can whole tomatoes, undrained and coarsely chopped
¾ teaspoon salt
½ teaspoon pepper

Cook ground beef, onion, and green pepper over medium heat until beef is browned, stirring to crumble meat; drain. Add remaining ingredients; bring to a boil, reduce heat, and simmer 30 minutes, stirring often. Yield: 6 servings.

Ausy P. Brown,
San Antonio, Texas.

SOUTH-OF-THE-BORDER BLACK-EYED PEAS

1 (16-ounce) package dried black-eyed peas
5 cups water
¼ pound smoked ham hock
1 fresh jalapeño pepper
2 tablespoons onion soup mix
2 teaspoons chili powder
1 teaspoon salt
¼ teaspoon pepper
Sliced jalapeño pepper (optional)

Sort and wash peas; place in a large Dutch oven. Cover with water 2 inches above peas; let soak overnight. Drain peas. Add 5 cups water and next 6 ingredients. Bring to a boil; cover, reduce heat, and simmer 1 hour or until tender. Remove jalapeño pepper; garnish with sliced jalapeño pepper, if desired. Yield: 8 to 10 servings.

Doris H. Davis,
Fort Valley, Georgia.

BLACK-EYED PEA SPECIAL

3 slices bacon
2 stalks celery, sliced
1 small onion, chopped
2 tablespoons chopped green pepper
1 (16-ounce) can tomatoes, undrained
1½ cups water
2 (10-ounce) packages frozen black-eyed peas
1 teaspoon Worcestershire sauce
½ teaspoon salt
¼ teaspoon pepper
1 small bay leaf

Fry bacon in a Dutch oven until crisp. Remove bacon, reserving drippings in pan. Crumble bacon, and set aside.

Sauté celery, onion, and green pepper in pan drippings for 5 minutes. Add remaining ingredients, and bring mixture to a boil. Cover, reduce heat, and simmer 1 hour and 10 minutes or until peas are tender. Remove bay leaf; stir in crumbled bacon before serving. Yield: 8 servings.

Debbie Whitlock,
Liberty, South Carolina.

BLACK-EYED PEAS WITH SAUSAGE

½ pound hot bulk pork sausage
2 cups water
½ teaspoon salt
¼ teaspoon pepper
¼ teaspoon dry mustard
2 (10-ounce) packages frozen black-eyed peas

Brown sausage in a large skillet; drain. Add water and seasonings, and bring to a boil. Add peas, and return to a boil. Cover, reduce heat, and simmer 40 to 45 minutes. Yield: 6 to 8 servings.

Cheryl Leveque,
Athens, Texas.

BLACK-EYED PEA VINAIGRETTE

1 (16-ounce) package dried black-eyed peas
2 quarts water
1 large onion, chopped
2 cloves garlic, minced
3 bay leaves
2 teaspoons salt
2 teaspoons ground cumin
1 teaspoon marjoram
½ cup plus 2 tablespoons vegetable oil
¼ cup red wine vinegar
3 tablespoons chopped fresh parsley
2 tablespoons freeze-dried cilantro
1 teaspoon freshly ground pepper

Sort and wash peas; place in a large Dutch oven. Add water, onion, garlic, bay leaves, salt, cumin, and marjoram, and bring to a boil. Cover, reduce heat, and simmer 40 to 45 minutes or until peas are tender. Drain and let cool. Remove bay leaves.

Add remaining ingredients to peas; toss well. Serve at room temperature. Yield: 10 servings.

Mrs. John Andrew,
Winston-Salem, North Carolina.

Desserts Your Family Will Love

Rich banana pudding and an old-fashioned chocolate cake are just a sampling of what we have to offer to capture your family's attention at dessert time. Other favorites include a custard, an applesauce cake, and oatmeal cookies that look like lace.

CREAMY BAKED CUSTARD

1 (13-ounce) can evaporated milk
1⅔ cups milk
5 eggs
½ cup sugar
1 teaspoon vanilla extract

Combine all ingredients, beating well. Pour into an 8-inch square dish. Place dish in a 13- x 9- x 2-inch baking dish. Pour 1 inch of hot water into larger dish. Bake at 350° for 45 minutes or until a knife inserted in center comes out clean. Remove from water; cool. Yield: 9 servings.

Carol S. Noble,
Burgaw, North Carolina.

SURPRISE BANANA PUDDING

⅔ cup sugar
⅔ cup all-purpose flour
¼ teaspoon salt
4 cups milk
5 egg yolks
1 tablespoon peanut butter
1 teaspoon vanilla extract
1 (12-ounce) package vanilla wafers
6 medium-size ripe bananas, sliced
1 (8-ounce) carton frozen whipped topping, thawed (optional)

Combine sugar, flour, and salt in top of a double boiler; stir in milk. Bring water to a boil. Reduce heat to low; cook, stirring constantly, 10 to 12 minutes or until slightly thickened.

Beat egg yolks until thick and lemon colored. Gradually stir about one-fourth of hot mixture into yolks; add to remaining hot mixture, stirring constantly. Cook, stirring constantly, until mixture thickens. Remove from heat, and gently stir in peanut butter and vanilla.

Layer one-fourth of vanilla wafers in a 3-quart casserole; top with one-third of bananas. Pour one-third of filling over bananas. Repeat layers twice, ending with remaining vanilla wafers. Spread top with whipped topping, if desired. Chill. Yield: 8 to 10 servings.

Suzanne Thomas,
Trafford, Alabama.

APPLESAUCE CAKE SQUARES

1½ (1-ounce) squares unsweetened
  chocolate
½ cup butter or margarine
1 cup firmly packed brown sugar
½ cup unsweetened applesauce
2 eggs, beaten
1 teaspoon vanilla extract
1 cup all-purpose flour
½ teaspoon baking powder
¼ teaspoon baking soda
¼ teaspoon salt
Nutty Coconut Frosting

Place unsweetened chocolate and butter in a heavy saucepan over low heat; stir until chocolate melts. Set aside.

Combine sugar, applesauce, eggs, and vanilla in a large bowl; mix well. Combine flour, baking powder, soda, and salt; add to applesauce mixture, stirring well. Stir in chocolate mixture.

Spoon the batter into a greased 9-inch square baking pan. Bake at 350° for 30 minutes.

Cool completely. Top with Nutty Coconut Frosting, and cut into squares. Yield: 1½ dozen.

Nutty Coconut Frosting:

⅓ cup sugar
⅓ cup milk
2 tablespoons plus 1 teaspoon butter or
  margarine
1 egg yolk
½ teaspoon vanilla extract
½ cup flaked coconut
½ cup chopped walnuts or pecans

Combine first 5 ingredients in top of a double boiler; bring water to a boil. Reduce heat to low; cook, stirring constantly, until mixture thickens. Stir in coconut and walnuts; beat until mixture reaches spreading consistency. Yield: enough frosting for a 9-inch cake.
Jayne Penn Hollar,
Chesapeake, Virginia.

RICH CHOCOLATE-NUT CAKE

½ cup butter or margarine, softened
2½ cups sugar
3 eggs
4 (1-ounce) squares unsweetened chocolate,
  melted
2 cups sifted cake flour
2 teaspoons baking powder
½ teaspoon salt
1½ cups milk
2 teaspoons vanilla extract
1 cup chopped pecans
Chocolate frosting (recipe follows)
Pecan halves (optional)

Cream butter; gradually add sugar, beating well. Add eggs, one at a time, beating well after each addition. Add melted chocolate.

Combine flour, baking powder, and salt; add to creamed mixture alternately with milk, beginning and ending with flour mixture. Mix well after each addition. Stir in vanilla and chopped pecans.

Pour batter into 3 greased and floured 9-inch round cakepans. Bake at 350° for 30 to 35 minutes or until a wooden pick inserted in center comes out clean. Cool in pans 10 minutes; remove layers from pans, and cool completely on wire racks.

Spread chocolate frosting between layers and on top and sides of cake. Garnish with pecan halves, if desired. Yield: one 3-layer cake.

Chocolate Frosting:

¼ cup butter or margarine
2 (1-ounce) squares unsweetened chocolate
About ½ cup half-and-half, scalded
1 teaspoon vanilla extract
3 cups sifted powdered sugar

Melt butter and chocolate. Add half-and-half and vanilla. Stir in powdered sugar; beat until smooth and mixture reaches spreading consistency. Yield: enough for one 3-layer cake.
Elaine Cooley,
Louisville, Kentucky.

LACE COOKIES

1 cup quick-cooking oats, uncooked
1 cup sugar
2 tablespoons plus 1 teaspoon all-purpose
  flour
¼ teaspoon salt
1 egg, slightly beaten
½ cup butter or margarine, melted
2 teaspoons vanilla extract

Combine oats, sugar, flour, and salt; mix well. Stir in remaining ingredients. Drop by ½ teaspoonfuls 3 inches apart onto aluminum foil-lined cookie sheets. Bake at 350° for 6 to 8 minutes or until edges are brown. Cool completely before removing. Yield: about 6½ dozen.
Ann McDowell,
Clayton, Georgia.

Tip: Use shiny cookie sheets and cakepans for baking. Dark pans absorb more heat and cause baked products to overbrown.

Make A Homemade Bread Mix

When you put together food mixes and tasty goodies this year, here's one you'll want to make for yourself as well as others. In Hubbard, Texas, Margot Foster keeps a batch of Quick Bread Mix on hand to bake waffles, muffins, coffee cake, or a loaf of bread at a moment's notice.

The mix is simply a combination of flour, baking powder, sugar, salt, and shortening. It can be stored at room temperature in an airtight container for several weeks. For longer storage, the mix may be kept in the refrigerator or freezer.

QUICK BREAD MIX

10 cups all-purpose flour
⅓ cup baking powder
¼ cup sugar
1 tablespoon plus 1 teaspoon salt
2 cups shortening

Combine dry ingredients in a large bowl; mix well. Divide flour mixture and shortening in half. Cut 1 cup shortening into half of flour mixture with a pastry blender until mixture resembles coarse meal. Repeat with remaining shortening and flour mixture. Combine mixtures. Store in an airtight container at room temperature up to 6 weeks. Refrigerate or freeze for longer storage. Yield: 13 cups.

BANANA-NUT BREAD

1 (8-ounce) package cream cheese,
  softened
1 cup sugar
2 eggs
1 cup mashed banana
2 cups Quick Bread Mix
½ cup chopped pecans

Beat cream cheese until light and fluffy; gradually add sugar, beating well. Add eggs, one at a time, beating well after each addition. Add banana; mix well. Stir in Quick Bread Mix and pecans.

Spoon batter into a greased 9- x 5- x 3-inch loafpan. Bake at 350° for 55 minutes or until a wooden pick inserted in center comes out clean. Cool completely in pan. Yield: 1 loaf.

SUNSHINE MUFFINS

1 (8½-ounce) can crushed pineapple, undrained
About ½ cup milk
1 egg, beaten
1¾ cups Quick Bread Mix
3 tablespoons sugar
1½ teaspoons grated orange rind

Drain pineapple, reserving juice. Add milk to juice to equal ¾ cup. Add egg to milk mixture; set aside.

Combine Quick Bread Mix, sugar, and orange rind in a medium bowl; make a well in center of mixture. Add milk mixture and pineapple to dry ingredients, stirring just until moistened. Spoon batter into greased muffin pans, filling two-thirds full. Bake at 400° for 25 minutes. Yield: 1 dozen.

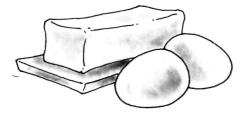

MARBLED COFFEE CAKE

2 cups Quick Bread Mix
¼ cup sugar
¾ cup milk
1 egg, beaten
2 tablespoons shortening, melted
2 tablespoons molasses
½ teaspoon ground cinnamon
¼ teaspoon ground nutmeg
¼ teaspoon ground cloves
¼ cup firmly packed brown sugar
2 tablespoons Quick Bread Mix
¼ teaspoon ground cinnamon
1 tablespoon butter or margarine

Combine 2 cups Quick Bread Mix and sugar in a mixing bowl; add milk, egg, and shortening, and beat at medium speed of an electric mixer until smooth. Remove 1 cup batter; combine with molasses, ½ teaspoon cinnamon, nutmeg, and cloves. Place spoonfuls of plain batter into a greased 8-inch square baking pan in a checkerboard pattern. Spoon spiced batter in spaces around plain batter; gently swirl with a knife.

Combine brown sugar, 2 tablespoons Quick Bread Mix, and ¼ teaspoon cinnamon in a small bowl. Cut in butter with a pastry blender until mixture resembles coarse meal. Sprinkle mixture over batter. Bake at 375° for 25 to 30 minutes. Serve warm. Yield: 9 servings.

QUICK MIX WAFFLES

2 eggs, separated
1⅓ cups milk
2 tablespoons vegetable oil
2 cups Quick Bread Mix

Beat egg yolks in a medium mixing bowl; add milk and oil. Add Quick Bread Mix, stirring until mixture is smooth.

Beat egg whites (at room temperature) until stiff peaks form, and gently fold into the batter.

Pour about ⅓ cup batter into a hot, lightly oiled waffle iron. Bake about 5 minutes or until steaming stops. Repeat procedure until all batter is used. Yield: 12 (4-inch) waffles.

Rely On Frozen Vegetables

Fresh vegetables can't be beat, but frozen foods come in handy when the fresh are out of season. Often the prices of frozen vegetables are lower than their fresh or canned counterparts. There is another advantage to frozen vegetables—you can rely on their speed and convenience in cooking.

TOMATO-VEGETABLE SOUP

1 pound ground beef
1 (46-ounce) can tomato juice
1 (14½-ounce) can beef broth, undiluted
¾ cup water
1 (10-ounce) package frozen green beans
1 (10-ounce) package frozen English peas
1 (10-ounce) package frozen chopped broccoli
2 medium potatoes, unpeeled and cubed
3 large carrots, scraped and sliced
1 medium onion, chopped
1 cup sliced fresh mushrooms
½ cup quick-cooking oats, uncooked
1 clove garlic, minced
2 teaspoons dried whole oregano
½ teaspoon salt
¼ teaspoon pepper

Brown ground beef in a large Dutch oven; drain. Add remaining ingredients; bring to a boil. Cover, reduce heat, and simmer 1 hour, stirring occasionally. Yield: about 4 quarts.

Meg Mordecai,
Nashville, Tennessee.

GREEN BEAN SURPRISE

2 (10-ounce) packages frozen green beans
4 slices bacon, diced
⅔ cup chopped onion
1 tablespoon all-purpose flour
1 tablespoon sugar
½ cup milk
¼ cup mayonnaise
¼ cup (1 ounce) shredded Cheddar cheese
½ cup buttered cracker crumbs

Cook green beans according to package directions, omitting salt; drain.

Cook bacon in a large skillet until crisp. Remove bacon with a slotted spoon, reserving drippings. Sauté onion in drippings until tender; remove onion, and set aside.

Add flour and sugar to bacon drippings; cook over low heat 1 minute, stirring well. Add milk, and cook, stirring constantly, until thickened. Stir in mayonnaise, green beans, bacon, and onion. Spoon into a lightly greased 1½-quart casserole. Sprinkle top evenly with shredded cheese and buttered cracker crumbs. Bake at 350° for 20 minutes. Yield: 6 servings.

Mary Rudolph,
Fort Worth, Texas.

LIMA-BACON BAKE

2 (10-ounce) packages frozen Fordhook lima beans
1½ cups water
6 slices bacon, diced
1 cup chopped onion
½ cup chopped celery
1 cup (4 ounces) shredded Monterey Jack cheese
¼ teaspoon Worcestershire sauce
¼ teaspoon pepper

Combine lima beans and water; bring to a boil. Cover, reduce heat, and simmer 15 minutes. Drain, reserving ½ cup liquid.

Cook bacon in a large skillet until limp; remove bacon with a slotted spoon, reserving 1 tablespoon of drippings in skillet. Set bacon aside.

Sauté onion and celery in reserved drippings until tender. Stir in beans, cheese, Worcestershire sauce, and pepper, and reserved liquid. Spoon mixture into a lightly greased 2-quart casserole; sprinkle with bacon. Bake, uncovered, at 350° for 25 minutes or until bacon is browned. Yield: 6 to 8 servings.

Debbie Dockery,
Brevard, North Carolina.

CAULIFLOWER CASSEROLE

2 (10-ounce) packages frozen cauliflower
1 cup water
1 cup (4 ounces) shredded Cheddar cheese
½ cup corn flake crumbs
⅓ cup minced green pepper
¼ cup finely chopped onion
1 (8-ounce) carton sour cream
½ cup grated Parmesan cheese
Paprika

Cook cauliflower in 1 cup boiling water until crisp-tender. Drain.

Combine cauliflower, Cheddar cheese, corn flake crumbs, green pepper, and onion. Spoon mixture into a lightly greased 2-quart casserole. Spread top with sour cream; sprinkle with Parmesan cheese and paprika. Bake at 350° for 35 minutes. Yield: 6 servings.

Jodie McCoy,
Tulsa, Oklahoma.

GREEK SPINACH QUICHE

Pastry for 9-inch pie
1 (10-ounce) package frozen chopped
**   spinach**
1 cup milk
1 cup crumbled feta cheese
3 eggs, beaten
¼ cup butter or margarine, melted
2 tablespoons grated Romano cheese
2 tablespoons all-purpose flour
½ teaspoon white pepper
¼ teaspoon salt
Dash of ground nutmeg

Line a 9-inch quiche dish with pastry; trim excess pastry around edges. Prick bottom and sides of pastry with a fork. Bake at 400° for 3 minutes; remove from oven, and prick with a fork. Bake 5 minutes.

Cook spinach according to package directions, omitting salt. Drain spinach thoroughly, pressing out excess water.

Combine spinach and remaining ingredients in a mixing bowl; mix well. Pour mixture into prepared pastry shell. Bake at 350° for 30 to 35 minutes or until set. Let stand 10 minutes before serving. Yield: one 9-inch quiche.

Frances Berga-Rigsby,
Daphne, Alabama.

Hot Salads
For Chilly Days

If you enjoy eating potato, chicken, or seafood salads chilled, you might also want to try some of our hot versions for colder months. Just add some fresh fruit or steamed winter vegetables and bread to the menu, and that's all you'll need.

You can cook Baked Seafood Salad in a casserole dish, but to serve company, use au gratin dishes or scallop shells to make it more attractive.

BAKED SEAFOOD SALAD

2½ cups water
¾ pound unpeeled fresh shrimp
1 cup fresh crabmeat, drained and flaked
1 cup thinly sliced celery
½ cup chopped pecans
½ cup mayonnaise
3 tablespoons grated onion
1 tablespoon lemon juice
1 tablespoon Worcestershire sauce
½ teaspoon salt
⅛ teaspoon pepper
⅓ cup breadcrumbs
Celery leaves

Bring water to a boil; add shrimp, and return to a boil. Reduce heat, and simmer 3 to 5 minutes. Drain well; rinse with cold water. Chill. Peel and devein shrimp. Set aside 4 shrimp for garnish.

Combine all ingredients except breadcrumbs, celery leaves, and shrimp for garnish. Spoon mixture into 4 baking shells. Sprinkle with breadcrumbs. Bake at 350° for 20 minutes or until hot. Garnish with celery leaves and reserved shrimp. Yield: 4 servings.

Dora S. Hancock,
Malakoff, Texas.

HOT TURKEY SALAD

2 cups diced cooked turkey
¼ cup beef consommé
1½ cups thinly sliced celery
1 cup coarsely chopped, roasted, salted
**   almonds**
1 cup mayonnaise
2 tablespoons grated onion
2 tablespoons lemon juice
1 pimiento, cut into strips
⅛ teaspoon pepper
6 baked patty shells
½ cup (2 ounces) shredded Cheddar
**   cheese (optional)**

Combine turkey and consommé in a saucepan; cook until turkey is thoroughly heated. Add celery, almonds, mayonnaise, onion, lemon juice, pimiento, and pepper, mixing well. Cook over low heat, stirring frequently, until mixture is thoroughly heated. Fill patty shells with hot turkey salad. Sprinkle with cheese, if desired, and bake at 350° for 5 minutes or until cheese melts. Serve immediately. Yield: 6 servings.

Sandra Russell,
Gainesville, Florida.

COUNTRY CLUB-STYLE HOT
CHICKEN SALAD

4 cups chopped cooked chicken
2 cups chopped celery
4 hard-cooked eggs, chopped
1 (2-ounce) jar diced pimiento, drained
1 tablespoon finely chopped onion
1 cup mayonnaise
2 tablespoons lemon juice
¾ teaspoon salt
1 cup (4 ounces) shredded Cheddar cheese
⅔ cup sliced almonds, toasted

Combine chicken, celery, eggs, pimiento, onion, mayonnaise, lemon juice, and salt; mix well. Spoon into a lightly greased 12- x 8- x 2-inch baking dish; cover and bake at 350° for 20 minutes. Sprinkle cheese over casserole; top with almonds. Bake, uncovered, an additional 3 minutes or until cheese melts. Yield: 6 to 8 servings.

J. Carroll Simms,
Richmond, Virginia.

HOT POTATO SALAD

4½ cups cooked, diced potatoes
1 cup (4 ounces) cubed Cheddar cheese
½ cup pickle relish
¼ cup sliced pimiento-stuffed olives
¼ cup chopped onion
⅓ cup mayonnaise
⅛ teaspoon celery salt
Dash of pepper
5 slices bacon, cooked and crumbled

Combine potatoes, cheese, pickle relish, olives, and onion in a large bowl; stir in mayonnaise and seasonings. Spoon mixture into a greased 8-inch square baking dish. Sprinkle with cooked bacon. Bake at 350° for 40 minutes. Yield: 6 servings.

Kim Varnadoe,
Cordele, Georgia.

Pick Canned Fruit For These Recipes

If you're wondering what to do with the cans of fruit sitting on your pantry shelf, take a look at these recipes. Canned fruit comes in handy, especially during months when most fresh fruit is not available.

Enhance the flavor of meats with Spicy Plum Sauce. And don't forget that many vegetables are even tastier with the addition of fruit. Our recipe for Sweet Potatoes and Peaches is a good example. Canned peach slices make this vegetable dish different.

Spicy Plum Sauce is an excellent complement to ham slices or roast pork.

SWEET POTATOES AND PEACHES

1 (16-ounce) can sliced peaches, undrained
1 (29-ounce) can sweet potatoes, drained
½ cup firmly packed brown sugar
3 tablespoons butter or margarine
Ground cinnamon

Drain peaches, reserving syrup. Combine peaches and sweet potatoes in a greased 2-quart casserole; set aside.

Combine reserved peach syrup, brown sugar, and butter in a small saucepan; bring to a boil. Reduce heat, and simmer 5 minutes, stirring occasionally. Pour over peaches and sweet potatoes; sprinkle with cinnamon. Bake at 325° for 30 minutes. Yield: 6 servings.
Susan Banaszak,
New Castle, Delaware.

PORT WINE-CHERRY SALAD

1 (16-ounce) can pitted dark sweet
** cherries, undrained**
2 (3-ounce) packages black cherry-flavored
** gelatin**
1 cup boiling water
¾ cup port wine
1 cup unsweetened applesauce
½ cup chopped pecans
Mayonnaise dressing (recipe follows)

Drain cherries, reserving syrup. Add enough water to syrup to make ¾ cup liquid, if necessary. Cut cherries in half, and set aside.

Dissolve gelatin in 1 cup boiling water. Add cherry liquid and wine; stir in applesauce. Chill until the consistency of unbeaten egg white; fold in cherry halves and chopped pecans.

Spoon mixture into a lightly oiled 4-cup mold. Chill until firm. Unmold salad and serve with mayonnaise dressing. Yield: 8 servings.

Mayonnaise Dressing:

1 cup mayonnaise or salad dressing
3 tablespoons orange juice
1 tablespoon port wine
1 tablespoon grated orange rind

Combine all ingredients; chill at least 1 hour. Yield: 1¼ cups.
Mrs. Frank J. Yount,
Baldwin, Maryland.

SPICY PLUM SAUCE

1 (16-ounce) can purple plums, undrained
1½ tablespoons cornstarch
¼ teaspoon ground cinnamon
¼ teaspoon ground allspice
2 tablespoons lemon juice
1 tablespoon butter or margarine

Drain plums, reserving juice. Seed and quarter plums; set aside.

Combine cornstarch, cinnamon, and allspice in a heavy saucepan, mixing well. Stir in plum juice. Cook over medium heat, stirring constantly, until smooth and thickened. Add lemon juice and butter; stir until butter melts. Stir in plums. Serve sauce warm with pork. Yield: 1½ cups.
Carol S. Noble,
Burgaw, North Carolina.

CINNAMON-BLUEBERRY SAUCE

1 (16½-ounce) can blueberries, undrained
¼ cup sugar
2 teaspoons cornstarch
½ teaspoon ground cinnamon
2 tablespoons lemon juice
Ice cream

Drain the blueberries, reserving ¼ cup juice.

Combine sugar, cornstarch, and cinnamon in a small saucepan. Stir in reserved blueberry juice and lemon juice; blend well. Bring to a boil over medium heat; reduce heat to low, and simmer 5 minutes, stirring occasionally. Stir in blueberries. Serve sauce warm over ice cream. Yield: 1¼ cups.
Jean McIntosh,
Spavinaw, Oklahoma.

MICROWAVE COOKERY

Add Flavor With Eggs And Cheese

If you've ever overcooked eggs or cheese in the microwave, you know how tough and rubbery they can get. Since microwaves are particularly drawn to foods high in protein and fat, eggs and cheese will cook faster than you might think. Cooking them at MEDIUM (50% power) to MEDIUM HIGH (70% power) for a short time, mixing them with heartier ingredients, and stirring occasionally are techniques that ensure the best product.

When egg yolk and white are mixed for scrambled eggs or used in casseroles, eggs can be cooked at HIGH with good results. In fact, scrambled eggs are even better cooked in the microwave than in a skillet. The eggs are fluffier and creamier, and they have more volume. They do need to be stirred every couple of minutes.

For baked eggs, such as our Baked Eggs Florentine, it's best to use MEDIUM (50% power). Since the egg yolk and white are not combined, the higher fat content in the yolk attracts microwaves and can overcook before the white cooks. Covering the egg and adding a small amount of water helps to distribute heat more evenly for a tender egg. One important point: Always pierce the yolk once and the whites several times with a wooden pick before cooking. This procedure allows steam to escape during cooking and prevents the egg from bursting.

Eggs and cheese make a popular combination for quiches and casseroles, such as Sausage-Egg Casserole. As with all egg dishes, it should be removed from the microwave and allowed to stand a few minutes. This allows the eggs to set without overcooking them. A knife inserted in the center will feel hot when the casserole is done.

When cooking with eggs and/or cheese in the microwave, keep the following tips in mind:

—To use cheese for a topping, sprinkle it on after the food is cooked and has been removed from the microwave. The heat from the food will melt it.

—Stir cheese into a sauce during the last few minutes of cooking to prevent it from becoming stringy.

—Never hard-cook an egg in the shell in the microwave. Steam will build up inside the shell, causing it to burst.

—To prepare a soufflé in the microwave, use only recipes designed for the microwave rather than trying to convert a conventional recipe. Puffy omelets and most soufflés are best cooked by conventional methods.

—Quiches and egg casseroles reheat well in the microwave. To reheat, place one serving on a microwave-safe plate, cover with heavy-duty plastic wrap, and cut a vent for steam to escape. Microwave at MEDIUM HIGH (70% power) for 1½ to 2 minutes.

—When converting conventional baked recipes, such as cheesecake or casseroles, for the microwave, reduce the number of eggs to prevent excess toughening.

BAKED EGGS FLORENTINE

4 slices bacon
1 (10-ounce) package frozen chopped spinach, thawed
3 tablespoons butter or margarine
¼ cup finely chopped onion
1 clove garlic, crushed
1 (2-ounce) jar diced pimiento, drained
½ cup commercial sour cream
¼ teaspoon pepper
¼ teaspoon ground nutmeg
4 eggs
¼ cup water, divided
3 tablespoons grated Parmesan cheese

Place bacon on a rack in a 12- x 8- x 2-inch baking dish; cover with paper towels. Microwave at HIGH for 4½ to 5½ minutes or until bacon is crisp; drain. Crumble bacon, and set aside.

Drain spinach well, and then pat dry. Set aside.

Combine butter, onion, and garlic in an 8-inch square dish. Cover and microwave at HIGH for 3 to 4 minutes or until onion is tender, stirring once. Stir in spinach, pimiento, sour cream, and seasonings, mixing well. Spread evenly in dish. Set aside.

Place 1 egg in each of four 6-ounce custard cups. Pierce each yolk one time with a wooden pick and pierce egg whites several times. Add 1 tablespoon of water to each egg, and cover tightly. Microwave on MEDIUM (50% power) for 4½ to 5½ minutes. Let stand covered 1 minute.

Microwave spinach mixture, uncovered, at HIGH for 4 to 5 minutes or until thoroughly heated. Drain eggs, and place over spinach. Sprinkle with Parmesan cheese and crumbled bacon. Yield: 4 servings.

SAUSAGE-EGG CASSEROLE

1 pound bulk pork sausage
¼ cup chopped green pepper
½ cup chopped onion
8 eggs, beaten
½ cup milk
¼ teaspoon pepper
1 cup (4 ounces) shredded Cheddar cheese
1 cup (4 ounces) shredded Swiss cheese

Crumble sausage into a 2-quart casserole; add green pepper and onion. Cover with waxed paper, and microwave at HIGH for 5 to 7 minutes or until sausage is done and vegetables are tender, stirring once. Remove sausage mixture from casserole, and drain on paper towels. Spread sausage mixture evenly in an 8-inch square baking dish; set aside.

Combine eggs, milk, and pepper in a 2-quart casserole, stirring well. Microwave at MEDIUM (50% power) for 7 to 8 minutes or until partially set, stirring at 2-minute intervals.

Stir in cheese. Pour egg mixture over sausage mixture. Cover with waxed paper, and microwave at MEDIUM for 4 to 6 minutes or until center is set, rotating dish at 3-minute intervals. Let stand, covered, 5 minutes before serving. Yield: 6 servings.

DENVER PITA SANDWICHES

3 tablespoons butter or margarine
3 tablespoons chopped green pepper
2 tablespoons chopped green onions
4 eggs, beaten
⅛ teaspoon salt
⅛ teaspoon pepper
½ cup chopped cooked ham
¼ cup commercial sour cream
2 pita bread rounds, cut in half
1 small tomato, chopped
½ cup (2 ounces) shredded Monterey Jack cheese

Place butter in a 10- x 6- x 2-inch baking dish. Microwave at HIGH for 1 minute or until butter melts. Add green pepper and onions; microwave at HIGH for 3 to 4 minutes or until vegetables are tender.

Combine eggs, salt, pepper, and ham; pour over vegetables. Cover tightly with heavy-duty plastic wrap. Make one slit in plastic wrap for steam to escape.

Microwave at MEDIUM HIGH (70% power) for 3½ to 4 minutes or until eggs are almost set, stirring 3 times. Stir in sour cream. Cover and microwave at MEDIUM HIGH for 1 minute or until thoroughly heated. Spoon mixture into pita halves. Top mixture with chopped tomato and shredded cheese. Serve hot. Yield: 4 sandwiches.

From Our Kitchen To Yours

You don't have to spend the whole day in the kitchen when you're preparing a meal. To make the job easier, here are some time-saving suggestions from our staff of home economists.

—Before beginning a recipe, gather all the necessary ingredients and utensils, and bring them to your work area. This speeds up the preparation time.

—If you're planning an entire menu, read through each recipe completely, and work out a schedule. Consider what can be done while ingredients or dishes are baking, cooking, or chilling. First, fix items that need to be frozen, marinated, or chilled. Leave time for last-minute chores, such as cooking fresh vegetables that will be served hot or garnishing your finished dishes.

—Common food ingredients, such as cheese, onions, and nuts, can be shredded or chopped in the food processor or blender in large quantities and held over for other recipes.

—Clean up as you go along. A sink or countertop full of dirty dishes can sometimes be overwhelming. Wash and reuse mixing bowls, measuring spoons and cups, and other utensils as you cook. This can also cut down on the time you spend cleaning up.

—For easier cleanup, place ingredients on or measure onto disposable products, such as waxed paper, aluminum foil, or paper plates.

—Keep your knives sharpened; slicing or chopping with a dull knife not only takes longer but can also be tiring.

—For a more efficient way of slicing, line up several similarly shaped ingredients, such as carrots, celery, or green onions, side-by-side, and slice through all pieces at one time.

—To chop elongated vegetables, such as carrots or celery, cut into 4 to 6 lengthwise pieces; then slice. An onion is easily chopped by slicing off both ends to make it level. Place one cut end down. Starting at either side, slice about halfway into onion; repeat all the way across. Give onion a quarter turn, and slice halfway through onion all the way across, forming a checkerboard design. Turn onion on its side, and slice down.

—Make the most of kitchen gadgets, such as an egg slicer for slicing mushrooms or an electric knife for cutting acorn or spaghetti squash.

—Keep kitchen equipment, such as wooden spoons, wire whisks, and spatulas, near your preparation area, and put beaters with your mixer.

—Preheat the oven while you're still involved in preparation; this keeps you from waiting for the oven to reach the correct temperature once the preparation is finished.

—To chill sauces or gelatin mixtures quickly, set mixing bowl into a larger bowl of ice water; then refrigerate.

—Measuring salt, pepper, brown sugar, and sifted powdered sugar can be messy as well as difficult. To measure food from packages or boxes more easily, transfer to wide-mouthed jars or containers with tight-fitting lids.

Cook Faster With A Processor

When seasoned cook Ann Hall of Macon, Georgia, received a food processor several years ago, she found that routine chopping and mixing tasks were quicker and left her with less cleanup.

Ann finds it handy to chop extra ingredients to freeze when she prepares a recipe. "It's been easy to have chopped onion, nuts, breadcrumbs, parsley, and other herbs in the freezer for a quick meal. I have those prepared ahead of time, and I always keep them on hand."

When she can, Ann likes to adapt regular recipes to use in the food processor. Her recipe for Strawberry-Cheese Ring involves shredding cheese, grating onion, and chopping pecans, so almost all the preparation can be done in the processor. "The recipe was originally from Jimmy Carter's wife, Rosalyn. She served it in Washington when he was President," says Ann. "I changed the recipe to make it in the processor." Ann suggests shredding the cheese coarsely by pressing firmly on the food pusher as the cheese goes through the shredding disc. For finely shredded cheese, push it through the blade slowly.

Ann says she enjoys the time savings the processor allows. She warns that overprocessing is one of the easiest mistakes to make. "You learn that pretty quickly when you start using a processor," she says.

Other cooks across the South have discovered the convenience of a food processor, too. You'll find some of their recipes along with Ann's favorites.

MINIATURE PECAN PIES

1 cup pecans
1 egg
¾ cup firmly packed brown sugar
1 tablespoon butter or margarine, melted
½ teaspoon vanilla extract
¼ teaspoon salt
Cream Cheese Pastry Shells

Position knife blade in food processor bowl; add pecans. Top with cover, and pulse 4 times or until pecans are evenly chopped. Remove pecans; set aside.

Position knife blade in processor bowl; add egg, sugar, butter, vanilla, and salt. Top with cover, and process until smooth. Fill each pastry shell three-fourths full with mixture. Sprinkle on pecans. Bake at 325° for 25 to 30 minutes. Remove immediately, and cool on rack. Yield: 2 dozen.

Cream Cheese Pastry Shells:

1 (3-ounce) package cream cheese, chilled and cubed
½ cup butter or margarine, chilled and cubed
1 cup all-purpose flour

Position knife blade in food processor bowl; add cream cheese and butter. Top with cover, and pulse 3 or 4 times or until combined. Add flour; process until dough forms a ball, leaving sides of bowl. Chill dough 2 hours.

Shape the dough into 24 balls; place each ball into greased 1¾-inch muffin tins, and shape into a shell. Yield: 2 dozen pastry shells.

STRAWBERRY-CHEESE RING

2 (8-ounce) packages sharp Cheddar
  cheese
1 small onion, peeled and cut in half
1 cup pecans
⅔ cup mayonnaise
¼ teaspoon garlic salt
¼ teaspoon pepper
Dash of red pepper
Strawberry preserves

Position shredding disc in food processor bowl, and top with cover. Cut cheese to fit food chute, if necessary. Place cheese in food chute; shred, applying firm pressure with food pusher.

Place onion in food chute; grate, applying firm pressure with food pusher. Remove shredded cheese and onion from processor bowl; set aside.

Position knife blade in processor bowl. Add pecans, and process until pecans are finely chopped. Add mayonnaise and seasonings; pulse 5 or 6 times or until ingredients are blended. Stir mayonnaise mixture into cheese and onion, mixing well. Shape mixture into a ring on a serving platter. Chill mixture several hours.

At serving time, fill center of ring with strawberry preserves. Serve with crackers. Yield: 3¼ cups.

SPINACH-STUFFED BAKED TOMATOES

4 medium tomatoes
⅛ teaspoon salt
1 (10-ounce) package frozen chopped
  spinach
½ cup grated Parmesan cheese, divided
2 tablespoons mayonnaise
2 teaspoons grated onion
⅛ teaspoon salt
⅛ teaspoon pepper

Slice off top of each tomato; scoop out some of the pulp, leaving shells intact. (Reserve pulp for other uses.) Sprinkle shells with ⅛ teaspoon salt; invert on paper towels to drain.

Cook spinach according to package directions; drain well, pressing out excess liquid with the back of a spoon. Position knife blade in food processor bowl; add spinach, ⅓ cup Parmesan cheese, mayonnaise, onion, salt, and pepper. Pulse several times or until mixture is blended.

Fill tomato shells with spinach mixture. Place in a 1-quart casserole, and sprinkle with remaining cheese. Bake, uncovered, at 400° for 15 minutes or until heated. Yield: 4 servings.

■ In Guntersville, Alabama, Nell H. Amador processes a peach glaze for spareribs. It's the fastest way to puree the canned peaches to get the right consistency for the glaze.

PEACH-GLAZED SPARERIBS

1 clove garlic
1 (15-ounce) can cling peach halves,
  drained
⅓ cup soy sauce
¼ cup vegetable oil
¼ cup honey
2 tablespoons brown sugar
1 teaspoon sesame seeds
¼ teaspoon ground ginger
3 to 4 pounds spareribs

Position knife blade in food processor bowl; top with cover. Drop garlic through food chute with processor running; process about 3 seconds or until garlic is finely chopped. Add peaches, and process until smooth. Add soy sauce, oil, honey, brown sugar, sesame seeds, and ginger; process 30 seconds. Set mixture aside.

Cut ribs into serving-size pieces; place in a large Dutch oven. Cover ribs with water. Bring water to a boil; cover, reduce heat, and simmer 30 minutes. Drain well.

Grill ribs, 5 inches from heat, over slow coals, 45 minutes or until desired degree of doneness, turning frequently. Brush ribs with sauce during last 15 minutes of grilling. Serve with remaining sauce. Yield: 3 to 4 servings.

■ Fresh herbs are easy to chop and combine using a processor. Margaret G. Quaadman of Roswell, Georgia, hollows out the center of a red cabbage to use as a container for fresh herb dip.

HERBAL DIP

1 clove garlic
1 cup mayonnaise
1 cup low-fat cottage cheese
¼ cup chopped chives
2 tablespoons chopped fresh parsley or 2
  teaspoons dried parsley flakes
2 tablespoons chopped fresh chervil or 2
  teaspoons dried whole chervil, crushed
1 tablespoon chopped fresh dillweed or 1
  teaspoon dried whole dillweed
1 tablespoon chopped fresh basil or 1
  teaspoon dried whole basil, crushed
Dash of Worcestershire sauce
Dash of hot sauce

Position knife blade in food processor bowl; top with cover. Drop garlic through food chute with processor running; process 3 to 5 seconds or until garlic is minced. Add remaining ingredients; process 2 minutes, scraping sides of bowl occasionally. Cover and chill at least 4 hours. Serve dip with assorted vegetables. Yield: about 2 cups.

■ Jan Bronson of Kissimmee, Florida, makes her easy Blueberry-Cream Cheese Muffins in the food processor. The key to successful processor muffins is to use the pulse button and be careful not to overprocess.

BLUEBERRY-CREAM CHEESE MUFFINS

1 cup fresh blueberries
2 cups all-purpose flour, divided
¾ cup sugar
1½ teaspoons baking powder
½ teaspoon baking soda
Pinch of salt
1 (3-ounce) package cream cheese, cut
  into cubes
2 teaspoons lemon juice
2 teaspoons vanilla extract
¼ cup butter or margarine, melted
½ cup milk
2 eggs

Toss blueberries with 2 tablespoons flour; set aside. Combine remaining flour with dry ingredients; set aside.

Position knife blade in food processor bowl. Add cream cheese, lemon juice, and vanilla; process until smooth. With processor running, pour butter and milk through chute; process several seconds. Scrape sides of bowl with spatula; process several seconds until smooth. Add eggs; pulse 4 or 5 times. Add flour mixture; pulse 6 times or until mixture is just moistened.

Remove knife blade; fold in the blueberries. Fill paper-lined muffin pans two-thirds full. Bake at 400° for 18 to 20 minutes. Remove from pans immediately. Yield: 16 muffins.

■ By using her food processor, Sherry Marr of Burke, Virginia, turns out Peach Ice Cream in minutes. She simply mixes sugar, frozen fruit, and whipped cream in the processor.

PEACH ICE CREAM

⅓ cup sugar
Rind from ½ lemon
1 (16-ounce) package frozen peaches
⅛ teaspoon ground nutmeg
1 cup whipping cream, chilled

Position knife blade in food processor bowl. Add sugar and lemon rind; process until rind is finely chopped. Add frozen peaches and nutmeg; process 10 to 15 seconds or until peaches are cut into small chunks. With machine running, pour whipping cream through food chute, and process 10 seconds or until mixture reaches a smooth, creamy consistency. (Some peach chunks may remain, if desired.) Serve immediately. Yield: about 5 cups.

Serve An Easy Morning Menu

A special breakfast is only fitting for overnight guests during their visit or for the family on a weekend morning. We've put together a menu you can assemble in about 45 minutes.

The secret to cutting your time in the kitchen is to organize your preparation. The entrée, Cheesy Egg Casserole, requires the longest baking time, so make it first. Then mix up the Breakfast Bites, and bake them with the casserole at the same temperature. The muffins bake 20 minutes, so put them in the oven 10 minutes after the casserole.

While the casserole and muffins bake, simmer canned peaches with spices for our Ginger Spiced Peaches. Frying the ham and making the gravy take just a few minutes too. Once the muffins are ready, dip the tops in butter, sprinkle with a sugar mixture, and serve.

**Fruit Juice
Cheesy Egg Casserole
Virginia Ham With Gravy
Ginger Spiced Peaches
Breakfast Bites
Coffee**

CHEESY EGG CASSEROLE

¼ cup all-purpose flour
¼ teaspoon salt
¼ cup butter or margarine, melted
4 eggs, beaten
1 cup cottage cheese
1 (4-ounce) can chopped green chiles, drained
2 cups (8 ounces) shredded Monterey Jack cheese
1 (4-ounce) jar whole pimientos
Green pepper

Combine flour, salt, and butter in a large bowl. Add eggs, cottage cheese, chiles, and cheese; mix well. Pour mixture into a lightly greased 10- x 6- x 2-inch baking dish. Garnish casserole with pimientos and green pepper. Bake, uncovered, at 375° for 30 minutes. Yield: 6 to 8 servings.

*Ella Huguley,
Lubbock, Texas.*

VIRGINIA HAM WITH GRAVY

4 slices country ham, cut in half
2 tablespoons butter or margarine, melted
1 (10-ounce) can beef gravy, undiluted
1 teaspoon instant coffee granules
3 tablespoons water
Fresh parsley sprigs (optional)

Cook ham in butter in a large skillet until browned on both sides; drain. Transfer ham to serving platter; set aside, and keep warm.

Stir remaining ingredients except parsley into pan drippings. Bring to a boil; reduce heat, and simmer 5 minutes, stirring occasionally. Serve gravy with ham. Garnish ham with parsley, if desired. Yield: 8 servings.

*Ruth Sherrer,
Fort Worth, Texas.*

GINGER SPICED PEACHES

2 (16-ounce) cans sliced peaches, undrained
1 teaspoon ground ginger
10 whole cloves

Drain peaches, reserving juice. Combine juice, ginger, and cloves in a large saucepan; bring to a boil. Reduce heat, and simmer 10 minutes. Add peaches to hot mixture; cook until thoroughly heated. Serve warm or chilled. Yield: 8 servings.

*Bettye Cortner,
Cerulean, Kentucky.*

BREAKFAST BITES

1½ cups all-purpose flour
½ cup sugar
1½ teaspoons baking powder
½ teaspoon salt
¼ teaspoon nutmeg
½ cup milk
⅓ cup vegetable oil
1 egg
1½ tablespoons butter or margarine, melted
¼ cup sugar
½ teaspoon ground cinnamon

Combine flour, ½ cup sugar, baking powder, salt, and nutmeg in a large bowl; make a well in center of mixture. Combine milk, oil, and egg; add mixture to dry ingredients, stirring just until moistened.

Spoon into greased muffin pans, filling two-thirds full. Bake at 375° for 20 minutes. Remove from pan immediately, and dip muffin tops in melted butter. Combine ¼ cup sugar and cinnamon; sprinkle sugar mixture over top of each muffin. Yield: about 1 dozen.

*Faye Poole,
Moneta, Virginia.*

Salads Sparkle With Citrus

One of the bright spots of winter is that citrus is at its best. So why not peel some oranges and grapefruit, and put them in a fresh salad? They'll add color, as well as taste and texture. In our Spinach-and-Orange Salad, the orange sections are a delicious contrast to the sliced onion rings.

SPINACH-AND-ORANGE SALAD

¾ pound fresh spinach, torn into bite-size pieces
3 medium-size oranges, peeled, sectioned, and seeded
1 medium-size red onion, sliced and separated into rings
¼ to ⅓ cup commercial French dressing

Combine spinach, orange sections, and sliced onion in a large salad bowl, tossing well.

Drizzle dressing over spinach mixture; toss gently. Yield: 6 servings.

*Mrs. R. E. Bunker,
Temple, Texas.*

COTTAGE CHEESE-AND-FRUIT SALAD

2 bananas, quartered
2 apples, unpeeled and cut into wedges
Lemon juice
1 (16-ounce) carton cream-style cottage cheese
Lettuce
2 oranges, peeled and sectioned
1 grapefruit, peeled and sectioned
Nutty topping (recipe follows)

Sprinkle bananas and apples with lemon juice, and toss lightly. Set aside.

Place cottage cheese in center of a lettuce-lined platter. Arrange the bananas, apples, oranges, and grapefruit around cottage cheese; sprinkle with topping. Yield: 6 servings.

Nutty Topping:
½ cup chopped walnuts
1 tablespoon poppy seeds
1 tablespoon sesame seeds

Combine all ingredients. Yield: about ⅔ cup.
Mary Pappas,
Richmond, Virginia.

Two For Soup

If you think homemade soup is impractical when you're only cooking for two, think again. Here are two recipes that may change your mind. They're quick and make just a few servings.

EGG DROP SOUP

1⅓ cups water
1 (10¾-ounce) can chicken broth
1 teaspoon soy sauce
1 tablespoon cornstarch
2 tablespoons water
1 egg, beaten
1 tablespoon dry sherry
Thinly sliced green onions

Combine 1⅓ cups water, broth, and soy sauce in a medium saucepan; bring to a boil. Combine cornstarch and 2 tablespoons water, stirring well; add to broth mixture. Boil 1 minute over medium heat, stirring occasionally. Combine egg and sherry; slowly pour egg mixture into boiling soup, stirring constantly. (The egg forms lacy strands as it cooks.) Ladle soup into bowls, and sprinkle with green onions. Serve immediately. Yield: 2⅔ cups. *Ashlyn Ritch, Forsyth, Georgia.*

THREE-POTATO SOUP

3 medium potatoes, cubed
2 green onions, sliced
1 stalk celery, chopped
1 cup water
¼ teaspoon salt
1 (12-ounce) can evaporated milk
¼ cup butter or margarine
1 teaspoon parsley flakes
Freshly ground pepper to taste (optional)
Sliced green onions (optional)

Combine potatoes, 2 green onions, celery, water, and salt in a saucepan. Cover and cook 10 minutes or until potatoes are tender. (Do not drain.) Mash vegetables slightly. Stir in milk, butter, parsley, and, if desired, pepper; heat. Garnish with green onions, if desired. Yield: 3½ cups.
Linda Lee Duke,
Corpus Christi, Texas.

Easy-To-Make Supper Breads

Don't let a busy schedule keep you from serving fresh bread. With these recipes you'll discover shortcuts to making loaves, muffins, and rolls.

Our Easy Cheese Bread, laced with rich Cheddar flavor, can be prepared in just minutes. And Sesame-Cheese Muffins are equally quick. They sport a sprinkling of sesame seeds for a crisp, nutty taste.

Yeast breads typically take hours to make, requiring several rising periods and kneading. But our Easy Yeast Rolls rise only once and don't have to be kneaded. They're also simple to form—just use a biscuit cutter; then fold one side over for the traditional Parker House shape.

EASY YEAST ROLLS

1 cup hot water
¼ cup plus 2 tablespoons shortening
¼ cup sugar
1 teaspoon salt
1 package dry yeast
2 tablespoons warm water (105° to 115°)
1 egg, beaten
3½ cups all-purpose flour, divided
2 tablespoons butter or margarine, melted

Combine 1 cup hot water, shortening, sugar, and salt in a large mixing bowl;

stir until shortening melts. Cool the mixture until lukewarm (105° to 115°).

Dissolve yeast in 2 tablespoons warm water; add to shortening mixture, stirring well. Add egg and 1¾ cups flour; beat vigorously with a wooden spoon for 1 minute. Stir in remaining flour.

Turn dough out onto a floured surface. Roll out to ¼-inch thickness. Cut into circles using a 2½-inch biscuit cutter, and brush with melted butter. Make a crease across each circle, and fold one half over. Gently press edges to seal. Place rolls on greased baking sheets, and let rise in a warm place (85°), free from drafts, 1 hour or until doubled in bulk. Bake at 425° for 12 to 15 minutes or until golden brown. Yield: about 3 dozen.
Mrs. John D. McMullen,
Georgetown, Kentucky.

MAYONNAISE MUFFINS

2 cups all-purpose flour
2 teaspoons baking powder
½ teaspoon salt
½ cup mayonnaise
¾ cup milk

Combine flour, baking powder, and salt in a small mixing bowl. Add mayonnaise and milk, stirring with a fork until dry ingredients are moistened. Spoon into lightly greased muffin pans, filling three-fourths full. Bake at 450° for 10 to 12 minutes. Yield: 8 muffins.
Mrs. Donald Heun,
Louisville, Kentucky.

SESAME-CHEESE MUFFINS

½ cup chopped onion
1 tablespoon butter or margarine, melted
1½ cups biscuit mix
1 cup (4 ounces) shredded sharp American cheese, divided
1 egg, beaten
½ cup milk
1 tablespoon sesame seeds, toasted
1 tablespoon butter or margarine, melted

Sauté onion in 1 tablespoon butter until tender. Combine onion, biscuit mix, and ½ cup cheese in a large bowl.

Combine egg and milk; add to biscuit mixture, stirring just until moistened. Spoon into lightly greased muffin pans filling two-thirds full. Sprinkle with remaining ½ cup cheese and sesame seeds; drizzle with 1 tablespoon butter. Bake at 400° for 15 minutes or until golden brown. Yield: 1 dozen.
Doug Baker,
Birmingham, Alabama.

EASY CHEESE BREAD

2½ cups biscuit mix
1 cup (4 ounces) shredded sharp Cheddar
   cheese
2 teaspoons poppy seeds
1 egg, beaten
1 cup milk

Combine biscuit mix, cheese, and poppy seeds in a large bowl.

Combine egg and milk; add to biscuit mixture, mixing vigorously for 1 minute. Spoon into a lightly greased 8½- x 4½- x 3-inch loafpan. Bake bread at 350° for 35 minutes or until golden brown. Yield: 1 loaf.
Margarine Smith,
Tyler, Texas.

HERB BREAD

3 cups all-purpose flour
2 tablespoons sugar
1 tablespoon baking powder
2 teaspoons caraway seeds
½ teaspoon ground nutmeg
½ teaspoon dried whole thyme
½ teaspoon salt
1 egg, beaten
1½ cups milk
½ cup vegetable oil

Combine flour, sugar, baking powder, and seasonings in a large mixing bowl; stir well.

Combine remaining ingredients; add to dry ingredients, stirring just until moistened. Spoon into a greased and floured 8½- x 4½- x 3-inch loafpan; bake at 350° for 50 to 55 minutes or until a wooden pick inserted in center comes out clean. Yield: 1 loaf.
Charlotte Watkins,
Lakeland, Florida.

Potatoes Are A Cook's Best Friend

No matter how you slice, dice, or mash them, potatoes are the anchor in any cook's pantry. Prepared home style and simple or fancy with a gourmet touch, they're standard fare for almost any menu. Potatoes offer a variety of ways to turn humdrum meals into something special—whether you use them in the fresh, frozen, or dehydrated form.

Choose potatoes that are firm, smooth, and free from blemishes and sprouts. A greenish color indicates sunburn or exposure to light and should be avoided or at least cut away before the potato is cooked. Select the right variety of potato for your intended purpose. Waxy potatoes with a high moisture content are better to boil or use in salads. To bake, mash, or fry, use potatoes that are dry and mealy.

Store potatoes in a dark, dry, cool place. Temperatures above 50°F encourage sprouting and shriveling, but refrigeration is not recommended. The starch will turn to sugar, and the potato will develop a sweet taste and turn dark when cooked. This process is only partially reversed when potatoes are taken from the refrigerator and returned to room temperature several days before they are cooked.

CHEESY CRAB-STUFFED POTATOES

4 medium baking potatoes
Vegetable oil
1 cup (4 ounces) shredded sharp Cheddar
   cheese
½ cup butter or margarine, melted
½ cup half-and-half
¼ cup diced onion
½ teaspoon salt
¼ teaspoon ground red pepper
1 (6-ounce) can crabmeat, drained, flaked,
   and chopped
Paprika

Scrub potatoes thoroughly, and rub skins with oil. Bake at 400° for 1 hour or until done.

Allow potatoes to cool to touch. Cut potatoes in half lengthwise; carefully scoop out pulp, leaving shells intact. Spoon pulp into a mixing bowl. Add remaining ingredients except paprika; mash with a potato masher. Stuff shells with potato mixture; sprinkle lightly with paprika. Bake at 425° for 15 to 20 minutes. Yield: 8 servings.
Jan Thompson,
Highland, Maryland.

BROCCOLI-TOPPED BAKED POTATOES

4 medium baking potatoes
Vegetable oil
1 (10-ounce) package frozen broccoli
   spears
1 (8-ounce) package process cheese with
   jalapeño peppers, cubed
2 teaspoons milk
Pepper to taste

Scrub potatoes thoroughly, and rub skins with oil. Bake at 400° for 1 hour or until done.

Cook broccoli according to package directions, omitting salt; coarsely chop broccoli spears.

Combine cheese and milk in a medium saucepan; cook over low heat, stirring until cheese melts. Stir in broccoli and pepper.

Split tops of potatoes lengthwise, and fluff pulp with a fork. Spoon topping over potatoes. Yield: 4 servings.
Mrs. Bernie Benigno,
Gulfport, Mississippi.

POTATO-TOMATO BAKE

1 (16-ounce) package frozen hash brown
   potatoes, thawed
1 small tomato, chopped
½ cup chopped onion
½ teaspoon dried whole oregano
¼ teaspoon salt
¼ teaspoon white pepper
1 cup (4 ounces) shredded mozzarella
   cheese
¼ to ½ cup milk
Parsley sprigs (optional)
Cherry tomato wedges (optional)

Layer half each of potatoes, tomato, onion, seasonings, and cheese in a greased 8-inch square baking dish. Repeat layers, ending with cheese. Pour milk over top. Cover and bake at 425° for 20 minutes. Uncover and bake an additional 5 minutes. Garnish with parsley and cherry tomato wedges, if desired. Yield: 6 servings.
Irene Murry,
Herculaneum, Missouri.

CHEESY CARAWAY POTATOES

¼ cup butter or margarine
½ teaspoon salt
¼ teaspoon white pepper
½ teaspoon caraway seeds
4 large baking potatoes, unpeeled and cut
   into 2- x ½-inch strips
1 medium onion, diced
1 cup (4 ounces) shredded sharp Cheddar
   cheese

Combine butter and seasonings in a large skillet; heat until butter melts. Add potatoes and onion, stirring well. Cover and cook over medium heat 15 to 20 minutes or until potatoes are tender and slightly browned. Sprinkle with cheese; cover and cook 1 minute or until cheese melts. Yield: 6 to 8 servings.
Nancy Oglesby,
Wilmington, Delaware.

POTATOES IN CREAM-WINE SAUCE

4 medium-size red potatoes, peeled and thinly sliced
¼ teaspoon salt
2 tablespoons butter or margarine, melted
1 medium onion, sliced
⅔ cup milk
¾ cup (3 ounces) shredded mozzarella cheese
1 tablespoon all-purpose flour
½ teaspoon sugar
½ teaspoon salt
¼ cup dry white wine

Sauté potatoes and salt in butter in a large skillet for 10 minutes, turning occasionally with a spatula.

Place remaining ingredients except wine in container of an electric blender; process until smooth. Pour mixture over potatoes in skillet; cover and cook over medium-low heat 5 minutes, stirring occasionally. Stir in wine, and cook an additional 5 minutes or until potatoes are tender. Yield: 6 servings.

Bruce Whitehouse,
Hockessin, Delaware.

PARSLIED POTATOES

1 large onion, chopped
1 large clove garlic, minced
2 tablespoons butter or margarine, melted
5 medium-size red potatoes, peeled and cubed
1 cup water
½ teaspoon salt
¼ teaspoon white pepper
⅓ cup chopped parsley

Sauté onion and garlic in butter in a large skillet until tender. Add potatoes, water, and seasonings. Cover and simmer 15 minutes or until tender. Drain liquid, and discard; top potatoes with parsley. Yield: 6 servings.

Corinne R. Gilder,
Crowley, Louisiana.

Make The Appetizers Special

If you want to get a party going in a hurry, serve an interesting appetizer—something new and different that has a little zip. We offer several suggestions.

Black-Eyed Pea Pinwheels are sure to be a conversation starter; guests will find it hard to believe that the base of the filling is actually black-eyed peas. It also contains cream cheese, garlic powder, and hot sauce. The mixture is rolled up inside a slice of ham with a green onion in the center. When the rolls are sliced, they make colorful hors d'oeuvres. This recipe was grand-prize winner at the 1985 Black-Eyed Pea Jamboree in Athens, Texas.

CHUNKY SHRIMP SPREAD

3 cups water
1 pound unpeeled fresh shrimp
½ cup minced onion
1 tablespoon fresh lemon juice
½ teaspoon curry powder
¼ cup plus 2 tablespoons mayonnaise
¼ teaspoon salt
⅛ teaspoon white pepper
Parsley sprig (optional)

Bring water to a boil; add shrimp, and cook 3 to 5 minutes. Drain well; rinse with cold water. Chill. Peel and devein shrimp; coarsely chop. Add remaining ingredients except parsley, mixing well; chill. Garnish with parsley, if desired. Serve spread with party-size rye or whole wheat bread. Yield: 2 cups.

Elizabeth M. Watts,
Panama City, Florida.

TERIYAKI CHICKEN WINGS

2½ pounds chicken wings
¾ cup soy sauce
¼ cup water
⅔ cup chopped onion
1 teaspoon grated fresh gingerroot

Cut chicken wings in half at joint; cut off tips of wings, and discard. Combine chicken and remaining ingredients in a shallow container. Cover and refrigerate 8 hours, turning occasionally.

Remove chicken from marinade, discarding marinade; place in a single layer on a lightly greased 15- x 10- x 1-inch jellyroll pan. Bake, uncovered, at 350° for 30 minutes. Turn each piece, and continue baking 15 minutes or until done. Yield: about 12 servings.

Betty Beske,
Arlington, Virginia.

BLUE CHEESE APPETIZER TARTS

1 cup (4 ounces) blue cheese, crumbled
1 tablespoon all-purpose flour
Tart shells (recipe follows)
1 egg, beaten
1 (5-ounce) can evaporated milk
Dash of salt
2 drops of hot sauce
¼ cup chopped walnuts

Combine blue cheese and flour; spoon evenly into tart shells.

Combine egg, milk, salt, and hot sauce; spoon evenly over blue cheese mixture in tart shells. Sprinkle with walnuts. Bake at 425° for 7 minutes. Reduce oven temperature to 300°, and bake an additional 17 minutes or until set. Yield: 2 dozen.

Tart Shells:

1 (3-ounce) package cream cheese, softened
½ cup butter or margarine, softened
1 cup all-purpose flour

Combine cream cheese and butter, mixing well. Stir in flour; chill. Shape dough into 24 (1-inch) balls. Place each ball into individual wells of ungreased 1¾-inch muffin pans, pressing dough onto bottom and sides to form shells. Yield: 2 dozen.

Note: Tarts can be made ahead, baked, and frozen. When ready to serve, bake, frozen and uncovered, on a baking sheet at 350° for 20 minutes or until thoroughly heated.

Gloria P. Different,
Harvey, Louisiana.

BLACK-EYED PEA PINWHEELS

1 (15-ounce) can black-eyed peas, drained
¼ cup butter or margarine
¼ teaspoon seasoned salt
Two dashes of hot sauce
Dash of garlic powder
2 (3-ounce) packages cream cheese, softened
1 (10-ounce) package 6- x 4-inch ham slices
10 green onions, cut into 6-inch lengths

Combine black-eyed peas, butter, seasoned salt, hot sauce, and garlic powder in a saucepan; bring to a boil. Reduce heat; simmer, uncovered, 15 minutes, stirring occasionally. Remove pan from heat, and let mixture cool.

Position knife blade in food processor bowl; add black-eyed pea mixture and cream cheese. Process 3 to 5 seconds. Stop processor, and scrape sides of bowl with a rubber spatula. Process an additional 5 seconds or until mixture is well blended.

Spread about 3 tablespoons of pea mixture on each slice of ham; place a strip of green onion lengthwise in middle of ham slice. Roll up ham lengthwise; chill. To serve, cut each roll into ½-inch slices, and arrange cut side up on a serving platter. Yield: about 6½ dozen. *Billy Archibald, Mexia, Texas.*

Give Everyday Entrées A Lift

Before you decide what to serve for dinner tonight, take a look at these creative entrées.

Glazed Beef Loaf is no ordinary meat loaf. It's filled with Cheddar cheese and shredded carrot; then it's baked with a sugar, catsup, and mustard glaze that makes it look just as special as it tastes.

Hamburgers take a new twist in Cheeseburger Loaves. These thick cheese-topped patties are served on Italian bread topped with tomato, onion, and bacon.

If Mexican food is a favorite at your house, then try our two offerings. In Tacos al Carbón, flour tortillas wrap up strips of flavorful grilled flank steak. And Matador Mania transforms an ordinary ground beef casserole into something special with refried beans, taco sauce, tortillas, sour cream, and cheese.

TACOS AL CARBÓN

4 pounds flank steak, tenderized
½ cup vegetable oil
½ cup burgundy
1 teaspoon garlic powder
1 teaspoon salt
1 teaspoon pepper
10 flour tortillas
1 avocado
Lime juice
1 (8-ounce) carton commercial sour cream
Pico de Gallo

Place steak in a large shallow container. Combine oil, burgundy, garlic powder, salt, and pepper, mixing well. Pour over steak; cover and marinate in the refrigerator 8 hours, occasionally turning the steak.

Wrap tortillas in aluminum foil, and heat in a 325° oven about 15 minutes. Cut avocado into cubes, and dip in lime juice; set aside.

Drain steak. Grill over hot coals 5 to 10 minutes on each side or until steak reaches desired degree of doneness.

Slice steak diagonally across grain into thin slices. Wrap tortillas around sliced steak and serve with avocado, sour cream, and Pico de Gallo. Yield: 8 to 10 servings.

Pico de Gallo:

1 tomato, cubed
½ medium onion, chopped
3 tablespoons fresh chopped cilantro or 1 teaspoon dried cilantro flakes
4 Serrano chiles, finely chopped

Combine all ingredients, mixing well. Cover and refrigerate overnight. Yield: about ¾ cup. *Joe Rich, Carrollton, Texas.*

MATADOR MANIA

1 pound ground beef
1 medium onion, chopped
½ cup water
3 tablespoons chili powder
1½ teaspoons salt
1 teaspoon ground cumin
⅛ teaspoon pepper
1 (16-ounce) can refried beans
2 (8-ounce) jars commercial taco sauce, divided
6 (7-inch) corn tortillas, divided
1 (8-ounce) carton commercial sour cream
1 cup (4 ounces) shredded Cheddar cheese

Cook ground beef in a large skillet until browned, stirring to crumble; drain well. Add chopped onion, water, chili powder, salt, cumin, and pepper to ground beef. Cook, uncovered, about 5 minutes, stirring occasionally. Remove skillet from heat; stir in refried beans, and set mixture aside.

Spread about ½ cup taco sauce in a greased 12- x 7½- x 2-inch baking dish. Arrange 2 tortillas on top of sauce; cover with half of meat mixture, sour cream, and an additional ½ cup taco sauce. Arrange 2 additional tortillas on top of sauce; cover with an additional ½ cup taco sauce, the remaining meat mixture, and half the cheese. Arrange remaining tortillas, taco sauce, and cheese on top. Cover and bake at 350° for 40 minutes. Let stand 5 minutes before serving. Yield: 6 servings.

Mary Rudolph, Fort Worth, Texas.

CHEESEBURGER LOAVES

1 pound ground beef
½ cup fine dry breadcrumbs
½ cup evaporated milk
1 tablespoon lemon juice
½ teaspoon dried whole oregano
½ teaspoon salt
½ teaspoon pepper
½ teaspoon Worcestershire sauce
⅛ teaspoon garlic powder
6 (1-ounce) slices process American cheese
1 (15-inch) loaf Italian bread
12 slices bacon, cooked
6 slices tomato
6 slices onion, separated into rings
Catsup
Mustard

Combine ground beef, breadcrumbs, milk, lemon juice, and seasonings, mixing well; shape into 6 patties about ¾ inch thick.

Place patties on a rack in a broiler pan. Broil 5 inches from heat for 5 minutes on each side or until burgers reach desired degree of doneness. Place a slice of cheese on each burger, and broil 20 seconds or until cheese melts.

Slice bread lengthwise, then into 6 equal portions. Place bacon on bottom half of bread portions; top with cheeseburgers, tomato, onion, and top half of bread portions. Serve with catsup and mustard. Yield: 6 servings.

Mary Lou Vaughn, Dallas, Texas.

GLAZED BEEF LOAF

2 eggs, beaten
3 slices bread, torn
½ cup milk
1 teaspoon salt
¼ teaspoon pepper
2 pounds ground beef
1½ cups (6 ounces) shredded Cheddar cheese
⅔ cup shredded carrot
⅔ cup diced onion
¼ cup firmly packed brown sugar
¼ cup catsup
1 tablespoon prepared mustard

Combine eggs, bread, milk, salt, and pepper in a large mixing bowl, mixing well. Add ground beef, cheese, carrot, and onion; mix well. Shape mixture into a loaf, and place on a lightly greased rack in a broiler pan. Bake at 350° for 45 minutes. Combine remaining ingredients, and spoon over loaf. Bake an additional 20 to 25 minutes or until done. Let stand 5 minutes before slicing. Yield: 8 servings. *Joanne Conway, Versailles, Kentucky.*

EASY BAKED RIBS

3 pounds spareribs
2 medium onions, chopped
2 tablespoons butter or margarine, melted
1 cup catsup
1 cup water
2 tablespoons brown sugar
2 tablespoons vinegar
2 tablespoons lemon juice
1 tablespoon plus 1 teaspoon hot sauce
1 tablespoon Worcestershire sauce

Cut ribs into serving-size pieces; place in a 13- x 9- x 2-inch baking pan. Bake, uncovered, at 400° for 30 minutes.

Sauté onion in butter over medium heat until tender. Remove from heat, and set onion aside.

Combine remaining ingredients in a small saucepan. Bring to a boil; cover, reduce heat, and simmer 15 minutes. Stir in onion. Pour mixture over ribs. Bake at 350° for 1½ hours or until tender. Yield: 3 to 4 servings.

Lucy J. Flynn,
Walpole, Massachusetts.

Molasses Is Still A Favorite Sweetener

In pioneer days, molasses was the staple sweetening ingredient used in most kitchens. Today, we still enjoy its old-fashioned flavor added to cakes, sauces, beans, and pies.

Capture the flavor of this dark syrup in Taffy Dessert Sauce. We recommend serving it over ice cream or waffles.

Our Molasses Snack Cake is rich with molasses and a fragrant blend of cinnamon, ginger, and raisins. You'll find Molasses Pie to be an extra-rich version of one of our favorite desserts—pecan pie. It's darker and thicker than traditional pecan pie because it's filled with molasses, rather than corn syrup.

MOLASSES PIE

3 eggs, beaten
1 cup firmly packed brown sugar
½ cup molasses
2 tablespoons butter or margarine, melted
1½ tablespoons all-purpose flour
Pinch of salt
½ cup chopped pecans
1 unbaked 8-inch pastry shell

Combine eggs, brown sugar, molasses, butter, flour, and salt; beat with an electric mixer until blended. Stir in pecans. Pour mixture into the pastry shell. Bake at 350° for 35 minutes. Yield: one 8-inch pie.

Sherry Allison,
Cookeville, Tennessee.

MOLASSES BAKED BEANS

2 (21-ounce) cans pork and beans
1 cup chopped onion
½ cup chopped green pepper
½ cup catsup
⅓ cup molasses
2 tablespoons brown sugar
2 tablespoons prepared mustard
2 teaspoons chili powder
⅛ teaspoon garlic powder
3 slices bacon, cooked and crumbled

Combine pork and beans, onion, green pepper, catsup, molasses, brown sugar, mustard, chili powder, and garlic powder; stir well. Spoon into a lightly greased shallow 2-quart casserole. Bake, uncovered, at 350° for 55 minutes. Sprinkle top with bacon; bake an additional 5 minutes. Yield: 8 servings.

Lynne Teal Weeks,
Columbus, Georgia.

MOLASSES SNACK CAKE

1 egg, beaten
1 cup molasses
½ cup boiling water
¼ cup all-purpose flour
¾ cup raisins
2 cups all-purpose flour
1 teaspoon baking soda
½ teaspoon salt
2 teaspoons ground cinnamon
2 teaspoons ground ginger
⅓ cup vegetable oil

Combine egg, molasses, and water; stir well. Combine ¼ cup flour and raisins, tossing well; set aside.

Combine 2 cups flour, soda, salt, cinnamon, and ginger; stir into molasses

mixture. Add raisin mixture and oil; mix well. Pour into a greased and floured 11- x 7- x 1½-inch baking pan; bake at 350° for 25 to 30 minutes or until a wooden pick inserted in the center comes out clean. Yield: 12 servings.

Debbie Baskin,
Shreveport, Louisiana.

MOLASSES COOKIES

¼ cup plus 2 tablespoons shortening
2 tablespoons butter or margarine, softened
¼ cup firmly packed brown sugar
1 cup molasses
3 cups all-purpose flour
1½ teaspoons baking soda
½ teaspoon salt
2 teaspoons ground allspice
½ teaspoon ground ginger
⅛ teaspoon anise seeds
½ cup sugar

Cream shortening and butter in a large mixing bowl; gradually add brown sugar, beating until light and fluffy. Add molasses, beating well.

Combine flour, soda, salt, allspice, ginger, and anise seeds. Add dry mixture to creamed mixture to make a stiff dough. Chill the dough several hours or overnight.

Shape chilled dough into 1½- x ½-inch logs; roll in sugar. Place cookie logs on a lightly greased cookie sheet; bake at 300° for 13 to 15 minutes. Cool cookies on wire racks. (Cookies will be crisp.) Yield: about 5 dozen.

Note: For softer molasses cookies, store them in an airtight container.

Marie H. Webb,
Roanoke, Virginia.

TAFFY DESSERT SAUCE

¾ cup butter or margarine
¾ cup sugar
¾ cup molasses
¾ cup evaporated milk
1½ teaspoons vanilla extract
1 cup chopped pecans

Melt butter in a medium saucepan; add sugar and molasses, stirring well. Bring to a boil; cook 2 minutes, stirring constantly. Remove from heat, and cool slightly. Stir in remaining ingredients. Serve warm over ice cream or waffles. Yield: 3¼ cups.

Jean Voan,
Shepherd, Texas.

These Entrées Start With Chicken

When you're looking for a main dish, chicken is always a favorite. It's economical, nutritious—and best of all from a cook's point of view—versatile. You can bake it, broil it, fry it, and still have choices left over. Take a look at some of these tasty alternatives.

Almond Chicken and Vegetables is a stir-fry dish that's practically a meal-in-one. For a foreign entrée with a completely different taste, try Chicken Curry. Piña Colada Chicken is a simple dish with a tropical flavor.

With so many ways to serve it, it makes sense to buy chicken on special and freeze it for later use. Use it within four to six months. With chicken on hand, you've always got a head start on planning the next meal.

ALMOND CHICKEN AND VEGETABLES

1 egg white
1 tablespoon soy sauce
1 teaspoon cornstarch
1 teaspoon sugar
⅛ teaspoon salt
⅛ teaspoon white pepper
1½ pounds boneless chicken breasts, skinned and cut into 1-inch pieces
¼ cup plus 2 tablespoons peanut or vegetable oil, divided
1 (2-ounce) package slivered almonds
1 (8-ounce) can sliced bamboo shoots, drained
3 green onions with tops, cut into 1-inch pieces
1 medium-size green pepper, cut into 1-inch pieces
1 tablespoon peanut or vegetable oil
1 tablespoon soy sauce
2 to 3 teaspoons grated fresh gingerroot
2 teaspoons white wine
Green onion top for garnish (optional)

Combine egg white, 1 tablespoon soy sauce, cornstarch, sugar, salt, and white pepper, stirring well. Add chicken breast pieces; mix well, and refrigerate 15 minutes.

Pour ¼ cup oil around top of preheated wok; allow to heat at high (350°) for 1 minute. Add chicken, and stir-fry 5 minutes or until lightly browned. Remove with slotted spoon; drain on paper towels.

Pour 2 tablespoons oil around top of wok; heat at medium high (325°) for 30 seconds. Add almonds, and stir-fry 2 minutes or until golden brown. Remove and drain on paper towels. Add bamboo shoots, green onions, and green pepper to wok. Stir-fry 1 to 2 minutes or until crisp-tender. (Add additional oil, if necessary.)

Combine 1 tablespoon oil, 1 tablespoon soy sauce, gingerroot, and wine, mixing well; add mixture to wok. Bring to a boil. Add chicken and almonds; stir-fry 30 seconds or until thoroughly heated. Garnish with green onion top, if desired. Serve immediately. Yield: 6 servings.

GOLDEN-BROWN OVEN-FRIED CHICKEN

1 (8-ounce) carton commercial sour cream
2 tablespoons lemon juice
2 tablespoons Worcestershire sauce
1 tablespoon celery salt
1 tablespoon paprika
½ teaspoon salt
Dash of pepper
8 chicken breast halves, skinned and boned
1½ cups herb-seasoned stuffing mix, crushed
¼ cup butter or margarine, melted

Combine sour cream, lemon juice, Worcestershire sauce, celery salt, paprika, salt, and pepper; mix well. Dip chicken breast halves in sour cream mixture, and dredge in stuffing mix. Place chicken in a lightly greased 13- x 9- x 2-inch baking dish.

Drizzle with butter, and bake, uncovered, at 350° for 1 hour. Yield: 8 servings.
Peggy C. Brown,
Winston-Salem, North Carolina.

EASY CHICKEN AND DUMPLINGS

1 (3- to 4-pound) broiler-fryer
3 quarts water
1 carrot, scraped and sliced
3 stalks celery, sliced
1 medium onion, quartered
¾ teaspoon salt
½ teaspoon pepper
5 (6-inch) flour tortillas, quartered

Place chicken, water, carrot, celery, and onion in a large Dutch oven; bring to a boil. Cover, reduce heat, and simmer 1 hour. Remove chicken, reserving broth, and let cool. Bone and chop chicken; set aside.
Strain broth to remove vegetables. Return strained broth and chicken to Dutch oven, and bring to a boil. Add salt and pepper. Drop tortilla quarters into broth, one at a time. Cover and cook 15 minutes. Yield: 6 to 8 servings.
Freida Stadelman,
Germantown, Tennessee.

CHICKEN CURRY

1 (2½- to 3-pound) broiler-fryer, cut up and skinned
¼ cup vegetable oil
2 cups chopped onion
2 cloves garlic, minced
1 tablespoon paprika
1½ teaspoons grated fresh gingerroot
1½ teaspoons ground coriander
1 teaspoon ground turmeric
1 teaspoon ground cumin
1 teaspoon salt
½ teaspoon ground cardamom
¼ teaspoon ground cinnamon
¼ teaspoon pepper
⅛ teaspoon ground cloves
1 cup yogurt
⅓ cup tomato paste

Brown chicken in hot oil in a large skillet. Remove chicken, reserving pan drippings; set aside.
Add onion and garlic to pan drippings in skillet; sauté until tender. Stir in seasonings, yogurt, and tomato paste. Add chicken, cover, and simmer 35 minutes or until chicken is tender. Yield: 4 servings.
Marietta Marx,
Louisville, Kentucky.

PIÑA COLADA CHICKEN

2 (8-ounce) cans sliced pineapple
1 (0.82-ounce) envelope commercial piña colada mix
¼ cup rum
¼ cup soy sauce
1 teaspoon ground ginger
1 clove garlic, minced
8 chicken thighs, skinned
8 maraschino cherries

Drain pineapple, reserving juice; set pineapple aside.
Combine pineapple juice and next 5 ingredients. Place chicken in a lightly greased 12- x 8- x 2-inch baking dish; add pineapple juice mixture. Marinate in refrigerator 1 hour.
Bake, uncovered, at 400° for 30 minutes. Reduce heat to 350°; bake 20 minutes. Top with pineapple slices and maraschino cherries; bake an additional 5 minutes. Remove to serving platter. Yield: 4 servings.
Janice Elder,
Spartanburg, South Carolina.

January 21

Give A New Twist To Salads

When you want the salad to be more than just tossed greens, these easy recipes will help you serve something different. They start with basic salad greens and boast some unique combinations of fruit, vegetables, and flavors.

In Spanish Sprout Salad, for instance, curly-edged leaf lettuce is tossed with celery, tomato, avocado, and alfalfa sprouts. Be sure that you add the avocado just before serving since it turns brown quickly.

Come up with your own salads by stirring spices into your favorite commercial dressings or mixing items from your pantry shelf into the salad. Don't forget about combining salad greens or trying different types of lettuce that may be new to you, such as romaine, Boston, and Bibb.

DIFFERENT COTTAGE CHEESE SALAD

2 cups cream-style cottage cheese
½ cup mayonnaise
2 tablespoons prepared horseradish
1 medium head iceberg lettuce, torn
3 green onions, chopped
1 medium-size green pepper, chopped
Tomato wedges (optional)
Minced green pepper (optional)

Combine cottage cheese, mayonnaise, and horseradish; chill well.

Combine lettuce, green onions, and green pepper; toss lightly. Arrange lettuce mixture on individual plates; top with the cottage cheese mixture. Garnish with tomato wedges and minced green pepper, if desired. Yield: 4 servings. *Cyndi Copenhaver, Virginia Beach, Virginia.*

HERBED GARDEN SALAD

1 head iceberg lettuce, torn
2 tomatoes, cut into wedges
½ cucumber, sliced
¼ green pepper, cut into strips
10 radishes, sliced
1 tablespoon chopped parsley
1 teaspoon salad herbs
½ teaspoon seasoned salt
⅛ teaspoon garlic powder
¼ teaspoon pepper
¼ cup vegetable oil
2 tablespoons cider vinegar
1 (3½-ounce) can French-fried onion rings

Combine lettuce, tomatoes, cucumber, green pepper, and radishes in a large salad bowl; sprinkle with seasonings. Combine oil and vinegar in a small jar; cover tightly, and shake vigorously until well blended. Pour over salad; toss gently. Sprinkle onion rings on top. Serve immediately. Yield: 8 servings.
Sue-Sue Hartstern, Louisville, Kentucky.

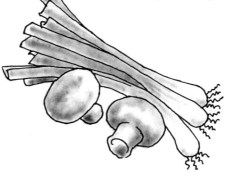

COMBINATION SPINACH SALAD

1 pound fresh spinach
5 small fresh mushrooms, sliced
3 green onions, sliced
1 (8-ounce) can pineapple chunks, drained
1 (14-ounce) can artichoke hearts, drained and quartered
1 (11-ounce) can mandarin oranges, drained
12 slices bacon, cooked and crumbled
Commercial ranch-style dressing

Remove stems from spinach; wash leaves, pat dry, and tear into bite-size pieces. Combine spinach, mushrooms, green onions, pineapple, artichoke hearts, and oranges in a large bowl. Sprinkle with bacon, and serve with dressing. Yield: 8 servings.
Arlene Margolis, Little Rock, Arkansas.

SPANISH SPROUT SALAD

1 small head leaf lettuce, torn
1 large tomato, diced
1 cup alfalfa sprouts
½ cup sliced celery
2 small avocados, cut into bite-size pieces
2 tablespoons lemon juice
Dash of red pepper
Commercial French dressing (optional)

Combine lettuce, tomato, sprouts, celery, and avocados in a large salad bowl. Combine lemon juice and pepper; sprinkle over salad, and toss gently. Serve with commercial French dressing, if desired. Yield: 6 servings.
Jan K. Sliwa, Temple, Texas.

This Chicken Soup Is Hot And Spicy

If you like chicken enchiladas, chances are you'll like Chicken Enchilada Soup. It has many of the same ingredients, but they're in a rich, satisfying soup instead.

CHICKEN ENCHILADA SOUP

1 dozen corn tortillas
Vegetable oil
1 small onion, chopped
1 clove garlic, crushed
2 tablespoons vegetable oil
1 (4-ounce) can chopped green chiles, undrained
1 (14½-ounce) can beef broth, undiluted
1 (10¾-ounce) can chicken broth, undiluted
1 (10¾-ounce) can cream of chicken soup, undiluted
1 (6¾-ounce) can chunk-style chicken
1½ cups water
1 tablespoon steak sauce
2 teaspoons Worcestershire sauce
1 teaspoon ground cumin
1 teaspoon chili powder
⅛ teaspoon pepper
3 cups (12 ounces) shredded Cheddar cheese
Paprika

Cut 6 tortillas into ½-inch-wide strips; set aside. Cut remaining tortillas into triangles, and fry in hot oil until crisp; set aside.

Sauté onion and garlic in 2 tablespoons hot oil in a Dutch oven. Add remaining ingredients except cheese and paprika; bring to a boil. Cover, reduce heat, and simmer 1 hour. Add tortilla strips and cheese; simmer, uncovered, 10 minutes. Sprinkle with paprika, and serve with reserved tortilla chips. Yield: 8 cups.

Tip: Read labels to learn the weight, quality, and size of food products. Don't be afraid to experiment with new brands. Store brands can be equally good in quality and nutritional value, yet lower in price. Lower grades of canned fruit and vegetables are as nutritious as higher grades. Whenever possible, buy most foods by weight or cost per serving rather than by volume or package size.

February

It's Time For Yummy Turnovers

Depending upon which area of the South you come from, you might call a turnover a fried pie, a half moon, or even a mule's ear. Turnovers can be filled with a variety of meats, vegetables, or dried fruit fillings.

Making turnovers takes some time, but it's easier than you might think. The crucial steps usually involve making the pastry. As you can see from the recipes shared here, some cooks encase their turnover fillings in traditional flour and shortening pastries. Others include special ingredients, such as cream cheese, spices, or buttermilk.

Usually, turnover fillings are partially or fully cooked before they are enclosed in pastry. Dried apples are chopped and plumped in water for our Delicious Apple Turnovers. A sprinkling of sugar and cinnamon adds the finishing touch.

Vegetable Turnovers are a nice addition to lunch or dinner. Hash brown potatoes, spinach, mushrooms, and cheese give them a hearty flavor. They're ideal with soup or salad.

Some of our turnovers are fried, but we've also included some that are baked. Of course, no matter how they are prepared, the end result is a delightful combination of flaky pastry and tasty filling.

VEGETABLE TURNOVERS

2 cups frozen hash brown potatoes
¼ cup chopped onion
2 tablespoons butter or margarine, melted
1 (10-ounce) package frozen spinach
5 large fresh mushrooms, sliced
2 tablespoons butter or margarine, melted
Pastry (recipe follows)
1 cup (4 ounces) shredded Cheddar cheese
1 egg yolk
1 teaspoon water
Mushroom-Wine Sauce

Cook hash browns and onion in 2 tablespoons butter until tender; set aside. Cook spinach according to package directions; drain well, and press dry. Set aside. Sauté mushrooms in 2 tablespoons butter until tender; set aside.

Roll pastry out into a 21- x 14-inch rectangle on a well-floured surface. Cut into six 7-inch squares.

Layer equal amounts of potato mixture, spinach, mushrooms, and cheese in center of each square.

Combine egg yolk and water; beat well. Moisten edges of squares with egg yolk mixture. Fold squares in half, diagonally, to make a triangle. Press edges together with a fork dipped in flour. Prick tops of turnovers with a fork. Place on lightly greased baking sheets; bake at 375° for 35 minutes. Serve turnovers with Mushroom-Wine Sauce. Yield: 6 turnovers.

Pastry:

3 cups all-purpose flour
2 teaspoons baking powder
1 teaspoon salt
1 cup shortening
½ to ¾ cup milk

Combine flour, baking powder, and salt; cut in shortening with pastry blender until mixture resembles coarse meal. Sprinkle milk over surface; stir with a fork until all ingredients are moistened. Shape into ball. Yield: enough for six 7-inch turnovers.

Mushroom-Wine Sauce:

½ pound fresh mushrooms, sliced
2 tablespoons butter or margarine, melted
3 tablespoons butter or margarine
3 tablespoons all-purpose flour
1½ cups milk
¼ cup dry white wine
½ teaspoon salt

Sauté mushrooms in 2 tablespoons butter until tender; set aside.

Melt 3 tablespoons butter in saucepan over low heat; add flour, stirring until smooth. Cook 1 minute; stir constantly. Stir in milk and wine; cook, stirring constantly, until thick and bubbly. Add salt and mushrooms. Yield: 2⅓ cups.
Louise Turpin,
Birmingham, Alabama.

TINY MUSHROOM TURNOVERS

3 tablespoons minced onion
1½ cups finely chopped fresh mushrooms
2 tablespoons butter or margarine, melted
1 tablespoon all-purpose flour
¼ teaspoon salt
⅛ teaspoon dried whole thyme
3 tablespoons commercial sour cream
Cream Cheese Pastry (recipe follows)

Sauté minced onion and chopped mushrooms in butter. Add flour, salt, and thyme, stirring until smooth; cook 1 minute, stirring constantly. Stir in sour cream; set mixture aside.

Roll pastry out to ⅛-inch thickness on a lightly floured board; cut into rounds with a 3-inch cutter. Place 1 teaspoonful mushroom mixture in center of each circle; moisten edges of circles with water. Fold circles in half; press edges together with a fork dipped in flour. Prick tops with a fork.

Place on ungreased baking sheets; bake at 425° for 10 to 12 minutes or until lightly browned. Yield: about 2½ dozen.

Cream Cheese Pastry:

½ cup butter, softened
3 (3-ounce) packages cream cheese, softened
1½ cups all-purpose flour

Combine butter and cream cheese; beat well. Add flour; mix until smooth. Chill several hours. Yield: enough for 2½ dozen miniature turnovers.
Sherry B. Phillips,
Knoxville, Tennessee.

FRIED APRICOT TURNOVERS

1 (6-ounce) package dried apricots
¾ cup sugar
1 teaspoon ground cinnamon
2 tablespoons butter or margarine, melted
1 tablespoon lemon juice
Pastry (recipe follows)
Vegetable oil

Combine apricots and just enough water to cover in a small saucepan; bring to a boil. Reduce heat and simmer, uncovered, 15 minutes or until tender. Drain well. Add sugar, cinnamon, butter, and lemon juice. Mash apricot mixture well.

Divide pastry into 2 portions; roll out each portion to ¼-inch thickness on a well-floured surface. Cut each portion into seven 5-inch circles. Spoon about 1 tablespoon fruit mixture on half of each circle; moisten edges of circles with water. Fold circles in half; press edges together with a fork dipped in flour.

Heat 1 inch of oil to 375° in a large skillet. Cook pies until golden, turning once; drain on paper towels. Yield: 14 turnovers.

Note: Turnovers can be refrigerated. To reheat them, bake, uncovered, at 350° for 15 minutes.

Pastry:

4 cups all-purpose flour
1 tablespoon baking powder
½ teaspoon baking soda
Dash of salt
⅓ cup shortening
1 egg, beaten
1 cup buttermilk

For one of the best turnovers you've ever had, try Delicious Apple Turnovers. It's surprisingly easy to make.

Combine flour, baking powder, soda, and salt; cut in shortening with pastry blender until mixture resembles coarse meal. Combine egg and buttermilk, stirring well. Add egg mixture to flour mixture, stirring with a fork until dry ingredients are moistened. Knead gently until smooth. Yield: enough for fourteen 5-inch turnovers.

DELICIOUS APPLE TURNOVERS

1 (8-ounce) package dried apples, chopped
6 cups water
¾ cup sugar
Dash of salt
½ teaspoon ground cinnamon
¼ teaspoon ground nutmeg
1 tablespoon butter or margarine
Pastry (recipe follows)
Vegetable oil
¼ cup sugar
¼ teaspoon ground cinnamon

Combine apples and water in a large saucepan; bring to a boil. Reduce heat to medium, and cook, uncovered, 30 to 35 minutes or until tender, stirring occasionally. Drain well. Slightly mash apples; add ¾ cup sugar, salt, ½ teaspoon cinnamon, nutmeg, and butter, stirring well.

Divide pastry into 9 portions; roll each portion into a 6-inch circle. Spoon ⅓ cup apple mixture on half of each circle; moisten edges of circles with water. Fold circles in half; press edges together with a fork dipped in flour.

Heat ½ inch of oil to 360° in a large skillet. Cook until golden, turning once; drain on paper towels. Combine ¼ cup sugar and ¼ teaspoon cinnamon; mix well. Sprinkle over hot turnovers. Yield: 9 turnovers.

Pastry:

2 cups all-purpose flour
1½ teaspoons baking powder
1 teaspoon salt
⅓ cup shortening
About ½ cup milk

Combine flour, baking powder, and salt; cut in shortening with pastry blender until mixture resembles coarse meal. Sprinkle milk (1 tablespoon at a time) evenly over surface; stir with a fork until all ingredients are moistened. Shape into a ball. Yield: enough for nine 6-inch turnovers.

Tip: For an easy job of measuring shortening, use the water-displacement method if the water that clings to the shortening will not affect the product. (Keep in mind this important point: Do not use this method for measuring shortening for frying.) To measure ¼ cup shortening using this method, put ¾ cup water in a measuring cup; then add shortening until the water reaches the 1-cup level. Just be sure that the shortening is completely covered with water. Drain off the water before using the shortening in your cooking.

Chocolate Lovers, Take Heart

As Valentine's Day draws near, lovers everywhere take notice. They price flowers, search for cards, and flip through recipe files for the right dessert to make for that special person.

In the latter category, we think we have just what you're looking for—a beautiful Mocha-Pecan Torte. Heart-shaped chocolate cutouts that you make yourself dance across the top.

Be sure not to confuse this torte with a cake; it looks like a cake, but the texture is firmer. Tortes typically contain ground nuts, little or no flour, and more eggs.

The piped frosting and chocolate garnishes lend a festive touch. (If you don't have the equipment needed for piping, spoon the frosting in dollops.) Be sure to make 12 dollops—one for each serving. Nestle a cherry half and a chocolate heart in each mound; then slice the torte between dollops.

MOCHA-PECAN TORTE
(pictured on facing page)

8 eggs, separated
⅔ cup sifted powdered sugar
1 teaspoon baking powder
⅓ cup cocoa
⅓ cup soft breadcrumbs
1 teaspoon vanilla extract
2 cups ground pecans
Mocha Buttercream Frosting
Chocolate hearts and shavings (recipe follows)
6 maraschino cherries, halved

Line the bottom of 4 (8-inch) round cakepans with waxed paper. Grease and flour waxed paper; set aside.

Combine egg yolks, sugar, and baking powder; beat at high speed of an electric mixer 2 to 3 minutes or until mixture is thick and lemon colored. Combine cocoa and breadcrumbs, and stir into the yolk mixture. Stir in vanilla; fold in ground pecans.

Beat egg whites (at room temperature) in a large mixing bowl until stiff peaks form; gently fold one-fourth of egg whites into yolk mixture. Fold remaining egg whites into yolk mixture. Pour batter evenly into the prepared pans, spreading top smoothly.

Bake at 350° for 15 minutes or until layers spring back when they are lightly touched. Do not overbake. Cool in pans 5 minutes. Invert layers onto wire racks, and gently peel off waxed paper. Let cool completely.

Measure and set aside 1½ cups Mocha-Buttercream Frosting for piping. Spread remaining frosting between layers and on top and sides of torte.

Spoon reserved frosting into a large decorating bag fitted with large metal tip No. 5. Pipe 12 decorative mounds of frosting evenly around top edges of torte. Fit decorating bag with large metal tip No. 1. Pipe remaining frosting around base of torte in a shell design.

Gently nestle a chocolate heart at an angle into each mound of frosting on top of torte; place a maraschino cherry half at base of each. Sprinkle chocolate shavings in center of the torte. Chill. Yield: one 8-inch torte.

Mocha-Buttercream Frosting:

2½ teaspoons instant coffee powder
2 tablespoons water
¾ cup plus 2 tablespoons butter, softened
1 tablespoon plus 2 teaspoons cocoa
7 cups sifted powdered sugar
⅓ cup half-and-half
1 teaspoon vanilla extract

Dissolve instant coffee powder in water; set aside. Cream butter in a large mixing bowl; add coffee mixture and cocoa. Gradually add powdered sugar alternately with half-and-half, beating until mixture is light and fluffy. Beat in vanilla. Yield: 4½ cups.

Chocolate Hearts and Shavings:

4 (1-ounce) squares semisweet chocolate

Melt chocolate in top of a double boiler over hot water. Line a baking sheet with aluminum foil; pour chocolate onto baking sheet.

For rippled chocolate hearts, gently shake baking sheet until chocolate is level and about ¼ inch thick. Let chocolate cool 5 to 10 minutes. Gently run a metal decorating comb over chocolate to achieve a rippled effect and to flatten chocolate to about ⅛-inch thickness. Let stand until chocolate is firm.

Firmly press a 1-inch heart-shaped cutter into chocolate, cutting through chocolate completely. Lift cutter up, and remove cutout by gently pressing through the cutter with a small wooden utensil. (Fingers leave prints.) Cut 12 chocolate hearts.

Break remaining chocolate into small pieces. Shave edges of chocolate with a vegetable peeler, holding chocolate with paper towels so that heat from hand doesn't melt chocolate. Yield: 12 hearts and about ⅓ cup shavings.

To make heart-shaped chocolate cutouts, pour melted chocolate onto a foil-lined baking sheet. For rippled design, pull a metal decorating comb across chocolate. Let chocolate stand until firm.

Make 12 chocolate hearts by firmly pressing a heart-shaped cutter into the chocolate. Remove cutouts by pressing through the cutter with a small wooden utensil. (Your fingers would leave prints).

To make chocolate shavings, break remaining chocolate into smaller pieces. Shave edges with a vegetable peeler, holding chocolate with a paper towel so that heat from your hand doesn't melt it.

Right: Present your valentine with stately Mocha-Pecan Torte (recipe on this page); for each serving, slice between piped dollops of frosting adorned with a cherry half and a chocolate heart.

Page 30: Colorful Almost Strawberry Cheesecake makes a spectacular ending to diet meals. (Recipe is on page 32.)

Above: *The feathery leaves of dill, also known as dillweed, perk up the flavor in Rice-and-Vegetable Salad (page 42). Serve it on radicchio for extra color.*

Left: *Take the chill off winter days with a hot drink made from our Spiced Tea Mix (page 32). You can enjoy this bracing beverage for only 3 calories per serving.*

Far left: *Cook a ham and enjoy it. Then with leftover slices of the ham, put together a dressy brunch or luncheon sandwich, Ham-Asparagus Delight (page 48).*

COOKING Light

Take A Positive Step Toward Better Eating

Good nutrition and physical fitness are popular trends as we try to make our lives as pleasant and full as possible. And southerners know that nutrition and fitness go hand in hand in promoting well-being and good health. As a matter of fact, that's just how our "Cooking Light"® feature came about. Readers began to write and tell us how much they enjoyed our food stories, but they needed help in the "battle of the bulge." So in January 1982, the "Cooking Light" feature was started to offer a healthier way of eating.

The phrase "Cooking Light" means several different things. It can mean a reduction in serving size, resulting in weighing or measuring foods. Or it can mean changing cooking methods, such as baking rather than frying.

Light cooking can also mean the reduction or substitution of fats; for example, skim milk can be used instead of heavy cream, or yogurt substituted for sour cream. Or it may mean a reduction or substitution in sugar, perhaps by using unsweetened fruit juice rather than granulated sugar.

Reduction or substitution of high-sodium products is another method used in "Cooking Light." For example, you might use herbs and spices instead of salt, or garlic powder rather than garlic salt. But the concept of light eating doesn't mean just reducing fat, sugar, and sodium. In fact, we often use the term when substituting an ingredient to increase nutritional value.

The popularity of our monthly "Cooking Light" feature has been overwhelming. In an effort to better meet your needs and requests, we proudly give you this first "Cooking Light" special section. You'll find tasty, appealing ideas for using convenience products in calorie-trimmed recipes as well as low-calorie dishes cooked totally from scratch. We've also included a detailed analysis of six nutrients along with the calorie count for each recipe.

Make It Sweet With Few Extra Calories

The newest alternative sweetener is aspartame, a generic term better known by two common names. Nutrasweet®, the brand name for aspartame, is found in several foods and beverages now on the market. Equal® is the only tabletop sweetener containing aspartame now available.

Made from two naturally occurring but commercially produced amino acids (building blocks of proteins), aspartame is not the same as sugar, which is a carbohydrate. At the same time, it is not an artificial sweetener.

Aspartame tastes like sugar and has the same nutritional value, 4 calories per gram. But because aspartame is 200 times sweeter than granulated sugar, the amount we eat is so small it's almost calorie free. For only 1/10 of a calorie, aspartame provides the same sweetness as 1 teaspoon of sugar (16 calories).

Unlike sugar, aspartame doesn't promote tooth decay. But unfortunately, it does not provide the volume, tenderizing, or browning effect as sugar does in baked products. In fact, aspartame breaks down at prolonged high heat and loses its sweetness in baking, cooking, or home-canning.

Aspartame is also different from sweeteners that contain saccharin, such as Sweet'N Low® and Sugar Twin®. Saccharin, an artificial sweetener, does not break down upon heating like aspartame and may have more application in cooking. Like aspartame, however, saccharin does not provide the bulk and other structural functions of sugar required in baked foods.

When using aspartame sweeteners in recipes, keep these tips in mind.
—Add aspartame sweetener to recipes after cooking.
—Sour, tart, and acid foods tend to require less sweetening with aspartame than with sugar.
—Bitter foods, such as chocolate, usually need more sweetening with aspartame than with sugar.
—Aspartame does not draw out the juice of fruit as sugar does.
—Aspartame sweetener does not provide the bulk and other structural functions needed in baking.

Try our recipes using aspartame. After that, let your imagination be your guide.

CHERRY-APPLE SALAD

1½ cups unsweetened applesauce
1 tablespoon lemon juice
1 (0.3-ounce) package cherry-flavored gelatin sweetened with aspartame
1 (8-ounce) can unsweetened crushed pineapple, undrained
¾ cup lemon-lime carbonated beverage sweetened with aspartame
Lettuce leaves (optional)

Combine applesauce and lemon juice in a saucepan; bring to a boil. Remove from heat; add gelatin, stirring until dissolved. Cool. Add pineapple and carbonated beverage; spoon into six ½-cup molds. Chill until firm. Unmold on lettuce, if desired. Yield: 6 servings (about 56 calories, 1.1 grams protein, 0.1 gram fat, 13.2 grams carbohydrate, 0 milligrams cholesterol, 49.4 milligrams sodium, and 126 milligrams potassium per serving).
Elena Wellinghoff,
Little Rock, Arkansas.

SWEET-AND-SOUR BEANS WITH SPROUTS

1 (9-ounce) package frozen cut green beans
1¼ cups thinly sliced cucumber, halved
¾ cup sliced celery
½ cup fresh bean sprouts
½ cup coarsely chopped green pepper
¼ cup sliced fresh mushrooms
1½ tablespoons chopped onion
1 tablespoon diced pimiento
¼ cup plus 2 tablespoons white wine vinegar
¼ cup plus 2 tablespoons water
3 envelopes tabletop sweetener with aspartame
¼ teaspoon salt
¼ teaspoon seasoned salt
¼ teaspoon garlic powder
¼ teaspoon pepper

Cook green beans according to package directions, omitting salt; drain. Let beans cool.

Combine beans, cucumber, celery, sprouts, green pepper, mushrooms, onion, and pimiento; set aside.

Combine remaining ingredients; mix well. Pour over vegetables; toss gently. Cover and chill 8 hours, stirring occasionally. Yield: 5 servings (about 37 calories, 1.7 grams protein, 0.3 gram fat, 7.8 grams carbohydrate, 0 milligrams cholesterol, 205 milligrams sodium, and 249 milligrams potassium per serving).
Letha Burdette,
Greenville, South Carolina.

SPICED TEA MIX
(pictured on page 29)

1 cup lemon-flavored iced tea mix sweetened with aspartame
3 tablespoons orange-flavored breakfast beverage crystals sweetened with aspartame
1 tablespoon apple pie spice
1 (0.49-ounce) package lemonade-flavored drink mix sweetened with aspartame

Combine all ingredients in a bowl, and mix well. Store mixture in an airtight container. Stir well before using.

For each serving, place 1¼ to 1½ teaspoons mix in a cup. Add ¾ cup hot water, stirring well. Serve hot. Yield: 48 servings (about 3 calories, .04 gram protein, .03 gram fat, 0.4 gram carbohydrate, 0 milligrams cholesterol, 0.3 milligram sodium, and 22.3 milligrams potassium per serving).

ALMOST STRAWBERRY CHEESECAKE
(pictured on page 30)

1 (0.3-ounce) package lemon-flavored gelatin sweetened with aspartame
1 cup boiling water
¾ cup cold water
5 envelopes tabletop sweetener with aspartame
1 cup 1% low-fat cottage cheese
1 envelope whipped topping mix sweetened with aspartame
Graham cracker crust (recipe follows)
Strawberry topping (recipe follows)
Strawberry halves
Mint sprigs

Dissolve gelatin in boiling water; add cold water and sweetener, stirring well. Chill mixture until consistency of unbeaten egg white.

Place cottage cheese in container of an electric blender; process until smooth. Fold into gelatin mixture.

Prepare whipped topping mix according to package directions; fold into gelatin mixture. Spoon mixture into graham cracker crust; chill until slightly set. Spoon strawberry topping on cheesecake, and chill until firm. Garnish with strawberry halves and mint sprigs. Yield: one 8-inch cheesecake or 6 servings (about 235 calories, 8 grams protein, 8 grams fat, 33.3 grams carbohydrate, 1.5 milligrams cholesterol, 358.6 milligrams sodium, and 388.3 milligrams potassium per serving).

Graham Cracker Crust:

⅔ cup graham cracker crumbs
3 tablespoons reduced-calorie margarine, melted

Combine crumbs and margarine; press into bottom of an 8-inch springform pan, and bake at 350° for 8 minutes. Cool. Yield: one 8-inch graham cracker crust.

Strawberry Topping:

½ cup low-sugar strawberry spread
½ cup sliced strawberries, pureed

Combine ingredients, and stir well. Yield: enough for one 8-inch cheesecake. *Nancy Byers, West Monroe, Louisiana.*

Cut Sodium, Not Flavor, In This Menu

If a diet low in salt and sodium is standard at your house, you're bound to welcome this menu. It's scrumptious enough to serve guests, yet low enough in sodium to help you stick to your sodium-restricted diet.

Golden-baked Cornish Hens in Vermouth makes an appetizing entrée. Let Calico Brown Rice, which is high in dietary fiber content, and Asparagus With Basil Sauce be the accompaniments. Tart Sesame-Citrus Green Salad rounds out the meal.

A loaf of Salt-Free Raisin Batter Bread is sure to win the hearts of your homemade bread lovers. And it's as simple to make as one, two, three: Mix all ingredients, let rise, and bake.

For dessert, serve Tropical Snow.

You can enjoy this entire menu for only 282 milligrams sodium per serving. A diet this low in sodium is not necessary for everyone, but it's still a good idea to become more aware of how much sodium you consume. And if you're watching calories, simply leave off the bread or the dessert.

Cornish Hens in Vermouth
Calico Brown Rice
Asparagus with Basil Sauce
Sesame Citrus Green Salad
Salt-free Raisin Batter Bread
Tropical Snow

CORNISH HENS IN VERMOUTH

2 (1¼-pound) Cornish hens
¼ cup chopped green onions
Vegetable cooking spray
¼ cup dry vermouth
2 tablespoons lemon juice
1 tablespoon reduced-sodium soy sauce
Paprika
Freshly ground pepper

Remove giblets from hens, and reserve for other uses. Rinse hens with cold water, and pat dry; split hens lengthwise using an electric knife.

Sprinkle green onions in a 12- x 8- x 2-inch baking dish coated with cooking spray; place split hens over onions. Combine vermouth, lemon juice, and soy sauce; pour over hens. Sprinkle lightly with paprika and pepper; bake at 450° for 15 minutes. Reduce heat to 350°, and bake an additional 25 minutes or until done. Yield: 4 servings (about 254 calories, 28.5 grams protein, 14.5 grams fat, 2.4 grams carbohydrate, 52.5 milligrams cholesterol, 211.3 milligrams sodium, and 284 milligrams potassium per serving). *Linda Mierley,*
Smyrna, Georgia.

CALICO BROWN RICE

3 tablespoons chopped carrots
2 tablespoons chopped celery
2 tablespoons chopped onion
1 tablespoon unsalted margarine, melted
1¼ cups water
1 cup low-sodium chicken broth
½ teaspoon salt-free 14 herb-and-spice blend
⅔ cup uncooked brown rice
1 tablespoon chopped fresh parsley

Sauté carrots, celery, and onion in margarine in a large skillet 1 minute.

Add water, chicken broth, and herb-and-spice seasoning; bring to a boil. Add rice. Cover, reduce heat, and simmer 1 hour or until liquid is absorbed and rice is tender. Stir in chopped parsley. Yield: 4 servings (about 149 calories, 2.7 grams protein, 3.7 grams fat, 26 grams carbohydrate, 0 milligrams cholesterol, 10 milligrams sodium, and 303 milligrams potassium per serving). *Bettye Jones,*
Yulee, Florida.

ASPARAGUS WITH BASIL SAUCE

1 (10-ounce) package frozen asparagus spears
1¼ teaspoons cornstarch
¼ teaspoon dried whole basil
Dash of garlic powder
Dash of white pepper
½ cup unsweetened apple juice
1 tablespoon lemon juice
8 cherry tomato halves

Cook asparagus according to package directions, omitting salt. Drain well, and place on a serving platter.

Combine cornstarch, basil, garlic powder, and white pepper in a small saucepan. Gradually add apple juice and lemon juice; cook, stirring constantly, until mixture is smooth and thickened. Pour sauce over asparagus; garnish with cherry tomato halves. Yield: 4 servings (about 40 calories, 3 grams protein, 0.2 gram fat, 8 grams carbohydrate, 0 milligrams cholesterol, 4 milligrams sodium, and 257 milligrams potassium per serving).

SESAME-CITRUS GREEN SALAD

1 clove garlic, split
2 cups Boston lettuce
2 cups romaine lettuce
6 leaves Belgium endive
1 cup fresh grapefruit sections, drained
½ cup fresh orange sections, drained
1 tablespoon sesame seeds, toasted
2 tablespoons vegetable oil
1 tablespoon tarragon-flavored vinegar

Rub inside of a medium salad bowl with garlic; discard garlic. Combine lettuce and endive in bowl; chill.

Top lettuce mixture with fruit; sprinkle with sesame seeds.

Combine oil and vinegar; pour over salad, tossing gently. Yield: 4 servings (about 115 calories, 2 grams protein, 8 grams fat, 10 grams carbohydrate, 0 milligrams cholesterol, 6.5 milligrams sodium, and 301 milligrams potassium per serving). *Wilmina R. Smith,*
St. Petersburg, Florida.

SALT-FREE RAISIN BATTER BREAD

2½ cups all-purpose flour
1 cup whole wheat flour
½ cup raisins
1 tablespoon sugar
½ teaspoon grated orange rind
1 package dry yeast
1 cup warm water (105° to 115°)
¼ cup vegetable oil
1½ tablespoons unsweetened orange juice
1 egg, beaten
Vegetable cooking spray

Combine flour, raisins, sugar, and orange rind.

Dissolve yeast in warm water in a medium bowl. Stir in oil, orange juice, and egg. Pour into flour mixture, blending well. Place dough in a 9- x 5- x 3-inch loafpan coated with cooking spray. Cover and let rise in a warm place (85°), free from drafts, 1 hour or until doubled in bulk. Bake at 350° for 40 minutes or until golden brown. Yield: 18 (½-inch) slices (about 112 calories, 3.2 grams protein, 1.8 grams fat, 21 grams carbohydrate, 15 milligrams cholesterol, 6 milligrams sodium, and 98 milligrams potassium per slice). *Helen F. Perreault,*
Stuart, Florida.

Tip: To protect the natural flavor of whole wheat flour and ensure a long shelf life, store in a moisture-proof bag in the refrigerator or freezer.

TROPICAL SNOW

1 egg, separated
1 cup unsweetened pineapple juice
⅔ cup skim milk
1 envelope unflavored gelatin
2 tablespoons sugar, divided
¼ teaspoon coconut extract
1 tablespoon flaked coconut, toasted

Beat egg yolk in a heavy saucepan; stir in pineapple juice and milk. Add gelatin and 1 tablespoon sugar; mix well. Let stand 1 minute. Bring to a boil, stirring constantly. Remove from heat; stir in coconut extract. Chill.

Beat egg white (at room temperature) until foamy; add remaining 1 tablespoon sugar. Beat until stiff peaks form; fold into chilled mixture. Pour into 4 individual dessert dishes; chill until firm. Before serving, sprinkle with coconut. Yield: 4 servings (about 105 calories, 5 grams protein, 2 grams fat, 17 grams carbohydrate, 69 milligrams cholesterol, 44 milligrams sodium, and 181 milligrams potassium per serving).

Serve Soup And Salad For Light Luncheon Fare

Soup and salad make an ideal luncheon combination that can be light yet satisfying. Nourishing to the body and spirit, soup is filling. Salads, chock-full of fruits and vegetables, add bulk or fiber to the diet. And if they're raw, the extra chewing that is necessary helps slow down the eating process. This allows more time for the stomach to signal the brain that you are getting full before overeating occurs. Protein items in salads, such as cheese, cottage cheese, eggs, meat, fish, and poultry, contain some fat, which also aids in the feeling of fullness.

Serve any of our soup-and-salad recipes together. Carrot-Leek Soup is a smooth vegetable puree thinned with chicken broth. It's especially nutritious since the carrot cooking liquid is used in the soup, retaining valuable water-soluble nutrients that otherwise would be drained away. A hint of fresh ginger makes this soup go especially well with Salad Niçoise.

For a palette of color, try Curried Chicken Soup with our Layered Salad. The mild-flavored soup complements the tart salad dressing made from plain low-fat yogurt and reduced-calorie buttermilk salad dressing mix.

CURRIED CHICKEN SOUP

2 (14½-ounce) cans chicken broth, divided
1 cup chopped onion
½ cup chopped carrots
½ cup chopped celery
1 teaspoon curry powder
1 bay leaf
⅛ teaspoon dry mustard
Dash of ground turmeric
Dash of ground cloves
½ pound boneless, skinless chicken breasts, cut into ½-inch pieces
¼ cup cold water
1 tablespoon plus 1 teaspoon cornstarch
¾ cup skim milk

Combine 1 can chicken broth, onion, carrots, and celery in a Dutch oven. Bring to a boil, and cook 10 minutes. Add remaining can of broth, curry powder, bay leaf, mustard, turmeric, and cloves; simmer 10 minutes. Remove bay leaf; add chicken, and return to a boil. Cover, reduce heat, and simmer 15 minutes or until chicken is tender.

Combine water and cornstarch; mix until smooth. Add cornstarch mixture and milk to soup; bring to a boil, and cook 1 minute. Yield: 5 cups (about 98 calories, 14.6 grams protein, 1.6 grams fat, 8.7 grams carbohydrate, 27 milligrams cholesterol, 408 milligrams sodium, and 392 milligrams potassium per 1-cup serving). *Maureen E. Murphy, Charlottesville, Virginia.*

Tip: Use baking soda on a damp cloth to shine up your kitchen appliances.

CARROT-LEEK SOUP

3¼ cups canned chicken broth, divided
3 cups sliced carrots
1 cup sliced leeks
¾ to 1 teaspoon grated fresh ginger
Dash of red pepper
Minced fresh parsley (optional)

Combine 1½ cups broth, carrots, leeks, and ginger in a large saucepan; bring to a boil. Cover, reduce heat, and simmer about 20 minutes or until the carrots are tender.

Remove from heat; pour vegetable mixture into container of an electric blender; process until smooth. Return pureed mixture to saucepan; add remaining 1½ cups broth. Cook over medium heat, stirring occasionally, until thoroughly heated. Stir in red pepper.

To serve, ladle soup into serving bowls; garnish with minced parsley, if desired. Yield: 5 cups (about 67 calories, 4.2 grams protein, 1.1 grams fat, 10.3 grams carbohydrate, 0 milligrams cholesterol, 531.8 milligrams sodium, and 388.7 milligrams potassium per 1-cup serving). *Ruby Kirkes, Tuskahoma, Oklahoma.*

COLD MINTED CUCUMBER SOUP

4 cups peeled, seeded, chopped cucumbers
1 teaspoon minced fresh mint
1¼ cups low-fat buttermilk
1 cup plain low-fat yogurt
¼ teaspoon salt
¼ teaspoon white pepper
Cucumber slices (optional)
Mint sprigs (optional)

Combine chopped cucumbers, mint, and buttermilk in container of an electric blender; process until smooth. Stir in yogurt, salt, and pepper; chill.

To serve, ladle soup into soup bowls; garnish with cucumber slices and mint sprigs, if desired. Yield: 5 cups (about 62 calories, 4.8 grams protein, 0.9 gram fat, 9.4 grams carbohydrate, 4 milligrams cholesterol, 219 milligrams sodium, and 354 milligrams potassium per 1-cup serving).

Carrie B. Bartlett, Gallatin, Tennessee.

CHEF'S FRUIT SALAD

1 cup fresh orange sections
1 cup unsweetened pineapple chunks, drained
½ cup unpeeled chopped apple
¼ cup raisins
4 cups chopped lettuce
2 cups 1% low-fat cottage cheese
2 tablespoons commercial low-calorie French dressing
¼ cup coarsely chopped walnuts

Combine orange sections, pineapple chunks, chopped apple, and raisins in a small bowl; set aside.

Layer lettuce and cottage cheese in a large bowl. Drizzle with French dressing. Spoon fruit mixture over dressing; top with walnuts. Yield: 6 servings (about 145 calories, 10.9 grams protein, 4.5 grams fat, 16.9 grams carbohydrate, 3 milligrams cholesterol, 355 milligrams sodium, and 293 milligrams potassium per serving). *Dorothy L. Driggers, Claxton, Georgia.*

LAYERED SALAD

3 cups torn iceberg lettuce
1 (15-ounce) can kidney beans, drained and rinsed
2 cups broccoli flowerets
2 cups sliced carrots
2 cups 1-inch green pepper chunks
3 hard-cooked eggs, sliced
1 (8-ounce) carton plain low-fat yogurt
1 tablespoon plus 2 teaspoons reduced-calorie buttermilk salad dressing mix
Sliced green onions
Cherry tomatoes, halved
Parsley sprigs

Layer lettuce, beans, broccoli, carrots, green pepper, and eggs in a large salad bowl.

Combine yogurt and salad dressing mix; stir well. Spread over top of salad. Garnish with green onions, cherry tomato halves, and parsley sprigs. Yield: 6 servings (about 150 calories, 10.2 grams protein, 3.9 grams fat, 19.6 grams carbohydrate, 139 milligrams cholesterol, 284.9 milligrams sodium, and 469 milligrams potassium per serving).

SALAD NIÇOISE

1½ cups fresh green beans, cut into 1½-inch pieces
2 (6½-ounce) cans 60% less-salt tuna packed in water, drained
½ cup sliced radishes
2 tablespoons sliced green onions
2 tablespoons no-salt-added Dijon mustard
2 tablespoons olive oil
2 tablespoons white wine vinegar
1 medium-size head Bibb lettuce, washed and drained

Arrange green beans in a steaming rack. Place rack over boiling water in a Dutch oven; cover and steam 5 minutes or until beans are crisp-tender. Set beans aside to cool.

Combine beans and remaining ingredients except lettuce; toss well. Chill at least 1 hour. Serve over lettuce leaves. Yield: 4 servings (about 189 calories, 23.1 grams protein, 8.7 grams fat, 5.3 grams carbohydrate, 48.1 milligrams cholesterol, 251.4 milligrams sodium, and 500.5 milligrams potassium per 1-cup serving). *Lynn Lockwood, Glencoe, Missouri.*

Make Seafood Part Of Good Eating Habits

Seafood is a popular item on most restaurant menus, and the choices have broadened in recent years. It's no mystery why people are eating more delicacies from the sea. Nutrition is a key to good health, and seafood is a key to good nutrition.

A low-calorie source of protein, seafood is also low in fat and cholesterol. In a 4-ounce serving of lean fish, you get half the daily protein requirement for adults. Still, some people are timid about preparing seafood at home. The secret is to avoid overcooking the delicate, lean flesh.

Our lighter version of Clam Chowder uses canned minced clams and their juice plus skim milk for the liquid. Hundreds of calories are saved by eliminating high-fat, high-calorie half-and-half.

The cod fillets in Fish Florentine are cooked by steaming—a low-calorie, nutritious method. The fish is arranged on a cheesecloth-lined steaming rack. After it is cooked, the fish is topped with spinach mixed with Parmesan cheese, yogurt, and seasonings.

Basque Fish Chowder uses frozen flounder fillets that cook in minutes. For safety's sake, remember to thaw fish in the refrigerator, allowing 18 to 24 hours per pound. This thick chowder gets its flavor from garlic, tomatoes, white wine, and thyme. And it has only 99 calories per 1-cup serving.

FISH FLORENTINE

1 (10-ounce) package frozen chopped spinach
¼ cup grated Parmesan cheese, divided
¼ cup plain low-fat yogurt
1 egg yolk
1 small onion, finely diced
2 teaspoons lemon juice
⅛ teaspoon salt
⅛ teaspoon ground nutmeg
4 cod fillets (about 1¼ pounds)
Lemon wedges (optional)

Cook spinach according to package directions; drain well. Combine spinach, 2 tablespoons Parmesan cheese, yogurt, egg yolk, onion, lemon juice, salt, and nutmeg; mix well.

Line a steaming rack with cheesecloth; arrange fish on cheesecloth. Place rack in a Dutch oven; cover and steam fish 5 minutes or until fish flakes easily when tested with a fork.

Carefully transfer fish to an ovenproof serving platter. Spoon spinach mixture evenly over each fillet. Sprinkle with remaining 2 tablespoons cheese; broil 3 minutes or until the cheese melts. Garnish with lemon wedges, if desired. Yield: 4 servings (about 187 calories, 32.1 grams protein, 3.7 grams fat, 7.5 grams carbohydrate, 118 milligrams cholesterol, 448 milligrams sodium, and 883 milligrams potassium per serving). *Alinda G. Fahrenkopf, Memphis, Tennessee.*

CLAM CHOWDER

2 cups water
2 medium potatoes, peeled and diced
1 medium onion, chopped
2 carrots, scraped and chopped
1 stalk celery, chopped
½ teaspoon salt
1 (6½-ounce) can minced clams,
  undrained
1 cup skim milk

Combine water, potatoes, onion, carrots, celery, and salt in a large saucepan; bring to a boil. Cover, reduce heat, and simmer 20 minutes or until vegetables are tender.

Add clams and milk; cover and simmer 5 minutes. Yield: 6 cups (about 88 calories, 5.2 grams protein, 0.4 gram fat, 16.3 grams carbohydrate, 10.7 milligrams cholesterol, 409 milligrams sodium, and 391.7 milligrams potassium per 1-cup serving). *Iris Allen, Effingham, South Carolina.*

BASQUE FISH CHOWDER

1 medium onion, chopped
½ cup chopped celery
1 clove garlic, minced
2 teaspoons margarine, melted
2 (16-ounce) cans whole tomatoes,
  undrained and coarsely chopped
½ cup Chablis or other dry white wine
1 tablespoon dried parsley flakes
¼ teaspoon salt
¼ teaspoon pepper
¼ teaspoon dried whole thyme
1 (16-ounce) package frozen flounder
  fillets, thawed and cut into 1-inch
  pieces

Sauté onion, celery, and garlic in margarine in a Dutch oven until tender. Add tomatoes and remaining ingredients except fish. Cover, reduce heat, and simmer 20 minutes.

Add fish; cover and simmer for 5 to 10 minutes or until fish flakes easily when tested with a fork. Yield: 7 cups (about 99 calories, 12.4 grams protein, 2 grams fat, 8.3 grams carbohydrate, 32 milligrams cholesterol, 365 milligrams sodium, and 585 milligrams potassium per 1-cup serving). *Mrs. Jack Proctor, Jeffersontown, Kentucky.*

Classics With Low-Calorie Appeal

Don't give up favorite recipes just because you're dieting. Instead, change them. A simple modification in cooking method or substitution of lower-calorie ingredients can mean the difference of whether or not a special dish will ever legitimately fit into your diet plan. All it takes is a little imagination and practice.

For example, you can put Individual Spinach Quiches on the menu for 384 calories less per serving than the higher-calorie classic quiche Lorraine. The traditional entrée calls for a standard 9-inch pastry shell at 150 calories per pastry serving. But we substituted six 6-inch crêpes for the pastry, trimming calories to 56 per crêpe serving. Hundreds of unnecessary calories from fat were shaved by using skim milk instead of heavy cream, and by substituting spinach for the bacon.

Pasta Primavera is nothing more than a fantasy on most weight-reduction diets. But you can enjoy our counterpart without a twinge of guilt. Almost Pasta Primavera uses strands of spaghetti squash rather than linguine as the base. And instead of the usual butter and olive oil, reduced-calorie margarine and butter flavoring give a rich taste.

Our Lean Lasagna starts with a change in pasta. We substituted wonton wrappers, another type of pasta, for the lasagna noodles and saved 1,350 calories in pasta alone! But we didn't stop there. Ground turkey (sold as a frozen poultry product), which is lower in fat than ground beef, was used, and 1% low-fat cottage cheese replaced regular creamed cottage cheese, eliminating even more calories. Spinach was added to the cheese mixture. We also used a lighter hand with the mozzarella and Parmesan cheese, bringing the total calories down from 837 per serving for the regular version to a mere 237 per serving for its alternative.

In the chart on page 38 you'll find the calorie and nutrient analysis of our lighter recipes compared to a regular version of the same classic recipe. We think you'll be pleased with the tasty results, and the savings in calories is sure to delight you.

LIGHT BEEF STROGANOFF

1 pound lean, boneless round steak
½ cup chopped onion
1 clove garlic, minced
1 teaspoon reduced-calorie margarine,
  melted
2 cups sliced fresh mushrooms
3 tablespoons dry red wine
1 tablespoon cornstarch
¾ cup beef broth
¼ teaspoon pepper
¼ teaspoon dried whole dillweed
1 (8-ounce) carton plain low-fat yogurt
2 tablespoons chopped fresh parsley
2 cups hot cooked noodles (cooked without
  salt or fat)

Partially freeze round steak; slice diagonally across the grain into 3- x ½-inch strips. Set aside.

Sauté onion and garlic in margarine until tender. Add steak and mushrooms; cook, stirring constantly, until steak is browned. Add wine; cover and simmer 10 minutes. Dissolve cornstarch in broth; stir into beef mixture. Cook, stirring constantly, until smooth and thickened. Remove from heat; stir in pepper, dillweed, and yogurt.

Toss parsley with noodles. Serve beef mixture over noodles. Yield: 4 servings (about 291 calories, 30.6 grams protein, 8.1 grams fat, 21 grams carbohydrate, 110 milligrams cholesterol, 267 milligrams sodium, and 758 milligrams potassium per serving).

LEAN LASAGNA

½ (1-pound) package raw ground turkey
1 (15-ounce) can tomato sauce with tomato bits
3 (8-ounce) cans no-salt-added tomato sauce
⅓ cup chopped green pepper
⅓ cup chopped onion
1 clove garlic, crushed
1 bay leaf
1¼ teaspoons Italian seasoning
½ teaspoon dried whole oregano
¼ teaspoon fennel seeds
⅛ teaspoon red pepper
Dash of ground nutmeg
1 (12-ounce) carton 1% low-fat cottage cheese
1 (10-ounce) package frozen chopped spinach, thawed and pressed dry
2 tablespoons grated Parmesan cheese
Vegetable cooking spray
18 wonton wrappers
1 cup (4 ounces) shredded part-skim mozzarella cheese

Cook turkey in skillet over medium heat until brown; drain well on paper towels. Combine turkey, tomato sauce, green pepper, onion, and seasonings in a large saucepan; cover and cook over low heat 30 minutes, stirring occasionally. Remove bay leaf from sauce.

Combine cottage cheese, spinach, and Parmesan cheese; set aside.

Coat a 12- x 8- x 2-inch baking dish with cooking spray. Spoon 1 cup turkey sauce into baking dish. Top with 6 wonton wrappers laid in a single layer; 1 cup spinach mixture, and 1½ cups turkey sauce. Repeat layers twice, ending with sauce mixture.

Bake at 350° for 40 minutes or until thoroughly heated. Remove from oven; top with mozzarella cheese, and bake an additional 5 minutes. Yield: 8 servings (about 237 calories, 18.7 grams protein, 8.4 grams fat, 22.6 grams carbohydrate, 30 milligrams cholesterol, 636 milligrams sodium, and 646 milligrams potassium per serving).

Tip: Revive the flavor of long-dried herbs by soaking them for 10 minutes in lemon juice.

SOUTHERN OVEN-FRIED CHICKEN

1 cup corn flake crumbs
1 teaspoon paprika
½ teaspoon garlic powder
¼ teaspoon ground thyme
¼ teaspoon red pepper
6 chicken breast halves, skinned
¼ cup low-fat cultured buttermilk
Vegetable cooking spray

Combine corn flake crumbs and seasonings in a plastic bag, mixing well. Brush both sides of chicken breasts with buttermilk; place chicken in bag with crumb mixture, shaking to coat. Place chicken on a broiler pan coated with cooking spray; bake, uncovered, at 400° for 45 minutes or until done. Yield: 6 servings (about 188 calories, 27.9 grams protein, 3.1 grams fat, 10.3 grams carbohydrate, 73.3 milligrams cholesterol, 181.5 milligrams sodium, and 261 milligrams potassium per serving).

OVEN-BAKED CHICKEN KIEV

4 ounces Neufchâtel cheese
1 tablespoon freeze-dried chives
8 chicken breast halves, skinned and boned
¾ teaspoon butter-flavored salt
½ teaspoon dried whole thyme
½ teaspoon dried whole marjoram
¼ teaspoon pepper
1 egg
1 tablespoon skim milk
½ cup seasoned dry breadcrumbs
Vegetable cooking spray

Slice cheese into 8 equal pieces, and place on waxed paper; sprinkle with chives. Cover and freeze 30 minutes or until firm.

Place each chicken breast between 2 sheets of waxed paper; flatten chicken to ¼-inch thickness, using a meat mallet or rolling pin.

Combine salt, thyme, marjoram, and pepper; sprinkle over both sides of chicken breasts. Place 1 slice of cheese mixture in center of each chicken breast. Fold long sides of chicken over cheese; tuck ends, and secure with wooden picks.

Combine egg and skim milk in a shallow dish. Dip chicken rolls in egg mixture; roll in breadcrumbs.

Place chicken seam side up in a 2-quart baking dish coated with cooking spray. Bake at 425° for 15 minutes; turn chicken rolls, and bake an additional 25 minutes. Yield: 8 servings (about 214 calories, 29.7 grams protein, 7.4 grams fat, 5.3 grams carbohydrate, 118.5 milligrams cholesterol, 396 milligrams sodium, and 260 milligrams potassium per serving). *Rose Marie Waggener, Knoxville, Tennessee.*

CHICKEN CORDON BLEU

6 chicken breast halves, skinned and boned
6 (¾-ounce) slices lean, cooked ham
6 (¾-ounce) slices Swiss cheese
2 tablespoons chopped fresh parsley
⅓ cup seasoned dry breadcrumbs
¼ teaspoon paprika
⅛ teaspoon salt
¼ teaspoon pepper
⅓ cup skim milk
Vegetable cooking spray
Chopped fresh parsley (optional)

Place each chicken breast between 2 sheets of waxed paper; flatten to ¼-inch thickness, using a meat mallet or rolling pin. Place 1 slice of ham and 1 slice of cheese in the center of each chicken piece. Sprinkle centers with 2 tablespoons parsley. Roll up lengthwise, and secure with wooden picks.

Combine breadcrumbs, paprika, salt, and pepper. Dip each chicken breast in milk; roll in breadcrumb mixture.

Place chicken in a 12- x 8- x 2-inch baking dish coated with cooking spray. Bake, uncovered, at 350° for 30 minutes. Sprinkle with chopped parsley, if desired. Yield: 6 servings (about 277 calories, 38.1 grams protein, 10.3 grams fat, 5.9 grams carbohydrate, 103 milligrams cholesterol, 520 milligrams sodium, and 362 milligrams potassium per serving).

CALORIE AND NUTRIENT ANALYSIS OF CLASSIC RECIPES
(LIGHT VS. REGULAR VERSIONS PER SERVING)

	Calories	Grams Protein	Grams Fat	Grams Carbohydrate	Milligrams Cholesterol	Milligrams Sodium	Milligrams Potassium
Individual Spinach Quiches	**251**	**19.1**	**13**	**15.1**	**211**	**402**	**343**
Classic Quiche Lorraine	635	16.2	56.5	16.6	324	849	188
Almost Pasta Primavera	**77**	**4.5**	**2.5**	**10.3**	**7**	**171**	**331**
Classic Pasta Primavera	574	15.2	33.5	55.4	92.25	1508	708.3
Lean Lasagna	**237**	**18.7**	**8.4**	**22.6**	**30**	**636**	**646**
Classic Lasagna	837	54.2	42.6	57.4	183	1378	788
Southern Oven-Fried Chicken	**188**	**27.9**	**3.1**	**10.3**	**73.3**	**181.5**	**261**
Southern Fried Chicken	383	31.8	22.5	11.3	96.8	873.2	344.1
Light Beef Stroganoff	**291**	**30.6**	**8.1**	**21**	**110**	**267**	**758**
Classic Beef Stroganoff	724.3	32	63.5	6.1	202	811	994
Chicken Cordon Bleu	**277**	**38.1**	**10.3**	**5.9**	**103**	**520**	**362**
Classic Chicken Cordon Bleu	580	70	29.6	5.1	229.2	870	613.7
Oven-Baked Chicken Kiev	**214**	**29.7**	**7.4**	**5.3**	**118.5**	**396**	**260**
Classic Chicken Kiev	354	28.9	22.5	8	138.7	529	268.2

blender; process 10 seconds. Scrape down sides of blender container with a rubber spatula; process 10 seconds or until smooth. Refrigerate batter 1 hour. (This allows flour particles to swell and soften so that the crêpes will be light in texture.)

Coat the bottom of a 6-inch crêpe pan or nonstick skillet with cooking spray; place pan over medium heat until just hot, not smoking.

Pour 2 tablespoons batter into pan. Quickly tilt pan in all directions so batter covers pan in a thin film; cook about 30 seconds.

Lift edge of crêpe to test for doneness. Crêpe is ready for flipping when it can be shaken loose from pan. Flip and cook 30 seconds on the other side.

When crêpe is done, place on a towel to cool. Stack between layers of waxed paper to prevent sticking. Repeat with remaining batter. Yield: six to eight 6-inch crêpes.

INDIVIDUAL SPINACH QUICHES

1 (10-ounce) package frozen chopped spinach
1 cup (4 ounces) shredded Swiss cheese
1 cup (4 ounces) shredded part-skim mozzarella cheese
2 tablespoons all-purpose flour
1⅓ cups skim milk
3 eggs, beaten
¼ cup diced onion
¼ teaspoon salt
⅛ teaspoon pepper
¼ teaspoon dried whole thyme
¼ teaspoon dried whole rosemary, crushed
⅛ teaspoon hot sauce
Vegetable cooking spray
6 (6-inch) Basic Crêpes (recipe follows)

Cook spinach according to package directions, omitting salt. Drain well, and press spinach between paper towels until barely moist. Set aside.

Combine cheese and flour; toss well, and set aside. Combine milk, eggs, onion, salt, pepper, thyme, rosemary, and hot sauce in a mixing bowl, stirring well. Stir in spinach and cheese mixture, mixing well.

Coat six 6-ounce custard cups with cooking spray. Line each cup with a crêpe. Spoon spinach mixture into each crêpe-lined custard cup.

Place cups on a cookie sheet; bake at 325° for 45 to 50 minutes or until set. (Place a piece of foil over quiches after baking 15 minutes to prevent edges from getting too brown.) Let stand 5 minutes before serving. Yield: 6 servings (about 251 calories, 19.1 grams protein, 13 grams fat, 15.1 grams carbohydrate, 211 milligrams cholesterol, 402 milligrams sodium, 343 milligrams potassium per serving).

Basic Crêpes:
1 egg
½ cup skim milk
¼ cup plus 3 tablespoons all-purpose flour
⅛ teaspoon salt
¾ teaspoon vegetable oil
Vegetable cooking spray

Combine all ingredients except cooking spray in container of an electric

ALMOST PASTA PRIMAVERA

1 medium spaghetti squash (about 3½ pounds)
1 cup fresh broccoli flowerets
1 cup sliced small zucchini
1 cup sliced fresh mushrooms
1 cup sliced carrot
1 small garlic clove, crushed
¾ teaspoon reduced-calorie margarine, melted
1 tablespoon skim milk
½ cup part-skim ricotta cheese
1 tablespoon Parmesan cheese
½ teaspoon imitation butter flavoring
¼ teaspoon salt
½ teaspoon Italian seasoning
⅛ teaspoon coarsely ground pepper

Wash squash; cut in half lengthwise, and discard seeds. Place squash, cut side down, in a Dutch oven; add 2 inches water. Bring water to a boil; cover and cook 20 minutes or until squash is tender.

Drain squash, and cool. Using a fork, remove spaghetti-like strands. Measure 3 cups of strands; set aside. Reserve remaining strands for other uses.

Steam vegetables 5 to 7 minutes or until crisp-tender; drain well. Combine squash strands and vegetables, tossing gently. Cover to keep warm; set aside.

Sauté garlic in margarine in a small saucepan; remove from heat. Add milk, cheese, butter flavoring, and seasonings to saucepan. Cook over low heat, stirring constantly, until mixture is hot (do not boil). Spoon cheese mixture over vegetable mixture, tossing gently. Yield: 6 servings (about 77 calories, 4.5 grams protein, 2.5 grams fat, 10.3 grams carbohydrate, 7 milligrams cholesterol, 171 milligrams sodium, and 331 milligrams potassium per serving).

Serve Baked Fruit With Any Meal

If you're watching your weight, you're probably eating lots of salads and vegetables. And for nutritional value and taste, they can't be beat. But if you're tired of vegetables as the side dish, consider warm baked fruit.

Warm Spiced Fruit presented this attractively can even be served as an appetizer.

SPICY BAKED PEACHES

1 (16-ounce) can peach halves in juice, undrained
¼ cup sugar
3 tablespoons reduced-calorie margarine
2 tablespoons lemon juice
6 (3-inch) sticks cinnamon, broken into pieces
12 whole cloves

Drain peaches, reserving ⅔ cup juice. Place peach halves in a 1½-quart baking dish; set aside.

Combine peach juice, sugar, margarine, and lemon juice in a small saucepan. Place over medium heat, stirring until margarine melts. Tie spices in a cheesecloth bag; add to juice mixture, and bring to a boil. Reduce heat, and simmer 15 minutes. Discard spice bag. Pour syrup over peach halves; bake, uncovered, at 350° for 20 minutes. Yield:

4 servings (about 131 calories, 0.4 gram protein, 4 grams fat, 24 grams carbohydrate, 0 milligrams cholesterol, 105 milligrams sodium, and 140 milligrams potassium per serving).

Susan Bradberry,
Texarkana, Arkansas.

WARM SPICED FRUIT

1 (16-ounce) can peach halves in light syrup, drained
1 (16-ounce) can pear halves in light syrup, drained
1 (8-ounce) can unsweetened pineapple slices, drained
1 cup unsweetened apple juice
¼ teaspoon ground cinnamon
¼ teaspoon ground mace
2 tablespoons chopped pecans, toasted

Combine fruit in a 1½-quart baking dish. Pour apple juice over fruit, and sprinkle with spices; stir gently. Bake at 325° for 45 minutes. Spoon into 6 individual compotes; top each with 1 teaspoon toasted pecans. Serve warm. Yield: 6 servings (about 109 calories, 0.6 gram protein, 2 grams fat, 24 grams carbohydrate, 0 milligrams cholesterol, 2.8 milligrams sodium, and 202.3 milligrams potassium per serving).

Elizabeth Griffin,
Louisville, Kentucky.

Tip: Mix liquid from canned fruit in a jar as you acquire it; use it in a gelatin dessert or as a punch drink.

BAKED APPLES

4 medium-size cooking apples (about 1
  pound)
2 teaspoons sugar
1 teaspoon ground cinnamon
2 tablespoons plus 2 teaspoons nutlike
  cereal nuggets
¼ cup vanilla low-fat yogurt

Core apples three-fourths through;
peel top third of each apple. Place
apples in an 8-inch square baking dish.
Combine sugar and cinnamon; sprinkle
cavity of each apple with ¾ teaspoon
cinnamon mixture.

Cover and bake at 350° for 45 minutes. Remove from oven; spoon 2 teaspoons cereal in each apple. Top each
with 1 tablespoon of yogurt. Serve
warm. Yield: 4 servings (about 117 calories, 1.5 grams protein, 0.8 gram fat,
28.5 grams carbohydrate, 1 milligram
cholesterol, 49 milligrams sodium, and
170 milligrams potassium per serving).
Mrs. Fred S. Clark,
Savannah, Georgia.

Trim Calories With These Salad Dressings

It's easy to see that one of the best
ways to lose weight is to cut down on
the amount of fat we eat since each
gram of fat is 9 calories. Traditionally,
salad dressings have a high-fat, high-calorie content. Fat—in the form of oil,
mayonnaise, and sour cream—adds
body and thickness to salad dressings.

But our light recipes explore alternatives. And you can enjoy any of them
for fewer than 22 calories per tablespoon. That's quite a savings from regular salad dressings, which scale in at 57
to 99 calories for the same amount.

Stay Trim Dressing has a fresh taste
that goes well with leaf lettuce and spinach greens. It gets its flavor from dry
mustard, horseradish, garlic, and Worcestershire sauce.

Sweet-Hot Yogurt Dressing may surprise you. Honey adds the slightly sweet
touch, but it's still only 16 calories per
tablespoon. Plain low-fat yogurt makes
it just the right consistency.

If an Italian-style dressing is your favorite, try our Herb Salad Dressing. It's
seasoned with oregano, thyme, and
parsley, but it gets its thickness from
unsweetened applesauce and powdered
fruit pectin. This dressing is only 18 calories per tablespoon.

STAY TRIM DRESSING

1 tablespoon cornstarch
½ teaspoon dry mustard
1 cup cold water
2 tablespoons vinegar
¼ cup catsup
½ teaspoon paprika
½ teaspoon Worcestershire sauce
½ teaspoon prepared horseradish
⅛ teaspoon salt
1 small clove garlic, crushed

Combine cornstarch and mustard in a
small saucepan; gradually stir in water.
Place mixture over medium heat; cook,
stirring constantly, until smooth and
thickened. Cool.

Add remaining ingredients; stir well.
Pour dressing into an airtight container,
and chill. Shake well before using.
Yield: 1⅓ cups (about 6 calories, 0.1
gram protein, 0 grams fat, 1.4 grams
carbohydrate, 0 milligrams cholesterol,
49 milligrams sodium, and 15 milligrams
potassium per tablespoon).
Pam Barber,
Nashville, Georgia.

SWEET-HOT YOGURT DRESSING

1 (8-ounce) carton plain low-fat yogurt
2 tablespoons honey
1 tablespoon Chinese-style hot mustard
1 tablespoon dried parsley flakes

Combine all of the ingredients, and
mix well.

Pour dressing into an airtight container, and chill. Yield: 1 cup plus 2
tablespoons (about 16 calories, 0.7 gram

protein, 0.2 gram fat, 3 grams carbohydrate, 1 milligram cholesterol, 20 milligrams sodium, and 33 milligrams
potassium per tablespoon).
Traci Myers,
Boca Raton, Florida.

HERB SALAD DRESSING

½ cup water
⅓ cup vinegar
1 tablespoon powdered fruit pectin
½ cup unsweetened applesauce
3 tablespoons vegetable oil
1 clove garlic, minced
1 tablespoon dried parsley flakes
½ teaspoon salt
½ teaspoon onion powder
½ teaspoon dry mustard
½ teaspoon dried whole oregano
½ teaspoon dried whole thyme

Combine water, vinegar, and fruit
pectin in a jar. Cover tightly, and shake
vigorously.

Add remaining ingredients to the jar;
cover tightly, and shake vigorously. Refrigerate. Yield: 1¾ cups dressing
(about 18 calories, .04 gram protein, 1.5
grams fat, 2 grams carbohydrate, 0 milligrams cholesterol, 43 milligrams sodium, and 6 milligrams potassium per
tablespoon). *Bernadine Olenick,*
Weirton, West Virginia.

SALAD DRESSING FOR FRUIT

¼ cup unsweetened pineapple juice
2 tablespoons frozen orange juice
  concentrate, thawed and undiluted
2 tablespoons lemon juice
2 tablespoons honey
1 egg, beaten
3 tablespoons instant nonfat dry milk
  powder
2 tablespoons plus 1 teaspoon ice water

Combine pineapple juice, undiluted
orange juice, lemon juice, honey, and
egg in a small heavy saucepan. Cook
over medium-low heat, stirring constantly, until mixture thickens and coats
a spoon. Set mixture aside to cool.

Pour dry milk powder into a small mixing bowl; place bowl and beaters in freezer to chill. Pour ice water over dry milk powder; beat at high speed of an electric mixer until stiff peaks form. Fold egg mixture into whipped milk mixture.

Pour dressing into an airtight container, and chill. Yield: 1¼ cups (about 21 calories, 0.8 gram protein, 0.3 gram fat, 3.9 grams carbohydrate, 14 milligrams cholesterol, 10 milligrams sodium, and 49 milligrams potassium per tablespoon).

Note: If refrigerated overnight, the salad dressing will separate. Stir well before serving.
Louise Ellis,
Talbott, Tennessee.

Aromatic Dillweed Lends Flavor

Nutrition-conscious cooks know the value of using herbs and spices to season food. Whereas butter, margarine, and vegetable oil have a high-fat, high-calorie content, and flavored salts have a high-sodium content, herbs and spices are low in both calories and sodium. And they make a world of difference in how foods taste.

It's apparent from the wide variety of herbs and spices now available on your grocer's shelves that Southerners are using these seasonings more today. To get the best of what herbs have to offer, consider growing your own. There's nothing that will compare to the wonderful look, aroma, and taste of fresh herbs grown right in your own garden. And best of all, it's easy to do. (See "Growing Dill at Home.")

Our Winter Vegetable Salad makes use of fresh dillweed with cauliflower and broccoli. A dressing made of low-fat buttermilk, part-skim ricotta cheese, reduced-calorie mayonnaise, and dry mustard adds a special dimension; cherry tomato halves lend color.

DILLED CHICKEN PAPRIKA

Vegetable cooking spray
1 tablespoon vegetable oil
2 whole chicken breasts (about 14½ ounces), skinned, boned, and cut into 1-inch pieces
1 cup sliced fresh mushrooms
½ cup chopped onion
½ cup chicken broth
2 teaspoons paprika
2 teaspoons chopped fresh dillweed
¼ teaspoon pepper
1 tablespoon cornstarch
2 tablespoons cold water
1 (8-ounce) carton plain low-fat yogurt
2 cups hot cooked noodles (cooked without salt or fat)
1 tablespoon chopped fresh parsley (optional)

Coat a large heavy skillet with cooking spray; add 1 tablespoon oil. Place skillet over medium heat until hot; add chicken. Heat 3 to 5 minutes, stirring occasionally, until chicken is lightly browned. Remove chicken from skillet; reserve drippings.

Add mushrooms and onion; sauté until vegetables are tender. Return chicken to skillet.

Add broth, paprika, dillweed, and pepper; cover and simmer 15 minutes or until chicken is tender.

Combine cornstarch and water; stir until smooth. Add to chicken, and cook over medium heat, stirring constantly, until mixture comes to a boil. Cook mixture 1 minute. Remove from heat, and stir in yogurt.

Serve immediately over noodles. Garnish with parsley, if desired. Yield: 4 servings (about 328 calories, 38.1 grams protein, 9.4 grams fat, 19.6 grams carbohydrate, 91 milligrams cholesterol, 218 milligrams sodium, and 563.2 milligrams potassium per serving).
Monnie Sandra Richmond,
Friendly, West Virginia.

Growing Dill At Home

Dill is an annual that grows 2 to 3 feet tall with leaves branching from a single hollow stem. Plant dill in full sun and well-drained soil in a spot where the stalks will be protected from strong winds. Sow seeds 2 to 4 weeks before the last frost. Make successive sowings every 2 weeks until seeds stop germinating in summer. For a fall crop, sow again about 2 months before frost, when the nights have cooled.

You will need to water dill when the weather is dry. Harvest it any time from seedling stage until plants bloom. Foliage is most aromatic just as the flowers open.

Material taken from *Growing Vegetables & Herbs,* copyright 1984, *Oxmoor House, Inc.* Reprinted by permission.

MUSHROOM-DILL-TOPPED POTATOES

4 small baking potatoes (about 1⅓ pounds)
1 cup sliced fresh mushrooms
¼ cup diced onion
½ teaspoon vegetable oil
½ cup part-skim ricotta cheese
2 teaspoons chopped fresh dillweed
⅛ teaspoon salt
⅛ teaspoon pepper

Scrub potatoes; bake at 400° for 50 to 60 minutes or until done.

Sauté mushrooms and onion in oil until tender; set aside. Combine cheese, dillweed, and seasonings, mixing well.

Split tops of potatoes lengthwise, and fluff pulp with a fork. Spoon mushroom mixture over potatoes, and top with a dollop of cheese mixture. Yield: 4 servings (about 221 calories, 7.5 grams protein, 3.3 grams fat, 41.5 grams carbohydrate, 9.5 milligrams cholesterol, 125 milligrams sodium, and 759.5 milligrams potassium per serving).
Annette Allerhand,
Miami Beach, Florida.

RICE-AND-VEGETABLE SALAD
(pictured on page 29)

2 tablespoons red wine vinegar
2¼ teaspoons vegetable oil
2¼ teaspoons water
¼ teaspoon salt
⅛ teaspoon pepper
⅓ cup uncooked regular rice
¾ cup diced raw, unpeeled zucchini
¼ cup sliced radishes
3 tablespoons plain low-fat yogurt
1 tablespoon thinly sliced green onions
1½ teaspoons chopped fresh dillweed

Combine vinegar, oil, water, salt, and pepper in a small bowl; set aside.

Cook rice according to package directions, omitting salt and fat. Pour vinegar mixture over hot rice; toss gently to coat. Let cool.

Add zucchini, radishes, yogurt, green onions, and dillweed to rice mixture. Toss gently; cover and refrigerate 8 hours. Yield: 6 servings (about 61 calories, 1.3 grams protein, 1.9 grams fat, 9.5 grams carbohydrate, 0 milligrams cholesterol, 105 milligrams sodium, and 86.7 milligrams potassium per serving).
Mrs. H. G. Drawdy,
Spindale, North Carolina.

WINTER VEGETABLE SALAD

⅓ cup low-fat cultured buttermilk
¼ cup part-skim ricotta cheese
2 tablespoons reduced-calorie mayonnaise
¼ teaspoon dry mustard
⅛ teaspoon salt
2 tablespoons diced onion
1 tablespoon chopped fresh parsley
1½ teaspoons chopped fresh dillweed
⅛ teaspoon pepper
2¼ cups cauliflower flowerets
2¼ cups broccoli flowerets
¼ cup sliced water chestnuts
6 Boston lettuce leaves
5 cherry tomatoes, halved
Dillweed sprigs (optional)

Combine buttermilk and cheese in container of an electric blender; process 1 minute or until smooth. Add mayonnaise, mustard, and salt; process 15 seconds or until combined. Stir in onion, parsley, dillweed, and pepper; chill 30 minutes.

Combine cauliflower, broccoli, and water chestnuts in a bowl; top with cheese mixture, tossing gently. Spoon mixture into a lettuce-lined bowl; garnish with cherry tomatoes. Add dillweed sprigs, if desired. Yield: 6 servings (about 60 calories, 3.7 grams protein, 2.4 grams fat, 7.2 grams carbohydrate, 5 milligrams cholesterol, 132 milligrams sodium, and 343 milligrams potassium per serving).
Ruby Kirkes,
Tuskahoma, Oklahoma.

International Chicken Favorites

Food is different around the world, but one thing almost every country has in common is a love of chicken. Americans ate about 56 pounds per person in 1985, and there's a good reason for it. The delicate flavor of low-fat, low-calorie chicken makes it compatible with a variety of seasonings, both regionally and internationally inspired. So put an end to mealtime monotony and taste the cuisine of faraway places without ever leaving home.

CHICKEN CACCIATORE

1 small onion, chopped
¼ cup water
1 cup canned whole tomatoes, undrained and chopped
½ cup tomato puree
1 teaspoon dried whole oregano
½ teaspoon garlic powder
⅛ teaspoon pepper
4 chicken breast halves (about 2 pounds), skinned
2 cups hot cooked spaghetti (cooked without salt or fat)

Combine onion and water in a 10-inch skillet; cover and cook over medium heat 3 to 4 minutes or until onion is tender. Stir in tomatoes, tomato puree, and seasonings. Cover, reduce heat, and simmer 10 minutes.

Add chicken to skillet; spoon tomato mixture over chicken. Cover and simmer 30 minutes; uncover and simmer an additional 15 minutes. Serve over spaghetti. Yield: 4 servings (about 255 calories, 30.6 grams protein, 3.6 grams fat, 24.6 grams carbohydrate, 73 milligrams cholesterol, 288 milligrams sodium, and 579 milligrams potassium per serving).
Betty Manente,
Lighthouse Point, Florida.

ORIENTAL CHICKEN WITH PINEAPPLE

4 chicken breast halves (about 2 pounds), skinned and boned
2 tablespoons margarine
½ cup sliced celery
1 medium onion, sliced
1 medium-size green pepper, cut into ½-inch pieces
1 (8-ounce) can unsweetened pineapple tidbits, undrained
1 (8-ounce) can no-salt-added tomato sauce
1 tablespoon cornstarch
¼ cup soy sauce
2 tablespoons sherry
¼ teaspoon ground ginger
3 cups hot cooked rice (cooked without salt or fat)

Cut chicken into bite-size pieces. Allow wok to heat at medium-high (325°) for 2 minutes. Melt margarine in wok; add chicken, and stir-fry 4 to 5 minutes or until lightly browned. Stir in

vegetables; cover, reduce heat, and simmer 5 minutes or until vegetables are crisp-tender.

Drain pineapple tidbits, reserving ¼ cup liquid. Set pineapple aside. Combine the reserved pineapple juice and remaining ingredients except rice; pour over chicken mixture. Cook until mixture is slightly thickened.

Combine rice and pineapple. Serve chicken mixture over pineapple-rice mixture. Yield: 6 servings (about 311 calories, 21.9 grams protein, 6.1 grams fat, 243.8 grams carbohydrate, 49 milligrams cholesterol, 785.5 milligrams sodium, and 376.7 milligrams potassium per serving).
Clarine Spetzler,
Salem, Virginia.

CURRIED CHICKEN

¼ cup all-purpose flour
1½ teaspoons curry powder
1½ teaspoons onion powder
½ teaspoon turmeric
¼ teaspoon ground ginger
¼ teaspoon dry mustard
Pinch of ground red pepper
1 (3-pound) broiler-fryer, cut up and skinned
¼ cup vegetable oil
½ cup Chablis or other dry white wine
½ cup water

Combine flour and seasonings; dredge chicken lightly in flour mixture. Reserve remaining flour mixture.

Heat oil in a large skillet; add chicken, and cook over medium heat until lightly browned, turning once. Remove chicken, and set aside.

Add reserved flour mixture to pan drippings, and cook 1 minute, stirring constantly. Gradually add wine and water; cook over medium heat, stirring constantly, until mixture is thickened and bubbly.

Add chicken; cover and cook 30 minutes or until tender. Yield: 6 servings (about 192 calories, 16.1 grams protein, 11.5 grams fat, 5.4 grams carbohydrate, 51 milligrams cholesterol, 57 milligrams sodium, and 207 milligrams potassium per serving).
Beverly George,
Metairie, Louisiana.

Fresh Ideas With High-Fiber Cereals

Eating whole grains and whole grain cereals is a way of getting more fiber in your diet. The outer layer of whole grains, or bran layer, is an excellent source of this important dietary component. We feature wheat bran cereal and oats, two popular choices, in these high-fiber, reduced-calorie recipes. Sample our dishes, and we think you'll agree that these two cereals are too tasty and versatile to eat only at breakfast.

Tease your taste buds with a loaf of Caraway-Raisin Oat Bread for dinner. We've teamed caraway seeds, raisins, and a small amount of honey for a terrific flavor. A combination of oats, whole wheat flour, and bread flour gives the bread its perfect shape and texture. Bread flour is higher in gluten content (the substance that makes dough smooth and elastic) than the whole wheat flour or oats and helps give the loaf a better structure.

Bake up a batch of piping-hot Spicy Apple-Oat Muffins for any meal. We used unsweetened apple juice instead of a lot of sugar.

For a new idea with wheat bran cereal, try Vegetable-Filled Bran Crepes. They're an elegant way to get more fiber in your low-calorie diet. They're filled with a mixture of vegetables and wheat bran cereal. A tasty sauce tops the vegetables and crepes.

CURRIED MEAT LOAF

1 pound ground round
⅔ cup peeled, diced cooking apple
⅓ cup diced onion
⅓ cup quick-cooking oats, uncooked
1 tablespoon prepared brown mustard
1 tablespoon prepared horseradish
½ teaspoon curry powder
¼ teaspoon garlic powder
½ teaspoon salt
¼ teaspoon pepper
¼ cup skim milk
1 egg, beaten
Chopped fresh parsley (optional)

Combine all ingredients except parsley; mix well. Place in an 8½- x 4½- x 3-inch loafpan; bake at 350° for 1 hour and 10 minutes.

Remove meat loaf from pan immediately. Garnish with chopped parsley, if desired. Yield: 6 servings (about 183 calories, 22.6 grams protein, 9.1 grams fat, 6.5 grams carbohydrate, 95 milligrams cholesterol, 298 milligrams sodium, and 354 milligrams potassium per serving).
Mrs. John R. Hendricks,
Martinsville, Virginia.

MEAL-IN-ONE SALAD

½ cup uncooked regular rice
½ teaspoon chicken-flavored bouillon granules
¼ teaspoon dried whole basil
¾ cup shreds of wheat bran cereal
¼ cup thinly sliced celery
¼ cup sliced green onions
¼ cup chopped green pepper
½ cup unsweetened apple juice
¼ cup cider vinegar
5 leaf lettuce leaves
8 ounces boned, skinned, cooked turkey breast, thinly sliced and cut into ½-inch strips
1 medium-size yellow grapefruit, peeled, sliced, and halved
2 medium-size oranges, peeled and sliced
¼ cup seedless red grapes, halved

Cook rice according to package directions, omitting salt, and adding bouillon granules and basil. Let cool. Add cereal, celery, green onions, and green pepper to rice, tossing well. Chill.

Combine apple juice and vinegar; add half of juice mixture to rice mixture just before serving, tossing well.

Line a serving platter with lettuce leaves; spoon rice mixture into center of platter. Arrange turkey strips around rice mixture. Place grapefruit and orange slices around turkey. Garnish with grapes around rice mixture. Pour remaining dressing over turkey and fruit. Yield: 6 servings (about 205 calories, 16 grams protein, 2 grams fat, 34.4 grams carbohydrate, 6.8 milligrams cholesterol, 226 milligrams sodium, and 557 milligrams potassium per serving).

RATATOUILLE-BRAN STUFFED EGGPLANT

3 small eggplant (about 2 pounds)
3 cups thinly sliced zucchini
Vegetable cooking spray
⅔ cup chopped green pepper
⅓ cup chopped onion
1 teaspoon minced garlic
1 (8¼-ounce) can tomatoes, drained and chopped
1 (8-ounce) can tomato sauce with onion bits
½ cup shreds of wheat bran cereal
⅓ cup dry white wine
1 tablespoon chopped fresh parsley
¾ teaspoon dried whole basil
¼ teaspoon dried whole thyme
¼ teaspoon salt
¼ teaspoon pepper
¼ cup plus 2 tablespoons (1½ ounces) shredded mozzarella cheese

Wash eggplant, and cut in half lengthwise. Remove pulp, leaving a ¼-inch shell; set shells aside. Chop pulp, and measure out 4 cups.

Sauté eggplant pulp and zucchini in a large skillet coated with cooking spray over medium heat 5 minutes, stirring occasionally. Add green pepper, onion, and garlic; cook 5 minutes, stirring occasionally. Add remaining ingredients except cheese. Cover, reduce heat, and simmer 5 minutes.

Place eggplant shells in a 13- x 9- x 2-inch baking dish. Spoon hot mixture into shells. Add water to ½-inch depth in dish. Bake, uncovered, at 350° for 15 minutes. Sprinkle with cheese, and bake an additional 5 minutes. Yield: 6 servings (about 91 calories, 4.7 grams protein, 2 grams fat, 18 grams carbohydrate, 5.5 milligrams cholesterol, 469 milligrams sodium, and 486 milligrams potassium per serving).

Tip: When selecting onions, consider all of the flavor possibilities. The large Spanish or Bermuda onion and the small white onion are usually mild in flavor, while Globe types, such as red, brown, and small yellow onions, are stronger flavored.

VEGETABLE-FILLED BRAN CRÊPES

1 cup chicken broth
3 cups broccoli flowerets
1 cup thinly sliced carrots
⅔ cup sliced fresh mushrooms
2 tablespoons thinly sliced green onions
2 tablespoons shreds of wheat bran cereal
Bran Crêpes
Zippy Sauce
Thinly sliced green onions (optional)

Heat chicken broth in a heavy skillet; add broccoli and carrots, and cook, uncovered, 5 minutes. Add sliced mushrooms and 2 tablespoons sliced green onions; cook 2 minutes or until vegetables are crisp-tender and liquid is evaporated. Stir in cereal.

Spoon about ⅔ cup of vegetable mixture in center of each crêpe. Spoon 1 tablespoon plus 1 teaspoon Zippy Sauce over vegetables; roll up. Place on serving dish; spoon 1 tablespoon plus 1 teaspoon sauce on top. Garnish with green onions, if desired. Yield: 6 servings (about 118 calories, 6.9 grams protein, 3.2 grams fat, 17.1 grams carbohydrate, 48.7 milligrams cholesterol, 375.5 milligrams sodium, and 424 milligrams potassium per serving).

Bran Crêpes:

1 egg
½ cup skim milk
⅓ cup all-purpose flour
2 tablespoons shreds of wheat bran cereal
1 teaspoon sugar
Dash of salt
¾ teaspoon vegetable oil
Vegetable cooking spray

Combine all ingredients except cooking spray in container of an electric blender; process 30 seconds. Scrape down sides of blender container with rubber spatula; process an additional 30 seconds or until smooth. Refrigerate the batter for 1 hour. (This allows flour particles to swell and soften so crêpes are light in texture.)

Coat the bottom of a 6-inch crêpe pan or nonstick skillet with cooking spray; place pan over medium heat until just hot, not smoking.

Pour about 2 tablespoons batter into pan. Quickly tilt pan in all directions so batter covers the pan in a thin film; cook crêpe about 1 minute.

Lift edge of crêpe to test for doneness. Crêpe is ready for flipping when it can be shaken loose from pan. Flip the crêpe, and cook about 30 seconds. (This side is rarely more than spotty brown, and it is the side on which the filling is placed.)

When crêpe is done, place on a towel to cool. Stack crêpes between layers of waxed paper to prevent sticking. Repeat procedure until all batter is used, stirring batter occasionally. Yield: six 6-inch crêpes.

Zippy Sauce:

1 (8-ounce) carton plain low-fat yogurt
1 tablespoon Dijon mustard
½ teaspoon prepared horseradish

Combine all ingredients; mix well. Yield: 1 cup.

CARAWAY-RAISIN OAT BREAD

½ cup regular oats, uncooked
1 tablespoon margarine
1 cup boiling water
1 package dry yeast
2 tablespoons plus 2 teaspoons warm water (105° to 115°)
¼ cup honey
1 teaspoon salt
⅓ cup raisins
1 teaspoon caraway seeds
1½ cups bread flour
¾ cup whole wheat flour
Vegetable cooking spray

Combine oats, margarine, and 1 cup boiling water in a large bowl; stir to melt margarine. Set aside until mixture is lukewarm.

Dissolve yeast in 2 tablespoons plus 2 teaspoons warm water in a small bowl; let stand 5 minutes.

Add honey, salt, and yeast mixture to lukewarm oat mixture, mixing well. Stir in raisins and caraway seeds. Stir in bread flour and whole wheat flour.

Turn dough out onto a heavily floured surface, and knead until smooth and elastic (5 to 8 minutes), adding extra flour as needed to keep from sticking. Place in a bowl coated with

cooking spray, turning to coat top. Cover and let rise in a warm place (85°), free from drafts, 1 hour or until doubled in bulk.

Punch dough down; turn out onto a floured surface, and knead 4 or 5 times. Shape into a loaf, and place in an 8½- x 4½- x 3-inch loafpan coated with cooking spray. Cover and let rise in a warm place (85°), free from drafts, about 30 minutes or until doubled in bulk.

Bake at 350° for 30 to 35 minutes or until loaf sounds hollow when tapped. Cool on wire racks. Yield: 16 (½-inch) slices (about 101 calories, 2.7 grams protein, 1.2 grams fat, 20.7 grams carbohydrate, 0 milligrams cholesterol, 157 milligrams sodium, and 76.3 milligrams potassium per slice).

SPICY APPLE-OAT MUFFINS

1 cup all-purpose flour
1 cup quick-cooking oats, uncooked
2 tablespoons sugar
2 teaspoons baking powder
½ teaspoon salt
¼ teaspoon apple pie spice
¾ teaspoon grated lemon rind
1 egg, beaten
½ cup unsweetened apple juice
¼ cup skim milk
3 tablespoons vegetable oil
Vegetable cooking spray

Combine dry ingredients and lemon rind; make a well in center of mixture.

Combine egg, apple juice, milk, and oil; add to dry ingredients, stirring just until moistened. Spoon into muffin pans coated with cooking spray, filling three-fourths full. Bake at 425° for 15 minutes. Yield: 10 muffins (about 136 calories, 3.2 grams protein, 5.4 grams fat, 18.8 grams carbohydrate, 28 milligrams cholesterol, 205 milligrams sodium, and 72 milligrams potassium per muffin).

Chicken Fits Any Meal

Today's active life-styles and demanding schedules leave little time for cooking a nutritious, low-calorie lunch. But you don't have to abandon your diet and give in to the temptation of fast-food calories to save time and energy.

Our Marinated Chicken Sandwiches make it easy to fix a hurry-up lunch for two in just 10 minutes. The convenience of this entrée comes from marinating boneless chicken breast halves in reduced-calorie Italian salad dressing for 6 to 8 hours. Then you cook them quickly in the microwave oven.

Chicken is an ideal food for your diet and for the microwave oven. High in protein and low in fat (when the skin is removed), it is lower in calories than many other popular meats. Two-thirds of the fat in chicken is unsaturated, making it another plus.

And because cooking in the microwave oven helps keep moisture in foods, you can cook this lean meat without added fat and still count on it being juicy and tender.

Just be sure that you place the larger, meatier parts of the chicken breasts near the outside of the dish, don't overcook, and remember that standing time is important since the chicken will continue to cook for a while after the microwave oven is turned off.

MARINATED CHICKEN SANDWICHES

2 chicken breast halves (about 1 pound), skinned and boned
⅓ cup Italian reduced-calorie salad dressing
Vegetable cooking spray
2 whole wheat hamburger buns, split
2 teaspoons reduced-calorie mayonnaise
2 teaspoons prepared mustard
Leaf lettuce

Place chicken in a shallow dish. Pour salad dressing over chicken; cover and marinate 6 to 8 hours in refrigerator.

Remove chicken from marinade. Place a browning grill or skillet in microwave oven; preheat at HIGH for 4 to 5 minutes.

Coat grill with cooking spray; place chicken on grill. Microwave at HIGH 2 minutes. Turn chicken over, and give dish a half-turn; then microwave at HIGH for 2½ to 3 minutes or until chicken is lightly browned and done.

Spread each bun half with ½ teaspoon mayonnaise and ½ teaspoon mustard. Place 1 lettuce leaf on each of 2 bun halves; top with chicken and remaining bun halves. Yield: 2 servings (about 329 calories, 31.9 grams protein, 8.4 grams fat, 30.4 grams carbohydrate, 92 milligrams cholesterol, 597 milligrams sodium, and 386 milligrams potassium per serving).

Walk Your Way To Better Health

Southerners these days are changing recent patterns. Folks no longer spend a lazy weekend in front of the television. Instead, they're out walking, swimming, biking, hiking, playing tennis or golf—and for good reasons. Exercise strengthens the heart and other muscles, while it makes you feel better and helps you lose weight.

Some people cannot stand the constant pounding on their joints that jogging may cause. Others may not have an indoor swimming pool near their home for year-round exercise. And biking is not always practical for people who live near busy streets or highways or for those who don't have access to stationary bikes.

But consider this: An hour of brisk walking burns off about 330 calories (for a 150-pound person). Vigorous daily exercise in combination with a lower calorie diet can help you lose 1 to 2 pounds of fat a week. You also strengthen muscles and increase your work endurance level.

One of the most important benefits of a walking program is the increased strength and efficiency of your heart. It becomes stronger and is able to pump more blood out to the body with each beat; therefore, it beats fewer times. This is why athletes may have resting heart rates of 40 to 60 beats per minute. In addition, blood pressure may be lowered during exercise and possibly at rest. This is especially true if you cut back on the amount of salt you eat. Physically active people tend to have fewer cases of osteoporosis (a crippling bone disease) as exercise may help reduce the loss of calcium, especially in post-menopausal women.

Exercise and diet go hand in hand in the battle against excess pounds. Weight loss depends on a deficit of calories in the diet. In other words, you lose weight when you burn off more calories than you take in. And exercise increases the number of calories burned in a day. During walking, the body's need for energy is raised, causing it to burn more calories. This higher energy need lasts even longer than the actual exercise period. For several hours after vigorous exercise, your metabolism is raised above normal, and you burn more calories than you do at rest.

Walking is easy for most people, and it's inexpensive. All you need are comfortable, loose-fitting clothes and a good pair of walking or running shoes. Walking can be done in your neighborhood or in a local park or indoor mall. It can be done any time of day, so it's easy to fit into your schedule. It's a good way to be with old friends and meet new ones. Many communities have exercise or walking groups for young people on up to senior citizens.

How do you get started? First, if you have any medical problems, are overweight, or are over 35 years old, see your physician for a checkup and a recommendation about a walking program. Start slowly with a progressive program that will be beneficial to your heart and not harmful to your body. Many muscle pulls and strains can be avoided by proper stretching and starting out slowly. You may be a little sore

at first, but this is normal. The best way to work out this soreness is to repeat the same exercise at a slower pace and for a shorter duration. If you think you're injured, check with a doctor.

Warm up properly. This includes slow walking and stretching exercises for about 10 minutes—even longer when the weather is cold.

Your program should consist of about 30 minutes of actual walking time. Walk at a brisk pace that is somewhat hard for you. Many people have the misconception that they should be exhausted at the end of a workout, but this is not true. All you're doing is needlessly tiring yourself. If you find that you can't walk for 30 minutes at a brisk pace, alternate slow walking with brisk walking and slowly build up until you can walk briskly for the full half hour.

To gain the most benefits, plan to walk 3 to 4 times per week—preferably every other day. As you progress, you may be able to walk for longer periods of time or more often. Be sure to check with your doctor when you feel you're ready for more.

Remember to cool down carefully after each workout. Walk slowly for several minutes; then stretch again. People who don't cool down long enough after exercising may cause unnecessary stress on the heart. Walk slowly until your breathing and heart rates return to near normal.

Walking is fun and good for your heart and body. So why not get back to the old Southern tradition of an after-dinner walk with friends and family? You'll also have time for another tradition—a leisurely visit.

These Cookies Are For Dieters

For dieters who don't want to give up chocolate chip cookies, the solution is Light Chocolate Chip Cookies. These

tasty treats have 21% fewer calories, 63% less fat, 97% less cholesterol, and 20% less sodium per cookie than regular chocolate chip cookies made from package directions. Besides good flavor, there's over twice as much protein and potassium and over five times more fiber in this version.

LIGHT CHOCOLATE CHIP COOKIES

1 tablespoon plus 2 teaspoons butter-flavored shortening
3 tablespoons light corn syrup
3 tablespoons plus 1 teaspoon brown sugar
½ teaspoon vanilla extract
2 egg whites
2 tablespoons water
⅔ cup all-purpose flour
½ cup instant nonfat dry milk powder
½ teaspoon baking soda
¼ teaspoon salt
1 cup quick-cooking oats, uncooked
½ cup semisweet chocolate minimorsels
3 tablespoons shreds of wheat bran cereal
Vegetable cooking spray

Combine shortening, syrup, brown sugar, and vanilla in a mixing bowl; beat at medium speed of an electric mixer until blended.

Add egg whites and water to corn syrup mixture, mixing well.

Add flour, dry milk powder, soda, and salt to corn syrup mixture; beat at medium speed of an electric mixer until well blended. Stir in oats, chocolate morsels, and bran cereal.

Drop by rounded teaspoonfuls onto cookie sheets coated with cooking spray. Bake at 375° for 8 to 9 minutes or until lightly browned. Yield: 3 dozen (about 52 calories, 1.5 grams protein, 1.5 grams fat, 8.4 grams carbohydrate, 0.3 milligram cholesterol, 45 milligrams sodium, and 59 milligrams potassium per cookie).
Gerry Spradlin,
Russellville, Arkansas.

Make Two Meals From One

When you serve ham, turkey, or a beef roast for dinner, do the leftovers usually find their way into sandwiches for the rest of the week? If so, see how our recipe combinations offer tasty ways to serve leftovers.

With just a little planning, your family won't recognize the meat when you serve it a second time. And you'll save hours in the kitchen by using already cooked meat to make an entrée.

When selecting an entrée that will work well in a second dish, choose one that isn't highly seasoned so that the flavor of the leftover meat won't compete with the flavors in the second entrée. It should use just a few spices, have a simple glaze, or be served with a sauce or relish, if extra flavor is needed. Chicken or turkey makes a good first-time entrée because the meat flavor takes well to most seasonings.

Casseroles are always an easy solution for using leftover pork, poultry, or beef, but you may come up with some creative recipes of your own. Chunks of meat make a tasty addition to salads. Omelets, quiches, meat pies, fritters or hush puppies, soups, crêpe fillings, and hot or cold pasta salads are other savory ways to serve a second meal.

■ After serving Bloody Mary Pot Roast, save the remaining beef. Tear it into chunks, and toss it into Combination Chef's Salad for either a light supper or tasty lunch.

BLOODY MARY POT ROAST

1 (3-pound) boneless chuck roast
1 (6-ounce) can Bloody Mary mix
½ cup red wine
2 tablespoons all-purpose flour
¼ teaspoon pepper
1 (1⅓-ounce) envelope dry onion soup mix
8 small onions
3 medium carrots, cut into 1-inch slices
1 stalk celery, cut into 1-inch slices

Place a 22- x 18-inch piece of aluminum foil in an ungreased 13- x 9- x 2-inch pan. Place beef in pan, and add Bloody Mary mix and wine. Sprinkle with flour, pepper, and onion soup mix. Arrange vegetables around beef. Fold foil over, and seal. Bake at 350° for 2 hours or until tender. Yield: 6 servings.
Janet M. Filer,
Arlington, Virginia.

COMBINATION CHEF'S SALAD

1 medium head iceberg lettuce, torn
8 radishes, thinly sliced
4 green onions, thinly sliced
3 medium tomatoes, cut into thin wedges
2 cups cubed cooked ham
2 cups coarsely chopped cooked roast beef
2 cups (8 ounces) shredded Cheddar cheese
Garlic-Flavored Croutons
Commercial salad dressing

Combine all ingredients except croutons and dressing in a large salad bowl; toss lightly. Sprinkle with Garlic-Flavored Croutons. Serve with your favorite salad dressing. Yield: 8 servings.

Garlic-Flavored Croutons:

3 slices bread
2 teaspoons butter or margarine, softened
¼ teaspoon garlic salt
Paprika

Trim crust from bread. Combine butter and garlic salt; spread on both sides of bread. Cut bread into ½-inch cubes. Place on baking sheet; sprinkle with paprika. Bake at 300° for 20 minutes or until golden brown. Cool. Serve on salad. Yield: 1½ cups.
Mrs. Robert L. Humphrey,
Palestine, Texas.

■ When company comes, prepare our Roast Turkey for an impressive entrée. Later, put together a family main dish of Herbed Turkey Tetrazzini using the leftover turkey. (If you don't use the leftover meat in a couple of days, just freeze it for later use.)

ROAST TURKEY

1 (12-pound) turkey
Salt and pepper
1 apple, halved
1 small onion, halved
4 celery tops
1 clove garlic, halved
Melted butter, margarine, or vegetable oil
Green onion brushes
Radish roses

Remove giblets and neck from turkey; reserve for gravy, if desired. Rinse turkey with cold water; pat dry. Sprinkle cavity and outside of turkey with salt and pepper. Place apple, onion, celery tops, and garlic into cavity. Close cavity with skewers or wooden picks, and truss. Tie ends of legs to tail with cord; lift wingtips up and over back so that they are tucked under bird. Brush entire bird with melted butter; place on a roasting rack, breast side up.

Insert meat thermometer in breast or meaty part of thigh, making sure it does not touch bone. Bake at 325° until meat thermometer reaches 185° (about 3 to 3½ hours). If turkey starts to brown too much, cover loosely with aluminum foil. When turkey is two-thirds done, cut the cord or band of skin holding the drumstick ends to the tail; this procedure will ensure that the insides of the thighs are cooked. Test the turkey for doneness: the turkey is done when the drumsticks are easy to move up and down.

Remove to serving platter; let stand 20 to 30 minutes before carving. Garnish with green onion brushes and radish roses. Yield: 12 to 14 servings.
Lora Blocker,
Dade City, Florida.

HERBED TURKEY TETRAZZINI

¼ cup chopped onion
¼ cup chopped fresh mushrooms
¼ cup butter or margarine, melted
¼ cup all-purpose flour
1 cup milk
1 cup chicken broth
1 tablespoon chopped fresh parsley
1 teaspoon dried whole tarragon
⅛ teaspoon pepper
Dash of ground nutmeg
2½ cups cooked spaghetti or fettuccine
1½ cups chopped cooked turkey
½ cup (2 ounces) shredded Swiss or Gruyère cheese, divided
Chopped parsley
Lemon slice halves
Red pepper strips

Sauté onion and mushrooms in butter in a large heavy saucepan until just tender. Add flour, stirring well. Cook 1 minute, stirring constantly. Gradually add milk and chicken broth; cook over medium heat, stirring constantly, until mixture is thickened and bubbly. Stir in parsley, tarragon, pepper, and nutmeg. Stir in spaghetti, turkey, and ¼ cup cheese, mixing well.

Pour into a greased 1½-quart casserole. Bake at 350° for 20 minutes. Sprinkle remaining ¼ cup cheese over top, and bake an additional 5 minutes. Garnish with parsley, lemon slices, and pepper strips. Yield: 4 servings.
Mrs. James S. Stanton,
Richmond, Virginia.

■ Pineapple-Baked Ham is the perfect size entrée for a crowd. You can entertain again for brunch using leftover ham slices for Ham-Asparagus Delight.

PINEAPPLE-BAKED HAM

1 (4-pound) fully cooked canned ham
⅓ cup firmly packed brown sugar
1 (8-ounce) can pineapple slices, undrained
Green grapes
Fresh watercress

Place ham in a lightly greased 12- x 8- x 2-inch baking dish; sprinkle evenly with brown sugar.

Drain pineapple, reserving 3 tablespoons juice. Arrange pineapple slices over sugar; sprinkle with reserved pineapple juice. Bake at 300° for 1 hour and 45 minutes or until a meat thermometer reaches 130° to 140°. Transfer to a serving platter, and garnish with grapes and watercress. Yield: 16 servings.

Gladys Stout,
Elizabethton, Tennessee.

HAM-ASPARAGUS DELIGHT
(pictured on page 28)

2 (10-ounce) packages frozen asparagus spears
4 English muffins, split and toasted
8 (3- x 3- x ¼-inch) slices cooked ham
Mushroom-Cheese Sauce
1 cup (4 ounces) shredded Cheddar cheese
Paprika

Cook asparagus according to package directions; drain.

Place English muffin halves, cut side up, on a 15- x 10- x 1-inch jellyroll pan. Place one slice ham on each English muffin half; arrange 4 asparagus spears on top. Spoon about 2 tablespoons Mushroom-Cheese Sauce over each; sprinkle with 2 tablespoons cheese and paprika. Broil 6 inches from heat for 3 to 5 minutes or until cheese melts. Serve immediately. Yield: 8 servings.

Mushroom-Cheese Sauce:

¾ cup fresh mushrooms, sliced
2 tablespoons finely chopped onion
2 tablespoons butter or margarine, melted
1 tablespoon all-purpose flour
¼ cup plus 2 tablespoons milk
2 tablespoons dry white wine
1 egg yolk, beaten
½ cup half-and-half
½ cup grated Parmesan cheese
Pinch of ground nutmeg
Dash of ground red pepper

Sauté mushrooms and onion in butter in a heavy saucepan until tender; add flour, stirring until smooth. Cook 1 minute, stirring constantly. Gradually add milk and wine; cook over medium heat, stirring constantly, until mixture is thick and bubbly.

Beat egg yolk; gradually stir about one-fourth of hot mixture into yolk; add to remaining hot mixture, stirring constantly. Cook over medium heat 3 minutes, stirring constantly. Stir in half-and-half, Parmesan cheese, nutmeg, and pepper; cook over medium heat until thoroughly heated, stirring constantly. Remove from heat. Yield: 1½ cups.

Mrs. Dina Walker,
Garland, Texas.

Valentine Sweets To Make

Parties and remembering special people are all part of Valentine's Day. With these cookie and candy recipes, you'll be sure to have some treats to serve or give away.

TIGER BUTTER

1 pound white chocolate
1 (12-ounce) jar chunky peanut butter
1 pound semisweet chocolate, melted

A tasty way to show your affection on Valentine's Day is with a batch of homemade Peanut Butter-Chocolate Kiss Cookies or thick, rich chunks of Tiger Butter.

Combine white chocolate and peanut butter in top of a double boiler; bring water to a boil. Reduce heat to low, and cook until chocolate and peanut butter melt, stirring constantly. Spread mixture onto a waxed paper-lined 15- x 10- x 1-inch jellyroll pan. Pour semisweet chocolate over peanut butter mixture, and swirl through with a knife. Chill until firm.

Cut into 1½- x 1-inch pieces. Store in refrigerator. Yield: about 6 dozen.
Yvonne Bennett,
Greenville, South Carolina.

PEANUT BUTTER-CHOCOLATE KISS COOKIES

½ cup shortening
½ cup peanut butter
½ cup sugar
½ cup firmly packed brown sugar
1 egg
2 tablespoons milk
1 teaspoon vanilla extract
1¾ cups all-purpose flour
1 teaspoon baking soda
½ teaspoon salt
¼ cup sugar
48 chocolate kisses

Cream shortening and peanut butter; gradually add ½ cup sugar and brown sugar, beating until light and fluffy. Add egg, milk, and vanilla; beat well.

Combine flour, soda, and salt; add to creamed mixture.

Roll dough into 1-inch balls; then roll in ¼ cup sugar. Place balls 2 inches apart on a lightly greased cookie sheet. Bake at 375° for 8 minutes. Remove from oven; press a chocolate kiss into the center of each cookie. Return to oven for an additional 2 minutes or until lightly browned. Yield: 4 dozen.
Peggy Wilson Witherow,
Meridian, Mississippi.

PINK DIVINITY

2 cups sugar
¾ cup water
¼ cup light corn syrup
2 egg whites
1 teaspoon vanilla extract
3 to 4 drops red food coloring
3 dozen pecan halves

Combine sugar, water, and corn syrup in a 3-quart saucepan; cook over low heat, stirring constantly, until sugar

dissolves. Cook over high heat, without stirring, until mixture reaches hard ball stage (260°).

Place egg whites (at room temperature) in a large mixing bowl; beat until stiff peaks form. Pour hot sugar mixture in a very thin stream over egg whites while beating constantly at high speed of an electric mixer. Add vanilla and food coloring. Continue beating 3 to 5 minutes or until mixture holds its shape.

Quickly drop mixture by heaping teaspoonfuls onto waxed paper; press a pecan half on top of each. Cool. Yield: 3 dozen.
Inez Vann,
Birmingham, Alabama.

ALMOND ROCA

2 cups butter
2 cups sugar
2 cups finely chopped almonds, toasted and divided
1 pound milk chocolate

Melt butter in a Dutch oven; add sugar and cook over medium-high heat until mixture comes to a boil. Reduce heat to medium, and boil mixture 5 minutes, stirring frequently. Add 1 cup almonds and cook, stirring constantly, until mixture reaches hard crack stage (300°). Remove from heat, and immediately pour onto two buttered aluminum foil-covered cookie sheets, spreading to about ¼-inch thickness. Let cool until candy is hard.

Melt chocolate in top of a double boiler over hot water. Working quickly, spread half of chocolate over cooled candy; sprinkle ½ cup almonds evenly on top. Lightly press almonds into chocolate. Let stand, or refrigerate until chocolate is firm. Invert candy onto foil, and repeat procedure.

When chocolate is firm, break candy into pieces. If stored in refrigerator, allow candy to stand at room temperature 5 minutes before serving. Yield: about 3¾ pounds.
Mrs. Howard E. Erdman,
Denton, Texas.

A Champagne Dinner For Two

If you're planning a cozy dinner for two and are looking for just the right menu, you'll find our champagne dinner is made to order. It starts and ends elegantly, but nothing on the menu requires elaborate preparation.

Chicken Breasts
With Champagne Sauce
Almond Wild Rice
Steamed Vegetable Medley
Garden Dew Dressing for Tossed Salad
Amaretto-Chocolate Mousse
Champagne   Coffee

CHICKEN BREASTS WITH CHAMPAGNE SAUCE

2 tablespoons butter or margarine
4 chicken breast halves, skinned and boned
½ cup sliced fresh mushrooms
⅓ cup champagne
⅓ cup commercial sour cream
⅛ teaspoon salt
⅛ teaspoon white pepper

Heat butter in a medium skillet. Add chicken, and brown on both sides. Remove chicken to a 1-quart baking dish, reserving drippings in skillet. Add mushrooms to skillet, and sauté; remove mushrooms, and set aside.

Stir champagne into drippings in skillet; simmer until thoroughly heated, stirring occasionally. Pour over chicken; cover and bake at 350° for 20 minutes or until chicken is done.

Remove chicken to platter, reserving liquid. Add sour cream, salt, and pepper to reserved liquid; whisk until smooth. Pour over chicken, and top with mushrooms. Yield: 2 servings.
Mrs. M. E. Natto,
Locust Grove, Virginia.

Tip: After purchasing fresh mushrooms, refrigerate immediately in their original container. If mushrooms are in a plastic bag, make a few holes in the bag for ventilation.

ALMOND WILD RICE

½ cup uncooked wild rice
2 tablespoons chopped onion
2 tablespoons slivered almonds
2 tablespoons butter or margarine,
   melted
1½ cups boiling water
1 teaspoon chicken-flavored bouillon
   granules

Sauté rice, onion, and almonds in butter 5 minutes or until almonds are browned. Stir in water and bouillon granules.

Pour into an ungreased 2½-cup casserole. Cover and bake at 350° for 1 hour and 15 minutes. Yield: 2 servings.

Pam Shifflett,
Bridgeport, West Virginia.

STEAMED VEGETABLE MEDLEY

½ cup sliced carrots
½ green pepper, cut into strips
1 cup sliced yellow squash
2 teaspoons butter or margarine
1½ teaspoons lemon juice
¼ teaspoon salt
¼ teaspoon pepper
Chopped chives

Place sliced carrots, green pepper strips, and sliced squash in steaming rack. Place rack over boiling water; cover and steam 3 to 5 minutes or until vegetables are crisp-tender.

Transfer vegetables to serving dish. Add butter, lemon juice, salt, and pepper, and toss gently. Sprinkle with chives. Yield: 2 servings.

Alice Goins,
Greenville, North Carolina.

GARDEN DEW DRESSING

¼ cup vegetable oil
2 tablespoons vinegar
2 tablespoons minced parsley
1½ teaspoons chopped chives
1½ teaspoons minced green pepper
½ teaspoon sugar
½ teaspoon dry mustard
¼ teaspoon salt
Dash of red pepper

Combine all ingredients in a jar. Cover tightly, and shake vigorously. Chill several hours. Serve over salad greens. Yield: ⅓ cup.

Jean McIntosh,
Spavinaw, Oklahoma.

AMARETTO-CHOCOLATE MOUSSE

2 tablespoons water
¼ cup sugar, divided
2 (1-ounce) squares unsweetened chocolate,
   coarsely chopped
2 eggs, separated
⅛ teaspoon cream of tartar
1½ tablespoons Amaretto
Sliced almonds (optional)

Combine water and 2 tablespoons sugar in a small heavy saucepan; bring to a boil, and stir until sugar dissolves. Remove from heat, add chocolate, and cover. Let mixture stand 5 minutes or until chocolate melts. Cool.

Beat egg whites (at room temperature) until foamy. Add cream of tartar and 2 tablespoons sugar, 1 tablespoon at a time, beating until stiff peaks form. Set aside.

Add egg yolks to chocolate mixture; beat until smooth. Stir in Amaretto. Fold about one-fourth of egg white mixture into chocolate mixture; fold chocolate mixture into remaining egg white mixture. Spoon mousse into 2 dessert dishes and chill. To serve, garnish each serving with an almond slice, if desired. Yield: 2 servings.

Mrs. Herbert W. Rutherford,
Baltimore, Maryland.

From Our Kitchen To Yours

Many of you depend on freezers for long-term food storage and often have questions about successful freezing. It's helpful to know the foods that freeze well, those that don't, and the dishes you can make ahead and freeze. Here are some answers to your questions on freezing.

What are some foods that can be frozen successfully? Bacon, baked bread, breadcrumbs, butter, buttercream frostings, and baked cakes usually freeze well. If a cake is frosted, freeze it unwrapped until the frosting is set; then store it in an airtight container to keep it from drying out. You can also freeze unbrewed coffee, fresh fish, deep-dish meat pies, baked meat, or vegetable casseroles. If you are freezing a casserole that calls for a cracker or crumb topping, sprinkle it on just before baking to prevent sogginess. A casserole with meat or pasta on top should be covered with sauce before freezing to keep ingredients from drying out. Hard cheeses and all types of nuts can be frozen, too.

What foods should you avoid freezing? Milk, cream, buttermilk, sour cream, yogurt, and cottage cheese lose their quality when frozen at home. However, some dishes that use cottage cheese or sour cream as an ingredient, such as lasagna and beef stroganoff, do freeze well. Raw eggs should be removed from the shell before freezing.

For easy storage and measuring, try freezing beaten eggs, egg yolks, or egg whites in ice cube trays. When frozen, cubes may be transferred to a freezer bag. Be sure to record how many cubes equal one egg, egg yolk, or egg white. Plain cooked pasta, hard-cooked eggs, and stuffed turkey don't freeze well. You should freeze poultry unstuffed, and stuff before cooking.

Raw potatoes get mushy if they are frozen. You can freeze cooked French fries or potatoes that have been baked or mashed. Potato salad, however, doesn't freeze well.

Avoid freezing unblanched vegetables, sandwiches filled with crisp vegetables, mayonnaise, egg white frostings, custard pies, pies with meringue, or unbaked yeast dough.

How important is it to maintain a constant freezer temperature? To freeze food successfully so that it will keep its vitamin content, color, taste, and texture, food needs to be stored at 0°F. If it's stored at a higher temperature, the food will lose quality. Buy a refrigerator/freezer thermometer. To get an accurate reading, place the thermometer toward the top and front of the freezer for at least 8 hours before checking the temperature. If the temperature is above 0°F, adjust your freezer controls, and check the temperature reading again the next day.

What types of wraps or containers are best for freezing? When freezing foods that are not already packaged as commercial frozen products, choose moisture- and vapor-proof materials for packaging. Heavy plastic wrap, aluminum foil, and freezer paper work well. For suitable containers, use strong plastic containers, heat-sealed cooking pouches, and waxed paper or plastic-lined paperboard cartons.

Avoid freezing foods in thin plastic film or bags, butcher wrap, or plain cardboard boxes (untreated).

What is "freezer burn" and how do you prevent it? Freezer burn is caused by improper wrapping of food. With dry air circulating in the freezer, moisture is removed from the food. Foods with freezer burn will have grayish dry spots and, as a result, may not be as tender as the fresh or properly frozen product. Foods should be protected with airtight wrapping.

Is there a need to label items frozen at home? It's important to label and date every item put in the freezer, especially if identical items are bought at different times. Always use the items marked with the earliest date first.

Wok Cooking— Southern Style

If you think a wok is just for stir-frying, then you're not taking advantage of one of the most versatile small appliances in your kitchen. One of the best ways to save money and kitchen space is to use appliances in as many ways as possible. See how easily you can adapt some of your favorite Southern recipes to the wok and make it a more useful cooking tool. You can, for instance, use the wok for deep-fat frying, braising, steaming, and simmering dishes.

Its unique shape helps the wok heat faster and use less energy to maintain a high heat, so that it's ideal for deep-fat frying chicken, doughnuts, or our recipe for pear fritters. A flat-bottomed wok works best since a traditional cone-shaped one may easily be knocked off balance and cause a spill. The wok's shape helps prevent spatters and uses less oil than other types of equipment for frying; about three cups of oil is all you'll need for a 14- or 16-inch wok. A good rule of thumb is to add oil to a depth no higher than half the depth of the wok. Be sure to use a deep-fat thermometer when heating the oil unless your wok is a temperature-controlled electric model.

Steaming puddings or vegetables becomes simple in a wok. Our Sweet Potato Pudding is a good example. It's spooned into a cake pan and placed over simmering water on a steaming rack. If your wok doesn't have a steaming rack, try using a wire cake-cooling rack. Although the size of the wok will determine the size dishes you can use,

several containers found in most kitchens work well. A shallow glass or metal container, such as a casserole dish, pieplate or piepan, a four- to six-cup ring mold, or a high-edged dish can be used for wok steaming.

To steam, fill the wok with water to 1 inch below the rack. Heat to simmering; then place the food on the rack, and cover with the wok lid.

Since a wok holds heat well, long-simmering soups and stews and a wok are great companions. Beef Stew is easy to prepare. After the meat is browned in the wok, vegetables and seasonings are added; then the stew simmers in the wok for 1½ hours.

Braising is one of the oldest methods of cooking, especially for tough cuts of meat. Traditionally, it's done in the oven or in a skillet, but the wok works well for braising, too. The meat is usually dredged in flour, browned in oil or butter, and simmered with a small amount of liquid until done. By braising in the wok, you'll find that cleanup is even easier because of the smooth, crease-free interior.

BEEF STEW

¼ cup all-purpose flour
2½ teaspoons salt
½ teaspoon pepper
2 pounds boneless beef chuck, cut into 1-inch cubes
2 medium onions, sliced
⅓ cup vegetable oil
1 (12-ounce) can light beer
1 tablespoon soy sauce
1 tablespoon Worcestershire sauce
1 tablespoon steak sauce
1 clove garlic, crushed
2 bay leaves
½ teaspoon dried whole thyme
4 medium potatoes, peeled and quartered
1 (10-ounce) package frozen English peas
2 tablespoons chopped parsley

Combine flour, salt, and pepper; dredge beef in flour mixture. Cook beef and onion in hot oil in wok over medium-high heat until beef is brown. Stir in beer, soy sauce, Worcestershire sauce, steak sauce, garlic, bay leaves, and thyme; cover, reduce heat, and simmer 1½ hours.

Stir in potatoes; cover and simmer over low heat 20 minutes or until potatoes are tender. Add peas; cook an additional 5 to 8 minutes. Remove bay leaves. Garnish each serving with chopped parsley. Yield: 11 cups.

M. DeMello,
Hollywood, Florida.

BRAISED BOURBON CHICKEN

½ teaspoon salt
⅛ teaspoon pepper
4 chicken breast halves
¼ cup all-purpose flour
3 tablespoons butter or margarine
2 tablespoons brown sugar
2 tablespoons cornstarch
⅛ teaspoon ground allspice
1 cup hot water
¼ cup orange juice
2 tablespoons bourbon
¼ cup currants or chopped raisins
4 (½-inch-thick) orange slices

Sprinkle salt and pepper on chicken breasts; dredge in flour. Melt butter in wok over medium heat; brown chicken breasts on both sides. Remove chicken, and set aside.

Add brown sugar, cornstarch, and allspice to wok; gradually stir in hot water. Reduce heat, and simmer, stirring constantly, about 5 minutes or until mixture is smooth and thickened. Stir in orange juice, bourbon, and currants.

Add chicken breasts to wok; place orange slice on each piece of chicken. Cover and simmer about 35 minutes or until fork can be inserted in chicken with ease. Serve bourbon sauce with chicken. Yield: 4 servings.

T. O. Davis,
Waynesboro, Mississippi.

OL' TIMEY PEAR FRITTERS

2 tablespoons sifted powdered sugar
1 tablespoon lemon juice
4 large pears, peeled and cored
1 cup all-purpose flour
1 teaspoon baking powder
¼ teaspoon salt
1 egg, beaten
⅔ cup milk
Vegetable oil
Sifted powdered sugar

Combine 2 tablespoons powdered sugar and lemon juice in a small bowl. Slice pears ⅜ inch thick. Dip each slice in lemon juice mixture.

Combine flour, baking powder, and salt in a small mixing bowl. Combine beaten egg and milk; add to flour mixture, mixing well.

Fill wok with oil half the depth of wok; heat to 360°. Dip pear slices in batter. Fry 1 to 2 minutes on each side or until golden. Drain on paper towels. Dust with powdered sugar; serve hot. Yield: about 2 dozen.

Mrs. Thomas Lee Adams,
Kingsport, Tennessee.

SWEET POTATO PUDDING

4 cups peeled, grated raw sweet potatoes
1⅓ cups milk
1 cup sugar
4 eggs, beaten
¾ teaspoon ground allspice
¾ teaspoon ground cinnamon

Combine all ingredients, mixing well. Pour into a greased, 9-inch, deep-dish pieplate or quiche dish. Place steaming rack in wok; fill wok with water to about 1 inch below rack. Heat water to boiling; set pudding on steaming rack.

Cover wok, and reduce heat; simmer 1 hour, adding more water if necessary. Remove dish from wok; let stand 5 minutes before serving. Yield: 8 servings.

Mrs. Joseph Laux,
Toney, Alabama.

One-Dish Dinners

If you're like most cooks, you probably have several recipes for one-dish meals that you use on a regular basis. They're ideal when you're running short of time. If you would like some new ideas, try these unusual recipes.

EASY OVEN POT ROAST

1 (2- to 3-pound) boneless chuck roast
1 tablespoon all-purpose flour
1 tablespoon vegetable oil
1 tablespoon soy sauce
⅛ teaspoon pepper
½ cup water
1 bay leaf
2 medium potatoes, peeled and cut into
   1-inch pieces
3 medium carrots, scraped and cut into
   2-inch pieces

Dredge roast in flour; brown on all sides in hot oil in a Dutch oven. Sprinkle soy sauce and pepper on all sides of roast. Add water and bay leaf; cover and bake at 350° for 45 minutes. Add potatoes and carrots; cover and cook an additional 30 minutes or until roast is done and vegetables are tender. Remove bay leaf before serving. Yield: 4 servings.

Louise Osborne,
Lexington, Kentucky.

SAUSAGE-BEAN SUPPER

1 cup dried large lima beans
3 cups water
1 pound bulk pork sausage
½ cup chopped onion
½ cup chopped celery
¼ cup chopped green pepper
1 (16-ounce) can whole tomatoes,
   undrained and coarsely chopped
½ cup tomato sauce
¼ teaspoon salt
⅛ teaspoon pepper

Sort and wash lima beans; place in a large saucepan with 3 cups water. Bring to a boil; cook 2 minutes. Remove beans from heat; cover and let beans soak 1 hour. Place beans over medium heat; cover and simmer 1 hour or until beans are tender, adding more water if necessary.

Combine sausage, onion, celery, and green pepper in a large skillet; cook until sausage is browned, stirring to crumble. Drain off pan drippings. Add beans, tomatoes, tomato sauce, and seasonings; stir well. Spoon into a lightly greased shallow 2-quart casserole dish; bake at 350° for 20 minutes or until thoroughly heated. Yield: 6 servings.

Louise Denmon,
Silsbee, Texas.

CHICKEN-PECAN FETTUCCINE

¼ cup butter or margarine
1 pound boneless chicken breasts, cut into
   ¾-inch pieces
3 cups sliced mushrooms
1 cup sliced green onions with tops
½ teaspoon salt
¼ teaspoon pepper
¼ teaspoon garlic powder
10 ounces uncooked fettuccine noodles
½ cup butter or margarine, melted
1 egg yolk
⅔ cup half-and-half
2 tablespoons fresh chopped parsley
¼ teaspoon salt
¼ teaspoon pepper
¼ teaspoon garlic powder
½ cup grated Parmesan cheese
1 cup chopped pecans, toasted

Melt ¼ cup butter in a large skillet; add chicken, and sauté until lightly browned. Remove chicken from skillet, and set aside. Leave pan drippings in skillet. Add mushrooms, green onions, ½ teaspoon salt, ¼ teaspoon pepper, and ¼ teaspoon garlic powder to skillet; sauté until vegetables are tender. Add chicken; simmer 20 minutes or until chicken is done.

Cook fettuccine according to package directions, omitting salt. Drain noodles. Combine ½ cup melted butter and remaining ingredients except cheese and pecans; stir into fettuccine. Add cheese, tossing until mixed well. Add chicken-and-vegetable mixture, and toss. To serve, arrange on a serving platter, and sprinkle with pecans. Serve immediately. Yield: 6 servings.

Chris Tortorici,
Pelham, Alabama.

CHICKEN-RICE CASSEROLE

1 (6-ounce) package long-grain and wild
   rice mix
3 cups chopped cooked chicken
1 (16-ounce) can French-style green beans,
   drained
1 (10¾-ounce) can cream of celery soup,
   undiluted
¾ cup mayonnaise
½ cup minced onion
1 (4-ounce) jar sliced pimiento, drained
¼ teaspoon pepper
Pimiento strips (optional)
Parsley (optional)

Prepare the rice mix according to package directions.

Combine prepared rice, chicken, beans, soup, mayonnaise, minced onion, sliced pimiento, and pepper; spoon into a lightly greased 2½-quart casserole. Cover and bake at 350° for 25 to 30 minutes or until bubbly.

To serve, garnish with pimiento strips and parsley, if desired. Yield: 6 servings.

Nelda Griffing,
Gilbert, Louisiana.

Ever Tried Papaya?

What looks like a melon, but grows on a tree? A papaya. This tropical fruit with its sweet, juicy golden flesh tastes delicious, and it's a good source of vitamins A and C and potassium. If this is still not enough to convince you to try it, note that it has only 54 calories in a 1-cup serving.

Let skin color be your guide to ripeness. A yellow-orange speckled skin indicates that the papaya is ready to eat. Choose green or only partially yellow fruit if you don't plan to eat the fruit for a few days. Papayas will ripen in three to five days at room temperature.

When ripe, they can be refrigerated up to a week.

Papayas work well in make-ahead fruit recipes. Unlike many other soft-fleshed fruits, they do not darken upon standing.

PAPAYA PIE

¼ cup sugar
2 tablespoons cornstarch
1 cup orange juice
1 tablespoon lemon juice
1 large papaya, peeled and sliced
1 baked 9-inch pastry shell
¾ cup whipping cream, whipped
½ cup chopped macadamia nuts

Combine sugar and cornstarch in a heavy saucepan; stir well to remove lumps. Gradually add orange juice and lemon juice, stirring until blended. Cook over medium heat, stirring constantly, until mixture thickens and comes to a boil. Cook 1 minute, stirring constantly. Remove mixture from heat.

Place papaya slices in pastry shell; pour orange juice mixture over papaya. Let cool. Cover and refrigerate several hours. Spread entire surface of pie with whipped cream, and sprinkle with nuts. Yield: one 9-inch pie.　*T. O. Davis,*
Waynesboro, Mississippi.

TROPICAL MEDLEY OF FRUIT

1 medium papaya, peeled, seeded, and cubed
¼ teaspoon grated lime rind
2 tablespoons fresh lime juice
2 cups sliced strawberries
2 medium kiwifruit, peeled and sliced
Sweetened whipped cream

Combine papaya, lime rind, and lime juice; toss gently. Add strawberries and kiwifruit, tossing gently. Cover and chill. To serve, spoon fruit into individual serving dishes; top with a dollop of whipped cream. Yield: 8 servings.
Jo Ann Maupin,
Fort Payne, Alabama.

Feature Italian Sausage

Southerners enjoy eating sausage almost as much as turnip greens and cornbread, and no wonder. The many interesting types now in the supermarket provide a wide range of choices. Among these you'll find Italian sausage. And while it may sound like a foreign food, our readers have come up with ideas for giving the spicy sausage down-home appeal.

Made from uncured meat, Italian sausage is considered a fresh sausage. It requires refrigeration and should be fully cooked before serving. Since freezing sausage for long periods of time increases the chances of rancidity, you should freeze Italian sausage for no longer than three months.

EGGPLANT PARMESAN

1 pound hot Italian sausage
½ pound ground beef
1 cup chopped onion
1 cup chopped celery
3 cloves garlic, minced
2 (14½-ounce) cans whole tomatoes, undrained and chopped
1 (6-ounce) can tomato paste
1 medium eggplant, unpeeled and thinly sliced
2 eggs, beaten
1 cup cracker crumbs
¼ cup plus 1 tablespoon vegetable oil, divided
½ cup grated Parmesan cheese

Remove casings from sausage. Cook sausage, ground beef, onion, celery, and garlic in a large skillet until meat is browned and vegetables are tender. Stir to crumble meat. Drain well. Stir in tomatoes and tomato paste. Cover, reduce heat, and simmer 1 hour.

Dip eggplant slices in eggs; coat with cracker crumbs. Heat 2 tablespoons oil in a heavy skillet. Arrange a single layer of eggplant slices in skillet, and brown on both sides. Drain eggplant on paper towels; set aside. Repeat procedure with remaining eggplant slices, adding more oil as needed.

Layer half the eggplant in a lightly greased 13- x 9- x 2-inch baking dish. Spoon half of sauce mixture over eggplant slices; repeat layers. Top with Parmesan cheese. Bake at 350° for 45 minutes. Yield: 8 servings.
Nellie Trosclair,
Marrero, Louisiana.

ITALIAN SAUSAGE AND RICE

1 pound mild Italian sausage
1 (28-ounce) can whole tomatoes, undrained
1 (6-ounce) can tomato paste
1 large onion, chopped
1 clove garlic, crushed
1½ teaspoons Italian seasoning
1 teaspoon sugar
⅛ teaspoon ground red pepper
2 medium-size green peppers, coarsely chopped
3 cups sliced fresh mushrooms
Hot cooked rice

Remove casings from sausage. Cook sausage in a skillet until browned. Stir to crumble; drain well. Add tomatoes, tomato paste, onion, garlic, Italian seasoning, sugar, and red pepper, and bring to a boil. Cover, reduce heat, and simmer 30 minutes. Stir in green pepper and mushrooms. Cover, and simmer 10 minutes. Serve over hot cooked rice. Yield: 6 servings.
David P. Bronikowski,
St. Albans, West Virginia.

PIZZA QUICHE

½ pound hot Italian sausage
Pastry for double-crust 9-inch pie, divided
1 cup ricotta or cream-style cottage cheese
3 eggs
1 cup (4 ounces) shredded mozzarella cheese
1 (3-ounce) package sliced pepperoni, chopped
¼ cup grated Parmesan cheese
2 tablespoons milk
Commercial pizza sauce

Remove casings from sausage. Cook sausage in a medium skillet until browned, stirring to crumble; drain well, and set aside.

Line a 9-inch pieplate with half of pastry; flute edges. Bake at 450° for 5 minutes. Remove from oven; reduce oven temperature to 350°.

Combine ricotta cheese and eggs; beat well. Stir in sausage, mozzarella cheese, pepperoni, and Parmesan cheese. Spoon into partially baked piecrust. Roll out remaining pastry to an 8-inch circle; cut into 6 wedges. Arrange on top of filling. Bake at 350° for 20 minutes. Brush milk over top of pastry; bake an additional 20 minutes or until golden brown. Let cool 10 minutes; serve with warm pizza sauce. Yield: 6 servings.
Margaret L. Hunter,
Princeton, Kentucky.

STUFFED ZUCCHINI

4 medium zucchini
½ pound hot Italian sausage
¼ cup diced onion
1 clove garlic, crushed
⅓ cup Italian breadcrumbs
¼ cup grated Parmesan cheese
½ cup (2 ounces) shredded mozzarella
   cheese

Cook zucchini in boiling water to cover 10 minutes; drain. Let cool to touch. Cut zucchini in half lengthwise; scoop out pulp leaving ¼-inch shells. Place shells in a lightly greased 13- x 9- x 2-inch baking dish. Mash pulp; drain well, and set aside.

Remove casings from sausage. Cook sausage, onion, and garlic in a skillet until sausage is browned, stirring to crumble meat; drain well.

Combine sausage mixture, zucchini pulp, breadcrumbs, and Parmesan cheese; mix well. Spoon sausage mixture into zucchini shells; bake at 350° for 10 minutes. Sprinkle with shredded mozzarella cheese; bake at 350° for an additional 5 minutes. Yield: 4 servings.
Jan Crenshaw,
Warrenton, North Carolina.

Oldtime Beaten Biscuits

Beat the dough 300 times for family, 500 times for company—that was the rule when it came to preparing beaten biscuits years ago. The original recipe consisted only of flour, shortening or butter, salt, and ice water and was born in a time when leavening was a precious commodity. Beating the dough added air to the mixture and resulted in thin, hard biscuits with tender, flaky insides.

Southerners have continued to make beaten biscuits through the years, changing only the method of beating the dough. It was once done with a special wooden mallet on a smooth-surfaced tree stump before the biscuit brake was invented. This machine worked like an old-fashioned clothes wringer—the dough was folded and passed between rollers over and over.

Today, a food processor can take the place of physically beating the dough. Experts say that the food-processor method produces beaten biscuits that aren't as flaky, but it's a good substitute if you're short on time or energy.

BEATEN BISCUITS

4 cups all-purpose flour
1 teaspoon salt
⅔ cup shortening
½ cup milk
½ cup ice water

Combine flour and salt; mix well. Cut in shortening with a pastry blender until mixture resembles coarse meal.

Add milk and ice water, stirring until dry ingredients are moistened. Turn dough out onto a lightly floured surface. Beat with a rolling pin or mallet for 20 to 30 minutes or until blisters appear in dough, folding dough over frequently. Roll dough to ¼-inch thickness; cut with a 1½-inch biscuit cutter. Place on ungreased baking sheets; prick each biscuit 3 times with the tines of a fork. Bake at 325° for 20 to 22 minutes or until biscuits are very lightly browned. Yield: 1½ dozen. *Margaret Wilson,*
Fayetteville, Arkansas.

Note: To use a food processor, work with half the ingredients at a time. Position knife blade in processor bowl. Add flour, salt, and shortening; cover. Process 5 seconds or until the mixture resembles coarse meal.

With processor running, add milk and ice water in a steady stream through food chute until dough forms a ball. Process dough an additional 2 minutes. Repeat with remaining ingredients, and proceed as for hand-beaten biscuits.

These Potatoes Are Stuffed

Stuffed potatoes have been around for a while, but that doesn't make them any less popular. They're a regular item on many restaurant menus; some people even order them as a meal-in-one. And judging by the number of recipes we get from our readers, they're a favorite for at-home meals, too. Here are some new ways you can serve them.

SOUTH-OF-THE-BORDER STUFFED POTATOES

4 medium baking potatoes
Vegetable oil
1 (8-ounce) carton commercial sour cream
1 (16-ounce) can chili with beans
1 hot green pepper, finely chopped
½ cup (2 ounces) shredded Cheddar
   cheese

Scrub potatoes thoroughly, and rub skins with oil; bake at 400° for 1 hour or until done.

Allow potatoes to cool to touch. Cut a ½-inch-thick slice from top of each potato; carefully scoop out pulp, leaving shells intact. Mash pulp; stir in sour cream. Stuff shells with potato mixture, leaving a well in center. Place potatoes on a baking sheet. Bake at 350° for 25 minutes; remove from the oven.

Combine chili and chopped hot green pepper in a small saucepan; simmer 10 minutes or until mixture is thoroughly heated. Spoon chili mixture over potatoes. Sprinkle each potato with 2 tablespoons Cheddar cheese; bake an additional 5 minutes or until the cheese melts. Yield: 4 servings.
Mrs. Bernie Benigno,
Gulfport, Mississippi.

PATCHWORK POTATOES

4 large baking potatoes
Vegetable oil
¾ to 1 cup evaporated milk
¼ cup grated Parmesan cheese
¼ teaspoon salt
¼ teaspoon pepper
2 small onions, sliced and separated into
   rings
1 medium-size green pepper, chopped
1 clove garlic, minced
¼ cup butter or margarine, melted
1 medium tomato, peeled and chopped

Scrub potatoes thoroughly, and rub skins with oil; bake at 400° for 1 hour or until done.

Allow potatoes to cool to touch. Cut potatoes in half lengthwise; carefully scoop out pulp, leaving shells intact. Mash pulp; stir in milk, cheese, salt, and pepper. Stuff shells with potato mixture.

Sauté onion, green pepper, and garlic in butter until vegetables are tender. Add tomato, and cook until thoroughly heated. Spoon tomato mixture over potatoes. Serve immediately. Yield: 8 servings.
Ann Elsie Schmetzer,
Madisonville, Kentucky.

CHICKEN-CHEESE STUFFED POTATOES

3 large baking potatoes
Vegetable oil
1 cup finely chopped cooked chicken
½ cup (2 ounces) shredded Swiss cheese
1 (2-ounce) jar diced pimiento, drained
¼ cup commercial sour cream
½ teaspoon salt
Dash of pepper
Paprika

Scrub potatoes thoroughly, and rub skins with oil; bake at 400° for 1 hour or until done.

Allow potatoes to cool to touch. Cut potatoes in half lengthwise; carefully scoop out pulp, leaving shells intact. Mash pulp; stir in remaining ingredients except paprika. Stuff the shells with potato mixture; sprinkle with paprika. Place on a baking sheet, and bake at 400° for 15 minutes or until thoroughly heated. Yield: 6 servings.
Libby Winstead,
Nashville, Tennessee.

CREAMY STUFFED BAKED POTATOES

4 large baking potatoes
Vegetable oil
½ cup butter or margarine
1 (8-ounce) carton commercial sour cream
1½ teaspoons prepared horseradish (optional)
½ teaspoon salt
Dash of pepper
¼ cup (1 ounce) shredded Cheddar cheese

Scrub potatoes thoroughly, and rub skins with oil; bake at 400° for 1 hour or until done.

Allow potatoes to cool to touch. Cut a ¼-inch-thick slice from top of each potato; carefully scoop out pulp, leaving shells intact. Mash pulp; add remaining ingredients except cheese; mix well. Stuff shells with potato mixture; place on a baking sheet. Bake at 350° for 25 minutes. Sprinkle 1 tablespoon cheese on top of each potato; bake an additional 5 minutes or until cheese melts. Yield: 4 servings.
George Barr,
Birmingham, Alabama.

Tip: Baked stuffed potatoes can be prepared ahead of time. Simply bake the potatoes, scoop out the pulp, mix the filling, stuff the potato, top with cheese, and wrap for freezing. Unwrap the potatoes before heating.

Spotlight Broccoli And Brussels Sprouts

Don't give up fresh vegetables just because it's winter. Broccoli and brussels sprouts are plentiful and at their tastiest during cold-weather months.

The key to tasty brussels sprouts is to use smaller sprouts and cook them only until done. Overcooking results in flavor change and loss of color.

Broccoli turns a vibrant green when steamed. That's why we recommend this gentle cooking technique.

BROCCOLI POLONAISE

1 (1½-pound) bunch broccoli
2 tablespoons finely chopped shallots
¼ cup butter or margarine, melted
¼ cup soft breadcrumbs
1 hard-cooked egg, sieved
2 tablespoons chopped fresh parsley

Trim off large leaves of broccoli; remove tough ends of lower stalks. Wash broccoli thoroughly, and separate into spears.

Arrange broccoli in steaming rack with stalks to center of rack. Place over boiling water; cover and steam 10 to 15 minutes or to desired degree of doneness. Arrange broccoli spears in serving dish; keep warm.

Sauté shallots in butter; add breadcrumbs, stirring well. Spoon mixture over broccoli; sprinkle with egg and parsley. Serve immediately. Yield: 6 servings.
Shirley Draper,
Winter Park, Florida.

QUICK-AND-EASY BROCCOLI

1 (1-pound) bunch broccoli
¾ cup mayonnaise
⅓ cup milk
Dash of salt
Dash of pepper
Pinch of grated lemon rind
2 tablespoons lemon juice
1 to 2 tablespoons diced pimiento (optional)

Trim off large leaves of broccoli; remove tough ends of lower stalks. Wash broccoli thoroughly, and separate into spears.

Arrange broccoli in steaming rack with stalks to center of rack. Place over boiling water; cover and steam 10 to 15 minutes or to desired degree of doneness. Arrange broccoli spears in serving dish; keep warm.

Combine mayonnaise, milk, salt, and pepper in a small saucepan; cook just until thoroughly heated, stirring constantly. (Do not boil.) Remove from heat; add lemon rind and juice, stirring well. Spoon sauce over broccoli; sprinkle with pimiento, if desired. Yield: 4 servings.
Stella Williams,
Jewett, Texas.

BRUSSELS SPROUTS IN ORANGE SAUCE

1½ pounds fresh brussels sprouts
¼ teaspoon ground nutmeg
1 tablespoon cornstarch
1 tablespoon grated orange rind
⅛ teaspoon ground cardamom
1 cup orange juice
½ teaspoon lemon juice
2 tablespoons butter or margarine
⅛ teaspoon dried whole basil
2 oranges, peeled and sliced

Wash brussels sprouts thoroughly, and remove discolored leaves. Cut off stem ends, and slash bottom of each sprout with a shallow X. Place sprouts in a small amount of boiling water; add nutmeg. Cover, reduce heat, and simmer 8 minutes or until sprouts are tender; drain and set aside.

Combine cornstarch, orange rind, and cardamom in a small saucepan. Slowly stir in orange juice and lemon juice. Cook over medium heat until thick, stirring constantly. Stir in butter and basil.

Make a border of orange slices on a platter. Spoon brussels sprouts in center; top with hot orange sauce. Yield: 6 servings.
Eunice Palmer,
Morris Chapel, Tennessee.

SESAME BRUSSELS SPROUTS

1 pound fresh brussels sprouts
2 tablespoons sesame seeds
1 tablespoon vegetable oil
¼ cup soy sauce
2 tablespoons sugar
Dash of salt

Wash brussels sprouts thoroughly, and remove discolored leaves. Cut off stem ends, and slash bottom of each sprout with a shallow X. Place sprouts in a small amount of boiling water. Cover, reduce heat, and simmer 8 minutes or until tender. Drain; set aside.

Brown sesame seeds in hot oil. Remove from heat; add soy sauce, sugar, and salt, stirring well. Pour over warm brussels sprouts, tossing gently. Yield: 4 servings.
Oberia J. Reudelhuber,
Lighthouse Point, Florida.

Break-Away Bread gets its distinctive shape from a Bundt pan; the tender buttery rolls, which can be pulled apart easily, are delicious served warm.

Try These Delicious Yeast Breads

If you've ever baked a yeast bread, you know the magnetic effect it can have on your household; everyone gathers in the kitchen and waits expectantly for a handout. The home economists in our test kitchens had the same experience when they began making these recipes; the rest of the staff stood by, eager to sample the results.

Our favorite was Break-Away Bread, a buttery pull-apart bread that bakes in a Bundt pan. Allow plenty of time to make it because you need to mix the dough ahead and refrigerate it for at least 8 hours; then it still has to double in bulk. However, we thought the final product was well worth the wait.

If you want a more standard yeast bread, try Special White Bread. It makes two loaves. Old-Fashioned Potato Bread starts with a mashed potato

and uses the liquid the potato is cooked in to dissolve the yeast. It has a light, even texture.

Honey-Granola Bread has a somewhat coarser texture, thanks to the granola in it, but it's still light for a granola bread. We liked it plain, but you may want to try it toasted, too.

BREAK-AWAY BREAD

2 packages dry yeast
1 cup warm water (105° to 115°)
1 cup boiling water
1 cup shortening
¾ cup sugar
2 eggs, beaten
1½ teaspoons salt
6 to 6½ cups all-purpose flour
¾ cup butter or margarine, melted

Dissolve yeast in warm water; let stand 5 minutes.

Combine boiling water and shortening in a large mixing bowl; beat with a wire whisk until shortening dissolves. Add sugar, eggs, salt, and yeast mixture; mix well. Gradually stir flour into batter. (Dough will be very soft.) Cover and refrigerate at least 8 hours.

Turn dough out onto a well-floured surface, and knead about 5 minutes or until smooth and elastic. Divide dough in half; shape each half into 24 (1½-inch) balls. Dip each ball into melted butter. Using 2 greased 10-inch Bundt pans, arrange 24 balls in each.

Cover and let rise in a warm place (85°), free from drafts, 1 hour or until doubled in bulk. Bake loaves at 350° for 40 minutes or until loaves sound hollow when tapped. Cool 15 minutes in pans; remove loaves from the pans, and serve warm. Yield: 2 loaves. *Bonnie Taylor, Jackson, Tennessee.*

HONEY-GRANOLA BREAD

6 to 6½ cups all-purpose flour, divided
2 packages dry yeast
1 tablespoon salt
1¼ cups water
1 cup milk
½ cup honey
¼ cup shortening
2 eggs
2 cups granola cereal, crushed

Combine 3 cups flour, yeast, and salt in a large mixing bowl. Combine water, milk, honey, and shortening in a saucepan, and heat until very warm (120° to 130°). Add to flour mixture.

Add eggs to flour mixture; beat with an electric mixer at low speed until well blended. Continue beating 3 minutes at medium speed. Gradually stir in cereal and enough remaining flour to make a stiff dough.

Turn dough out onto a floured surface, and knead until smooth and elastic (5 to 10 minutes). Place dough in a greased bowl, turning to grease top. Cover and let rise in a warm place (85°), free from drafts, 1 hour or until doubled in bulk.

Punch dough down; turn out onto a lightly floured surface, and knead 4 or 5 times. Divide dough in half; shape each half into a loaf. Place in two well-greased 9- x 5- x 3-inch loafpans.

Cover and let rise in a warm place (85°), free from drafts, 40 minutes or until doubled in bulk. Bake at 375° for 25 to 30 minutes or until bread sounds hollow when tapped. Yield: 2 loaves.
Martha Edington, Knoxville, Tennessee.

SPECIAL WHITE BREAD

1 package dry yeast
½ cup warm water (105° to 115°)
¼ cup shortening
¼ cup butter or margarine
1 cup milk, scalded
½ cup sugar
¾ teaspoon salt
4¼ to 4½ cups bread flour

Dissolve yeast in warm water; let stand 5 minutes. Combine shortening, butter, milk, sugar, and salt in a large mixing bowl; mix well. Cool to 105° to 115°. Add yeast mixture and 1 cup flour, mixing well. Gradually stir in enough remaining flour to make a slightly stiff dough.

Turn dough out onto a floured surface, and knead until smooth and elastic (about 8 to 10 minutes). Place in a well-greased bowl, turning to grease top. Cover and let rise in a warm place (85°), free from drafts, 1½ hours or until doubled in bulk.

Punch dough down, and divide in half; shape each half into a loaf. Place in two well-greased 8- x 4- x 3-inch loaf-pans. Cover and let rise in a warm place (85°), free from drafts, 50 to 60 minutes or until doubled in bulk. Bake at 350° for 25 to 30 minutes or until loaves sound hollow when tapped. Yield: 2 loaves.
Dee Buchfink,
Oologah, Oklahoma.

OLD-FASHIONED POTATO BREAD

1 medium potato, peeled and diced
2 packages dry yeast
2 tablespoons butter or margarine, softened
2 tablespoons sugar
2 teaspoons salt
1 cup milk
5½ to 6 cups all-purpose flour

Cook potato in a small amount of boiling water 10 to 15 minutes or until tender; drain and reserve liquid. Mash potato, and measure ¾ cup; set aside. Add enough water to reserved liquid to make 1 cup; cool to 105° to 115°.

Dissolve yeast in potato liquid in a large mixing bowl. Add butter, and stir well. Stir in sugar, salt, milk, mashed potatoes, and 1 cup flour. Gradually stir in enough of the remaining flour to make a stiff dough.

Turn dough out onto a floured surface, and knead until smooth and elastic (about 8 to 10 minutes). Place in a well-greased bowl, turning to grease top.

Cover and let rise in a warm place (85°), free from drafts, 1 hour or until doubled in bulk.

Punch dough down, and divide in half; shape each half into a loaf. Place in two well-greased 8- x 4- x 3-inch loaf-pans. Cover and let rise in a warm place (85°), free from drafts, 30 minutes or until doubled in bulk. Bake at 375° for 25 minutes or until loaves sound hollow when tapped. Yield: 2 loaves.
Elsie Fitzgerald,
Staunton, Virginia.

MICROWAVE COOKERY

Using Your Temperature Probe

Almost everyone who buys a microwave oven wants the added feature of a temperature probe. But more often than not, the probe is never used, hidden away in a drawer. To help you understand how the temperature probe operates, we've decided to share some recipes and tips on using this feature in your microwave cooking.

Designed to measure internal temperature, the probe allows food to be cooked to a specific temperature without overcooking. The probe actually cooks by computer; as the food heats, it automatically lowers the power level.

The probe is easy to set and use. After inserting it into the food, plug the probe into the receptacle inside the oven. On most ovens, the desired temperature is then pressed into the cook pad. Now you are ready to press "Start." If a lower power setting is used, press this into the cook pad before pressing "Start."

Some microwave ovens have a "temperature hold" feature that, along with the probe, lets you maintain a specific temperature for a period of time. This feature is especially useful when preparing items that need to simmer, such as soups or stews. In some models, the probe indicates the temperature during cooking so you know how close the food is to being done.

While testing our recipes, we discovered both advantages and disadvantages of using the probe. We found that it took some of the guesswork out of microwave cooking. However, there were occasions when the probe temperature was not representative of the rest of the food. That's why we always suggest looking at the food along with the probe to determine degree of doneness.

It's important to insert the probe near the center of the food. It is also helpful to check the internal temperature of a cooked item in several different areas to make sure it is the same temperature throughout. Casserole lids help retain heat but may not allow for correct probe placement. Instead of using casserole lids, try heavy-duty plastic wrap or waxed paper, and insert the probe through the covering.

CHICKEN IN A BAG

1 small onion, chopped
¼ cup chopped celery
¼ cup butter or margarine
4 cups bread cubes
½ cup chopped water chestnuts
2 teaspoons parsley flakes
1½ teaspoons poultry seasoning
½ teaspoon salt
¼ teaspoon pepper
1 (4-pound) broiler-fryer
½ cup water

Combine onion, celery, and butter in a 2-quart bowl. Microwave at HIGH, uncovered, for 3 to 3½ minutes. Stir in bread cubes, chestnuts, and seasonings, mixing well.

Remove giblets and neck from chicken; reserve for other uses. Rinse chicken with cold water; pat dry. Lift wing tips up and over back, and tuck under chicken. Stuff bread cube mixture into cavity of chicken; close cavity with wooden picks. Tie legs together with nylon tie or string.

Place chicken in a regular oven cooking bag; secure with nylon tie or string. Place chicken and bag in a 12- x 8- x 2-inch baking dish, breast side down. Cut 4 slits in top of bag. Pour ½ cup water into dish. Microwave at HIGH for 5 minutes. Reduce to MEDIUM (50% power), and microwave 15 minutes. Turn chicken, breast side up, and cut 4 slits in top of bag. Insert temperature probe through bag into meaty portion of chicken thigh; set probe at 190°. Microwave at MEDIUM (50% power) until temperature is reached (5 minutes). Let stand in bag 5 to 10 minutes. Remove chicken to serving platter. Yield: 4 servings.

SEAFOOD SPREAD

1 (8-ounce) package cream cheese
1 (6½-ounce) can lump crabmeat, rinsed, drained, and flaked
½ cup commercial sour cream
½ cup chopped celery
¼ cup chopped green onions
¼ cup chili sauce
¼ teaspoon garlic powder
⅛ teaspoon onion powder
¼ cup sliced almonds
Paprika
1 tablespoon chopped fresh parsley

Place cream cheese in a 9-inch pieplate; microwave at HIGH for 45 seconds or until soft. Stir until cream cheese is smooth and creamy. Stir in crabmeat, sour cream, celery, green onions, chili sauce, garlic powder, and onion powder, mixing well.

Spread mixture evenly in pieplate. Sprinkle with almonds and paprika. Insert temperature probe into center of mixture; set probe at 140°. Microwave at MEDIUM HIGH (70% power), uncovered, until temperature is reached (4 minutes).

Sprinkle top evenly with chopped parsley, and serve spread with crackers. Yield: about 3 cups.

EASY BEEF CASSEROLE

1 pound ground beef
½ cup chopped onion
½ cup chopped green pepper
1 cup macaroni, cooked and drained
1 (12-ounce) can whole kernel corn, drained
2 cups commercial spaghetti sauce
½ teaspoon pepper
½ cup (2 ounces) shredded American cheese
2 tablespoons grated Parmesan cheese

Crumble ground beef into a 2-quart casserole; stir in chopped onion and green pepper. Cover with heavy-duty plastic wrap, and microwave at HIGH for 6 to 7 minutes or until done, stirring twice. Drain off drippings.

Add cooked macaroni, corn, spaghetti sauce, and pepper to meat mixture, mixing well. Cover with heavy-duty plastic wrap; insert the temperature probe through plastic wrap into center of dish. Set probe at 140°. Microwave at HIGH until temperature is reached (12 to 18 minutes).

Sprinkle casserole evenly with cheese. Cover and microwave at MEDIUM HIGH (70% power) for 1 minute. Yield: 6 servings.

QUICK CHOCOLATE MINT SAUCE

1 (6-ounce) package chocolate-covered mint patties
⅓ cup whipping cream
Vanilla ice cream

Combine patties and whipping cream in a 2-quart glass measure. Cover with heavy-duty plastic wrap. Insert temperature probe through wrap so it rests on bottom of cup. Set probe at 140°. Microwave at MEDIUM (50% power) until temperature is reached (3 to 4 minutes), stirring twice. Serve sauce over ice cream. Yield: 1 cup.

Start With Phyllo Or Puff Pastry

Even if you've never used phyllo or puff pastry before, we think you'll be inspired by these two unusual recipes. Spanakópita, a classic Greek dish, makes a wonderful entrée for many different occasions. Camembert Bars are ideal when you want a sophisticated appetizer for a party.

Although phyllo and puff pastry are both found in the frozen foods section of your supermarket, they're handled very differently. Be sure to follow package directions on thawing, rolling out, and refreezing.

CAMEMBERT BARS

1 egg, beaten
1 (4½-ounce) package Camembert cheese, cubed, with rind removed
½ (8-ounce) package cream cheese, softened
1½ tablespoons fresh chopped chives
1½ teaspoons lemon juice
1 (17¼-ounce) package frozen puff pastry, thawed

Combine all ingredients except puff pastry in a mixing bowl; beat at medium speed of an electric mixer until blended.

Roll one sheet puff pastry to a 14- x 10-inch rectangle on a lightly floured surface. Place on a lightly greased baking sheet. Spread cheese mixture over pastry, leaving a ½-inch border on all sides. Roll out remaining sheet of puff pastry to a 14- x 10-inch rectangle, and set aside. Dip fingers in water, and moisten borders of puff pastry on baking sheet. Place remaining puff pastry sheet on top. Using a fork dipped in flour, press pastry edges firmly together. Cut horizontal slits, 2 inches apart, in top pastry. Bake at 400° for 20 to 25 minutes or until golden brown. Using horizontal slits as a guide, slice horizontally 2 inches apart; then slice vertically 2 inches apart. Serve warm. Yield: about 3 dozen.   *Brenda Clark, Auburn, Alabama.*

SPANAKÓPITA

2 (10-ounce) packages frozen chopped spinach
2 cups cottage cheese
1⅓ cups crumbled feta cheese
3 eggs, beaten
4 green onions with tops, chopped
1 teaspoon dried whole dillweed
1 teaspoon Greek seasoning
¼ teaspoon pepper
¼ teaspoon dried whole thyme
1 (1-pound) package frozen phyllo pastry, thawed
1 cup butter, melted

Cook spinach according to package directions, omitting salt. Drain well, and press spinach in paper towels until barely moist.

Combine spinach, cottage cheese, feta cheese, eggs, green onions, dillweed, Greek seasoning, pepper, and thyme. Mix well, and set aside.

Cut phyllo sheets in half crosswise, and cut each half to fit a 13- x 9- x 2-inch baking pan. Cover with a slightly damp towel.

Lightly butter bottom and sides of a 13- x 9- x 2-inch baking pan. Layer half of phyllo sheets in pan, brushing each sheet with melted butter. (Keep remaining sheets covered with damp towel as you work to keep dough from drying out.) Spread spinach mixture evenly over phyllo in pan. Top with remaining phyllo, brushing each sheet with butter. Bake at 350° for 40 to 45 minutes or until golden brown. Yield: 8 servings.
Mary I. Newsom, Etowah, North Carolina.

March

Easter Cakes Welcome Spring

You've pulled out the linens and lace, cut fresh flowers, and planned a festive menu for a traditional Easter meal. What's better to serve for dessert than a cake that glows with soft pastels or boasts a delicate texture that reflects the new, light feeling of the season?

Long-standing tradition compels Southerners to bake a cake for company, and these recipes are just suited to a spring holiday that draws family and friends together. Choose from delicate flavors that complement any menu—orange, lemon, pineapple, strawberry, and more.

CHOCOLATY SPONGE CAKE

2 cups super-fine sugar
¾ cup all-purpose flour
½ cup cocoa
12 egg whites
1 teaspoon cream of tartar
1 teaspoon vanilla extract
Cocoa Frosting
Ground almonds
Chocolate shavings
Crystallized violets

Sift the sugar, flour, and cocoa together; set aside.

Beat egg whites (at room temperature) until foamy. Add cream of tartar and vanilla; continue beating 5 minutes or until stiff peaks form.

Sprinkle one-fourth of flour mixture over egg whites; gently fold in with a rubber spatula. Repeat procedure with remaining flour mixture, adding one-fourth of the mixture at a time. Spoon into an ungreased 10-inch tube pan with removable bottom. Bake at 375° for 40 minutes or until cake springs back when touched lightly with fingers. Invert pan on funnel or bottle for 2 hours or until cake is completely cooled.

Loosen cake from sides of tube pan, using a small metal spatula. Remove from pan; split cake horizontally into 2 layers.

Reserve 1 cup Cocoa Frosting; set aside. Spread remaining frosting between layers and on top and sides of cake. Garnish with alternating bands of ground almonds and chocolate shavings. Spoon reserved frosting into a decorating bag fitted with No. 5B star tip. Pipe a row of stars around base of cake. Arrange crystallized violets on top of cake. Yield: one 10-inch cake.

Cocoa Frosting:

2 cups whipping cream
¾ cup sifted powdered sugar
3 tablespoons cocoa
1 teaspoon vanilla extract

Beat cream until foamy; gradually add powdered sugar, cocoa, and vanilla, beating until stiff peaks form. Yield: enough for one 10-inch cake.

Mildred Bickley,
Bristol, Virginia.

TOASTED COCONUT CAKE

1 (18.25-ounce) package white cake mix without pudding
1 (3⅛-ounce) package vanilla instant pudding mix
1⅓ cups water
¼ cup vegetable oil
4 eggs
1⅓ cups flaked coconut
1 cup chopped pecans or walnuts
Coconut Cream Cheese Frosting
Toasted flaked coconut (reserved from Coconut Cream Cheese Frosting recipe)

Combine cake mix, pudding mix, water, oil, and eggs; beat 4 minutes at medium speed of an electric mixer. Stir in 1⅓ cups coconut and pecans.

Pour batter into 3 greased and floured 9-inch round cakepans. Bake at 350° for 20 to 25 minutes or until a wooden pick inserted in center comes out clean. Cool in pans 10 minutes; remove layers from pans, and let cool completely. Spread Coconut Cream Cheese Frosting between layers and on top and sides of cake. Sprinkle top with ½ cup toasted coconut reserved from frosting recipe. Yield: one 3-layer cake.

Coconut Cream Cheese Frosting:

2 tablespoons butter or margarine
2½ cups flaked coconut
2 tablespoons butter or margarine, softened
1 (8-ounce) package cream cheese, softened
3½ cups sifted powdered sugar
2 teaspoons milk
½ teaspoon vanilla extract

Melt 2 tablespoons butter in a large skillet; stir in coconut. Cook, stirring

constantly, over medium heat until golden brown. Set aside.

Combine 2 tablespoons butter and cream cheese, beating until light and fluffy. Add powdered sugar, milk, and vanilla; beat until smooth. Stir in 2 cups toasted coconut; reserve ½ cup toasted coconut for garnish. Yield: enough for one 3-layer cake.

Note: Refrigerate cake several hours or overnight for easier slicing.

Betty G. Pritchard,
Huntingdon, Tennessee.

LEMON-PINEAPPLE CAKE

1 cup shortening
2 cups sugar
6 egg whites
3½ cups all-purpose flour
2 teaspoons baking powder
1 cup milk
1 teaspoon vanilla extract
Lemon-Pineapple Topping

Cream shortening; gradually add sugar, beating well at medium speed of an electric mixer. Add egg whites (at room temperature), one at a time, beating well after each addition.

Combine flour and baking powder; add to creamed mixture alternately with milk, beginning and ending with flour mixture. Mix just until blended after each addition. Stir in vanilla.

Pour batter into 3 greased and floured 9-inch round cakepans. Bake at 350° for 15 to 20 minutes or until a wooden pick inserted in center comes out clean. Cool in pans 10 minutes; remove layers from pans, and let cool completely.

Spread Lemon-Pineapple Topping between layers and on top and sides of cake. Yield: one 3-layer cake.

Lemon-Pineapple Topping:

1½ cups sugar
¼ cup all-purpose flour
¾ cup butter
6 egg yolks, beaten
¼ cup lemon juice
1 (20-ounce) can crushed pineapple, drained

Combine sugar and flour in a heavy saucepan; mix well. Stir in remaining ingredients; bring to a boil. Boil 1 to 2 minutes or until the mixture has thickened; cool completely. Yield: enough for one 3-layer cake.

Note: The texture of these cake layers is similar to pound cake.

Nell Jones,
Ariton, Alabama.

LUSCIOUS LEMON LAYER CAKE

½ cup shortening
1¾ cups sugar
6 egg yolks
2½ cups sifted cake flour
2½ teaspoons baking powder
½ teaspoon salt
1 cup plus 3 tablespoons milk
1 tablespoon grated lemon rind
Lemon Buttercream Frosting

Cream shortening; add sugar, beating well. Add egg yolks to mixture, one at a time, beating at medium speed of an electric mixer.

Combine flour, baking powder, and salt; add to creamed mixture alternately with milk, beginning and ending with flour mixture. Stir in lemon rind.

Pour batter into 2 greased and floured 9-inch round cakepans. Bake at 350° for 25 to 30 minutes or until a wooden pick inserted in center comes out clean. Cool in pans 10 minutes; remove layers from pans, and let cool completely.

Spread Lemon Buttercream Frosting between layers and on top and sides of cake. Yield: one 2-layer cake.

Lemon Buttercream Frosting:

½ cup butter or margarine, softened
1 egg yolk
1 (16-ounce) package powdered sugar, sifted
1 teaspoon grated lemon rind
5 to 6 tablespoons lemon juice

Cream butter; add egg yolk, and beat well. Add powdered sugar, beating well. Add remaining ingredients, beating until smooth. Yield: enough for one 2-layer cake.
Marcella Burns,
Athens, Alabama.

ORANGE CAKE

½ cup butter or margarine, softened
¼ cup shortening
1½ cups sugar
3 eggs
2¾ cups all-purpose flour
1½ teaspoons baking soda
¾ teaspoon salt
1½ cups buttermilk
1½ teaspoons orange extract
1 cup chopped dates
½ cup chopped pecans
1 tablespoon grated orange rind
Orange Frosting
Grated orange rind (optional)
Orange segments (optional)
Orange rind strips (optional)

Cream butter and shortening; gradually add sugar, beating well at medium speed of an electric mixer. Add eggs, one at a time, beating well after each addition.

Combine flour, soda, and salt; add to creamed mixture alternately with buttermilk, beginning and ending with flour mixture. Beat at high speed of an electric mixer for 3 minutes. Stir in orange extract, dates, pecans, and 1 tablespoon orange rind.

Pour cake batter into 3 greased and floured 9-inch round cakepans. Bake at 350° for 30 minutes or until a wooden pick inserted in center comes out clean. Cool cake layers in pans 10 minutes; remove layers from pans, and let cool completely.

Spread Orange Frosting between layers and on top and sides of cake. Garnish with grated orange rind, orange segments, and orange rind strips, if desired. Yield: one 3-layer cake.

Orange Frosting:

¼ cup plus 2 tablespoons butter or margarine, softened
6 cups sifted powdered sugar
¼ cup plus 1 to 2 tablespoons orange juice
1 teaspoon orange extract
1 teaspoon grated orange rind
2 drops red food coloring (optional)
3 to 4 drops yellow food coloring (optional)

Cream butter; add powdered sugar alternately with ¼ cup plus 1 tablespoon orange juice. Add orange extract and orange rind; beat until smooth. Add more juice, if necessary, to reach desired spreading consistency. Add food coloring, if desired. Yield: 3 cups.
Kathryn Elmore,
Demopolis, Alabama.

STRAWBERRY CREAM CAKE

1 (14.5-ounce) package white angel food cake mix
1 (8-ounce) package cream cheese, softened
1 (14-ounce) can sweetened condensed milk
⅓ cup lemon juice
1 teaspoon almond extract
2 cups sliced fresh strawberries
1 (8-ounce) carton frozen whipped topping, thawed
Additional strawberries (optional)

Prepare angel food cake mix according to package directions, using a 10-inch tube pan. Invert pan on funnel or bottle for 2 hours or until cake is completely cooled.

Loosen cake from sides of pan using a small metal spatula. Remove from pan; cut a 1-inch slice crosswise from top of cake, and set top aside. Cut 1 inch from center hole and outer edge of cake with a sharp knife. Carefully remove center of cake, gently pulling cake pieces out with fingers, leaving a 1-inch layer of cake on bottom. Reserve cake pieces.

Beat cream cheese until light and fluffy. Add milk; mix well. Stir in lemon juice and almond extract. Fold in cake pieces and strawberries; spoon into tunnel in center of cake. Top with reserved cake slice. Chill 8 hours or overnight. Frost with whipped topping, and garnish with additional strawberries, if desired. Yield: one 10-inch cake.
Mrs. John R. Allen,
Dallas, Texas.

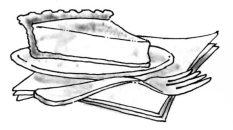

BUTTER PECAN CHEESECAKE

1½ cups graham cracker crumbs
⅓ cup sugar
⅓ cup butter or margarine, melted
½ cup finely chopped pecans
3 (8-ounce) packages cream cheese, softened
1½ cups sugar
3 eggs
2 (8-ounce) cartons commercial sour cream
1 teaspoon vanilla extract
½ teaspoon butter flavoring
1 cup finely chopped pecans, toasted

Combine cracker crumbs, ⅓ cup sugar, butter, and ½ cup pecans, mixing well. Reserve ⅓ cup mixture; firmly press remaining mixture on bottom of a 9-inch springform pan.

Beat cream cheese with an electric mixer until light and fluffy; gradually add 1½ cups sugar, mixing well. Add eggs, one at a time, beating well after each addition. Add sour cream and flavorings; mix well. Stir in 1 cup pecans.

Spoon into prepared pan; sprinkle with reserved crumb mixture. Bake at 475° for 10 minutes; reduce temperature to 300°, and bake an additional 50 minutes. Let cool to room temperature on a wire rack; chill. Yield: one 9-inch cheesecake.
Eunice Bradley,
Experiment, Georgia.

Celebrate The Vegetables Of Spring

One sure sign of spring is supermarkets and produce stands coming alive with garden vegetables. There are many vegetables to choose from—delicate asparagus spears, tiny English peas, or crisp snow peas. And this is the best time of year to savor the nutty flavor of artichokes and the mild taste of leeks.

These vegetables require only gentle preparation techniques, such as steaming or glazing. The end results are vegetables with more flavor, brighter color, and better texture.

If you have never purchased these vegetables before, there are some things you need to know. For instance, the most valued asparagus spears are those that have thin, crisp, straight stems and tightly closed tips. The stately artichoke should be firm, heavy, and green; avoid those with leaves already spreading.

Small to medium-size leeks are usually best. The base should be long, white, and straight, rather than bulbshaped. Leeks that have not been trimmed excessively will stay fresh longer. Always examine the center of a leek's leaves to determine that no tough flower stalk is present.

There is one main rule of thumb for selecting peas: They *must* be fresh. Peas are like sweet corn; their sugar begins to convert to starch immediately after picking. Peas, therefore, cannot taste perfectly fresh and sweet unless they are rushed from the vine to the table. In a supermarket, look for those that have bright green, glossy pods and fresh stem ends. Avoid dull, faded, yellowish, scarred, or limp pods. If your English peas are beginning to age, add a pinch of sugar to improve the taste.

FRENCH LETTUCE PEAS

2 cups water
½ teaspoon salt
1½ pounds shelled fresh English peas
8 green onions, chopped
1 cup coarsely shredded iceberg lettuce
¼ cup butter or margarine
1 teaspoon sugar

Combine water and salt in a saucepan; bring to a boil. Add peas; cover, reduce heat, and simmer 8 to 12 minutes. Drain. Stir in remaining ingredients; cook, uncovered, 5 minutes or until lettuce is slightly wilted. Yield: 8 servings.
Harriet O. St. Amant,
Vienna, Virginia.

HONEY-GLAZED LEEKS

6 medium leeks
¼ cup butter or margarine, melted
¼ cup plus 2 tablespoons honey
3 tablespoons lemon juice

Remove roots, tough outer leaves, and tops from leeks, leaving 1½ to 2 inches of dark leaves. Split leeks in half lengthwise to within 1 inch of bulb end. Place in a large skillet. Cook leeks, covered, in a small amount of boiling water 8 minutes or until barely tender; drain.

Combine butter, honey, and lemon juice in skillet; add leeks to mixture, and simmer 6 to 8 minutes or until leeks are glazed and thoroughly heated. Yield: 6 servings.

CRUNCHY SNOW PEAS AND DIP

4 to 5 dozen fresh snow peas
1 cup mayonnaise
1 (8-ounce) carton commercial sour cream
2½ teaspoons beef-flavored bouillon granules
¼ teaspoon garlic powder
½ teaspoon Worcestershire sauce
1 (8-ounce) can water chestnuts, drained and finely chopped
2 tablespoons chopped pimiento
1 tablespoon chopped green onions

Trim ends from snow peas. Place snow peas in a steaming basket. Plunge basket into boiling water, and remove immediately. Place snow peas in a bowl of ice water to cool quickly. Remove from water, and refrigerate.

Combine mayonnaise, sour cream, bouillon granules, garlic powder, and Worcestershire sauce; mix well. Stir in water chestnuts, pimiento, and green onions. Chill 1 to 2 hours. Serve with snow peas. Yield: 8 to 10 servings.
Mrs. Quentin Bierman,
Dunwoody, Georgia.

SPRING ARTICHOKES

6 medium artichokes
1 lemon, cut into wedges
2 egg yolks
1 to 1½ tablespoons lemon juice
1 tablespoon minced fresh parsley
1 clove garlic, crushed
1 teaspoon minced fresh chives
½ teaspoon dry mustard
⅛ teaspoon red pepper
1 cup butter or margarine, softened and divided

Wash artichokes by plunging up and down in cold water. Cut off stem ends, and trim about 1 inch from top of each artichoke. Remove any loose bottom leaves. With scissors, trim away about a fourth of each outer leaf. Rub top of artichoke and cut edges of leaves with a lemon wedge to prevent discoloration.

Place artichokes in 2 Dutch ovens; cover artichokes with water. Squeeze juice from lemon wedges into water. Discard wedges. Cover artichokes, and bring water to a boil; reduce heat to low, and cook 45 minutes. Place artichokes upside down on a rack to drain; let cool.

Spread center leaves apart; scrape out the fuzzy thistle center (choke) with a spoon. Chill artichokes, if desired.

Combine egg yolks and remaining ingredients except butter in top of a double boiler; beat with a wire whisk until blended.

Add one tablespoon butter. Bring water to a boil. (Water in bottom of double boiler should not touch pan.) Reduce heat to low; cook, stirring constantly, until butter melts. Continue adding butter, 1 tablespoon at a time, stirring constantly, until sauce is smooth and thickened. Remove from heat. Pour sauce into a serving bowl; let cool slightly. Serve as a dip with artichokes. Yield: 6 servings.

ASPARAGUS WITH LEMON SAUCE
(pictured at right)

1½ pounds fresh asparagus spears
1 egg, beaten
⅓ cup butter or margarine
2 teaspoons sugar
½ teaspoon cornstarch
¼ cup fresh lemon juice
2 teaspoons grated lemon rind

Snap off tough ends of asparagus. Remove scales with knife or vegetable peeler, if desired. Cook asparagus, covered, in a small amount of boiling water 6 to 8 minutes or until crisp-tender; drain. Arrange in serving dish.

Combine egg, butter, sugar, and cornstarch in top of double boiler; bring water to a boil. Cook 3 minutes or until butter melts and mixture begins to thicken. Add lemon juice; cook, stirring constantly, an additional 2 to 3 minutes or until slightly thickened. Pour over asparagus. Sprinkle with lemon rind. Yield: 4 to 6 servings.

Right: *One of the most prized and elegant of all spring vegetables is asparagus. The young, tender spears are delicious in Asparagus With Lemon Sauce (above).*

Above: *Pastry-wrapped Pâté en Croûte (page 65) and Vegetable-Chicken Pâté (page 66) make an elegant appetizer or entrée. Serve pâté with spicy mustard and tiny cucumber pickles.*

Right: *Tomato-Shrimp Bisque (page 66) has a wonderful flavor and takes just a few minutes to make. Served with breadsticks, crackers, or hot bread, it's a good choice to serve for lunch or dinner.*

Pack Pâtés With Flavor

You may have noticed pâté listed on a lot of restaurant menus lately and assumed it was difficult to make. But just a splash of spirits and a few extra twists of the pepper mill help turn plain ground chicken, pork, or other meat into a flavorful blend you can serve as an appetizer or entrée.

Pâté is actually just a fancy meat loaf. It is more highly seasoned, however, than the version of meat loaf you might normally serve for dinner. It can be made from any type of ground or chopped meat, fish, or seafood—not necessarily liver, as some people think. It's frequently made from a combination of meats, which adds flavor variety and also helps use up the leftovers you have been storing in the refrigerator.

In traditional versions of pâté, the loaf is encased in pastry, although today's cooking authorities no longer hold to that. Unwrapped pâté is just as common and is frequently served with crusty French bread or crackers. Spicy mustard and *cornichons* (tiny cucumber pickles) often accompany pâté. The loaf is usually served chilled or at room temperature, but it can also be offered hot.

When making Pâté en Croûte, or any other pâté with a crust, you'll need a pâté pan or a pan with removable sides. Line the pan first with pastry, pack in the meat mixture, and then cover with additional pastry.

Because pâté will shrink a little as it bakes, a small gap between the meat and crust usually forms. A flavored gelatin mixture poured in through vent holes in the top of the pastry commonly will fill that gap and bind the meat and pastry together.

Pâtés baked without a crust, such as our Country Pâté and Vegetable-Chicken Pâté, are often weighted down while cooling. This compresses the meat, and gives the pâté its characteristic close, even texture.

Refrigerate the pâté at least a day or two before serving to let flavors blend. When making it ahead or storing leftover pâté, you can keep it up to a week in the refrigerator.

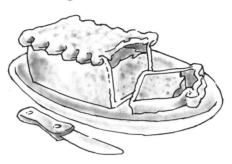

PÂTÉ EN CROÛTE
(pictured at left)

Pâté pastry (recipe follows)
¾ pound ground pork
¾ pound boneless chicken, ground
¼ pound bacon, ground (about 6 slices)
½ cup minced onion
3 cloves garlic, minced
2 tablespoons brandy
2 eggs, beaten
1 teaspoon dried whole basil
1 teaspoon dried whole thyme
½ teaspoon salt
½ teaspoon freshly ground pepper
Milk
Madeira Aspic

Roll about three-fourths of pastry on a lightly floured surface into a 14- x 9-inch rectangle. Lightly grease bottom and sides of an 8- x 4- x 3-inch loafpan with removable sides. Carefully fit rectangle of pastry into loafpan, gently pressing against bottom and sides of pan so that pastry is an even thickness. Trim excess pastry so that it is even with the top of the pan, and reserve scraps.

Combine meat, onion, garlic, brandy, eggs, and seasonings, mixing well. Spoon meat mixture into pastry-lined pan, pressing with the back of a spoon to firmly pack mixture. Roll half of remaining pastry to ¼-inch thickness; cut into a rectangle ½ inch larger than top dimensions of pan. Transfer pastry to pan; moisten and pinch edges of pastry to seal. Flute edges.

Roll remaining pastry and reserved scraps to ⅛-inch thickness. Using a small canapé cutter, cut about 40 shells or flowers. Press the dull side of a knife into the pastry cutouts to make indentations, if desired.

Working with one at a time, moisten back side of each cutout lightly with water. Starting at edges, arrange pastry cutouts over top pastry, letting each subsequent row slightly overlap previous row. Place 2 metal cake decorating tips in top pastry to release steam as pâté bakes. Brush pastry lightly with milk.

Place loafpan in a greased shallow baking pan to catch possible drippings. Bake at 375° for 1 hour or until done. Remove cake decorating tips.

Cool the pâté in pan, and refrigerate at least 8 hours. Insert a small funnel into steam holes, and slowly pour in enough Madeira Aspic to fill the empty spaces. Chill at least 4 hours. Carefully remove pâté from pan just before serving. Cut into slices, and serve with *cornichons* (tiny pickles) and spicy mustard. Yield: 12 servings.

Pâté Pastry:

2½ cups all-purpose flour
½ teaspoon salt
¾ cup shortening
1 egg, beaten
7 to 8 tablespoons cold water

Combine flour and salt; cut in shortening with pastry blender until mixture resembles coarse meal. Add beaten egg; stir briskly until blended. Sprinkle cold water (1 tablespoon at a time) evenly over surface; stir with a fork until the dry ingredients are moistened. Shape dough into a ball; chill at least 1 hour. Yield: enough for one 8-inch pâté.

Madeira Aspic:

2 envelopes unflavored gelatin
1 cup cold water
1 cup Madeira wine
¼ cup plus 2 tablespoons tarragon vinegar

Soften gelatin in cold water in a saucepan. Cook over medium heat until gelatin dissolves; stir in wine and vinegar. Let mixture cool slightly. Yield: about 2½ cups.

Tip: Stains or discolorations inside aluminum utensils can be removed by boiling a solution of 2 to 3 tablespoons cream of tartar, lemon juice, or vinegar to each quart of water in the utensil for 5 to 10 minutes.

Pâté en Croûte requires a special loafpan with removable sides; inverting the pâté from a standard loafpan would mar the decorative pastry on top.

COUNTRY PÂTÉ

1 pound ground pork
¼ pound calves liver, ground
¼ pound boneless pork, cut into ⅜-inch cubes
¼ pound boneless ham, cut into ⅜-inch cubes
½ cup finely chopped onion
1 large clove garlic, minced
¼ cup brandy
2 eggs, beaten
½ teaspoon salt
¼ teaspoon freshly ground pepper
8 to 10 slices bacon
1 bay leaf

Combine all ingredients except bacon and bay leaf, mixing until blended; set mixture aside.

Line the bottom and sides of a 1-quart soufflé dish or casserole with bacon, letting excess bacon hang over edges of dish. Spoon meat mixture into dish, pressing with the back of a spoon to firmly pack mixture. Place bay leaf on top of pâté. Cover pâté with overhanging bacon strips; cover dish with aluminum foil.

Set dish in a larger baking pan. Pour enough hot water into larger pan to reach one-third the way up sides of dish. Bake at 350° for 1½ hours or until done. Pâté will be slightly firm. Do not overcook.

Remove dish from water. Set another dish, slightly smaller, on top of pâté, and fill dish with pastry weights or cans to pack pâté as it cools. Drain off pan drippings as pâté cools.

When cool, remove top dish and weights; wrap pâté securely, and refrigerate at least 8 hours. Unmold pâté onto serving dish. Peel away bacon and bay leaf, smoothing surface of pâté with the back of a spoon, if necessary. Serve with crackers and commercial mustard sauce. Yield: 14 to 16 servings.

VEGETABLE-CHICKEN PÂTÉ

(pictured on page 64)

2 medium carrots, scraped
¾ pound fresh spinach
1 pound boneless chicken breasts, coarsely ground
¼ pound bacon, ground (about 6 slices)
1 medium carrot, shredded
½ cup ground pecans
1 large clove garlic, minced
2 eggs, lightly beaten
¼ cup milk
½ teaspoon salt
1 teaspoon dried herbes de Provence
½ teaspoon freshly ground pepper
Carrot curls (optional)

Cook 2 carrots in a small amount of boiling water 8 minutes or until tender. Drain and set aside.

Trim stems from spinach; cook leaves in boiling water 1 minute or until pliable. Remove spinach with a slotted spoon. Carefully spread on paper towels, and pat dry; set aside. Line the bottom and sides of an oiled 9- x 5- x 3-inch loafpan with enough spinach to cover pan, placing spinach smooth side down, and allowing some leaves to hang over sides of pan. Coarsely chop remaining spinach, and squeeze until barely moist. Combine chopped spinach and remaining ingredients except carrot curls; mix well.

Spoon half of meat mixture into spinach-lined pan. Place whole carrots lengthwise over the meat mixture; top with remaining meat mixture, packing firmly. Fold overhanging spinach leaves over meat mixture. Cover loafpan tightly with aluminum foil.

Set loafpan in a larger baking pan. Pour enough hot water into larger pan to reach one-third the way up sides of loafpan. Bake at 325° for 1 hour or until done. Do not overcook.

Remove dish from water. Set another loafpan on top of pâté, and fill loafpan with pastry weights or cans to pack pâté as it cools. Drain off pan drippings.

When cool, remove top pan and weights; wrap pâté securely, and refrigerate at least 8 hours. Unmold pâté onto serving dish. Garnish with carrot curls, if desired. Slice and serve with crackers. Yield: 14 to 16 servings.

Serve A Steaming Bisque

The traditional definition of a bisque was simple—a thick, rich, creamy soup with a shellfish base. Today the term is used to describe a variety of thick soups that may be made with vegetables and/or seafood. Modern versions may also contain small bits of food instead of always being creamy.

No matter how you define them, bisques are popular in the South, both as a first course with dinner or as a light lunch all by themselves. They may be served simply or dressed up with a sophisticated garnish, such as watercress, lemon twists, or fresh herbs. This versatility adds to their appeal.

TOMATO-SHRIMP BISQUE

(pictured on page 64)

1 (11-ounce) can tomato bisque soup, undiluted
1 (10¾-ounce) can cream of shrimp soup, undiluted
¾ cup water
½ cup milk
2 tablespoons chopped parsley
1 tablespoon minced onion
Freshly ground pepper to taste
⅓ cup dry sherry
Parsley sprigs or avocado wedges (optional)

Combine soups in a medium saucepan, stirring well; gradually add water and milk, stirring until smooth. Add chopped parsley, onion, and pepper; cook over medium-high heat, stirring constantly, until bisque comes to a boil. Reduce heat, and simmer 5 minutes. Stir in sherry, and cook an additional minute. Garnish each serving with parsley sprigs or avocado wedges, if desired. Yield: 3½ cups. *Lenora Blaylock, Little Rock, Arkansas.*

SEAFOOD BISQUE

¼ cup chopped green onions with tops
¼ cup butter or margarine, melted
¼ cup all-purpose flour
4 cups milk
¼ teaspoon hot sauce
¼ teaspoon salt
¼ teaspoon white pepper
¾ cup fresh crabmeat, drained and flaked
¾ cup shrimp, peeled, uncooked, and chopped
3 tablespoons chopped parsley

Sauté green onions in butter in a heavy saucepan until tender. Add flour, stirring until smooth. Cook 1 minute, stirring constantly. Gradually add milk; cook over medium heat, stirring constantly, until thickened and bubbly. Stir in hot sauce, salt, and pepper.

Stir in crabmeat and shrimp; cook over low heat until shrimp turns pink. Stir in parsley. Yield: 5 cups.

SPINACH-POTATO BISQUE

4 cups chicken broth
2 cups fresh spinach, washed and stemmed
6 green onions with tops, sliced
2 cups mashed potatoes
2 cups half-and-half
½ teaspoon hot sauce
½ teaspoon freshly ground black pepper
Lemon twists (optional)

Bring broth to a boil in a Dutch oven; add spinach and onions. Cover, reduce heat, and simmer 3 to 5 minutes.

Place about one-fourth of broth mixture in container of electric blender; process until smooth. Repeat procedure with remaining mixture. Return to Dutch oven; stir in mashed potatoes with a wire whisk until soup is smooth. Stir in remaining ingredients except lemon twists. Cook on low until soup is thoroughly heated. Garnish each serving with a lemon twist, if desired. Yield: about 7 cups.   *Dorsella Utter, Louisville, Kentucky.*

SPICY PUMPKIN BISQUE

1 cup finely chopped onion
1 clove garlic, minced
2 tablespoons butter or margarine, melted
2 cups chicken broth
1 teaspoon salt
½ teaspoon ground nutmeg
½ teaspoon ground allspice
½ teaspoon ground coriander
¼ teaspoon pepper
2 cups half-and-half
1 (16-ounce) can pumpkin
1 (7½-ounce) can whole tomatoes, drained and chopped

Sauté onion and garlic in butter in a 2-quart saucepan. Add broth and seasonings; bring to a boil. Cover, reduce heat, and simmer 15 minutes.

Combine half-and-half and pumpkin; mix well. Stir in pumpkin mixture and tomatoes; cook, stirring constantly, until heated. (Do not boil.) Yield: about 2 quarts.   *Kathleen Stone, Houston, Texas.*

A Roundup Of Hard-Cooked Eggs

Hard-cooked eggs can be eaten with a sprinkling of salt and pepper. Or try them in any of the recipes suggested here. Stuffed, chopped, pickled, or sauced, you'll find they are a delicious source of protein.

Before attempting any of these recipes, take a moment to review the directions for preparing perfect hard-cooked eggs. The American Egg Board recommends placing a layer of eggs in a saucepan, and covering them with enough water to come at least 1 inch above the eggs. Then cover the pan, and bring the water to a boil. Turn off the heat, and let the eggs stand for 15 to 17 minutes.

OPEN-FACED CHEESY EGG SANDWICHES

6 hard-cooked eggs, peeled and chopped
1 cup (4 ounces) shredded Cheddar cheese
¼ cup chopped green onions
3 tablespoons mayonnaise
2 tablespoons sweet pickle relish
1 teaspoon prepared mustard
¼ teaspoon Worcestershire sauce
Dash of salt
Dash of pepper
¼ cup butter or margarine, softened
6 English muffins, split

Combine all ingredients except butter and muffins; mix well. Spread butter on each muffin half; toast. Spread about 2 tablespoons egg mixture on each muffin half; broil 3 minutes or until cheese melts. Yield: 6 servings.   *Mrs. C. Robert Bauer, Charlottesville, Virginia.*

BEDEVILED EGGS

2 tablespoons butter or margarine
2 tablespoons all-purpose flour
1 cup milk
2 tablespoons minced onion
2 tablespoons shredded Cheddar cheese
1 tablespoon mayonnaise
1 tablespoon grated Parmesan cheese
1 teaspoon Worcestershire sauce
1 teaspoon prepared mustard
½ teaspoon salad seasoning
½ teaspoon salt
¼ teaspoon pepper
¼ teaspoon garlic powder
⅛ teaspoon hot sauce
4 hard-cooked eggs, peeled and coarsely chopped
4 slices bread, toasted

Melt butter in a heavy saucepan over low heat; add flour, stirring until smooth. Cook 1 minute, stirring constantly. Gradually add milk; cook over medium heat, stirring constantly, until mixture is thickened and bubbly.

Stir in onion, Cheddar cheese, mayonnaise, Parmesan cheese, Worcestershire sauce, mustard, seasonings, and hot sauce; mix well. Add eggs. Serve over toast. Yield: 4 servings.   *Rosa M. Hinton, Augusta, Georgia.*

CREAMED EGGS

8 hard-cooked eggs
½ cup finely chopped ham
¼ cup butter or margarine, melted
1 tablespoon finely chopped green onions
1 teaspoon minced fresh parsley
½ teaspoon Worcestershire sauce
¼ teaspoon prepared mustard
1 chicken-flavored bouillon cube
½ cup boiling water
3 tablespoons butter or margarine
3 tablespoons all-purpose flour
1 cup half-and-half
½ cup (2 ounces) shredded American cheese

Peel eggs; slice in half lengthwise, and carefully remove yolks. Mash yolks; add ham, ¼ cup butter, green onions, parsley, Worcestershire sauce, and mustard. Stir well; stuff egg whites with yolk mixture. Place eggs in a lightly greased 12- x 8- x 2-inch casserole.

Combine bouillon cube and water; stir until dissolved. Set aside.

Melt 3 tablespoons butter in a heavy saucepan over low heat; add flour, stirring until smooth. Cook 1 minute, stirring constantly. Gradually add bouillon mixture and half-and-half. Cook over medium heat, stirring constantly, until thickened and bubbly. Pour over eggs. Bake at 325° for 20 minutes. Sprinkle with cheese, and bake an additional 5 minutes. Yield: 8 servings.   *Linda C. Hawkins, Cushing, Oklahoma.*

CRUNCHY STUFFED EGGS

6 hard-cooked eggs
¼ cup commercial sour cream
¼ teaspoon salt
⅛ teaspoon coarsely ground pepper
1 teaspoon parsley flakes
2 slices bacon, cooked and crumbled
Paprika
6 pimiento-stuffed olives, halved

Peel eggs; slice in half lengthwise, and carefully remove yolks. Mash yolks, and stir in sour cream, salt, pepper, and parsley flakes; mix until smooth. Stir in bacon. Stuff egg whites with yolk mixture; sprinkle with paprika, and top with an olive half. Yield: 12 servings.   *Lynne Teal Weeks, Columbus, Georgia.*

ROSY PICKLED EGGS

12 hard-cooked eggs
4 cups water
1 cup beet juice
1 cup vinegar
1 small onion, sliced
1 clove garlic
1 bay leaf
2 teaspoons mixed pickling spices
½ teaspoon salt

Peel eggs, and place loosely in a jar. Combine remaining ingredients in a saucepan; place over low heat just until thoroughly heated. Remove onion; pour hot mixture over eggs. Seal with an airtight lid. Refrigerate 2 days before serving. Store in refrigerator up to 2 weeks. Yield: 12 servings.

Wanda Dooley Gaines,
Homewood, Alabama.

COOKING LIGHT®

These Dishes Have A Low-Sodium Bonus

From early childhood on, our taste buds are trained to expect salt in the food we eat. So it's no wonder that diets low in sodium taste bland. But we can re-educate ourselves to enjoy food without salt. The secret to this is using ingenious low-sodium seasonings to perk up flavors.

Table salt and sodium are not the same. Salt is a sodium-containing compound (sodium chloride). The sodium in our diet comes from three sources: medications, water, and food. Food is the main source of sodium in the diet. A small amount is naturally present in food, but the majority is added as table salt or other sodium-containing compounds in seasonings and processed foods. Therefore, the sodium you add to food can be as important as the food you choose.

Sodium is an essential nutrient, but it is needed in less amounts than what we presently consume. Moderation is the best advice for most people.

Sodium has received a lot of attention in recent years. The relationship of sodium in the diet to the development of hypertension (high blood pressure) has been suggested. However, new research indicates other factors—obesity, alcohol consumption, and the amount of potassium, calcium, and magnesium in the diet—may also play an important role.

Our recipes are full of punch and flavor, but they use sodium-containing ingredients sparingly. We think you'll enjoy them, even if you're not on a low-sodium diet.

CORNY MEAT LOAF

1 pound ground chuck
½ cup quick cooking oats, uncooked
¼ cup diced onion
2 tablespoons chopped fresh parsley
½ cup frozen corn, thawed and drained
2 tablespoons salt-free 14-herb-and-spice blend
1½ teaspoons reduced-sodium soy sauce
1 egg, beaten
2 tablespoons plain low-fat yogurt
¼ cup plus 1 tablespoon no-salt-added catsup, divided
Vegetable cooking spray

Combine ground chuck, oats, onion, parsley, corn, herb-and-spice blend, and soy sauce in a mixing bowl; mix lightly.

Combine egg and yogurt, blending until smooth; add to meat mixture. Stir in ¼ cup catsup. Shape into an 8½- x 4½-inch loaf. Place on a broiler pan coated with cooking spray. Bake, uncovered, at 350° for 40 to 45 minutes. Spread remaining 1 tablespoon catsup on top of meat loaf; bake an additional 5 minutes. Yield: 6 servings (about 235 calories and 111.3 milligrams sodium per 1¼-inch slice). *Sheree McIntosh,*
Flag Pond, Tennessee.

STIR-FRY CHICKEN-AND-VEGETABLES

2 tablespoons vegetable oil
1 pound chicken breasts, boned and skinned, and cut into 1½-inch cubes
1⅓ cups broccoli flowerets
1 cup (1-inch) carrot sticks
½ cup (1-inch) celery sticks
⅓ cup green pepper strips
⅓ cup sliced fresh mushrooms
½ cup water
2 tablespoons unsweetened pineapple juice
2 tablespoons chopped fresh parsley
1 tablespoon plus 1 teaspoon cornstarch
2 teaspoons dry mustard
2 teaspoons ground ginger
2 teaspoons dried whole tarragon
⅛ teaspoon white pepper
3 cups hot cooked rice (cooked without salt or fat)

Heat oil in wok at medium high (325°) for 1 to 2 minutes. Add chicken; stir-fry 6 to 8 minutes. Remove chicken from wok; reserve pan drippings.

Add broccoli, carrot sticks, celery sticks, green pepper strips, mushrooms, and water to wok; stir-fry 6 minutes or until vegetables are crisp-tender. Remove vegetables from wok.

Combine pineapple juice, parsley, cornstarch, mustard, ginger, tarragon, and pepper in a small bowl. Add to wok; cook until thickened, stirring occasionally. Add chicken and vegetables to the sauce in wok.

Reduce heat to low (225°), and simmer 2 to 3 minutes. Serve over hot rice. Yield: 5 cups (about 234 calories and 69 milligrams sodium per 1-cup serving plus about 90 calories and 1 milligram sodium per ½ cup cooked rice).

Elaine Murdock,
Hendersonville, Tennessee.

MUSHROOM-AND-PEPPER SALAD

1 medium-size red pepper, cut into 1½- x ¼-inch strips
1 medium-size green pepper, cut into 1½- x ¼-inch strips
¾ cup diagonally sliced celery
2 cups sliced fresh mushrooms
¼ cup olive oil
1 tablespoon plus 1 teaspoon red wine vinegar
1 tablespoon plus 1 teaspoon lemon juice
½ teaspoon sugar
2 medium Belgium endive, separated
¼ cup sliced green onions

Drop red pepper strips into boiling water for 45 seconds; remove with a slotted spoon, and drop into a bowl of ice water. Repeat procedure with green pepper and celery. Drain vegetables; add mushrooms and chill.

Combine oil, vinegar, lemon juice, and sugar in a jar; cover tightly, and shake vigorously. Chill.

Combine vegetables and dressing, mixing well. Arrange vegetables over endive on a large serving platter. Sprinkle with green onions. Pour any remaining dressing over salad. Yield: 8 servings (about 96 calories and 40.4 milligrams sodium per 1 cup serving).

Lydia Michalsen,
Jacksonville, Florida.

Tip: To slice mushrooms quickly and uniformly, use an egg slicer.

ASPARAGUS-AND-NEW POTATO SALAD

1¼ pounds fresh asparagus
1 pound small new potatoes
½ cup water
¼ cup white wine vinegar
¼ cup diced purple onion
1½ teaspoons salt-free Dijon mustard
½ teaspoon dried whole dillweed
⅛ teaspoon freshly ground pepper
Bibb lettuce leaves
1 hard-cooked egg, separated

Snap off tough ends of asparagus. Remove scales with a knife or vegetable peeler, if desired. Cook asparagus, covered, in a small amount of boiling water 6 to 8 minutes or until crisp-tender; drain. Let cool completely. Cut asparagus into 2-inch pieces.

Wash potatoes; cook in boiling water 15 to 20 minutes or until tender; drain. Cool and slice thin; combine potatoes with asparagus.

Combine water, vinegar, onion, Dijon mustard, dillweed, and pepper in a small bowl; pour over vegetables. Cover and marinate vegetables in refrigerator 3 hours.

With a slotted spoon, place salad on a lettuce-lined plate; top salad with sieved egg yolk. (Reserve egg white for other uses.) Yield: 8 servings (about 85 calories and 9.7 milligrams sodium per ½ cup serving).

SUNSHINE LEMON COOKIES

½ cup vegetable shortening
¼ cup sugar
1 egg, separated
1½ teaspoons grated lemon rind
1 tablespoon plus 1 teaspoon fresh lemon juice
1¼ cups all-purpose flour
⅔ cup finely chopped pecans
Vegetable cooking spray

Cream shortening; gradually add sugar, beating at medium speed of an electric mixer until light and fluffy. Add egg yolk, lemon rind, and lemon juice; beat well. Gradually add flour; mix just until blended. Cover and chill dough at least 1 hour.

Shape dough into 1-inch balls; dip in beaten egg white, and roll in pecans. Place 2 inches apart on cookie sheets coated with cooking spray; bake at 325° for 25 minutes or until lightly browned. Cool on wire racks. Yield: 2 dozen (about 93 calories and 3 milligrams sodium per cookie).

Note: Cookies will be fragile.
Beverly George,
Metairie, Louisiana.

ORANGE MOUSSE

⅔ cup evaporated skim milk
1 envelope unflavored gelatin
½ cup unsweetened orange juice
2 teaspoons honey
¼ teaspoon grated orange rind
⅛ teaspoon ground nutmeg
1½ cups fresh orange sections, divided
Vegetable cooking spray

Thoroughly chill milk in a small stainless steel or glass mixing bowl.

Sprinkle gelatin over orange juice in a small saucepan; cook over low heat, stirring constantly, just until gelatin dissolves. Cool slightly.

Add honey, grated orange rind, and nutmeg to gelatin mixture, mixing well; set aside.

Beat chilled milk at high speed of an electric mixer until milk begins to thicken. Gradually add gelatin mixture in a slow, steady stream, beating constantly, just until thickened. Coarsely chop 1 cup orange sections; fold into whipped mixture. Spoon into a 4-cup mold coated with cooking spray; chill until set. Unmold on a serving platter; garnish with remaining ½ cup orange sections. Yield: 8 servings (about 50 calories and 26 milligrams sodium per ½-cup serving).
Doris Garton,
Shenandoah, Virginia.

Food Is For Giving All Year Long

How many times have you wished you had a little something to take along when you went to visit a friend, meet a new neighbor, or check on an elderly relative? You can quickly prepare Granola with Chocolate Morsels to take with you. A gift of food is a thoughtful gesture that's always appreciated.

Food is the answer for many other occasions as well. Bake a loaf of Apple Butter Bread as a bon voyage present for friends going on vacation. Or welcome someone home from the hospital with a Glazed Lemon Cake. (Our recipe makes two half-size cakes, so you can keep one and still have one to give away.) If you include the recipe, the gift means even more.

When it comes to packaging, the possibilities are endless. For example, you can find a variety of inexpensive containers at garage sales and flea markets. (Just be sure to wash them in hot,

soapy water or line them with something to protect the food.) Keep an eye out for baskets, old-fashioned canning jars, cookie tins, and glass canisters; they're good containers for many different food items.

The pantry is another good place to look for containers. Many foods, including shortening, breadcrumbs, and potato chips, now come in round, metal or cardboard cans with plastic lids. Once these are empty, they can be recycled to hold cookies, candy, and other goodies. The plastic lids help keep the contents fresh. To wrap, just cut a length of gift paper as wide as the depth of the can, and glue it to the outside.

GRANOLA WITH CHOCOLATE MORSELS

3 cups fruit-and-nut granola cereal
¾ cup unsalted peanuts
½ cup semisweet chocolate morsels
½ cup raisins
½ cup diced dried apricots

Combine all ingredients. Store in an airtight container. Yield: about 5 cups.
Louise Holmes,
Winchester, Tennessee.

APPLE BUTTER BREAD

½ cup butter or margarine, softened
1 cup firmly packed brown sugar
1 egg
¾ cup buttermilk
2 teaspoons baking soda
2 cups all-purpose flour
1 teaspoon ground cinnamon
1 teaspoon ground nutmeg
1 teaspoon ground allspice
½ teaspoon ground cloves
1 cup apple butter
½ cup chopped pecans

Cream butter and brown sugar; add egg to mixture, and beat well. Combine buttermilk and soda.

Combine flour, cinnamon, nutmeg, allspice, and cloves; add to creamed mixture alternately with buttermilk mixture, beginning and ending with flour. Stir in apple butter and chopped pecans.

Pour into a greased 9- x 5- x 3-inch loafpan. Bake at 350° for 1 hour and 5 minutes or until a wooden pick inserted in center comes out clean. Cool in pan 5 minutes; remove to wire rack, and cool completely. Yield: one 9- x 5- x 3-inch loaf.
Louise Turpin,
Birmingham, Alabama.

BANANA-NUT BREAD

½ cup shortening
1 cup sugar
2 eggs
1½ cups mashed ripe banana
2 cups all-purpose flour
1 teaspoon baking soda
½ cup chopped pecans

Cream shortening; gradually add sugar, beating at medium speed of an electric mixer until light and fluffy. Add eggs, one at a time, beating well after each addition. Stir in banana. Combine flour and soda; add to creamed mixture, mixing well. Stir in pecans.

Spoon batter into 2 greased 7½- x 3½- x 2¼-inch loafpans. Bake at 350° for 35 to 40 minutes or until a wooden pick inserted in center comes out clean. Cool in pans 5 minutes; remove to wire rack, and cool completely. To store, wrap in plastic wrap or aluminum foil. Yield: 2 loaves.
Jane Moss,
Victoria, Texas.

GLAZED LEMON CAKE

1 cup shortening
2 cups sugar
4 eggs
3 cups all-purpose flour
½ teaspoon salt
¾ cup buttermilk
1 teaspoon butter flavoring
1 teaspoon vanilla extract
1 tablespoon lemon extract
1 teaspoon baking soda
1 tablespoon vinegar
1 cup sifted powdered sugar
2 tablespoons lemon juice

Cream shortening; gradually add sugar, beating at medium speed of an electric mixer until light and fluffy. Add eggs, one at a time, beating well after each addition.

Combine flour and salt; add to creamed mixture alternately with buttermilk, beginning and ending with flour mixture. Mix just until blended after each addition. Stir in flavorings. Combine soda and vinegar; mix well. Stir into batter.

Pour batter into two greased and floured 6-cup (8-inch) Bundt pans. Bake at 325° for 40 to 45 minutes or until a wooden pick inserted in center comes out clean. Cool cakes in pans 10 to 15 minutes; remove from pans. Combine powdered sugar and lemon juice; drizzle over the cakes while they are still warm. Yield: two 8-inch Bundt cakes.
Pamela Nordyke,
San Angelo, Texas.

GINGERBREAD ANIMAL COOKIES

½ cup shortening
½ cup sugar
½ cup molasses
¼ cup water
2½ cups all-purpose flour
¾ teaspoon salt
½ teaspoon baking soda
¾ teaspoon ground ginger
¼ teaspoon ground nutmeg

Cream shortening and sugar; add molasses and water. Beat well. Combine remaining ingredients; add to creamed mixture. Cover and refrigerate dough several hours.

Working with one-fourth of dough at a time (store remainder in refrigerator), roll dough to ¼-inch thickness on a floured surface. Cut dough with assorted (2- to 3-inch) cookie cutters, and place on ungreased cookie sheets. Bake at 375° for 8 to 9 minutes. Cool 2 minutes. Remove to wire racks; cool. Repeat procedure with remaining dough. Yield: about 2½ dozen.

A Menu For Seafood Lovers

If you live near the coast or have access to fresh seafood, you'll love this menu featuring crabmeat, shrimp, fish, and clams. A trip to your favorite coastal fishing spot or market will provide you with the makings for one of the best meals you've ever had.

Hot Crab Canapés
Chilled Seafood Mold
Quick Shrimp Gumbo
Gourmet Fish
Broccoli With Lemon Sauce and Pecans
Clam Fritters
Quick Pear Sundaes

HOT CRAB CANAPÉS

8 slices white bread
½ cup flaked crabmeat
½ cup (2 ounces) shredded Cheddar cheese
¼ cup plus 2 tablespoons mayonnaise
1 tablespoon grated onion
½ teaspoon curry powder
¼ teaspoon salt
Chopped fresh parsley

Cut each slice of bread into 4 decorative shapes using 1½-inch cutters. Place cutouts on ungreased baking sheets; broil 6 inches from heat for 1 minute or until lightly browned. Cool.

Combine remaining ingredients except parsley; mix well. Spread crabmeat mixture on bread cutouts. Sprinkle with parsley. Bake at 425° for 5 to 7 minutes or until bubbly. Yield: about 2½ dozen.
Anita Bosch,
Springfield, Virginia.

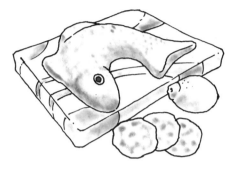

CHILLED SEAFOOD MOLD

1½ cups water
½ pound medium shrimp
1 cup mayonnaise
½ cup flaked crabmeat
½ cup diced celery
½ cup grated carrot
2 tablespoons diced onion
2 tablespoons prepared horseradish
2 tablespoons lemon juice
⅛ teaspoon salt
⅛ teaspoon pepper
1 envelope unflavored gelatin
¼ cup water
Pimiento (optional)
Lemon slices (optional)
Carrot curls (optional)
Fresh parsley (optional)

Bring 1½ cups water to a boil in a saucepan; add shrimp, and cook 3 to 5 minutes. Drain well; rinse with cold water. Peel, devein, and chop shrimp.

Combine shrimp, mayonnaise, crabmeat, celery, carrot, onion, horseradish, lemon juice, salt, and pepper; mix well, and set aside.

Combine gelatin and ¼ cup water in a saucepan; let stand 5 minutes. Place saucepan over low heat, stirring until gelatin dissolves. Pour gelatin mixture into shrimp mixture; stir well. Pour mixture into a greased 3-cup mold. Chill until firm. Unmold and garnish with pimiento, lemon slices, carrot curls, and parsley, if desired. Yield: 2⅔ cups.
Mrs. John Montgomery,
Pensacola, Florida.

QUICK SHRIMP GUMBO

2 tablespoons vegetable oil
2 tablespoons all-purpose flour
1½ cups chopped onion
½ cup sliced celery
1 (28-ounce) can whole tomatoes,
    undrained and chopped
1 quart water
1 bay leaf
3 cloves garlic, minced
2 teaspoons salt
½ teaspoon pepper
3 cups sliced okra
1½ pounds medium shrimp, peeled and
    deveined
2 tablespoons filé powder
Hot cooked rice (optional)

Heat oil in a Dutch oven; add flour, and cook over medium heat, stirring constantly, until roux is the color of a copper penny (about 10 minutes).

Stir onion and celery into roux; cook over medium heat 5 minutes, stirring often. Add tomatoes, water, bay leaf, garlic, salt, and pepper; bring to a boil. Cover, reduce heat, and simmer 20 minutes. Add sliced okra; cover and simmer 15 minutes.

Add shrimp to mixture; cook 3 minutes. Remove from heat; stir in filé powder. Remove bay leaf; serve gumbo over hot cooked rice, if desired. Yield: about 3½ quarts.

Christine Jones,
Boone, North Carolina.

GOURMET FISH

¾ cup grated Parmesan cheese
½ cup butter or margarine, softened
3 tablespoons chopped green onions
3 tablespoons mayonnaise
2 teaspoons chives
6 (¾-inch-thick) grouper fillets
3 tablespoons lemon juice
¼ teaspoon pepper

Combine cheese, butter, green onions, mayonnaise, and chives in a small bowl; mix well, and set aside.

Place grouper fillets in a single layer in a lightly greased 13- x 9- x 2-inch baking dish. Pour lemon juice over fish; sprinkle with pepper.

Broil fillets 6 to 8 minutes or until fish flakes easily when tested with a fork. Remove from oven; spread top of fillets with cheese mixture. Broil fillets an additional 2 to 3 minutes or until cheese is lightly browned and bubbly. Yield: 6 servings.

Martin Golubow,
Charleston, South Carolina.

BROCCOLI WITH LEMON SAUCE AND PECANS

2 teaspoons cornstarch
½ cup chicken broth
¼ cup lemon juice
1 tablespoon sugar
1 teaspoon grated lemon rind
¼ teaspoon pepper
1 (1½-pound) bunch fresh broccoli
⅓ cup chopped pecans
1 tablespoon butter or margarine, melted

Combine cornstarch, chicken broth, and lemon juice in a small saucepan. Cook over medium heat, stirring constantly, until thickened. Stir in sugar, lemon rind, and pepper.

Trim off large leaves of broccoli. Remove tough ends of lower stalks, and wash broccoli thoroughly. Cook broccoli, covered, in a small amount of boiling water 10 to 12 minutes or until tender; drain and arrange on serving platter. Spoon sauce over broccoli.

Sauté pecans in butter until golden. Sprinkle over broccoli before serving. Yield: 6 servings.

Kathleen Stone,
Houston, Texas.

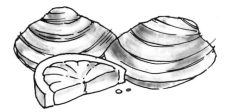

CLAM FRITTERS

1 (11-ounce) container minced fresh clams,
    drained
¼ cup chopped onion
¼ cup chopped green pepper
2 eggs, beaten
2 tablespoons butter or margarine, melted
½ teaspoon lime juice
½ teaspoon hot sauce
½ teaspoon salt
⅛ teaspoon pepper
⅔ cup all-purpose flour
1 teaspoon baking powder
Vegetable oil

Combine clams, onion, green pepper, eggs, butter, lime juice, hot sauce, salt, and pepper in a mixing bowl; mix well.

Combine flour and baking powder; add to clam mixture, and stir until moistened.

Heat ¾ inch oil in a skillet to 350°. Drop clam mixture into hot oil by level tablespoonfuls. Fry until light golden brown, turning once. Drain on paper towels. Serve immediately. Yield: about 1½ dozen fritters. *Hank Boerner,*
Homewood, Alabama.

QUICK PEAR SUNDAES

6 scoops vanilla ice cream
3 Bartlett pears, peeled, halved, and
    cored or 6 canned pear halves, drained
¾ cup commercial caramel or butterscotch
    sauce
¼ cup slivered almonds, toasted

Place a scoop of ice cream in each pear cavity; top with caramel sauce. Sprinkle with almonds. Yield: 6 servings.
Libby Winstead,
Nashville, Tennessee.

Tomatoes Make It Flavorful

To anyone who does a lot of cooking, tomatoes are favorite ingredients. Plump, ripe, and juicy, they're wonderful in their natural state, eaten all by themselves. But they also make a nice addition to many dishes just sliced or chopped. Canned tomatoes, tomato juice, tomato sauce, and tomato paste round out the possibilities. But no matter what their form, they add a rich, distinctive taste. Here's a variety of recipes to demonstrate the possibilities.

SPICY CHILI SALAD

1½ pounds ground beef
1 medium onion, chopped
1 small green pepper, chopped
1 (15-ounce) can tomato sauce with
    tomato bits
2 tablespoons chili powder
2 tablespoons Italian seasoning
1½ teaspoons celery salt
1½ teaspoons pepper
1 teaspoon garlic powder
1 small head lettuce, shredded
¾ cup (3 ounces) shredded Cheddar
    cheese
2 medium tomatoes, cut in wedges

Cook beef, onion, and green pepper in a large skillet until meat is browned, stirring to crumble meat; drain. Stir in tomato sauce, chili powder, and other seasonings; cook over low heat 5 minutes. Cool slightly.

Place lettuce on a serving dish; top with meat mixture. Sprinkle with cheese; garnish with tomato wedges. Yield: about 6 servings. *Janie Lamb,*
Paducah, Kentucky.

BEEF-EATER SANDWICHES

1 (16-ounce) loaf French bread
Butter or margarine, softened
1 pound ground beef
1 (10¾-ounce) can tomato soup, undiluted
¼ cup chopped onion
1 tablespoon prepared mustard
2 teaspoons Worcestershire sauce
¼ teaspoon salt
12 slices process American cheese

Slice French bread in half lengthwise; lightly spread cut sides with butter. Cut each half into 6 pieces. Place the pieces on a baking sheet, and bake at 350° for 10 to 12 minutes.

Cook ground beef in a large skillet until browned, stirring to crumble; drain. Add remaining ingredients except cheese, and heat thoroughly.

Spoon meat mixture over each piece of bread; top with cheese. Bake at 350° for 3 to 5 minutes or until cheese melts. Yield: 12 servings. *Sandi Morris, Elk City, Oklahoma.*

TASTY CABBAGE AND TOMATOES

2 tablespoons bacon drippings
1 small onion, chopped
1 tablespoon chopped green pepper
1 cup canned tomatoes, undrained and coarsely chopped
3 cups coarsely shredded cabbage
½ teaspoon sugar
½ teaspoon salt

Heat bacon drippings in a heavy skillet; add onion and green pepper, and sauté until tender. Add tomatoes; cook vegetables over medium heat 5 minutes, stirring often.

Stir in remaining ingredients; cover, and simmer 10 minutes, stirring occasionally. Yield: about 4 servings. *Ruby Bonelli, Bastrop, Texas.*

TOMATO BISCUITS

2 cups all-purpose flour
1 tablespoon plus 1 teaspoon baking powder
1 teaspoon sugar
½ teaspoon salt
¼ teaspoon baking soda
Dash of ground ginger
¼ cup shortening
1 cup (4 ounces) shredded sharp Cheddar cheese
1 cup tomato juice

Combine dry ingredients; stir well. Cut in shortening with a pastry blender until mixture resembles coarse meal. Stir in cheese; add juice, stirring until dry ingredients are moistened. Turn dough out onto floured surface; knead lightly 3 or 4 times.

Roll dough to ½-inch thickness; cut with a 1½-inch biscuit cutter. Place the biscuits on a greased baking sheet and bake at 400° for 10 to 12 minutes or until biscuits are lightly browned. Yield: 2½ dozen. *Mrs. James L. Twilley, Macon, Georgia.*

MICROWAVE COOKERY

Make Soup In 20 Minutes

If you don't have time to simmer a soup all day, whip up a quick one in the microwave. With these recipes, you'll find the cooking time is only about 20 minutes.

By using the microwave, you'll also eliminate scorching and sticking problems sometimes associated with conventionally cooked cream-based soups, such as our Mushroom Soup and New England Clam Chowder. In addition, microwave soups don't have to be stirred constantly; just stir every couple of minutes to blend the ingredients and ensure even cooking. One word of caution: Always be sure to use a container that holds twice the volume of the soup mixture because liquids boil much higher in the microwave.

Just about any soup recipe can be adapted to the microwave oven. For soups that need thickening, you might need to reduce the liquid or increase the thickening agents for the correct consistency. This adjustment is necessary since liquids are not reduced as they cook in the microwave.

Microwave soup made with milk may be cooked at HIGH without curdling. But if the recipe calls for cream, it's best to microwave at MEDIUM (50% power) unless the mixture contains flour or cornstarch. Keep in mind that these thickening agents help to stabilize the cream mixture and allow the soup to be cooked at HIGH.

When converting your favorite recipes for the microwave, look for extra ways to trim cooking time as we did for

Quick Chicken Soup. Instead of cooking chicken, we used a canned version and canned broth to shorten cooking time about 10 minutes. We also substituted instant rice for regular rice.

NEW ENGLAND CLAM CHOWDER

4 slices bacon, chopped
3 cups diced potatoes
1 medium onion, minced
2 (6½-ounce) cans minced clams, undrained
3 tablespoons all-purpose flour
2 cups milk, divided
¾ teaspoon salt
¼ teaspoon pepper
⅔ cup half-and-half

Place bacon in a deep 3-quart casserole. Cover and microwave at HIGH for 3 minutes. Drain off drippings, reserving 2 tablespoons in casserole. Add potatoes and onion.

Drain clams, reserving liquid. Set clams aside. Stir clam liquid into potato mixture. Microwave at HIGH for 7 to 9 minutes or until potatoes are tender, stirring after 4 minutes.

Combine flour and ¼ cup milk, stirring well; stir into potato mixture. Add remaining 1¾ cups milk, salt, and pepper. Microwave at HIGH 7 to 9 minutes or until thickened, stirring after 4 minutes. Stir in clams and half-and-half. Microwave at HIGH for 1 to 2 minutes or just until chowder is thoroughly heated. Yield: 5 cups.

QUICK CHICKEN SOUP

1 (10¾-ounce) can chicken broth, undiluted
1 cup water
½ cup diced carrot
¼ cup diced celery
¼ cup diced onion
⅛ teaspoon garlic powder
2 (5-ounce) cans chunk chicken
1 cup frozen English peas
¼ to ½ teaspoon pepper
⅓ cup uncooked instant rice

Combine broth, water, carrot, celery, onion, and garlic powder in a 3-quart casserole. Cover and microwave at HIGH for 8 minutes, stirring after 4 minutes.

Add chicken, English peas, and pepper. Cover and microwave at HIGH for 6 to 8 minutes. Stir in uncooked instant rice; cover and microwave 2 to 3 minutes. Yield: 5 cups.

MUSHROOM SOUP

¾ cup chopped green onions
2 cups chopped fresh mushrooms
2 tablespoons butter or margarine
¼ cup all-purpose flour
3 teaspoons chicken-flavored bouillon
   granules
⅛ teaspoon white pepper
1½ cups water
1½ cups milk

Combine onions, mushrooms, and butter in a 2-quart casserole. Microwave at HIGH for 6 to 7 minutes or until vegetables are tender, stirring once.

Stir in flour, bouillon granules, and pepper. Gradually stir in water and milk. Microwave, uncovered, at HIGH for 10 to 15 minutes or until thickened. Yield: 4 cups.

Stuffed Avocados Add Variety

Avocados are a versatile fruit—they can be sliced for a salad, mashed for a dip, or even pureed for a soup. To the creative cook who likes to add a little flair to the menu, they offer imaginative serving possibilities as well. Sliced in half with the seeds removed, avocados provide natural containers for a number of interesting fillings.

You may notice that we included instructions in our recipes for brushing the avocado halves with lemon juice. Be sure to include this step if you don't want the cut surfaces of the avocados to turn brown.

Shrimp Salad on the Half Shell is a delightful combination that includes shrimp, celery, and green onions served on avocado halves. It's as eye-catching as it is delicious.

SHRIMP SALAD ON THE HALF SHELL

9 cups water
3 pounds unpeeled shrimp, uncooked
2 tablespoons sliced green onions with
   tops
2 tablespoons diced celery
⅓ cup vegetable oil
3 tablespoons lemon juice
1½ teaspoons minced parsley
1 clove garlic, crushed
¼ teaspoon dry mustard
¼ to ½ teaspoon salt
Dash of pepper
2 medium avocados
Lemon juice
Bibb lettuce leaves

Bring water to a boil; add unpeeled shrimp, and cook 3 to 5 minutes. Drain well; rinse with cold water. Allow shrimp to chill thoroughly. Peel and devein shrimp.

Combine shrimp, green onions, and celery in a medium bowl; set aside.

Combine oil, lemon juice, minced parsley, garlic, dry mustard, salt, and pepper in a jar. Cover tightly, and shake vigorously. Pour lemon mixture over shrimp mixture, stirring well. Cover and chill at least 2 hours, stirring shrimp occasionally.

Cut avocados in half lengthwise; remove seeds. Brush avocado halves with lemon juice, and fill with shrimp mixture. To serve, arrange avocado halves on lettuce leaves. Yield: 4 servings.
Mary Ealey,
Smithfield, Virginia.

CRAB-STUFFED AVOCADOS

2 cups fresh crabmeat, drained and flaked
1 (11-ounce) can mandarin oranges,
   drained
¼ cup plus 1 tablespoon vegetable oil
½ cup sliced green onions with tops
2 tablespoons wine vinegar
½ teaspoon garlic salt
3 small avocados, peeled
2 tablespoons lemon juice
Lettuce leaves

Combine fresh crabmeat, mandarin oranges, oil, green onions, vinegar, and garlic salt; mix well.

Cut avocados in half lengthwise; remove seeds. Brush avocado halves with lemon juice, and fill with crabmeat mixture. Arrange avocado halves on lettuce leaves. Yield: 6 servings. *Betty Beske,*
Arlington, Virginia.

SALMON-STUFFED AVOCADOS

1 (7¾-ounce) can boned and skinned pink
   salmon, drained and flaked
½ cup chopped celery
½ cup frozen English peas, thawed
¼ cup chopped green onions
1 hard-cooked egg, chopped
¼ cup mayonnaise
2 large avocados, peeled
Lemon juice
Paprika
Bibb lettuce leaves

Combine salmon, celery, peas, green
onions, chopped egg, and mayonnaise;
toss well. Chill.

Cut avocados in half lengthwise; remove seeds. Brush avocado halves with
lemon juice, and fill with salmon mixture. Sprinkle with paprika. Arrange
avocado halves on lettuce leaves. Yield:
4 servings.　　　　　*Jan Crenshaw,*
Warrenton, North Carolina.

TOMATO-AVOCADO SALAD

3 medium tomatoes, chopped
3 green onions with tops, chopped
½ cup vegetable oil
¼ cup wine vinegar
½ teaspoon salt
½ teaspoon paprika
¼ teaspoon freshly ground pepper
1 clove garlic, crushed
3 medium-size avocados, peeled
2 tablespoons lemon juice
Lettuce leaves

Combine tomatoes and green onions
in a small bowl; set aside.

Combine oil, vinegar, salt, paprika,
pepper, and garlic in a jar. Cover
tightly, and shake vigorously. Pour mixture over vegetables. Cover and marinate 1 hour.

Cut avocados in half lengthwise; remove seeds. Brush avocado halves with
lemon juice, and fill with tomato mixture. Arrange avocado halves on lettuce
leaves. Yield: 6 servings.
Rita Hastings,
Edgewater, Maryland.

GUACAMOLE IN SHELLS

2 medium-size ripe avocados
1 small tomato, seeded and chopped
¼ cup mayonnaise
¼ cup chopped celery
¼ cup sliced green onions
3 tablespoons diced green pepper
1 tablespoon plus 1 teaspoon lemon juice
1 clove garlic, crushed
¼ teaspoon chili powder
⅛ teaspoon salt
⅛ teaspoon pepper
Dash of hot sauce
Tortilla chips

Cut avocados in half lengthwise; remove seeds, and scoop out avocado. Set
aside avocado shells.

Position knife blade in food processor
bowl; add avocado. Top with cover;
process until smooth.

Combine avocado puree and remaining ingredients except tortilla chips in a
medium bowl; blend well. Chill.

Spoon guacamole into reserved avocado shells, and serve with tortilla
chips. Yield: 3½ cups.
Aimee Goodman,
Knoxville, Tennessee.

Popcorn With Pizzazz

If you always serve popcorn the same
way—with butter and salt—you're in for
a treat. Next time you make a batch of
popcorn, give it new flavor by tossing it
with various spices or seasonings. We
think you will agree that popcorn can
be one of the most versatile and enjoyable snacks around.

BACON-CHEESE POPCORN

4 quarts freshly popped popcorn, unsalted
⅓ cup butter or margarine, melted
½ teaspoon seasoned salt
¼ teaspoon hickory-smoked salt
⅓ cup grated Parmesan cheese
⅓ cup bacon-flavored bits

Pour popcorn into a large mixing
bowl. Combine butter and salt; pour
over popcorn, stirring well. Add cheese
and bacon bits; stir well. Pour into a 15-
x 10- x 1-inch jellyroll pan. Bake at 350°
for 8 minutes, stirring once. Store in an
airtight container. Yield: 4 quarts.
Cheryl Blakney,
Sandersville, Georgia.

ORIENTAL POPCORN

2 quarts freshly popped popcorn, unsalted
1 (6¼-ounce) can cashew nuts
1 (5-ounce) can chow mein noodles
¼ cup butter or margarine, melted
1½ tablespoons soy sauce
¾ teaspoon ground ginger

Combine popcorn, nuts, and noodles.
Combine butter, soy sauce, and ginger,
stirring well; pour over popcorn mixture. Toss well. Pour into a 15- x 10- x
1-inch jellyroll pan. Bake at 350° for 5
to 10 minutes. Store in an airtight container. Yield: about 2½ quarts.

A Hint Of Coffee
Flavors
These Desserts

A steaming cup of coffee is always a
favorite beverage, but too often its appearance in a menu ends there. Once
you try these recipes, you'll find that
coffee also adds a flavorful touch to different kinds of desserts.

COFFEE-CHIP FUDGE

1½ cups firmly packed brown sugar
1½ cups sugar
1 cup milk
½ cup half-and-half
2 tablespoons light corn syrup
2 tablespoons instant coffee granules
⅛ teaspoon salt
3 tablespoons butter or margarine,
   softened
1 teaspoon vanilla extract
1 (6-ounce) package semisweet chocolate
   morsels
½ cup chopped pecans

Combine sugar, milk, half-and-half,
corn syrup, coffee granules, and salt in
a large heavy saucepan. Bring to a boil
over medium heat, stirring constantly.
Continue cooking, without stirring, to
the soft ball stage (234°).

Remove from heat; add butter and
vanilla; do not stir. Cool to 110°; beat
until fudge loses gloss and begins to
thicken. Add chocolate morsels and
pecans; stir just to mix. Pour into a
buttered 9-inch square pan. Cool and
cut into 1½-inch squares. Yield: 3
dozen.　　　　*Mrs. Evelyn Weisman,*
Kingsville, Texas.

MOCHA CHIFFON

1 envelope unflavored gelatin
¼ cup cold water
¾ cup milk
⅓ cup semisweet chocolate morsels
3 tablespoons cocoa
2 eggs, separated
½ cup sugar
2 teaspoons instant coffee granules
1 teaspoon vanilla extract
1 cup whipping cream, whipped
Additional whipped cream (optional)
Chocolate shavings (optional)

Soften gelatin in cold water; let stand 5 minutes.

Combine milk, chocolate morsels, and cocoa in a heavy saucepan; cook over low heat until chocolate melts.

Combine egg yolks and sugar in a small mixing bowl; blend well. Gradually stir about one-fourth of hot mixture into egg yolk mixture; add to remaining hot mixture, stirring constantly.

Add coffee granules to hot mixture. Cook, stirring constantly, until mixture thickens. Remove from heat and stir in softened gelatin and vanilla. Chill until mixture is the consistency of unbeaten egg white.

Beat egg whites (at room temperature) until stiff peaks form. Gently fold egg whites into coffee mixture.

Gently fold whipped cream into egg white mixture. Spoon into a 1-quart casserole, and chill until firm.

To serve, top with additional whipped cream and chocolate shavings, if desired. Yield: 4 to 6 servings.
Mrs. Ronald D. Smith,
Houston, Texas.

TWO-DAY COFFEE SPONGE CAKE

2 cups all-purpose flour
2 teaspoons baking powder
8 eggs, separated
2 cups sugar
½ cup boiling water
Filling (recipe follows)
1 cup strong coffee, cooled and divided
1¼ cups whipping cream
2 tablespoons sifted powdered sugar

Sift flour and baking powder together; set aside.

Combine egg yolks and sugar in a large mixing bowl; beat at high speed of an electric mixer until thick and lemon colored. Reduce speed to medium, and gradually add boiling water. Add flour mixture; mix until well blended. Set mixture aside.

Beat egg whites (at room temperature) until stiff peaks form. Fold egg whites into batter. Pour batter into 3 ungreased, waxed paper-lined, 9-inch round cakepans. Bake at 350° for 20 minutes or until cake springs back when lightly touched. Invert cake layers on racks; cool about 30 minutes. Loosen cake from sides of pan, using a small metal spatula. Remove cake from pan, and peel off waxed paper.

Spread filling between layers; drizzle ½ cup coffee over top layer. Cover and refrigerate at least 5 hours. Place a serving plate on top of cake; invert cake onto serving plate. Drizzle remaining coffee over top; cover and chill.

Beat whipping cream until foamy; add sugar, beating until peaks hold their shape. Spread whipped cream on sides and top of cake. Chill up to 1½ hours before serving. Yield: one 3-layer cake.

Filling:

2 teaspoons instant coffee granules
1 to 2 tablespoons water
¼ cup butter or margarine, softened
3 cups sifted powdered sugar

Dissolve coffee granules in 2 tablespoons water; set aside. Cream butter; add sugar and 1 tablespoon coffee mixture. Beat until smooth, adding more coffee mixture until filling reaches desired consistency. Yield: 1½ cups.
Helen Boatman,
Chapel Hill, North Carolina.

Applause For Pork

Farmers are producing leaner pork these days. And that's good news because it means the meat has less fat than before. The leanest cut of all, succulent tenderloin, is always a favorite. Smoked and cured, you may have enjoyed it as Canadian bacon. But have you tried the fresh version, which lends itself to broiling, grilling, or sautéing?

Apple-Ginger Pork Tenderloin boasts a smooth transparent sauce delicately flavored with apple juice and ginger, two flavors that are particularly complementary to pork. Serve this dish with baked sweet potatoes, steamed fresh broccoli, and sautéed apples.

Pork Tenderloin Towers are pork tenderloin slices topped with onion and bacon before grilling. And just before they're done, you add a slice of tomato and Swiss cheese. Serve the towers in a bun or with rye bread.

APPLE-GINGER PORK TENDERLOIN

1 tablespoon all-purpose flour
1¼ teaspoons garlic salt
1 teaspoon ground ginger
1 (1½-pound) pork tenderloin
¼ cup vegetable oil
1 tablespoon cornstarch
1 tablespoon water
1¼ cups apple juice
Chopped fresh parsley (optional)
Apple wedges (optional)

Combine flour, garlic salt, and ginger; dredge tenderloin in flour mixture.

Cook tenderloin, uncovered, in hot oil in a skillet over low heat 10 minutes, turning occasionally. Insert meat thermometer. Cover and cook an additional 35 minutes or until thermometer registers 170°.

Combine cornstarch and water in a small saucepan, stirring until smooth; stir in apple juice. Bring to a boil, and cook 1 minute or until thickened, stirring constantly. Serve sauce over sliced tenderloin. Garnish with parsley and apple wedges, if desired. Yield: 4 servings.
Sherry Hilliard,
Rhine, Georgia.

PORK TENDERLOIN TOWERS

8 slices bacon
4 slices onion
1 (¾-pound) pork tenderloin, cut into 4 (1-inch) slices
Salt
Pepper
4 (½-inch) tomatoes slices
4 slices Swiss cheese

Layer 2 slices bacon to form an X. Place 1 slice onion in center of bacon; top with 1 slice tenderloin. Sprinkle with salt and pepper. Bring ends of bacon over tenderloin, and secure with a wooden pick. Repeat procedure with remaining bacon, onion, and tenderloin.

Place meat on grill over medium coals, and grill 40 minutes, turning frequently. Turn meat wooden pick side up; remove wooden picks. Top each with a slice of tomato and cheese, and grill an additional 10 minutes. Yield: 4 servings.
Lilyan Oulehla,
New Port Richey, Florida.

PORK TENDERLOIN WITH BLUE CHEESE

2 tablespoons vegetable oil
1 (1½-pound) pork tenderloin, cut into
    1-inch slices
½ teaspoon salt
¼ teaspoon pepper
3 tablespoons butter or margarine
3 tablespoons all-purpose flour
2 cups milk
4 ounces blue cheese, crumbled
Hot cooked noodles
Chopped fresh parsley (optional)

Heat oil in a large skillet. Add pork, and cook over medium heat until browned; add salt and pepper. Cover and cook 10 minutes. Drain well, and set aside.

Melt butter in a skillet over low heat; add flour, stirring until smooth. Cook 1 minute, stirring constantly. Gradually add milk; cook over medium heat, stirring constantly, until mixture is thickened and bubbly. Stir in pork and blue cheese. Serve over hot noodles. Garnish with chopped parsley, if desired. Yield: 4 servings.

Ruby Vineyard,
Rutledge, Tennessee.

PORK TENDERLOIN PICATTA

1 (1-pound) pork tenderloin, diagonally
    cut into ¼-inch slices
1 egg, beaten
¼ cup milk
⅔ cup all-purpose flour
½ teaspoon salt
¼ teaspoon pepper
¼ cup butter or margarine, divided
1 tablespoon lemon juice
Lemon slices (optional)

Place tenderloin between 2 sheets of waxed paper, and flatten to ⅛-inch thickness with a meat mallet or rolling pin. Set aside.

Combine egg and milk in a shallow dish; mix well. Combine flour, salt, and pepper in a shallow dish; stir well. Dip pork into egg mixture, and dredge in flour mixture.

Heat 2 tablespoons butter in a large skillet; add meat, and cook over medium heat until golden brown, turning once. Keep warm on a serving platter.

Add remaining 2 tablespoons butter and lemon juice to skillet; cook 1 minute, stirring to loosen pan particles. Pour over pork; garnish with lemon slices, if desired. Yield: 4 servings.

Shirley W. Hodge,
Delray Beach, Florida.

CURRIED PORK TENDERLOIN

1 (20-ounce) can pineapple chunks,
    undrained
1 tablespoon cornstarch
¼ teaspoon salt
½ teaspoon curry powder
¼ cup cider vinegar
2 tablespoons soy sauce
3 tablespoons vegetable oil, divided
1 (1½- to 2-pound) pork tenderloin, cut
    into 1-inch cubes
1 large green pepper, cut into strips
2 small onions, sliced and separated into
    rings
1 (8-ounce) can sliced water chestnuts,
    drained
Hot cooked rice
½ cup chopped dates (optional)
½ cup flaked coconut (optional)
¼ cup commercial bacon bits (optional)

Drain pineapple, reserving liquid; set pineapple aside.

Combine pineapple liquid, cornstarch, salt, curry powder, vinegar, and soy sauce; mix well, and set aside.

Add 2 tablespoons oil to a preheated wok, coating sides; allow to heat at medium high (325°) for 1 minute. Add pork; stir-fry 8 to 10 minutes or until done. Remove pork from wok.

Add remaining 1 tablespoon oil, green pepper, onion, and water chestnuts to wok; stir-fry 2 minutes or until crisp-tender. Return pork to wok. Add cornstarch mixture to wok; cook, stirring constantly, until thickened.

Add pineapple to wok; cook, stirring gently, until thoroughly heated. Serve over hot cooked rice. Sprinkle with dates, coconut, and bacon, if desired. Yield: 6 servings. *Janice Elder,*
Spartanburg, South Carolina.

Start With A Soup Mix

Tear open a package of dry soup mix, and let your imagination take over. These handy pouches of flavor offer a multitude of ideas for perking up dishes without the need for many different spices and herbs.

Piquant Chicken is as tasty as its name indicates. Onion soup mix, stewed tomatoes, green pepper, and lemon juice make up the tangy sauce. And best of all, the dish is low in calories.

For an appetizer that is out of the ordinary, try Black-eyed Pea Spread.

Southerners will delight in this ingenious use of their favorite peas. Combined with chopped spinach, sour cream, mayonnaise, dry vegetable soup mix and just a bit of garlic powder, this tasty spread is served on pumpernickel party bread slices. Water chestnuts add crunch to this colorful appetizer spread.

APRICOT-STUFFED PORK CHOPS

1 (16-ounce) can apricot halves, drained
6 (1-inch-thick) rib pork chops
2 tablespoons vegetable oil
½ cup uncooked rice
1 (1¼-ounce) package dry onion soup mix
1⅓ cups water
¼ cup chopped pecans
¼ teaspoon ground mace
¼ cup apricot preserves
1 tablespoon plus 1 teaspoon lemon juice
¼ teaspoon ground cloves

Chop enough apricots to make ½ cup; reserve remaining apricot halves.

Make pockets in pork chops, cutting from rib side to fat edge of each chop. (Do not cut through fat edge.)

Heat oil in a skillet over medium heat; brown pork chops on both sides. Set aside.

Combine rice, soup mix, and water in a saucepan; cover and cook over medium heat 10 minutes. Add chopped apricots, pecans, and mace, mixing well. Spoon about ⅓ cup rice mixture into each pork chop pocket. Place chops in a 13- x 9- x 2-inch baking pan; cover and bake at 350° for 1 hour or until pork chops are done.

Combine apricot preserves, lemon juice, and cloves. Brush chops with mixture; bake, uncovered, an additional 15 minutes. Transfer to a serving platter, and garnish with reserved apricot halves. Yield: 6 servings.

Dorothy Nieman,
Dunnellon, Florida.

PIQUANT CHICKEN

1 (16-ounce) can stewed tomatoes,
    undrained and chopped
1 (1¼-ounce) package dry onion soup mix
½ cup chopped green pepper
2 tablespoons chopped onion
1½ teaspoons dried whole oregano
4 chicken breast halves, skinned
Juice of 1 lemon
¼ teaspoon salt
¼ teaspoon pepper
Green pepper rings (optional)

Combine tomatoes, soup mix, ½ cup green pepper, chopped onion, and oregano; set aside.

Dip chicken in lemon juice; sprinkle with salt and pepper. Place chicken in a lightly greased 13- x 9- x 2-inch baking pan, meaty side down. Cover and bake at 400° for 10 minutes. Turn chicken meaty side up, and cover with tomato mixture. Cover and bake an additional 40 minutes. Garnish with green pepper rings, if desired. Yield: 4 servings.

Mrs. Robert S. Henderson,
Virginia Beach, Virginia.

CREAMY LEEK DIP

1 (8-ounce) carton commercial sour cream
1 cup cream-style cottage cheese
½ (2.4-ounce) package dry leek soup mix

Combine all ingredients, mixing well. Chill 3 to 4 hours. Serve with fresh vegetables. Yield: 2 cups.

Eileen R. MaCutchan,
Largo, Florida.

BLACK-EYED PEA SPREAD

1 (10-ounce) package frozen chopped spinach, thawed and pressed dry
1 (16-ounce) can black-eyed peas, drained
1 (8-ounce) can sliced water chestnuts, drained and chopped
1 (8-ounce) carton commercial sour cream
½ cup mayonnaise
⅓ cup dry vegetable soup mix
⅛ teaspoon garlic powder
About 40 pumpernickel party bread slices

Combine all ingredients except bread; mix well. Spread mixture on bread slices. Yield: about 40 appetizer servings.

Michele Burger,
Euless, Texas.

Dishes Rich With Cheese

Judging by the recipes we receive from our readers, Southern cooks use cheese in just about everything. It's added to soups, salads, main dishes, casseroles—even desserts. To give you a sampling, we've chosen a number of recipes that have an extra helping of rich cheese flavor.

If you're a pizza fan, you'll want to try Double Cheesy Beef-and-Sausage Pizza. It has both mozzarella cheese and provolone in the filling as well as ground beef, sausage, and bacon. The result is a tasty combination that was a big hit in our test kitchens.

Another cheesy entrée with Italian roots is Chicken Marinara. Chicken breasts are baked in a savory, tomato-base sauce and are topped with mozzarella, Swiss, and Parmesan cheese. We suggest serving it with noodles.

For an unusual side dish, try Rice au Gratin Supreme, Hominy With Chiles and Cheese, or Baked Cheese Pudding.

CHICKEN MARINARA

¾ cup fine dry breadcrumbs
½ teaspoon salt
¼ teaspoon pepper
6 chicken breast halves, skinned and boned
2 eggs, beaten
¼ cup butter or margarine
1 (15½-ounce) jar marinara sauce or spaghetti sauce
½ cup half-and-half
3 (1-ounce) slices mozzarella cheese, cut in half crosswise
6 (1-ounce) slices Swiss cheese
1 tablespoon grated Parmesan cheese
Cooked noodles (optional)

Combine breadcrumbs, salt, and pepper; mix well, and set aside.

Dip each chicken breast half in eggs; coat with breadcrumb mixture, and set aside. Melt butter in a large skillet over medium heat. Add chicken, and cook about 2 minutes on each side or until light-golden brown. Remove chicken, and drain.

Combine marinara sauce and half-and-half, mixing well; reserve ¼ cup plus 2 tablespoons, and set aside. Pour remaining sauce mixture into a lightly greased 13- x 9- x 2-inch baking dish, and top with chicken. Cover and bake at 350° for 25 minutes.

Place a slice of mozzarella and Swiss cheese on each chicken breast half; top with a tablespoon of reserved sauce, and sprinkle with Parmesan cheese. Cover and bake an additional 5 minutes. Serve over cooked noodles, if desired. Yield: 6 servings.

Mrs. Harold Wagner,
Hendersonville, North Carolina.

DOUBLE CHEESY BEEF-AND-SAUSAGE PIZZA

1 (8-ounce) can tomato sauce
Pizza crust (recipe follows)
¼ teaspoon garlic powder
1 to 2 teaspoons dried whole oregano
1 pound ground beef
1 pound bulk pork sausage
½ pound bacon, cooked and crumbled
2 (4-ounce) cans sliced mushrooms, drained
4 cups (16 ounces) shredded mozzarella cheese
2 cups (8 ounces) shredded provolone cheese

Spread tomato sauce evenly over each partially baked pizza crust, leaving a ½-inch border around pizza edges. Sprinkle garlic powder and oregano evenly over each pizza.

Cook ground beef and sausage until browned, stirring occasionally to crumble; drain well. Sprinkle meat mixture and bacon over each pizza; top with mushrooms. Combine mozzarella and provolone cheese; sprinkle over each pizza. Bake at 375° for 20 to 25 minutes. Yield: two 12-inch pizzas.

Pizza Crust:

1 package dry yeast
1¼ cups warm water (105° to 115°)
2 tablespoons vegetable oil
Dash of salt
4 cups all-purpose flour, divided
2 tablespoons cornmeal

Dissolve yeast in water in a large bowl; let stand 5 minutes. Stir in oil and salt. Stir in enough flour to make a soft dough.

Turn dough out onto a lightly floured surface, and knead about 8 to 10 minutes or until smooth and elastic. Sprinkle cornmeal over 2 lightly greased 12-inch pizza pans. Divide dough in half. Lightly grease hands, and pat dough evenly into pizza pans. Bake at 425° for 8 to 10 minutes or until pizza crust is lightly browned. Yield: two 12-inch pizza crusts.

Lou Lowery,
Atlanta, Georgia.

CHEESE RAREBIT

¼ cup butter or margarine
¼ cup all-purpose flour
2 cups milk
3 cups (12 ounces) shredded Cheddar
  cheese
¼ teaspoon salt
¼ teaspoon dry mustard
⅛ teaspoon paprika
1 egg, beaten
Toast points

Melt butter in a heavy saucepan over low heat; add flour, stirring until smooth. Cook 1 minute, stirring constantly. Gradually add milk; cook over medium heat, stirring constantly, until mixture is thickened and bubbly. Stir in Cheddar cheese, salt, dry mustard, and paprika.

Gradually stir about one-fourth of hot mixture into beaten egg; add to remaining hot mixture. Cook mixture over low heat 1 minute. Serve over toast points. Yield: 6 to 8 servings.

Doris Garton,
Shenandoah, Virginia.

MACARONI-AND-CHEESE WITH WINE

1½ cups uncooked elbow macaroni
¼ cup chopped onion
3 tablespoons butter or margarine,
  melted
3 tablespoons all-purpose flour
1¾ cups milk
¼ cup dry white wine
½ teaspoon salt
Pinch of pepper
1½ cups (6 ounces) shredded sharp
  Cheddar cheese
Paprika

Cook macaroni according to package directions, omitting salt; then drain and set aside.

Sauté onion in butter in a heavy saucepan; add flour, stirring until smooth. Cook 1 minute, stirring constantly. Gradually add milk and wine; cook over medium heat, stirring constantly, until mixture is thickened and bubbly.

Remove from heat; add salt, pepper, and Cheddar cheese. Stir until cheese melts. Add macaroni; mix well. Pour into a lightly greased 2-quart casserole. Sprinkle top with paprika.

Cover and bake at 350° for 15 minutes; uncover and continue baking 15 minutes. Yield: 6 servings.

Jane Grace,
Cyril, Oklahoma.

RICE AU GRATIN SUPREME

4 cups cooked rice
½ cup chopped onion
½ cup chopped green pepper
1 (2-ounce) jar diced pimiento, drained
1 (10¾-ounce) can cream of mushroom
  soup, undiluted
⅓ cup mayonnaise
2 cups (8 ounces) shredded Cheddar
  cheese, divided
½ cup milk

Combine rice, onion, green pepper, and pimiento in a large bowl; mix well. Combine soup, mayonnaise, 1 cup cheese, and milk. Stir soup mixture into the rice mixture.

Spoon mixture into a lightly greased 2-quart casserole. Bake at 350° for 25 minutes; sprinkle top with remaining 1 cup cheese, and bake an additional 5 minutes. Yield: 8 servings.

Jill Rorex,
Dallas, Texas.

HOMINY WITH CHILES AND CHEESE

2 (15-ounce) cans hominy, rinsed, drained,
  and divided
1 (4-ounce) can chopped green chiles,
  drained, and divided
½ cup commercial sour cream, divided
2 teaspoons butter or margarine, divided
Salt and pepper to taste
½ cup (2 ounces) shredded Monterey Jack
  cheese
¼ cup milk

Layer half of hominy and half of chiles in a lightly greased 1½-quart casserole. Dot with ¼ cup sour cream and 1 teaspoon butter. Sprinkle lightly with salt and pepper. Repeat layering procedure with remaining hominy, green chiles, sour cream, and butter. Sprinkle with cheese, and pour milk over the casserole. Bake, uncovered, at 350° for 30 minutes. Yield: 6 servings.

Mrs. Robert Collins,
Fairfax, Missouri.

BAKED CHEESE PUDDING

3 eggs, beaten
1 cup half-and-half
1⅓ cups soft breadcrumbs
1 cup (4 ounces) shredded sharp Cheddar
  cheese
3 tablespoons butter, melted
Paprika

Combine eggs and half-and-half; beat well. Stir in breadcrumbs, cheese, and butter. Pour mixture into a lightly greased 1-quart casserole. Sprinkle with paprika. Bake at 350° for 30 minutes or until set. Serve immediately. Yield: 4 servings.

Mrs. Robert Wilkinson,
Dothan, Alabama.

GERMAN PASTRIES

1 egg yolk
2 tablespoons sugar
1 (8-ounce) package cream cheese,
  softened
½ teaspoon vanilla extract
¼ cup raisins
Cream Cheese Pastry
1 cup sifted powdered sugar
1 tablespoon plus 1 teaspoon milk

Beat egg yolk; gradually add sugar, beating until thick and lemon colored. Add cream cheese; beat until smooth. Stir in vanilla and raisins.

Roll pastry to ⅛-inch thickness; cut into 2-inch squares. Place about 1 teaspoon filling in center of each square. Moisten edges of pastry with water. Fold corners to center; press edges together, sealing well.

Place pastries on lightly greased baking sheets, and bake at 375° for 15 to 20 minutes or until the pastries are lightly browned.

Combine powdered sugar and milk; mix well. Spoon over warm pastries. Yield: about 3 dozen.

Cream Cheese Pastry:

½ cup butter or margarine
1 cup all-purpose flour
1 (8-ounce) package cream cheese,
  softened

Cut butter into flour with a pastry blender until mixture resembles coarse meal. Add cream cheese; beat with an electric mixer until smooth. Shape pastry into a ball; chill 1 to 2 hours. Yield: enough for 3 dozen pastries.

Donna Anderson,
Pottsboro, Texas.

Make A Layered Salad

Colorful ingredients are stacked in layers and tossed right before serving for most layered salads. But Kelly Carlton of Birmingham, Alabama, cuts her version into squares.

"I make it mostly when we have company," says Kelly, "because I can make it overnight and not be in the kitchen all day the next day." Kelly says her Layered Salad easily serves as a meal in itself. "When I have some left over, my husband and I have it for lunch the next day. It seems to taste even better after it's been in the refrigerator again."

Since the salad contains some chunky ingredients, use an electric knife to cut it into squares. If you don't have an electric knife, a regular knife with a serrated blade will make cutting easier.

LAYERED SALAD

½ head romaine lettuce
6 hard-cooked eggs, sliced
1 cup (4 ounces) shredded Swiss cheese, divided
1 pound fresh spinach, torn into bite-size pieces
1 (10-ounce) package frozen baby English peas, thawed and drained
1 small red onion, thinly sliced and separated into rings
1 pound bacon, cooked and crumbled
1 cup mayonnaise
1 cup salad dressing
1 teaspoon sugar
1 cup (4 ounces) shredded Cheddar cheese

Arrange romaine lettuce leaves in a 13- x 9- x 2-inch dish. Then layer ingredients over romaine in the following order: eggs, ¼ cup Swiss cheese, spinach, ¼ cup Swiss cheese, peas, ¼ cup Swiss cheese, red onion, ¼ cup Swiss cheese, and bacon.

Combine mayonnaise, salad dressing, and sugar in a small bowl; mix well. Spread over top of salad, sealing to edge of dish. Sprinkle with Cheddar cheese. Cover salad tightly, and refrigerate several hours or overnight. To serve, cut salad into squares. Yield: 12 servings.

Tip: Don't add salt to green salad until just before serving. The salt wilts and toughens salad greens.

Serve A Green Salad

Spinach, romaine, and iceberg lettuce are just a few of the leafy greens that make crisp salads taste so refreshing. Fruit, vegetables, cheese, and seasonings blend well with them, making the flavor combinations endless.

Add variations to salads by experimenting with different leafy green vegetables. Try mixing two or three kinds and adding new seasonings to come up with a new recipe. (See "From Our Kitchen To Yours" on page 80 for information on lettuce.)

PARTY VEGETABLE SALAD

8 cups torn iceberg lettuce
⅔ cup chopped green onions with tops
⅔ cup chopped celery
1 medium-size green pepper, cut into strips
1 (8-ounce) can sliced water chestnuts, drained
1 (10-ounce) package frozen green peas, thawed
Parmesan Mayonnaise
1 tablespoon herb salad seasoning
2 medium tomatoes, cut into wedges
3 hard-cooked eggs, sliced
⅓ cup (1.33 ounces) shredded Cheddar cheese
6 slices bacon, cooked and crumbled

Layer lettuce, chopped green onions, celery, green pepper strips, water chestnuts, and green peas in a large salad bowl. Pour Parmesan Mayonnaise over top of salad. Sprinkle with herb salad seasoning. Cover salad tightly, and refrigerate overnight.

To serve, top salad with remaining ingredients in order listed. Yield: 10 servings.

Parmesan Mayonnaise:

1 egg
2 tablespoons grated Parmesan cheese
⅓ cup mayonnaise
2 tablespoons cider vinegar
½ teaspoon prepared mustard
½ teaspoon salt
½ teaspoon pepper
1 cup vegetable oil

Combine all ingredients except oil in container of an electric blender. With blender running, gradually add oil in a slow, steady stream, mixing just until well blended and thickened. Yield: about 1½ cups.

Joann Wilson,
Silverhill, Alabama.

HEARTY LAYERED SALAD

2 cups torn iceberg lettuce
2 cups torn fresh spinach
1 cup (4 ounces) shredded Cheddar cheese, divided
¼ cup chopped purple onion
¼ cup chopped celery
½ cup cottage cheese
1 (5-ounce) can boned chicken, drained
1 (8.5-ounce) can English peas, drained
¼ cup slivered almonds, toasted
Egg Dressing
2 slices bacon, cooked and crumbled

Combine lettuce and spinach. Place 2 cups of salad green mixture in a 2-quart salad bowl. Layer with ½ cup cheese, onion, celery, cottage cheese, chicken, peas, remaining ½ cup cheese, almonds, and remaining salad green mixture. Spread Egg Dressing over top of salad, sealing to edge of bowl. Cover salad tightly, and refrigerate several hours. Sprinkle with bacon before serving. Yield: 4 servings.

Egg Dressing:

⅓ cup mayonnaise
⅓ cup commercial sour cream
2 teaspoons lemon juice
1 hard-cooked egg, chopped

Combine all ingredients; mix thoroughly. Yield: ⅔ cup.

Roxanne Menees,
White Pines, Tennessee.

MAJESTIC LAYERED SALAD

¾ pound fresh spinach, torn into bite-size pieces
2 cups sliced fresh mushrooms
1 small purple onion, sliced and separated into rings
1 (10-ounce) package frozen English peas, thawed and drained
1 cup mayonnaise
½ teaspoon sugar
½ teaspoon curry powder
2 slices bacon, cooked and crumbled

Layer torn spinach, sliced mushrooms, onion rings, and English peas in a 2½-quart salad bowl.

Combine mayonnaise, sugar, and curry powder; mix well. Spread over top of salad, sealing to edge of bowl. Cover salad tightly, and refrigerate 8 hours or overnight.

Uncover salad and sprinkle with crumbled bacon before serving. Yield: 6 to 8 servings.

Charlotte Farmer,
Richmond, Virginia.

CAESAR SALAD

1 clove garlic, peeled and halved
2 tablespoons vegetable oil
2 cups water
1 egg
1½ teaspoons anchovy paste
1 large head romaine lettuce, torn
2½ teaspoons red wine vinegar
1 teaspoon Worcestershire sauce
¾ teaspoon lemon juice
2 tablespoons grated Parmesan cheese
¼ teaspoon freshly ground pepper
1 cup seasoned croutons

Combine garlic and vegetable oil in a small mixing bowl; cover and let stand several hours.

Bring water to a boil in a small saucepan; remove from heat. Carefully lower egg into water using a slotted spoon; cover, and let stand 1½ minutes. Remove egg from water, and then set aside to cool.

Rub the inside bottom half of a large salad bowl with anchovy paste. Remove garlic from oil; place romaine in salad bowl, and drizzle with garlic oil. Sprinkle with vinegar, Worcestershire sauce, lemon juice, cheese, and pepper. Break coddled egg over romaine, and toss lightly. Add croutons, and toss well. Serve immediately. Yield: 4 to 6 servings.   *Bonnie Neely,*
Woodbridge, Virginia.

From Our Kitchen To Yours

With many types of lettuce to choose from today, your tossed salads need never be dull. **Iceberg** or **crisphead** is the most popular. It has a firm, crisp-textured head of green leaves on the outside and a pale green core. Iceberg leaves are lighter green and crisper than most types of lettuce.

Bibb or **butterhead** is a small cup-shaped head of lettuce with deep-green leaves. The veins and ribs of Bibb lettuce are less prominent than in other lettuces. Like iceberg, the inner leaves of Bibb are whitish green. Its slightly nutty taste makes it unique.

Romaine or **cos** lettuce is a long loaf-shaped head with coarse, crisp leaves and heavy ribs. Romaine has a more pronounced flavor than iceberg.

Boston, another type of butterhead lettuce, has delicate leaves that are easily separated. It's usually lighter and softer and not as crisp in texture as either iceberg or Romaine.

Leaf or **"bunching"** lettuce has delicate leaves that grow loosely, rather than form heads. Leaves are just pressed together and clustered at the core. Leaf lettuce can be all green or have red-tipped leaves. The ruffled leaves are usually sweet in flavor and crisp textured.

When selecting lettuce, choose a head that gives slightly when squeezed and has a bright green color. Lettuce doesn't ripen on the way to the store; it's picked just after it has matured. A pale-brown head of lettuce is too mature and tasteless.

Lettuce that looks fresh and crisp has usually been stored properly and kept cool. If the core is brown, it's just a sign of oxidation. After lettuce is cut during harvesting, the core naturally turns brown as the cut surface seals to keep the head fresh and hold in the nutrients.

Although most refrigerators maintain a temperature of 36° to 38° F., it's best to store lettuce at 32° F. or as close to freezing as possible. If bought fresh and stored at 32° F., lettuce may keep two to three weeks.

The crisper drawer in the refrigerator is the best spot for storing any kind of lettuce. Store lettuce away from apples, pears, melons, or bananas because these kinds of fruit give off a gas called ethylene, causing brown spots to form on the lettuce.

Extra Tips

—To core a head of lettuce, hold it core end down, and hit it on the kitchen counter. Then twist, and lift out the core with your fingers. Follow this procedure because if the core is cut out with a knife, the surrounding area will discolor more quickly.

—For extra-crisp lettuce, put washed and drained leaves in a plastic bag, and place in the freezer for a few minutes. Immediately mix with other salad ingredients, and serve.

—Loose outer leaves on a head of lettuce or "wrappers" shouldn't be thrown away; they're very high in nutritive value.

—One medium head of lettuce will yield about 4 cups shredded lettuce, 3 to 4 crosswise slices, about 4 cups bite-size chunks, or 4 wedges.

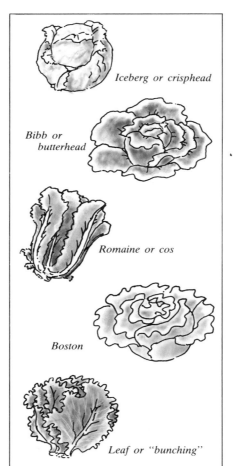

Iceberg or crisphead

Bibb or butterhead

Romaine or cos

Boston

Leaf or "bunching"

Make A Meal With Appetizers

It's easy to make a meal from appetizers at most restaurants today, so why not try it at home, too? With the recipes for appetizers you'll find here, no one will leave hungry.

If you are planning to have an informal get-together with friends, have several appetizers prepared to serve; then let guests help themselves. This easy, relaxed way of serving is a good solution for entertaining when your eating area is small or when folks want to stay gathered around the television.

If you plan to serve platters of appetizers for an informal meal at the table, you may want to start with a crisp green salad. Be sure to plan the appetizer recipes to serve as you would a meal—plan for variation in food temperature, color, and shape. You'll also want to include a mixture of meat and vegetable appetizers. Fresh fruit pieces are cool and refreshing, especially if several of the appetizers are served hot.

CHILI CON QUESO DIP

1 pound hot bulk pork sausage
1 (2-pound) package process cheese
1 (10¾-ounce) can cream of mushroom
    soup, undiluted
1 (8-ounce) jar picante sauce
¼ cup plus 2 tablespoons milk or water
Tortilla chips

Cook sausage in a large skillet until meat is browned, stirring to crumble. Drain well; set aside.

Combine cheese and undiluted soup in a heavy Dutch oven; cook mixture over medium heat, stirring until cheese melts. Add crumbled sausage, picante sauce, and milk; mix well.

To serve, transfer mixture to a chafing dish. Serve dip warm with tortilla chips. Yield: about 2 quarts.

Barbara Davis,
Lilburn, Georgia.

EGG ROLLS

2 tablespoons vegetable oil
3 cups shredded cabbage
½ cup diced onion
½ cup diced celery
3½ pounds boneless pork, cooked and
    diced
2 boneless chicken breast halves, cooked
    and diced
1 (8-ounce) package frozen cooked shrimp,
    thawed, drained, and diced
1 (8-ounce) can bamboo shoots, drained
    and chopped
1 (8-ounce) can water chestnuts, drained
    and chopped
3 medium carrots, scraped and
    shredded
¾ cup bean sprouts, chopped
¼ cup soy sauce
¼ teaspoon dry mustard
¼ teaspoon ground ginger
¼ teaspoon pepper
½ cup cornstarch
½ cup water
2 (1-pound) packages egg roll wrappers
Vegetable oil
Commercial sweet-and-sour sauce
    (optional)
Commercial hot mustard sauce (optional)

Heat 2 tablespoons oil in a preheated wok, coating sides; add cabbage, onion, and celery. Stir-fry 2 minutes on medium-high heat. Turn off heat; add pork, chicken, shrimp, bamboo shoots, water chestnuts, carrots, sprouts, soy sauce, mustard, ginger, and pepper, and stir well.

Combine cornstarch and water, and set mixture aside.

Mound 3 heaping tablespoonfuls of filling in center of each egg roll wrapper. Fold top corner of wrapper over filling, tucking tip of corner under filling. Fold left and right corners over filling. Lightly brush exposed corner with cornstarch mixture. Tightly roll the filled end of the wrapper toward the exposed corner; gently press to seal.

Heat 1 inch vegetable oil to 375° in wok. Place 2 egg rolls in hot oil, and fry 35 to 45 seconds on each side or until golden brown; drain on paper towels. Repeat with remaining egg rolls. Serve with sweet-and-sour sauce and hot mustard sauce, if desired. Yield: about 2 dozen egg rolls.

Note: Two (4½-ounce) cans shrimp may be substituted for one (8-ounce) package frozen, cooked shrimp. Remaining egg roll wrappers may be frozen and reserved for later use.

Cindie King,
Sherman, Texas.

SPINACH-STUFFED MUSHROOMS

1½ pounds fresh mushrooms
¼ cup plus 1 tablespoon butter or
    margarine, melted and divided
1 (10-ounce) package frozen chopped
    spinach
¼ cup minced onion
¼ cup minced celery
1 clove garlic, minced
1 (4-ounce) jar diced pimiento, drained
1 teaspoon Worcestershire sauce
¼ teaspoon salt
¼ teaspoon pepper
¼ cup grated Parmesan cheese

Clean mushrooms with damp paper towels. Remove mushroom stems, and finely chop; set aside. Brush caps with 2 tablespoons butter, and set aside.

Cook spinach according to package directions; drain well, and squeeze out excess liquid. Set aside.

Sauté mushroom stems, onion, celery, and garlic in remaining butter until tender. Remove from heat; add spinach, pimiento, Worcestershire sauce, salt, and pepper, mixing well. Spoon mixture into mushroom caps. Place on a lightly greased baking sheet; sprinkle with cheese. Bake mushrooms at 350° for 10 to 15 minutes. Yield: about 2 dozen.

Tony Jones,
Atlanta, Georgia.

BAKED POTATO SKINS

6 large baking potatoes
3 to 4 tablespoons butter or margarine,
    melted
1¼ teaspoons freshly ground pepper
½ teaspoon onion salt
½ teaspoon garlic salt
¼ cup grated Parmesan cheese
Commercial sour cream

Scrub potatoes thoroughly, and prick several times with a fork. Bake at 400° for 1 to 1¼ hours or until done.

Allow to cool to touch. Cut potatoes in half lengthwise; carefully scoop out pulp, leaving about ¼-inch-thick shells. (Reserve pulp for other uses.) Cut each shell lengthwise into 1-inch-wide strips, and place on ungreased baking sheets. Brush tops of strips with butter; sprinkle with seasonings and cheese. Bake at 400° for 10 to 12 minutes or until crisp; serve warm with sour cream. Yield: 3 dozen. *Mrs. J. Russell Buchanan,*
Monroe, Louisiana.

Feast On Rice Anytime

Rice is a staple that's found in almost every kitchen. As all good cooks know, it's the perfect accompaniment to round out a meal. It's versatile and goes with almost any entrée or vegetable. Here are some interesting rice side dishes.

QUICK CURRIED RICE

1 tablespoon butter or margarine
⅓ cup finely chopped onion
1 cup uncooked instant rice
1 chicken-flavored bouillon cube
1 cup boiling water
1 (2.5-ounce) jar sliced mushrooms,
    drained
½ teaspoon curry powder
Dash of pepper

Melt butter in a heavy skillet; add onion and rice; cook over medium heat, stirring constantly, until rice is lightly browned. Dissolve bouillon cube in boiling water; stir into rice mixture. Cover, remove from heat, and let stand 5 minutes or until all liquid is absorbed. Stir in remaining ingredients. Yield: 3 to 4 servings. *Jo Novotny,*
Robertsdale, Alabama.

Combine cooked rice, ½ cup Cheddar cheese, sour cream, and red pepper; mix well. Spoon mixture into a lightly greased 1½-quart casserole. Cover and bake at 350° for 15 to 20 minutes. Sprinkle top with remaining ¼ cup cheese, and bake, uncovered, an additional 5 minutes. Yield: 4 servings.

Camilla C. Hudson,
Denton, Texas.

MADRAS SALAD

2 cups cooked rice
1 (10-ounce) package frozen English peas, thawed
2 medium tomatoes, peeled, seeded, and coarsely chopped
⅓ cup olive oil
¼ cup minced onion
¼ cup minced fresh parsley
3 tablespoons white wine vinegar
1 tablespoon chopped fresh basil
¼ teaspoon salt
¼ teaspoon pepper

Combine all ingredients in a large salad bowl; toss well. Refrigerate and allow to chill thoroughly before serving. Yield: 8 to 10 servings.

Sharon McClatchey,
Muskogee, Oklahoma.

WILD RICE BELVEDERE

½ pound fresh mushrooms, sliced
¼ cup butter or margarine, melted
1 tablespoon lemon juice
1 (4-ounce) package wild rice
2 cups water
1 tablespoon beef-flavored bouillon granules
1 tablespoon minced fresh parsley
1 tablespoon minced onion
⅛ teaspoon garlic powder
½ cup pecan halves

Sauté fresh mushrooms in butter and lemon juice.

Wash wild rice in 3 changes of hot water; drain.

Combine rice, 2 cups water, and bouillon granules in a medium saucepan; bring to a boil. Cover, reduce heat to low, and simmer 30 to 45 minutes or until rice is tender. Stir in sautéed mushrooms, minced parsley, minced onion, garlic powder, and pecan halves. Serve immediately. Yield: 4 servings.

Chris Adkins,
Austin, Texas.

Rice Pilaf is a mouth-watering accompaniment to any meat dish.

RICE PILAF

¼ cup butter or margarine
1½ cups uncooked regular rice
3¼ cups chicken broth
¼ cup plus 2 tablespoons chopped celery
¼ cup plus 2 tablespoons chopped fresh parsley
¼ cup plus 2 tablespoons chopped carrots
¼ cup plus 2 tablespoons sliced almonds
¼ teaspoon pepper
Whole natural almonds (optional)
Carrot sticks (optional)
Fresh parsley sprig (optional)

Melt butter in a heavy skillet; add rice and cook, stirring often, until light brown. Stir in chicken broth, and heat to boiling. Pour into a lightly greased 2½-quart casserole; cover and bake at 375° for 30 minutes.

Remove casserole from oven, and stir in ¼ cup plus 2 tablespoons each of chopped celery, chopped parsley, chopped carrots, and sliced almonds; stir in ¼ teaspoon pepper. Cover and bake an additional 20 minutes. Garnish with whole almonds, carrot sticks, and parsley sprigs, if desired. Yield: 6 servings.

Romanza Johnson,
Bowling Green, Kentucky.

RICE CHANTILLY

3 cups cooked rice
¾ cup (3 ounces) shredded Cheddar cheese, divided
½ cup commercial sour cream
3 dashes of red pepper

Hurrah For Jicama

If you've seen something in the grocery store that looks similar to a giant turnip, it's probably a jicama (pronounced heé-cah-mah). Pale brown and thin skinned, this root vegetable varies in size and weight from 1 to 6 pounds.

Jicama flesh is white, crisp, and slightly sweet. Served raw, it goes well combined with citrus fruit as in our Jicama-Fruit Salad. Or serve it plain with your favorite vegetable dip. Cooked, the vegetable can be prepared like potatoes or added at the last minute to Oriental stir-fry dishes.

Choose jicamas that are firm to the touch and without blemishes. Count on 1 pound to yield 4 to 6 servings. Avoid very large jicamas because they may have a "woody" texture.

Unpeeled and unwashed, jicamas will keep several weeks in the refrigerator. As you peel and use the vegetable, store any remaining raw jicama in plastic wrap.

Jicamas have about 45 calories per 3½-ounce serving. This is less than potatoes and most other starchy vegetables. They are a fairly good source of vitamin C.

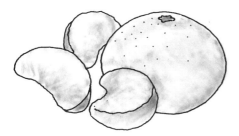

JICAMA-ORANGE SALAD

1 medium jicama, peeled and cut into ¼-inch strips
3 large oranges, peeled, seeded, and sectioned
1 medium-size purple onion, thinly sliced and separated into rings
1 cup orange juice
¼ cup lime juice
1 teaspoon ground coriander
Lettuce leaves
1 lime, thinly sliced

Combine jicama, oranges, onion, orange juice, lime juice, and coriander in a bowl; cover and refrigerate 1 hour. Spoon onto lettuce leaves with a slotted spoon, and garnish with lime slices. Yield: about 6 servings.
Carrie Byrne Bartlett,
Gallatin, Tennessee.

JICAMA-FRUIT SALAD

2 cups jicama, peeled, thinly sliced, and cut into 1-inch pieces
1 (20-ounce) can pineapple chunks, undrained
1 tablespoon lemon juice
1 teaspoon anise seeds
¼ teaspoon salt
½ medium head iceberg lettuce, shredded
2 bananas, sliced
2 large oranges, peeled, seeded, and sectioned
¼ cup salted peanuts
2 tablespoons pomegranate seeds (optional)
½ cup mayonnaise

Combine jicama, pineapple chunks, lemon juice, anise seeds, and salt in a mixing bowl; mix well. Cover and chill 3 to 4 hours.

Line a large serving platter with lettuce. Add banana to chilled mixture; toss gently. Drain, reserving 2 tablespoons liquid. Arrange orange sections and fruit pieces on lettuce leaves; sprinkle with peanuts and pomegranate seeds, if desired.

Combine reserved liquid and mayonnaise; mix well. Serve with salad. Yield: 8 servings.
Mrs. Earl L. Faulkenberry,
Lancaster, South Carolina.

Try Savory Sauces For Meat

When there isn't time to cook, consider reaching for a cooked ham or deli meats. Sound boring? It doesn't have to be if you add one of our hot sauces.

Deli corned beef will never be the same once you serve it with our distinct but mild Horseradish Sauce.

Royal Cherry Sauce goes well with ham or poultry. Its rich, regal color is topped only by its delicious flavor. And no one will ever know you made it in a matter of minutes.

ROYAL CHERRY SAUCE

1 (16-ounce) can pitted dark cherries
3 tablespoons brown sugar
2 tablespoons cornstarch
½ cup Sauterne wine or other dry white wine
1 tablespoon lemon juice
2 teaspoons grated orange rind

Drain cherries, reserving liquid. Set cherries aside. Combine sugar, cornstarch, and reserved cherry liquid in a saucepan; stirring until smooth. Add wine, lemon juice, and orange rind. Cook over medium heat, stirring occasionally, until mixture thickens. Stir in cherries; cook until thoroughly heated. Serve sauce hot with ham or poultry. Yield: 2 cups.
Mrs. Earl L. Faulkenberry,
Lancaster, South Carolina.

CRANBERRY JUICE SAUCE

1 cup firmly packed brown sugar
1½ tablespoons cornstarch
¼ teaspoon ground allspice
1 cup cranberry juice
1 tablespoon lemon juice
½ cup golden raisins

Combine sugar, cornstarch, and allspice in a small saucepan. Stir in cranberry juice and lemon juice; cook over medium heat, stirring constantly, until mixture thickens. Stir in raisins. Serve hot with ham or pork. Yield: 1½ cups.
Mrs. Thomas Lee Adams,
Kingsport, Tennessee.

HORSERADISH SAUCE

¼ cup butter or margarine
¼ cup all-purpose flour
¼ teaspoon salt
⅛ teaspoon pepper
Dash of red pepper
2 cups milk
3 to 4 tablespoons prepared horseradish
1 tablespoon lemon juice

Melt butter in a large saucepan over low heat; add flour, salt, and both peppers, stirring until smooth. Cook 1 minute, stirring constantly. Gradually add milk; cook over medium heat, stirring constantly, until the mixture is thickened and bubbly. Stir in the horseradish and lemon juice; cook until sauce is thoroughly heated. Serve hot with corned beef or roast beef. Yield: 2 cups.
Mrs. Bernie Benigno,
Gulfport, Mississippi.

Tip: Submerge an unpeeled lemon or orange in hot water for 15 minutes before squeezing to yield more juice.

ONION-MUSHROOM SAUCE

½ clove garlic
¼ cup butter or margarine, melted
1 (¾-ounce) package brown gravy mix
½ cup water
½ cup Burgundy or other dry red wine
Pinch of pepper
½ pound mushrooms, sliced
1 cup thinly sliced green onions

Sauté garlic in butter in a large skillet. Add gravy mix, water, wine, and pepper; bring to a boil. Cook over medium heat, stirring constantly, until smooth and thickened. Add mushrooms and green onions; cook until thoroughly heated. Serve sauce hot with beef patties or steak. Yield: about 3 cups.
Maggie Cates,
Orlando, Florida.

MILD MUSTARD SAUCE

1 tablespoon butter or margarine
1½ teaspoons all-purpose flour
¼ teaspoon salt
1 cup evaporated milk
1 tablespoon plus 1 teaspoon prepared mustard
1 tablespoon diced pimiento
½ teaspoon lemon juice

Melt butter in a heavy saucepan over low heat. Add flour and salt, stirring until smooth. Cook 1 minute, stirring constantly. Gradually add milk; cook over medium heat, stirring constantly, until mixture thickens. Stir in remaining ingredients; cook until thoroughly heated. Serve hot with roast beef or ham. Yield: about 1 cup.
Janis Moyer,
Farmersville, Texas.

Cottage Cheese Makes It Rich

Does the mention of cottage cheese conjure up memories of being on a diet and eating the creamy white curds stuffed in a tomato? If so, then we hope these recipes will give you a different opinion of cottage cheese.

Cottage cheese is very nutritious. Made from milk, it contains all the wholesome goodness of the beverage but in a concentrated form. It's a source of high-quality protein and calcium for bones and teeth.

SPINACH-AND-HAM ROLLUPS

1 (10¾-ounce) can cream of celery soup, undiluted
1 (8-ounce) carton commercial sour cream
2 teaspoons Dijon mustard
1 (10-ounce) package frozen chopped spinach, thawed and drained
1 cup cooked rice
1 cup small-curd cottage cheese
2 eggs, beaten
½ cup diced onion
¼ cup all-purpose flour
24 (4-inch square) slices boiled ham
½ cup dry breadcrumbs
1 tablespoon butter or margarine, melted
½ teaspoon parsley flakes

Combine soup, sour cream, and mustard, mixing well. Divide soup mixture in half.

Combine half of soup mixture, spinach, rice, cottage cheese, eggs, onion, and flour; stir well. Spoon a heaping tablespoonful on each ham slice; roll up. Place ham rolls seam side down in a lightly greased 13- x 9- x 2-inch baking dish. Spoon remaining mixture over ham rolls.

Combine breadcrumbs, butter, and parsley flakes; mix well, and sprinkle over ham rolls. Bake, uncovered, at 350° for 30 to 35 minutes. Let rollups stand 10 minutes before serving. Yield: 8 to 10 servings.
Clota Engleman,
Spur, Texas.

HAM-AND-EGG POTATO SALAD

2 cups cubed cooked ham
2 cups peeled, cubed, cooked potatoes
4 hard-cooked eggs, chopped
1 (12-ounce) carton small-curd cottage cheese
¼ cup chopped onion
2 tablespoons sugar
2 tablespoons cider vinegar
2 teaspoons prepared mustard
1 teaspoon salt
1 teaspoon celery seeds

Combine ham, potatoes, and eggs in a large mixing bowl; set aside.

Combine remaining ingredients in a small bowl, and mix well. Pour over potato mixture; toss gently. Cover and refrigerate 6 hours or overnight. Yield: 6 to 8 servings.
Phyllis F. Purvis,
Avondale Estates, Georgia.

SHRIMP DIP

1 (12-ounce) carton small-curd cottage cheese
¼ cup mayonnaise
2 tablespoons chili sauce
1 tablespoon lemon juice
1 (4¼-ounce) can tiny shrimp, drained and rinsed
2 tablespoons diced onion
Salt and pepper to taste

Combine cottage cheese, mayonnaise, chili sauce, and lemon juice; beat until smooth. Stir in remaining ingredients; chill thoroughly. Serve with assorted crackers. Yield: 2½ cups.
Patsy Layer,
Galveston, Texas.

CHEESE KUCHEN

1 cup all-purpose flour
¼ cup sugar
¼ cup butter or margarine, melted
1 egg, beaten
2 cups cream-style cottage cheese
½ cup sugar
⅓ cup golden raisins
2 eggs, beaten
2 tablespoons all-purpose flour
2 tablespoons butter or margarine, melted
½ teaspoon vanilla extract
¼ teaspoon salt
¼ teaspoon almond extract
¼ teaspoon ground cinnamon

Combine 1 cup flour, ¼ cup sugar, ¼ cup melted butter, and 1 beaten egg, mixing well; press mixture firmly into bottom and 1 inch up sides of a 9-inch springform pan.

Combine cottage cheese, ½ cup sugar, raisins, 2 beaten eggs, 2 tablespoons flour, 2 tablespoons melted butter, vanilla, salt, and almond extract; mix well. Pour into prepared pan, and sprinkle with cinnamon. Bake at 425° for 10 minutes. Reduce heat to 350°, and bake an additional 30 to 35 minutes or until knife inserted in center comes out clean. Serve warm. Yield: one 9-inch pie.
Jane Weber,
Port Richey, Florida.

GREEN CHILE-COTTAGE CHEESE SQUARES

4 eggs, beaten
¼ cup all-purpose flour
1 tablespoon butter or margarine, melted
½ teaspoon baking powder
¼ teaspoon salt
¼ teaspoon pepper
1 cup cream-style cottage cheese
1 cup (4 ounces) shredded Cheddar cheese
1 cup (4 ounces) shredded Monterey Jack cheese
1 (4-ounce) can diced green chiles, drained
Pimiento strips (optional)

Combine eggs, flour, butter, baking powder, salt, and pepper; mix until smooth. Stir in all cheese and chiles; pour into a greased 8-inch square baking dish. Bake at 350° for 30 minutes. Let stand 10 minutes; cut into squares. Garnish with pimiento strips, if desired. Yield: about 3 dozen appetizer servings.
Barbara Davis,
Lilburn, Georgia.

DAIRY LAND SALAD DRESSING

1 cup cream-style cottage cheese
½ cup commercial sour cream
3 tablespoons milk
2 teaspoons Worcestershire sauce
¼ teaspoon salt
2 to 3 drops of hot sauce
½ cup crumbled blue cheese
¼ cup diced onion
2 tablespoons chopped pimiento

Combine cottage cheese, sour cream, milk, Worcestershire sauce, salt, and hot sauce in container of electric blender, and blend until smooth. Stir in remaining ingredients. Yield: 2½ cups.
L. K. Klomfar,
Gulfport, Florida.

Puffy Doughnut Treats

Fry a batch of Doughnut Puffs; they're a delicious treat sprinkled with powdered sugar. It's easy to make them if you follow this recipe. The puffy pillows of pastry are quite similar to the delicious beignets served in the French Quarter of New Orleans.

DOUGHNUT PUFFS

5 cups all-purpose flour, divided
¼ cup sugar
1 package dry yeast
½ teaspoon salt
1¾ cups milk
2 tablespoons butter or margarine, softened
2 tablespoons shortening
1 egg
Vegetable oil
Sifted powdered sugar

Combine 1½ cups flour, sugar, yeast, and salt in a large bowl; mix well.

Combine milk, butter, and shortening in a saucepan; heat until very warm (120° to 130°), stirring until butter and shortening melt. Add milk mixture to flour mixture; beat at medium speed of an electric mixer 2 minutes. Add egg and 1½ cups flour. Beat 2 minutes. Stir in remaining flour.

Turn dough out onto a lightly floured surface, and knead 3 or 4 times. Place mixture in a well-greased bowl, turning to grease top. Cover and let rise in a warm place (85°), free from drafts, about 1 hour and 10 minutes or until doubled in bulk.

Punch dough down; turn out onto a lightly floured surface. Knead 3 or 4 times. Divide dough into thirds. Cover 2 sections, and set aside. Roll remaining section out to ½- to ¼-inch thickness; cut into 2-inch squares. Repeat with remaining sections.

Heat ¾ to 1 inch of oil to 375°. Gently pull outside edges of each square so center is thinner than edges. Drop 4 dough squares at a time into hot oil. Cook on each side until golden. Drain, and sprinkle with powdered sugar. Yield: 3 dozen.
Charyl Safley,
Raleigh, North Carolina

The Best Of Homemade Breads

Anyone who has the time to make homemade breads—piping hot rolls from the oven or a warm coffee cake spread with sweet frosting—knows that their flavors and aromas are worth the extra effort.

Bran fans will cheer over our Quick Bran Muffins. These muffins require fewer ingredients than most bran muffins, and in this recipe, the bran doesn't have to soak before mixing.

QUICK BRAN MUFFINS

1½ cups shreds of wheat bran cereal
1¼ cups self-rising flour
½ cup sugar
½ cup butter or margarine, melted
½ cup milk
1 egg, beaten

Combine cereal, flour, and sugar in a mixing bowl; make a well in center of mixture. Add butter, milk, and egg; stir just until moistened. Spoon batter into greased muffin pans, filling two-thirds full. Bake at 400° for 18 minutes. Yield: 1 dozen.
Martha A. Hardeman,
Gadsden, Alabama.

HARD ROLLS

1 package dry yeast
1 cup warm water (105° to 115°), divided
2 tablespoons shortening, melted
1 tablespoon sugar
1 teaspoon salt
½ teaspoon cardamom
3½ to 4 cups all-purpose flour, divided
2 egg whites
1 tablespoon cornmeal
1 egg yolk
2 tablespoons water

Dissolve yeast in ¼ cup warm water. Combine remaining ¾ cup water, shortening, sugar, salt, and cardamom in a large bowl. Add 1 cup flour, and beat well; set mixture aside.

Beat egg whites (at room temperature) until soft peaks form; stir egg whites and yeast mixture into flour mixture. Stir in enough of the remaining flour to make a soft dough.

Turn dough out onto a floured surface; knead 5 minutes or until smooth and elastic. Place dough in a well-greased bowl, turning to grease top. Cover and let rise in a warm place (85°), free from drafts, 1 hour or until doubled in bulk.

Punch dough down, and divide in half; divide each half into 12 portions. Shape each portion into ovals. Place ovals on 2 ungreased baking sheets sprinkled with cornmeal. Cover and let rise in a warm place (85°), free from drafts, 30 minutes or until doubled in bulk. Combine 1 egg yolk and 2 tablespoons water; lightly brush rolls with yolk mixture. Bake at 450° for 18 to 20 minutes or until rolls are golden brown. Yield: 2 dozen.

Note: For crustier rolls, place a shallow pan filled with boiling water in bottom of oven just before placing rolls in oven to bake. *Mrs. Hugh F. Mosher,*
Huntsville, Alabama.

SEASONED POPOVERS

2 eggs
1 cup milk
1 cup all-purpose flour
1 teaspoon poultry seasoning
½ teaspoon salt

Beat eggs at medium speed of an electric mixer until frothy. Add remaining ingredients; continue beating just until smooth.

Place a well-greased muffin pan in a 450° oven for 3 minutes or until a drop of water sizzles when dropped in muffin cup. Remove pan from oven; fill each muffin cup two-thirds full with batter. Bake at 450° for 15 minutes; reduce heat to 350°, and bake an additional 25 minutes. Remove pan from oven, and serve popovers immediately while warm. Yield: 10 to 12 popovers.

Virginia B. Stalder,
Nokesville, Virginia.

ORANGE-PECAN COFFEE CAKE

½ cup milk, scalded
¼ cup sugar
¼ cup shortening
½ teaspoon salt
1 package dry yeast
¼ cup warm water (105° to 115°)
1 teaspoon sugar
1 egg, beaten
1 teaspoon grated orange rind
¼ teaspoon fresh grated nutmeg
About 2½ cups all-purpose flour
Pecan Frosting

Combine milk, ¼ cup sugar, shortening, and salt in a small mixing bowl; stir until shortening melts. Cool to lukewarm (105° to 115°).

Dissolve yeast in warm water in a large mixing bowl; stir in 1 teaspoon sugar, and let stand 10 minutes. Add milk mixture, egg, orange rind, and nutmeg; mix well. Stir in enough flour to form a soft dough.

Turn dough out onto a lightly floured surface, and knead about 4 minutes until smooth and elastic. Place dough in a greased bowl, turning to grease top. Cover and let rise in a warm place (85°), free from drafts, 1 hour or until doubled in bulk.

Punch dough down, and turn out onto a lightly floured surface. Cover and let dough rest 5 minutes.

Divide dough in half; pat into two well-greased 8-inch round cakepans. Cover and let rise in a warm place (85°), free from drafts, about 35 minutes or until doubled in bulk.

Bake at 375° for 15 minutes or until cakes sound hollow when tapped. Spread Pecan Frosting evenly on warm cakes; serve coffee cakes warm. Yield: two 8-inch coffee cakes.

Pecan Frosting:

¼ cup butter or margarine, softened
1⅔ cups sifted powdered sugar, divided
1 tablespoon dark corn syrup
½ teaspoon vanilla extract
Pinch of salt
2 tablespoons half-and-half
1 cup chopped pecans

Cream butter and ⅓ cup powdered sugar; add corn syrup, vanilla, and salt, mixing well. Add half-and-half alternately with remaining powdered sugar, beginning and ending with sugar. Mix well after each addition. Stir in pecans. Yield: about 1 cup.

Mrs. James S. Stanton,
Richmond, Virginia.

HOBO BREAD

¾ cup chopped dates
¾ cup raisins
1 cup boiling water
2 teaspoons baking soda
3 tablespoons shortening
1 cup sugar
1 egg
2 cups all-purpose flour
Pinch of salt

Combine dates, raisins, water, and soda in mixing bowl; set aside.

Cream shortening and sugar, beating well at medium speed of an electric mixer. Add egg, and beat well; stir in flour and salt. Add date mixture, stirring until well blended.

Spoon batter into 2 greased and floured 1-pound coffee cans. Bake at 350° for 50 to 55 minutes. Cool in cans 10 minutes; remove to wire racks, and cool completely. Yield: 2 loaves.

Vickie Mangum,
Fuquay-Varina, North Carolina.

Enchanting Tabletops For Easter

If you have a collection of baskets, figurines, lace, or other collectibles, use them to set your Easter table. Depending on the items, you can create a holiday tabletop with whimsical charm, elegant style, or traditional warmth.

In Mobile, Penny Coleman uses her treasured linens, antique doilies, hand-painted eggs, and floral china to make each year's Easter dinner memorable. To make the occasion even more personal, she also includes special mementos for each family member.

The decorating approach will differ with the types of collectibles you have. Just be sure to define the total theme first. Not everything has to match or look alike, but the overall arrangement should make a statement.

Keep these finishing touches in mind for your holiday tabletops and turn special occasions into family traditions. Friends and family will treasure the times you share your collectibles with them in such a unique way.

Top: Linens, lace, crystal, and collectibles create an enchanting mood for Easter dinner. Below: Hand-painted ostrich eggs arranged in an antique silver basket make a beautiful, yet simple, centerpiece.

April

Cook With Personality With Fresh Herbs

Getting to know fresh herbs is like getting to know people—each one has its own distinct personality. Some herbs have bold flavors and must be used with care; others are subtle and can be added more freely.

Deciding which herb to use and how much to add is as personal as the use of salt and pepper. We've found that herbs are best used to enhance the natural flavor of food, not to disguise or change it. Too much of a robust herb can be objectionable. On the other hand, a mild-flavored herb can add magic to one dish but lose impact in another.

When experimenting with a new herb, pull off a leaf and crush it, letting it warm in your hand. If it has a delicate aroma, you can add it adventurously. If it is strong and pungent, be cautious. It is easier to add more of an herb than to subtract.

In simplest terms, herbs can be divided into two categories—accent herbs and character herbs. Parsley, chives, and dillweed are a few of the accent herbs. They are milder in flavor and are often combined within the same recipe. The character herbs, such as basil, bay leaves, marjoram, oregano, rosemary, tarragon, thyme, and sage, impart strong, dominant flavors to dishes. To blend these herbs, select one as the leading herb flavor and combine it with smaller amounts of other herbs, or even let it stand alone.

Most herbs are bitter when cooked too much, but a little heat releases their flavors. Try adding accent herbs during the last few minutes of cooking time. Character herbs, such as bay leaves, can withstand longer cooking times and may be added from the beginning.

Once you've tasted fresh herbs, it will seem a crime to go back to using the dried variety. But most of us must do this if the fresh are not available. When cooking with dried herbs, keep in mind that their flavor is much more concentrated than the fresh, so use about one-third of the dried leaves to replace the fresh. For example, one teaspoon of dried leaves is equal to one tablespoon of fresh. The exception is rosemary; the fresh leaves are more pungent than the dried ones.

You will not want to overlook the garnishing possibilities that fresh herbs offer. Add eye appeal by garnishing with herbs already in the recipe.

Fresh herbs bring out the flavors of poultry and seafood. Taste the magic they work in Dilled Sauced Shrimp and Roast Cornish Hens.

DILLED SAUCED SHRIMP

2 tablespoons chopped onion
1 tablespoon butter or margarine, melted
1½ pounds medium shrimp, peeled and deveined
¾ cup Chablis or other dry white wine
⅛ teaspoon garlic powder
3 tablespoons butter or margarine
3 tablespoons all-purpose flour
1⅓ cups skim milk
2 tablespoons lemon juice
1 tablespoon chopped fresh dillweed or 1 teaspoon dried whole dillweed
¼ to ½ teaspoon salt
Hot cooked rice

Sauté onion in 1 tablespoon butter in a large skillet until tender; add shrimp, wine, and garlic powder. Bring to a boil. Cook 5 minutes, stirring constantly. Remove skillet from heat, and set aside.

Melt 3 tablespoons butter in a medium saucepan over low heat; add flour, stirring until mixture is smooth. Cook 1 minute, stirring constantly. Gradually add milk; cook over medium heat, stirring constantly, until mixture is thickened and bubbly. Add lemon juice, dillweed, and salt, stirring well.

Stir flour mixture into shrimp mixture, and cook 5 minutes, stirring well. Spoon shrimp sauce over rice, and serve immediately. Yield: 4 to 6 servings.

Janet M. Filer,
Arlington, Virginia.

ALL-SEASONS POT ROAST

1 (3½-pound) boneless chuck roast, trimmed
1 tablespoon chopped fresh rosemary or 1 teaspoon dried whole rosemary
1½ teaspoons chopped fresh thyme or ½ teaspoon dried whole thyme
¾ teaspoon chopped fresh marjoram or ¼ teaspoon dried whole marjoram
¾ teaspoon chopped fresh oregano or ¼ teaspoon dried whole oregano
¾ teaspoon chopped fresh tarragon or ¼ teaspoon dried whole tarragon
1 teaspoon salt
1 teaspoon pepper
1 teaspoon paprika
½ teaspoon dry mustard
¼ teaspoon red pepper
¼ teaspoon seasoned salt
2 cloves garlic, minced
2 tablespoons all-purpose flour
2 tablespoons vegetable oil
3 cups water
4 medium carrots, scraped and cut into 2-inch pieces
4 stalks celery, cut into 2-inch pieces
2 medium onions, quartered
1 green pepper, cut into ½-inch strips
2 cloves garlic
4 medium potatoes, peeled and quartered
1½ tablespoons cornstarch
3 tablespoons water

Cut roast lengthwise three-fourths way through center. Combine herbs, seasonings, and 2 cloves minced garlic; sprinkle half of herb mixture on inside of cut portion of roast. Close roast, and sprinkle remaining herb mixture and flour on outside. Brown roast on all sides in hot oil in a large Dutch oven.

Add 3 cups water, carrots, celery, onion, green pepper, and 2 cloves garlic; cover, reduce heat, and simmer 1½ hours. Add potatoes; cover and simmer 1 hour or until potatoes and meat are tender.

Remove roast and vegetables to serving platter. Combine cornstarch and 3 tablespoons water; stir until smooth. Pour cornstarch mixture into roast liquid; cook over high heat, stirring constantly, until mixture boils. Boil 1 minute. Serve gravy with roast. Yield: 6 servings.
W. E. Parker,
Prattville, Alabama.

Tip: Use finely chopped fresh herbs whenever possible. Dried whole herbs are usually the next best choice since they maintain their strength longer than the commercially ground form.

ROASTED ROSEMARY LAMB

1 (6- to 6½-pound) leg of lamb
½ cup minced fresh parsley
2 tablespoons minced fresh rosemary or ¼ cup dried whole rosemary
¼ cup vegetable oil, divided
4 cloves garlic, finely chopped
½ teaspoon ground cardamom
Salt and pepper to taste
1 cup Chablis or other dry white wine

Make several deep slits on outside of lamb; set aside. Combine parsley, rosemary, 1 tablespoon oil, garlic, and cardamom. Stuff slits with herb mixture. Brush outside of lamb with one tablespoon of oil, and sprinkle with salt and pepper.

Place lamb in a roasting pan; bake at 450° for 5 to 10 minutes. Combine remaining 2 tablespoons oil and wine; set aside. Reduce heat to 325°; bake lamb for 2½ hours or until meat thermometer reaches 160°, basting occasionally with wine mixture. Let stand 10 minutes before carving. Yield: 6 to 8 servings.
Norma Zeigler,
Huntsville, Alabama.

STUFFED PORK CHOPS

6 (1-inch-thick) pork chops
2 tablespoons vegetable oil
1 cup cornbread crumbs
1 cup soft breadcrumbs
1 egg, beaten
¼ cup minced fresh parsley
1 tablespoon minced fresh sage or 1 teaspoon dried rubbed sage
1 tablespoon instant minced onion
2 teaspoons celery flakes
½ teaspoon salt

Make pockets in pork chops, cutting from rib side just to beginning of fat edge of each chop. Brown chops on both sides in hot oil. Remove chops, and set aside.

Add enough water to pan drippings to make ¾ cup liquid. Combine liquid and remaining ingredients, mixing well. Stuff pockets of pork chops with cornbread mixture. Place stuffed chops in a lightly greased 13- x 9- x 2-inch baking dish. Bake, uncovered, at 350° for 1 hour. Yield: 6 servings.
Marian Johnson,
Jackson, Tennessee.

FRENCH HERBED CHICKEN

2 tablespoons shortening
1 (3-pound) broiler-fryer, cut up and skinned
½ teaspoon salt
¼ teaspoon pepper
½ cup coarsely chopped carrot
1 clove garlic, minced
2 tablespoons minced fresh parsley
¾ teaspoon chopped fresh thyme or ¼ teaspoon dried whole thyme
1 cup sauterne
2 stalks celery, sliced
1 cup peeled pearl onions
1 (2-ounce) can sliced mushrooms, undrained
1 medium bay leaf

Melt shortening in a large skillet. Sprinkle chicken with salt and pepper; brown on both sides in hot shortening. Remove chicken, and place in a lightly greased shallow 2-quart casserole.

Drain excess shortening from skillet; add carrot, garlic, parsley, and thyme. Cook over low heat until carrot is tender, stirring often. Add carrot mixture and remaining ingredients to chicken; cover and bake at 350° for 1 hour or until chicken is tender. Remove bay leaf before serving. Yield: 4 servings.
Teresa Cox,
Caney, Kentucky.

ROAST CORNISH HENS

2 (1-pound) Cornish hens
Salt
¼ cup butter or margarine, softened
1½ teaspoons chopped fresh marjoram or ½ teaspoon dried whole marjoram
¼ teaspoon hot sauce
Salt
Watercress
Preserved kumquats

Remove giblets from hens, and reserve for other uses. Rinse hens with cold water, and pat dry. Lift wingtips up and over back so they are tucked under hen. Sprinkle cavities with salt. Close cavities, and tie leg ends together with string; set aside.

Combine butter, marjoram, and hot sauce; spread on hens. Sprinkle lightly with salt. Place hens, breast side up, in a shallow roasting pan.

Bake at 350° for 1 hour, basting often with pan drippings. Serve hens on a bed of watercress; garnish with kumquats. Yield: 2 servings.

Viola Beauchamp,
Winston-Salem, North Carolina.

COQUILLES SAINT CYRANO

1 cup Chablis or other dry white wine
1 tablespoon minced fresh parsley
1½ teaspoons chopped fresh thyme or ½ teaspoon dried whole thyme
1 bay leaf
¼ teaspoon coarsely ground pepper
1½ pounds bay scallops
¼ cup butter or margarine
¼ cup all-purpose flour
½ cup milk
1 teaspoon lemon juice
1 tablespoon chopped fresh chives
2 tablespoons grated Parmesan cheese

Combine wine, parsley, thyme, bay leaf, and pepper in a large saucepan; bring to a boil. Add scallops; cook 2 minutes, stirring often. Remove bay leaf. Drain scallops, reserving liquid.

Melt butter in a saucepan over low heat; add flour, stirring until smooth. Cook 1 minute, stirring constantly. Gradually add reserved scallop liquid and milk; cook over medium heat, stirring constantly, until mixture is thickened and bubbly. Stir in scallops, lemon juice, and chives. Pour into 4 lightly greased individual baking dishes or scallop shells. Sprinkle each with 1½ teaspoons Parmesan cheese; bake at 350° for 15 to 20 minutes or until thoroughly heated. Yield: 4 servings.

Chris Adkins,
Austin, Texas.

Lamb Tastes Great!

The delicate flavor of lamb requires just the right seasoning to keep it from being overpowered. These recipes contain ingredients that make prized choices.

Keep in mind that low to moderate heat is best for cooking lamb. The meat will taste better if not overcooked.

LEG OF LAMB

1 (6- to 7-pound) leg of lamb
1 small onion, halved
1¾ cups cider vinegar
1 cup firmly packed brown sugar
1 cup water
½ teaspoon salt
¼ teaspoon pepper
Dash of hot sauce
4 medium onions, quartered
4 large potatoes, quartered
Commercial mint sauce (optional)

Remove the fell (tissue-like covering) from lamb with a sharp knife. Rub surface with small onion halves. Place lamb in a large roasting pan. Insert meat thermometer, being careful not to touch bone or fat.

Combine vinegar, sugar, water, salt, pepper, and hot sauce in a small bowl; pour over lamb. Cover and bake at 325° for 1½ hours. Add quartered onions and potatoes; cover and bake 1 hour. Uncover and bake until thermometer registers 140° (rare) or 160° (medium).

Transfer lamb and vegetables to a warm serving platter; discard drippings. Serve with mint sauce, if desired. Yield: 6 to 8 servings.

Bethell Pritchett,
Memphis, Tennessee.

GLAZED LEG OF LAMB

1 (10¾-ounce) can consommé, undiluted
1 small clove garlic, minced
½ cup peach preserves
2 tablespoons lemon juice
1 (3- to 4-pound) half of leg of lamb
½ teaspoon dried whole rosemary, crushed
½ teaspoon salt
⅛ teaspoon pepper
1 tablespoon cornstarch
1 tablespoon water

Combine consommé, garlic, preserves, and lemon juice; mix well. Reserve 1 cup mixture; set aside.

Cut small slits in lamb with tip of knife. Press rosemary into slits. Sprinkle lamb with salt and pepper; place fat side up on a rack in a roasting pan. Insert meat thermometer, being careful not to touch bone or fat. Bake, uncovered, at 325° for 25 to 30 minutes per pound or until thermometer registers 140° (rare) or 160° (medium), basting with reserved 1 cup consommé mixture every 30 minutes.

Dissolve cornstarch in water in a saucepan. Add remaining consommé mixture; cook over medium heat, stirring constantly, until mixture comes to a boil. Boil 1 minute. Serve with lamb. Yield: 4 to 6 servings.

Mrs. Roderick W. McGrath,
Orlando, Florida.

HALF OF LEG OF LAMB

1 (3- to 4-pound) half of leg of lamb
1 (8-ounce) can whole tomatoes, undrained and chopped
½ cup dry sherry
½ cup honey
2 tablespoons soy sauce
2 tablespoons diced onion
1 clove garlic, minced
1 teaspoon sugar
1 teaspoon dried parsley flakes
¼ to ½ teaspoon salt
½ teaspoon pepper

Place lamb fat side up on a rack in a 13- x 9- x 2-inch baking pan. Insert meat thermometer, being careful not to touch bone or fat. Bake, uncovered, at 325° for 40 minutes. Drain off drippings, and discard.

Combine remaining ingredients; mix well, and pour mixture over lamb. Bake an additional 50 to 80 minutes or until thermometer registers 140° (rare) or 160° (medium), basting often with drippings. Yield: 4 to 6 servings.

Mrs. M. L. Shannon,
Fairfield, Alabama.

LAMB KABOBS

⅓ cup cider vinegar
⅓ cup vegetable oil
2 cloves garlic, crushed
2 teaspoons dried whole basil
1 teaspoon salt
⅛ teaspoon pepper
1 pound boneless lamb, cut into 1-inch cubes
3 stalks celery, cut into 1-inch pieces
1 large sweet red pepper, cut into 24 pieces

Combine vinegar, oil, garlic, basil, salt, and pepper in a saucepan. Bring to a boil; reduce heat, and simmer 5 minutes. Let cool.

Pour half of marinade over lamb in a shallow container; pour remaining marinade over vegetables in a separate shallow container. Cover containers, and let marinate in refrigerator 6 hours.

Remove lamb and vegetables from marinade, reserving vegetable marinade. Alternate lamb, celery, and red pepper on 12 (7-inch) skewers. Place kabobs on a rack in a lightly greased broiling pan. Broil about 4 inches from heat 6 to 8 minutes, turning kabobs once and basting occasionally with marinade. Yield: 4 servings.

Tammy Smith,
Talbott, Tennessee.

BREAKFASTS & BRUNCHES®

Fresh Ideas For Morning Meals

Southern hospitality comes in many different forms. Some folks delight in giving intimate little dinners; others prefer to host cocktail parties for large groups of people. Still others are apt to go a more casual route and have friends over for steaks or hamburgers they grill in the backyard. We've also found a growing number who like to do their entertaining in the morning with breakfast or brunch.

Come to Brunch Under the Gazebo

In Chattanooga, Tennessee, Peter and Ann Platt are famous for their brunches. Entertaining friends and family under their backyard gazebo, Ann often does what she calls a "theme party," such as an Italian brunch, complete with an Italian menu and Italian wine. For all of her parties, she makes as much food ahead as she can. "I also like to make a list and be rather organized; I find that works better for me than trying to be impromptu," she says.

Another secret of Ann's success may be the personal attention she gives to the menu. She says, "I always think about the people who are coming while I'm cooking. I visualize them and try to remember what they like and dislike. For example, someone who doesn't like vegetables—is he going to have enough to eat with just meat or dessert?"

On the day we dropped in, the organization and personal attention were apparent. Peter had smoked the ham the night before, and Ann had the rest of the food ready by the time the guests arrived. They were welcomed with bullshots and mimosas, and Ann passed around Shrimp Toast as an appetizer. Brunch was served buffet style on one side of the gazebo.

After a leisurely meal that included a delicious variety of meat, fruit, vegetables, and bread, Ann served coffee, and one of her friends passed around Potato Chip Cookies and Fudge Bars. The sweet ending topped off a delightful meal as guests took in the last of the morning.

Bullshots   Mimosas
Shrimp Toast
Smoked Ham
Sausage Grits
Orange Cups
Tomato-Artichoke Aspic
Marinated Asparagus
Zucchini Bread
Potato Chip Cookies
Fudge Bars
Coffee

BULLSHOTS

6 cups beef consommé
6 cups commercial Bloody Mary mix
Dash of hot sauce
Dash of Worcestershire sauce
Dash of celery salt
Dash of lemon-pepper seasoning
Celery tops

Combine all ingredients except celery tops; mix well. Chill at least 1 hour. To serve, pour in individual glasses, and garnish each serving with a celery top. Yield: 12 cups.

MIMOSAS

2 (12-ounce) cans frozen orange juice concentrate, thawed and divided
1 (16-ounce) jar maraschino cherries with stems, drained
6 cups extra dry champagne, chilled
Mint sprigs

Prepare 1 can orange juice concentrate according to can directions. Pour into ice cube trays. Place a cherry in each cube; freeze 8 hours or overnight.

Prepare remaining can orange juice concentrate according to can directions. Stir in the champagne just before serving. Add ice cubes, and garnish with mint. Yield: 3 quarts.

SHRIMP TOAST

1½ cups water
½ pound unpeeled fresh shrimp
6 whole water chestnuts
2 tablespoons chopped green onion tops
½ teaspoon salt
½ teaspoon sugar
1 egg white
11 slices white bread

Bring water to a boil; add shrimp, and cook 3 to 5 minutes. Drain. Rinse with cold water. Chill. Peel and devein shrimp.

Position knife blade in food processor bowl; add shrimp, water chestnuts, onion tops, salt, and sugar. Top with cover, and process 30 seconds or until finely ground.

Beat egg white (at room temperature) until stiff peaks form; fold into the shrimp mixture.

Trim crust from bread; cut each slice into 4 triangles. Broil 6 inches from heat 1 to 2 minutes. Cool. Spread shrimp mixture on bread sections; bake at 425° for 5 minutes or until lightly browned. Yield: about 44 appetizers.

Note: Appetizers can be made ahead, baked, and frozen. To reheat, bake at 400° for 5 minutes.

SMOKED HAM

Hickory chips
1 (10- to 12-pound) uncooked fresh ham
1½ cups firmly packed brown sugar
2 tablespoons dry mustard
About 50 whole cloves
1 (12-ounce) can cola beverage
Cherry tomato halves (optional)
Parsley sprigs (optional)

Soak hickory chips in water 30 minutes. Prepare charcoal fire in smoker, and let burn 10 to 15 minutes. Place hickory chips on coals. Place water pan in smoker, and fill with water.

Place ham on food rack. Insert meat thermometer, making sure it does not touch fat or bone. Cover with smoker lid; cook 9 to 10 hours or until meat thermometer reaches 170°. Refill water pan, and add charcoal as needed.

Remove ham from food rack. Remove skin and score fat in a diamond design. Combine brown sugar and mustard; pat over ham. Insert cloves at 1-inch intervals. Return ham to rack; pour cola over ham, and cook 15 minutes. Slice ham; garnish with cherry tomatoes and parsley, if desired. Yield: about 20 servings.

SAUSAGE GRITS

1 pound bulk pork sausage
3 cups hot cooked grits
2½ cups (10 ounces) shredded Cheddar
  cheese
3 tablespoons butter or margarine
3 eggs, beaten
1½ cups milk
Pimiento strips (optional)
Parsley (optional)

Cook sausage until browned in a heavy skillet; drain well. Spoon sausage into a lightly greased 13- x 9- x 2-inch baking dish.

Combine hot grits, cheese, and butter. Stir until cheese and butter melt.

Combine eggs and milk; stir into grits. Pour over sausage. Bake at 350° for 1 hour. Garnish casserole with pimiento strips and parsley, if desired. Yield: about 15 servings.

Note: This can be made and refrigerated overnight, and baked next day.

ORANGE CUPS

8 medium-size oranges
3 cups seedless green grapes
2 cups blueberries
¼ cup finely chopped fresh mint leaves
½ cup Kirsch or other cherry-flavored
  brandy
1 (8-ounce) carton commercial sour cream
¼ cup firmly packed brown sugar

Cut oranges in half crosswise. Clip membranes, and carefully remove pulp. (Do not puncture bottom.) Set the orange cups aside, and reserve orange pulp for other uses.

Combine grapes, blueberries, and mint leaves in a medium bowl. Pour Kirsch over fruit; cover and marinate in refrigerator 2 hours.

Combine sour cream and brown sugar in a small bowl. Before serving, pour ½ cup sour cream sauce over marinated fruit; blend well.

Using slotted spoon, fill orange cups with fruit. Top with remaining sauce. Yield: 16 servings.

TOMATO-ARTICHOKE ASPIC

4 cups cocktail vegetable juice, divided
2 (3-ounce) packages lemon-flavored
  gelatin
1 teaspoon Worcestershire sauce
1 (14-ounce) can artichoke hearts, drained
  and halved
3 green onions with tops, cut into 1-inch
  pieces
1 (8-ounce) package cream cheese, cut
  into 1-inch pieces
1 (12-ounce) carton small-curd cottage
  cheese
2 cups mayonnaise
½ cup capers
Bibb lettuce
1 (2-ounce) jar black caviar
8 to 9 lemon slices, halved (optional)

Bring 2 cups vegetable juice to a boil in a medium saucepan; remove from heat, and add gelatin, stirring until dissolved. Stir in remaining 2 cups juice and Worcestershire sauce. Pour 2 cups gelatin mixture into an oiled 11-cup ring mold. Let remaining juice mixture stand at room temperature. Chill mixture in mold until the consistency of unbeaten egg white. Press artichoke halves into thickened mixture around outside of mold; chill until gelatin is firm.

Position knife blade in food processor bowl. Add green onions. Top with cover, and process, pulsing 5 or 6 times until onions are chopped. Add cream cheese and cottage cheese; process 15 seconds or until smooth.

Spread cheese mixture evenly over chilled aspic, spreading to edge of ring mold. Gently pour remaining gelatin mixture over cheese layer; chill until gelatin is firm.

Combine mayonnaise and capers; mix well. Chill until serving time.

Run a thin metal spatula between ring mold and aspic all the way around; unmold onto serving platter. Surround aspic with Bibb lettuce leaves. Place half of caper mayonnaise in a small serving bowl; place in center of aspic mold. Place a heaping tablespoonful of caviar onto center of caper mayonnaise. Gently press lemon slices around outside of aspic mold, if desired. Serve remaining caper mayonnaise topped with remaining caviar in a separate bowl. Yield: 14 servings.

MARINATED ASPARAGUS

4 pounds fresh asparagus spears
1 cup olive oil
⅓ cup tarragon vinegar
3 tablespoons chopped parsley
3 tablespoons sweet pickle relish
1 (2-ounce) jar chopped pimiento
1½ tablespoons chopped fresh chives
1 teaspoon salt
⅛ teaspoon pepper
1 hard-cooked egg, sieved (optional)
Parsley sprigs (optional)

Remove tough ends of asparagus. Remove scales from stalks with a knife or vegetable peeler, if desired. Cook asparagus, covered, in boiling salted water 6 to 8 minutes or until asparagus is crisp-tender; drain.

Combine oil, vinegar, parsley, pickle relish, pimiento, chives, salt, and pepper in a jar; cover tightly, and shake vigorously. Place asparagus in a shallow container; pour marinade over spears. Cover and chill at least 2 hours. Drain off marinade; arrange asparagus on a serving platter. Garnish asparagus with sieved egg and parsley sprigs, if desired. Yield: 16 servings.

ZUCCHINI BREAD

3 cups all-purpose flour
2 teaspoons baking soda
1 teaspoon salt
½ teaspoon baking powder
¾ cup finely chopped pecans
3 eggs
2 cups sugar
1 cup vegetable oil
2 teaspoons vanilla extract
2 cups shredded zucchini
1 (8-ounce) can crushed pineapple, well drained

Combine dry ingredients and pecans; set aside.

Beat eggs lightly in a large mixing bowl; add sugar, oil, and vanilla; beat until creamy. Stir in zucchini and pineapple. Add dry ingredients, stirring only until dry ingredients are moistened.

Spoon batter into 2 well-greased and floured 8- x 4- x 3-inch loafpans. Bake at 350° for 1 hour or until done. Cool 10 minutes in pans; turn out on rack, and allow bread to cool completely. Yield: 2 loaves.

POTATO CHIP COOKIES

1 cup butter, softened
½ cup sugar
1¾ cups all-purpose flour
¾ cup coarsely crushed potato chips
1 teaspoon vanilla extract
⅔ cup sifted powdered sugar

Cream butter and sugar, beating until light and fluffy. Add flour, potato chips, and vanilla; beat well. Drop dough by rounded teaspoonfuls onto ungreased cookie sheets. Bake at 350° for 10 to 12 minutes or until edges are lightly browned. Cool 5 minutes on cookie sheets; remove to wire racks. When cookies are cool, roll in powdered sugar. Yield: 4 dozen.

FUDGE BARS

1 cup butter or margarine
4 (1-ounce) squares unsweetened chocolate
2 cups sugar
4 eggs
1 cup all-purpose flour
½ teaspoon salt
1 cup chopped pecans
2 teaspoons vanilla extract
Chocolate frosting (recipe follows)

Combine butter and chocolate in a medium saucepan over low heat. Cook until chocolate and butter melt.

Combine sugar and eggs in a mixing bowl; beat at medium speed of an electric mixer until well blended. Add chocolate mixture; beat well. Stir in flour and salt just until blended. Stir in pecans and vanilla.

Pour into a greased 12- x 8- x 2-inch baking dish. Bake at 325° for 45 minutes or until a wooden pick inserted in center comes out clean. Let cool slightly. Spread with chocolate frosting while slightly warm. Let cool completely. Cut into 2- x ¾-inch bars. Yield: 4½ dozen.

Chocolate Frosting:

¼ cup butter or margarine
¼ cup water
3 cups sifted powdered sugar
¼ cup cocoa
¾ teaspoon vanilla extract
⅛ teaspoon salt

Combine butter and water in a medium saucepan over low heat; cook until butter melts. Combine remaining ingredients in a mixing bowl; add butter mixture, and beat until smooth. Yield: about 1½ cups.

Put Fruit On The Menu

Serving chilled fruit as an appetizer provides a colorful introduction to the meal. Or use it as a supplement to any morning menu. Baked fruit recipes, such as Honey-Baked Apple Quarters, make good side dishes or desserts.

HONEY-BAKED APPLE QUARTERS

3 large baking apples, cored, and quartered
⅔ cup honey
2 tablespoons water
1 tablespoon sugar
1½ teaspoons ground cinnamon
3 tablespoons butter or margarine
½ cup half-and-half (optional)

Place apples in a shallow buttered 2-quart casserole. Combine honey, water, sugar, and cinnamon, mixing well; pour over apples, turning apples to coat. Dot with butter. Cover, and bake at 350° for 20 minutes or until apples are tender, basting twice. Serve apples with half-and-half, if desired. Yield: 4 servings.
Imogene Narmore,
Russellville, Alabama.

BERRY-FILLED MELON

1 small cantaloupe
3 tablespoons Kirsch or other cherry-flavored brandy
3 tablespoons sifted powdered sugar
1 teaspoon lime juice
1½ cups fresh strawberries, capped and halved

Cut cantaloupe in half, and remove seeds; prick cavities with a fork. (Do not puncture rind.)

Combine brandy, sugar, and lime juice in a medium-sized bowl. Add strawberries; toss lightly. Spoon into cantaloupe halves. Chill at least 2 hours. Yield: 2 servings.
Mrs. Homer Baxter,
Charleston, West Virginia.

PINEAPPLE-HONEY PEARS

4 medium pears, peeled, halved, and
  cored
¾ cup pineapple juice
⅓ cup chopped pecans
¼ cup firmly packed brown sugar
½ teaspoon vanilla extract
⅛ teaspoon lemon extract
¼ cup honey

Place pear halves, cut side up, in a
9-inch square baking dish. Pour pineapple juice over pears. Combine pecans,
sugar, and flavorings; stir well, and
spoon evenly over pears. Pour honey on
top of each pear. Cover and bake at
350° for 55 minutes, basting once during
baking. Serve warm. Yield: 8 servings.
Alida Garrison,
Johnson City, Tennessee.

PINEAPPLE SPRITZ

2 (20-ounce) cans pineapple chunks,
  drained and chilled
1 (12-ounce) can ginger ale, chilled
½ cup loosely packed fresh mint leaves,
  bruised
Additional mint sprigs
Maraschino cherries (optional)

Combine first 3 ingredients. Chill 30
minutes. Before serving, remove and
discard mint leaves. Spoon pineapple
mixture into individual compotes, and
garnish with additional mint and cherries, if desired. Yield: 6 to 8 servings.
Mrs. Harry H. Lay Jr.,
Fairmount, Georgia.

Wake Up To These Main Dishes

If you think Marinated Baked Ham,
New Orleans Veal With Crabmeat, and
Quail With Currant Jelly Sauce sound
appetizing, you're right. Each of these
main dish recipes will liven up any
breakfast or brunch, turning it into a
delicious occasion.

MARINATED BAKED HAM

1 cup unsweetened pineapple juice
1 cup orange juice
3 tablespoons vegetable oil
1 tablespoon wine vinegar
2 teaspoons dry mustard
¾ teaspoon ground ginger
½ teaspoon ground cloves
1 (2-pound) fully cooked ham slice

Combine all ingredients except ham;
mix well. Pour over ham slice; cover
and chill 8 hours or overnight, stirring
occasionally.

Drain ham, reserving marinade. Place
ham in a shallow baking pan; bake, uncovered, at 325° for 35 to 40 minutes,
basting every 10 minutes with reserved
marinade. Yield: 6 servings.
John L. Wood,
Memphis, Tennessee.

NEW ORLEANS VEAL WITH CRABMEAT

3 tablespoons all-purpose flour
½ teaspoon salt
¼ teaspoon pepper
1½ to 1¾ pounds (¼-inch-thick) boneless
  veal cutlets
⅓ cup butter or margarine
¼ cup lemon juice
¾ pound lump crabmeat
1 tablespoon chopped fresh parsley
  (optional)
Hollandaise sauce (recipe follows)
Paprika

Combine flour, salt, and pepper;
dredge veal in flour mixture. Melt butter in a large skillet over medium heat.
Add veal, and cook 1 minute on each
side or until lightly browned. Add
lemon juice to skillet; cook an additional 30 seconds. Remove veal to serving platter. Discard all but 1 tablespoon
of pan drippings. Add crabmeat to reserved drippings; sprinkle with parsley,
if desired. Sauté crabmeat just until

heated; spoon evenly over veal cutlets.
Top with hollandaise sauce, and sprin-
kle with paprika. Serve immediately.
Yield: 6 servings.

Hollandaise Sauce:

3 egg yolks
⅛ teaspoon salt
Dash of red pepper
2 tablespoons lemon juice
½ cup butter or margarine, softened and
  divided

Beat egg yolks, salt, and red pepper
in top of a double boiler; gradually add
lemon juice, stirring constantly. Add
about one-third of butter to egg mixture. Cook over hot, but not boiling,
water; stir constantly, until butter melts.

Add another third of butter, stirring
constantly. As sauce thickens, stir in remaining third of butter. Cook until
thickened. Yield: ¾ cup.

QUAIL WITH CURRANT JELLY SAUCE

8 quail, dressed
½ teaspoon salt
¼ teaspoon pepper
3 tablespoons butter or margarine, melted
½ cup chicken broth
½ teaspoon grated orange rind
½ cup orange juice
⅓ cup currant jelly
¼ teaspoon ground ginger
2 teaspoons cornstarch
2 teaspoons lemon juice

Sprinkle quail with salt and pepper.
Brown quail on both sides in butter in a
large skillet over medium heat. Add
chicken broth; cover, reduce heat, and
simmer 40 minutes or until tender.
Place quail on serving platter.

Combine orange rind, orange juice,
currant jelly, and ginger in a small
saucepan; cook mixture over medium
heat until jelly melts.

Combine cornstarch and lemon juice
in a small bowl. Add to jelly mixture;
cook over low heat, stirring constantly,
until thickened and bubbly. Spoon over
quail. Yield: 4 servings.
Frances Simmons,
Vardaman, Mississippi.

SCRAMBLED EGG TOSTADAS
(pictured on page 100)

½ cup chopped onion
2 tablespoons butter or margarine, melted
8 eggs, slightly beaten
1 (8-ounce) carton commercial sour cream, divided
½ cup (2 ounces) shredded Monterey Jack cheese
2 tablespoons commercial mild taco sauce
½ teaspoon garlic salt
¼ teaspoon ground cumin
6 commercial tostadas
2 cups shredded lettuce
1 large tomato, chopped
1 medium-size green pepper, chopped
2 to 3 tablespoons sliced ripe olives
Additional mild taco sauce (optional)

Sauté onion in butter in a large skillet until tender. Combine eggs, ½ cup sour cream, cheese, 2 tablespoons taco sauce, garlic salt, and cumin, mixing well; pour over onion in skillet. Cook egg mixture over medium heat, stirring often, until eggs are firm but still moist. Set aside, and keep warm.

Bake tostadas according to package directions. Place tostadas on serving plates; top with lettuce, egg mixture, tomato, green pepper, remaining ½ cup sour cream, and olives. Serve immediately with additional taco sauce, if desired. Yield: 6 servings. *Jean Voan,*
Shepherd, Texas.

CHEESY PICANTE OMELET

4 eggs
1 tablespoon butter or margarine
1 cup (4 ounces) shredded Cheddar cheese
1 to 2 teaspoons ground cumin
Picante sauce

Beat eggs well. Heat a 10-inch omelet pan or heavy skillet until hot enough to sizzle a drop of water. Add 1 tablespoon butter; tilt pan to coat bottom. Pour eggs into pan. As eggs begin to cook, gently lift edges of omelet with a spatula to allow uncooked portion to flow underneath.

When eggs are set, sprinkle with cheese and cumin. Loosen omelet with a spatula, and fold in half; remove from heat. Cover and let stand 1 minute or until cheese melts. Gently slide omelet onto serving plate. Top omelet with picante sauce, and serve immediately. Yield: 2 servings.

Bronwen M. Gibson,
Birmingham, Alabama.

Morning Dishes To Make Ahead

If you're having guests over for breakfast or brunch, you know that anything you prepare the night before will make things go smoother the next morning. With that in mind, we've selected several make-ahead recipes.

SAUSAGE-MUSHROOM BREAKFAST CASSEROLE
(pictured on page 100)

2¼ cups seasoned croutons
1½ pounds bulk pork sausage
4 eggs, beaten
2¼ cups milk
1 (10¾-ounce) can cream of mushroom soup, undiluted
1 (4-ounce) can sliced mushrooms, drained
¾ teaspoon dry mustard
2 cups (8 ounces) shredded Cheddar cheese
Cherry tomato halves (optional)
Parsley sprigs (optional)

Spread croutons in a lightly greased 13- x 9- x 2-inch baking dish; set aside.

Cook sausage until browned, stirring to crumble; drain well. Sprinkle sausage over croutons. Combine eggs, milk, soup, mushrooms, and mustard; mix well, and pour over sausage. Cover and refrigerate at least 8 hours or overnight.

Remove from refrigerator; let stand 30 minutes. Bake, uncovered, at 325° for 50 to 55 minutes. Sprinkle cheese over top; bake an additional 5 minutes or until cheese melts. Garnish with tomatoes and parsley, if desired. Yield: 8 servings. *Eileen Wehling,*
Austin, Texas.

FRUITED RICE PUDDING

⅓ cup currants
2 cups milk
1 (3-ounce) package vanilla pudding mix
2 cups cooked rice
⅓ cup pineapple preserves
1 teaspoon vanilla extract
½ teaspoon ground cinnamon
Whipped cream (optional)

Pour enough boiling water over currants to cover; let stand 10 minutes. Drain and set currants aside.

Combine milk and pudding in a large saucepan. Cook over medium heat, stirring frequently, until mixture comes to a boil. Remove from heat, and stir in currants and remaining ingredients except whipped cream. Pour mixture into a 1½-quart serving dish; chill at least 6 hours or overnight. Serve with whipped cream, if desired. Yield: 6 servings.
Sandy Hayes,
Morristown, Tennessee.

OMELET SANDWICH

Vegetable cooking spray
16 slices white bread, crust removed
8 (1-ounce) slices process American cheese
8 (1-ounce) slices ham
6 eggs, beaten
3 cups milk
½ teaspoon salt
½ teaspoon dry mustard
1 cup corn flakes, crushed
2 tablespoons butter or margarine, melted

Coat bottom and sides of a 13- x 9- x 2-inch baking dish with cooking spray. Line bottom of dish with 8 bread slices, cutting them to fit. Arrange the cheese, ham, and remaining bread slices over top; set aside.

Combine eggs, milk, salt, and dry mustard, mixing well; pour over bread mixture. Cover and refrigerate at least 8 hours or overnight.

Remove from refrigerator; let stand 30 minutes. Sprinkle crushed corn flakes over top bread layer; drizzle with butter. Bake at 350° for 45 to 50 minutes; let stand 5 minutes before cutting into squares. Yield: 8 servings.
Joyce Petrochko,
St. Albans, West Virginia.

Pass The Syrup!

Pancakes, waffles, and French toast are the dishes we favor when we have a little extra time to enjoy the morning. Drenched with syrup, they seem more of a treat than anything else.

APPLE-FILLED PANCAKE

4 cups peeled, thinly sliced apples
¼ cup butter or margarine, melted
⅓ cup sugar
¼ teaspoon ground cinnamon
⅛ teaspoon ground nutmeg
½ cup all-purpose flour
¼ teaspoon salt
2 eggs
½ cup milk
3 tablespoons butter or margarine, melted and divided
2 tablespoons powdered sugar, divided
Sautéed apple slices (optional)

Combine apples and ¼ cup butter in a medium saucepan; cook over medium heat 5 minutes. Stir in sugar, cinnamon, and nutmeg; cover and simmer an additional 10 minutes. Set aside.

Combine flour and salt in a mixing bowl; gradually beat in eggs and milk, mixing well. Pour 1 tablespoon melted butter in a 10-inch ovenproof skillet. Add egg mixture to skillet; bake at 450° for 10 minutes.

Watch pancake closely after 5 minutes baking time; as pancake puffs up, immediately puncture it with a fork. Repeat puncturing as pancake continues to puff up. Lower temperature to 350°; bake an additional 5 minutes. (Pancake will have lumpy appearance.)

Remove pancake from oven; drizzle with 1 tablespoon butter, and sprinkle with 1 tablespoon powdered sugar. Spoon apple mixture onto half of pancake; fold other half over apples. Drizzle top with remaining 1 tablespoon butter, and sprinkle with 1 tablespoon powdered sugar. Garnish with apple slices sautéed in butter, if desired. Yield: 4 servings.   *Lynn Koenig, Charleston, South Carolina.*

BANANA-GINGER WAFFLES

1½ cups all-purpose flour
2 teaspoons baking powder
¾ teaspoon salt
1 teaspoon ground cinnamon
¾ teaspoon ground ginger
2 eggs, beaten
⅓ cup brown sugar
¾ cup milk
1 ripe banana, mashed
¼ cup molasses
¼ cup butter or margarine, melted
2 large bananas, sliced (optional)

Combine flour, baking powder, salt, cinnamon, and ginger in a medium mixing bowl; mix well.

Combine eggs, sugar, milk, banana, and molasses; beat until smooth. Add to dry ingredients, stirring just until moistened; stir in butter.

Bake in a preheated lightly oiled waffle iron about 5 minutes. Serve with sliced bananas, if desired. Yield: 12 (4-inch) waffles.   *Lilly S. Bradley, Salem, Virginia.*

MACADAMIA FRENCH TOAST

4 eggs, beaten
⅔ cup orange juice
⅓ cup milk
¼ cup sugar
½ teaspoon vanilla extract
¼ teaspoon ground nutmeg
8 (½-inch) slices Italian or French bread
⅓ cup butter or margarine, melted
½ cup chopped macadamia nuts

Combine eggs, juice, milk, sugar, vanilla, and nutmeg in a medium bowl; mix well. Set aside.

Arrange bread slices in a 13- x 9- x 2-inch baking dish; pour egg mixture over bread. Cover and refrigerate.

Pour butter evenly in a jellyroll pan; arrange bread in a single layer in pan. Sprinkle with nuts; bake at 400° about 25 minutes. Yield: 8 servings.
Brenda Clark, Auburn, Alabama.

PUMPKIN-NUT WAFFLES

2 cups sifted cake flour
1 tablespoon plus 1 teaspoon baking powder
1 teaspoon salt
¾ teaspoon ground cinnamon
¼ teaspoon ground nutmeg
3 eggs, separated
1¾ cups milk
½ cup shortening, melted
½ cup canned pumpkin
¾ cup chopped pecans
Butter curls (optional)

Combine cake flour, baking powder, salt, cinnamon, and nutmeg in a medium mixing bowl; mix well. Combine egg yolks, milk, shortening, and pumpkin; add pumpkin mixture to dry ingredients, stirring just until moistened.

Beat egg whites (at room temperature) at high speed of an electric mixer until stiff peaks form. Fold into pumpkin mixture.

Pour one-fourth of batter into a preheated, lightly oiled waffle iron. Sprinkle 3 tablespoons chopped pecans evenly over batter. Cook about 5 minutes or until done. Repeat procedure with remaining batter and pecans. Serve with butter curls, if desired. Yield: 16 (4-inch) waffles.

Mrs. John Shoemaker, Louisville, Kentucky.

Right: Stately Almond-Butter Wedding Cake looks impressive but is not difficult to make. A fresh garland of ivy and miniature nosegays trim the table. (Suggestions for planning a wedding reception begin on page 104, with the cake recipe and how-to photographs on pages 106 and 107.)

Above: *Set a beautiful Fruit Cascade on a side table. Shells of cantaloupe hold melon balls, strawberries, and Pineapple-Ginger Dip. (Directions for making a Fruit Cascade, as well as the Pineapple-Ginger Dip recipe, are given on page 104. The photograph on page 105 shows how a Fruit Cascade is constructed.)*

Left: *Offer several appetizers from a dining room buffet (from left), Country Ham in Heart Biscuits, Shrimp Salad in Pastry, Crudité Dip with cut vegetables. Foliage arrangements were composed entirely from the greenery in one backyard. (Recipes are on page 105.)*

Above: *Add interest to Four-Fruit Cooler by serving it from an attractive pitcher and glass. (Recipe on facing page.)*

Above right: *Sausage-Mushroom Breakfast Casserole (page 95) can be mixed in the evening and baked the next morning. It's garnished with cherry tomatoes and parsley for extra color.*

Right: *Everyone will warm up to Scrambled Egg Tostadas (page 95). They're fun to make and eat.*

Fill Your Cup With A Flavorful Beverage

Coffee, tea, and orange juice are standard at most morning meals. But you don't have to settle for ordinary beverages. Instead, you can turn a simple menu into a special occasion by serving your family or guests one of our tasty drinks made from the recipes below.

Four-Fruit Cooler combines pineapple juice, orange juice concentrate, lemon juice, and bananas. Lemon-lime carbonated beverage adds sparkle and fizz. Serve it chilled or as an icy slush.

If a warm drink is what it takes to get you going, make some Minted Tea. This recipe has been in the family of Vida Duke, of Paris, Texas, for over 50 years. The beverage has been served at many luncheons, bridge parties, and brunches she has hosted. Chopped fresh mint makes the drink's aroma as pleasant as its flavor.

FOUR-FRUIT COOLER
(pictured at left)

3 cups water
1½ cups sugar
3 cups pineapple juice
1 (6-ounce) can frozen orange juice
   concentrate, thawed and undiluted
2 tablespoons fresh lemon juice
3 ripe bananas, mashed
2 quarts plus 1 cup lemon-lime
   carbonated beverage, chilled

Combine water and sugar in a large saucepan; bring to a boil. Boil 3 minutes. Remove from heat; add fruit juices and bananas, mixing well. Chill. To serve, combine fruit juice mixture with lemon-lime beverage, stirring well. Yield: about 1 gallon.

Note: This drink may also be prepared as a slush. Freeze mixture 8 hours or until firm. Remove from freezer 45 minutes before serving; combine with lemon-lime beverage, stirring well.
Jo Novotny,
Robertsdale, Alabama.

ORANGE FROSTY

1 (6-ounce) can frozen orange juice
   concentrate, thawed and undiluted
¼ cup sifted powdered sugar
8 pineapple chunks
1 ripe banana, cut into chunks
3 cups crushed ice

Combine all ingredients except ice in container of an electric blender; process until smooth. Add ice; process until frothy. Serve immediately. Yield: about 4 cups.
T. G. Lovelace,
Roanoke, Virginia.

MINTED TEA

4 cups boiling water
4 regular tea bags
1½ cups sugar
1 (6-ounce) can frozen orange juice
   concentrate, thawed and undiluted
1 (6-ounce) can frozen lemonade
   concentrate, thawed and undiluted
¾ cup chopped fresh mint
11½ cups water
Lemon slices (optional)
Fresh mint sprigs (optional)

Pour 4 cups boiling water over tea bags; cover. Let stand 12 minutes. Discard bags.

Combine sugar, orange juice concentrate, and lemonade concentrate in a saucepan; bring to a boil, stirring constantly. Remove from heat; add mint. Let stand 15 minutes. Strain mint from fruit juice mixture; discard mint. Add tea and 11½ cups water to fruit juice mixture. Serve hot, garnished with lemon slices and mint sprigs, if desired. Yield: 1 gallon.
Vida Duke,
Paris, Texas.

SPIKED TEA PUNCH

2 quarts water
3¼ cups Burgundy or other red wine
1 cup bourbon
2 oranges, sliced
2 lemons, sliced
3 (3-inch) sticks cinnamon
1½ teaspoons whole cloves
2 family-size tea bags
1½ cups sugar

Combine water, wine, bourbon, oranges, lemons, cinnamon, and cloves in a large Dutch oven; bring to a boil. Remove from heat; add tea bags. Cover and let stand 5 minutes; remove tea bags. Add sugar; heat tea mixture just until the sugar dissolves, stirring occasionally. Serve hot. Yield: 3½ quarts.
Cindy Wallis,
Lawton, Oklahoma.

CHAMPAGNE PUNCH

2 (33.8-ounce) bottles ginger ale, chilled
1 (6-ounce) can frozen lemonade
   concentrate, thawed and undiluted
12 maraschino cherries
1 (12-ounce) can frozen orange juice
   concentrate, diluted
1 (25.4-ounce) bottle dry champagne,
   chilled

Pour 1 bottle of ginger ale and lemonade concentrate into an 11-cup ring mold; add cherries, and freeze until firm. Unmold ice ring in a punch bowl; add remaining ginger ale, orange juice, and champagne. Stir well. Yield: 18 cups.
Linda Gellatly,
Winston-Salem, North Carolina.

Tip: It is best to store most fruit in the refrigerator. Allow melons, avocados, and pears to ripen at room temperature; then refrigerate. Berries should be sorted to remove imperfect fruit before refrigerating; then wash and hull just before serving.

Make Breakfast One Of Your Healthy Habits

Dieting is a poor excuse for missing breakfast. Studies show that eating a good breakfast everyday is one of several key habits linked to good health—whether you are on a diet or not. And people who start the day with a nutritious meal are more alert, and they perform better mentally and physically at work and at school. Most nutritionists consider breakfast the most important meal of the day. It literally breaks the 10- to 12-hour fast from the night meal and provides the body with fuel. It's a good idea to plan ¼ to ⅓ of your daily calories to be eaten at this time.

If your waistline says "lighter," but your appetite cries for more substantial fare, make Asparagus Roulade your choice. It's delicious proof that breakfast need not be high calorie in order to satisfy. Prepare this beautiful and delicious entrée when there's lots of time to enjoy the morning meal.

When a quick breakfast is important, try Slender French Toast and Apple Julep. The beverage and the egg white mixture that coats the toast can be made the night before serving. Then all that's left to do the next morning is to dip the bread in the prepared coating and brown it, which takes less than 15 minutes.

Elegance prevails when you serve Asparagus Roulade.

ASPARAGUS ROULADE

Vegetable cooking spray
1 tablespoon all-purpose flour
1 (10-ounce) package frozen asparagus spears
¼ cup plus 2 tablespoons low-calorie margarine
¾ cup all-purpose flour
3½ cups skim milk, divided
1 teaspoon dry mustard
½ teaspoon salt
4 eggs, separated
1 cup (4 ounces) shredded Swiss cheese
Tomato rose (optional)
Asparagus tips (optional)

Coat a 15- x 10- x 1-inch jellyroll pan with cooking spray. Line with waxed paper, allowing paper to extend beyond ends of pan; coat the waxed paper with cooking spray; dust lightly with 1 tablespoon flour.

Cook asparagus according to package directions; drain well. Cut into 1-inch pieces; set aside.

Melt margarine in a heavy saucepan over low heat; add ¾ cup flour, stirring until smooth. Cook 1 minute, stirring constantly. Gradually add 3 cups skim milk; cook over medium heat, stirring constantly, until mixture is thickened and bubbly. Stir in dry mustard and salt. Measure 1 cup white sauce into a small saucepan; set aside.

Place egg yolks in a large bowl, and beat slightly. Gradually stir about one-fourth of the remaining hot white sauce into egg yolks; add to remaining hot mixture, stirring constantly.

Beat egg whites (at room temperature) in a medium bowl at high speed of an electric mixer until stiff peaks form. Fold one-third of egg whites into yolk mixture; carefully fold in remaining egg whites. Spoon into jellyroll pan, spreading evenly to sides of pan.

Bake at 325° for 40 minutes or until puffed and firm to the touch. (Do not allow roulade to overbake.) Remove from oven and set aside.

Combine remaining ½ cup skim milk, Swiss cheese, and reserved white sauce. Heat slowly, stirring constantly, until cheese melts and sauce is smooth.

Loosen edges of roulade with a metal spatula. Place 2 lengths of waxed paper (longer than jellyroll pan) on a large tray. Quickly invert jellyroll pan onto waxed paper; remove pan, and carefully peel waxed paper from roulade.

Place asparagus over roulade; spoon ¾ cup cheese sauce over asparagus.

Starting at short end, carefully roll roulade jellyroll fashion; use waxed paper to help support roulade as it is rolled. Top with half of remaining cheese sauce. Garnish with tomato rose and asparagus tips, if desired. To serve, cut into 8 equal slices. Top with remaining cheese sauce. Yield: 8 servings (about 219 calories per 1-inch slice).

Joyce Andrews,
Washington, Virginia.

CRUSTLESS GRITS-AND-HAM PIE

⅓ cup quick-cooking grits, uncooked
1 cup water
1 cup evaporated skim milk
¾ cup (3 ounces) shredded reduced-calorie Cheddar cheese
¾ cup cooked, lean chopped ham
3 eggs, beaten
1 tablespoon fresh chopped parsley
½ teaspoon dry mustard
½ teaspoon hot sauce
¼ teaspoon salt
Vegetable cooking spray

Cook grits in water according to package directions, omitting salt.

Combine cooked grits, milk, cheese, ham, eggs, parsley, mustard, hot sauce, and salt, mixing well. Pour grits mixture into a 9-inch pieplate coated with cooking spray.

Bake at 350° for 30 to 35 minutes or until set. Let stand 5 to 10 minutes before serving. Yield: 6 servings (about 181 calories per 1½-inch wedge).

ZUCCHINI FRITTATA

6 cups water
½ teaspoon salt
1¾ cups unpeeled, diced zucchini
¼ cup soft breadcrumbs
¼ cup plus 2 tablespoons skim milk
6 eggs, beaten
Vegetable cooking spray
2 tablespoons reduced-calorie margarine, melted
¼ cup grated Parmesan cheese
Zucchini slices (optional)
Parsley (optional)

Combine water and salt in a large saucepan; bring to a boil. Add diced zucchini, and cook about 2 minutes. Drain, and set aside.

Combine breadcrumbs and milk in a large bowl; let stand 5 minutes. Stir in cooked zucchini and eggs. Coat a 9-inch pieplate with cooking spray; drizzle with margarine. Pour zucchini mixture into pieplate; sprinkle with cheese. Bake at 350° for 25 minutes or until set. Garnish with zucchini slices and parsley, if desired. Yield: 6 servings (about 137 calories per 1½-inch wedge). *Shelley Field, Houston, Texas.*

SLENDER FRENCH TOAST

2 egg whites
2 tablespoons frozen orange juice concentrate, thawed and undiluted
¼ teaspoon vanilla extract
2 drops of butter flavoring
Dash of ground cinnamon
Dash of ground nutmeg
Vegetable cooking spray
4 slices whole wheat bread
1 teaspoon sifted powdered sugar

Combine egg whites, orange juice concentrate, flavorings, and spices in a shallow bowl; beat well.

Coat a large skillet with vegetable cooking spray; place over medium heat until hot. Dip bread, one slice at a time, into egg white mixture, coating well. Arrange in skillet, and cook on medium heat 4 minutes on each side or until browned. Sprinkle with powdered sugar. Yield: 4 servings (about 96 calories per slice).

MUFFINS MADE OF BRAN

1¼ cups all-purpose flour
1 cup shreds of wheat bran cereal
2½ teaspoons baking powder
1 egg, beaten
¾ cup skim milk
¼ cup molasses
3 tablespoons vegetable oil
Vegetable cooking spray

Combine dry ingredients in a medium bowl; make a well in center of mixture. Combine egg, milk, molasses, and oil; add to dry ingredients, stirring just until moistened. Spoon into muffin pans coated with cooking spray, filling two-thirds full. Bake at 400° for 20 minutes. Yield: 1 dozen (about 120 calories per muffin).

C. R. Heminger,
Doraville, Georgia.

APPLE JULEP

1 quart unsweetened apple juice
2 cups unsweetened pineapple juice
1 cup unsweetened orange juice
¼ cup lemon juice
Mint sprigs (optional)

Combine fruit juices, stirring well. Chill. Before serving, garnish with mint sprigs, if desired. Yield: 7¼ cups (about 120 calories per 1-cup serving).

Patsy Taylor,
Hartsville, Tennessee.

PEACH REFRESHER

2 (16-ounce) cans peach slices in extra light syrup, drained
1⅔ cups skim milk
2 teaspoons honey
½ teaspoon vanilla extract

Freeze peach slices 2 hours or until partially frozen.

Combine peaches and remaining ingredients in container of an electric blender; process until smooth. Serve immediately. Yield: 5 cups (about 107 calories per 1-cup serving). *Eva Kellogg, Houston, Texas.*

Ring The Wedding Bells At Home

The time, place, and style of weddings are no longer predictable. Today's brides look for ways to individualize their weddings, and one way is by having part or all of the festivities in their own homes.

Planning for the Crowd

It's perfectly acceptable to serve only cake, party nuts, and punch at a wedding reception, but many hosts add a dip or spread or as much as an entire dinner buffet. For our menu, we planned a lavish appetizer spread. Our recipes make up an entire menu, but they also work well singularly or any way you'd like to group them.

Decide on your menu two months early, if possible. Stay away from recipes that require last-minute cooking or preparation, unless you have someone to help you in the kitchen. Choose dishes that guests will be able to serve themselves, so that you can mingle.

Once your menu is established, check to be sure you have enough serving containers, plates, flatware, and glassware, as well as equipment and storage containers. Make sure there is enough space in your refrigerator and oven.

If you decide you need to rent some things, make your reservations two months in advance, if possible. And be sure to verify your order and delivery arrangements two weeks before the wedding to avoid any mix-ups.

If you'll need to hire people to serve, reserve their services at least two months in advance. About a week before the event, give the servers verbal and written instructions, and post an instruction list in the kitchen. Give every helper a particular task, such as refilling platters, refilling glasses, or removing used glassware. Appoint at least one floater to survey the crowd and take care of needs that you'll be too busy to worry about.

As soon as your menu is planned, begin making out grocery lists. Make two lists: one for items to be bought weeks in advance, and the other for perishables to be purchased a couple of days beforehand.

Along with your grocery lists, make two time schedules that specify exactly when you will prepare each recipe. Also make a list of when you will take care of extra jobs, such as polishing silver and washing and ironing linens.

Plan to place your reception foods in several different rooms to keep the crowd dispersed and to encourage guests to circulate. A few days before the wedding, set out serving platters exactly where you plan to serve them to see if your serving locations work.

The Wedding Reception

If you're planning to prepare some or all of the food for your own wedding or a friend's, we hope you'll enjoy our ideas on the subject.

We've prepared a time schedule for you to work by when preparing this menu. As early as two months ahead, you can make and freeze the ice ring and fruit juice base for Wedding Punch. Thaw the fruit juice base a day or two ahead of time, and refrigerate it until ready to serve. Stir the chilled champagne and tonic water into the fruit juice mixture just before serving.

You can bake the cake layers up to a month in advance and freeze them. You can also bake the biscuits for Country Ham in Heart Biscuits a month early. When biscuits cool, wrap them in freezer bags, and place in an airtight container in the freezer. Thaw the biscuits at room temperature in the plastic bags the night before the wedding. There's no need to reheat them.

One to two weeks ahead of time, prepare the Mint Twists; store them in an airtight container at room temperature. No more than a week ahead, prepare the tart shells for Shrimp Salad in Pastry, and store in an airtight container. Also make Layered Cheese Pâté; cover pan with plastic wrap, and chill. Unmold paté the wedding day.

Two to three days before the wedding, fill and frost the cake. Stir up the Crudité Dip, Pineapple-Ginger Dip, and Mustard Spread for ham biscuits. Cook and chop shrimp; combine with marinade, and chill.

The day before the wedding, make melon balls, and scoop out cantaloupe shells. Wash the grapes, and assemble the base for the Fruit Cascade. Arrange the fruit on the base a day ahead if you have room to store the large arrangement in your refrigerator. Wrap it well with plastic wrap. Prepare vegetables for the dip and refrigerate.

The morning of the wedding, place a waterproof liner and tablecloth on table; then position the wedding cake, and place the top tier on the divider plates. Arrange the flowers on and around the cake. Place nosegays on small squares of waxed paper around table edge; pin strands of miniature ivy between nosegays.

Ask a helper to spoon the shrimp filling into the tart shells no more than an hour or two before the time you serve. This menu serves about 25 guests. Multiply the recipes to accommodate your particular guest list.

**Pineapple-Ginger Dip   Fruit Cascade
Layered Cheese Pâté   Crackers
Crudité Dip   Cut Vegetables
Shrimp Salad in Pastry
Country Ham in Heart Biscuits
Mint Twists
Almond-Butter Wedding Cake
Wedding Punch**

PINEAPPLE-GINGER DIP
(pictured on page 99)

**2 (8-ounce) packages cream cheese, softened
¼ cup plus 1 tablespoon pineapple juice
1 tablespoon lemon juice
1 tablespoon grated orange rind
1½ to 2 teaspoons ground ginger
¼ cup flaked coconut, toasted
2 tablespoons powdered sugar (optional)**

Beat cream cheese until light and fluffy. Stir in remaining ingredients. Serve with fresh fruit. Yield: 2 cups.

FRUIT CASCADE
(pictured on page 99)

Stack 3 rigid plastic foam rounds (each 12 inches in diameter and 2 inches thick) on a base several inches larger than the rounds. Cut another plastic foam round in half vertically; stack both pieces on top of rounds. (See photo at right.) Insert several thin dowels through top to secure stack.

Slice 2 pineapples in half lengthwise. Scoop out pulp, leaving shells intact. Reserve pulp for other recipes, or cut into chunks and serve with dip. Place shells randomly on plastic foam; secure with florist picks.

Cut 2 or 3 cantaloupes in half using a scalloped-edge knife. Discard seeds. Using melon baller, scoop out balls from pulp, and set aside. Scoop out excess pulp from shells, leaving shells intact. Place cantaloupes randomly on form, and secure with florist picks.

Fill in empty spaces around plastic foam with clusters of grapes (about 12 to 15 pounds), securing with florist picks. Set arrangement on table where it is to be served. Fill one cantaloupe shell with dip, and fill others with fruit.

You can construct the frame and cut and arrange fruit a day ahead. Wrap with plastic wrap and refrigerate.

LAYERED CHEESE PÂTÉ

2 (8-ounce) packages cream cheese,
   softened
1¼ teaspoons dried Italian seasoning
⅛ teaspoon pepper
½ cup (2 ounces) shredded Gruyère
   cheese
¼ cup finely chopped pecans
¾ cup chopped fresh parsley, divided
1 (3-ounce) package Roquefort cheese,
   crumbled
Fresh spinach leaves

Combine cream cheese, Italian seasoning, and pepper in a mixing bowl;
beat at medium speed of an electric
mixer until smooth.

Line a lightly oiled 6- x 4- x 2-inch
loafpan with plastic wrap, leaving a 2-
inch overhang on each side.

Carefully spread about one-third of
cream cheese mixture in loafpan,
smoothing to corners of pan. Next,
layer Gruyère cheese and chopped
pecans; top with half of remaining
cream cheese mixture. Then layer ½
cup parsley and Roquefort cheese; top
with remaining cream cheese mixture,
pressing mixture firmly. Cover with
overhanging plastic wrap, and allow
cheese loaf to chill at least 8 hours.

To unmold, lift cheese loaf out of pan
using the plastic wrap, and invert onto a
serving plate lined with a bed of spinach. Remove plastic wrap, and sprinkle
loaf with remaining ¼ cup chopped
parsley. Let cheese loaf come to room
temperature before serving. Serve with
crackers. Yield: 1 (6-inch) loaf.

*Stack three (12-inch) rigid plastic foam
rounds. Cut another 12-inch round in half;
stack on top and to one side of rounds.
Insert dowels through the stack. Attach
pineapple halves and cantaloupe shells with
florist picks. Cover exposed form with
grapes. (See photo, page 99.)*

CRUDITÉ DIP
(pictured on page 98)

1 (8-ounce) carton commercial sour cream
1 cup mayonnaise
½ cup chopped fresh parsley
3 tablespoons minced fresh chives
1 teaspoon lemon juice
¼ teaspoon salt
1 clove garlic, minced
1 large cabbage
Chopped fresh parsley

Combine sour cream, mayonnaise, ½
cup parsley, chives, lemon juice, salt,
and garlic; mix well. Allow dip mixture
to chill thoroughly.

Trim core end of cabbage to form a
flat base. Fold back several outer leaves
of cabbage. Cut a crosswise slice from
the top, making it wide enough to remove about a fourth of the head; then
cut and lift out enough inner leaves
from the cabbage to form a shell about
1 inch thick. (Reserve the slice and
inner leaves of the cabbage for use in
other recipes.)

Spoon chilled dip into cavity of cabbage, and sprinkle top of dip with
chopped parsley. Serve dip with snow
peas, green onion fans, and blanched
asparagus. Yield: 2 cups.

SHRIMP SALAD IN PASTRY
(pictured on page 98)

2 cups water
½ pound unpeeled fresh shrimp
3 tablespoons finely chopped celery
2 tablespoons finely chopped green pepper
3 tablespoons finely chopped pecans
1 tablespoon chopped sweet pickle
¼ cup plus 2 tablespoons commercial
   Italian salad dressing
Tart shells (recipe follows)
Alfalfa sprouts

Bring water to a boil; add shrimp,
and cook 3 to 5 minutes. Drain well;
rinse with cold water. Chill. Peel, devein, and coarsely chop shrimp.

Combine shrimp, celery, green pepper, pecans, pickle, and salad dressing,
tossing well. Chill 8 hours.

Line each tart shell with a small
amount of alfalfa sprouts. Drain chilled
shrimp salad well. Spoon about 1 teaspoon salad into each of the tart shells.
Yield: about 3½ dozen.

Tart Shells:

1¼ cups all-purpose flour
½ teaspoon salt
¼ cup plus 2 tablespoons shortening
2½ to 3 tablespoons cold water

Combine flour and salt; cut in shortening with pastry blender until mixture
resembles coarse meal. Sprinkle cold
water (1 tablespoon at a time) evenly
over surface; stir with a fork until all
dry ingredients are moistened. Shape
into a ball, and chill.

Divide pastry into 42 equal portions.
Place each portion in a 1½-inch pastry
mold, and press pastry to fit mold. Bake
at 400° for 10 minutes or until browned.
Cool slightly, and remove from molds.
Store shells in an airtight container.
Yield: 3½ dozen.

COUNTRY HAM
IN HEART BISCUITS
(pictured on page 98)

3 cups all-purpose flour
1½ tablespoons baking powder
¾ teaspoon baking soda
¼ teaspoon salt
½ cup butter or margarine
1½ cups buttermilk
3 tablespoons butter or margarine, melted
About 1½ pounds sliced country ham
Mustard Spread

Combine flour, baking powder, soda,
and salt; cut in butter with a pastry
blender until mixture resembles coarse
meal. Add buttermilk, stirring just until
dry ingredients are moistened. Turn
dough out onto a lightly floured surface,
and knead lightly 4 or 5 times.

Roll dough to ½-inch thickness; cut
with a 2-inch heart-shaped cutter. Place
biscuits on a lightly greased baking
sheet; bake at 450° for 10 to 12 minutes
or until golden. Brush with melted butter. Serve with country ham and Mustard Spread. Yield: about 2½ dozen.

Mustard Spread:

½ cup mayonnaise
2 tablespoons Dijon mustard
2 tablespoons tangy mustard-mayonnaise-
   flavored sandwich sauce
2 tablespoons sweet pickle relish

Combine all ingredients, mixing well.
Chill until served. Yield: about 1 cup.

*Tip: When preparing finger sandwiches
in advance, keep them from drying out
by placing them in a shallow container
lined with a damp towel and waxed
paper. Separate sandwich layers with
waxed paper, and cover with another
layer of waxed paper and a damp
towel; refrigerate.*

MINT TWISTS

2 cups sugar
1 cup water
¼ cup butter or margarine
⅛ teaspoon oil of peppermint
4 drops of desired food coloring

Combine sugar and water in a large saucepan; bring to a boil, and add butter. Cover and cook, without stirring, over high heat 5 minutes. Uncover and continue cooking until mixture reaches hard ball stage (260°). Remove from heat, and immediately pour syrup onto a buttered marble slab.

Sprinkle oil of peppermint and food coloring over surface of hot syrup; let rest 3 minutes or until edges begin to set. Begin scraping syrup with metal spatula into a central mass. Continue scraping and folding until color is evenly distributed.

Pull mixture with fingertips, allowing a spread of about 15 inches between hands; then fold mixture in half. Repeat pulling and folding until consistency of mixture changes from sticky to elastic.

Begin twisting while folding and pulling. Continue pulling until ridges on the twists begin to hold their shape. This takes 5 to 10 minutes, depending on the weather and your skill.

Shape mint mixture into a 1-inch-thick rope. Using kitchen shears, cut the rope into 1-inch segments. Leave mints in 1-inch pillows, or pull segments and tie into love knots. Place mints on waxed paper to cool, and cover with a linen towel. Let mints sit overnight or until they become creamy. Store in an airtight container. Yield: about 4 dozen.

Note: You can divide the mixture in half and make 2 colors of mints; the resting time will be shortened to about 1 minute. You may need someone to help knead and pull the second color so it doesn't harden too quickly.

Do not double recipe. If more mints are needed, make 2 batches.

ALMOND-BUTTER WEDDING CAKE
(pictured on page 97)

2 to 3 recipes Almond-Butter Frosting
2 recipes Almond-Butter Cake
Apricot Filling

Cover 8- and 12-inch sturdy cardboard circles with aluminum foil. Spread a small amount of Almond-Butter Frosting on the 12-inch circle, and place one 12-inch cake layer on top. Spread about ⅓ cup Apricot Filling on top of cake layer, spreading to

Photo A

Photo B

Photo C

Photo D

within ½ inch of edge. Top with remaining 12-inch cake layer. Spread sides and top of 12-inch cake with Almond-Butter Frosting. Smooth top of cake with a wet metal spatula. Insert 4 wooden sticks cut the depth of 12-inch tier in 12-inch layers about 3 inches from sides, spacing evenly to support weight of other layers.

Gently insert ruffled skirting around edge of cake, if desired, between foil and cake, lifting the cake slightly with metal spatula as you work.

Assemble 8-inch tier on its cardboard base, filling and frosting as described above, using about two-thirds of remaining Apricot Filling. Position 8-inch tier in center of 12-inch tier (See **Photo A** above).

Spread small amount of frosting on 6-inch plastic divider plate; fill and frost 6-inch layers as described in frosting procedure for 12-inch tier, using remaining Apricot Filling. Set aside.

Prepare a large decorating bag with large coupler and large metal tip No. 4 or 1B. Spoon frosting into bag. Fold corners of bag over, and crease until all air is pressed out. Starting with bottom tier, pipe vertical lines of frosting using a zigzag motion all around sides of cake, refilling decorating bag with frosting as needed. Pipe a top border around

bottom tier using a zigzag mot[...] peat piping procedure for re[...] tiers (**Photo B**), piping the top [...] fully because it is on a smaller [...]

Assemble columns on secon[...] plastic divider plate. If plastic [...] for cake divider are taller [...] depth of 8-inch tier, cut of[...] length. Insert supports on bott[...] vider plate. Center divider pl[...] inch tier (**Photo C**).

Spread a small amount of fr[...] center of serving platter. P[...] stacked tiers carefully in cente[...] ing platter. (Frosting on servi[...] will help hold finished cake [...] you carefully transfer cake t[...] location.)

Transport cake at this stage [...] location. Then attach 6-inch ti[...] umns of divider plate (**Photo [...]**

Make flower centerpiece fo[...] cake no more than 4 hours be[...] ing time. Cut a plastic foam pl[...] 5-inch circle. Center a 2-inch [...] soaked florist foam on plate; a[...] florist picks inserted up throug[...] of plate. Insert flowers (condit[...] day before) into foam to form [...] arrangement.

Insert wooden picks partiall[...] bottom of flower arrangemen[...] half of each pick exposed o[...]

Position centerpiece on cake, using exposed picks to brace arrangement.

Arrange additional flowers (conditioned and refrigerated the day before) as desired on cake and serving plate. When inserting the flowers directly into the cake, first wrap all stem ends of flowers with florist tape or aluminum foil. Yield: about 75 servings.

Almond-Butter Frosting:

¾ cup butter, softened
¾ cup shortening
3 (16-ounce) packages powdered sugar, sifted and divided
1 egg white
½ teaspoon salt
1½ teaspoons almond extract
½ to ¾ cup whipping cream

Cream butter and shortening in a large mixing bowl at medium speed of an electric mixer; gradually add about one-third of sugar. Cream until light and fluffy.

Add egg white, salt, and almond extract; mix well. Gradually add remaining sugar and ½ cup whipping cream alternately, beginning and ending with sugar; add more whipping cream, if necessary, to make frosting a good piping consistency. Mix well after each addition. Continue beating until mixture is fluffy and creamy. Yield: about 7 cups.

Almond-Butter Cake:

1 cup butter, softened
½ cup shortening
3 cups sugar
4½ cups all-purpose flour
1 tablespoon baking powder
½ teaspoon salt
1½ cups cold water
2 teaspoons vanilla extract
1½ teaspoons almond extract
9 egg whites

Grease bottoms of one 6-inch, one 8-inch, and one 12-inch round cake pans. Do not grease the sides. Line bottoms of pans with waxed paper; grease and flour waxed paper, and set aside.

Cream butter and shortening in a large mixing bowl; gradually add sugar, beating well. Combine dry ingredients; add to creamed mixture alternately with cold water, beginning and ending with flour mixture. Mix well after each addition. Stir in flavorings.

Beat egg whites (at room temperature) until soft peaks form; fold into batter. Pour 1¾ cups batter into 6-inch pan, 2¾ cups batter into 8-inch pan, and remaining batter into 12-inch pan. Bake layers at 325° for 30 to 35 minutes or until a wooden pick inserted in center comes out clean. Cool in pans 10

minutes; remove from pans, peel off waxed paper, and let cool on wire racks. Brush excess crumbs from cake. Yield: one 6-inch cake, one 8-inch cake, and one 12-inch cake.

Now prepare recipe again to make a second cake layer of each size.

Note: Cake layers may be frozen up to 1 month. To freeze, tightly seal each layer in plastic wrap, and then in aluminum foil. Thaw layers in wrapping the night before you decorate.

Four (18½-ounce) packages any flavor cake mix may be used instead of 2 recipes Almond-Butter Cake. Prepare 1 package of mix, and spoon to a depth of 1 inch in 6- and 8-inch pans. Spoon any remaining batter into 12-inch pan. Bake 6- and 8-inch layers at 325° for 18 to 20 minutes. Prepare another package of mix, and spoon into 12-inch pan. Bake 28 to 30 minutes or until cake tests done. Repeat procedure with 2 remaining packages of mix to make a second layer of each size.

Apricot Filling:

1 (8¾-ounce) can apricot halves, drained
¼ cup Amaretto

Combine apricots and Amaretto in container of an electric blender. Blend well. Yield: ¾ cup.

To cut cake, use knife with serrated edges. Remove top tier. (It is usually saved for first wedding anniversary, although it is part of the yield.) Cut a circle in second tier, slicing vertically 2 inches from edge. From this, cut 1-inch-wide slices. Cut another circle 2 inches from edge, and continue procedure to cut both tiers.

WEDDING PUNCH

2 small oranges, sliced and seeded
1 (6-ounce) jar maraschino cherries
1 (33.8-ounce) bottle ginger ale
1 (12-ounce) can frozen orange juice concentrate, diluted
1 (46-ounce) can pineapple juice
¼ cup lime juice
¾ cup sugar
1 (28-ounce) bottle tonic water, chilled
2 (25.4-ounce) bottles champagne or 2 (33.8-ounce) bottles ginger ale, chilled

Cut orange slices in half. Line bottom of a 6½-cup ring mold with half of orange slices and cherries. Pour in a thin layer of ginger ale, and freeze until firm. Arrange remaining orange slices and cherries along side of ring mold, and pour in another thin layer of ginger ale. Freeze until firm. Pour in remainder of bottle of ginger ale, and freeze until firm.

Combine orange juice, pineapple juice, lime juice, and sugar, stirring until sugar dissolves. Chill mixture.

Just before serving, pour chilled juice mixture into punch bowl; add tonic water, champagne, and ice ring. Yield: 6 quarts.

Preparing the Flowers

To decorate our cake, we used stephanotis, miniature carnations, Dendrobium orchids, baby's breath, roses, and maidenhair fern.

Condition flowers the day before. With maidenhair fern, place stems directly into hot tap water, and let stand until water cools to room temperature. Wrap in a plastic bag, and chill until ready to decorate. Split the stem ends of garden roses, remove thorns and lower leaves, and place stems in warm water up to the base of the flower head. Cut stems of carnations at an angle and place in warm water overnight. Cover orchids with plastic wrap, and store in refrigerator. Wire stephanotis by piercing the base of each flower with floral wire, pulling the wire through the flower and carefully twisting it down the stem. Mist the prepared flowers, and place in a plastic bag in the refrigerator. Baby's breath needs no conditioning. Cover all stem ends of flowers you plan to insert directly into cake with floral tape or aluminum foil.

For nosegays, cut stems the desired length, and remove excess foliage. Plunge stems in warm water, and let stand for eight hours. Soak small squares of florist foam in water 10 to 15 minutes; arrange flowers and greenery in them. Mist the nosegays and place in plastic bag in refrigerator.

A Dieter's Best Buys

Have you ever strolled through the grocery store wondering which foods give you the most nutrition for the least calories, and at the best price?

A recent study shows that good nutritional buys do exist, and you don't have to turn to specially formulated foods or bizarre health foods to find them. Instead, they may already be some of your favorites: spinach, beef liver, tomatoes, canned tuna in water, skim and low-fat milk, tofu, dry-roasted peanuts, eggs, and fresh carrots. We've featured these nutritional all-stars in tasty low-calorie dishes you're sure to like. (You'll also save money on these standard foods while you gain nutrition.)

Protein-packed Tuna Croquettes With Parsley Sauce contains plenty of niacin, vitamin B-12, and vitamin B-6. In addition, they're chock-full of vegetables, with a lemony sauce.

You'll never miss the salt in Marinated Carrots. Mixed pickling spices and cider vinegar provide all the seasoning needed. The key nutrients you'll find in this colorful side dish include vitamin A, vitamin C (ascorbic acid), vitamin B-6, and copper.

Spinach Soufflé makes an impressive show. And best of all, our version tastes similar to a popular frozen variety, but without the extra calories. We made it "light" by substituting additional egg whites for whole eggs, skim milk for whole milk, and farmer cheese for Cheddar cheese. The lead nutrients in this dish are vitamin A, vitamin C, magnesium, and folic acid.

CREOLE LIVER

Vegetable cooking spray
1½ pounds baby beef liver
¼ teaspoon salt
¼ teaspoon pepper
2 small onions, sliced and separated into rings
2 stalks celery, sliced
2 medium tomatoes, peeled and cut into wedges
1 large green pepper, cut into thin strips
½ cup vegetable juice cocktail

Coat a large skillet with cooking spray; add liver. Sprinkle each side with salt and pepper. Cook liver over medium heat until lightly browned on both sides. Add remaining ingredients. Cover and cook 15 minutes or until liver is tender. Yield: 6 servings (about 158 calories per 3-ounce serving).
Sherry L. Cooler,
Beaufort, South Carolina.

TUNA CROQUETTES WITH PARSLEY SAUCE

1 cup dry breadcrumbs
1 (6½-ounce) can water-packed tuna, drained
1 cup grated carrots
½ cup skim milk
½ cup diced celery
1 egg, beaten
1 tablespoon minced onion
¼ teaspoon salt
⅛ teaspoon pepper
Vegetable cooking spray
Parsley Sauce

Combine breadcrumbs, tuna, carrots, milk, celery, egg, onion, salt, and pepper; mix well. Divide mixture into 6 equal portions, shaping each into a cone. Place on a baking sheet coated with cooking spray. Bake at 400° for 20 minutes. Serve with Parsley Sauce. Yield: 6 servings (about 119 calories per croquette, plus 14 calories per tablespoon sauce).

Parsley Sauce:

1 cup skim milk, divided
1 tablespoon cornstarch
2 tablespoons reduced-calorie margarine
⅛ teaspoon pepper
¼ cup chopped fresh parsley
1½ tablespoons lemon juice

Combine ¼ cup skim milk and cornstarch in a small saucepan; stir until smooth. Add remaining milk, margarine, and pepper. Cook over medium heat, stirring constantly, until mixture comes to a boil; boil 1 minute, and remove from heat. Stir in parsley and lemon juice. Yield: 1 cup.
Mrs. Roy D. Simpson,
Fort Myers, Florida.

CHEESE HERBED-TOPPED TOMATOES

9 tomato slices, cut ¾-inch thick
3 tablespoons reduced-calorie Italian salad dressing
Vegetable cooking spray
¾ cup (3 ounces) shredded part-skim mozzarella cheese
2 tablespoons Italian seasoned breadcrumbs
1 tablespoon chopped fresh basil

Brush tomato slices on bo[th] with salad dressing; place in layer in a 9-inch square bak[ing] coated with cooking spray. Spr[inkle to]mato slices evenly with shredd[ed moz]zarella cheese.

Combine breadcrumbs an[d] sprinkle mixture over cheese. [Bake at] 350° for 8 to 10 minutes or un[til cheese] melts. Yield: 3 servings (about [ ] ries per 3 slices).

MARINATED CARR[OTS]

1 teaspoon whole mixed picklin[g spices]
¾ cup cider vinegar
¼ cup water
2 teaspoons sugar
4 medium carrots, scraped and [cut into] julienne strips

Place pickling spices in a [ ] cheesecloth bag. Combine [with] remaining ingredients in [a] saucepan; bring to a boil. C[over, reduce] heat, and simmer 5 minutes [until car]rots are crisp-tender.

Remove carrot mixture [and] pour into a shallow dish. [Cover and] chill 2 to 3 hours. Remove [spices be]fore serving. Yield: 5 servin[gs (about] calories per ½-cup serving).
Eleanor [ ]
Arlin[gton,]

SPINACH SOUFF[LÉ]

1 (10-ounce) package frozen ch[opped] spinach
¼ cup chopped onion
Vegetable cooking spray
2 tablespoons all-purpose flour
¾ cup skim milk
1 egg yolk
½ cup (2 ounces) shredded far[mer cheese]
¼ teaspoon salt
⅛ teaspoon pepper
¼ teaspoon ground nutmeg
⅛ teaspoon hot sauce
3 egg whites

Cook spinach according to package directions, omitting salt. Drain and squeeze dry on paper towels.

Sauté onion in a small saucepan coated with cooking spray until tender. Add flour, and cook 1 minute, stirring constantly. Gradually add milk; cook over medium heat, stirring constantly, until thickened.

Combine spinach, onion mixture, egg yolk, cheese, seasonings, and hot sauce in the container of an electric blender; process until mixture is smooth.

Beat egg whites (at room temperature) until stiff peaks form; fold into spinach mixture. Pour spinach mixture into a 1-quart soufflé dish coated with cooking spray. Place dish in a 9-inch square baking pan. Pour hot water to depth of 1 inch into pan. Bake at 325° for 1 hour or until puffed and knife inserted in center comes out clean. Serve immediately. Yield: 4 cups (about 118 calories per 1-cup serving).

Virginia Bennack,
San Antonio, Texas.

TOFU DIP

1 cup tofu, drained and mashed
½ cup diced green onions
1 teaspoon chopped fresh parsley
1 teaspoon Dijon mustard
½ cup plain low-fat yogurt
¼ teaspoon plus ⅛ teaspoon garlic salt
⅛ teaspoon freshly ground pepper

Combine all ingredients in the container of an electric blender; process until smooth. Chill. Serve with raw vegetables. Yield: 1½ cups (about 6 calories per tablespoon).

Mrs. Fred H. Lofland,
Williston, Florida.

COCONUT CUSTARD

2 eggs, slightly beaten
2 cups evaporated skim milk
¼ cup sugar
1 teaspoon coconut extract
⅛ teaspoon salt
Vegetable cooking spray
1 tablespoon flaked coconut, toasted

Combine eggs, milk, sugar, coconut extract, and salt, mixing well. Pour mixture evenly into five custard cups coated with cooking spray. Place cups in a 13- x 9- x 2-inch baking pan. Pour hot water to depth of 1 inch into pan.

Bake at 325° for 45 to 50 minutes or until knife inserted in center comes out clean. Remove cups from water; let cool. Chill. Sprinkle with toasted coconut. Yield: 5 servings (about 164 calories per ½ cup serving).

Mrs. Gilbert Cyrus,
La Grange, Georgia.

Start With A Jar Of Peanut Butter

As soon as a child is old enough to lick peanut butter from a cracker, the creamy spread is usually one of his favorite things to eat. It has one of those flavors we never seem to outgrow the desire for, as evidenced by these four recipes sent to us by readers.

PEANUT BUTTER PIE

1 (12-ounce) jar crunchy peanut butter
1 (8-ounce) container frozen whipped topping, thawed
1 quart vanilla ice cream, softened
2 (9-inch) commercial chocolate crumb crusts
Frozen whipped topping, thawed (optional)

Combine peanut butter, whipped topping, and ice cream; stir until blended. Spoon into crumb crusts. Freeze at least 8 hours.

Garnish tops of pies with dollops of additional whipped topping, if desired. Yield: two 9-inch pies.

Martha Heun,
Louisville, Kentucky.

PEANUT BUTTER SWIRL CAKE

½ cup creamy peanut butter
¼ cup butter or margarine
1½ cups firmly packed brown sugar
2 eggs
2 cups sifted cake flour
2 teaspoons baking powder
½ teaspoon baking soda
½ teaspoon salt
⅔ cup milk
1 teaspoon vanilla extract
Peanut Butter Swirl Frosting

Cream peanut butter and butter; gradually add brown sugar, beating at medium speed of an electric mixer until blended. Add eggs, one at a time; beat after each addition.

Combine flour, baking powder, soda, and salt; add to creamed mixture alternately with milk, beginning and ending with flour mixture. Mix well after each addition. Stir in vanilla.

Pour batter into 2 greased and floured 8-inch round cakepans. Bake at 350° for 28 to 30 minutes or until a

wooden pick inserted in center comes out clean. Cool in pans 10 minutes; remove layers from pans, and let cool completely on wire racks.

Spread Peanut Butter Swirl Frosting between layers and on top and sides of cake. Dollop small portions of frosting blended with peanut butter onto top of cake, and swirl with a knife. Yield: one 2-layer cake.

Peanut Butter Swirl Frosting:

1½ cups sugar
2 egg whites
⅓ cup water
2 teaspoons light corn syrup
⅛ teaspoon salt
1 teaspoon vanilla extract
1½ tablespoons creamy peanut butter

Combine sugar, egg whites, water, syrup, and salt in top of a double boiler; beat at low speed of an electric mixer 30 seconds or just until blended.

Place over boiling water, and beat constantly at high speed for 6 minutes or until stiff peaks form; remove from heat. Add vanilla; beat an additional 1 minute or until frosting is thick enough to spread. Remove ¼ cup of frosting and combine with peanut butter, stirring well. Set peanut butter mixture aside to swirl on top of frosted cake. Yield: enough for one 2-layer cake.

Jean Voan,
Shepherd, Texas.

QUICK PEANUT BUTTER COOKIES

1 (11-ounce) package piecrust mix
1 cup firmly packed brown sugar
½ cup creamy peanut butter
3 tablespoons water

Combine all ingredients; stir until thoroughly blended. Shape dough into 1-inch balls; place 2 inches apart on ungreased cookie sheets. Flatten cookies to ¼-inch thickness with a fork, making a crisscross pattern. Bake at 375° for 8 to 10 minutes. Let cool 2 minutes on cookie sheets. Remove to wire rack, and let cool completely. Yield: about 4½ dozen.

Thelma Peedin,
Newport News, Virginia.

Tip: Let cookies cool completely before storing. To keep cookies fresh, store soft and chewy ones in an airtight container, and crisp cookies in a jar with a loose-fitting lid.

CHOCOLATE-TOPPED OATMEAL BARS

1 (9.9-ounce) package coconut-pecan
  frosting mix
3 cups regular oats, uncooked
1 cup butter or margarine, melted
½ cup sugar
1 (6-ounce) package semisweet chocolate
  morsels
¾ cup crunchy peanut butter

Combine frosting mix, oats, butter, and sugar; stir until blended. Press into an ungreased 13- x 9- x 2-inch baking pan; bake at 350° for 18 to 20 minutes.

Combine chocolate morsels and peanut butter in top of a double boiler; bring water to a boil. Reduce heat to low; cook until chocolate melts. Spread over oat layer. Cover and chill at least 2 hours. Cut into bars. Yield: 4 dozen.

Lynn McLeod,
Huntington, West Virginia.

Keep Serving Those Vegetables

A typical Southern dinner includes at least two vegetables—maybe three or four if Grandmother is cooking. It's no wonder that our readers send us so many vegetable recipes. We've put together this assortment of family favorites that all use fresh vegetables.

CABBAGE-AND-TOMATO SKILLET

2 slices bacon
4 cups chopped cabbage
2 medium onions, chopped
2 medium tomatoes, chopped
1 green pepper, chopped
1 teaspoon salt

Cook bacon in a large skillet until crisp; remove bacon, reserving drippings in skillet. Crumble bacon, and set aside. Add remaining ingredients to drippings in skillet; cook over medium heat, uncovered, for 15 minutes, stirring occasionally. Stir in bacon. Yield: 6 servings. *Susan Boren,*
Gonzalez, Florida.

EGGPLANT CREOLE

2 medium eggplant, peeled and cut into
  1-inch cubes
3 tablespoons butter or margarine
3 tablespoons all-purpose flour
3 large tomatoes, peeled and chopped
1 medium onion, chopped
1 medium-size green pepper, chopped
1 bay leaf
1 tablespoon brown sugar
½ teaspoon salt
¼ teaspoon pepper
½ cup soft breadcrumbs
½ cup (2 ounces) shredded sharp Cheddar
  cheese

Cook eggplant, covered, in a small amount of water 10 minutes or until tender. Drain well.

Melt butter in a medium saucepan; add flour, stirring until smooth. Cook 1 minute, stirring constantly. Add tomatoes, onion, green pepper, bay leaf, sugar, salt, and pepper. Simmer mixture 5 to 7 minutes, stirring often. Remove bay leaf.

Layer half of eggplant in a lightly greased 2½-quart casserole; top with half of tomato mixture. Repeat layers; sprinkle with breadcrumbs.

Bake at 350° for 25 minutes; sprinkle with cheese, and bake an additional 5 minutes. Yield: 8 to 10 servings.

Joe Howard,
Lakeland, Florida.

CRISPY ONION RINGS

3 medium Spanish onions
1⅓ cups all-purpose flour
2 tablespoons grated Parmesan cheese
1 tablespoon dried parsley flakes
1 teaspoon salt
½ teaspoon garlic powder
Dash of pepper
1¼ cups beer
1 tablespoon vegetable oil
2 eggs, separated
Vegetable oil

Peel onions; cut into ¼-inch slices, and separate into rings.

Combine flour, Parmesan cheese, parsley flakes, salt, garlic powder, pepper, beer, 1 tablespoon oil, and egg yolks; beat well. Beat egg whites (at room temperature) until stiff peaks form; fold into batter. Dip onion rings into batter; fry in deep hot oil (375°) until golden brown. Drain on paper towels. Yield: 8 servings.

Mrs. C. L. Goldsmith,
Crewe, Virginia.

CREAMED SPINACH

1 pound fresh spinach
1 small onion, diced
1 tablespoon butter or margarine, melted
3 slices bacon
1 tablespoon butter or margarine, melted
1 tablespoon all-purpose flour
1 cup half-and-half
⅛ teaspoon salt
Pinch of ground nutmeg

Remove stems from spinach; wash leaves thoroughly. Cook spinach, covered, in a large Dutch oven 3 to 5 minutes. (Do not add water.) Drain spinach well; chop and set aside.

Sauté onion in 1 tablespoon butter for 3 to 5 minutes or until onion is tender; set aside.

Cook bacon until crisp, reserving 2 teaspoons drippings. Crumble bacon, and set aside.

Combine bacon drippings and 1 tablespoon butter in a heavy saucepan over low heat; add flour, stirring until smooth. Cook 1 minute, stirring constantly. Gradually add half-and-half; cook over medium heat, stirring constantly, until mixture is thickened and bubbly. Add salt, nutmeg, spinach, and onion, stirring well. Serve immediately. Yield: 3 to 4 servings.

Mrs. C. D. Marshall,
Culpeper, Virginia.

PEPPY SKILLET POTATOES

4 slices bacon
1 large potato, peeled and cut into thin
  strips
1 small onion, sliced into thin rings
1 green pepper, cut into thin strips

Fry bacon until crisp in a large skillet. Remove bacon, and set aside; reserve 2 tablespoons pan drippings in skillet. Add potato and onion to skillet and cook, uncovered, over medium heat 3 to 4 minutes, stirring occasionally. Add green pepper and cook, stirring occasionally, an additional 10 to 12 minutes or until potatoes are tender. Crumble bacon, and stir into potato mixture. Yield: 2 servings. *Grace Shrader,*
Trenton, Georgia.

Tip: Leftover vegetables may be folded into a cream sauce to serve over a plain omelet, added to fritter batter, or marinated with French dressing for a delicious salad.

Cook Vegetables For Two

If your favorite vegetable recipes yield more than you can eat, give these versions a try. Fresh vegetables are easy to tailor for a couple of servings. And there are canned versions that are a size small enough to keep you from eating leftovers for a week.

Italian Stuffed Yellow Squash can be a main dish or a side dish. The recipe makes six squash halves filled with a sausage-cheese mixture.

If you're planning a menu to make ahead, you'll want to include Marinated Carrots. The carrots chill overnight, so serve them right from the refrigerator.

With a yellow squash, a zucchini, and about 10 minutes, you can stir up a vegetable side dish that's ideal for two. If you have a garden, it's an excellent way to use squash as it begins to appear. Our recipe calls for two small squash, but you may want to use larger produce and savor the fresh flavor that will soon be at its peak.

MARINATED CARROTS

½ cup water
½ pound carrots, scraped and sliced
    diagonally
1 tablespoon vegetable oil
1 tablespoon tarragon wine vinegar
1 tablespoon sugar
1 teaspoon parsley flakes
1 teaspoon dry onion flakes
¼ teaspoon garlic powder

Bring water to a boil in saucepan; add carrots. Return to a boil; cover, reduce heat, and simmer 8 to 10 minutes or just until tender. Drain carrots, reserving 1 tablespoon liquid. Combine liquid and remaining ingredients; mix well. Pour over carrots; cover and chill 8 hours or overnight. Yield: 2 servings.
Nellie Bywaters,
Warrensburg, Missouri.

SCALLOPED CORN

1 (8-ounce) can whole kernel corn,
    drained
½ cup milk
1 egg, beaten
⅛ teaspoon salt
⅛ teaspoon pepper
¼ cup round buttery cracker crumbs
1 tablespoon butter or margarine, melted
    and divided

Combine corn, milk, egg, salt, and pepper, mixing well. Pour into a lightly greased 2-cup baking dish. Combine cracker crumbs and half of butter; mix well, and sprinkle over corn mixture. Drizzle with the remaining butter. Bake at 375° for 30 minutes. Yield: 2 servings.
Jeanette Green,
Apopka, Florida.

ITALIAN STUFFED YELLOW SQUASH

3 large yellow squash
¼ pound hot bulk pork sausage
⅓ cup chopped onion
½ cup chopped green pepper
½ cup chopped tomato
½ cup grated Parmesan cheese
¾ cup (3 ounces) shredded mozzarella
    cheese

Cut squash in half lengthwise; scoop out pulp and seeds, leaving a ¼-inch shell. Set squash shells aside.

Cook sausage, onion, and green pepper in a skillet over medium-high heat until sausage is browned; drain well. Stir in tomato and Parmesan cheese. Spoon mixture into squash shells; place squash in a shallow dish. Bake, uncovered, at 350° for 20 minutes. Sprinkle with mozzarella; bake an additional 5 minutes or until cheese melts. Yield: 2 to 3 servings.
James A. Mitchell,
Lilburn, Georgia.

CREAMY SPINACH CASSEROLE

1 (10-ounce) package frozen chopped
    spinach
1 (3-ounce) package cream cheese,
    softened
¼ cup butter or margarine, melted and
    divided
⅛ teaspoon salt
⅛ teaspoon pepper
½ cup soft breadcrumbs
¼ teaspoon ground sage
1 hard-cooked egg, sliced (optional)

Cook spinach according to package directions. Drain and squeeze dry.

Combine spinach, cream cheese, 2 tablespoons butter, salt, and pepper; mix well. Spoon into a greased 1-quart baking dish. Combine breadcrumbs and sage; sprinkle over spinach mixture. Drizzle remaining 2 tablespoons butter over breadcrumbs. Bake, uncovered, at 350° for 20 minutes. Garnish with egg slices, if desired. Yield: 3 servings.
Marge Killmon,
Annandale, Virginia.

TOMATO SQUASH

1 (6-ounce) can tomato juice
1 clove garlic, minced
1 small zucchini, cut into julienne strips
1 small yellow squash, cut into julienne
    strips
Grated Parmesan cheese

Combine tomato juice and garlic in a small saucepan; bring to a boil, and add zucchini and yellow squash. Reduce heat, and simmer, uncovered, 5 to 6 minutes or until crisp-tender. Remove zucchini and yellow squash with a slotted spoon. Bring tomato juice to a boil over high heat; boil 4 to 5 minutes or until juice is reduced. Return zucchini and yellow squash to saucepan; cook about 1 minute or until thoroughly heated. Remove to serving dish; sprinkle with cheese. Yield: 2 servings.
Eugenia W. Bell,
Louisville, Kentucky.

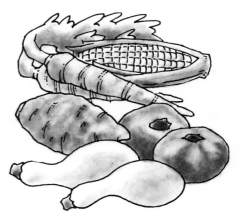

CANDIED SWEET POTATOES

2 small sweet potatoes
¼ cup firmly packed brown sugar
2 tablespoons chopped pecans
1 tablespoon pineapple juice
1 teaspoon lemon juice
⅛ teaspoon ground cinnamon
1 tablespoon butter or margarine

Cook sweet potatoes in boiling water 20 to 25 minutes or until tender. Let sweet potatoes cool; peel and cut into ¾-inch-thick slices.

Arrange sweet potatoes in a lightly greased shallow 1-quart casserole. Combine sugar, pecans, juices, and cinnamon, mixing well; pour over sweet potatoes, tossing gently. Dot with butter. Bake, uncovered, at 350° for 30 minutes, spooning glaze over potatoes occasionally. Yield: 2 servings.
Vera Hanley,
Georgetown, South Carolina.

Microwave Fish In Minutes

Fish that is cooked in a microwave oven can be outstanding. With fish's natural tenderness and moisture, the rapid cooking action of microwaves helps retain the delicate flavor and texture. On the other hand, it is easy to overcook fish. Always test for doneness after the minimum time suggested in the recipe for fish.

When fish turns opaque, it's done. Sometimes, with thick fish fillets or steaks, the outer areas may be opaque, while the centers are still translucent. But the underdone parts will finish cooking after the fish is taken out of the oven. If after a few minutes, the fish doesn't appear done, put it back in the microwave, but only for a few seconds, not minutes.

For best results, always pay special attention to the quantity and shape of the fish, the size and shape of the container it is cooking in, and the power setting of the oven.

Generally, fish is microwaved at HIGH power to quickly seal in juices and flavor. Arrange thicker portions to outside of dish so that they cook without overcooking thinner areas.

We've found fish microwaves better in shallow, flat containers. Most of our recipes call for 2-quart baking dishes. Round or square dishes will be easier to rotate, but a rectangular dish can be used if it is taken out of the oven and turned around.

Frozen fillets, should be defrosted at LOW (10% power) or MEDIUM LOW (30% power) just until the pieces can be separated, and then plunged into cold water. Be sure that the fish is free of ice crystals before going ahead with the recipe because ice can throw the cooking time off considerably.

EASY ITALIAN FISH

4 (6-ounce) orange roughy or grouper
  fillets, about ¾ inch thick
⅔ cup tomato juice
2 tablespoons vinegar
1 (1.3-ounce) envelope Italian salad
  dressing mix
¼ cup chopped green onions
¼ cup chopped green pepper

Arrange fish in a shallow 2-quart casserole with thickest portions to outside of dish. Combine tomato juice, vinegar, and salad dressing mix; pour over fish. Cover and marinate in refrigerator 30 minutes, turning once.

Sprinkle green onions and green pepper over fish. Cover with heavy-duty plastic wrap, and microwave at HIGH for 6 to 7 minutes, turning dish around after 3 minutes, or until fish flakes easily when tested with a fork. Let stand 1 minute. Yield: 4 servings.

HERB-COATED FISH

4 (7-ounce) skinless grouper fillets, about
  ¾ inch thick
½ cup crushed corn flakes
½ cup grated Parmesan cheese
⅓ cup minced fresh parsley
½ teaspoon garlic powder
½ teaspoon paprika
¼ teaspoon salt
¼ teaspoon pepper
2 egg whites, lightly beaten

Pat fish dry. Combine remaining ingredients except egg whites in a shallow dish, mixing well. Dip fillets in egg whites, then in crumb mixture, coating well. Arrange in a shallow 2-quart baking dish, with thickest portions to outside of dish. Cover with paper towels, and microwave at HIGH for 8 to 10 minutes, turning dish around every 2 minutes, or until fish flakes easily when tested with a fork. Yield: 4 servings.

PARMESAN FILLETS

4 (6-ounce) skinless grouper fillets, about
  ¾ inch thick
1 tablespoon lemon juice
½ cup grated Parmesan cheese
3 tablespoons chopped green onion
1 (2-ounce) jar chopped pimiento, drained
2 tablespoons butter or margarine,
  softened
1 tablespoon mayonnaise
¼ teaspoon salt
⅛ teaspoon hot sauce

Arrange fish in a shallow 2-quart casserole with thickest portions to outside of dish. Brush with lemon juice. Cover with heavy-duty plastic wrap, and microwave at HIGH for 4 minutes.

Combine remaining ingredients, mixing well; spread over fillets. Microwave, uncovered, at HIGH for 4 to 6 minutes or until fish flakes easily when tested with a fork. Let stand 1 minute before serving. Yield: 4 servings.

SPANISH-STYLE FILLETS

1 medium onion, chopped
⅛ teaspoon garlic powder
1 tablespoon vegetable oil
1 tablespoon cornstarch
¾ teaspoon chili powder
1 (16-ounce) can whole tomatoes,
  undrained and chopped
¼ cup sliced green olives
2 teaspoons chopped green chiles
4 (6-ounce) skinless red snapper fillets,
  about ½ inch thick
1 teaspoon lemon juice
¼ teaspoon salt

Combine onion, garlic, and oil in a bowl; cover and microwave at HIGH for 3 to 3½ minutes, stirring once. Stir in cornstarch, chili powder, and tomatoes; cover and microwave at HIGH 3 to 3½ minutes, stirring once.

Stir in olives and chiles. Spoon half of sauce into a lightly greased 12- x 8- x 2-inch baking dish. Arrange snapper fillets over sauce with thickest portions to outside. Drizzle lemon juice over fish; sprinkle tops with salt. Top fish with remaining sauce.

Cover with heavy-duty plastic wrap, and microwave at HIGH for 7 to 9 minutes, turning dish after 3 minutes, or until fish flakes easily when tested with a fork. Let stand 3 minutes before serving. Yield: 4 servings.

SOY FISH STEAKS

4 (6-ounce) swordfish steaks, about 1 inch
  thick
3 tablespoons orange juice
3 tablespoons soy sauce
1 tablespoon catsup
1 tablespoon vegetable oil
1 tablespoon minced fresh parsley
1 tablespoon lemon juice
½ teaspoon dried whole basil
¼ teaspoon pepper
⅛ teaspoon garlic powder
Orange slices (optional)

Arrange fish in a shallow 2-quart baking dish with thickest portions to outside of dish. Combine remaining ingredients except orange slices, mixing well; pour over fish. Cover and marinate in refrigerator 30 minutes, turning fish once.

Cover with heavy-duty plastic wrap, and microwave at HIGH for 8 to 10 minutes, turning dish around every 3 minutes, or until fish flakes easily when tested with a fork. Let stand 2 minutes. Garnish with orange slices, if desired. Yield: 4 servings.

From Our Kitchen To Yours

Microwave ovens have become popular in many kitchens because they provide a cool, fast, convenient way of cooking. If you're buying a microwave oven for the first time or replacing one, consider the space available and the features that are right for you.

Available Sizes

Microwave ovens vary in size from about .4 cubic feet to 1.6 cubic feet. The larger, full-size ovens are usually countertop types or are built in, using a trim kit. They have cube-shaped interiors and tend to cook more evenly than the space-saving ovens with long, narrow cavities.

Smaller models include over-the-range, under-the-counter, or compact. These smaller models work best for reheating and defrosting, but because of their lower wattages, food takes longer to cook. Because most microwave owners use their ovens for reheating and defrosting, the smaller models are becoming more popular. When selecting a size, consider your space, the foods you'll be microwaving, and the size of the dishes you'll use.

Wattages

Although you can purchase microwave ovens with up to 1,000 watts, most are 600 to 700 watts. And, of course, the higher the wattage, the faster the food will cook. Because ovens are not standardized, you'll often see microwave recipes that include ranges in cooking time to prevent undercooking or overcooking your food.

Features

Microwave ovens are available with some basic features, such as variable power and defrost cycle, as well as some special options. When you're looking for a microwave, consider what you'll be using the oven for—whether it's just reheating or preparing whole meals. If the microwave is going to be your main cooking appliance, the following features will be helpful.

Variable power refers to the different power levels that let you cook foods that need less heating than the HIGH setting provides. These levels can be selected by dial or touch controls. Touch controls may be slightly difficult to master and more expensive, but they are usually more accurate and allow you more cooking options.

Defrost cycle lets you defrost food without cooking it at the same time. The way the defrost cycle works varies; some ovens decrease power as the food defrosts, while others cycle on and off to defrost and prevent cooking.

A **turntable** is a tray or shelf in the microwave that automatically rotates during cooking to allow for even cooking or browning. This feature speeds up cooking and makes it easier, but often limits space in the oven cavity.

A **browning unit** is available at the top of the oven cavity on some microwave models. You can also buy a browning dish that will brown foods.

A **temperature probe** is placed in a food or beverage, and the plug is inserted into a socket on the oven wall. Set the final temperature you want, and when it is reached, the oven automatically turns off. Some ovens will maintain a specific internal temperature for an hour if the food is kept in the oven with the temperature probe inserted.

Humidity and weight sensors select the power level and cooking time. By just setting controls for the type and amount, or weight of food, the cooking is done automatically. Or after pressing a control, a burst of steam from the food being cooked will be used to calculate the right power level and cooking time needed.

The **memory control feature** can be used to key in several steps that will work in sequence without continually reprogramming your oven.

Delay start lets you preset your oven to start cooking at a certain time without you being there.

Oven shelves are racks in the oven cavity that allow you more food space. They will help if reheating several foods but will lengthen cooking time because of the increased amount of food.

Microwave Oven Variations

Combination convection/microwave joins the speed of microwave cooking with the browning capability of convection cooking. A convection oven heats or browns by blowing hot air around the oven cavity, so that it's best for food to be baked uncovered in pans with low sides. Converting conventional recipes to a convection oven may involve some experimenting.

Conventional/microwave is a combination oven that lets you use the oven conventionally or as a microwave. With this combination, a continuous or self-cleaning feature is usually not an option. And often, the microwave feature has lower wattage and doesn't allow a faster cooking time.

Marinades For Any Meat

Ask any chef what gives his grilled specialty that savory flavor, and you're likely to hear that it's the secret marinade. Besides adding flavor, marinades tenderize meat. Our Tangy Beef Marinade, flavored with horseradish, is particularly good for tenderizing chuck roasts and other tougher cuts of meat.

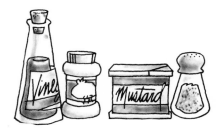

TANGY BEEF MARINADE

¾ cup vegetable oil
¼ cup red wine vinegar
2 teaspoons dry minced onion
2 teaspoons celery salt
1 teaspoon powdered horseradish
1 teaspoon dry mustard
1 teaspoon pepper
⅛ teaspoon garlic powder

Combine all ingredients in a jar. Cover tightly; shake vigorously. Place desired cut of beef in a shallow dish; pour marinade over beef. Cover and marinate 6 hours or overnight in refrigerator, turning meat occasionally.

Baste meat with marinade during grilling. Yield: 1 cup.

Beverly Jones,
Starkville, Mississippi.

SWEET-AND-SOUR MARINADE

1 cup soy sauce
½ cup vinegar
½ cup pineapple juice
½ cup firmly packed brown sugar
1 teaspoon garlic powder

Combine all ingredients in a saucepan; bring to a boil, stirring frequently. Place desired cut of lamb or beef in a shallow dish; pour marinade over meat. Cover and marinate for at least 4 hours, turning meat occasionally.

Baste meat with marinade during grilling. Yield: about 2 cups.

Lucille James,
New Orleans, Louisiana.

TERIYAKI MARINADE

½ cup soy sauce
¼ cup firmly packed brown sugar
2 tablespoons lemon juice
1 tablespoon vegetable oil
½ teaspoon ground ginger
⅛ teaspoon garlic powder

Combine all ingredients, stirring well. Place chicken, beef, or pork in a shallow dish; pour marinade over meat. Cover and marinate several hours or overnight in the refrigerator, turning meat occasionally.

Baste meat with marinade during grilling. Yield: ¾ cup. *Jan M. Avery, Raleigh, North Carolina.*

Feature A Tex-Mex Favorite

Add a bit of spice to your menus by cooking up one of these Tex-Mex recipes. All across the South, our readers regularly enjoy the lively flavor of popular favorites, such as burritos, fajitas, and chimichangas. Here four of our readers share their Tex-Mex recipes—some of the best we've come across.

FAVORITE FAJITAS

Juice of 2 to 3 limes
1 to 1½ teaspoons garlic salt
½ teaspoon pepper
1 pound flank or skirt steak
4 flour tortillas
Sauce or vegetable toppings (optional)

Combine lime juice, salt, and pepper in a zip-top heavy-duty plastic bag. Place steak in bag, and secure tightly, turning bag to coat each side thoroughly. Refrigerate 6 to 8 hours.

Remove steak from marinade, and drain well. Grill steak over medium-hot mesquite coals 5 to 6 minutes on each side or until desired degree of doneness. Slice steak diagonally across grain into thin slices.

Wrap tortillas in aluminum foil, and heat at 325° for 15 minutes. Wrap tortillas around meat, and top with any of the following, if desired: chopped tomato, green onions, guacamole, sour cream, picante sauce, or taco sauce. Yield: 4 servings. *Mary K. Sweeten, College Station, Texas.*

FIESTA BURRITOS

10 (8-inch) flour tortillas
1 (1¼-ounce) envelope taco seasoning mix
1½ cups tomato juice
1 tablespoon vegetable oil
½ pound ground beef
1 (15-ounce) can refried beans
2 cups (8 ounces) shredded Cheddar cheese, divided
1½ cups shredded lettuce
1 small avocado, peeled and cubed

Wrap tortillas in aluminum foil; heat at 350° for 15 minutes.

Combine seasoning mix, tomato juice, and oil; mix well, and set aside.

Cook ground beef in a skillet until browned, stirring to crumble; drain. Stir in beans and ½ cup tomato juice mixture. Bring to a boil; cover, reduce heat, and simmer 5 minutes, stirring occasionally, or until mixture is thoroughly heated. Remove from heat.

Place about ¼ cup beef mixture and about 2½ tablespoons cheese on center of each tortilla. Roll up tortillas, and place seam side down in a lightly greased 13- x 9- x 2-inch baking dish. Pour remaining tomato juice mixture over top. Cover and bake at 350° for 15 minutes. Uncover and sprinkle with remaining cheese; bake an additional 5 minutes or until cheese melts.

Sprinkle lettuce and avocado on top; serve immediately. Yield: 5 servings. *Mrs. David Williams, Baton Rouge, Louisiana.*

CHIMICHANGAS

2 pounds beef stew meat
1½ cups water
2 cloves garlic, minced
2 tablespoons chili powder
1 tablespoon vinegar
2 teaspoons dried whole oregano
1 teaspoon ground cumin
¾ teaspoon salt
⅛ teaspoon pepper
12 (10-inch) flour tortillas
Vegetable oil
1 (6-ounce) carton frozen guacamole, thawed
Shredded lettuce
Taco sauce (optional)

Combine meat, water, and all seasonings in a heavy saucepan; bring to a boil. Cover, reduce heat, and simmer 2 hours or until meat is tender. Uncover and cook until liquid evaporates, about 15 minutes, stirring frequently. Using two forks, shred meat very fine; set shredded meat aside.

Wrap tortillas in aluminum foil; heat at 350° for 15 minutes.

Place ¼ cup meat mixture just below center of each tortilla. Fold in left and right sides of tortilla to partially enclose filling. Fold up bottom edge of tortilla to partially cover filling; roll up, and secure with a wooden pick.

Gently place filled tortillas, 1 or 2 at a time, in deep hot oil (375°); fry 1 to 2 minutes or until golden brown, turning once. Remove from oil, and drain on paper towels. Remove wooden picks.

Serve immediately with guacamole, shredded lettuce and, if desired, taco sauce. Yield: 6 servings.

D'Etta Coit, Clinton, Oklahoma.

SWEET-HOT PINTO BEANS

1 (16-ounce) package dried pinto beans
2 to 3 dried red chiles, washed, stemmed, and seeded
4 slices bacon, chopped
2 teaspoons salt
1 large onion, quartered
1 medium-size green pepper, chopped
¼ cup firmly packed brown sugar

Sort and wash beans; place in a large Dutch oven. Cover with water 2 inches above beans; let soak overnight.

Add chiles, bacon, salt, and enough additional water to cover beans. Bring to a boil; cover, reduce heat, and simmer 1½ hours. Add remaining ingredients and additional water, if needed; cover and simmer 30 minutes or until beans are tender. Remove chiles before serving. Yield: 8 to 10 servings.

Note: To make refried beans, heat 1 tablespoon vegetable oil per cup of cooked beans in a large, heavy skillet. Add beans, and mash to desired consistency, stirring as needed until thoroughly heated. Add additional cooking liquid from beans, if necessary.

Helen McKey, Edna, Texas.

Suit Your Taste With Sugar Snap Peas

In the Orient, snow peas are commonly used in cooking, but here in the South, it's Sugar Snap peas. Meant to be eaten pod and all, these crisp, sweet delights taste good raw or cooked. Versatile, too, they can serve as side dishes or as part of salads and appetizers.

When you shop for these peas, choose pods that are tiny and tender, with little to no pea formed. You can store them in a plastic bag in the refrigerator crisper for up to 4 days.

The fresh flavors in Spring Vegetable Medley are highlighted with a hint of garlic powder.

SUGAR SNAP PEA SALAD

½ pound fresh Sugar Snap peas
1 cup sliced celery
2 (4-ounce) cans sliced mushrooms, drained
1 small onion, thinly sliced
1 (4-ounce) jar diced pimiento, drained
1 cup commercial Italian salad dressing

Trim ends from peas. Arrange peas in a steaming rack. Place rack over boiling water; cover and steam 3 to 5 minutes. Pour cold water over peas to cool; drain. Combine peas and remaining ingredients, tossing well. Chill 2 hours before serving. Yield: 6 servings.

*Jacqueline Dorn,
Leesville, South Carolina.*

SPRING VEGETABLE MEDLEY

½ pound fresh Sugar Snap peas
8 small new potatoes, unpeeled
⅛ teaspoon garlic powder
1 teaspoon salt
8 green onions, trimmed, leaving 1½ inches of green tops
2 tablespoons butter or margarine
Pepper to taste

Trim ends from peas; set peas aside.

Place potatoes in a large saucepan; add garlic powder, salt, and water to cover; bring to a boil. Cover and cook 6 to 7 minutes; add peas and green onions. Cook an additional 5 minutes or until potatoes are tender.

Drain vegetables, reserving 2 tablespoons cooking liquid. Return reserved liquid to saucepan; add butter and pepper, and cook over low heat until butter melts. Return vegetables to saucepan. Heat gently, tossing vegetable mixture in butter sauce.

Arrange vegetables on a serving platter; pour on any remaining sauce. Yield: 4 servings.

*Mrs. F. W. Armstrong,
Dallas, Texas.*

SUGAR SNAP PEA APPETIZERS

1 (3-ounce) package cream cheese, softened
1 teaspoon prepared horseradish
¼ pound small fresh Sugar Snap peas
1 medium carrot, cut into 1¼-inch thin julienne strips

Combine cream cheese and horseradish, mixing well; set aside.

Trim ends from peas. Using a sharp knife, carefully slit inside curve of each pea pod. Spoon cream cheese mixture into a small decorating bag fitted with a tip. Pipe cream cheese mixture into each pod. Place one strip of carrot on filling. Cover and chill. Yield: 3 dozen.

Tip: Remember that overcooking destroys the nutrients in vegetables. So next time you have leftovers, either warm them carefully in a double boiler or microwave, or, even better, just mix them cold into a salad.

It's The Season For Fresh Pineapple

Colonial seamen traveled to tropical islands for fresh pineapple years ago, and since then, Southerners have enjoyed the fruit's sweet flavor. A symbol of hospitality, pineapple blends deliciously with an array of spices, vegetables, meat, and other fruit.

One of the easiest ways to enjoy pineapple flavor anytime is to preserve it in jam and pickles as in the recipes you'll find here.

If you'd rather enjoy fresh pineapple, mix up tropical-tasting Creamy Piña Coladas. Chunks of pineapple also perk up salads. Be sure to mix fresh pineapple into fruit salads right away—it will help keep fruit, such as bananas, apples, and pears, from browning. On the other hand, we suggest waiting until the last minute to stir the juicy fruit into meat salads because fresh pineapple contains an enzyme that breaks down protein. It's this same enzyme that prevents gelatin mixtures from congealing when fresh pineapple is used. Heat deactivates it, so canned pineapple is better suited for congealed mixtures.

When selecting fresh pineapple, look for large fruit with deep-green crown leaves. Because pineapples are harvested when fully ripe, shell color is only an indication of variety, not ripeness. Fragrance, a good sign of quality, will be helpful only if the pineapple is at room temperature.

HAWAIIAN CHICKEN SALAD

2 cups coarsely chopped cooked chicken
½ cup chopped celery
½ cup chopped pecans, toasted
¼ cup mayonnaise
¼ teaspoon curry powder
¼ teaspoon salt
Dash of pepper
1 medium fresh pineapple

Combine all ingredients except pineapple; stir well. Cover and refrigerate at least 2 hours.

Cut pineapple in half lengthwise; remove core. Cut pineapple pulp into ½-inch cubes; set 1 cup aside. (Reserve remaining pineapple for other uses.)

Combine 1 cup cubed pineapple with chicken salad, mixing well. To serve, spoon into pineapple shells. Yield: 4 servings. *Frances Bowles, Mableton, Georgia.*

PINEAPPLE PICKLES

2 medium fresh pineapples
1½ cups sugar
¾ cup water
⅓ cup vinegar (5% acidity)
10 whole cloves
1 (3-inch) stick cinnamon

Peel and trim eyes from pineapples; remove core. Cut pineapples crosswise into ¼-inch slices; quarter slices. Set pineapple aside.

Combine remaining ingredients in a saucepan; bring to a boil. Add the pineapple; reduce heat, and simmer, uncovered, 30 minutes.

Continue simmering while packing hot pineapple into hot sterilized pint jars, leaving ½-inch headspace. Remove cinnamon stick from syrup; pour hot syrup over pineapple, leaving ½-inch headspace. Cover at once with metal lids, and screw on bands. Process pickles in boiling-water bath 10 minutes. Yield: 3 pints. *Libby Winstead, Nashville, Tennessee.*

PINEAPPLE JAM

1 quart finely chopped fresh pineapple
2½ cups sugar
1 cup water
½ lemon, thinly sliced

Combine all ingredients in a large saucepan, stirring well. Bring to a boil over high heat, stirring frequently. Cook 30 minutes or until the sugar dissolves and mixture thickens, stirring frequently.

Quickly ladle jam into hot jars, leaving ¼-inch headspace; cover at once with metal lids, and screw on bands. Process in boiling-water bath 15 minutes. Yield: 4 half pints.

PINEAPPLE-ORANGE SAUCE FLAMBÉ

½ cup orange marmalade
2 tablespoons brown sugar
2 tablespoons light corn syrup
2 cups finely chopped fresh pineapple
¼ cup Cointreau or other orange-flavored liqueur

Combine marmalade, sugar, syrup, and pineapple in a saucepan; cook over medium heat, stirring occasionally, until thoroughly heated.

Heat Cointreau in a small long-handled pan just until warm; remove from heat. Ignite fumes with a long match, and pour over pineapple mixture. Stir gently until flames die down. Serve sauce immediately over ice cream. Yield: 2 cups. *Patricia Boschen, Ashland, Virginia.*

CREAMY PIÑA COLADAS

1 fresh pineapple
2 cups vanilla ice cream
1 (8½-ounce) can cream of coconut
¾ cup light rum (optional)
1 large banana
4 cups crushed ice
Toasted flaked coconut (optional)

Peel and trim eyes from pineapple; remove core. Cut pineapple crosswise into ½-inch slices; quarter the slices. Position knife blade in food processor bowl; add half of pineapple, and replace processor cover. Process 25 seconds or until pureed. Add half each of ice cream, cream of coconut, rum, and banana; process until smooth. Add half of ice, processing until mixture reaches desired consistency. Repeat procedure with remaining half of ingredients. Garnish each serving with flaked coconut, if desired. Serve immediately. Yield: about 10 cups.

Churn A Fruity Ice Cream

When Bessie Lamb of Winchester, Virginia, tried to duplicate her favorite commercial ice cream, she came up with an original recipe she calls Orange-Pineapple Ice Cream. Our foods staff loved the bright color and delicious flavor. We think you will, too.

If you can't eat the ice cream all at once, store what is left in an airtight container in the freezer. The texture stays smooth and creamy. And you'll have an outstanding dessert on hand to serve drop-in guests.

ORANGE-PINEAPPLE ICE CREAM

1 (6-ounce) package orange-flavored
    gelatin
2 cups boiling water
4 eggs
1½ cups sugar
1 (20-ounce) can crushed pineapple,
    undrained
1 (14-ounce) can sweetened condensed
    milk
1 (13-ounce) can evaporated milk
1 (8-ounce) carton frozen whipped
    topping, thawed
1 (6-ounce) can frozen orange juice
    concentrate, thawed

Dissolve the gelatin in boiling water, and let cool.

Beat eggs in a large bowl at medium speed of an electric mixer until frothy. Add sugar, mixing well. Stir in gelatin and remaining ingredients.

Pour into freezer can of a 1-gallon freezer. Freeze according to manufacturer's directions. Let ice cream ripen at least 1 hour. Yield: about 1 gallon.

Add Nuts To Salad For Flavor

Tossing a few nuts into a fruit, vegetable, or meat salad can make it even more appealing. The salad recipes here were selected because of the added crunch and flavor of peanuts, pecans, almonds, or walnuts.

Green Bean-Peanut Salad makes an unusually tasty combination. The beans are chilled in a dillweed marinade, and roasted peanuts are stirred in just before serving. It's important not to add the nuts before marinating since peanuts will absorb liquid and become soft. Remember, too, that using roasted nuts helps preserve the crispness.

Pecans and almonds lend a nuttier and more aromatic flavor to salads when they are toasted. To toast pecans, spread them in a shallow pan in a single layer, and bake at 400° for 5 to 8 minutes. Stir occasionally to ensure even

browning. Toast almonds at 350° for about 10 minutes. If the recipe calls for chopped nuts, chop before toasting.

Because of the mild flavor of pecans and almonds, you can easily substitute them for other nuts or add them to just about any salad without worrying about a conflict in flavor. Walnuts and peanuts offer more distinctive tastes; use them with milder flavored ingredients so their unique flavors are highlighted.

TURKEY SALAD WITH SAUTÉED WALNUTS

1 cup coarsely chopped walnuts
2 tablespoons butter or margarine, melted
4 cups diced cooked turkey
1 cup chopped celery
½ cup mayonnaise
1 to 2 tablespoons tarragon-flavored wine
    vinegar
½ teaspoon salt
⅛ teaspoon pepper
Lettuce leaves (optional)

Sauté walnuts in butter; set aside.

Combine turkey and celery in a medium bowl. Combine mayonnaise, vinegar, salt, and pepper in a small bowl; add to turkey mixture, mixing well. Stir in ¾ cup sautéed walnuts.

Spoon salad on lettuce leaves, if desired. Sprinkle with remaining ¼ cup walnuts. Yield: 4 to 6 servings.
                                        Kathleen Stone,
                                        Houston, Texas.

CHICKEN SALAD WITH GRAPES

2 cups cubed cooked chicken or turkey
½ cup chopped cucumber
½ cup chopped celery
¼ cup vegetable oil
¼ cup vinegar
1 cup seedless green grapes, halved
1 (11-ounce) can mandarin oranges,
    drained
⅓ cup slivered almonds, toasted
2 green onions, minced
½ cup mayonnaise
Lettuce cups

Combine chicken, cucumber, and celery in a bowl. Combine oil and vinegar; pour over chicken mixture. Cover and chill 1 hour. Drain.

Add grapes, oranges, almonds, green onions, and mayonnaise to chicken mixture; mix well. Chill at least 2 hours. Serve in lettuce cups. Yield: 4 to 6 servings.
                                        Lorraine G. Bennett,
                                        Virginia Beach, Virginia.

SUNSHINE DELIGHT

1 (6-ounce) package orange-flavored
    gelatin
2 cups boiling water
1 (11-ounce) can mandarin oranges,
    drained and chopped
1 (8¾-ounce) can fruit cocktail, drained
½ cup chopped pecans
1 medium banana, sliced
1 (3-ounce) package cream cheese,
    softened
¼ cup commercial sour cream
Lettuce leaves

Dissolve gelatin in boiling water; add oranges, fruit cocktail, pecans, and banana, stirring gently. Pour half of gelatin mixture into a lightly oiled, 9-inch square dish; chill until firm.

Combine cream cheese and sour cream in a small mixing bowl; beat at medium speed of an electric mixer until smooth. Spread evenly over gelatin layer; chill slightly. Pour remaining half of gelatin mixture on top; chill until firm. Cut into squares, and serve on lettuce leaves. Yield: 9 servings.
                                        Sherry S. Thompson,
                                        Hendersonville, North Carolina.

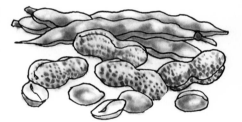

GREEN BEAN-PEANUT SALAD

2 (9-ounce) packages frozen French-cut
    green beans
½ cup finely chopped onion
¼ cup white wine vinegar
¼ cup peanut oil
1 tablespoon lemon juice
1½ teaspoons dried whole dillweed
1 teaspoon salt
½ teaspoon pepper
⅓ cup chopped, dry-roasted peanuts

Cook green beans according to package directions; drain well. Combine green beans and onion in a shallow dish; toss gently.

Combine remaining ingredients except peanuts in a jar; cover tightly, and shake vigorously. Pour over green bean mixture, and toss gently. Cover and refrigerate overnight. Spoon green bean mixture into a serving container; sprinkle with dry-roasted peanuts. Yield: 6 servings.
                                        Jennie Kinnard,
                                        Mabank, Texas.

VEGETABLE SALAD WITH WALNUTS

1½ cups chopped green pepper
3¾ cups chopped tomatoes
¼ cup sliced onions, separated into rings
½ cup coarsely chopped walnuts
2 tablespoons red wine vinegar
2 tablespoons olive oil
¼ teaspoon salt
⅛ teaspoon pepper
Leaf lettuce (optional)

Combine green pepper, tomatoes, onions, and walnuts in a bowl.

Combine vinegar, oil, salt, and pepper in a small bowl; pour mixture over vegetable mixture, mixing well. Cover and chill 1 hour.

Serve on leaf lettuce, if desired. Yield: 6 servings.

Dorothy D. Warner,
Whispering Pines, North Carolina.

Entrées That Feature Fruit

Fruit can liven up many meats. Take Lemon Veal Piccata, for example; freshly squeezed lemon juice gives this mild-flavored meat a zesty new flavor. Pork Chops Fiesta is another tasty entrée that combines the flavor of pork with citrus; orange slices and raisins make it look pretty, too.

We've been teaming turkey with cranberry sauce for years, but how about trying Cornish Hens With Cranberry-Orange Sauce? It's perfect when it's just the two of you for dinner. And don't forget that avocados are fruit, too. They dress up any salad or mixture. You'll love them stuffed with our tasty crab-meat mixture and then topped with Herbed-Mayonnaise Dressing.

LEMON VEAL PICCATA

⅓ cup all-purpose flour
1 teaspoon salt
¼ teaspoon pepper
⅛ teaspoon garlic powder
6 veal scallops or thin cutlets (about ½ pound)
¼ cup butter or margarine
3 to 4 tablespoons lemon juice
1 tablespoon chopped fresh parsley
Lemon slices (optional)

Combine flour, salt, pepper, and garlic; set aside.

Remove and discard any excess fat from veal; dredge in flour mixture.

Melt butter in a large skillet over medium heat. Add veal, and cook about 1 minute on each side; remove and drain on paper towels. Add lemon juice to skillet; cook until thoroughly heated. Return veal to skillet; add parsley, and heat briefly. To serve, spoon lemon mixture over veal. Garnish with lemon slices, if desired. Yield: 2 servings.

Betty Chason,
Tallahassee, Florida.

PEACHY HAM ROAST

1 (2-inch-thick) fully cooked ham slice (about 4 pounds)
2 dozen whole cloves
2 tablespoons dry mustard
1 cup firmly packed brown sugar
½ cup peach nectar
1 (21-ounce) can peach pie filling
⅓ cup raisins
⅓ cup chopped pecans
Juice of 1 lemon
Juice of 1 orange

Score ham on top and bottom sides, and insert cloves at 1-inch intervals. Sprinkle both sides of ham with mustard; place in a lightly greased 13- x 9- x 2-inch baking pan. Combine brown sugar and peach nectar; pour over ham. Bake at 325° about 1½ hours or until meat thermometer registers 140°, basting often. Slice and arrange on platter.

Combine remaining ingredients in a saucepan; cook over low heat until thoroughly heated. Serve over ham. Yield: 8 to 10 servings.

Mary Evelyn Hollaway,
Hanceville, Alabama.

PORK CHOPS FIESTA

2 tablespoons sugar
2 tablespoons cornstarch
⅛ teaspoon ground allspice
1 cup water
¼ cup orange juice
2 tablespoons lemon juice
¼ cup raisins or currants
¼ cup all-purpose flour
½ teaspoon salt
¼ teaspoon pepper
4 (1-inch-thick) pork chops
1 tablespoon shortening
4 orange slices

Combine sugar, cornstarch, and allspice in a small saucepan; add water

and cook over low heat, stirring constantly, until mixture thickens. Stir in fruit juice and raisins. Remove from heat, and set aside.

Combine flour, salt, and pepper. Dredge pork chops in flour mixture. Heat shortening in a skillet over medium high heat; brown chops quickly on both sides. Pour juice mixture over chops; cover. Reduce heat, and simmer 45 minutes or until chops are tender. Top with orange slices. Yield: 4 servings.

T. O. Davis,
Waynesboro, Mississippi.

SWEET-AND-PUNGENT PORK

1 egg, beaten
⅔ cup all-purpose flour
¼ cup water
½ teaspoon salt
1 pound boneless pork, cut into ½-inch cubes
Vegetable oil
1 (20-ounce) can pineapple chunks, undrained
1 large green pepper, cut into strips
¾ cup vinegar
½ cup firmly packed brown sugar
2 tablespoons molasses
3 tablespoons cornstarch
¼ cup water
2 medium tomatoes, peeled and cut into wedges
2 teaspoons soy sauce
Hot cooked rice

Combine egg, flour, ¼ cup water, and salt; mix well. Add pork, stirring to coat. Heat 1 inch of oil in a large skillet to 375°; add pork, and fry 6 minutes. Drain on paper towels.

Drain pineapple, reserving juice. Add enough water to juice to make 1 cup. Combine pineapple, pineapple juice mixture, green pepper, vinegar, sugar, and molasses in a saucepan; bring to a boil. Boil 1 minute, stirring gently. Dissolve cornstarch in ¼ cup water; add to saucepan. Cook over medium heat for 1 minute, stirring constantly, until thickened. Stir in tomatoes, soy sauce, and pork; cook, uncovered, for 5 minutes. Serve over rice. Yield: 4 to 6 servings.

Mrs. Joseph D. Schauer, Jr.,
Merritt Island, Florida.

Tip: Prices of fresh vegetables and fruit change with the seasons. Buy seasonal fresh foods when most plentiful and at peak quality in your area.

CORNISH HENS WITH CRANBERRY-ORANGE SAUCE

2 (1- to 1¼-pound) Cornish hens
Pepper
2 tablespoons butter or margarine
½ teaspoon chicken-flavored bouillon granules
¼ cup water
2 tablespoons sugar
½ teaspoon cornstarch
⅛ teaspoon ground ginger
Dash of garlic powder
¼ cup water
½ cup fresh cranberries
2 tablespoons orange marmalade

Remove giblets from hens; reserve for another use. Rinse hens with cold water, and pat dry; sprinkle with pepper. Close cavities, and secure with wooden picks; then truss.

Melt butter in a heavy Dutch oven; brown hens for 10 minutes, turning once. Combine bouillon granules and ¼ cup water; add to hens. Cover, reduce heat, and simmer 50 minutes or until hens are done.

Combine sugar, cornstarch, ginger, and garlic powder in a small saucepan; add ¼ cup water, mixing well. Bring mixture to a boil; cook until thickened, stirring constantly. Add cranberries and marmalade; cook 3 to 5 minutes or until cranberry skins pop.

Arrange Cornish hens on serving platter; then spoon sauce over hens. Yield: 2 servings.
Wanda Cline,
Augusta, Georgia.

CRISPY MANDARIN CHICKEN

1 egg white
2 tablespoons cornstarch
2 tablespoons soy sauce
4 boneless chicken breast halves, skinned and cut into ¾-inch pieces
½ cup biscuit mix
⅓ cup water
1 tablespoon sesame seeds
Vegetable oil
1 (8-ounce) can mandarin oranges, undrained
2 medium carrots, scraped and thinly sliced
2 medium-size green peppers, cut into ¼-inch-wide strips
½ cup catsup
¼ cup sugar
2 tablespoons cornstarch
2 tablespoons vinegar
1 teaspoon chicken-flavored bouillon granules
Hot cooked rice

Combine egg white, 2 tablespoons cornstarch, and soy sauce in a large bowl; mix well. Add chicken, coating well; set aside.

Combine biscuit mix, water, and sesame seeds; mix well. Add to chicken mixture, stirring to coat. Heat 3 to 4 inches of oil to 370°; drop 4 to 5 pieces of chicken, one at a time, into hot oil. Fry chicken 1 to 1½ minutes on each side or until golden brown. Drain on paper towels; set aside.

Drain oranges, reserving juice. Add enough water to juice to make 1¼ cups. Pour juice mixture into a skillet and bring to a boil; add carrots. Cover, reduce heat, and simmer 4 to 5 minutes or until crisp-tender. Add green pepper; cover, and cook 1 minute. Combine catsup, sugar, cornstarch, vinegar, and bouillon granules, mixing well. Stir into vegetables, and bring to a boil. Add oranges and chicken; cook over medium heat until chicken is thoroughly heated. Serve over rice. Yield: 4 servings.
Barbara Davis,
Lilburn, Georgia.

AVOCADO WITH CRABMEAT

2 avocados
Lemon juice
1 (6-ounce) package frozen crabmeat, thawed and drained
¼ cup finely chopped celery
¼ cup mayonnaise
1 teaspoon lemon juice
¼ teaspoon salt
⅛ teaspoon pepper
Dash of hot sauce
2 cups shredded iceberg lettuce
2 hard-cooked eggs, sliced
4 anchovy fillets (optional)
1 tomato, cut into wedges
1 lemon, cut into wedges
4 ripe olives
Parsley sprigs
Herbed-Mayonnaise Dressing

Cut avocados in half lengthwise; remove seed, and peel. Brush with lemon juice, and set aside.

Combine crabmeat, celery, mayonnaise, 1 teaspoon lemon juice, salt, pepper, and hot sauce; mix well. Fill avocados with crabmeat mixture.

Place lettuce on a serving platter. Arrange avocados, eggs, anchovies, if desired, with tomato wedges, lemon wedges, olives, and parsley sprigs on lettuce. Serve with Herbed-Mayonnaise Dressing. Yield: 4 servings.

Herbed-Mayonnaise Dressing:

1 cup mayonnaise
3 tablespoons tomato puree
2 tablespoons chopped chives
⅛ teaspoon dried whole chervil
⅛ teaspoon dried whole tarragon

Combine all ingredients; stir well. Yield: 1¼ cups.
Helen J. Wright,
Leesville, South Carolina.

Start With A Candy Bar

If you think candy bars are strictly for snacking, take a look at these ingenious recipes from our readers. They all use candy bars as a cooking ingredient. The same rich taste that tempts us between meals is a wonderful addition to cakes, pies, and other desserts.

You can use candy bars in other ways, too. Melted milk chocolate bars make a great frosting for brownies or snack cakes. A grated chocolate bar works well as a garnish for chocolate desserts. And crunchy candy bars can be crushed and used as a topping for ice cream and frozen desserts.

CREAMY CHOCOLATE PIE

6 (1.45-ounce) milk chocolate with almonds candy bars
2 tablespoons hot water
1 (8-ounce) carton frozen whipped topping, thawed
1 (9-inch) baked pastry shell

Place candy bars and water in top of a double boiler; bring water to a boil. Reduce heat to low; cook until candy bars melt. Cool about 20 minutes. Gradually fold in whipped topping. Spoon into pastry shell. Chill 8 hours. Yield: one 9-inch pie.
Salli Ball,
Atlanta, Georgia.

CHOCOLATE CHUNK-PEANUT BUTTER ICE CREAM

3 eggs
1½ cups sugar
2 tablespoons peanut butter
6 (2.16-ounce) chocolate-covered crispy
   peanut butter candy bars, crushed
3 (13-ounce) cans evaporated milk
3 cups milk

Beat eggs at high speed of an electric mixer; add sugar and peanut butter, and beat well. Stir in candy bars and evaporated milk, mixing until combined. Stir in milk.

Pour mixture into freezer can of a 5-quart hand-turned or electric freezer. Freeze according to manufacturer's instructions. Let ice cream ripen at least 1 hour. Yield: about 1 gallon.

Kim Wilkerson,
Birmingham, Alabama.

CANDY BAR CHEESECAKE

¾ cup graham cracker crumbs
⅔ cup finely chopped walnuts
2 tablespoons sugar
2 tablespoons butter or margarine,
   melted
1 (8-ounce) milk chocolate candy bar
4 (3-ounce) packages cream cheese,
   softened
¾ cup sugar
2 tablespoons cocoa
Dash of salt
2 eggs
½ cup commercial sour cream
½ teaspoon vanilla extract
Sour Cream Topping
Chopped walnuts

Combine graham cracker crumbs, ⅔ cup chopped walnuts, 2 tablespoons sugar, and butter, and mix well; firmly press mixture onto bottom and sides of an 8-inch springform pan.

Break candy bar into several pieces, and place in top of a double boiler; bring water to a boil. Reduce heat to low; cook until chocolate melts. Set chocolate aside.

Beat cream cheese with an electric mixer until light and fluffy. Combine ¾ cup sugar, 2 tablespoons cocoa, and dash of salt; gradually add to cream cheese, mixing well. Add eggs, one at a time, beating well after each addition. Add melted chocolate; beat until blended. Stir in ½ cup sour cream and ½ teaspoon vanilla, blending well.

Pour into prepared pan. Bake at 325° for 40 minutes. Turn off oven, and let cheesecake stand in closed oven 30 minutes. Let cheesecake cool to room temperature; then chill. Remove sides of springform pan; spread with Sour Cream Topping, and sprinkle on walnuts. Yield: one 8-inch cheesecake.

Sour Cream Topping:

½ cup commercial sour cream
2 tablespoons sugar
½ teaspoon vanilla extract

Combine all ingredients; stir well. Yield: ½ cup.

W. N. Cottrell II,
New Orleans, Louisiana.

Tip: Use odd pieces of candy to make a topping for ice cream. Plain chocolate, mints, or cream candies may be placed in top of a double boiler with a little cream and heated until well blended. Serve hot over ice cream or cake, or store in refrigerator and use later cold.

Pasta Salad is full of colorful vegetables and two kinds of pasta.

Pasta Salad At Its Best

The next time you're asked to bring a covered dish to feed a crowd, prepare a bowl of Pasta Salad. Served with deli meats and warm French bread, it makes a filling meal. Almost as important, it's a dish you can make ahead and transport easily.

PASTA SALAD

2 cups fresh snow peas
2 cups broccoli flowerets
2½ cups cherry tomato halves
2 cups fresh mushrooms, sliced
1 (7.75-ounce) can whole pitted ripe
   olives, drained
1 (8-ounce) package cheese-stuffed
   tortellini, uncooked
3 ounces fettuccine, uncooked
1 tablespoon grated Parmesan cheese
Pasta Salad Dressing (recipe follows)
Grated Parmesan cheese (optional)

Drop snow peas into boiling water; boil 1 minute, and remove with a slotted spoon. Place broccoli in boiling water; boil 1 minute, and drain. Combine peas, broccoli, tomatoes, mushrooms, and olives.

Cook pasta according to package directions; drain and let cool slightly. Combine vegetables, pasta, and 1 tablespoon Parmesan cheese in a large bowl; add salad dressing, and toss well. Chill several hours before serving. Garnish with additional Parmesan cheese, if desired. Yield: 10 to 12 servings.

Pasta Salad Dressing:

½ cup sliced green onions
⅓ cup red wine vinegar
⅓ cup vegetable oil
⅓ cup olive oil
2 tablespoons chopped fresh parsley
2 cloves garlic, minced
2 teaspoons dried whole basil
1 teaspoon dried whole dillweed
1 teaspoon salt
½ teaspoon pepper
½ teaspoon sugar
½ teaspoon dried whole oregano
1½ teaspoons Dijon mustard

Combine all ingredients in a jar, and cover tightly. Shake vigorously until well mixed. Yield: 1¼ cups.

Whip Up Leftover Egg Whites

When making sauces or baking, you may find yourself with leftover egg whites after using the yolks in other recipes. So what do you do with extra whites? Try adding them to these recipes or storing for later use.

Egg whites can be stored for a week to 10 days in a tightly covered container in the refrigerator. For longer storage, they may be frozen in sealed freezer bags. If you like, freeze the whites individually in ice cube trays; then transfer to sealed freezer bags. To use, thaw overnight in the refrigerator or under cold running water.

Here are several tips. First, bring them to room temperature before beating. Second, bear in mind that the type of bowl you use for beating the whites can make a difference—a copper bowl produces frothier results. And finally, beware of making meringues on humid days; it's best to do this during dry weather.

SWEET POTATO SOUFFLÉ

3 medium unpeeled sweet potatoes
½ cup half-and-half
⅓ to ½ cup firmly packed brown sugar
2 tablespoons butter or margarine, melted
¼ teaspoon salt
⅛ teaspoon ground nutmeg
⅛ teaspoon ground cinnamon
3 egg whites
1 teaspoon baking powder

Cook sweet potatoes in boiling water 20 to 25 minutes or until tender. Let cool to touch; peel and mash. Combine potatoes, half-and-half, sugar, butter, salt, nutmeg, and cinnamon, mixing well; set aside.

Beat egg whites (at room temperature) until foamy; add baking powder, beating until stiff but not dry. Gently fold into sweet potato mixture. Spoon into a greased 5-cup soufflé dish. Bake at 325° for 45 minutes. Yield: 6 servings.
Glyna Meredith Gallrein,
Anchorage, Kentucky.

SUGAR-AND-SPICE PECANS

1 cup sugar
1 tablespoon ground cinnamon
2 teaspoons ground nutmeg
½ teaspoon salt
2 egg whites
3 tablespoons water
5 cups pecan halves

Combine sugar, cinnamon, nutmeg, and salt; set aside.

Beat egg whites (at room temperature) and water until foamy. Gradually add the sugar mixture, 1 tablespoon at a time, beating until stiff peaks form. Fold in pecan halves.

Pour pecans on a well-greased 15- x 10- x 1-inch jellyroll pan. Bake at 300° for 30 minutes, stirring every 10 minutes. Cool and store in an airtight container. Yield: 5 cups.
Iris Brenner,
Fort McCoy, Florida.

MERINGUE KISS COOKIES

2 egg whites
1 cup sugar
½ cup semisweet chocolate morsels
½ cup chopped pecans
½ teaspoon vanilla extract
½ teaspoon grated lemon rind

Beat egg whites (at room temperature) until foamy. Gradually add sugar, beating until stiff peaks form. Gently fold remaining ingredients into egg

whites. Drop by teaspoonfuls onto cookie sheets lined with brown paper. Bake at 200° for 1½ hours. Cool slightly on cookie sheets; remove cookies to wire racks to cool completely. Yield: about 3 dozen.
Elizabeth Grimes,
Fremont, North Carolina.

DELUXE ANGEL FOOD CAKE

12 egg whites
½ teaspoon salt
1½ teaspoons cream of tartar
1½ cups sugar, divided
1 cup sifted cake flour
½ teaspoon almond extract
1 teaspoon vanilla extract

Beat egg whites (at room temperature) and salt until foamy. Add cream of tartar; beat until soft peaks form. Add 1 cup sugar, 2 tablespoons at a time, beating until stiff peaks form.

Sift remaining ½ cup sugar and flour together. Gently fold into egg whites. Add flavorings.

Spoon the batter into an ungreased 10-inch tube pan. Bake at 375° for 30 to 35 minutes. Invert cake; cool 1 hour or until completely cool. Remove cake from pan. Yield: one 10-inch cake.
Juanita Lowery,
McRae, Georgia.

CHOCOLATE-FILLED MERINGUE PIE

20 round buttery crackers, crushed
1 cup sugar, divided
1 cup chopped pecans
3 egg whites
6 (1.45-ounce) milk chocolate bars
1 (8-ounce) container frozen whipped topping, thawed

Combine cracker crumbs, ½ cup sugar, and pecans; mix well. Beat egg whites (at room temperature) until soft peaks form. Gradually add remaining ½ cup sugar, 1 tablespoon at a time; beat until stiff peaks form. Fold crumb mixture into egg white mixture. Spread meringue on bottom and sides of a greased 9-inch deep-dish pieplate. Bake at 350° for 30 minutes. Cool.

Place chocolate bars in top of a double boiler; bring water to a boil. Reduce heat to low; cook until chocolate melts. Let cool slightly. Fold chocolate into whipped topping; spoon into shell. Chill. Yield: one 9-inch pie.
Barbara O. Broxson,
Gulf Breeze, Florida.

Chicken—Plain Or Fancy

Chicken is such a versatile meat that it finds its way into the fanciest menus, yet it also works well for everyday meals. If you're like many of our readers, you're always looking for a new chicken recipe to serve family and guests. We offer some here that should satisfy just about any occasion.

If you're watching your budget, chicken is an ideal entrée. But remember that the more work the butcher does, the more you'll pay. For the best savings, buy a whole broiler-fryer, and cut it into pieces; or try boning chicken breasts yourself.

To save time when preparing boneless chicken breast entrées, pound chicken breast halves; then freeze. Be sure to place waxed paper between each breast half so that you can easily separate the number you'll need. The chicken will thaw quicker when it's pounded into thin pieces, and one preparation step will be out of the way.

PRINCESS CHICKEN

2 tablespoons cornstarch
2 tablespoons soy sauce
1 pound boneless chicken breasts, skinned and cut into 1-inch pieces
2 tablespoons soy sauce
1 tablespoon sugar
1 tablespoon rice wine or white wine
1 teaspoon cornstarch
1 teaspoon sesame oil
¼ cup peanut or vegetable oil
5 to 6 dried whole red peppers
2 teaspoons grated fresh gingerroot
½ cup chopped roasted peanuts

Combine 2 tablespoons each of cornstarch and soy sauce; stir well. Add chicken pieces, mixing well. Let stand 30 minutes.

Combine soy sauce, sugar, wine, cornstarch, and sesame oil; mix well, and set aside. Pour peanut oil around top of preheated wok; allow to heat at high (350°) for 1 minute. Add chicken, and stir-fry 2 minutes. Remove and drain on paper towels.

Reserve 2 tablespoons drippings in wok. Heat at medium high (325°) for 30 seconds. Add red peppers, and stir-fry until dark brown. Add gingerroot and chicken; stir-fry 1 minute. Add wine mixture. Cook until slightly thickened. Stir in peanuts. Yield: 4 servings.

ITALIAN CHICKEN

4 chicken breast halves, skinned and boned
3 tablespoons all-purpose flour
1 egg, beaten
⅓ cup fine, dry breadcrumbs
2 tablespoons vegetable oil
2 tablespoons butter or margarine, melted
2 tablespoons olive oil
1 tablespoon lemon juice
½ teaspoon salt
½ teaspoon dried whole basil
½ teaspoon dried whole oregano
¼ teaspoon garlic powder

Dredge each chicken breast half in flour; dip in egg, and coat with breadcrumbs. Heat vegetable oil in a skillet over medium-high heat; cook chicken about 2 minutes on each side or until golden brown. Place chicken in a 9-inch square baking dish; set aside.

Combine remaining ingredients, mixing well; pour over chicken. Cover and bake at 350° for 30 minutes. Yield: 4 servings.

Kathy B. Erskine,
Miami, Florida.

CHICKEN IN PASTRY

6 chicken breast halves, skinned and boned
2 green onions with tops, chopped
1 clove garlic, minced
½ pound fresh mushrooms, chopped
2 tablespoons butter or margarine, melted
⅛ teaspoon salt
1 (10-ounce) package frozen patty shells, thawed
1 egg, beaten
½ cup currant jelly
¼ cup cooking sherry

Place each chicken breast half between 2 sheets of waxed paper. Flatten chicken to ¼-inch thickness using a meat mallet or rolling pin; set aside.

Sauté onion, garlic, and mushrooms in butter until tender; drain. Stir in salt.

Roll out each patty shell to ⅛-inch thickness; spread 1 heaping tablespoon onion mixture on each, leaving a ½-inch border. Place 1 chicken breast half over vegetable mixture. Moisten edges of pastry with water; roll up jellyroll fashion. Place seam side down on a lightly greased 15- x 10- x 1-inch jellyroll pan, pressing edges to seal. Brush with egg; bake at 425° for 30 minutes or until golden brown.

Combine jelly and sherry, and cook over low heat, stirring constantly, until jelly melts. Serve with chicken. Yield: 6 servings.

Phyllis Garrett,
Monett, Missouri.

SESAME CHICKEN

1 teaspoon dry mustard
3 to 4 tablespoons water
2 teaspoons curry powder
1 teaspoon paprika
1 teaspoon garlic powder
4 chicken breast halves
4 chicken-flavored bouillon cubes
1 cup boiling water
1 tablespoon plus 1 teaspoon sesame seeds
Lemon slice halves (optional)

Dissolve dry mustard in 3 tablespoons water in a small bowl. Add curry powder, paprika, and garlic powder; mix well. Mixture should be the consistency of prepared mustard; add more water if needed.

Rub chicken breasts with mustard mixture, and place in a lightly greased 12- x 8- x 2-inch baking dish.

Combine bouillon cubes with 1 cup boiling water. Pour over chicken breasts. Bake, uncovered, at 350° for 45 minutes, turning frequently.

Increase oven temperature to 425°; turn chicken breasts skin side up, and sprinkle with sesame seeds. Bake 10 minutes or until golden brown. Remove to serving platter; garnish with lemon slice halves, if desired. Yield: 4 servings.

Ann Hall Harden,
Pleasant Garden, North Carolina.

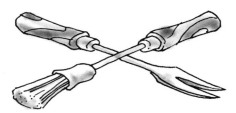

BARBECUE CHICKEN

1 (2½- to 3-pound) broiler-fryer, cut up
2 cups cola-flavored carbonated beverage
1 (6-ounce) can tomato paste
¼ cup vinegar
2 teaspoons instant minced onion
½ teaspoon celery seeds
¼ teaspoon dry mustard
¼ teaspoon salt
⅛ teaspoon ground cinnamon
⅛ teaspoon ground cloves

Place chicken in a lightly greased 12- x 8- x 2-inch baking dish.

Combine remaining ingredients in a medium saucepan; bring to a boil. Reduce heat, and simmer 5 minutes. Pour over chicken. Bake, uncovered, at 350° for 1 hour or until done, basting frequently. Yield: 4 servings.

Mildred Bickley,
Bristol, Virginia.

CREAMED CHICKEN IN PATTY SHELLS

4 to 6 frozen patty shells
3 tablespoons butter or margarine, divided
1½ cups sliced fresh mushrooms
3 tablespoons all-purpose flour
1 cup chicken broth
1 cup milk
¼ cup dry sherry
½ teaspoon salt
¼ teaspoon pepper
Dash of ground nutmeg
2 cups chopped cooked chicken

Bake patty shells according to package directions; cool. Pull out center of shells; set shells aside.

Melt 1 tablespoon butter in a small skillet; sauté mushrooms 4 to 5 minutes. Set aside.

Melt remaining 2 tablespoons butter in a heavy saucepan over low heat; add flour, stirring until smooth. Cook 1 minute, stirring constantly. Gradually add broth and milk; cook over medium heat, stirring constantly, until mixture is thickened and bubbly. Stir in mushrooms, sherry, seasonings, and chicken; heat thoroughly. Serve creamed chicken in patty shells. Yield: 4 to 6 servings.
Jean King,
Durham, North Carolina.

You Can't Beat Homemade Salad Dressing

A homemade dressing is all it takes to turn a simple tossed green salad into your favorite part of the meal. Our recipes offer some spicy new combinations as well as tried-and-true classics. The flavors of these dressings range from smooth and subtle to big and bold.

SPICY FRENCH DRESSING

½ cup sugar
½ cup plus 2 tablespoons catsup
¼ cup vinegar
2 teaspoons lime juice
¾ teaspoon onion juice
Dash of paprika
Dash of celery salt
1 cup vegetable oil

Combine all ingredients except oil in container of electric blender. Blend

until smooth. Add oil slowly while blender is running. Continue blending until mixture is thick. Cover and refrigerate until mixture is chilled. Yield: about 1¾ cups. *Mrs. Ed Stetz, Jr.,*
Johnstown, Pennsylvania.

THOUSAND ISLAND DRESSING

1 cup mayonnaise
½ cup catsup
1 tablespoon grated onion
1 tablespoon minced green pepper
2 tablespoons minced pimiento-stuffed olives
½ stalk celery, cut into 1-inch pieces
½ cup whipping cream
1 hard-cooked egg, chopped

Combine all ingredients except hard-cooked egg in container of an electric blender; blend 30 seconds. Stir in egg. Cover and refrigerate until chilled. Yield: 2½ cups. *Marie B. Matthews,*
Charlotte, North Carolina.

RÉMOULADE DRESSING

1½ cups mayonnaise
2 hard-cooked egg yolks, sieved
2 tablespoons minced fresh parsley
2 tablespoons vinegar
1 tablespoon paprika
1½ tablespoons prepared mustard
1½ teaspoons Worcestershire sauce
2 cloves garlic, crushed
Dash of hot sauce
Pinch of salt
Pinch of pepper

Combine all ingredients; mix well. Cover and refrigerate until chilled. Yield: 2 cups. *Mrs. Don L. Moore,*
Harrison, Arkansas.

GARLIC SALAD DRESSING

2 cups mayonnaise
⅓ cup buttermilk
⅓ cup vegetable oil
¼ cup water
1½ tablespoons garlic powder
1 tablespoon vinegar
1½ teaspoons lemon juice
1½ teaspoons honey
¾ teaspoon dry mustard
½ teaspoon salt

Combine mayonnaise and buttermilk; mix well, using a wire whisk. Stir in vegetable oil, water, garlic powder, vinegar, lemon juice, honey, dry mustard, and salt. Cover and refrigerate at least 8 hours. Yield: 3 cups. *Cynda A. Spoon,*
Broken Arrow, Oklahoma.

POPPY SEED DRESSING

1½ cups sugar
⅔ cup vinegar
3 tablespoons lemon juice
2 teaspoons dry mustard
1 teaspoon salt
2 cups vegetable oil
2 tablespoons poppy seeds

Combine sugar, vinegar, lemon juice, mustard, and salt in container of an electric blender; blend well. Add oil slowly while blender is running. Continue blending until mixture is thick.

Stir in poppy seeds. Cover and refrigerate until mixture is chilled; stir before serving. Yield: 3½ cups.
Rachel R. Mixon,
Kenedy, Texas.

CREAMY BLUE CHEESE SALAD DRESSING

2 cups mayonnaise
1 cup crumbled blue cheese
½ cup commercial sour cream
¼ cup vinegar
2 tablespoons sugar
1 clove garlic, minced

Combine mayonnaise, blue cheese, sour cream, vinegar, sugar, and garlic in a medium bowl. Beat with an electric mixer until smooth and fluffy. Cover and refrigerate until mixture is chilled. Yield: 3 cups. *Mrs. Don Walker,*
Delray Beach, Florida.

Sweet Strawberry Treats

When Louise Jones of Lithia Springs, Georgia, spots the first strawberries of the season, she knows it's time for her favorite dessert—Strawberry Shortcake Squares. Louise sweetens the plump berries and then sandwiches them between pieces of shortcake.

Another way to enjoy fresh strawberries is in Claire Buquoi's Stuffed Strawberries With Walnuts. Each berry is scooped out and filled with a rich walnut and cream cheese mixture.

STUFFED STRAWBERRIES WITH WALNUTS

18 extra-large strawberries
¾ cup whipped cream cheese
2 tablespoons finely chopped walnuts
1½ teaspoons powdered sugar
½ to 1½ teaspoons milk

Cut a thin slice from the stem end of strawberries, allowing the berries to stand upright. Cut ¼ inch off tip end of berries, reserving tips.

Carefully scoop out about half of the pulp from each berry, leaving shells intact. Combine pulp with cream cheese, walnuts, sugar, and milk, mixing well. Add extra milk if needed to make a creamy consistency. Spoon mixture into a decorating bag fitted with a large tip. Pipe mixture into strawberries, and top with reserved strawberry tips. Yield: 1½ dozen.
Claire Buquoi,
New Orleans, Louisiana.

STRAWBERRY-YOGURT PIE

1 envelope unflavored gelatin
¼ cup boiling water
1 (3-ounce) package cream cheese, softened
¼ cup sifted powdered sugar
1 teaspoon vanilla extract
1 cup whipping cream
¾ cup plain yogurt
1 (9-inch) graham cracker crust
2 cups strawberries, hulled and halved
⅓ cup strawberry jelly, melted

Dissolve gelatin in boiling water, and set aside.

Combine cream cheese, sugar, and vanilla; beat until light and fluffy. Add whipping cream; beat until soft peaks form. Add yogurt and gelatin mixture, mixing until smooth.

Spoon filling into graham cracker crust. Chill at least 4 hours. Arrange strawberries on top of pie; drizzle jelly over berries. Yield: one 9-inch pie.
Helen Maurer,
Christmas, Florida.

STRAWBERRY SHORTCAKE SQUARES

4 cups strawberries, hulled and sliced
¼ cup sugar
2 cups all-purpose flour
¼ cup sugar
1 tablespoon baking powder
¼ teaspoon salt
½ cup butter or margarine
⅔ cup half-and-half
1 egg, beaten
2 cups sweetened whipped cream
6 additional strawberries (optional)

Combine sliced strawberries and ¼ cup sugar; chill.

Combine flour, sugar, baking powder, and salt; cut in butter with a pastry blender until mixture resembles coarse meal. Combine half-and-half and egg, stirring well; add to flour mixture, stirring just until moistened. Spread mixture in a lightly greased 8-inch square baking pan. Bake at 450° for 15 minutes or until golden brown. Cool 5 minutes; turn out onto a wire rack.

Cut shortcake into 6 pieces; slice each piece crosswise in half. Place bottom half of shortcake, cut side up, on an individual serving plate; top with a dollop of whipped cream and 2½ tablespoons of strawberry mixture. Add second layer of shortcake, cut side down; top with a dollop of whipped cream and 2½ tablespoons of strawberry mixture. Garnish with an additional dollop of whipped cream. Add a strawberry, if desired. Repeat for each of remaining five shortcake squares. Yield: 6 servings.
Louise Jones,
Lithia Springs, Georgia.

Dainty Doilies Are All-Purpose

The old-fashioned doily is back. And it's frillier, fancier, and more formal than ever before. Years ago, a white paper doily was used mainly for lining a dessert plate. But today, with Victorian lace and freshly starched linen featured in fashion and interior design, these intricately cut paper accessories have become popular again. This time they have some brand new uses.

For a ladies' luncheon or a bridal shower, use the doily theme from beginning to end. Start with invitations handwritten on a doily; then use other shapes and sizes of doilies for place mats, plate liners, place cards, menus, name tags, and thank-you notes. You can pair paper doilies with everyday china for a soft, feminine look.

Add a special touch to your party with a fresh flower nosegay wrapped with a doily and tied with a pretty ribbon. Lay it at the guest of honor's place setting as a memento of the event. For other accents, wrap the frilly paper around a wine bottle, a marmalade jar, or a votive candle.

And since every table needs height to create a feeling of balance, try stacking cake stands for a tiered effect. Then add doily liners to tie the two stacked pieces together for a pretty touch.

There's no need to buy wrapping paper for gifts if you have a few paper doilies on hand. The lacy edge creates a delicate look, especially for bridal or Mother's Day gifts. To make food gifts extra special, place doilies on top of jars, and tie in place. Or wrap bread in the ruffled paper, and place in a basket.

Doilies offer some creative everyday uses as well. Use them as liners for shelves in closets, kitchen cabinets, and armoires. Let a portion of the scalloped edge hang over the shelf's end for a finishing touch.

Wrap gifts, favors, and flowers in frilly doilies. For a truly feminine touch, write invitations and thank-you notes on them; then add a touch of your favorite fragrance just before mailing.

May

Consider serving one of these party sandwiches at your next gathering: (from front) Bread Basket of Sandwiches, Stacking Sandwiches, and Party Canapés.

Fresh Ideas For Party Sandwiches

You won't have to apologize for serving sandwiches at a party when they look like these; the different shapes and various spreads make them anything but ordinary. They are, in fact, quite impressive. Choose from Stacking Sandwiches or Bread Basket of Sandwiches for casual gatherings; Party Canapés are just right for more formal occasions, such as teas and receptions.

The trick to making these sandwiches lies in cutting the bread neatly and evenly. Refer to our step-by-step photographs for explicit directions for each recipe. Remember to use a knife with a serrated edge when slicing the bread. If the bread is especially fresh, use an electric knife.

All the spreads and fillings for these sandwiches can be made a day or two ahead of time, but don't fill the sandwiches more than four hours before serving to keep the bread from getting soggy. When sandwiches are filled, cover them with plastic wrap, and chill until ready to serve.

BREAD BASKET OF SANDWICHES

1 large round loaf Italian or rye bread, about 8 inches in diameter
Leaf lettuce
Pineapple-Cheese Spread
Ham Spread

Slice off about ½ inch from top and bottom of loaf using a large serrated knife. Set aside both slices to use later as a bread basket base and lid.

Using a gentle sawing motion, cut vertically to bottom of loaf, ½ inch from edge. Lift out center for sandwiches, and trim ½ inch around outside of center portion to allow room for the sandwiches in the basket, and make serving easier. Slice the trimmed center into 8 equal wedges.

To assemble basket, set bread base on platter; replace bread shell on base, and line with lettuce.

Turn each wedge of bread on its side, and cut into 4 equal slices. Spread about 1½ tablespoons of Pineapple-Cheese Spread or Ham Spread between every 2 slices. Stack the sandwiches back into position in the basket, and then top with the reserved bread lid. Yield: 16 appetizer sandwiches.

Pineapple-Cheese Spread:

1 (3-ounce) package cream cheese, softened
½ cup drained crushed pineapple
¼ cup finely chopped pecans
½ teaspoon ground ginger

Beat cream cheese until light and fluffy. Stir in remaining ingredients. Yield: ¾ cup.

Ham Spread:

1 (3-ounce) package cream cheese, softened
¾ cup finely chopped cooked ham
1 tablespoon mayonnaise
½ teaspoon dry mustard
⅛ teaspoon red pepper

Beat cream cheese until light and fluffy. Stir in the remaining ingredients. Yield: ¾ cup.

Tip: Prevent soggy sandwiches by spreading butter or margarine all the way to the crusts of the bread before adding the filling.

To make Bread Basket of Sandwiches, slice off about ½ inch from top and bottom of loaf to use as basket base and lid.

Cut vertically to bottom of loaf about ½ inch from edge. Next, lift out the center portion of bread.

Slice center into eight equal wedges; cut each wedge into four equal slices. Spread filling on sandwiches, and restack loaf.

STACKING SANDWICHES

⅓ cup strong coffee (105° to 115°)
3 tablespoons molasses
1 package dry yeast
1 cup evaporated milk
2 tablespoons regular oats, uncooked
1½ tablespoons vegetable oil
½ teaspoon salt
¼ teaspoon ground ginger
2 cups all-purpose flour, divided
1 cup whole wheat flour
Mayonnaise
4 lettuce leaves
Pimiento Cheese Spread
About ½ cup alfalfa sprouts
Egg Salad Spread

Combine coffee, molasses, and dry yeast in a large mixing bowl; let mixture stand for 5 minutes. Add milk, oats, oil, salt, and ginger, stirring well. Stir in ¾ cup all-purpose flour and 1 cup whole wheat flour; beat at medium speed of an electric mixer 1 minute. Gradually add remaining 1¼ cups flour, stirring with a wooden spoon.

Spoon dough into 2 well-greased 1-pound coffee cans. Cover and let rise in a warm place (85°), free from drafts, 1 hour or until doubled in bulk.

Bake at 350° for 25 to 30 minutes. Remove bread from cans, and cool completely on wire racks.

Slice each loaf horizontally into 8 slices, counting the rounded top as a slice. Make a sandwich with the bottom 2 slices from one loaf using a small amount of mayonnaise, a lettuce leaf, and one-fourth of Pimiento Cheese

Spread. Make a sandwich with the next 2 slices of bread using a small amount of mayonnaise, sprouts, and one-fourth of Egg Salad Spread.

Place egg salad sandwich on top of pimiento cheese sandwich. Repeat filling and stacking sandwiches, alternating filling flavors, until both loaves are completed. Yield: 8 sandwiches.

Pimiento Cheese Spread:

1 cup (4 ounces) shredded sharp Cheddar cheese
1 (2-ounce) jar diced pimiento, drained
¼ cup chopped almonds, toasted
3 tablespoons mayonnaise
⅛ teaspoon white pepper
⅛ teaspoon hot sauce

Fill Stacking Sandwiches from the bottom of the loaf up. Alternate fillings, and stack sandwiches as you fill them.

Combine all ingredients, and stir well. Chill. Yield: 1 cup.

Egg Salad Spread:

4 hard-cooked eggs, finely chopped
3 tablespoons mayonnaise
2 tablespoons chopped chives
2 tablespoons sweet pickle relish
⅛ teaspoon salt
⅛ teaspoon white pepper

Combine all ingredients, and stir well. Chill. Yield: 1 cup.

Note: For smaller sandwiches, cut each filled sandwich in half or quarters before stacking. Alternate the directions in which the cuts are placed when stacking to make the stacks more sturdy.

Cut each round sandwich into halves or quarters. Alternate the directions of cuts as you stack the loaf to make it sturdy.

PARTY CANAPÉS

1 (1-pound) loaf unsliced sandwich bread
Tomato Butter
Herb Butter
Alfalfa sprouts
Ripe olive slices
4 to 5 ounces smoked salmon or cherry
tomato slices
Fresh dill or parsley sprigs

Trim crust from loaf of bread, making bread an even rectangle. Slice bread horizontally into 7 (³⁄₈-inch-thick) slices.

Spread a very thin layer of Tomato Butter over one side of 3 or 4 bread slices; spread a very thin layer of Herb Butter over one side of remaining bread slices. Spoon remaining Tomato Butter into a decorating bag fitted with metal tip No. 14; pipe a small border along the long sides of each piece spread with Tomato Butter. Repeat piping with remaining Herb Butter on remaining bread. Place bread slices on baking sheets, and cover loosely with plastic wrap. Chill at least 30 minutes or until ready to serve.

Just before serving, slice each portion of bread spread with Tomato Butter into 8 triangles; slice each portion of bread spread with Herb Butter into 7 rectangles. Garnish Tomato Butter canapés with alfalfa sprouts and ripe olive slices. Garnish Herb Butter canapés with tiny rolls of smoked salmon and dill sprigs. Yield: 4 to 4½ dozen.

Tomato Butter:

¼ cup butter, softened
2 teaspoons tomato paste
Dash of red pepper

Cream softened butter until light and fluffy. Stir in tomato paste and red pepper. Yield: ¼ cup.

Herb Butter:

¼ cup butter, softened
2 tablespoons finely minced fresh parsley
1½ teaspoons finely minced fresh basil
1 small clove garlic, minced
1 drop green food coloring (optional)

Cream butter until light and fluffy; stir in parsley, basil, and garlic. Press mixture through a sieve. (Not all the herbs will press through.) Stir in food coloring, if desired. Yield: ¼ cup.

It's Time For Homemade Ice Cream

Can you remember a backyard barbecue or lakeside cookout when homemade ice cream wasn't anticipated as the grand finale to a day of fun? A gathering during the summer is sure to mean this sweet cooler is ripening in a churn nearby.

In the *Southern Living* test kitchens, we've found that the results vary greatly according to the ingredients and the method of freezing. Naturally, ice cream made with whipping cream offers a richer flavor, while recipes using whole milk taste more like commercial ice milk. The ice cream seems to melt faster when whole milk is used, but it's cheaper than using whipping cream or half-and-half and saves calories, too. Using ginger ale instead of milk or cream turns the mixture into an icy sherbet as in our recipe for Fruit Punch Sherbet. But the texture is still as smooth as the frozen cream mixtures.

When freezing ice cream, you'll get the best results by following the manufacturer's directions for your freezer. If you've lost the instructions, use the following general tips.

■ Fill the freezer canister no more than two-thirds full before freezing. This gives the ice cream space to expand.

■ Use about 20 pounds of crushed ice and 3 to 4 cups of rock salt for a 1-gallon freezer. Alternate four thick layers of ice with four thin layers of salt. Add leftover ice and salt as the top layer of ice melts and during ripening.

■ When the churning process is finished (it will take about 30 minutes), drain off the brine, and wipe the canister top and cover to remove any traces of salt. Remove the canister cover, and take out the dasher, scraping ice cream back into the can. Top the canister with plastic wrap or foil, and replace the cover. Pack leftover ice and salt around the canister, and wrap the entire churn with a thick layer of newspaper or towels. Let the churn stand for 1 to 3 hours to allow the ice cream to harden and the flavors to blend.

To make Party Canapés, first trim crust from loaf of unsliced sandwich bread, making bread an even rectangular.

Slice horizontally into ³⁄₈-inch-thick slices. Spread each with flavored butter; pipe remaining butter along long sides.

Cut bread slices into triangles or rectangles, and garnish as desired. (See garnished canapés in photograph on page 126.)

TUTTI-FRUTTI ICE CREAM

1 (14-ounce) can sweetened condensed milk
¼ cup lemon juice
½ cup sugar
3 ripe bananas, mashed
1 (8-ounce) can crushed pineapple, undrained
1 (11-ounce) can mandarin oranges, drained and chopped
1 (6-ounce) jar maraschino cherries, drained and chopped
3 cups milk
1 cup water

Combine sweetened condensed milk, lemon juice, sugar, and fruit; blend well. Add 3 cups milk and water.

Pour mixture into freezer can of a 1-gallon hand-turned or electric freezer. Freeze according to manufacturer's instructions. Allow ice cream to ripen at least 1 hour. Yield: 2 quarts.

Sally Smith,
Rustburg, Virginia.

FRUIT PUNCH SHERBET

1 (67.6-ounce) bottle red fruit punch
2 (14-ounce) cans sweetened condensed milk
2 (10-ounce) bottles ginger ale

Combine all ingredients; mix well. Pour mixture into freezer can of a 5-quart hand-turned or electric freezer. Freeze according to manufacturer's instructions. Allow sherbet to ripen at least 1 hour. Yield: about 1 gallon.

Mike Hamilton,
Birmingham, Alabama.

CHERRY-NUT ICE CREAM

4 eggs, beaten
2 cups sugar
Dash of salt
2 (12-ounce) cans evaporated milk
5 cups milk
1 tablespoon vanilla extract
1 cup chopped pecans
1 (10-ounce) jar maraschino cherries, drained and chopped

Combine eggs, sugar, and salt; blend well. Add evaporated milk, milk, and vanilla. Stir in pecans and cherries.

Pour mixture into freezer can of a 5-quart hand-turned or electric freezer. Freeze according to manufacturer's instructions. Allow ice cream to ripen at least 1 hour. Yield: 1 gallon.

Cheryl Landreth,
Pleasant Grove, Alabama.

BUTTER PECAN ICE CREAM

1½ cups chopped pecans
¼ cup butter, melted
8 egg yolks, lightly beaten
3 cups milk, divided
1½ cups firmly packed light brown sugar
¼ cup butter
2 cups whipping cream

Sauté pecans in ¼ cup melted butter until lightly browned, stirring frequently. Drain pecans on paper towels.

Combine egg yolks, 1 cup milk, and brown sugar in top of a double boiler. Place over simmering water, and beat at high speed of an electric mixer 5 minutes. Beat in ¼ cup butter, ½ tablespoon at a time. Continue beating an additional 5 to 7 minutes or until mixture thickens.

Pour mixture into a deep bowl; place bowl in a larger container of ice water, and beat mixture until cool (about 5 minutes). Add whipping cream, and beat an additional 5 minutes. Stir in remaining 2 cups milk and pecans. Pour mixture into freezer can of a 1-gallon hand-turned or electric freezer. Freeze according to manufacturer's instructions. Allow ice cream to ripen at least 1 hour. Yield: about 3 quarts.

Charles Wolf,
Macon, Georgia.

VANILLA ICE CREAM

4 eggs
1 cup sugar
1 (14-ounce) can sweetened condensed milk
1 (3-ounce) package vanilla instant pudding mix
1 tablespoon vanilla extract
1½ quarts milk, divided

Beat eggs in a large bowl at medium-high speed of an electric mixer for 1 minute. Add sugar, and beat well. Add sweetened condensed milk, pudding mix, and vanilla; beat well. Stir in 1 quart milk. Pour mixture into freezer can of a 1-gallon hand-turned or electric freezer. Add remaining ½ quart milk.

Freeze mixture according to the manufacturer's instructions. Let ripen at least 1 hour. Yield: about 2½ quarts.

Chocolate Ice Cream Variation: Follow recipe for Vanilla Ice Cream, except for adding 1 (16-ounce) can chocolate-flavored syrup when adding sweetened condensed milk, pudding mix, and vanilla. Yield: 3 quarts.

Peppermint Ice Cream Variation: Follow recipe for Vanilla Ice Cream, except add ½ teaspoon peppermint extract when adding vanilla and 1 cup crushed peppermint candy when adding the last ½ quart of milk. Yield: about 3 quarts.

Ruth Ann Pool,
Palestine, Texas.

Pour On Lemon And Lime Juice

If there's only one lemon or lime in the refrigerator, save it for garnishing, and reach for the bottled juice for your recipes. It's a must to have lemon and lime juice handy since many foods are enhanced by the tart flavors. Our recipes calling for one of these citrus juices include entrées and side dishes, as well as salads and desserts.

MARINATED BRISKET

1 (10½-ounce) can beef consommé
½ cup soy sauce
¼ cup lemon juice
1 tablespoon liquid smoke
1 clove garlic, minced
1 (3-pound) beef brisket

Combine beef consommé, soy sauce, lemon juice, liquid smoke, and garlic in an 11- x 7- x 2-inch baking dish, mixing well. Place beef brisket in dish, turning once in marinade. Cover and refrigerate several hours or overnight, turning meat occasionally.

Cover beef brisket, and bake at 300° for 2 hours or until desired degree of doneness. Serve with gravy made from marinade. Yield: 6 servings.

Note: To thicken gravy, combine marinade and ¼ cup cornstarch in a heavy saucepan; mix well. Bring to a boil over medium heat, stirring occasionally; cook 1 minute. Yield: 4 cups.

D. J. Trickey,
Oklahoma City, Oklahoma.

VERACRUZ FISH WITH SHRIMP

3 cups water
1 pound unpeeled fresh shrimp
4 fish fillets
2 cloves garlic, crushed
¼ cup lime juice
1 medium onion, chopped
1 medium green pepper, chopped
3 tomatoes, peeled and chopped
1 to 2 jalapeño peppers, seeded and
  chopped
1½ tablespoons olive oil
1 bay leaf
½ teaspoon dried whole oregano
¼ teaspoon ground cinnamon
2 tablespoons capers

Bring water to a boil; add shrimp, and cook 3 to 5 minutes. Drain well; rinse with cold water. Chill. Peel and devein shrimp.

Place fish in a 2-quart casserole. Spread garlic and lime juice over fish; set aside.

Sauté onion, green pepper, tomatoes, and jalapeño peppers in olive oil in a skillet until vegetables are tender. Add bay leaf, oregano, and cinnamon; spoon over fish. Sprinkle with capers. Bake, uncovered, at 425° for 20 minutes. Add shrimp; heat an additional 2 to 4 minutes. Remove bay leaf before serving. Yield: 4 servings.   *Chris Blanton,*
Madison, Tennessee.

NEW POTATOES
WITH LEMON SAUCE

12 small new potatoes, unpeeled and
  sliced
2 tablespoons diced onion
½ cup butter or margarine, melted
¼ cup lemon juice
1 teaspoon caper juice
2 tablespoons chopped capers
2 tablespoons chopped fresh parsley
1 teaspoon salt
¼ teaspoon pepper
¼ cup grated Parmesan cheese
Lemon slices (optional)

Cover potatoes with water, and bring to a boil; reduce heat, and cook about 15 minutes or until potatoes are tender. Drain potatoes; arrange slices on platter, and keep warm.

Sauté onion in butter until tender. Reduce heat; stir in lemon juice, caper juice, capers, parsley, salt, and pepper. Cook just until mixture is thoroughly heated. Pour sauce over potatoes. Sprinkle with cheese; garnish with lemon slices, if desired. Yield: 8 servings.   *Norma Cowden,*
Shawnee, Oklahoma.

FRESH SPINACH SALAD

½ cup vegetable oil
¼ cup vinegar
3 tablespoons lemon juice
1 clove garlic, crushed
¼ teaspoon sugar
¼ teaspoon salt
Dash of pepper
6 slices bacon, cooked and crumbled
1 pound fresh spinach, torn into bite-size
  pieces
2 hard-cooked eggs, chopped
3 green onions, sliced

Combine oil, vinegar, lemon juice, garlic, sugar, salt, and pepper in a jar. Cover tightly, and shake vigorously. Add bacon, mixing well.

Combine spinach, eggs, and green onions in a serving bowl. Pour dressing over salad, tossing lightly. Yield: 4 to 6 servings.   *Edna E. Moore,*
Hueytown, Alabama.

CHUNKY SALSA

4 green onions, chopped
1 large tomato, finely chopped
½ cup tomato sauce
¼ cup plus 2 tablespoons chopped green
  olives
¼ cup sliced ripe olives
1½ tablespoons dried cilantro
1 tablespoon lime juice
2¼ teaspoons olive oil
1½ teaspoons minced jalapeño pepper
½ teaspoon white wine vinegar
½ teaspoon garlic powder
¼ teaspoon salt
⅛ teaspoon pepper

Combine all ingredients; cover and refrigerate 6 to 8 hours. Serve with meat or as a dip. Yield: 2½ cups.
Sally Murphy,
El Paso, Texas.

LEMON MERINGUE PIE

3 egg yolks
1½ cups water
½ cup lemon juice
1¼ cups sugar
⅓ cup cornstarch
3 tablespoons butter or margarine
2 teaspoons vinegar
1½ teaspoons lemon extract
1 (9-inch) baked pastry shell
Cooked Meringue

Combine egg yolks, water, lemon juice, sugar, and cornstarch in top of a double boiler; mix well. Bring water to a boil; reduce heat, and cook egg mixture over hot water, stirring constantly, until mixture thickens and comes to a boil. Boil 1 minute, stirring constantly. Remove from heat; stir in butter, vinegar, and lemon extract. Pour immediately into pastry shell. Spread meringue over warm filling, sealing to edge of pastry. Bake at 425° for 5 to 8 minutes or until lightly browned. Cool before serving. Yield: one 9-inch pie.

Cooked Meringue:

¾ cup water
¼ cup plus 2 tablespoons sugar
1 tablespoon cornstarch
3 egg whites
Pinch of salt
1 teaspoon vanilla extract

Combine water, sugar, and cornstarch in a small saucepan, stirring well. Cook over medium heat, stirring constantly, until transparent and thickened. Combine egg whites (at room temperature) and salt; beat until foamy. Add vanilla, and continue beating while gradually pouring cooked mixture into egg whites. Beat 3 minutes or until stiff, but not dry. Do not overbeat. Yield: enough for one 9-inch pie.   *Mrs. Joe D. Wilson,*
Pulaski, Virginia.

LIME CHIFFON PIE

1 envelope unflavored gelatin
1 cup sugar, divided
4 eggs, separated
½ cup lime juice
¼ cup water
¼ teaspoon salt
1 cup whipping cream, whipped
1 (9-inch) baked pastry shell
Chocolate shavings
Lime slices (optional)

Combine gelatin and ½ cup sugar in a heavy saucepan. In a small bowl lightly beat egg yolks; add lime juice and water. Add mixture to gelatin mixture; stir well. Cook over medium heat, stirring frequently, until mixture comes to a boil and thickens. Remove from heat.

Combine egg whites (at room temperature) and salt; beat until foamy. Gradually add remaining ½ cup sugar, 1 tablespoon at a time, beating until stiff peaks form. Fold meringue and whipped cream into gelatin mixture; spoon mixture into pastry shell. Chill until firm. Garnish pie with chocolate shavings and, if desired, lime slices. Yield: one 9-inch pie.   *Jenny Peebles,*
Miami Shores, Florida.

Enjoy A Spirited Refresher

When you want to offer guests something stronger than iced tea, try serving a light and refreshing Melon Ball Cooler. This drink has the distinctive color and taste of Midori, a bright green liqueur made with honeydew melon. Vodka gives it a little extra punch.

MELON BALL COOLER

¼ cup Midori (honeydew melon liqueur)
¼ cup vodka
¼ cup pineapple juice
¼ cup orange juice
1 cup ginger ale
Crushed ice
Watermelon or honeydew melon balls (optional)
Fresh mint sprigs (optional)

Combine first 5 ingredients; stir well. Pour over crushed ice. Garnish with melon balls and mint sprigs, if desired. Yield: 2 cups.

CREAMY DESSERT DRINK

2 cups vanilla ice cream
½ cup crème de cacao
¼ cup plus 2 tablespoons Galliano
1¾ cups crushed ice

Combine all ingredients in container of electric blender; process at high speed until frothy. Yield: 3¼ cups.

Warm-Weather Recipes For Two

When you want something that's not too filling for lunch or supper, these recipes are for you. And better yet, each recipe is scaled just for two, so that you won't have to worry about having any leftovers.

For a crisp main dish, try our Curried Chicken Salad. It's just right for an outdoor lunch at home with a friend or even for a light supper. To make it a full meal, serve slices of chilled tomato or marinated fresh yellow squash and zucchini slices and a hard roll. For dessert, a refreshing scoop of pineapple or lemon sherbet tops it off.

You can put together a menu from recipes here and keep from spending too much time in the kitchen. Serve our recipe for Appetizer Fruit Cup to start the meal, and offer Shrimp-Stuffed Peppers for the main course. Just add a vegetable and a dessert. If you're in a rush for time, cook the rice for Shrimp-Stuffed Peppers the day before; you'll save an extra 20 minutes. There's no need to reheat the rice before filling the peppers because they will be baked after they're stuffed.

SHRIMP-STUFFED PEPPERS

¼ cup uncooked regular rice
½ cup water
¼ teaspoon salt
2 medium-size green peppers, cored and seeded
1 (4½-ounce) can shrimp, drained and rinsed
⅓ cup mayonnaise
1 tablespoon chopped onion
2 drops of hot sauce
2 tablespoons cracker crumbs
1 tablespoon butter or margarine, melted

Combine rice, water, and salt in a saucepan; bring to a boil. Cover, reduce heat, and simmer 17 to 20 minutes or until done. Remove from heat; set aside.

Cook green peppers in boiling salted water 5 minutes; drain.

Set aside 2 shrimp. Combine rice, remaining shrimp, mayonnaise, onion, and hot sauce; mix well. Spoon into peppers; place in an 8½- x 4½- x 3-inch loafpan. Combine cracker crumbs and butter; mix well. Sprinkle on peppers; bake, uncovered, at 350° for 30 minutes. Garnish with reserved shrimp. Yield: 2 servings.
*Julie Earhart,
St. Louis, Missouri.*

CURRIED CHICKEN SALAD

¾ cup cubed cooked chicken
⅔ cup cooked rice
⅓ cup chopped celery
⅓ cup sliced water chestnuts
8 ripe olives, sliced
2 tablespoons sliced green onions
⅓ cup mayonnaise
1 teaspoon lemon juice
1 teaspoon curry powder
Lettuce leaves

Combine chicken, rice, celery, water chestnuts, olives, and green onions; toss well. Combine mayonnaise, lemon juice, and curry powder; add to chicken mixture, stirring well. Chill. Serve on lettuce leaves. Yield: 2 servings.
*Nellie Bywaters,
Warrensburg, Missouri.*

APPLE WEDGES WITH POPPYSEED DRESSING

2 tablespoons orange juice
2 teaspoons vegetable oil
1 teaspoon honey
⅛ teaspoon poppyseeds
Dash of salt
1 Red Delicious apple
Coarsely shredded lettuce

Combine orange juice, oil, honey, poppyseeds, and salt in a small bowl; stir well, and chill.

Cut apple into wedges; arrange on shredded lettuce. Serve with chilled poppyseed dressing. Yield: 2 servings.
*Mrs. C. D. Marshall,
Culpeper, Virginia.*

APPETIZER FRUIT CUP

½ cup honeydew balls
½ cup cantaloupe balls
½ cup fresh strawberries, halved
3 tablespoons Cointreau or other orange-flavored liqueur
Fresh mint leaves

Combine all ingredients except mint; toss gently to coat. Cover and chill 1 to 2 hours. Spoon into individual compotes; garnish with mint leaves. Yield: 2 appetizer servings.

FRUIT DELIGHT

2 tablespoons mayonnaise
2 tablespoons honey
1 apple, unpeeled, cored, and diced
1 banana, sliced
¼ cup chopped walnuts

Combine mayonnaise and honey; mix well. Combine remaining ingredients in a small mixing bowl. Add to dressing; toss gently until well coated. Yield: 2 servings.
*Mrs. Roy Sweeney,
Louisville, Tennessee.*

Oysters Are Big On Flavor

There are those who swear the best way to enjoy fresh oysters is on the half shell. But if you prefer your oysters cooked, here are some superb recipes.

There was a time when oysters were avoided during months without an "r." But thanks to modern refrigeration techniques and expanded harvesting, oysters can be enjoyed either fresh or frozen any time of the year.

You might notice when buying oysters that they are often labeled as being either Select or Standard. This is referring to the size of the oyster; Select oysters are large, while Standard oysters are medium to small.

Live oysters should have tightly closed shells. They will remain fresh for 7 to 10 days in their shells if they are stored in the refrigerator and covered with a moist cloth.

Home freezing of oysters isn't recommended unless they are frozen in the commercial packing in which they were purchased or in their own liquid in a container with little air space. You'll find they are better if used within two months. Thaw oysters in the refrigerator or in an airtight container under cold running water. Once thawed, they shouldn't be refrozen.

SCALLOPED OYSTERS

1 (12-ounce) container Standard oysters, undrained
¼ cup sliced celery
2 tablespoons minced onion
2 tablespoons butter or margarine, melted
1½ cups round buttery cracker crumbs
½ cup milk
1 tablespoon chopped fresh parsley
1 teaspoon lemon juice
½ teaspoon salt
¼ teaspoon garlic powder
⅛ teaspoon pepper
½ cup (2 ounces) shredded Cheddar cheese
Additional chopped fresh parsley (optional)

Pour oysters and oyster liquid into a medium saucepan; simmer 5 minutes or until edges of oysters begin to curl. Drain, reserving 2 tablespoons liquid; set aside.

Sauté celery and onion in butter until tender; add cracker crumbs, milk, 1 tablespoon parsley, lemon juice, salt, garlic powder, and pepper, mixing well.

Stir in oysters and 2 tablespoons reserved liquid. Spoon mixture into a lightly greased 1-quart casserole. Bake, uncovered, at 375° for 15 minutes. Sprinkle cheese over top; bake an additional 5 minutes or until cheese melts. Garnish with additional chopped parsley, if desired. Yield: 4 servings.

Diane Chapman,
Tallahassee, Florida.

SAUTÉED OYSTERS

1 (12-ounce) can beer
1 (8-ounce) bottle commercial Italian salad dressing
2 tablespoons minced fresh parsley
2 cloves garlic, crushed
1 tablespoon hot sauce
Red pepper to taste
3 (12-ounce) containers Standard oysters, drained
2 French rolls, split lengthwise and toasted

Combine beer, salad dressing, parsley, garlic, hot sauce, and red pepper in a shallow container; add oysters. Cover and refrigerate 6 to 8 hours.

Pour oyster mixture into a large skillet; cook over medium heat about 5 minutes or until edges of oysters begin to curl, stirring occasionally. Spoon oyster mixture over toasted rolls, and serve immediately. Yield: 4 servings.

Stanley Pichon, Jr.,
Slidell, Louisiana.

BACON-BAKED OYSTERS
(pictured at right)

2 dozen unshucked oysters
6 slices bacon, quartered
¾ to 1 cup round buttery cracker crumbs
½ cup mayonnaise
2 tablespoons chopped chives
1 teaspoon lemon juice
1 teaspoon hot sauce
½ teaspoon Dijon mustard
1 (4-pound) package rock salt
¼ cup grated Parmesan cheese

Wash and rinse oysters thoroughly in cold water. Shuck oysters, reserving deep half of shells; place oysters in colander to drain. Set aside.

Cook bacon until limp, but not brown; drain and set aside.

Combine cracker crumbs, mayonnaise, chives, lemon juice, hot sauce, and Dijon mustard; mix well, and set mixture aside.

Sprinkle rock salt in bottom of a 15- x 10- x 1-inch jellyroll pan; arrange reserved shells on rock salt. Place oysters in half shells. Spread crumb mixture over each oyster; top with a piece of bacon, and sprinkle with cheese. Bake at 400° for 8 to 10 minutes or until bacon is crisp. Yield: 4 to 6 servings.

Patsy Elrod,
Smyrna, Georgia.

GOLDEN OYSTER STEW
(pictured at right)

½ cup chopped onion
½ cup sliced celery
2 tablespoons butter or margarine, melted
2 cups sliced fresh mushrooms
2 tablespoons all-purpose flour
2 cups milk
1 cup (4 ounces) shredded sharp Cheddar cheese
1 (10½-ounce) can cream of potato soup, undiluted
1 (2-ounce) jar diced pimiento, undrained
¼ teaspoon salt
¼ teaspoon pepper
¼ teaspoon hot sauce
1 (12-ounce) container Standard oysters, undrained

Sauté onion and celery in butter until tender. Add mushrooms, and cook 2 minutes. Add flour, and cook 1 minute, stirring constantly. Gradually add milk; cook over medium heat, stirring frequently, until mixture is thickened and bubbly. Stir in cheese, soup, pimiento, and seasonings; cook over medium heat, stirring often, until cheese melts and mixture is thoroughly heated. Add oysters and oyster liquid; reduce heat, and simmer 5 to 8 minutes or until edges of oysters curl. Yield: 6½ cups.

Edna McDonald,
Bonifay, Florida.

Right: *Here are three favorite ways to enjoy this seafood: (front) Bacon-Baked Oysters, (middle) fresh oysters on the half shell, and (back) Golden Oyster Stew. (Recipes are on this page.)*

Page 134: *Pesto adds a splash of color and flavor to all types of food: (clockwise from top) Pesto Salad Dressing, hot pasta tossed with Fresh Pesto, Tomatoes Pesto, and Pesto-Stuffed Mushrooms. (Recipes are on page 150.)*

Appetizers Add To The Fun

Whether on the deck or around the dinner table, start the evening off right by serving Peanut Butter Dip and a tower of fresh fruit—it's the perfect appetizer for entertaining. Cheese Spread is another favorite with hungry guests; just add crackers, and you're set.

CURRIED SHRIMP CHEESE BALL

½ cup flaked coconut
¼ teaspoon curry powder
2 (8-ounce) packages cream cheese, softened
2 (4½-ounce) cans shrimp, rinsed, drained, and chopped
2 tablespoons minced onion

Combine coconut and curry powder; mix well. Spread mixture on a baking sheet; bake at 350° for 7 minutes, stirring every 2 minutes. Cool and set mixture aside.

Combine remaining ingredients; mix well. Shape into a ball (mixture will be sticky), and roll in coconut. Chill 1 to 2 hours. Serve with crackers. Yield: one 5-inch cheese ball. *Peggy Head, Ennis, Texas.*

MARINATED MUSHROOMS

¾ cup olive oil
⅓ cup wine vinegar
1 clove garlic, halved
1 bay leaf
¾ teaspoon sugar
½ teaspoon salt
½ teaspoon dried whole basil
6 peppercorns
1½ pounds medium mushrooms, halved

Combine all ingredients except mushrooms in a skillet; bring to a boil. Reduce heat, and simmer 10 minutes. Stir in mushrooms, and simmer 5 minutes. Let cool; cover and chill several hours or overnight. Drain before serving, removing garlic and bay leaf. Yield: 10 appetizer servings. *Merriane Sanford, San Antonio, Texas.*

GARDEN SPREAD

1 medium cucumber, seeded and cut into large pieces
1 medium-size green pepper, cut into pieces
1 small onion, quartered
1 carrot, scraped and cut into pieces
1 envelope unflavored gelatin
¼ cup cold water
1 cup mayonnaise
1 tablespoon Worcestershire sauce
½ teaspoon prepared mustard
1 large tomato, diced
1 teaspoon salt
1 teaspoon paprika

Place cucumber, green pepper, onion, and carrot in food processor bowl or container of electric blender; process just until coarsely ground.

Sprinkle gelatin over cold water in a saucepan; let stand 5 minutes. Place over low heat, stirring until dissolved.

Combine gelatin mixture, mayonnaise, Worcestershire sauce, and mustard; mix well. Stir in vegetable mixture, tomato, salt, and paprika. Chill before serving. Serve with party bread or crackers. Yield: 4 cups. *Mrs. John B. Wright, Greenville, South Carolina.*

CHEESE SPREAD

1 (8-ounce) package process cheese
1 (3-ounce) package cream cheese
⅓ cup mayonnaise
3 tablespoons evaporated milk
2 tablespoons sweet pickle juice
1 tablespoon chopped pimiento
½ teaspoon sugar

Place cheese in top of a double boiler; bring water to a boil. Reduce heat to low; cook, stirring frequently, until cheese melts. Stir in remaining ingredients, mixing well. Serve with crackers. Store in refrigerator. Yield: about 2 cups. *Mrs. Charles Hellem, Columbia, Missouri.*

Tip: Evaporated milk and sweetened condensed milk are two of the forms in which milk is sold. They are different and cannot be interchanged within a recipe. Evaporated milk is unsweetened milk thickened by removing some of its water content. Sweetened condensed milk is sweetened with sugar and thickened by evaporation of some of its water content.

PEANUT BUTTER DIP

½ cup peanut butter
½ cup commercial sour cream
¼ cup frozen orange juice concentrate, thawed and undiluted
¼ cup water

Combine all ingredients except water in a small bowl; beat until smooth. Stir in water until blended; cover and chill. Serve with fresh fruit. Yield: 1⅓ cups. *Mrs. J. W. Hopkins, Abilene, Texas.*

It's Time For A Picnic

When you want a change of pace at mealtime, head outdoors for a picnic. Whether it's a simple backyard affair or a more adventurous trek to the park or beach, take along some of our readers' picnic favorites.

Get a headstart on preparation with Vegetable-Chicken Vinaigrette Salad. You can make it the day before, and forget about it until it's time to eat. Serve Peanut Butter-Cheese Ball, another make-ahead idea, with crisp apple wedges for a great appetizer or dessert. Another tasty snack to take along is Cinnamon-Popcorn Crunch, a favorite with all ages.

VEGETABLE-CHICKEN VINAIGRETTE SALAD

2¼ cups chopped cooked chicken
1 pound fresh mushrooms, halved
1 pint cherry tomatoes, halved
2 small zucchini, sliced
1 green pepper, cut into thin strips
1 green onion with top, thinly sliced
½ cup vegetable oil
2 tablespoons lemon juice
2 tablespoons white wine vinegar
1 teaspoon salt
½ teaspoon sugar
½ teaspoon pepper

Combine chicken and vegetables in a large bowl. Combine remaining ingredients, and mix well. Pour over chicken mixture, tossing gently. Cover and chill several hours or overnight. Yield: 6 to 8 servings. *Charlotte Farmer, Richmond, Virginia.*

HAM HOT RODS

½ pound cooked ham, diced
1 cup (4 ounces) shredded Cheddar cheese
½ cup sliced ripe olives
½ cup catsup
3 tablespoons chopped onion
2 tablespoons mayonnaise
8 hot dog buns

Combine all ingredients except buns; mix well. Spoon mixture into buns. Wrap each bun separately in aluminum foil. Cook on grill for 20 minutes or until cheese melts. Yield: 8 servings.
Mrs. Roy Nieman,
Dunnellon, Florida.

BACON DEVILED EGGS

6 hard-cooked eggs
2 tablespoons mayonnaise or salad dressing
1 tablespoon commercial French or Thousand Island dressing
½ teaspoon dry mustard
¼ teaspoon lemon-pepper seasoning
3 slices bacon, cooked and crumbled

Slice eggs in half lengthwise; carefully remove yolks. Mash yolks, and stir in remaining ingredients. Stuff egg whites with yolk mixture. Yield: 6 servings.
Mary H. Gilliam,
Cartersville, Virginia.

MIXED VEGETABLE SALAD

3 medium zucchini, thinly sliced
1 cucumber, unpeeled and thinly sliced
1 green pepper, chopped
2 tomatoes, cut into wedges
2 green onions with tops, sliced
¾ cup vegetable oil
½ cup cider vinegar
1 teaspoon garlic salt
½ teaspoon pepper
¼ teaspoon dried whole dillweed
¼ teaspoon dried whole tarragon

Combine zucchini, cucumber, green pepper, tomatoes, and green onions; set aside. Combine remaining ingredients; mix well. Pour over vegetables; toss gently. Cover and chill several hours or overnight. Yield: 10 servings.
Nancy Beasley,
Orlando, Florida.

PEANUT BUTTER-CHEESE BALL

1½ cups peanut butter
1 (8-ounce) package cream cheese, softened
½ cup sifted powdered sugar
3 to 4 tablespoons milk
½ cup chopped peanuts

Combine peanut butter, cream cheese, sugar, and milk in a medium mixing bowl. Beat on medium speed of an electric mixer until smooth. Add more milk, if desired, for a creamier texture. Shape mixture into a ball; roll in peanuts. Chill several hours or overnight. Serve with apple wedges or whole wheat crackers. Yield: 3⅓ cups.
Susan S. Watkins,
Raleigh, North Carolina.

CINNAMON-POPCORN CRUNCH

1½ quarts popped corn
1 (6½-ounce) can salted mixed nuts
1 (16-ounce) package light brown sugar
1 cup light corn syrup
½ cup butter or margarine
½ cup water
1½ teaspoons ground cinnamon
½ teaspoon salt

Combine popped corn and mixed nuts in a large bowl; set aside.

Combine remaining ingredients in a heavy Dutch oven. Bring mixture to a boil, and cook over medium-high heat, stirring frequently, until mixture reaches soft crack stage (290°). Remove from heat, and pour over popcorn mixture; blend ingredients well.

Spoon mixture into greased jellyroll pans; press lightly to flatten. Separate into bite-size pieces; let cool. Yield: about 2½ quarts. *Mrs. W. J. Nichol,*
Knoxville, Tennessee.

ORANGE-CRUNCH SQUARES

½ cup butter or margarine, softened
1 tablespoon grated orange rind
1 cup firmly packed brown sugar
2 eggs
1 cup all-purpose flour
¼ teaspoon salt
1 cup chopped walnuts or pecans
½ cup firmly packed brown sugar
2 tablespoons grated orange rind
2 tablespoons orange juice
Powdered sugar (optional)

Cream butter and 1 tablespoon orange rind until fluffy. Add brown sugar,

mixing well. Add eggs, and beat until blended. Combine flour and salt; stir into creamed mixture. Stir in chopped walnuts or pecans.

Spoon mixture into a greased 9-inch square baking pan. Bake at 350° for 27 minutes. Combine remaining ingredients except powdered sugar; spoon over cooked mixture, spreading to edge of pan. Broil until bubbly; cool. Sprinkle with powdered sugar, if desired. Cut into squares. Yield: 16 squares.
Charlotte Watkins,
Lakeland, Florida.

Serve The Best Of Burgers

Ground beef is a staple in most family meals, and it's easy to see why. Layered in casseroles, baked in bread, or stirred into beans, its use is limited only by the cook's imagination. But burgers always seem to be a favorite way to serve this meat. Plain or fancy, with or without a bun, it's hard to match the great taste of a burger, whether hot from the oven or straight from the grill.

SEASONED STUFFED BURGERS

1 pound ground beef
½ teaspoon salt
¼ teaspoon pepper
¼ cup catsup
¼ cup chopped onion
3 tablespoons chopped green pepper
1 small clove garlic, minced
1 tablespoon butter or margarine, melted
¼ teaspoon salt
2 slices bread, cut into ½-inch cubes
⅓ cup mayonnaise
3 tablespoons milk

Combine ground beef, ½ teaspoon salt, pepper, and catsup in a bowl; mix well. Shape into 4 patties, and place on a broiler rack. Make a well in center of each patty, leaving ½-inch sides.

Sauté onion, green pepper, and garlic in butter until tender. Remove from heat; add ¼ teaspoon salt, bread, mayonnaise, and milk, stirring well. Spoon mixture into well of each patty. Bake at 350° for 30 to 35 minutes. Yield: 4 servings. *Mrs. Otis Jones,*
Bude, Mississippi.

MEXICALI BEEF PATTIES

2 medium onions
2 medium-size green peppers
2 pounds ground beef
1 (8-ounce) can whole tomatoes, drained and chopped
1 egg, beaten
½ cup crushed corn flakes
1 teaspoon salt
½ teaspoon dried whole oregano
½ teaspoon chili powder
4 (1-ounce) slices Cheddar cheese, cut diagonally in half

Cut four ¼-inch-thick slices from center of each onion and green pepper. Set slices aside.

Dice remainder of onion and green pepper. Combine diced onion, diced green pepper, ground beef, tomatoes, egg, corn flakes, salt, oregano, and chili powder in a large bowl; mix well. Shape meat into 8 patties, and place on a broiler rack. Bake at 350° for 20 minutes, turning once. Top each meat pattie with onion slice, green pepper ring, and cheese; bake an additional 5 minutes. Serve immediately. Yield: 8 servings.

Erma P. Ferdinard,
Houston, Texas.

BEEFBURGERS HAWAIIAN

¼ cup soy sauce
2 tablespoons catsup
1 tablespoon cider vinegar
2 cloves garlic, minced
¼ teaspoon pepper
1½ pounds ground beef
1 (8-ounce) can crushed pineapple, drained
⅛ teaspoon salt
¼ teaspoon pepper
6 slices bacon

Combine soy sauce, catsup, vinegar, garlic, and ¼ teaspoon pepper in a small mixing bowl; blend well. Set mixture aside.

Combine ground beef, pineapple, salt, and ¼ teaspoon pepper in a bowl. Shape into 6 patties. Wrap bacon around edge of each patty, and secure with a wooden pick. Place patties in a shallow 2-quart dish. Pour soy sauce mixture over patties; cover and marinate in refrigerator 30 minutes.

Place patties on broiler rack; spoon marinade over meat. Broil 5 inches from heat 12 minutes, turning once. Remove picks. Yield: 6 servings.

Carolyn Brantley,
Greenville, Mississippi.

APPLE BURGERS

¾ pound ground beef
⅓ cup seasoned dry breadcrumbs
¼ cup unsweetened applesauce
2 tablespoons diced onion
2 tablespoons catsup
⅛ teaspoon salt
⅛ teaspoon pepper
⅛ teaspoon garlic powder
⅛ teaspoon dried whole thyme
1 small apple, unpeeled and thinly sliced

Combine all ingredients except apple slices in a bowl; mix well. Shape into 4 patties about ½ inch thick. Place patties on a broiler rack. Broil 4 or 5 inches from heat 7 minutes, turning once. Top with apple slices; broil an additional 2 to 3 minutes. Yield: 4 servings.

Elnora Broady,
Fayetteville, North Carolina.

ITALIAN MEAT ROLLS

1 pound ground beef
¼ teaspoon pepper
1 tablespoon Worcestershire sauce
1 tablespoon dry spaghetti sauce mix
1 tablespoon lemon juice
½ teaspoon lemon-pepper seasoning
¼ teaspoon onion powder
¼ teaspoon garlic powder
2 eggs, beaten
1 cup corn flake crumbs

Combine all ingredients except egg and corn flake crumbs in a bowl; mix well. Shape into 4 (4-inch-long) rolls. Dip each roll in egg; dredge in corn flake crumbs. Place on a broiler rack. Bake at 350° for 30 to 35 minutes or until done. Yield: 4 servings.

Pam Hidalgo,
Iberville, Louisiana.

Wake Up To Breakfast Breads

You'll look forward to getting out of bed each morning for one of these breakfast breads. Our doughnuts, waffles, and pancakes are great choices to help your day get off to a good start.

BANANA DOUGHNUTS

¼ cup shortening
1 cup sugar
3 eggs, beaten
¾ cup mashed ripe banana
½ cup buttermilk
1½ teaspoons vanilla extract
5 cups all-purpose flour
1 tablespoon plus 1 teaspoon baking powder
2 teaspoons salt
1 teaspoon baking soda
1 teaspoon ground nutmeg
Vegetable oil
Sifted powdered sugar

Cream shortening; gradually add sugar, beating well. Add eggs, and beat mixture well. Set aside.

Combine banana, buttermilk, and vanilla in a small bowl. Set aside.

Combine flour, baking powder, salt, soda, and nutmeg; add flour mixture to creamed mixture alternately with banana mixture, beginning and ending with flour mixture. Mix ingredients well after each addition.

Place dough on a lightly floured surface, and roll out to ½-inch thickness. Cut dough with a floured 2½-inch doughnut cutter.

Heat 3 to 4 inches of oil to 375°; drop in 3 to 4 doughnuts at a time. Cook about 1 minute on each side or until golden brown. Drain on paper towels. Toss doughnuts in powdered sugar; cool. Yield: 2½ dozen.

Mrs. Bronwen M. Gibson,
Dallas, Texas.

FLUFFY PANCAKES

1¼ cups all-purpose flour
1 tablespoon sugar
1½ teaspoons baking soda
1 teaspoon baking powder
½ teaspoon salt
1 egg, beaten
1 cup buttermilk
2 tablespoons butter or margarine, melted

Combine flour, sugar, soda, baking powder, and salt. Combine egg, buttermilk, and butter; slowly stir into dry ingredients. (Pancake batter will be very thick.)

For each pancake, spoon about ¼ cup batter onto a hot, lightly greased griddle. Turn pancakes when tops are covered with bubbles and edges are brown. Serve pancakes with syrup. Yield: 10 (4-inch) pancakes.

Sallie Speights,
Lafayette, Louisiana.

FRENCH WAFFLES

1½ cups all-purpose flour
1 tablespoon baking powder
½ teaspoon salt
3 eggs, separated
1½ cups milk
⅓ cup butter or margarine, melted
1 tablespoon sugar
Vegetable cooking spray

Combine flour, baking powder, and salt in a medium mixing bowl. Combine egg yolks, milk, and melted butter; add to dry ingredients, stirring until mixture is smooth.

Beat egg whites (at room temperature) with sugar until stiff peaks form. Gently fold into flour mixture.

Coat an 8-inch square waffle iron with vegetable cooking spray; allow to preheat. Pour about 1 cup batter onto hot waffle iron. Bake 5 minutes or until steaming stops. Repeat procedure until all batter is used. Yield: 16 (4-inch) waffles.
Pankey Kite,
Macon, Georgia.

SOFT-AS-A-CLOUD SOUR CREAM BISCUITS

1 cup all-purpose flour
2 teaspoons baking powder
1 teaspoon sugar
¼ teaspoon baking soda
¼ teaspoon salt
½ cup commercial sour cream
¼ cup half-and-half

Combine flour, baking powder, sugar, soda, and salt; stir well. Combine sour cream and half-and-half; add to flour mixture, stirring with a fork until dry ingredients are moistened. Turn dough out onto a lightly floured surface, and knead lightly 4 or 5 times.

Roll dough to ½-inch thickness, and cut with a floured 2-inch biscuit cutter. Place biscuits on an ungreased baking sheet; bake at 425° for 8 to 10 minutes. Yield: 10 biscuits.
Mrs. A. L. Farber,
Marietta, Georgia.

Tip: Leftover thin pancakes can be spread with jelly or jam, rolled up, and frozen; reheat in oven and sprinkle with powdered sugar for dessert. Or spread them with a soft cheese or meat filling and serve with a sauce or gravy.

BABA AU ORANGE

1 (13¾-ounce) package hot roll mix
⅓ cup sugar
1 cup hot water
¼ cup plus 2 tablespoons butter or margarine, softened
2 eggs, beaten
1 (6-ounce) can frozen orange juice concentrate, thawed and undiluted
1 cup sugar
1 cup water
Toasted sliced almonds (optional)

Combine hot roll mix, ⅓ cup sugar, and 1 cup hot water in a large bowl. Stir in butter and eggs. Cover and let rise in a warm place (85°), free from drafts, about 1 hour or until doubled in bulk. (Batter will be very soft.)

Stir dough down; spoon evenly into a well-greased, 6½-cup, ovenproof ring mold. Cover with greased waxed paper, and let rise in a warm place (85°), free from drafts, 30 to 45 minutes or until doubled in bulk. (Dough will rise to the top of the pan.)

Bake at 400° for 30 minutes or until loaf sounds hollow when tapped. (If necessary, cover bread with foil the last 10 minutes. This will help to prevent the top from over browning.)

Combine orange juice concentrate, 1 cup sugar, and 1 cup water in a small saucepan. Bring mixture to a boil; reduce heat, and simmer, stirring constantly, until sugar dissolves.

Remove bread from pan, and place on a large platter; spoon hot orange syrup over bread. Let sit until most of syrup is absorbed. Garnish with almonds, if desired. Serve cool. Yield: 10 to 12 servings.
Mrs. Philip Davis,
Drexel, North Carolina.

Sweet Endings With Bananas

You've enjoyed bananas in fruit salads and moist breads before, and with these recipes bananas will become a favorite ingredient for dessert, too.

Chocolate cake is always a treat—but try our Chocolate-Banana Cake. For the fruitiest flavor, use ripe bananas for this recipe; they will mash easier than firm ones. Three medium bananas will equal 1 cup of mashed fruit.

In desserts such as Bananas Foster or banana pudding, it's best to use slightly underripe fruit.

It's a good idea to keep bananas at room temperature until you're ready to use them. You can stop the ripening process by refrigerating the fruit; the skins of the bananas will turn dark brown, but the fruit will keep its texture, firmness, and flavor.

CHOCOLATE-BANANA CAKE

2 (1-ounce) squares unsweetened chocolate
1 cup butter or margarine, softened
2¾ cups sugar
3 eggs
3 cups all-purpose flour
2 teaspoons baking powder
¼ teaspoon baking soda
¼ teaspoon salt
1 cup mashed banana
⅔ cup buttermilk
1 tablespoon vanilla extract
1 cup chopped pecans
Chocolate frosting (recipe follows)

Place chocolate in top of a double boiler; bring water to a boil. Reduce heat to low; cook until chocolate melts. Set aside to cool.

Cream butter; gradually add sugar, beating well with an electric mixer. Add eggs, one at a time, beating well after each addition.

Combine flour, baking powder, soda, and salt; add to creamed mixture alternately with banana, buttermilk, and melted chocolate, beginning and ending with flour mixture. Mix well after each addition. Stir in vanilla and pecans.

Spoon batter into 3 greased and floured 9-inch round cakepans. Bake at 350° for 30 minutes or until a wooden pick inserted in center comes out clean. Cool in pans 10 minutes; remove layers from pans, and let cool completely. Spread chocolate frosting between layers and on top and sides of cake. Yield: one 3-layer cake.

Chocolate Frosting:

⅓ cup butter or margarine, softened
5 cups sifted powdered sugar
⅓ cup cocoa
¼ teaspoon salt
½ cup to ½ cup plus 1 tablespoon evaporated milk

Combine butter, sugar, cocoa, and salt in a large mixing bowl; beat at low speed of an electric mixer. Gradually add milk until frosting reaches desired spreading consistency; beat until smooth. Yield: enough frosting for one 9-inch, 3-layer cake.
Mrs. J. O. Branson,
Thomasville, North Carolina.

BANANA-MALLOW PUDDING

1 (3⅛-ounce) package regular vanilla
    pudding mix
3½ cups milk, divided
2 cups miniature marshmallows, divided
1 (8-ounce) carton frozen whipped
    topping, thawed and divided
1 (12-ounce) package vanilla wafers
4 medium bananas, sliced
1 (3⅜-ounce) package instant vanilla
    pudding mix
Crushed vanilla wafers

Combine regular pudding mix and 2 cups milk in a small saucepan. Cook according to package directions. Add 1½ cups marshmallows; blend until marshmallows are melted. Add half of whipped topping.

Layer one-third of vanilla wafers in the bottom of a 3-quart bowl. Top with one-third of banana slices and half of pudding mixture. Repeat layers once. Top with remaining vanilla wafers and banana slices.

Combine instant pudding mix and remaining 1½ cups milk in a large mixing bowl; mix according to package directions. Stir in remaining ½ cup marshmallows and whipped topping. Pour over bananas. Garnish with crushed vanilla wafers. Yield: 10 servings.

Mary K. Quesenberry,
Dugspur, Virginia.

BANANAS FOSTER

4 bananas
1 tablespoon lemon juice
½ cup firmly packed brown sugar
¼ cup butter or margarine
Dash of ground cinnamon
⅓ cup light rum
Coffee or vanilla ice cream

Cut bananas in half lengthwise, and toss in lemon juice; set aside.

Combine brown sugar and butter in a large skillet; cook over low heat 2 minutes, stirring constantly until sugar melts. Add bananas; stir gently, and cook 1 to 2 minutes or until thoroughly heated. Remove from heat; sprinkle with cinnamon.

Place rum in a small, long-handled saucepan; heat just until warm. (Do not boil.) Remove from heat. Ignite rum with a long match, and pour over banana mixture. Let flames die down. Serve immediately over ice cream. Yield: 4 servings.

Louise E. Ellis,
Talbott, Tennessee.

MICROWAVE COOKERY

One-Serving Entrées In Minutes

If you feel it's not worth the effort to cook when you're eating alone, take a look at these recipes before you pull out the sandwich fixings.

Because microwave cooking time is increased when you add extra meat, you'll find our recipes particularly quick as each one is portioned for a single serving. If you decide to double the recipe, just remember to increase the cooking times at each stage of preparation to account for the extra food.

You can prepare our recipe for Orange Chicken in as little time as it takes to make a sandwich and less time than it takes to heat up a frozen dinner. Cooking time is only 5½ minutes. Chicken cooks quickly when the breast halves are pounded to a thin, even thickness. To save time and money, you can buy packages of boneless breast halves (or bone them yourself) and flatten each one. Then package them for the freezer, placing waxed paper between each piece. It will be easy to use only one at a time.

Pork chops are easy to prepare for one serving—see our recipe for Saucy Pork Chop. It takes at least 45 minutes to an hour to cook chops conventionally, so you'll save at least half the time by cooking one in the microwave. Because meat tends to toughen when cooked in the microwave, we used extra sauce and low power in this recipe for tender, moist results.

BEEF-STUFFED ZUCCHINI

1 medium zucchini
¼ pound ground beef
1 tablespoon chopped onion
1 tablespoon minced green pepper
3 tablespoons tomato sauce
2 tablespoons Parmesan cheese, divided
Dash of garlic powder
Dash of salt

Wash zucchini, and cut in half lengthwise. Scoop out pulp, leaving a ¼-inch shell. Chop pulp, and set aside.

Place ground beef, onion, and green pepper in a small casserole. Cover and microwave at HIGH for 1 to 2 minutes, stirring once, until beef is browned.

Drain. Add zucchini pulp, tomato sauce, 1 tablespoon Parmesan cheese, garlic powder, and salt to ground beef mixture. Place half of beef mixture in each zucchini shell; sprinkle top of mixture with remaining 1 tablespoon Parmesan cheese.

Place stuffed zucchini on a microwave roasting rack; cover tightly with heavy-duty plastic wrap. Microwave at HIGH for 1½ minutes. Give dish a half-turn, and microwave at HIGH for 1½ to 3½ minutes or until filling is set and zucchini is fork-tender. Serve immediately. Yield: 1 serving.

VEAL AND CARROTS IN WINE SAUCE

1 (4-ounce) veal cutlet
1 tablespoon all-purpose flour
⅛ teaspoon salt
⅛ teaspoon pepper
¼ teaspoon dried whole marjoram
Dash of garlic powder
¼ teaspoon dried parsley flakes
2 teaspoons butter or margarine
1 large carrot, scraped and thinly cut into
    diagonal slices
2 tablespoons lemon juice
2 tablespoons dry white wine

Remove and discard any excess fat from cutlet. Place cutlet between 2 sheets of waxed paper, and flatten to ⅛-inch thickness using a meat mallet or rolling pin.

Combine flour and seasonings; mix well. Dredge veal cutlet in flour mixture. Set aside.

Place butter in an 8-inch square baking dish. Microwave at HIGH for 35 seconds or until melted. Place cutlet in baking dish, cover tightly with heavy-duty plastic wrap, and microwave at HIGH for 1 minute. Turn cutlet over; add carrot, lemon juice, and wine; cover and microwave at MEDIUM (50% power) for 2½ to 3 minutes. Give dish a half-turn; cover and microwave at MEDIUM for an additional 2½ to 3 minutes or until veal is tender and carrot is crisp-tender. Yield: 1 serving.

SAUCY PORK CHOP

1 teaspoon butter or margarine
¼ cup sliced fresh mushrooms
1 tablespoon chopped onion
1 tablespoon chopped green pepper
1 small tomato, peeled and finely chopped
¼ cup water
½ teaspoon lemon juice
⅛ teaspoon garlic powder
⅛ teaspoon ground oregano
⅛ teaspoon dried whole thyme
⅛ teaspoon salt
⅛ teaspoon pepper
1 (½- to ¾-inch) pork chop
Hot cooked rice
Green pepper ring (optional)

Place butter in a shallow 1-quart casserole dish. Microwave at HIGH for 20 seconds or until melted. Add mushrooms, onion, and green pepper; cover and microwave at HIGH for 2 to 3 minutes or until vegetables are tender, stirring once. Stir in tomato, water, lemon juice, and seasonings. Place pork chop over mixture, and spoon a small amount of vegetable mixture over pork chop. Cover and microwave at MEDIUM (50% power) for 8 to 10 minutes; turn pork chop over. Cover and continue to microwave at MEDIUM for 5 to 10 minutes or until meat next to bone loses pink color.

Serve pork chop over rice, and garnish with green pepper ring, if desired. Yield: 1 serving.

ORANGE CHICKEN

1 boneless chicken breast half
3 tablespoons orange juice
¼ teaspoon chicken-flavored bouillon granules
Dash of salt
Dash of white pepper
2 tablespoons chopped green onions
1 orange, peeled and sectioned
Hot cooked rice

Place chicken between two sheets of waxed paper, and flatten to ¼-inch thickness using a meat mallet or rolling pin; set aside. Microwave orange juice in a shallow 1-quart casserole at HIGH for 1 minute; add bouillon granules, stirring until dissolved.

Sprinkle chicken with salt and pepper. Add chicken and green onions to bouillon; cover and microwave at MEDIUM (50% power) for 2 to 4 minutes or until chicken is tender, turning chicken over and giving dish a half-turn after 1 minute. Add orange; cover and microwave at HIGH for 30 seconds. Serve over rice. Yield: 1 serving.

Rosy Rhubarb Favorites

As rhubarb makes its way into the grocery store, be ready to take advantage of the tart, rosy vegetable with one of our tasty recipes.

Choose rhubarb that is firm and crisp. Young stalks will be the most tender. Avoid those that are wilted or flabby. Dark-red stalks with many leaves indicate a very tart flavor; bright-pink stalks with few small leaves are less acidic and will have a milder flavor. Be sure to keep these color differences in mind when adding sugar.

To store rhubarb, remove and discard leaves. Wash stalks, pat dry with a paper towel, and store in a plastic bag in the refrigerator.

RHUBARB CONGEALED SALAD

1 cup chopped rhubarb
¾ cup water
1 (3-ounce) package strawberry-flavored gelatin
½ cup sugar
1 cup pineapple juice
1 cup chopped unpeeled apple
½ cup chopped pecans
Lettuce leaves

Combine rhubarb and water in a saucepan; cover and cook 8 to 10 minutes or until tender. Remove from heat; add gelatin and sugar, stirring until dissolved. Add juice; chill until consistency of unbeaten egg white. Fold in apple and pecans. Spoon into a lightly oiled 4-cup mold; chill until firm. Serve on lettuce. Yield: 6 servings.

Catherine Bearden,
Bostwick, Georgia.

RHUBARB-STRAWBERRY BAVARIAN

3 cups coarsely chopped rhubarb
1 cup orange juice
1 (3-ounce) package strawberry-flavored gelatin
½ cup whipping cream
3 tablespoons sugar
Orange peel (optional)

Combine rhubarb and orange juice in a saucepan; cover and cook over medium heat 8 to 10 minutes or until crisp-tender. Remove from heat; add gelatin,

stirring until gelatin dissolves. Set aside to cool.

Beat whipping cream until foamy; gradually add sugar, beating until soft peaks form. Fold into gelatin mixture, and spoon into dessert dishes; chill until firm. Garnish with orange peel, if desired. Yield: 6 to 8 servings.

Mrs. Clayton Turner,
De Funiak Springs, Florida.

RHUBARB-PEACH PIE

Pastry for double-crust 9-inch pie
1 (8½-ounce) can sliced peaches, undrained
2 cups sliced rhubarb
¼ cup flaked coconut
1¼ cups sugar
3 tablespoons tapioca
1 teaspoon vanilla extract
3 tablespoons butter or margarine

Line a 9-inch pieplate with half of pastry; set aside.

Drain and chop peaches, reserving juice. Combine peaches, rhubarb, coconut, sugar, and tapioca; mix well. Add reserved peach juice and vanilla. Spoon into prepared pastry shell; dot with butter. Place remaining pastry over rhubarb mixture, sealing edges. Cut slits in pastry. Bake at 325° for 45 to 50 minutes or until golden brown. Yield: one 9-inch pie. *Mrs. Wilcie Leonharat,*
Virginia Beach, Virginia.

From Our Kitchen To Yours

The variety of fresh vegetables now available is increasing along with our consumption. You can gain nutritional value through the right selection, storage, and preparation of fresh vegetables. Here are some hints.

—While their calorie content is low, most fresh vegetables rate high nutritionally. Besides being high in vitamin A and vitamin C, some vegetables are also a good source of calcium, iron, potassium, folic acid, and fiber. Color can be a guide for judging nutritional value of vegetables—usually the darker and brighter, the better. Pale carrots, for example, are not as nutritious as bright orange carrots.

—When fresh vegetables are compared with processed types, high-quality fresh vegetables rate first nutritionally; frozen are second in rank, and canned, last. Sometimes, however, processing causes only a slight loss in nutrients. And if produce has been allowed to sit unrefrigerated or become bruised, vitamin levels will decrease substantially. When handled and stored properly, fresh vegetables are better than processed ones in taste and texture.

—Canned vegetables are often higher in salt content. For reduced-sodium variations, the cost may be higher.

—Most of us rely on supermarkets for fresh produce, but you may find better prices at a roadside stand or farmers' market. If you're unsure of where the closest market is, contact your local co-operative Extension office.

—The best way to save money on fresh vegetables is to buy them when they're in season. When a certain vegetable is popular and hard to find, which is often at the beginning of the season, the price tends to be higher.

—Because young, small vegetables are usually tastier and more tender, you shouldn't have to chop or peel them before cooking. Chopping and peeling exposes more surface area, and as a result, more nutrients will be lost. If chopping is necessary, such as for use in casseroles, wait until the last minute. Cut vegetables into uniform pieces so that they will cook evenly. Cut vegetables lose nutritional value if soaked too long. Nutrients are better retained by cooking vegetables with their jackets or peels. Then, if desired, you may peel vegetables after cooking them.

—Most fresh vegetables should be kept refrigerated or stored in a cool spot, out of direct light and away from air, to maintain quality and nutritional value. Onions and potatoes don't need refrigeration—just a cool, dark place, free of moisture. Buy an abundance of vegetables only if you plan to can or freeze. As storage time is lengthened, nutrients are lost.

—Fresh vegetables need to be washed before cooking to remove any dirt and insects. It's best to scrub hard-surfaced vegetables, such as potatoes and turnips, with a vegetable brush.

—Cooked vegetables need to be served immediately. Leftovers that are not used within two or three days may lose half their vitamin C content.

—If you choose to add an acid, such as vinegar or lemon juice, to fresh vegetables, it should be done after the vegetable is cooked. This will help prevent toughness.

—Adding baking powder to a fresh green vegetable when cooking can alter the quality of the finished product. You'll have a bright-green product, but it may be softer and contain less thiamine and vitamin C.

Pistachios For More Than Nibbling

Long favored as a snack to nibble on, pistachios have found their way into all types of recipes. They dress up everything from pasta salad to muffins.

There's practically no end to the ways you can use pistachios, because they can be substituted in recipes calling for almost any type of nut.

Pistachios were originally dyed red to mask stains that they got from sitting in their natural skins too long in processing. Today processing is done so quickly that the nuts no longer get stained, and so don't have to be dyed. Many consumers still prefer the familiar red color, however, so pistachios are marketed in both red and natural tan colors. Use tan ones in recipes, because dye from red ones may alter the color of some ingredients.

PISTACHIO-PASTA SALAD

1¾ cups uncooked corkscrew macaroni
Oregano Dressing
2½ ounces (1 cup) fresh snow peas
2 cups torn fresh spinach
1 cup chopped fresh tomato
⅓ cup chopped pistachios
1 tablespoon grated Parmesan cheese

Cook macaroni according to package directions; drain well. Pour Oregano Dressing over hot macaroni, stirring gently; let macaroni cool. Place snow peas in a wire basket; dip in boiling water about 10 seconds. Drain. Add snow peas, spinach, and tomato to macaroni, tossing gently. Sprinkle with pistachios and cheese; cover and chill at least 2 hours, stirring occasionally. Yield: 6 servings.

Oregano Dressing:

¼ cup red wine vinegar
¼ cup olive oil
¾ teaspoon dried whole oregano
⅛ teaspoon garlic powder
⅛ teaspoon freshly ground pepper

Combine all ingredients in a jar. Cover tightly, and shake vigorously. Yield: ½ cup.

PISTACHIO-STUFFED MUSHROOMS

20 medium-size fresh mushrooms
3 tablespoons minced onion
¼ cup butter or margarine, melted
⅓ cup fine dry breadcrumbs
¼ cup chopped pistachios
2 tablespoons diced pimiento, drained
¼ teaspoon dried whole thyme
⅛ teaspoon salt
2 tablespoons butter or margarine, melted

Clean mushrooms with damp paper towels. Remove and chop stems; set caps aside.

Sauté mushroom stems and onion in ¼ cup butter until tender; stir in remaining ingredients except butter. Spoon mixture into mushroom caps, and place in a lightly greased 11- x 7- x 2-inch baking pan. Drizzle 2 tablespoons butter over top; bake stuffed mushrooms at 350° for 10 minutes. Yield: 20 appetizer servings.

NUTTY MUFFINS

2 cups all-purpose flour
¾ cup sugar
2 teaspoons baking powder
½ teaspoon baking soda
½ teaspoon ground cinnamon
¼ teaspoon salt
1 cup buttermilk
1 egg, beaten
2 tablespoons vegetable oil
¾ cup coarsely chopped pistachios, toasted
½ cup raisins

Combine flour, sugar, baking powder, soda, cinnamon, and salt in a medium bowl; make a well in center of mixture.

Combine buttermilk, egg, and oil; add to dry ingredients, stirring just until moistened. Stir in pistachios and raisins. Spoon into greased muffin pans, filling three-fourths full. Bake at 400° for 20 minutes. Yield: about 17 muffins.

Cooking With Alcohol Is His Specialty

Curt Treloar, of Largo, Florida, has dreams of opening a restaurant someday, and no wonder. He's an excellent cook who has a number of special dishes to his credit.

Curt often uses wine, liquor, and liqueurs in his recipes. His favorites are brandy and a medium-dry white wine. "The key to cooking with alcohol is to make sure it's flambéed or something so it doesn't overpower the dish, but you still have the flavor," he explains as he shares some of his best recipes.

Curt's Veal Amelio is a perfect example of how wine can complement even a very mild-flavored meat when the alcohol has evaporated. But in his Grand Marnier Dip and Decadent Chocolate Cake, he shows us that there's a place for uncooked alcohol in food, especially when it comes to desserts.

VEAL AMELIO

1 pound veal cutlets
½ cup all-purpose flour
¼ teaspoon salt
¼ teaspoon pepper
⅓ cup butter or margarine, softened
1 tablespoon olive oil
¼ cup Chablis or other dry white wine
1½ teaspoons lemon juice
¾ cup sliced mushrooms
⅓ cup chopped green onions with tops
1 tablespoon capers, drained
Steamed green beans (optional)
Steamed yellow squash (optional)

Place veal on waxed paper, and flatten to ⅛-inch thickness using a meat mallet or rolling pin. Combine flour, salt, and pepper; dredge veal in flour mixture.

Heat butter and oil in a large skillet over medium-high heat. Add veal, several pieces at a time, and cook 2 minutes on each side; do not brown. Remove veal to a platter; keep warm. Repeat with remaining veal.

Add wine, lemon juice, mushrooms, and green onions to drippings in skillet. Cook over medium heat, stirring frequently, 5 minutes. Add capers, and cook until thoroughly heated. Pour mushroom sauce over veal. Serve with steamed green beans and yellow squash, if desired. Yield: 4 servings.

SMOKED CORNISH HENS

4 (1½-pound) Cornish hens
2 teaspoons Greek seasoning
4 slices bacon, cut in half
2 (12-ounce) cans beer
8 to 10 cups orange juice
Orange Liqueur Sauce
Dirty Rice
Orange slices (optional)
Parsley (optional)

Remove giblets from hens, and reserve for other uses. Rinse hens with cold water; pat dry. Lift wing tips over back; tuck under hen.

Sprinkle each hen with ½ teaspoon Greek seasoning. Lay 2 slices bacon to form an X across breast of hen.

Prepare charcoal fire in commercial meat smoker; let fire burn 15 to 20 minutes. Soak mesquite chips in water 15 minutes, and place chips on coals. Place water pan in smoker; fill pan with beer and orange juice.

Place hens on rack. Insert meat thermometer in breast so it doesn't touch bone or fat. Cover with smoker lid; cook 5 to 6 hours or until meat thermometer registers 185°. Refill water pan with orange juice, and add additional charcoal as needed.

Remove hens to serving platter; spoon Orange Liqueur Sauce over hens. Surround with Dirty Rice. Garnish with orange slices and parsley, if desired. Yield: 4 servings.
Note: An electric meat smoker cooks faster. Consult manufacturer's brochure for best results.

Orange Liqueur Sauce:

1 medium onion, chopped
1 clove garlic, minced
½ cup butter or margarine, melted
½ cup honey
⅔ cup orange liqueur
2 tablespoons lemon juice
1 tablespoon Worcestershire sauce
1 teaspoon ground ginger
½ teaspoon ground allspice
2 tablespoons cornstarch
½ cup orange juice

Sauté onion and garlic in butter in a saucepan. Add honey and next 5 ingredients, stirring well. Bring to a boil.

Dissolve cornstarch in orange juice. Add to onion mixture. Bring to a boil, and cook 1 minute, stirring constantly; remove from heat. Yield: 2½ cups.

Dirty Rice:

5 slices bacon
1 medium onion, chopped
1 (6-ounce) package long grain and wild rice
½ cup pecans, chopped

Cook bacon in skillet until crisp; remove bacon, crumble, and set aside. Sauté onion in drippings until tender.

Prepare rice according to package directions; cook 10 minutes. Stir in crumbled bacon, onion, and pecans. Cook an additional 15 minutes or until rice is done. Yield: 4 servings.

GRAND MARNIER DIP

3 egg yolks
¼ cup plus 2 tablespoons sugar
¼ teaspoon salt
¼ cup Grand Marnier
2 cups whipping cream

Combine egg yolks, sugar, and salt in a small saucepan; mix well. Cook over medium heat, stirring constantly, 2 or 3 minutes or until sugar dissolves. Remove from heat; stir in Grand Marnier. Let cool.

Beat whipping cream until stiff peaks form; fold into Grand Marnier mixture. Cover and chill 1 to 2 hours; serve with assorted fresh fruits. Yield: 2½ cups.

DECADENT CHOCOLATE CAKE

1 (18.5-ounce) package chocolate cake mix with pudding
1 (12-ounce) package semisweet chocolate morsels, divided
½ cup apricot brandy
½ cup apricot preserves
¾ cup commercial sour cream
½ cup chopped pecans

Prepare cake mix according to package directions, stirring in 1 cup chocolate morsels. Pour batter into 2 greased and floured 9-inch round cakepans. Bake at 350° for 30 minutes or until a wooden pick inserted in center comes out clean. Cool in pans 10 minutes; remove layers from pans, and let cool completely. Brush brandy over layers; allow to stand until brandy is absorbed. Spread preserves between cake layers.

Place remaining morsels in top of a double boiler; bring water to a boil. Reduce heat to low; cook until chocolate melts. Remove from heat; stir in sour cream, blending well. Spread on cake. Top with pecans; cover. Chill overnight. Yield: one 9-inch cake.

Tip: When a recipe calls for a "greased pan," grease the pan with solid shortening or an oil unless specified.

An Italian Feast Without All The Calories

Italian food is not just lasagna and spaghetti. And it doesn't have to be fattening if it's prepared the "Cooking Light" way. We've got some not-so-well-known Italian dishes (seasoned with a light Southern hand) to help dispel the myth that Italian fare isn't for dieters.

The skillful blend of quality ingredients plays an important part in good food. Our Cannelloni Crêpes are delicious. But the best part is that you can enjoy two of these crêpes as a serving for only 270 calories. Limiting fat and using skim milk instead of whole milk in the sauce are two ways we kept the calories low. But another calorie-saving attraction is the substitution of Light Crêpes (48 calories per crêpe) for the cannelloni pasta (70 calories per tube).

Minestrone Soup illustrates the Italian love of vegetables. And our recipe is brimming with eight vegetables, herbs, and pasta. We used whole wheat macaroni shells for added dietary fiber. If you can't find the plum tomatoes and cannellini beans, use regular tomatoes and white navy beans instead.

CANNELLONI CRÊPES

½ pound ground chuck
¼ cup chopped onion
¼ cup chopped celery
¼ cup shredded carrot
1 small clove garlic, minced
½ (10-ounce) package frozen chopped spinach, thawed and drained
2 tablespoons dry Italian white wine
2 tablespoons grated Parmesan cheese
1 egg, beaten
½ teaspoon dried whole basil
¼ teaspoon dried whole oregano
¼ teaspoon salt
Light Crêpes
Vegetable cooking spray
½ cup skim milk
2 tablespoons all-purpose flour
½ cup water
½ teaspoon chicken-flavored bouillon granules
⅛ teaspoon salt
Dash of white pepper
½ cup (2 ounces) shredded mozzarella cheese
Chopped fresh parsley (optional)

Combine meat, onion, celery, carrot, and garlic in a skillet; cook over medium heat until meat is browned, stirring to crumble beef. Drain mixture in a colander, and pat dry with paper towels. Wipe pan drippings from skillet; return beef mixture to skillet.

Press spinach between paper towels to remove excess liquid. Add spinach, Italian white wine, Parmesan cheese, egg, basil, oregano, and salt to meat mixture; stir well.

Spoon 3 tablespoons meat mixture down the center of each crêpe; fold sides over, and place seam side up in a 13- x 9- x 2-inch baking dish coated with cooking spray. Set aside.

Combine milk and flour in a small saucepan, stirring until smooth. Add water, bouillon granules, salt, and white pepper. Cook over medium heat, stirring constantly, until sauce thickens and comes to a boil. Pour sauce over crêpes. Cover and bake at 375° for 20 minutes. Sprinkle with mozzarella cheese; bake, uncovered, an additional 5 minutes. Garnish with parsley, if desired. Yield: 5 servings (about 270 calories per 2 crêpes).

Light Crêpes:

1 egg
¾ cup skim milk
⅔ cup all-purpose flour
¼ teaspoon salt
1 teaspoon vegetable oil
Vegetable cooking spray

Combine egg, milk, flour, salt, and oil in container of an electric blender; process 30 seconds. Scrape down sides of blender container with rubber spatula; process an additional 30 seconds. Refrigerate batter 1 hour.

Coat bottom of a 6-inch crêpe pan or nonstick skillet with cooking spray; place pan over medium heat until just hot, not smoking.

Pour 2 tablespoons batter into pan. Quickly tilt pan in all directions so batter covers pan in a thin film; cook about 1 minute.

Lift edge of crêpe to test for doneness. Crêpe is ready for flipping when it can be shaken loose from pan. Flip the crêpe, and cook 30 seconds on other side. (This side is usually spotty brown and is the side on which the filling is placed.)

When crêpe is done, place on a towel to cool. Stack between layers of waxed paper to prevent sticking. Repeat until all batter is used, stirring batter occasionally. Yield: 10 (6-inch) crêpes.

Lisa Bailey,
Gulf Breeze, Florida.

TUNA-AND-CANNELLINI BEAN SALAD

1 (15-ounce) can cannellini beans, drained and rinsed
1 (6½-ounce) can solid white tuna in water, drained
¼ cup sliced purple onion
2 tablespoons olive oil
2 tablespoons red wine vinegar
1 teaspoon chopped fresh parsley
1 teaspoon chopped fresh basil
1 teaspoon capers, drained
¼ teaspoon freshly ground pepper
3 leaf lettuce leaves
1 small tomato, cut into wedges

Combine beans, tuna, and onion in a medium bowl; set aside.

Combine oil, vinegar, parsley, basil, capers, and pepper in a jar. Cover tightly, and shake vigorously. Pour over bean mixture, and toss well. Chill. Serve on lettuce leaves. Garnish with tomato wedges. Yield: 3 servings (about 232 calories per 1-cup serving).

VERMICELLI AND SPROUTS WITH RED CLAM SAUCE

Vegetable cooking spray
½ teaspoon olive oil
1 clove garlic, minced
2 (6½-ounce) cans chopped clams, undrained
1 (8-ounce) can tomato sauce
2 tablespoons chopped fresh parsley
1 tablespoon chopped onion
1 tablespoon grated Parmesan cheese
½ teaspoon dried whole basil
½ teaspoon dried whole oregano
⅛ teaspoon freshly ground pepper
Dash of red pepper
1 cup hot cooked vermicelli
1 cup bean sprouts
1 tablespoon grated Parmesan cheese

Coat a skillet with cooking spray; add olive oil, and place over medium-high heat until hot. Add garlic, and sauté 2 minutes. Drain clams, reserving juice from 1 can. Add reserved juice to garlic; set clams aside. Add tomato sauce, parsley, onion, 1 tablespoon Parmesan cheese, and seasonings to skillet. Simmer, uncovered, 30 minutes. Stir in clams, and cook until clam sauce is thoroughly heated.

Combine hot vermicelli and bean sprouts; toss well. Pour clam sauce over pasta and sprouts. Sprinkle with 1 tablespoon Parmesan cheese. Yield: 2 servings (about 161 calories per ½ cup sauce and 112 calories per 1 cup vermicelli-sprout mixture).

MINESTRONE SOUP

Vegetable cooking spray
1 teaspoon olive oil
½ cup chopped onion
2 cloves garlic, minced
8 cups water
1 (14-ounce) can whole plum tomatoes,
    drained and chopped
½ (10-ounce) package frozen chopped
    spinach, thawed and drained
1 cup sliced carrots
1 cup coarsely chopped zucchini
¾ cup cubed potato
½ cup sliced celery
1 tablespoon plus 1 teaspoon
    chicken-flavored bouillon granules
1 bay leaf
1 teaspoon dried whole basil
1 teaspoon dried whole oregano
½ teaspoon freshly ground pepper
½ cup whole wheat pasta shells, uncooked
1 (15-ounce) can cannellini beans, drained

Coat a Dutch oven with cooking spray; add olive oil, and place over medium-high heat until hot. Add onion and garlic, and sauté 3 minutes. Add water, tomatoes, spinach, carrots, zucchini, potato, celery, bouillon granules, bay leaf, and seasonings; bring to a boil. Reduce heat and simmer, uncovered, 10 to 15 minutes.

Add pasta shells and beans to mixture; cook over medium heat 8 to 10 minutes or until pasta is done. Remove bay leaf. Yield: 11 cups (about 66 calories per 1-cup serving).

GREEN BEANS ITALIANO

1 pound fresh green beans
Vegetable cooking spray
1 teaspoon olive oil
1 medium-size green pepper, cut into
    strips
1 small onion, sliced and separated into
    rings
1 (14-ounce) can whole plum tomatoes,
    undrained and chopped
⅓ cup water
⅛ teaspoon freshly ground pepper
⅛ teaspoon dried whole oregano
1 tablespoon grated Parmesan cheese

Wash and trim beans; set aside.

Coat a skillet with cooking spray; add olive oil and place over medium-high heat until hot. Add green pepper and onion, and sauté until onion is tender. Add beans, tomatoes, water, pepper, and oregano. Cover and cook 30 minutes or until beans are tender. To serve, sprinkle with Parmesan cheese. Yield: 5 servings (about 71 calories per 1-cup serving).

WINE-POACHED PEARS WITH BERRY SAUCE

1 cup water
3 tablespoons lemon juice
6 medium-size firm, ripe pears
1½ cups dry Italian white wine
½ cup water
⅓ cup sugar
Rind of ½ lemon, cut into pieces
1 (3-inch) stick cinnamon
4 whole cloves
½ cup reduced-sugar strawberry spread
2½ teaspoons raspberry liqueur
Lemon rind curls (optional)

Combine 1 cup water and lemon juice; set aside. Peel pears, and cut a thin slice from bottoms so pears stand upright. Dip pears in lemon water, coating well.

Combine wine, ½ cup water, sugar, lemon rind, cinnamon stick, and cloves in a Dutch oven; cover and bring to a boil. Add pears; cover, reduce heat, and simmer 20 to 25 minutes or until pears are tender but still hold their shape. Let pears cool in wine mixture.

Combine strawberry spread and raspberry liqueur in a small saucepan. Cook over medium heat until strawberry spread melts and sauce is warm. (If sauce is too thin, let stand a few minutes to thicken slightly.) Drizzle sauce over pears. Garnish with lemon rind curls, if desired. Yield: 6 servings (about 114 calories per pear plus 17 calories per teaspoon sauce).

Papillote: It's Easier Than It Sounds

Papillote is the name given to a classic technique where food is cooked in parchment paper. Although the process sounds and looks dramatic, it's actually very simple. Parchment paper is cut, folded, and sealed to form a bag that allows food to steam in its own juices.

With our simple instructions, you can serve seafood or chicken papillote to raving reviews. Just imagine how impressed guests will be when parchment bags are taken from the oven and cut open at the table. The food may be removed from the bag or eaten right out of it.

Parchment paper should be available in kitchen specialty shops or art supply stores. If not, aluminum foil can be substituted and gives the same tasty results.

Step 1: *Cut parchment paper into 15- x 12-inch rectangles, and fold in half lengthwise. Trim each piece of paper into a large heart shape.*

FISH WITH SNOW PEAS EN PAPILLOTE

1 to 2 tablespoons vegetable oil
1 cup cherry tomatoes, cut into
    wedges
⅓ cup chopped green onions
2 tablespoons vegetable oil
2 tablespoons lemon juice
1 teaspoon dried whole oregano
½ pound fresh snow peas,
    trimmed
4 (4-ounce) orange roughy or
    grouper fillets
Salt
Freshly ground pepper

Cut four 15- x 12-inch pieces parchment paper or aluminum foil; fold in half lengthwise, creasing firmly. Trim each into a large heart shape. Place parchment hearts on baking sheets. Lightly brush one side of each heart with 1 to 2 tablespoons vegetable oil, leaving edges ungreased. Set aside.

Combine tomatoes, green onions, 2 tablespoons vegetable oil, lemon juice, and oregano; set aside.

Arrange snow peas attractively in a fan design on one greased half of each parchment heart, near the crease. Sprinkle fillets with salt and pepper; arrange fillets over snow peas. Spoon tomato mixture over fillets. Fold over remaining halves of hearts. Starting with rounded edge of each heart, pleat and crimp edges together to seal. Twist end tightly to seal.

Bake at 450° for 10 to 12 minutes or until bags are puffed and lightly browned and fish flakes easily when tested with a fork. Yield: 4 servings.

Step 2: *Place parchment hearts on baking sheets; brush inside surface with oil, leaving edges ungreased. Arrange food near the crease to the right.*

Step 3: *Fold and seal heart, beginning at rounded end. Keep edges together; crease firmly, leaving space for puffing. Twist tip end tightly.*

Step 4: *Cut open one bag to see if the food is done; then quickly transfer the remaining bags to serving plates. Your guests may open their own, or you can do it for them.*

SHRIMP WITH ASPARAGUS EN PAPILLOTE

2 to 3 tablespoons vegetable oil
1½ pounds fresh asparagus
¼ cup butter or margarine, softened
1 large clove garlic, crushed
2 tablespoons grated fresh gingerroot
2 teaspoons grated lemon rind
1½ tablespoons fresh lemon juice
¼ teaspoon salt
2 pounds medium-size fresh shrimp, peeled and deveined
6 lemon slices

Cut six 15- x 12-inch pieces of parchment paper or aluminum foil. Fold in half lengthwise, creasing firmly. Trim each into a large heart shape. Place hearts on baking sheets. Lightly brush one side of each heart with oil, leaving edges ungreased.

Trim tough ends of lower stalks of asparagus. Make stalks about the same length. Cook asparagus in boiling water 2 to 3 minutes. Drain and rinse in cold water. Drain well. Set aside.

Combine butter, garlic, gingerroot, lemon rind, lemon juice, and salt, stirring well. Set aside.

Arrange asparagus spears on one greased half of each heart near the crease. Arrange shrimp over asparagus. Dot with butter mixture, and top each with a lemon slice. Fold over remaining halves of hearts. Starting with rounded edge of each heart, pleat and crimp edges together to make a seal. Twist end tightly to seal. Bake at 400° for 9 to 11 minutes or until parchment bags are puffed and lightly browned and shrimp are cooked. Yield: 6 servings.

CHICKEN AND VEGETABLES EN PAPILLOTE

2 to 3 tablespoons vegetable oil
6 boneless chicken breast halves
3 tablespoons orange juice
3 tablespoons teriyaki sauce
1 tablespoon sesame oil
½ teaspoon grated fresh gingerroot
6 green onions, chopped
2 medium carrots, cut into thin julienne strips
2 small yellow squash, thinly sliced

Cut six 15- x 12-inch pieces parchment paper or aluminum foil; fold in half lengthwise, creasing firmly. Trim each into a large heart shape. Place hearts on baking sheets. Brush one side of each heart with vegetable oil, leaving edges ungreased.

Pound chicken breasts to ¼-inch thickness. Combine orange juice, teriyaki sauce, sesame oil, and gingerroot in a shallow dish; add chicken breasts to orange juice mixture, and marinate in refrigerator 30 minutes.

Drain chicken, reserving marinade; place a chicken breast half on one half of each parchment heart near the crease. Arrange vegetables over chicken. Spoon reserved marinade over vegetables.

Fold over remaining halves of parchment hearts. Starting with rounded edge of each heart, pleat and crimp edges together to make a seal. Twist end tightly to seal.

Bake chicken in parchment at 350° for 20 minutes or until bags are puffed and lightly browned and chicken is done. Yield: 6 servings.

Macaroons Make The Dessert

For an impressive dessert, give Elegant Ending a try. It teams the flavors of coffee ice cream and rum with the textures of macaroons and almonds. Irene Smith of Covington, Georgia, describes it as "a winning combination that always gets rave reviews at dinner parties." You're sure to agree with her.

ELEGANT ENDING

1 (13¾-ounce) package soft macaroons
¼ cup plus 1 tablespoon rum
½ gallon coffee ice cream, softened
1 (2-ounce) package slivered almonds, toasted
1 cup whipping cream
1 tablespoon powdered sugar

Crumble macaroons, and place on a baking sheet; bake at 400° for 5 to 8 minutes or until golden brown, stirring occasionally. Cool completely.

Set aside ⅓ cup macaroon crumbs. Combine remaining macaroon crumbs and rum; let stand 30 minutes.

Press into bottom and 1 inch up sides of a 9-inch springform pan. Combine coffee ice cream and slivered almonds; spoon into crust. Freeze for 8 hours or until firm.

Combine whipping cream and powdered sugar; beat until soft peaks form. Pipe whipped cream over ice cream. Sprinkle reserved crumbs into the center. Yield: 10 servings.

Offer Zucchini Year-Round

Zucchini is known not only for its low cost and delicious taste, but for its availability as well. Sold in grocery stores year-round, this dark green member of the squash family can also be seen in Southern gardens during the summer.

Zucchini is best if picked when small and immature. This ensures a delicate flavor and texture. Zucchini will keep for about a week if stored in a plastic bag in the refrigerator. When grated, a medium-size zucchini will yield one cup.

ZUCCHINI-BEEF BAKE

3 medium zucchini, sliced
1 cup sliced mushrooms
2 tablespoons vegetable oil
1 pound ground beef
1 small onion, chopped
2 (8-ounce) cans tomato sauce
1 tablespoon all-purpose flour
½ teaspoon dried whole oregano
½ teaspoon dried whole basil
¼ to ½ teaspoon salt
1 green pepper, diced
2 cups (8 ounces) shredded mozzarella
    cheese

Sauté zucchini and mushrooms in oil until tender; drain well, and set aside.

Cook ground beef and onion in a skillet until meat is browned, stirring to crumble. Drain off pan drippings; stir in tomato sauce, flour, and seasonings. Reduce heat, and simmer, uncovered, 5 minutes, stirring occasionally.

Layer half each of zucchini mixture and green pepper in a lightly greased 12- x 8- x 2-inch baking dish. Spoon half of ground beef mixture over vegetables. Sprinkle with half of cheese. Repeat layers of vegetables and ground beef. Bake, uncovered, at 350° for 30 minutes. Sprinkle with remaining cheese, and bake an additional 5 minutes. Yield: 6 servings. *Deborah Alford, Independence, Kentucky.*

ZUCCHINI PROVENÇAL

1 small onion, sliced
2 tablespoons vegetable oil
2 medium zucchini, cut into small cubes
2 tomatoes, peeled and quartered
⅓ cup diced green pepper
1 small clove garlic, crushed
Salt and pepper to taste
Grated Parmesan cheese
Chopped parsley (optional)

Sauté onion in oil in a skillet until tender. Stir in zucchini, tomatoes, green pepper, garlic, and seasonings; cover and cook over medium heat 10 to 12 minutes or until vegetables are tender, stirring occasionally. Transfer vegetables to a serving dish, and sprinkle with cheese and parsley, if desired. Yield: 4 to 6 servings. *Carol M. Snyder, Monroe, North Carolina.*

FRENCH FRIED ZUCCHINI WITH COCKTAIL SAUCE

½ cup catsup
1 tablespoon prepared horseradish
¾ cup all-purpose flour
¼ teaspoon salt
¼ to ½ teaspoon pepper
1 egg, beaten
2 tablespoons milk
2 medium zucchini, cut into ¼-inch slices
Vegetable oil

Combine catsup and horseradish, stirring well; set sauce aside.

Combine flour and seasonings; set aside. Combine egg and milk, mixing well. Dredge zucchini slices in flour mixture, and dip in egg mixture; roll in flour mixture again. Deep fry in hot oil (375°) until light golden brown. Drain slices on paper towels. Serve immediately with cocktail sauce. Yield: about 2½ dozen appetizer servings.
Betty Lyons, Madison, Tennessee.

ZUCCHINI MUFFINS

1 cup all-purpose flour
½ cup whole wheat flour
1½ teaspoons baking powder
¼ teaspoon baking soda
⅛ teaspoon salt
2 teaspoons ground cinnamon
1 egg, beaten
1 cup grated zucchini
⅔ cup honey
⅓ cup vegetable oil
1 teaspoon vanilla extract
¾ cup chopped walnuts

Combine dry ingredients in a mixing bowl; make a well in center. Combine egg, zucchini, honey, oil, and vanilla, mixing well; add to dry ingredients, stirring just until moistened. Stir in walnuts. Spoon into greased muffin pans, filling two-thirds full. Bake at 400° for 18 minutes. Yield: 14 muffins.
Julie King, Durham, North Carolina.

Crisp Cucumbers From The Garden

Don't panic if your garden is producing cucumbers faster than you can use them. If you need ideas about what to do with the harvest, try these recipes created by our readers to make the most of this crisp green vegetable. There's even a recipe for frying cucumber strips in deep fat.

MARINATED CUCUMBERS AND SQUASH

2 medium cucumbers, unpeeled and thinly
    sliced
2 small yellow squash, thinly sliced
1 (0.7-ounce) envelope Italian dressing mix
½ cup water
2 teaspoons vinegar
½ teaspoon sugar

Combine cucumber and squash in a medium bowl; set aside. Combine dressing mix, water, vinegar, and sugar; mix well. Pour over vegetables, tossing gently. Chill several hours. Yield: 4 to 6 servings. *Denise Smith, Oneonta, Alabama.*

FRIED CUCUMBER FINGERS

1 large cucumber
1 egg, beaten
¼ cup milk
½ cup biscuit mix
½ cup seasoned dry breadcrumbs
½ teaspoon salt
Vegetable oil

Peel cucumber. Slice in half lengthwise; scoop out pulp from each half. Cut cucumber into 2½- x ½-inch strips.

Combine egg and milk, mixing well; set aside. Combine biscuit mix, breadcrumbs, and salt, stirring well.

Dip cucumber strips in milk mixture, and dredge in breadcrumb mixture. Deep fry in 2 inches hot oil (375°) until golden brown. Drain on paper towels; serve immediately. Yield: 4 servings.

Renee S. Bradshaw,
Ashland, Virginia.

SIMPLE CUCUMBER COOLER

2 medium cucumbers, unpeeled
¼ cup diced onion
1 (12-ounce) carton small curd cottage cheese
2 tablespoons mayonnaise or salad dressing
Lettuce leaves
Chopped green onions (optional)

Chop cucumbers; pat with paper towels to remove the excess moisture. Combine cucumber, ¼ cup diced onion, cottage cheese, and mayonnaise, mixing well. Serve salad on lettuce leaves on individual salad plates. Garnish salad with chopped green onions, if desired. Yield: 4 to 6 servings.

Mrs. L. B. Shepler,
San Antonio, Texas.

CREAMY CUCUMBER SALAD

2 envelopes unflavored gelatin
1 cup cold water
1½ cups commercial creamy cucumber dressing
1 teaspoon instant minced onion
1 teaspoon dried whole dillweed
3 cups diced peeled cucumber
½ cup chopped celery
Lettuce (optional)
Cherry tomato halves (optional)

Sprinkle gelatin over water in a medium saucepan; let stand 5 minutes. Heat mixture over low heat, stirring constantly, until gelatin dissolves. Add dressing, onion, and dillweed to gelatin mixture, stirring well. Chill until the consistency of unbeaten egg white. Fold in cucumber and celery.

Pour mixture into a lightly oiled 5-cup mold. Chill until firm.

Unmold salad onto a serving platter; garnish with lettuce and cherry tomato halves, if desired. Yield: 8 servings.

Betty T. Burnside,
Newport, North Carolina.

CUCUMBER-ALMOND SALAD

2 large cucumbers
½ teaspoon salt
½ cup commercial sour cream
¼ cup chopped blanched almonds
2 tablespoons minced green onions
1 tablespoon lemon juice
¼ teaspoon coarsely ground pepper

Peel cucumbers, if desired, and thinly slice. Sprinkle with salt, and let stand 15 minutes.

Drain cucumbers, if necessary. Combine remaining ingredients; add to cucumbers, tossing gently. Chill at least 1 hour. Yield: 4 to 6 servings.

Claire Wash,
Greenwood, South Carolina.

Fresh Ideas For Vegetables

After you've fried, steamed, baked, and sautéed vegetables, it's time for a change. Why not enjoy them in a crisp, cool vinaigrette salad?

Cauliflower-Olive Toss combines the vegetable's flowerets with ripe olives, pimiento, and parsley. Red wine vinegar, which has a snappy flavor similar to the wine, and olive oil, with its nutty taste, give this colorful dish just the right amount of zest.

Try Cucumber-Vinaigrette Oriental for the flavor of fresh ginger spiked with the sharp, tart taste of fresh distilled vinegar. This vinegar goes well with light-colored vegetables to help keep their natural color.

Two types of vinegar combine with green beans and garbanzo beans in Sweet-and-Sour Bean Salad. Cider vinegar provides a smooth, mellow flavor while tarragon-wine vinegar adds a lively herb taste.

CAULIFLOWER-OLIVE TOSS

1 small head cauliflower, cut into flowerets
½ cup sliced ripe olives
1 (2-ounce) jar diced pimiento, drained
3 tablespoons chopped fresh parsley
⅓ cup olive oil
¼ cup red wine vinegar
1 teaspoon sugar
¼ teaspoon salt
⅛ teaspoon pepper

Arrange cauliflower on a steaming rack. Place over boiling water; cover and steam 5 to 6 minutes or until crisp-tender. Drain and cool.

Combine cauliflower, olives, pimiento, and parsley in a bowl. Combine remaining ingredients in a jar. Cover tightly, and shake vigorously. Pour over cauliflower mixture, tossing gently. Chill 8 hours, stirring occasionally. Yield: 4 servings.

Betty J. Moore,
Belton, Texas.

SWEET-AND-SOUR BEAN SALAD

2 pounds green beans
1 (15-ounce) can garbanzo beans, drained
1 medium-size purple onion, thinly sliced
1 (4-ounce) jar diced pimiento, drained
⅔ cup sugar
½ cup vegetable oil
½ cup cider vinegar
½ cup tarragon wine vinegar
1 clove garlic, crushed
½ teaspoon salt
½ teaspoon lemon-pepper seasoning

Remove strings from beans; wash. Cut beans into 1½-inch pieces. Cook, covered, in a small amount of water 8 to 10 minutes; drain. Toss beans with garbanzo beans, onion, and pimiento.

Combine remaining ingredients in a jar. Cover tightly, and shake vigorously. Pour over vegetables, tossing gently. Chill 8 hours, stirring occasionally. Yield: 10 to 12 servings.

Maude Crenshaw,
Lehigh Acres, Florida.

CUCUMBER-VINAIGRETTE ORIENTAL

2 large cucumbers, peeled and thinly sliced
⅓ cup white distilled vinegar
1 tablespoon plus 1 teaspoon sugar
½ teaspoon salt
1½ teaspoons minced fresh ginger

Place cucumbers in a bowl. Combine remaining ingredients in a jar. Cover tightly, and shake. Pour over cucumbers; toss gently. Chill 8 hours; stir occasionally. Yield: 6 servings.

Carole May,
Valley, Alabama.

Try These Vegetable Egg Rolls

Broccoli and spinach may not seem like typical ingredients for an Oriental egg roll filling, but they add color and flavor to Vegetarian Egg Rolls. Violet Moore of Montezuma, Georgia, says shredded cooked chicken, beef, pork, or turkey may be added to the filling.

The egg rolls make hearty appetizers or can be served as a meatless meal. Be sure to include sweet-and-sour sauce or hot mustard sauce.

VEGETARIAN EGG ROLLS

3 tablespoons peanut oil
4 cups shredded cabbage
2½ cups fresh bean sprouts, chopped
1 cup shredded carrots
½ cup minced green onions
½ cup chopped fresh spinach
½ cup chopped fresh broccoli
½ cup chopped green pepper
½ cup thinly sliced fresh mushrooms
1 (2-ounce) jar diced pimiento, drained
¼ cup soy sauce
2 tablespoons sugar
3 tablespoons cornstarch, divided
¼ teaspoon red pepper
¼ teaspoon garlic salt
2 tablespoons water
1 (1-pound) package egg roll wrappers
Peanut oil
Commercial sweet-and-sour sauce
    (optional)
Commercial mustard sauce (optional)

Heat 3 tablespoons oil in a preheated wok, coating sides; allow to heat at medium high (325°) for 2 minutes. Add vegetables and pimiento; stir-fry 3 minutes or until vegetables are crisp-tender. Turn off heat, and set wok aside.

Combine soy sauce, sugar, 2 tablespoons cornstarch, red pepper, and garlic salt in a small bowl. Add to vegetables in wok, stirring constantly; cook 1 minute.

Combine remaining 1 tablespoon cornstarch and water; set aside.

Spoon 1 heaping tablespoon filling in center of each egg roll wrapper. Fold top corner of wrapper over filling; then fold left and right corners over filling. Lightly brush exposed corner of wrapper with cornstarch mixture. Tightly roll the filled end of the wrapper toward the exposed corner; gently press to seal. Secure with wooden picks.

Heat 2 inches peanut oil to 375° in Dutch oven. Place 2 egg rolls in hot oil, and fry 35 to 45 seconds on each side or

until golden brown; drain on paper towels. Remove wooden picks. Repeat procedure with remaining egg rolls. Serve with sweet-and-sour sauce and mustard sauce, if desired. Yield: about 30 egg rolls.

Cake flour gives Mini Pound Cakes light texture; a glaze provides a sweet topping.

Pound Cakes To Share

Busy homemakers are always looking for ways to get more from the time they spend in food preparation. And batch cooking has become a popular idea.

For example, Katherine Mabry of Athens, Alabama, bakes Mini Pound Cakes. The recipe makes three small cakes, so you can enjoy one and freeze the others for later.

MINI POUND CAKES

1 cup unsalted butter or margarine,
    softened
1¼ cups sugar
4 eggs
2 cups sifted cake flour
1 teaspoon baking powder
¼ teaspoon salt
⅓ cup milk
1 tablespoon brandy
1 teaspoon vanilla extract
Glaze (recipe follows)
Pecan halves (optional)

Cream butter; gradually add sugar, beating at medium speed of an electric mixer until mixture is light and fluffy. Add eggs, one at a time, beating after each addition.

Combine cake flour, baking powder, and salt. Add to creamed mixture alternately with milk, beginning and ending with flour mixture. Mix just until blended after additions. Stir in brandy and vanilla.

Grease and flour 3 (6¾- x 3- x 2-inch) loafpans. Pour batter into pans, and bake at 325° for 35 to 40 minutes or until a wooden pick inserted in center comes out clean. Cool in pans 10 to 15 minutes; remove from pans, and cool on wire racks.

Spoon glaze over cakes. Garnish with pecan halves, if desired. Yield: 3 loaves.

Glaze:

2 cups sifted powdered sugar
2½ tablespoons milk
1 teaspoon vanilla extract

Mix all ingredients until smooth. Yield: about 1¼ cups.

Tip: Have your oven thermostat professionally checked at least once a year. Another way to occasionally check oven temperature is to prepare a cake mix according to package directions; the cake should cook the entire recommended time and test done. (A wooden pick inserted in the center should come out clean.)

June

Give Pesto A Southern Accent

That unusual green sauce you may have noticed tossed with pasta in restaurants is pesto. It originated in Italy, but it has been gaining popularity in Southern kitchens—with good reason.

Pesto adds a burst of flavor and color to tomatoes and salad greens that have been harvested from backyard gardens. It's also appealing with seafood.

The first pesto was made slowly with a mortar and pestle, but nowadays you can whip up the creamy sauce in a food processor in a matter of minutes.

Some sources define pesto strictly as a basil sauce. Although originally made with basil, pesto is a green sauce made from any leafy herb or green vegetable. Our test kitchens staff prepared three separate batches of pesto—one flavored with basil, one with parsley, and one with spinach. We found similar consistencies and a variety of flavors.

Our recipe for pesto yields 1¾ cups, so that one batch goes a long way. The mixture keeps well in an airtight container for up to a week in the refrigerator or freezes as long as six months. You might consider freezing the mixture in 1-tablespoon amounts in ice cube trays. Once the pesto is frozen, pop the cubes from the tray, and store them in a freezer bag.

Our recipes offer several ways to use pesto, and the following serving suggestions are so simple that you won't even need a recipe.

—Toss pesto over hot spaghetti, linguine, or fettuccine. Use 1 pound of pasta for 1 recipe of pesto.

—Stir 2 tablespoons pesto into one 8-ounce carton of commercial sour cream for an instant dip to serve with raw vegetables.

—Serve warmed pesto as a topper for baked potatoes. Allow about 1 tablespoon per potato.

—Spread a small amount of pesto over slices of French bread, and then toast before serving.

—Stir about 3 tablespoons pesto into a can of commercial tomato soup (diluted as the can directs). The soup with the pesto will taste homemade!

—Try pesto as an omelet filling. Spoon about 2 tablespoons of the sauce over half of a three-egg omelet; then fold it over, and serve.

—Stir 2 tablespoons pesto into ½ cup of softened unsalted butter. Serve the pesto butter as a bread spread, or toss it with hot vegetables. Melt the butter for dipping fresh shrimp or lobster.

FRESH PESTO
(pictured on page 134)

2 cups packed fresh basil, parsley, or
  coarsely chopped spinach
¾ cup grated Parmesan cheese
½ cup walnut pieces
2 large cloves garlic, cut in half
¼ teaspoon salt
¼ teaspoon freshly grated pepper
⅔ cup olive oil

Remove stems from basil. Wash leaves thoroughly in lukewarm water, and drain well.

Position knife blade in food processor bowl; add basil, Parmesan cheese, walnuts, garlic, salt, and pepper, and top with cover. Process until smooth. With processor running, pour olive oil through food chute in a slow, steady stream until combined. Use pesto immediately, or place in an airtight container; refrigerate up to 1 week, or freeze up to 6 months. Yield: 1¾ cups.

PESTO BROILED FLOUNDER

2 tablespoons butter or margarine, melted
4 (6-ounce) flounder fillets
1 tablespoon lemon juice
¼ cup Fresh Pesto

Line a shallow baking pan with aluminum foil; lightly brush foil with small amount of butter. Arrange fillets in prepared pan. Brush fish with remaining butter; sprinkle lightly with lemon juice, and spread with pesto. Broil 5 inches from heat for 10 minutes or until fish flakes easily when tested with a fork. Yield: 4 servings.

TOMATOES PESTO
(pictured on page 134)

4 medium tomatoes, sliced
2 tablespoons olive oil
2 tablespoons Fresh Pesto
1½ tablespoons lemon juice

Place tomatoes in a shallow dish. Combine remaining ingredients; stir well, and pour over tomatoes. Cover and refrigerate several hours, stirring once or twice. Yield: 6 to 8 servings.

PESTO-STUFFED MUSHROOMS
(pictured on page 134)

1¼ pounds large fresh mushrooms
3 tablespoons butter or margarine, melted
½ cup Fresh Pesto
About 1½ dozen pimiento strips

Clean mushrooms with damp paper towels; remove stems, and reserve for other uses.

Place butter in a shallow baking dish. Roll mushroom caps in butter, and arrange in dish, cap side down. Spoon pesto evenly into mushroom caps. Cover and bake at 350° for 15 to 20 minutes. Top each mushroom with a pimiento strip. Yield: about 1½ dozen.

PESTO SALAD DRESSING
(pictured on page 134)

¾ cup olive oil
½ cup vinegar
3 tablespoons sugar
¼ cup Fresh Pesto
2 tablespoons diced pimiento

Combine all ingredients in container of an electric blender or food processor. Process at low speed until blended. Serve dressing over salad greens. Yield: 1¾ cups.

Here At Last Summer Berries

Glistening like jewels in the morning dew, ripe raspberries, blackberries, strawberries, and blueberries bring the promise of a sweet combo of berries and cream, a hot cobbler topped with ice cream, a fresh lattice-topped pie, or a sumptuous mixture of fresh fruit for any meal of the day.

Raspberries are a sought-after delicacy during these summer months—you may pay a high price for them even during the peak season. That's why you'll want to use them in recipes in which the tangy-sweet flavor can be enjoyed to the fullest. You may want to stretch the taste by mixing them with strawberries and blueberries for a fresh fruit salad, or serve in delicate meringue cups for dessert.

In contrast to scarce raspberries, blackberries are one of the most abundant wild crops gracing our Southern landscape. If you plan to pick them yourself, wait until the dew dries. Dry berries will stay fresh longer than those picked moist and piled together.

Of course, strawberries are a must. Feature them in a dessert or salad, and use them to garnish everything from appetizers to desserts. They add a splash of vivid color and sweet flavor to any menu. Do not remove the caps from the berries before washing, but rather just before serving.

For the best blueberries, buy those with a dark-blue color and a silvery-gray coating called the bloom. As with all berries, store them unwashed in a shallow container in the refrigerator for 1 to 2 days. Washing removes a natural protective coating on the berries and will promote quicker spoilage. When you're ready to use, wash them quickly, and drain on paper towels.

FRUIT-FILLED MERINGUE SHELLS

3 egg whites
¼ teaspoon cream of tartar
⅛ teaspoon salt
¼ teaspoon vanilla extract
¼ teaspoon almond extract
½ cup superfine sugar
1⅓ cups sliced fresh strawberries
1⅓ cups fresh blueberries
1⅓ cups fresh raspberries
Sweetened whipped cream

Beat egg whites (at room temperature) at high speed of an electric mixer until foamy. Sprinkle cream of tartar, salt, and flavorings over egg whites; continue beating until soft peaks form. Gradually add sugar, 1 tablespoon at a time, beating until stiff peaks form.

Line a baking sheet with aluminum foil. Drop meringue mixture by rounded ½ cupfuls onto baking sheet. Working quickly, smooth meringues into 3½-inch circles using the back of a spoon. Form a well in center of each meringue by pushing excess meringue up to the edges. Bake at 225° for 1 hour. Turn off oven, and cool meringues in oven at least 8 hours.

Combine fruit; spoon ½ cup fruit into each meringue shell. Top with a dollop of whipped cream. Serve immediately. Yield: 8 servings. *Gwen Louer, Roswell, Georgia.*

Tip: Beware—a wet potholder used on a hot utensil may cause a steam burn.

FRESH FRUIT PUDDING COMPOTE

1¾ cups milk
1 tablespoon orange liqueur or orange juice
1 (3-ounce) package vanilla instant pudding
1 cup whipped topping
1½ cups fresh blueberries
1½ cups sliced fresh strawberries
1½ cups sliced bananas
1½ cups sliced peaches
Whipped topping (optional)

Combine first 3 ingredients in a bowl; beat at low speed of an electric mixer 1 minute. Add 1 cup whipped topping, and beat an additional minute. Combine fruit; arrange half of fruit mixture in 8 to 10 individual compotes; top with pudding mixture. Top with remaining fruit. Garnish with additional whipped topping, if desired. Yield: 8 to 10 servings. *Peggy H. Amos, Martinsville, Virginia.*

SURPRISE STRAWBERRY PARFAIT

1¼ cups sliced fresh strawberries
1 tablespoon sugar
1 (6-ounce) can frozen lemonade concentrate, partially thawed and undiluted
3 cups vanilla ice cream
Whipped cream (optional)
6 whole strawberries (optional)

Combine sliced strawberries and sugar, mixing well; set aside for 5 minutes. Combine lemonade concentrate and sliced strawberries; stir well. Spoon about 1½ tablespoons strawberry mixture into each of six 6-ounce parfaits; top with ½ cup ice cream. Repeat layers. Top with remaining strawberry mixture. Freeze until firm. Before serving, top each parfait with whipped cream and a whole strawberry, if desired. Yield: 6 servings. *Roberta E. McGrath, Hopkinsville, Kentucky.*

HAWAIIAN DREAM BOATS

1 large pineapple
6 peaches, peeled and sliced
1½ teaspoons lemon juice
1 pint fresh strawberries
1 (8-ounce) carton commercial sour cream
3 tablespoons brown sugar
4 macaroons, crushed

Cut pineapple in half from the bottom through the crown; keep leaves intact. Cut out core, and discard. Remove pineapple from the shell with a curved knife. Cut pineapple into chunks; set aside. Reserve pineapple shells.

Combine peaches and lemon juice; toss well. Add pineapple chunks and strawberries; toss gently. Spoon fruit into pineapple shells. Refrigerate until serving time.

Combine sour cream and brown sugar, mixing well. Just before serving, stir in macaroons. Spoon into a small serving bowl; serve as dip for fruit. Yield: 12 to 15 appetizer servings. *Kristina Simms, Montezuma, Georgia.*

HUCKLE-BUCKLE BLUEBERRY

¼ cup butter or margarine, softened
1 cup sugar, divided
1 egg
1⅔ cups all-purpose flour, divided
1 teaspoon baking powder
¼ teaspoon salt
½ cup milk
1 teaspoon vanilla extract
2½ cups fresh blueberries
½ teaspoon ground cinnamon
¼ cup butter or margarine

Cream softened butter; gradually add ½ cup sugar, beating well. Add egg; beat well.

Combine 1⅓ cups flour, baking powder, and salt; add to the creamed mixture alternately with milk, beginning and ending with the flour mixture. Mix well after each addition. Stir in vanilla.

Pour batter into a greased 8-inch square baking pan. Top with blueberries. Combine remaining ½ cup sugar, remaining ⅓ cup flour, and cinnamon. Cut ¼ cup butter into cinnamon mixture with a pastry blender until mixture resembles coarse meal. Sprinkle over berries. Bake at 375° for 45 to 50 minutes. Yield: 6 servings.

Ethel Jernegan, Savannah, Georgia.

AMARETTO CUSTARD
WITH RASPBERRIES
(pictured on page 167)

6 eggs, slightly beaten
½ cup sugar
2 cups milk, scalded
2 tablespoons amaretto
Sweetened whipped cream
2 cups fresh raspberries

Combine eggs and sugar, beating well; gradually add milk, stirring constantly. Stir in amaretto. Pour into 6 lightly greased 6-ounce custard cups. Place custard cups in a 13- x 9- x 2-inch baking pan; pour hot water into pan to a depth of 1 inch. Bake at 375° for 15 to 20 minutes or until knife inserted in center of custard comes out clean. Remove cups from water, and let cool. Chill custard thoroughly.

Run a knife around edge of custard cups; unmold onto serving plates. Top custard with a dollop of whipped cream, and then sprinkle with raspberries. Yield: 6 servings. *Jill Rorex, Dallas, Texas.*

FRESH RASPBERRY ICE CREAM

4 cups fresh raspberries
2 eggs
1⅓ cups sugar
1½ cups half-and-half
1 cup whipping cream
¼ cup light corn syrup
1 tablespoon lemon juice

Wash raspberries; drain. Place berries in container of an electric blender; process until almost smooth. Press puree through a sieve to remove seeds. Set puree aside.

Beat eggs and sugar at medium-high speed of an electric mixer 4 to 5 minutes or until thick and lemon colored. Stir in raspberry puree and remaining ingredients.

Pour mixture into freezer can of a 1-gallon hand-turned or electric freezer. Freeze, following manufacturer's instructions. Let ripen 1 hour. Yield: 2 quarts. *Mrs. A. J. Amador, Decatur, Alabama.*

BLACKBERRY SAUCE

5 cups fresh blackberries
1 cup water
¾ cup sugar
2 tablespoons water
1 tablespoon cornstarch
1 tablespoon lemon juice
Angel food or sponge cake

Combine berries, 1 cup water, and sugar in a large saucepan; bring to a boil. Combine 2 tablespoons water and cornstarch, mixing well; stir into blackberry mixture. Cook 1 minute over medium-high heat, stirring constantly. Remove from heat, and add lemon juice; cool. Chill.

Serve sauce over angel food or sponge cake. Yield: 4 cups.
Billie Jean Couch Coppage, Tulsa, Oklahoma.

BLACKBERRY PIE

Pastry for double-crust 9-inch pie
4 cups fresh blackberries
1 cup sugar
¼ cup all-purpose flour
1 to 1½ tablespoons lemon juice
¼ teaspoon salt
1 tablespoon butter or margarine

Line a 9-inch pieplate with half of pastry; set aside.

Combine berries, sugar, flour, lemon juice, and salt in a bowl; toss well. Spoon berry mixture into pastry-lined pieplate. Dot mixture with butter.

Roll out remaining pastry to ⅛-inch thickness, and cut into 10 (10- x ½-inch) strips. Arrange strips in lattice design over pie, and trim edges; seal and flute. Bake at 350° for 50 to 55 minutes (cover edges with foil to prevent overbrowning, if necessary). Yield: one 9-inch pie.

Note: The pie may be covered with a complete top crust rather than lattice strips, if desired. *Johnny Pierson, Tallulah, Louisiana.*

Enjoy The Taste Of Texas Barbecue

The Lone Star State is famous for many things, not the least of which is mouth-watering, succulent barbecue. This usually means beef. But just about any meat can be used. Pork is barbecued, but it doesn't enjoy the exalted position it holds in the Southeast.

While the actual origin of barbecue remains unclear, Anne Anderson, coordinator of the Beef Industry Council of Texas, says the roots of Texas barbecue can be traced back to the influence of two major groups—the Germans in Central Texas and the Mexicans in South and West Texas.

Anderson says it's important to know what you mean when you talk about Texas barbecue. "When people in other parts of the country talk about barbecue, they mean grilling. Real Texas barbecue is a much different process. It usually means big pieces of meat cooked 14 to 18 hours in a covered pit with the meat on one end and the fire at the other. This way the meat is cooked long and slow, and you get more of a smoked flavor. The wood is usually mesquite or pecan—it gives a sweeter flavor than oak."

Anderson says another common misconception about Texas barbecue is that barbecue sauce is applied to the meat while it's cooking. "True Texas barbecue is basted with a 'sop' to keep it moist, but it's not the same as the barbecue sauce that's put on the meat later. For one thing, it doesn't contain any tomatoes—they make the meat black. It's usually just a mixture of butter, lemon, beer, and onion. If barbecue sauce is applied to the meat at all, it's put on toward the end of the cooking time. Often the sauce is put on the meat after it's cooked or just served with the meat at the table."

We thought you may want to try cooking some Texas-style barbecue yourself, so we went to three Texans famous for their barbecue recipes and tips. If you don't have a limestone pit or a specially designed smoker, don't despair. Our test kitchens have adapted the recipes so they can be prepared on most home barbecue grills.

■ A barbecue at the H. C. Carter ranch near Dripping Springs usually features longhorn lean. We took the liberty of substituting boneless rib roast for the longhorn prime rib because the roast is generally more available. Both the longhorn lean and the boneless rib roast require the same cooking time of about 22 minutes per pound. Other Carter favorites are Barbecued Chicken and Barbecued Sausage.

BARBECUED RIB ROAST

2 tablespoons lemon-pepper seasoning, divided
1 (6- to 8-pound) boneless rib roast
Marinade (recipe follows)
Savory Barbecue Sauce
Additional lemon-pepper seasoning

Rub 1 tablespoon lemon-pepper seasoning into roast; place roast in a large container. Pour marinade over roast, and cover. Refrigerate 6 hours, turning roast occasionally. Remove roast from marinade, reserving 2 cups marinade for use in Savory Barbecue Sauce. Rub remaining 1 tablespoon lemon-pepper seasoning into roast.

Soak mesquite or oak chips in water 1 to 2 hours. Prepare fire in grill; let burn until coals are white. Rake coals to one end of grill; place wood chips over hot coals. Place roast at opposite end; cover with lid, and cook over indirect heat 2½ to 3 hours (approximately 22 minutes per pound).

Cook roast until the thermometer registers 140° to 170° or to desired degree of doneness, basting at 1-hour intervals with Savory Barbecue Sauce. Sprinkle roast with lemon-pepper seasoning before slicing. Yield: approximately 16 to 18 servings.

Marinade:

3½ cups water
1½ cups Burgundy or other dry red wine
¾ cup red wine vinegar
1 small onion, sliced
1 stalk celery
1 clove garlic, crushed

Combine all ingredients, and stir until blended. Yield: 6 cups.

Savory Barbecue Sauce:

2 cups reserved marinade
2 cups beer
1 cup vegetable oil
¼ cup plus 2 tablespoons seasoning blend

Combine all ingredients, and stir until blended. Yield: 5 cups.

BARBECUED CHICKEN

2 (2½- to 3-pound) chickens
1 tablespoon lemon-pepper seasoning
1 tablespoon seasoned pepper
¼ teaspoon garlic powder
Savory Barbecue Sauce (see Barbecued Rib Roast)

Sprinkle chickens with seasonings.
Soak mesquite or oak chips in water 1 to 2 hours. Prepare fire in grill; let burn until coals are white. Rake coals to one end of grill; place wood chips over hot coals. Place chickens at opposite end; cover with lid, and cook 45 minutes or until skin begins to turn brown and a little crusty. Baste chickens with Savory Barbecue Sauce; continue cooking an additional 1 hour and 45 minutes, basting every 30 minutes. Yield: 8 servings.

BARBECUED SAUSAGE

2 pounds fully cooked German sausage

Soak mesquite or oak chips in water 1 to 2 hours. Prepare fire in grill; let burn until coals are white. Rake coals to one end of grill; place wood chips over hot coals. Place sausage at opposite end; cover with lid, and cook over indirect heat 20 minutes or to desired degree of doneness. Yield: 6 to 8 servings.

■ When Don Small barbecues at his home in Fort Worth he often includes beef brisket or *cabrito* (goat) on the menu. Don cautions against putting *cabrito* over direct fire, stressing the importance of not overcooking the meat on the grill. "You can tell it's done when the meat has a darkened color or starts to pull away from the bone."

BARBECUED CABRITO

5 cloves garlic, chopped
4 cups vegetable oil
4 cups cider vinegar
2 cups water
1 cup Worcestershire sauce
2 bay leaves
2 lemons, halved
3 tablespoons seasoning salt
3 tablespoons pepper
1 tablespoon paprika
1 (8- to 10-pound) goat loin, split
1 (8- to 10-pound) goat hindquarter

Combine garlic, oil, vinegar, water, Worcestershire sauce, and bay leaves. Squeeze lemons; add juice and lemon halves to mixture. Set marinade aside.

Combine seasoning salt, pepper, and paprika; rub into goat, and place goat in a large shallow container. Add marinade. Cover and refrigerate 8 hours, turning meat once.

Place 2 pieces of oak (each the length of the grill) at front and back of grill. Place charcoal in middle. Start fire, and let burn until coals are white.

Remove goat from marinade, reserving marinade. Rake coals to one end of grill; place goat at opposite end with bone side down. Cover with lid, and cook over indirect heat 4 hours or until meat starts to shrink from bone, basting with marinade and turning every 20 minutes. Yield: 10 servings.

BARBECUED BEEF BRISKET WITH SAUCE

1½ tablespoons seasoning salt
1½ tablespoons pepper
1½ teaspoons paprika
1 (6-pound) beef brisket
2 cups vegetable oil
2 cups cider vinegar
½ cup Worcestershire sauce
2 bay leaves, crumbled
Barbecue sauce (recipe follows)

Combine seasoning salt, pepper, and paprika; rub into brisket. Place brisket in a shallow container. Combine oil, vinegar, Worcestershire sauce, and bay leaves; pour marinade mixture over brisket. Cover and refrigerate 8 hours, turning brisket occasionally.

Place 2 pieces of oak (each piece the length of the grill) at the front and back of the grill. Place charcoal in the middle. Start fire, and let fire burn until the coals are white.

Remove brisket from marinade, reserving marinade for basting. Rake coals to one end of grill; place brisket at opposite end. Cover with lid, and cook over indirect heat 3½ to 4 hours or until tender, basting with marinade every 30 minutes.

Coat both sides of brisket with barbecue sauce at the beginning of the last hour of cooking; continue to cook until tender, basting only top of brisket with sauce. Serve brisket with sauce. Yield: 14 servings.

Barbecue Sauce:

4 cups catsup
1 cup cider vinegar
1 cup Worcestershire sauce
1 medium onion, grated
½ cup butter or margarine
2 tablespoons seasoning salt
2 tablespoons brown sugar
1 tablespoon chili powder
1 tablespoon pepper
1 bay leaf

Combine all ingredients in a large saucepan; bring to a boil, stirring occasionally. Remove bay leaf from sauce. Yield: 6⅔ cups.

■ A backyard barbecue at Bob Cross's home in Kilgore may feature Cornish hens or Polish sausage and almost always includes brisket. "I usually cook briskets at 250° for approximately 12 hours," says Bob. "I have an electronically controlled damper on my firebox that really helps maintain a steady heat. It works on the same principle as the oven in a kitchen stove." You can get almost the same results even without a smoker if you follow the recipe below.

BARBECUED BRISKET

2 tablespoons coarsely ground pepper
2 teaspoons paprika
1 (5-pound) beef brisket

Sprinkle pepper and paprika on fat side of brisket only.

Soak oak, pecan, or mesquite chips in water 1 to 2 hours. Prepare fire in grill; let burn until coals are white. Rake coals to one end of grill; place wood chips over hot coals.

Place brisket, fat side up, at opposite end. Cover and cook over indirect heat 3½ to 4 hours or until tender. To test for doneness, press thumb into side of brisket. If meat feels spongy, it is done. Yield: 12 servings.

SMOKED CORNISH HENS

4 (1- to 1¼-pound) Cornish hens
1 teaspoon pepper

Remove giblets from hens; reserve giblets for other uses. Rinse hens with cold water, and pat dry; sprinkle hens with pepper.

Soak oak, pecan, or mesquite chips in water 1 to 2 hours.

Prepare fire in grill; let burn until coals are white. Rake coals to one end of grill; place wood chips over hot coals. Place hens at opposite end; cover and cook over indirect heat 2 to 2½ hours or until thermometer registers 185°. Yield: 4 servings.

Tip: When using your grill, never allow the coals to flame during cooking, as flames may either burn the food or cause it to dry out. Just remember to keep a container of water nearby, and douse flames as they appear.

SMOKED SAUSAGE

1 pound fully cooked Polish sausage

Soak oak, pecan, or mesquite chips in water 1 to 2 hours. Prepare fire in grill; let burn until coals are white. Rake coals to one end of grill; place wood chips over hot coals.

Place sausage at opposite end; cover with lid, and cook over indirect heat 20 minutes or to desired degree of doneness. Yield: 4 servings.

COOKING LIGHT®

Shellfish Nature's Gift From The Sea

Warm weather has many of us scurrying toward the coast to spend a leisurely vacation enjoying the sun and seafood. And to make the trip last a little longer, many will return home with an ice chest full of fresh shellfish.

The popularity of shellfish, like other seafood, has increased. Protein-packed and low in calories, shellfish also boast an impressive vitamin and mineral content. And these gems of the sea don't have to be deep-fried to taste good.

Start your meal with Scallop Appetizer. This lightly seasoned dish is colorful, but simple, and contains only 112 calories per serving. When buying scallops, choose those that are creamy white, light tan, or pink in color and that have a slightly sweet, fresh scent. If you are using packaged scallops, look for those that are practically free of liquid. Keep in mind that as scallops cook, they lose a great deal of moisture, so that other liquid in the recipe may need to be adjusted.

If you've ever made a traditional Louisiana-style gumbo, you know the secret to its success is in the roux (a mixture consisting of half flour and half fat). Slowly browned in a skillet on top of the stove, it gives gumbo flavor, thickness, and a deep, rich color, but it also adds many calories. Our Light Seafood-Okra Gumbo doesn't contain a bit of added fat. Instead of using a roux, we browned the flour in the oven to achieve the same great results.

Drawn butter for dipping may come to mind when you think of lobster. But extra fat is one of the first items to be eliminated when you're counting calories. We suggest Lobster Tails With Spiced Orange Sauce. Chicken bouillon, orange juice, lemon juice, ginger, and chili powder add zest to this basting and dipping sauce. A few drops of butter flavoring help satisfy the yearning for drawn butter.

To make Crabmeat au Gratin without all the calories, we substituted skim milk for half-and-half and reduced-calorie margarine for regular margarine. We also reduced the flour and cheese called for in regular recipes. You won't miss cheese flavor, though. We used a medium-sharp cheese (which has a more pronounced flavor), and seasoned the mixture with dry mustard, Worcestershire sauce, and red pepper. These ingredients help bring out cheese flavor without adding extra calories to the total count. In fact, a serving of this rich-tasting dish is only 179 calories.

CRABMEAT AU GRATIN

1½ cups skim milk
2 tablespoons all-purpose flour
1½ teaspoons reduced-calorie margarine
½ cup (2 ounces) shredded medium-sharp Cheddar cheese
1 pound fresh lump crabmeat, drained
⅓ cup chopped green onions
3 tablespoons grated Parmesan cheese
2 tablespoons minced fresh parsley
½ teaspoon dry mustard
½ teaspoon Worcestershire sauce
¼ teaspoon salt
¼ teaspoon red pepper
¼ teaspoon paprika
Dash of white pepper
2 (13¾-ounce) cans artichoke bottoms, drained

Combine skim milk and flour in container of an electric blender; process until smooth.

Melt margarine in a heavy saucepan over low heat; add flour mixture. Cook over medium heat, stirring constantly, until mixture is thickened and bubbly.

Add Cheddar cheese, stirring until cheese melts. Add fresh lump crabmeat, green onions, Parmesan cheese, parsley, mustard, Worcestershire sauce, salt, red pepper, paprika, and white pepper; stir mixture well.

To serve, spoon about ¼ cup crabmeat mixture over each artichoke bottom. Yield: 6 servings (about 179 calories per 2 artichoke bottoms with mixture).
Nancy S. Hughes,
Mobile, Alabama.

LOBSTER TAILS
WITH SPICED ORANGE SAUCE

¼ teaspoon chicken-flavored bouillon
    granules
¼ cup boiling water
¼ cup unsweetened orange juice
2 teaspoons lemon juice
1 teaspoon grated orange rind
4 drops imitation butter flavoring
Dash of ground ginger
Dash of chili powder
2 (7- to 8-ounce) lobster tails

Dissolve bouillon granules in boiling water. Add orange juice and remaining ingredients except lobster; stir well.

Split lobster tails lengthwise; cut through upper shell and meat to, but not through, bottom shell. Lift meat through split shell to rest on outside of shell, leaving meat attached to far end of shell.

Place lobster tails on a broiler rack, and brush with orange sauce. Broil 4 inches from heat 5 minutes; brush lobster with orange sauce, and broil an additional 5 minutes.

Serve lobster with remaining orange sauce. Yield: 2 servings (about 109 calories per tail with sauce).

Elda A. Caldwell,
San Antonio, Texas.

Scallop Appetizer and Light Seafood-Okra Gumbo get any meal off to a good start, or they can be enjoyed alone. Either dish will add variety to a low-calorie diet.

LIGHT SEAFOOD-OKRA GUMBO

¼ cup all-purpose flour
1 cup diced green pepper
1¾ cups diced celery
1⅓ cups chicken broth, divided
2⅔ cups beef broth, diluted
1 (8-ounce) can tomato sauce
½ cup water
4 cups sliced okra
2 tablespoons plus 1 teaspoon instant
    minced onion
1 tablespoon parsley flakes
2 cloves garlic, minced
1 bay leaf
¾ teaspoon dried whole thyme
½ teaspoon poultry seasoning
¼ teaspoon pepper
¼ teaspoon hot sauce
2 drops liquid smoke
Dash of ground allspice
Dash of ground mace
Dash of ground cloves
Dash of red pepper
1 pound peeled medium shrimp
1 (12-ounce) container fresh Standard
    oysters, drained
½ pound fresh crabmeat, drained and
    flaked
Gumbo filé (optional)

Place flour in a shallow baking pan. Bake at 400°, stirring every 4 minutes, for 12 to 15 minutes or until flour is browned.

Combine green pepper, celery, and ⅓ cup chicken broth in a Dutch oven. Cook over medium heat 10 to 12 minutes or until vegetables are tender. Stir in flour. Gradually stir in remaining 1 cup chicken broth, beef broth, tomato sauce, water, okra, onion, parsley flakes, garlic, bay leaf, and remaining seasonings. Reduce heat, and simmer, uncovered, 1 hour.

Stir shrimp, oysters, and crabmeat into mixture. Simmer 10 to 15 minutes or until shrimp are done and edges of oysters begin to curl.

Remove bay leaf from gumbo mixture. Serve the gumbo with gumbo filé, if desired. Yield: 12 cups (about 123 calories per 1-cup serving).

Joanne Champagne,
Covington, Louisiana.

SCALLOP APPETIZER

¾ cup Chablis or other dry white wine
½ cup water
1 pound bay scallops
½ cup red pepper strips
⅓ cup diced celery
¼ cup chopped green onions
3 tablespoons lemon juice
⅛ teaspoon white pepper
Leaf lettuce

Combine wine and water in a medium saucepan; bring to a boil. Add scallops, and cook 3 to 5 minutes. Drain and let cool. Combine scallops, red pepper, celery, green onions, lemon juice, and white pepper in a shallow dish. Cover and chill scallop mixture 3 to 4 hours, stirring occasionally.

To serve, line individual scallop shells with leaf lettuce; top with scallop mixture. Yield: 5 servings (about 112 calories per ½-cup serving). *Ella Stivers,*
Abilene, Texas.

FRUITED SHRIMP SALAD

3 cups water
1 pound unpeeled large fresh shrimp
2 (8-ounce) cans unsweetened pineapple
   tidbits, drained
1 (11-ounce) can mandarin oranges in
   extra light syrup, drained
½ cup chopped celery
3 tablespoons reduced-calorie mayonnaise
1½ teaspoons lemon juice
Bibb lettuce leaves (optional)

Bring water to a boil; add shrimp, and cook 3 to 5 minutes. Drain well; rinse with cold water. Chill. Peel and devein shrimp.

Combine shrimp, pineapple, mandarin oranges, celery, mayonnaise, and lemon juice, tossing gently; chill. Serve on lettuce leaves, if desired. Yield: 3 servings (about 271 calories per ¾-cup serving). *Gwen Louer, Roswell, Georgia.*

CRAWFISH ÉTOUFFÉE

¾ cup chopped onion
½ cup chopped celery
½ cup chopped green pepper
1 tablespoon reduced-calorie margarine,
   melted
1 (10¾-ounce) can chicken broth
¼ cup plus 1 tablespoon tomato paste
1½ tablespoons lemon juice
¼ teaspoon Worcestershire sauce
¼ teaspoon hot sauce
⅛ teaspoon pepper
1 pound peeled crawfish tails
2 cups hot cooked rice (cooked
   without fat)

Sauté onion, celery, and green pepper in margarine until tender. Add chicken broth, tomato paste, lemon juice, Worcestershire sauce, hot sauce, and pepper. Cook over medium-high heat, stirring until smooth and bubbly.

Add crawfish; reduce heat and simmer 5 minutes or until mixture is thoroughly heated. Serve over hot rice. Yield: 4 servings (about 143 calories per 1 cup étouffée plus 90 calories per ½ cup rice). *Jane Butterworth, St. Francisville, Louisiana.*

Depend On Chicken For Versatility

Chicken is the ideal entrée—it's versatile, simple to prepare, and nutritious. Whether you're planning a picnic or elegant seated dinner, you can count on it.

For a fun-filled outing or casual meal, we suggest Delicious Fried Chicken, coated in a spicy, crisp crust. If you want more formality, turn to Chicken Scaloppine With Lemon Sauce.

DELICIOUS FRIED CHICKEN

1 cup all-purpose flour
1 teaspoon paprika
1 teaspoon dry mustard
½ teaspoon garlic powder
½ teaspoon ground nutmeg
3 pounds chicken pieces, skinned
Salt and pepper
Vegetable oil

Combine flour, paprika, mustard, garlic powder, and nutmeg in a plastic bag; shake to mix, and set aside.

Sprinkle chicken pieces with salt and pepper. Place 2 or 3 pieces of chicken in bag; shake well. Repeat procedure with remaining chicken.

Heat 1 inch of oil in a large skillet to 325°; add chicken, and fry 30 to 35 minutes or until golden brown, turning once. Drain chicken on paper towels. Yield: 4 servings. *Linda Heath, Roswell, Georgia.*

CHICKEN SCALOPPINE WITH LEMON SAUCE

6 chicken breast halves, skinned, boned,
   and halved
1 cup all-purpose flour
¼ teaspoon pepper
2 eggs, beaten
¼ cup butter or margarine
¼ cup vegetable oil
½ to ¾ pound fresh mushrooms, thinly
   sliced
¼ cup water
½ cup Chablis or other dry white wine
½ cup lemon juice
½ cup chopped fresh parsley

Place each chicken piece between 2 sheets of waxed paper; flatten to ¼-inch thickness using a meat mallet or a rolling pin.

Combine flour and pepper; stir well. Dredge chicken in eggs and then in

flour mixture, shaking off excess flour; set chicken aside.

Heat butter and oil in a heavy skillet. Cook chicken in skillet over medium heat about 4 minutes on each side or until golden brown. Remove chicken to serving platter; keep warm.

Add mushrooms and ¼ cup water to pan drippings; cook over medium heat, stirring often, about 3 minutes. Spoon mushrooms over chicken.

Add wine and lemon juice to skillet; heat thoroughly. Pour sauce over chicken; sprinkle with parsley. Yield: 6 servings. *Marian Celletti, Englewood, Florida.*

SUNNY HERBED CHICKEN

½ teaspoon salt
½ teaspoon paprika
¾ teaspoon chopped fresh basil or
   ¼ teaspoon dried whole basil
½ teaspoon chopped fresh rosemary leaves
   or 1 teaspoon dried whole rosemary,
   crushed
¼ teaspoon pepper
6 chicken breast halves, skinned and
   boned
1 tablespoon butter or margarine
¼ cup Chablis or other dry white wine
3 tablespoons lemon juice
3 tablespoons lime juice
3 tablespoons orange juice
3 tablespoons low-fat banana yogurt

Combine salt, paprika, basil, rosemary, and pepper, mixing well. Sprinkle over chicken. Melt butter in a large skillet; add chicken, and sauté about 5 minutes on each side or until golden.

Combine wine and juices, mixing well; pour over chicken. Cover, reduce heat, and simmer 20 minutes or until chicken is done. Remove chicken to serving platter. Add yogurt to pan drippings, stirring well. Cook yogurt over low heat until thoroughly heated. Pour sauce over chicken. Yield: 6 servings. *Shirley Draper, Winter Park, Florida.*

SOY-CHICKEN KABOBS

1 (15¼-ounce) can pineapple chunks
½ cup soy sauce
⅓ cup sugar
1 clove garlic, minced
½ teaspoon ground ginger
5 chicken breast halves, skinned, boned,
   and cut into 1-inch cubes
1 green pepper, cut into 1-inch pieces
Vegetable cooking spray
Hot cooked rice (optional)

Drain pineapple, reserving ⅓ cup juice; set pineapple aside. Combine pineapple juice, soy sauce, sugar, garlic, and ginger in a dish; mix. Add chicken; cover and marinate in refrigerator 1 hour, turning occasionally.

Remove chicken from marinade, reserving marinade. Alternate chicken, green pepper, and pineapple on skewers. Coat grill with cooking spray. Grill kabobs over medium-hot coals for 15 minutes or until done, turning and basting frequently with marinade. Serve over rice, if desired. Yield: 4 servings.
Linda Gellatly,
Winston-Salem, North Carolina.

Simple Meals To Tote

Everyone occasionally needs to help out by taking a simple meal to a friend's home. We've put together a small collection of recipes that can be mixed and matched to serve various needs. When you just want to carry something simple, we suggest a combination of Crunchy Chicken Salad, Marinated Broccoli, and Favorite Brownies.

If more substantial food is needed, turn to Biscuit-Topped Chicken Pie, Dilled Green Beans, and Favorite Brownies. Of course, the vegetables can be switched, and fresh fruit, a relish tray, or bread added to help round out either menu.

Before preparing the recipes, consider the containers in which they will be transported. Aluminum disposable pans, paper products, and zip-top plastic bags are ideal. We found that Biscuit-Topped Chicken Pie can be baked and carried in an 8-inch square disposable pan.

BISCUIT-TOPPED CHICKEN PIE
¼ cup butter or margarine
⅓ cup all-purpose flour
1 (13¾-ounce) can chicken broth, undiluted or 1¾ cups chicken broth
⅔ cup milk
2 cups diced cooked chicken
1 (8.5-ounce) can English peas, drained
1 (16-ounce) can mixed vegetables, drained
¼ teaspoon salt
⅛ teaspoon pepper
Biscuit topping (recipe follows)

Melt butter in a large saucepan over low heat; add flour, stirring until smooth. Cook 1 minute, stirring constantly. Gradually add chicken broth and milk; cook over medium heat, stirring constantly, until mixture is thickened and bubbly. Stir in chicken, peas, vegetables, salt, and pepper; heat thoroughly. Pour mixture into a greased 8-inch square pan; cover with biscuit topping. Bake at 425° for 35 minutes. Yield: 4 to 6 servings.

Biscuit Topping:
1 cup all-purpose flour
1 teaspoon ground celery seeds
½ teaspoon salt
½ teaspoon paprika
⅓ cup shortening
¼ cup cold water

Combine flour, celery seeds, salt, and paprika; cut in shortening until mixture resembles coarse meal. Add water, 1 tablespoon at a time, stirring with a fork until dry ingredients are moistened. Turn dough out onto a well-floured surface, and knead 3 or 4 times.
Roll dough to ¼-inch thickness; cut with a 2½-inch biscuit cutter. Yield: 9 biscuit rounds.
Julia Wood,
Paducah, Kentucky.

CRUNCHY CHICKEN SALAD
5½ cups chopped cooked chicken
3 hard-cooked eggs, chopped
1 cup chopped celery
1 cup cubed sweet pickles
1 cup chopped pecans, toasted
1 cup seedless green grapes, halved
1 cup mayonnaise
1 (8-ounce) can water chestnuts, drained and chopped
1 (8-ounce) can pineapple tidbits, drained and chopped
½ cup pimiento-stuffed olives, chopped
1 small onion, chopped
1 (2-ounce) jar diced pimiento, drained
1 tablespoon lemon juice

Combine all ingredients; blend well. Chill. Serve on lettuce cups, or use for sandwiches. Yield: 12 servings.
Mrs. J. O. Branson,
Thomasville, North Carolina.

DILLED GREEN BEANS
1½ pounds fresh green beans
⅓ cup olive oil
¼ cup minced green onions
3 tablespoons minced fresh dillweed or 1 tablespoon dried whole dillweed
2 tablespoons sugar
2 tablespoons lemon juice
2 tablespoons Dijon mustard
1 tablespoon chopped fresh parsley
1 tablespoon cider vinegar
Pinch of salt
Pinch of coarsely ground pepper
⅓ cup sliced radishes
⅓ cup chopped walnuts

Remove strings from green beans, and wash thoroughly. Cut beans into 1½-inch pieces. Cook green beans, covered, in a small amount of boiling water 10 minutes or until crisp-tender. Drain beans, and set aside to cool.

Combine oil, green onions, dillweed, sugar, lemon juice, mustard, parsley, vinegar, salt, and pepper in a jar; cover tightly, and shake vigorously. Pour over green beans; toss well. Cover and refrigerate 8 hours. Stir in radishes and walnuts before serving. Yield: 6 servings. *Mrs. C. M. Shackelford,*
Florence, South Carolina.

MARINATED BROCCOLI
2 pounds fresh broccoli
1½ cups cider vinegar
½ cup vegetable oil
¼ cup cold water
2 tablespoons sugar
1 tablespoon dillseeds
1 teaspoon salt
½ teaspoon pepper
1 clove garlic, minced

Trim off large leaves of broccoli. Remove tough ends of lower stalks, and wash broccoli. Cut into flowerets, reserving stalks for use in another recipe. Place flowerets in a large shallow dish, and set aside.

Combine remaining ingredients, and pour over broccoli. Cover and refrigerate for 8 hours, stirring occasionally. Yield: 8 servings. *Carol Van Sickle,*
Versailles, Kentucky.

FAVORITE BROWNIES

3 (1-ounce) squares semisweet chocolate
1 cup butter or margarine
2 cups sugar
4 eggs
2 cups all-purpose flour
1 cup chopped pecans
1 tablespoon vanilla extract

Melt chocolate and butter in a medium saucepan. Add sugar. Remove from heat; add eggs, one at a time, mixing well after each addition. Stir in flour, pecans, and vanilla. Pour into a greased and floured 13- x 9- x 2-inch baking pan. Bake at 350° for 30 minutes. Cool. Cut into squares. Yield: 2 dozen.

Lynda Marshall,
Slaton, Texas.

Add Pasta On The Side

Tired of serving rice or potatoes? Then consider a pasta side dish. In each of these recipes, hot pasta is tossed with a dressing or sauce—just right for serving alongside a variety of main dishes.

FETTUCCINE ALFREDO

1 (12-ounce) package uncooked fettuccine
1 cup grated Parmesan cheese
½ cup butter or margarine, softened
½ cup whipping cream
2 tablespoons chopped fresh parsley
¼ teaspoon white pepper

Cook fettuccine according to package directions, omitting salt. Drain well; place in a large bowl. Add remaining ingredients. Toss until fettuccine is coated. Yield: 6 servings.

Patricia Pashby,
Memphis, Tennessee.

ANCHOVY-GARLIC SAUCE OVER VERMICELLI

1 (8-ounce) package vermicelli
1 (2-ounce) can anchovy fillets, minced
3 cloves garlic, minced
½ cup olive oil
3 tablespoons seasoned breadcrumbs
2 tablespoons chopped fresh parsley

Cook vermicelli according to package directions, omitting salt. Drain well, and set aside.

Sauté anchovies and garlic in hot olive oil for 2 minutes. Pour over hot vermicelli. Stir in breadcrumbs and parsley. Serve immediately. Yield: 6 servings.

Bob Barletta,
Marietta, Georgia.

MUSHROOM SAUCE SUPREME ON VERMICELLI

1 beef-flavored bouillon cube
½ cup boiling water
1 cup fresh mushrooms, sliced
½ cup chopped onion
¼ cup butter or margarine, melted
1 (10¾-ounce) can cream of mushroom soup, undiluted
¼ cup white wine
½ teaspoon Italian seasoning
¼ teaspoon pepper
6 ounces vermicelli

Dissolve bouillon cube in ½ cup boiling water; set aside.

Sauté mushrooms and onion in butter in a skillet. Stir in dissolved bouillon, undiluted soup, wine, Italian seasoning, and pepper.

Cook vermicelli according to package directions, omitting salt. Drain well; stir in mushroom sauce. Yield: 4 servings.

Karen A. O'Neal,
Muskogee, Oklahoma.

SPAGHETTI WITH HERBAL DRESSING

1 (8-ounce) package spaghetti
½ cup mayonnaise
½ cup commercial sour cream
2 teaspoons minced fresh basil or ⅔ teaspoon dried whole basil
2 teaspoons minced fresh dillweed or ⅔ teaspoon dried whole dillweed
½ teaspoon garlic powder
½ teaspoon salt
Dash of pepper

Cook spaghetti according to package directions, omitting salt; drain well, and set aside.

Combine mayonnaise and sour cream in a small saucepan; stir in remaining ingredients. Blend well. Cook over low heat just until thoroughly heated. (Do not boil.) Pour over hot spaghetti, and serve immediately. Yield: 4 servings.

Kathy Richards,
Blackville, South Carolina.

LINGUINE WITH TOMATO-CREAM SAUCE

1 medium onion, chopped
1 small clove garlic, minced
2 tablespoons olive oil
1 (14-ounce) can Italian-style tomatoes, undrained and chopped
1 tablespoon dried whole basil
¾ teaspoon sugar
¼ teaspoon dried whole oregano
¼ teaspoon salt
⅛ teaspoon pepper
½ cup whipping cream
1 tablespoon butter or margarine
8 ounces uncooked linguine
¼ cup grated Parmesan cheese

Sauté onion and garlic in oil in a large skillet over medium heat. Add tomatoes, basil, sugar, oregano, salt, and pepper. Bring mixture to a boil; continue to boil 5 minutes or until most of liquid evaporates. Remove from heat; stir in whipping cream and butter. Reduce heat, and simmer 5 minutes. Set sauce aside.

Cook linguine according to package directions, omitting salt. Drain well. Pour tomato sauce over hot linguine, and toss well. Sprinkle with Parmesan cheese. Yield: 4 to 6 servings.

Linda Keith,
Dallas, Texas.

Pick Up Tips From This Processor Cook

Merijoy Lantz Rucker, caterer and cooking instructor of Alpharetta, Georgia, says she couldn't cook without her food processor. "It saves a great deal of time. And you don't have to have lots of other equipment in the kitchen."

Merijoy started using her processor more than seven years ago when she began catering parties. At that time, she began looking for recipes that involved two or three procedures that could all be done in the processor.

From her collection of make-ahead food processor recipes, one of Merijoy's favorites is Olive Quiche Appetizers. "I dump everything in at once, and by the time you beat the eggs, the olives are chopped." By preparing the quiche in a jellyroll pan, it's easy to cut into small squares to serve at parties. She suggests serving it hot or cold.

Party food is Merijoy's specialty, but any recipe that can be made ahead of time is a hit with her. "My idea behind every recipe for a cocktail party is that it shouldn't be something you worry about," she says. "One thing I tell people about giving parties is to put out small amounts of food and replenish during the party—it looks prettier. For example, instead of making one large pâté, I make small ones so I can put out a fresh one later on."

Over the years, Merijoy has practiced trimming time from recipes by using the food processor. You may find some of her following hints helpful.

—Remember to use the pulse button. The processor is so quick that before you know it, the food is overprocessed.

—"I think people wash the work bowl too much," states Merijoy. "Process dry food first, wet food next, and combinations last."

—Process together only foods of similar textures, such as onions and green peppers. Don't chop nuts and a soft food, such as bananas, at the same time.

—Because the processor is fast, foods such as cream cheese and butter don't need to be at room temperature before mixing unless your recipe specifically states that it must.

—Don't overbeat mixtures that are to be baked. Once again, pulse only to blend mixture.

—Finally, clean a space on your counter for your machine. "My processor stays on my counter," says Merijoy, "and I use it all the time. If I had to pull it out every time, I would probably use it much less."

Enjoy Merijoy's recipes below.

PÂTÉ WITH COGNAC

1 small onion, quartered
1 small clove garlic, crushed
1 tablespoon butter or margarine, melted
1 pound chicken livers
¼ cup cognac
¼ teaspoon salt
⅛ teaspoon pepper
⅛ teaspoon ground allspice
⅛ teaspoon ground nutmeg
1 (8-ounce) package cream cheese, cut into cubes
2 tablespoons chopped fresh parsley
1 tablespoon chopped fresh chives
Chopped fresh parsley (optional)
Ripe olives (optional)

Position knife blade in food processor bowl; add onion. Top with cover, and pulse 4 or 5 times or until onion is coarsely chopped. Sauté onion and garlic in butter for 5 minutes. Add livers,

and cook over medium heat 3 to 4 minutes, stirring frequently. Add cognac, salt, pepper, and spices. Cook an additional 5 minutes or until livers are slightly pink. Drain livers.

Add cream cheese and livers to processor bowl. Process mixture 20 seconds or until smooth, stopping to scrape sides of bowl with a spatula. Stir in 2 tablespoons parsley and 1 tablespoon chives, mixing well. Line a 7½- x 3½-inch loaf pan with plastic wrap; pour liver mixture into pan. Cover and chill pâté at least 8 hours.

Remove pâté from pan; peel off plastic wrap. Smooth surface of pâté with a knife if necessary. Garnish with parsley and olives, if desired. Serve with crackers. Yield: 3½ cups.

SPINACH DIP

6 green onions
1 cup low-fat cottage cheese
1 cup plain yogurt
1 (10-ounce) package frozen chopped spinach, thawed and well drained
2 tablespoons fresh lime juice
1 teaspoon curry powder
¼ teaspoon salt
Pinch of pepper
1 large purple cabbage
Assorted fresh vegetables

Cut onions into 1-inch pieces. Position knife blade in food processor bowl; add green onions. Top with cover; process until chopped. Remove cover; add cottage cheese and yogurt. Top with cover; process 1 minute or until smooth. Remove top; add spinach, lime juice, and seasonings. Top with cover, and pulse 2 or 3 times or until mixed well. Chill until serving time.

Cut off base of cabbage to set securely. Peel back largest leaves, and leave attached to cabbage. Cut off top one-third of cabbage, and hollow out center. (Reserve cabbage from center for other uses.) Fill hollowed center with dip, and serve with assorted fresh vegetables. Yield: 1⅔ cups.

OLIVE QUICHE APPETIZERS

Pastry for double-crust 9-inch pie
6 ounces Monterey Jack cheese
6 eggs
1 cup pimiento-stuffed olives
2 cups commercial sour cream
1 teaspoon dried whole oregano
Sliced pimiento-stuffed olives (optional)

Roll pastry to ⅛-inch thickness on a lightly floured surface; fit in bottom and up sides of a 15- x 10- x 1-inch jellyroll pan. Set aside.

Position shredding disc in food processor bowl; top with cover. Cut cheese to fit food chute, and shred, using firm pressure. Remove cheese, and set aside.

Position knife blade in processor bowl; add eggs. Top with cover. Process 5 seconds. Add olives, sour cream, oregano, and shredded cheese; process 5 seconds. Pour into prepared crust. Bake at 425° for 15 minutes. Reduce temperature to 375°, and continue baking for 20 to 25 minutes or until center is set. Cool slightly, and cut into 1½- x 1¼-inch bars. Garnish with sliced pimiento-stuffed olives, if desired.

Note: Quiche may be baked a day ahead and refrigerated. To reheat, bake at 375° for 10 minutes or until thoroughly heated. Yield: about 6 dozen.

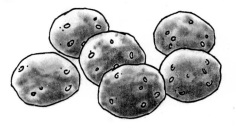

PROCESSOR POTATO CASSEROLE

14 medium-size red potatoes, unpeeled
6 ounces Cheddar cheese
3 green onions
½ cup butter or margarine, melted
1½ cups commercial sour cream

Cook potatoes in boiling salted water to cover 15 minutes or until almost tender. Drain and chill well. Quarter potatoes.

Position coarse shredding disc in food processor bowl; top with cover. Closely pack potatoes into food chute. Shred, applying medium pressure with food pusher. Remove potatoes, and place in a large mixing bowl.

Cut cheese to fit food chute. Shred, applying medium pressure with food pusher; add to potatoes. Set aside.

Cut onions into 1-inch pieces. Position knife blade in processor bowl; add green onions. Pulse 3 or 4 times until onions are evenly chopped, scraping bowl as needed. Sauté onions in butter until tender; add onions to potatoes. Stir in sour cream.

Spoon potato mixture into a shallow 2-quart casserole. Bake at 325° for 35 minutes or until bubbly. Yield: 8 to 10 servings.

Best Bets For Lunch

In the middle of a busy day, it's a challenge to fix a lunch that's simple, but appetizing. So take a break, and put together one of these proven favorites.

QUICK PAN PIZZA

1 (10-ounce) can refrigerated flaky biscuits
⅓ cup grated Parmesan cheese
1 pound ground beef
½ cup chopped green pepper
½ cup chopped onion
1 (8-ounce) can tomato sauce
1 (2½-ounce) can sliced mushrooms, drained
¼ cup water
2 tablespoons Italian-style spaghetti sauce mix
1 (3½-ounce) package sliced pepperoni
1½ cups (6 ounces) shredded mozzarella cheese

Separate biscuit dough into 10 biscuits. Arrange in a lightly greased 13- x 9- x 2-inch baking pan; press biscuits to form crust. Sprinkle Parmesan cheese over biscuits.

Combine ground beef, green pepper, and onion in a skillet; cook over medium heat until meat is browned, stirring to crumble. Drain well. Add tomato sauce, mushrooms, water, and spaghetti sauce mix; simmer 5 minutes. Spoon mixture over crust; top with pepperoni. Bake at 400° for 20 minutes; sprinkle with mozzarella cheese. Bake an additional 5 minutes or until cheese melts. Yield: 6 servings. *Joy M. Hall, Lucedale, Mississippi.*

ITALIAN SAUSAGE SLOPPY JOES

1½ pounds mild Italian sausage
½ cup chopped green pepper
½ cup chopped onion
1 (2.2-ounce) can sliced black olives, drained
1 (28-ounce) can whole tomatoes, drained and chopped
1 tablespoon chopped fresh parsley
1½ teaspoons dried whole basil
⅛ teaspoon salt
¼ teaspoon pepper
Biscuits or hamburger buns, split
½ cup (2 ounces) shredded mozzarella cheese

Remove casings from sausage. Combine sausage, green pepper, and onion in a large skillet; cook over medium heat until meat is browned, stirring to crumble. Drain well. Add olives, tomatoes, and seasonings; cover and simmer 30 minutes.

Serve meat mixture over split biscuits or hamburger buns, and sprinkle with mozzarella cheese. Yield: 6 servings.
Peggy Fowler Revels, Woodruff, South Carolina.

DRIED BEEF PITA SANDWICHES

2 cups shredded lettuce
1 cup chopped tomato
1 cup (4 ounces) shredded mozzarella cheese
1 (2½-ounce) jar dried beef, rinsed, drained, and cut into strips
½ cup chopped celery
½ cup chopped onion
½ cup chopped cucumber
¼ cup sliced pitted ripe olives
½ cup commercial Italian salad dressing
3 (6-inch) pita bread rounds, cut in half

Combine all ingredients except bread; toss gently. Spoon into pita bread halves. Yield: 3 servings.
Mrs. Wesley Hull, Dallas, Texas.

CHICKEN CLUB SANDWICHES

12 slices whole wheat bread, toasted
¼ to ½ cup mayonnaise
8 lettuce leaves, divided
8 (1½-ounce) slices smoked chicken breast
8 slices tomato
8 slices bacon, cooked

Spread one side of each slice of bread with mayonnaise. Top 4 slices of bread with a lettuce leaf and 2 slices of chicken; cover each with another slice of bread. Top each with a lettuce leaf, 2 tomato slices, and 2 slices of bacon; cover each with remaining slices of bread, mayonnaise side down. Cut each sandwich into 4 triangles. (Insert a wooden pick in each triangle, if necessary.) Yield: 4 servings.
Pamela Barber, Nashville, Georgia.

OPEN-FACE EGG SANDWICHES

2 English muffins, split and toasted
1 tablespoon plus 1 teaspoon prepared brown mustard
4 lettuce leaves
4 slices bacon, cooked and halved
4 slices tomato
4 poached eggs
¼ cup (1 ounce) shredded Cheddar cheese, divided

Spread each muffin half with 1 teaspoon mustard. Top each with a lettuce leaf, 2 bacon halves, 1 tomato slice, and a poached egg. Sprinkle each with 1 tablespoon cheese. Serve immediately. Yield: 4 servings. *Alice Higdon, Quincy, Florida.*

Vegetable Soups For Summer

Vegetable soups are ideal for summer menus; fresh produce offers peak flavor, and canned vegetables give you the option of making soup in just minutes. Our Garden Vegetable Soup celebrates the season's best with carrots, tomatoes, green beans, and zucchini.

GARDEN VEGETABLE SOUP

2 tablespoons butter or margarine
2 tablespoons vegetable oil
1 cup thinly sliced carrots
1 cup sliced celery with leaves
1 cup chopped onion
1 clove garlic, crushed
9 medium tomatoes, peeled and chopped
1 teaspoon dried whole oregano
1 teaspoon dried whole basil
2 teaspoons salt
¼ teaspoon pepper
1 (14½-ounce) can beef broth, undiluted
⅓ pound fresh green beans, washed and cut into 1-inch pieces
1 medium zucchini, halved lengthwise and sliced
¼ cup chopped fresh parsley
Grated Parmesan cheese (optional)

Heat butter and oil in a large Dutch oven. Add carrots, celery, onion, and garlic; sauté until onion is tender. Add tomatoes, oregano, basil, salt, and pepper; bring to a boil. Reduce heat and simmer vegetable mixture 15 minutes, stirring occasionally.

Add broth and green beans; simmer 20 minutes. Add zucchini and parsley; simmer 10 minutes. Spoon into soup bowls; sprinkle with Parmesan cheese, if desired. Yield: 9 cups.

Mrs. Kenneth B. Waldron,
Mountain Rest, South Carolina.

WATERCRESS-AND-LEEK SOUP

1 tablespoon butter or margarine
3 tablespoons water
3 leeks, sliced
1 medium onion, sliced
1 bunch watercress, divided
2 large potatoes, peeled and sliced
3 cups chicken broth
2½ cups milk
¼ teaspoon salt
⅛ teaspoon freshly ground pepper

Melt butter in a Dutch oven; add water, leeks, and onion. Cover and cook about 8 minutes or until tender, stirring occasionally. (Do not brown.)

Set aside ¾ cup watercress. Add remaining watercress and remaining ingredients to Dutch oven. Cover, and bring to a boil. Reduce heat, and simmer 30 minutes or until vegetables are soft.

Spoon one-third of soup mixture into container of an electric blender, and puree; continue blending until all mixture is pureed. Return puree to Dutch oven, reserving ⅓ cup in blender. Add reserved ¾ cup watercress to blender, and puree; set aside.

Simmer pureed soup mixture until thoroughly heated. Just before serving, stir in the pureed watercress mixture. Yield: 7 cups.

Mrs. Herbert W. Rutherford,
Baltimore, Maryland.

CREAM OF TOMATO SOUP WITH PARMESAN CHEESE

2 (14-ounce) cans Italian plum tomatoes, undrained
1 cup whipping cream
¼ cup chopped fresh basil
¼ cup chopped fresh parsley
1 teaspoon freshly ground pepper
¼ teaspoon salt
½ cup freshly grated Parmesan cheese

Position knife blade in food processor bowl; add all ingredients except cheese. Top with cover, and pulse until mixture is smooth.

Pour mixture into a saucepan; cook over medium heat until thoroughly heated. Stir in cheese; heat until cheese melts. Yield: 4½ cups. *Lynn Rollins,*
Mechanicsville, Virginia.

BROCCOLI SOUP

2 tablespoons grated onion
½ cup butter or margarine, melted
¼ cup all-purpose flour
1 cup milk
1 cup half-and-half
2 cups chicken broth
½ teaspoon salt
⅛ teaspoon garlic powder
¼ to ½ teaspoon dried whole basil
3 cups chopped fresh broccoli

Sauté onion in butter in a Dutch oven. Add flour, stirring until smooth. Cook 1 minute, stirring constantly. Gradually add milk, half-and-half, and chicken broth; cook over medium heat, stirring constantly, until the mixture is thickened and bubbly.

Stir in salt, garlic powder, and basil. Add broccoli; cover and cook over medium heat 15 minutes or until broccoli is tender. Yield: 5 cups. *Sandy DeRose,*
Marietta, Georgia.

Favorite Fruit And Vegetable Breads

Cooks have known the benefits of stirring fruit and vegetables into bread doughs and batters for years. For that reason, the recipes you'll find here are mostly old favorites you're sure to recognize and want to try.

DEEP-DISH APPLE DANISH

8 medium-size cooking apples, peeled and sliced
⅔ cup sugar
2 teaspoons lemon juice
¼ teaspoon ground cinnamon
¼ teaspoon ground nutmeg
1 package dry yeast
¼ cup warm water (105° to 115°)
2 cups all-purpose flour
2 tablespoons sugar
1 cup butter or margarine
1 egg, beaten
1 teaspoon vanilla extract
Sugar Glaze

Combine apples, ⅔ cup sugar, lemon juice, cinnamon, and nutmeg in a large saucepan or skillet. Bring to a boil; cover, reduce heat, and simmer 25 minutes or until apples are almost tender. Let apples cool.

Dissolve yeast in warm water; let stand 5 minutes. Combine flour and 2 tablespoons sugar in a medium mixing bowl; cut in butter with a pastry blender until mixture resembles coarse meal. Combine egg, vanilla, and dissolved yeast; stir into flour mixture.

Pat two-thirds of dough in bottom of a greased 9-inch square pan. Spread apple filling evenly over dough. Roll remaining one-third of dough into a 9-inch square on a well-floured surface; place over apple mixture, sealing edges to sides of pan. Bake at 375° for 35 minutes; reduce heat to 300°, and bake an additional 25 minutes. (Cover edges with foil to prevent overbrowning, if necessary.) Drizzle with Sugar Glaze. Serve warm or at room temperature. Yield: 12 servings.

Sugar Glaze:

1 cup sifted powdered sugar
1½ tablespoons butter or margarine, melted
About 2 tablespoons milk
½ teaspoon vanilla extract
½ teaspoon lemon juice

Combine all ingredients in a small mixing bowl; beat until smooth. Yield: ½ cup. *Sandra Souther,*
Gainesville, Georgia.

OLD-FASHIONED BLUEBERRY MUFFINS

2 cups all-purpose flour
⅔ cup sugar
1 tablespoon baking powder
½ teaspoon salt
½ teaspoon ground nutmeg
2 eggs, beaten
½ cup milk
½ cup butter or margarine, melted
1½ cups fresh blueberries
¼ cup sliced almonds
1 tablespoon sugar

Combine flour, ⅔ cup sugar, baking powder, salt, and nutmeg in a large bowl, reserving 1 tablespoon to toss with blueberries. Make a well in the center of the mixture.

Combine eggs, milk, and butter; add to dry ingredients, stirring just until moistened. Toss blueberries with reserved flour mixture to coat; stir into batter. Spoon mixture into greased muffin pans, filling two-thirds full. Sprinkle with almonds and 1 tablespoon sugar. Bake at 400° for 15 to 18 minutes. Yield: 18 muffins. *Myrtice Hartman,*
Montezuma, Georgia.

POTATO LOAVES

1 medium potato, peeled and chopped
1 package dry yeast
1 cup milk, scalded
5 cups all-purpose flour, divided
¼ cup shortening
¼ cup butter or margarine, softened
½ cup sugar
2 eggs, beaten
2 teaspoons salt
Melted butter or margarine

Cook potato in unsalted boiling water to cover 10 minutes or until tender. Drain potato, reserving ½ cup liquid. Mash potato, and set aside.

Dissolve yeast in warm potato water (105° to 115°); let stand 5 minutes, and set aside.

Cool milk to 105° to 115°; stir into yeast mixture. Add 1½ cups flour and mashed potato, mixing well. Cover and let rise in a warm place (85°), free from drafts, 1 hour or until doubled in bulk.

Cream shortening and ¼ cup butter; gradually add sugar, beating until light and fluffy. Add eggs and salt; blend well. Stir creamed mixture into yeast mixture. Gradually add remaining 3½ cups flour to make a soft dough. Place in a well-greased bowl, turning to grease top. Cover and let rise in a warm place (85°), free from drafts, 1 hour or until doubled in bulk.

Punch dough down, and divide in half. Place in two well-greased, 9- x 5- x 3-inch loafpans. Brush with melted butter. Cover and let rise in a warm place (85°), free from drafts, 50 to 60 minutes or until doubled in bulk. Bake at 350° for 50 minutes or until loaves sound hollow when tapped. Yield: 2 loaves.
Rena Nixon,
Mount Airy, North Carolina.

SPICED ZUCCHINI BREAD

⅓ cup shortening
1 cup sugar
2 eggs
1 cup shredded zucchini
⅓ cup water
1½ cups plus 2 tablespoons all-purpose flour
1 teaspoon baking soda
¼ teaspoon baking powder
½ teaspoon salt
½ teaspoon ground cinnamon
½ teaspoon ground cloves
⅓ cup chopped pecans

Cream shortening at medium speed of an electric mixer; gradually add sugar,

beating well. Add eggs, zucchini, and water; mix thoroughly.

Combine flour, soda, baking powder, salt, and spices; add to creamed mixture, stirring well. Stir in pecans.

Spoon batter into an 8- x 4- x 3-inch loafpan greased only on bottom. Bake at 350° for 50 minutes or until a wooden pick inserted in center comes out clean. Cool in pan 10 minutes; remove from pan, and cool completely. Yield: 1 loaf.

Note: For variety, substitute 1 cup shredded carrot or 1 cup mashed banana for 1 cup shredded zucchini.
Sandra Russell,
Gainesville, Florida.

For The Love Of Ladyfingers

Have you ever wondered what you can do with ladyfingers? These long and narrow, delicate sponge confections have many uses and bring a new dimension to desserts.

Rich and dreamy best describe Chocolate Ladyfinger Dessert. Serve this specialty at your next dinner party. It's a great make-ahead idea.

CHOCOLATE LADYFINGER DESSERT

1 cup cocoa
½ cup sugar
4 eggs, separated
¼ cup water
½ cup butter or margarine, softened
1 cup sifted powdered sugar
1 teaspoon vanilla extract
½ cup chopped walnuts
2 tablespoons sugar
16 ladyfingers, split
1 cup whipping cream
1½ tablespoons powdered sugar
½ teaspoon vanilla extract

Combine cocoa and ½ cup sugar in top of a double boiler; mix well. Stir in egg yolks and water; bring water in bottom of double boiler to a boil. Cook mixture, stirring constantly, for 5 minutes; set aside to cool.

Cream butter, 1 cup powdered sugar, and 1 teaspoon vanilla in a large bowl; beat in cooled cocoa mixture until smooth. Stir in walnuts; set aside.

Beat egg whites (at room temperature) until foamy; gradually add 2 tablespoons sugar, beating until peaks are stiff, but not dry. Fold egg white mixture into cocoa mixture; set aside.

Line bottom and sides of an 8-inch springform pan with ladyfingers, placing rounded sides of ladyfingers toward outside of pan. Spoon chocolate mixture into pan; cover and chill 8 hours.

Combine whipping cream, 1½ tablespoons powdered sugar, and ½ teaspoon vanilla; beat at medium speed of an electric mixer until stiff peaks form. Spread whipped cream over chocolate mixture before serving. Yield: 6 to 8 servings. *Mrs. Marshall M. DeBerry,*
Franklin, Virginia.

STRAWBERRY-LEMON DESSERT

1 (3-ounce) package ladyfingers, split
1 (14-ounce) can sweetened condensed milk
1 tablespoon grated lemon rind
⅓ cup lemon juice
1 pint whipping cream, whipped and divided
8 to 10 strawberries, sliced

Line bottom and sides of a 2½-quart soufflé dish or straight-sided bowl with ladyfingers, placing rounded sides of ladyfingers toward outside of soufflé dish; set dish aside.

Combine sweetened condensed milk, lemon rind, and lemon juice in a large mixing bowl; stir well. Fold in two-thirds of whipped cream; spoon into dish. Spread remaining whipped cream on top; cover and chill 3 to 4 hours. Arrange the strawberry slices on top before serving. Yield: 8 servings.
Carole May,
Shawmut, Alabama.

FRESH PEACH CUSTARD DESSERT

½ cup lemon juice
½ cup orange juice
1 envelope unflavored gelatin
1 cup sugar
¼ cup all-purpose flour
1 cup milk
3 eggs, separated
3 cups frozen peach slices, thawed, drained, and mashed
1 teaspoon grated lemon rind
3 tablespoons sugar
18 ladyfingers, split
¾ cup whipping cream, whipped

Combine lemon juice and orange juice; sprinkle gelatin over juice, and let stand 5 minutes.

Combine 1 cup sugar and flour in a saucepan; stir in milk. Bring mixture to a boil over medium-high heat; reduce heat, and cook until thickened, stirring constantly. Beat egg yolks until thick and lemon colored. Gradually stir about one-fourth of hot mixture into yolks; add to remaining hot mixture, stirring constantly. Cook over medium-low heat, stirring constantly, for 2 minutes. Remove from heat; add gelatin mixture, stirring until gelatin dissolves. Stir in peaches and lemon rind; let cool.

Chill peach mixture until thickened. Beat egg whites (at room temperature) until foamy; add 3 tablespoons sugar, one tablespoon at a time, beating until soft peaks form. Fold egg whites into peach mixture; set aside.

Line bottom and sides of a 13- x 9- x 2-inch dish with ladyfingers, placing rounded sides of ladyfingers toward outside of dish. Spoon peach mixture into dish; cover and chill 8 hours. Spread whipped cream over top before serving. Yield: 10 to 12 servings.
Mrs. Farmer L. Burns,
New Orleans, Louisiana.

Desserts To Make Ahead

Do you need something to perk up appetites? You won't even have to turn on the oven with no-bake desserts. Our chilled selections let you get a head-start on meal preparation.

You'll always have room for Peachy-Apricot Cream. It's delectable, airy, light, and not too sweet. And since most of the ingredients come from a can or package, you can keep them on hand to make the dessert anytime.

PEACHY-APRICOT CREAM

1 (12-ounce) can apricot nectar, divided
1 (3-ounce) package lemon-flavored gelatin
2 (16-ounce) cans unsweetened peach halves, drained
2 (16-ounce) cans unsweetened apricot halves, drained
1 (8-ounce) carton commercial sour cream
Whipped cream (optional)
Mint sprigs (optional)

Bring 1 cup apricot nectar to a boil in a saucepan. Remove from heat; add gelatin, stirring until dissolved. Stir in remaining apricot nectar; set aside.

Place peaches and apricots in container of an electric blender; process until smooth. Add fruit and sour cream to gelatin mixture. Spoon mixture into dessert dishes; chill until firm. Garnish with whipped cream and mint, if desired. Yield: 8 servings. *T. O. Davis, Waynesboro, Mississippi.*

CANTALOUPE PIE

1 medium cantaloupe
1 (3-ounce) package cream cheese, softened
¼ cup sugar
2 envelopes unflavored gelatin
½ cup orange juice
1 (9-inch) graham cracker crust, chilled
Sweetened whipped cream (optional)
Cantaloupe balls (optional)

Cut melon in half; remove the seeds, and peel. Cut into chunks, and place in container of electric blender; process until smooth.

Combine ½ cup melon puree and cream cheese in container of an electric blender; process until smooth. Add to remaining melon puree; set aside.

Combine sugar, gelatin, and orange juice in a small saucepan; let stand 2 minutes. Cook over low heat, stirring until sugar and gelatin dissolve. Slowly add to melon mixture, stirring well. Pour into chilled crust; chill until firm. Garnish pie with a dollop of whipped cream and cantaloupe balls, if desired. Yield: one 9-inch pie. *Alta W. Perry, Fredericksburg, Virginia.*

TOASTED ALMOND PIE

1 tablespoon instant-coffee granules
¼ cup boiling water
¼ cup cold water
¼ cup plus 2 tablespoons sugar
1 envelope plus 1 teaspoon unflavored gelatin
3 eggs, separated
¼ cup plus 2 tablespoons amaretto
¼ cup Kahlúa or other coffee-flavored liqueur
¼ cup plus 2 tablespoons sugar
1 cup whipping cream, whipped
1 (9-inch) graham cracker crust, chilled
Sliced toasted almonds

Dissolve coffee in boiling water; add ¼ cup cold water, and set aside.

Combine ¼ cup plus 2 tablespoons sugar and gelatin in a medium saucepan. Add coffee mixture; let stand 1 minute. Cook over low heat until gelatin dissolves.

Beat egg yolks until thick and lemon colored. Gradually stir about one-fourth of hot mixture into yolks; add to remaining hot mixture, stirring constantly. Cook, stirring constantly, until mixture thickens. Remove from heat, and stir in amaretto and Kahlúa; set aside.

Beat egg whites (at room temperature) until frothy. Gradually add remaining sugar, 1 tablespoon at a time, beating until soft peaks form; fold into coffee mixture. Fold in whipped cream. Spoon mixture into chilled crust; top with toasted almonds. Chill until firm. Yield: one 9-inch pie. *Patricia Flint, Staunton, Virginia.*

LAYERED ICE CREAM DESSERT

1 (16-ounce) can dark sweet pitted cherries, drained
¼ cup bourbon
1½ cups macaroon crumbs (about 16 macaroons)
¾ cup chopped pecans
½ gallon vanilla ice cream, softened
½ gallon raspberry sherbet, softened

Combine cherries and bourbon in a large mixing bowl; cover and refrigerate overnight.

Remove cherries from bourbon; set cherries aside. Add crumbs to bourbon, mixing until all liquid is absorbed. Stir in pecans, cherries, and vanilla ice cream. Spread half of ice cream mixture in a chilled two-piece 10-inch tube pan. Return both portions of ice cream mixture to freezer for 30 minutes. Spread raspberry sherbet evenly over ice cream in tube pan; freeze 30 minutes. Top with remaining ice cream mixture; freeze until firm.

Let stand at room temperature 10 minutes before serving. Remove outer portion of tube pan, and slice. Yield: 16 to 18 servings. *Mrs. Hoyt C. Taylor, Palm City, Florida.*

The Best Chocolate Crêpes

Dessert connoisseurs and chocolate lovers are sure to be pleased when you serve them Chocolate Dream Crêpes. This rich dessert has an elegant look, but the best part is that it is actually fairly easy to make.

Start with a thin, delicate chocolate crêpe pancake. Wrap it around a chocolate ice cream filling, and then cover it with a special chocolate sauce and pecans. The end result is one of the most luscious crêpes you'll ever taste.

CHOCOLATE DREAM CRÊPES

½ cup semisweet chocolate morsels
2 tablespoons butter or margarine
½ cup sifted powdered sugar
¼ cup light corn syrup
2 tablespoons crème de cacao
2 tablespoons water
½ teaspoon vanilla extract
1 quart chocolate ice cream
Chocolate Crêpes
½ cup chopped pecans

Combine chocolate morsels and butter in top of a double boiler; bring water to a boil. Reduce heat to low; cook, stirring often, until chocolate melts. Remove from heat. Add powdered sugar, syrup, crème de cacao, water, and vanilla, and stir until mixture is smooth.

Spoon about 3 tablespoons ice cream down center of each Chocolate Crêpe; fold sides over, and place seam side down on serving dishes. Spoon warm chocolate sauce over each Chocolate Crêpe; sprinkle with chopped pecans. Yield: 10 servings.

Chocolate Crêpes:

½ cup all-purpose flour
1 tablespoon cocoa
2 teaspoons sugar
Dash of salt
¾ cup milk
¼ teaspoon almond extract
1 egg
2 teaspoons butter or margarine, melted
Vegetable oil

Combine flour, cocoa, sugar, and salt. Add milk and almond extract; beat until smooth. Add egg, and beat well; stir in butter. Refrigerate 2 hours. (This allows flour particles to swell and soften so that crêpes are light in texture.)

Brush bottom of a 6-inch crêpe pan or heavy skillet with oil; place over me-

With each bite of Chocolate Dream Crêpes, you enjoy delicate crêpe, chocolate ice cream, chocolate sauce, and pecans.

dium heat until just hot, not smoking.

Pour 2 tablespoons batter into pan; quickly tilt pan in all directions so batter covers pan in a thin film. Cook 1 minute or until lightly browned.

Lift edge of crêpe to test for doneness. Crêpe is ready for flipping when it can be shaken loose from pan. Flip crêpe, and cook about 30 seconds on other side. (This side is rarely more than spotty brown and is the side on which the filling is placed.)

Place crêpes on a towel to cool. Stack between layers of waxed paper to prevent sticking. Repeat until all batter is used. Yield: 10 (6-inch) crêpes.

Tip: When melted, semisweet chocolate morsels and semisweet chocolate squares can be used interchangeably.

Team Pears With Chocolate

Rublelene Singleton of Scotts Hill, Tennessee, thinks that a special meal merits a grand finale like Pears Belle Helene. Poached pears are luscious alone, but when drizzled with a rich orange-flavored chocolate sauce, they're outstanding.

PEARS BELLE HELENE

6 medium-size firm ripe pears
2 cups water
½ cup sugar
1 vanilla bean, split, or 1 teaspoon vanilla extract
Chocolate-Orange Sauce

Peel pears, and cut a thin slice from bottoms so pears stand upright.

Combine water, sugar, and vanilla in a Dutch oven; bring to a boil over medium heat, stirring until sugar dissolves. Add pears; cover, reduce heat, and simmer 25 minutes or until pears are tender but still hold their shape. Let pears cool in sugar mixture.

To serve, drain pears well, and spoon into individual dessert dishes. Top pears with Chocolate-Orange Sauce. Yield: 6 servings.

Chocolate-Orange Sauce:
½ cup whipping cream
1 (4-ounce) package sweet baking chocolate
½ teaspoon orange extract
¼ teaspoon grated orange rind

Heat whipping cream in a heavy saucepan until hot. (Do not boil.) Remove from heat. Add chocolate; stir until melted. Stir in orange extract and orange rind. Chill. Yield: ¾ cup.

MICROWAVE COOKERY

Simplify Dessert With The Microwave

If your schedule is hectic and you need a dessert that's ready and waiting, take a look at these recipes. Each one features a custard or pudding-type filling that can be microwaved and chilled several hours before serving.

In addition to faster cooking, microwaving also eliminates the constant stirring that most cream and custard fillings require, as well as the scorching and sticking.

Our recipes offer a variety of chill-ahead desserts, from pudding and pie to an airy Bavarian Cream. Although the desserts are fairly easy to make and don't demand a lot of time, they look elegant and are bound to make quite an impression on your guests.

Along with these impressive recipes, we would like to pass on several hints to make certain you succeed with our microwaved desserts.

—Use HIGH power when microwaving most custard or creamy fillings; however, fillings with lots of eggs, sugar, sour cream, or cream cheese will often work better if they are microwaved at MEDIUM HIGH or MEDIUM. These

ingredients have a high-fat content, making them attract more energy; thus, they cook faster.

—It's important to stir fillings or custards occasionally to mix the cooked with the uncooked portions. This way you'll end up with a more evenly cooked product.

—Sometimes fillings or custards will not be thick enough after microwaving is complete; however, they will thicken more as they cool or stand.

—As with conventional cooking, when adding a hot mixture to egg yolks, always start by stirring a small amount of the hot mixture gradually into the egg yolks. Then slowly stir the yolk mixture back into the hot mixture. If you carefully follow this procedure, you will prevent the mixture from curdling.

—A glass measure or casserole dish is perfect for making custards or fillings in the microwave. A word of caution: Be sure that the container you choose is large enough to prevent the mixture from boiling over.

CARAMEL-BANANA PIE

⅓ cup firmly packed brown sugar
1 tablespoon cornstarch
⅛ teaspoon salt
1 cup milk
1 egg yolk
1½ tablespoons butter or margarine
½ teaspoon vanilla extract
2 medium bananas, peeled and sliced
1 (9-inch) graham cracker crust
½ cup whipping cream
¼ cup sifted powdered sugar

Combine brown sugar, cornstarch, and salt in a 1-quart casserole. Gradually stir in milk. Microwave at HIGH 3 to 4 minutes until smooth and thickened, stirring with a wire whisk every 2 minutes.

Beat egg yolk until thick and lemon colored. Gradually stir about one-fourth of hot mixture into yolk; add to remaining hot mixture, stirring constantly. Microwave at MEDIUM HIGH (70% power) 1 minute. Add butter and vanilla, stirring until butter melts.

Arrange bananas in bottom of graham cracker crust. Pour filling mixture over bananas; cover with waxed paper, and let cool 30 minutes.

Beat whipping cream until foamy; gradually add powdered sugar, beating until soft peaks form. Spread whipped cream mixture over pie. Chill at least 3 hours. Yield: one 9-inch pie.

BROWN SUGAR-PECAN PUDDING

½ cup firmly packed light brown sugar
2 tablespoons cornstarch
1 tablespoon all-purpose flour
¼ teaspoon salt
2 cups milk
4 egg yolks
2 tablespoons butter or margarine
1 teaspoon vanilla extract
⅓ cup chopped pecans, toasted
½ cup frozen whipped topping, thawed
Additional chopped toasted pecans

Combine brown sugar, cornstarch, flour, and salt in a 1½-quart glass mixing bowl; mix well. Gradually stir in milk. Microwave at HIGH 6 to 8 minutes or until thickened and bubbly, stirring every 2 minutes.

Beat egg yolks slightly. Gradually stir about one-fourth of hot mixture into yolks; add to remaining hot mixture, stirring constantly. Microwave at HIGH for 1 to 2 minutes or until thickened, stirring after 1 minute.

Stir in butter. Cool slightly; stir in vanilla and ⅓ cup pecans. Spoon into stemmed glasses; cover and chill 2 to 3 hours. Garnish with whipped topping and pecans. Yield: about 3 cups.

BAVARIAN CREAM

½ cup sugar
3 tablespoons cornstarch
2 envelopes unflavored gelatin
¼ teaspoon salt
2¾ cups milk
2 eggs, separated
1 teaspoon vanilla extract
¼ cup sugar
1 cup whipping cream, whipped
Strawberries

Combine ½ cup sugar, cornstarch, gelatin, and salt in a 2-quart casserole. Gradually add milk, stirring until blended. Microwave at HIGH 8 to 10 minutes, stirring every 3 minutes or until smooth and slightly thickened.

Beat egg yolks slightly. Gradually stir about one-fourth of hot mixture into yolks; add to remaining hot mixture, stirring constantly. Microwave at MEDIUM HIGH (70% power) 2 to 4 minutes, stirring after every minute. Cool in refrigerator until mixture mounds slightly (about 1 hour). Stir in vanilla.

Beat egg whites until foamy. Gradually add ¼ cup sugar, beating until soft peaks form. Fold egg whites and whipped cream into gelatin mixture. Spoon into a lightly oiled 5-cup mold. Chill until set. Unmold and garnish with strawberries. Yield: 10 servings.

Try These Unusual Loaf Breads

If you're looking for a special bread to serve with a meal, consider these loaf bread recipes from our readers. Each adds a distinctive touch to a menu.

Loaf breads take on extra glamour if they are served in baskets lined with pretty tea towels or napkins; the covering also helps keep the bread warm. For a casual meal, it's sometimes fun to pass the loaf around on a small bread board, restaurant-style.

Pull-Apart Maple Wheat Bread is especially easy to serve; just let guests pull off their own portions.

PULL-APART MAPLE WHEAT BREAD

1¼ cups water
¾ cup maple-flavored syrup
⅓ cup vegetable oil
3 cups all-purpose flour
2 packages dry yeast
1 teaspoon salt
1 teaspoon ground cinnamon
2 eggs, beaten
1 cup raisins
3 to 3½ cups whole wheat flour
1 tablespoon butter or margarine, melted

Combine water, syrup, and oil in a small saucepan; heat until very warm (120° to 130°). Set aside.

Combine all-purpose flour, yeast, salt, and cinnamon in a large mixing bowl; stir in syrup mixture and eggs, mixing well. Stir in raisins and enough whole wheat flour to make a soft dough.

Turn dough out onto a lightly floured surface, and knead until smooth and elastic (about 5 minutes). Place in a greased bowl, turning to grease top. Cover and let rise in a warm place (85°), free from drafts, 1 hour.

Punch dough down; divide into 20 pieces, and shape each piece into a ball.

Place 10 balls, in rows of 5, in each of two greased 9- x 5- x 2-inch loafpans. Brush each loaf with melted butter. Cover and let rise in a warm place (85°), free from drafts, 45 minutes.

Bake at 375° for 30 minutes or until loaves sound hollow when tapped. Remove loaves from pans, and cool thoroughly on wire racks. Yield: 2 loaves.
Deborah Alford,
Independence, Kentucky.

HERBED FRENCH BREAD

1 (1.6-ounce) package buttermilk-style salad dressing mix, divided
5 to 6 cups all-purpose flour, divided
2 packages dry yeast
1 tablespoon plus 2 teaspoons sugar
½ teaspoon salt
1½ cups buttermilk
½ cup water
¼ cup shortening
1 egg
Melted butter or margarine

Set aside 1 teaspoon buttermilk-style salad dressing mix.

Combine 2 cups flour, yeast, remaining salad dressing mix, sugar, and salt in a large mixing bowl. Set aside. Combine buttermilk, water, and shortening in a small saucepan; cook over low heat until very warm (120° to 130°). Gradually add buttermilk mixture to flour mixture, mixing at low speed of an electric mixer. Add egg, and beat 3 minutes at medium speed. Stir in enough remaining flour to make a soft dough.

Turn dough out onto a lightly floured surface, and knead until smooth and elastic (5 to 10 minutes). Place in a greased bowl, turning to grease top. Cover and let rise in a warm place (85°), free from drafts, 45 minutes or until doubled in bulk.

Punch dough down, and divide in half. Place dough on a lightly floured surface. Roll each half into a 12- x 7-inch rectangle. Starting at long end, roll up each rectangle jellyroll fashion; pinch edges together to seal. Place dough seam side down on a greased cookie sheet; turn ends under. Cut diagonal slashes, 2 inches apart, in top of each loaf. Brush with butter, and sprinkle each loaf with ½ teaspoon salad dressing mix. Cover and let rise in a warm place (85°), free from drafts, 30 minutes or until doubled in bulk.

Bake at 375° for 30 to 40 minutes or until golden brown. Yield: 2 loaves.
Martha Edington,
Knoxville, Tennessee.

PIMIENTO-CHEESE BREAD

3 tablespoons all-purpose flour
2 tablespoons butter or margarine, melted
1 tablespoon sugar
1 teaspoon salt
½ teaspoon ground marjoram
¼ teaspoon ground thyme
1 cup milk
⅓ cup (1½ ounces) shredded sharp Cheddar cheese
¼ cup finely chopped pimiento
1 package dry yeast
2 tablespoons warm water (105° to 115°)
3¼ to 3¾ cups all-purpose flour
1 tablespoon butter or margarine, melted

Combine first 6 ingredients in a medium saucepan; gradually stir in milk. Cook over medium heat, stirring constantly, until mixture is thickened and smooth. Remove from heat; add cheese and pimiento, stirring until cheese melts. Cool mixture to lukewarm (105° to 115°).

Dissolve yeast in warm water; add to cooled cheese mixture. Gradually add 3 cups flour, beating at medium speed of an electric mixer until dough is smooth. Stir in enough remaining flour to form a stiff dough.

Turn dough out onto a lightly floured surface, and knead until smooth and elastic (about 5 to 10 minutes). Place dough in a greased bowl, turning to grease top. Cover and let rise in a warm place (85°), free from drafts, 1 hour or until doubled in bulk.

Punch dough down, and shape into a loaf. Place in a greased 9- x 5- x 3-inch loafpan. Cover and let rise in a warm place, free from drafts, 1 hour or until doubled in bulk.

Brush top with 1 tablespoon melted butter. Bake at 350° for 35 to 40 minutes or until loaf sounds hollow when tapped. Remove loaf from pan, and cool on a wire rack. Yield: 1 loaf.
Mary M. Hoppe,
Kitty Hawk, North Carolina.

Right: *Enjoy the full flavor of raspberries in a serving of elegant Amaretto Custard With Raspberries (page 152). And try our recipes using strawberries and blueberries, shown here in baskets, as well as blackberries. (Recipes begin on page 150.)*

Page 168: *(Clockwise from front) Make a simple summer meal with Company Buttermilk Fried Chicken, Green Beans With Cherry Tomatoes, fresh fruit, Lemon-Steamed Potatoes, and Cornmeal Yeast Rolls. (Recipes, page 177.)*

Main Dish Salads Minus The Meat

The primary source of protein in a meal usually comes from a main dish containing meat, fish, or poultry. But it's possible to have a meatless entrée and still meet this important nutrient need. In addition to supplying protein, our main dish salads are tailored for stretching your food dollars.

Cottage cheese, walnuts, and granola add protein to Cottage-Fruit Split. And you can get even more protein benefit by serving this colorful salad with crackers or rolls.

Pasta-Bean Salad gets a protein boost from red kidney beans and macaroni. Carrots and peas add color, while garlic and lemon juice add flavor.

A combination of eggs, rice, and cheese make Egg-Rice Salad a high-protein choice. Green chiles, sour cream, and picante sauce season the mixture and add south-of-the-border appeal.

EGG-RICE SALAD

4 hard-cooked eggs, chopped
1½ cups cooked regular rice
½ cup (2 ounces) shredded sharp Cheddar cheese
½ cup sliced celery
¼ cup sliced green onions with tops
2 tablespoons chopped green chiles
½ cup commercial sour cream
2 tablespoons commercial picante sauce
1½ teaspoons lemon juice
¼ teaspoon seasoned pepper
⅛ teaspoon salt
Lettuce leaves (optional)
Tomato wedges (optional)

Combine eggs, rice, cheese, celery, green onions, and green chiles in a large bowl; toss gently. Combine sour cream, picante sauce, lemon juice, seasoned pepper, and salt, mixing well; add to egg mixture, tossing gently to coat. Cover and chill 2 hours. Serve on lettuce leaves, and garnish with tomato wedges, if desired. Yield: 4 servings.
Sara A. McCullough,
Broaddus, Texas.

PASTA-BEAN SALAD

2 cups cooked, drained macaroni
1 (15-ounce) can red kidney beans, rinsed and drained
1 cup frozen peas, thawed and drained
1 cup diced carrots
½ cup mayonnaise
¼ cup chopped fresh parsley
¼ cup grated Parmesan cheese
2 tablespoons lemon juice
1 clove garlic, pressed
1 teaspoon dried whole basil
Lettuce leaves (optional)

Combine macaroni, beans, peas, and carrots in a large bowl; toss gently. Combine mayonnaise, parsley, cheese, lemon juice, garlic, and basil, mixing well; add to macaroni mixture, tossing gently to coat. Cover and chill 2 hours. Serve on lettuce leaves, if desired. Yield: 4 servings.
Cathy Williams,
Vale, North Carolina.

PINTO SALAD

2 (16-ounce) cans pinto beans, drained
4 hard-cooked eggs, chopped
1 cup (4 ounces) shredded Monterey Jack cheese
½ cup sliced purple onion
½ cup vegetable oil
2 tablespoons cider vinegar
2 tablespoons red wine vinegar
2 tablespoons picante sauce
1 tablespoon plus 1 teaspoon Dijon mustard
Lettuce leaves
4 slices bacon, cooked and crumbled

Combine beans, eggs, cheese, and onion in a large bowl; toss gently. Combine oil, vinegars, picante sauce, and mustard in a jar. Cover tightly, and shake vigorously. Pour over bean mixture, tossing gently to coat. Cover and chill 2 hours. Serve on lettuce leaves, and sprinkle with bacon. Yield: 8 servings.
Eileen Wehling,
Austin, Texas.

COTTAGE-FRUIT SPLIT

1 medium cantaloupe
Lettuce leaves
2 cups cream-style cottage cheese
½ cup raisins
¼ cup chopped walnuts
¼ cup granola
2 kiwifruit, peeled and sliced
¼ cup commercial Catalina French salad dressing

Cut cantaloupe into four wedges; peel skin, and place cantaloupe wedges on lettuce leaves.

Combine cottage cheese, raisins, and walnuts; spoon over cantaloupe wedges. Sprinkle with granola, and top with kiwifruit. Drizzle dressing over each salad. Yield: 4 servings. *Iris Brenner,*
Fort McCoy, Florida.

Readers Share Their Vegetable Favorites

Whether or not you have a garden, you can enjoy summer's finest vegetables. Here's a collection of recipes from traditional to unusual to help you plan for the season's best.

QUICK-AND-EASY BROILED ZUCCHINI

3 small zucchini, cut in half lengthwise
1½ tablespoons butter or margarine, melted
Salt and pepper
3 tablespoons grated Parmesan cheese
Paprika

Place zucchini, cut side up, in a lightly greased broiler pan. Brush tops of zucchini with melted butter, and sprinkle with salt, pepper, cheese, and paprika. Broil 6 to 8 inches from heat 12 minutes or until tender. Yield: 3 servings. *Judith U. Spaeth,*
Burlington, North Carolina.

CRISPY FRIED OKRA

1 pound fresh okra
1 egg, beaten
1 cup yellow cornmeal
1 teaspoon salt
⅛ teaspoon pepper
Vegetable oil

Wash okra, and drain well. Remove tip and stem end; cut okra into ½-inch slices. Add egg to okra, and toss to coat. Combine cornmeal, salt, and pepper. Dredge okra pieces in cornmeal mixture.

Deep fry okra in hot oil (375°) until golden brown. Drain on paper towels. Yield: 4 servings. *Nell C. Weems,*
Pioneer, Louisiana.

GREEN BEANS
AND PEPPER STRIPS

1¼ pounds fresh green beans
2 scallions, sliced
2 tablespoons olive oil
1 clove garlic, minced
1 red or green pepper, cut into strips
1 to 1½ tablespoons minced fresh
    marjoram or 1 teaspoon dried whole
    marjoram
2 tablespoons water
¼ teaspoon salt
Pinch of black pepper
Pinch of red pepper

Wash beans; trim ends and remove strings, if necessary. Cut beans into 1½-inch pieces; set aside.

Sauté scallions in hot oil in a large skillet 1 minute. Stir in green beans and remaining ingredients; bring to a boil. Cover, reduce heat, and simmer 15 minutes. Yield: 4 servings.
Charlotte Farmer,
Richmond, Virginia.

BAKED CORN
WITH SOUR CREAM

2 tablespoons chopped onion
2 tablespoons butter or margarine, melted
2 tablespoons all-purpose flour
1 (8-ounce) carton commercial sour cream
2 (12-ounce) cans shoe peg corn, drained
¼ teaspoon salt
6 slices bacon, cooked and crumbled,
    divided

Sauté onion in butter in a large skillet until tender. Stir in flour, and cook 1 minute over low heat, stirring constantly. Gradually stir in sour cream, corn, and salt; cook over medium-low heat, stirring constantly, until thoroughly heated. (Do not boil.) Stir in half the bacon; pour corn mixture into a greased, shallow 2-quart casserole. Sprinkle remaining bacon over top. Bake at 350° for 25 to 30 minutes. Yield: 6 servings.   *Ann Thomas,*
Huntsville, Alabama.

SUMMER SUCCOTASH

1½ cups fresh corn cut from cob
1 (10-ounce) package frozen lima beans
4 slices bacon
1 medium onion, chopped
1 tablespoon all-purpose flour
1 (16-ounce) can tomatoes, undrained

Cook corn and lima beans in a small amount of boiling water 12 minutes or until tender; drain and set aside.

Cook bacon in a large skillet until crisp; remove bacon, reserving drippings in skillet. Crumble bacon, and set aside.

Sauté chopped onion in bacon drippings until onion is tender; remove onion, and set aside.

Add flour to bacon drippings, stirring until smooth. Cook 1 minute, stirring constantly. Add tomatoes, corn and lima bean mixture, bacon, and onion. Cook until heated. Yield: 6 servings.
Mrs. Rodger Giles,
Augusta, Georgia.

TOMATOES AND OKRA

½ cup diced onion
2 tablespoons bacon drippings
4 cups (about 1 pound) sliced okra
2½ cups peeled, chopped tomatoes
1 teaspoon salt
½ teaspoon paprika
2 teaspoons brown sugar
1 clove garlic, minced
¼ teaspoon curry powder
3 tablespoons chopped green pepper

Sauté onion in bacon drippings in a Dutch oven until tender. Add okra, and cook 5 minutes, stirring occasionally. Add remaining ingredients, stirring well. Cover and simmer 15 minutes or until okra is tender. Yield: 6 to 8 servings.   *Marjorie Henson,*
Benton, Kentucky.

EGGPLANT SUPREME

1 large eggplant
⅔ cup chopped celery
1 large onion, chopped
1 small green pepper, chopped
¼ cup butter or margarine, melted
1 cup (4 ounces) shredded sharp Cheddar
    cheese
1 teaspoon Worcestershire sauce
¼ teaspoon salt
⅛ teaspoon pepper
Dash of hot sauce
½ cup cracker crumbs

Peel eggplant, and cut into ½-inch cubes. Cook in boiling water 8 minutes or until eggplant is tender; drain well, and set aside.

Sauté celery, onion, and green pepper in butter in a large skillet until vegetables are tender. Stir in eggplant, Cheddar cheese, Worcestershire sauce, salt, pepper, and hot sauce.

Spoon eggplant mixture into a lightly greased 1½-quart baking dish; sprinkle with cracker crumbs. Bake at 350° for 30 minutes. Yield: 4 to 6 servings.
Betty Walton,
Opelika, Alabama.

SUGAR PEAS WITH DIP

½ pound Sugar Snap peas or snow peas
1 cup cream-style cottage cheese
1 tablespoon chopped fresh chives
1 (3-ounce) package cream cheese,
    softened
2 tablespoons cocktail sauce
1 teaspoon dry mustard
3 drops of hot sauce

Wash pea pods, and remove strings; drain and set aside.

Combine remaining ingredients in container of electric blender; process until thoroughly blended. Chill. Serve dip with peas. Yield: 15 to 18 appetizer servings.   *Alice McNamara,*
Eucha, Oklahoma.

It's Ground Turkey—
Not Ground Beef

Looking for an alternative to ground beef? Ground turkey is one answer. It is lower in fat and costs less, too. Made primarily from the dark meat, ground turkey has 50% less fat than is allowed in regular ground beef, but the taste and appearance are similar. Use it in your favorite burger, meat loaf, or casserole recipes, or try one of our recipes specially created for the product.

Ground turkey has a milder flavor than ground beef, so that herbs, spices, and other seasonings can be used to full advantage. Our Stuffed Ground Turkey Patties are a good example. Green pepper, onion, garlic powder, and celery salt season the meat; then Cheddar cheese and bacon are added for even more flavor.

When buying ground turkey, look for it alongside other frozen poultry products. It comes in 1-pound packages and may be stored, unopened, in the home freezer up to one month after purchase. To use, thaw ground turkey in the refrigerator overnight, and use within one or two days just as you would other ground meat.

GROUND TURKEY LOAF

2 (1-pound) packages raw ground turkey
1½ cups soft breadcrumbs
⅔ cup chopped celery
⅔ cup chopped onion
⅔ cup chopped green pepper
2 eggs, beaten
⅓ cup evaporated milk
⅓ cup chicken broth
½ teaspoon dried whole marjoram
¼ teaspoon dried whole rosemary
1 (10¾-ounce) cream of chicken soup, undiluted
½ cup milk
3 tablespoons chopped pimiento-stuffed olives

Combine turkey, breadcrumbs, celery, onion, green pepper, eggs, ⅓ cup evaporated milk, chicken broth, marjoram, and rosemary in a medium bowl; mix well. Place mixture on a greased broiler rack, and shape into a slightly rounded loaf. (Mixture will be soft.) Bake at 350° for 1 hour or until done.

Combine soup, ½ cup milk, and olives in a saucepan; cook over medium heat, stirring constantly, until thoroughly heated. To serve, transfer loaf to serving platter; spoon sauce over top. Yield: 8 servings. *Doris Phillips, Springdale, Arkansas.*

STUFFED GROUND TURKEY PATTIES

2 (1-pound) packages raw ground turkey
¼ teaspoon garlic powder
¼ teaspoon celery salt
⅛ teaspoon white pepper
⅓ cup chopped green pepper
⅓ cup chopped green onions
⅓ cup chopped fresh mushrooms
3 (1-ounce) slices Cheddar cheese, halved
6 slices bacon

Combine turkey, garlic powder, celery salt, and white pepper; mix well, and shape into 12 thin patties. Combine green pepper, green onions, and mushrooms; spoon 2 rounded tablespoons of vegetable mixture on top of half the patties. Top each with half a Cheddar cheese slice and a remaining turkey patty, sealing edges.

Wrap bacon around each patty, tucking ends under bottom. Place patties on greased broiler rack; bake at 350° for 20 minutes or until done. Place under broiler for an additional 2 minutes or until bacon is browned. Yield: 6 servings. *Hazel Slucher, Taylorsville, Kentucky.*

CRANBERRY-GLAZED TURKEY LOAF

¼ pound bulk pork sausage
1 cup diced onion
¼ cup diced celery
1½ (1-pound) packages raw ground turkey
1 cup herb-seasoned stuffing mix
½ cup evaporated milk
¼ cup chopped fresh parsley
2 eggs
¾ teaspoon salt
¼ teaspoon pepper
Cranberry Glaze

Cook sausage in a heavy skillet until browned, stirring to crumble. Add onion and celery; cook 1 minute, stirring constantly. Drain well.

Combine sausage mixture, turkey, stuffing mix, milk, parsley, eggs, salt, and pepper in a large mixing bowl; mix well. Shape mixture into a loaf; place in a lightly greased 8- x 4- x 3-inch loafpan. Bake at 350° for 55 to 60 minutes or until loaf is done. Pour off excess liquid. Transfer loaf to serving platter; spoon ½ cup Cranberry Glaze over top of loaf. Serve remaining glaze with loaf. Yield: 6 servings.

Cranberry Glaze:

1 cup whole cranberry sauce
2 tablespoons light corn syrup
2¼ teaspoons grated orange rind

Combine all ingredients in a small saucepan; cook over medium heat, stirring constantly, until bubbly. Yield: about 1¼ cups. *Jo Ann Maupin, Fort Payne, Alabama.*

Bake Peanut Butter Bread

Here's a new twist to yeast bread— stir chunky peanut butter into the dough. This recipe starts with an old-fashioned potato bread recipe, and it uses brown sugar and chunky peanut butter for extra flavor.

Peanut Butter Bread will be a hit. Of course, the kids will love this bread for jelly sandwiches to make a traditional flavor combination. Adult tastes will find it blends well served with crisp salads, especially those with fruit. It makes a good dinner bread, too. Because the bread offers just a hint of peanut butter taste, it won't overpower any strong flavors in the menu.

These loaves are also good for gift giving. Since each recipe makes two loaves, you'll have one to keep and one to give away.

PEANUT BUTTER BREAD

3 medium potatoes, peeled and chopped
5 to 6 cups all-purpose flour or bread flour, divided
¼ cup firmly packed brown sugar
2 teaspoons salt
2 packages dry yeast
¼ cup shortening
1 egg, beaten
½ cup chunky peanut butter

Cook potatoes in boiling water to cover 10 minutes or until tender. Drain potatoes, reserving 2 cups liquid. (Add water to make 2 cups, if necessary.) Reserve potatoes for another use; set potato liquid aside.

Combine 2 cups flour, sugar, salt, and yeast; mix well. Set aside.

Combine potato water and shortening in a saucepan; cook, stirring constantly, until shortening melts. Cool to 105° to 115°; pour over flour mixture. Mix at low speed of an electric mixer until blended. Add egg and peanut butter, mixing until ingredients are well blended. Gradually stir in enough of remaining flour to make a soft dough.

Turn dough out on a floured surface, and knead until smooth and elastic (about 8 to 10 minutes). Place in a well-greased bowl, turning to grease top. Cover and let rise in a warm place (85°), free from drafts, 1 hour or until doubled in bulk.

Punch dough down, and divide in half. Turn each portion of dough out on a lightly floured surface, and roll out to a 14- x 7-inch rectangle; fold and reroll. Starting with the narrow end, roll tightly as for a jellyroll.

Pinch seams together to seal edges. Place loaves, seam side down, in two well-greased 9- x 5- x 3-inch loafpans. Cover and let rise in a warm place (85°), free from drafts, 45 to 55 minutes or until doubled in bulk.

Bake at 375° for 40 to 50 minutes or until loaves sound hollow when tapped. Yield: 2 loaves.

From Our Kitchen To Yours

While some people fire up the outdoor grill on the patio, others venture out to a campsite to cook. Whether you're preparing hot dogs and baked beans or beef Stroganoff and steamed broccoli served with a favorite wine, cooking at a campsite can be simple as well as special. The basic hints we offer on planning, packing, cooking, and cleaning up should help make your camping experience pleasant.

Plan Ahead

—Each meal you prepare at the campsite should be fully planned before leaving home. Making a checklist helps ensure that nothing is forgotten. When considering what to prepare, choose fancy as well as simple foods. Remember that campers work up a hearty appetite, so have enough food.

—Do as much preparation as you can before you leave home. Chop or slice vegetables; combine spices or herbs to be used for a dish; or make meat patties, and store them in a plastic bag. When finished preparing, try storing all ingredients for a dish together, possibly in the pot you'll use for cooking.

—Be sure to include all the necessary cooking equipment and supplies. Have a checklist for these items, too. Some items have no substitute, such as a corkscrew, a can opener, or aluminum foil. Keep in mind that foil works well for packaging leftovers or cooking vegetables and meat on the grill.

Packing

—Pack lightly by taking disposable plates and cups. Have a dual purpose for cooking containers, and use heavy plastic bags as mixing bowls. Use dishwashing pans for storage of ingredients and equipment. Don't include any unnecessary items.

—If you bring eggs along, you may want to break them at home and store them in a plastic container.

—If you camp often, keep the basics, such as nonperishable condiments, paper products, hot pads, common cooking equipment, and utensils, packed to cut down on the packing time when you head for the campsite.

—Include freeze-dried and dehydrated foods or instant breakfast foods in your menus. Carry powdered milk instead of fresh to reduce bulk.

—If original containers of foods are too large or bulky, repackage them to reduce the volume.

Cooking and Cleanup

—Whatever type of heat source you use, know how to start and control it. Fires should never be larger in size than what is needed. Besides wasting fuel, large fires can be hard to control and difficult to work over.

—The pan or kettle you're using should be raised above the fire so that air can circulate beneath. The more air the fire gets, the more heat you'll have.

—When you're cooking large amounts of meats that need to be basted frequently, use a good quality paintbrush for basting; the brush works well to speed up the basting process.

—When you're grilling, first brush the grill with oil or vegetable cooking spray to prevent meat from sticking. Take along utensils coated with a nonstick surface for easy cleanup. To keep pots and pans from blackening over the campfire, remember to rub the outside of them with a thin layer of bar soap.

Garden Vegetables Add Variety

When the garden harvest provides you with a variety of vegetables, a few at a time, mix and match them in a vegetable medley. With just an ear of corn, a couple of tomatoes, or an eggplant, you can create some tasty homestyle dishes that are sure to please family and guests alike.

VEGETABLE-BEEF SKILLET

½ pound ground beef
1 large onion, chopped
1 cup lima beans
1 cup corn cut from cob
1 cup cut green beans
¾ to 1 teaspoon garlic salt
¾ teaspoon pepper
4 medium tomatoes, peeled and cubed

Cook ground beef until browned in a large skillet, stirring to crumble; drain. Return beef to skillet; add onion, lima beans, corn, green beans, garlic salt, and pepper. Cover and cook over low heat 20 minutes. Add tomatoes, and heat. Yield: 6 to 8 servings.
Cindy Turner Overall,
Baton Rouge, Louisiana.

RATATOUILLE SUPREME

4 cups peeled, cubed eggplant
4 cups cubed zucchini
½ cup olive oil
½ cup coarsely chopped green pepper
¼ cup coarsely chopped sweet red pepper
½ cup chopped onion
1 tablespoon minced garlic
4 medium tomatoes, peeled and cut into wedges
½ cup pitted small ripe olives
½ cup dry white wine
1 teaspoon salt
1 teaspoon white pepper
1 teaspoon dried whole basil
⅛ teaspoon dried whole thyme
⅛ teaspoon dried whole rosemary
1 bay leaf
2 tablespoons chopped fresh parsley

Sauté eggplant and zucchini in oil in a large skillet over medium heat 6 to 8 minutes, stirring occasionally. Add peppers and onion; cook 6 minutes, stirring occasionally. Add garlic, and cook 2 minutes. Add remaining ingredients except parsley; cover and reduce heat. Simmer 5 minutes. Sprinkle with parsley. Remove bay leaf. Yield: 8 servings.
Mrs. Pitts Hinson,
Columbia, Tennessee.

GARDEN COMBO

½ cup sliced, fresh mushrooms
¼ cup chopped onion
½ teaspoon dried whole basil
2 tablespoons butter or margarine, melted
¾ cup chicken broth
2½ cups cut green beans
1 cup scraped, sliced carrots
2 teaspoons cornstarch
1 tablespoon water
1 tomato, cut into wedges

Sauté mushrooms, onion, and basil in butter in a skillet just until vegetables are tender. Add broth, and bring to a boil; add beans and carrots. Cover and cook 8 to 10 minutes or until the vegetables are crisp-tender.

Combine cornstarch and water, blending well; stir into vegetable mixture. Add tomato; cook 1 minute or until sauce thickens and tomato is thoroughly heated. Yield: 4 to 6 servings.
Ginger Barker,
Mesquite, Texas.

Tip: Depending on the condition when purchased, fresh mushrooms can be refrigerated for 7 to 10 days.

GARDEN GREEK SALAD

3 large tomatoes, cut into wedges
1 cucumber, unpeeled and thinly sliced
1 medium-size green pepper, cut into
    1-inch pieces
1 small onion, thinly sliced
8 pitted ripe olives
¼ cup plus 1 tablespoon olive oil
¼ cup red wine vinegar
½ teaspoon dried whole oregano
½ teaspoon salt
¼ teaspoon pepper
⅔ cup crumbled Feta cheese

Combine tomatoes, cucumber, green pepper, onion, and olives in a large bowl; set aside.

Combine remaining ingredients except cheese in a jar. Cover tightly, and shake. Pour over vegetables; toss. Chill several hours. To serve, toss and sprinkle with cheese. Yield: 6 servings.

Mary Pappas,
Richmond, Virginia.

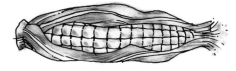

FRESH MARINATED VEGETABLE SALAD

1½ cups field peas
1 cup water
1½ cups corn cut from cob
¼ cup water
½ cup thinly sliced carrots
½ cup chopped celery
½ cup chopped dill pickle
⅓ cup vegetable oil
⅓ cup cider vinegar
1 tablespoon sugar
1 teaspoon diced onion
½ teaspoon salt
⅛ teaspoon pepper

Combine peas and 1 cup water in a medium saucepan. Bring to a boil; cover and reduce heat. Cook 30 to 35 minutes or just until peas are tender; drain. Chill.

Combine corn and ¼ cup water in a medium saucepan. Bring to a boil; cover and reduce heat. Simmer 7 to 8 minutes or just until corn is tender; drain. Chill.

Combine peas, corn, carrots, celery, and pickle in a bowl; set aside.

Combine remaining ingredients in a jar. Cover tightly, and shake. Pour over vegetables; toss. Cover and chill 3 hours. Yield: 6 to 8 servings.

Jeanette Guess,
Edinburg, Virginia.

Stir-Fry For Quick, Fresh Cooking

To cook fresh vegetables and entrées with a light summer touch, get out your wok or large skillet and try stir-frying. It's one of the best ways to preserve the flavor and color of fresh ingredients. At the same time, you'll be preparing the food in a nutritious way.

To stir-fry, just heat a small amount of oil or butter; then add your ingredients, stirring continuously to ensure even cooking.

Potato-Snow Pea Stir-Fry is a brightly colored side dish, which like all stir-fry recipes proceeds rapidly. Just gather your ingredients before you begin to heat the wok.

LEMON CHICKEN

2 lemons
3 medium-size dried Chinese mushrooms
1½ cups warm water
¼ cup vegetable oil
4 boneless chicken breast halves, skinned
    and cut into ¼-inch strips
½ teaspoon salt
⅛ teaspoon pepper
1 sweet red pepper, cut into ¼-inch strips
6 green onions, cut diagonally into ½-inch
    pieces
½ teaspoon freshly grated gingerroot
½ cup chicken broth
2 tablespoons dry sherry
2 tablespoons soy sauce
2 teaspoons cornstarch
1½ teaspoons sugar
Hot cooked rice
Lemon slices (optional)

Peel 1 lemon; cut rind into ⅛-inch pieces. Set aside 2 tablespoons rind. Squeeze lemons to yield 3 tablespoons juice; set juice aside.

Cover mushrooms with warm water, and soak 30 minutes. Drain mushrooms; cut into ⅛-inch pieces, and set aside.

Pour oil around top of preheated wok, coating sides; allow to heat at medium high (325°) for 2 minutes.

Sprinkle chicken with salt and pepper. Add chicken to wok; stir-fry 2 minutes. Remove chicken from wok to platter; keep warm. Add mushrooms, 2 tablespoons lemon rind, red pepper, green onions, and gingerroot to wok; stir-fry 1 minute.

Combine 3 tablespoons lemon juice, chicken broth, sherry, soy sauce, cornstarch, and sugar; mix well. Add mix-

ture to wok, and stir-fry 3 minutes or until mixture is thickened. Return chicken to wok and stir-fry 1 minute. Serve over rice. Garnish with lemon slices, if desired. Yield: 4 servings.

Mildred Bickley,
Bristol, Virginia.

SZECHUAN SHRIMP

½ cup catsup
¼ cup chili sauce
½ cup water
¼ cup sugar
2 tablespoons cornstarch
3 tablespoons dry sherry
1 tablespoon soy sauce
2 teaspoons sesame oil
¼ cup vegetable oil
6 scallions or green onions, chopped
3 cloves garlic, minced
1 (8-ounce) can water chestnuts, drained
    and chopped
1 to 2 teaspoons crushed red pepper
1 teaspoon minced fresh gingerroot
1 teaspoon cracked black pepper
2 pounds medium-size fresh shrimp,
    peeled and deveined
Hot cooked rice

Combine catsup, chili sauce, water, sugar, cornstarch, sherry, soy sauce, and sesame oil; mix well, and set aside.

Pour vegetable oil around top of preheated wok or large skillet, coating sides; allow to heat at medium high (325°) for 1 minute. Add scallions, garlic, water chestnuts, red pepper, gingerroot, and cracked black pepper; stir-fry 2 to 3 minutes. Add shrimp; stir-fry 3 minutes or until shrimp turn pink.

Add catsup mixture to wok, and cook 1 minute, stirring constantly, until thickened. Serve over rice. Yield: 6 to 8 servings.

POTATO-SNOW PEA STIR-FRY

2 tablespoons butter or margarine
4 small new potatoes, quartered
1 pound fresh snow peas
1 small onion, sliced and separated into
    rings
½ teaspoon salt

Melt butter in a wok or heavy skillet; add potatoes. Stir-fry on medium heat 10 minutes or until potatoes are golden and crisp-tender. Add snow peas, onion, and salt; stir-fry 5 to 7 minutes or until peas are crisp-tender. Serve immediately. Yield: 6 servings.

Stacey Wilson,
Reidsville, North Carolina.

TWO-SQUASH STIR-FRY

2 tablespoons vegetable oil
2 tablespoons butter or margarine
6 green onions, sliced
4 carrots, scraped, quartered and sliced
2 medium zucchini, sliced
2 large yellow squash, halved and sliced
1 medium-size green pepper, chopped
1 teaspoon lemon-pepper seasoning
½ teaspoon salt

Pour oil around top of a preheated wok or large skillet; add butter, and allow to heat at medium high (325°) for 2 minutes. Add vegetables and seasonings; stir-fry 5 minutes. Cover and simmer an additional 5 minutes or until vegetables are crisp-tender. Serve immediately. Yield: 8 servings.

Jan Perrin,
Fort Worth, Texas.

THREE-VEGETABLE STIR-FRY

1 pound fresh green beans
⅓ cup olive oil
2 cloves garlic, minced
1 pound yellow squash, sliced
1 pound zucchini, sliced
½ teaspoon dried whole oregano
½ teaspoon salt
⅛ teaspoon pepper

Wash green beans; trim ends, and remove strings. Cut beans into 1-inch pieces; set aside.
Pour oil around top of a preheated wok or large skillet; allow to heat at medium high (325°) for 2 minutes. Add green beans and garlic; stir-fry 8 minutes. Add yellow squash and zucchini; stir-fry 5 to 6 minutes or until tender. Sprinkle with oregano, salt, and pepper. Serve immediately. Yield: 8 servings.

Ella C. Stivers,
Abilene, Texas.

Plums Make Sweet Finales

Take advantage of the fresh plums that are so plentiful now, and try one of these easy desserts that promise a sweet finale to any meal. Most of the preparation is done ahead, so the recipes work well for a family meal as well as casual entertaining.

EASY PLUM CREAM PIE

1 (8-ounce) package cream cheese, softened
½ cup light corn syrup
1 (3¾-ounce) package vanilla instant pudding mix
1 cup cold milk
1 (9-inch) graham cracker crust
1½ cups unpeeled sliced fresh plums
¼ cup red currant jelly

Beat cream cheese until fluffy; gradually add corn syrup, mixing well. Set mixture aside.
Combine pudding mix and milk; beat 2 minutes at medium speed of electric mixer. Stir pudding mixture into cream cheese mixture, and beat until smooth. Pour into graham cracker crust. Refrigerate 2 hours or until filling is set.
Arrange plums over filling. Melt jelly in a small saucepan over low heat; spoon over plums. Refrigerate until serving time. Yield: one 9-inch pie.

Jodie McCoy,
Tulsa, Oklahoma.

LAYERED PLUM CRUNCH

1 cup unsweetened apple juice
1½ tablespoons cornstarch
1 tablespoon lemon juice
½ teaspoon ground cinnamon
⅛ teaspoon ground ginger
3 cups peeled, sliced fresh red plums
¼ cup crushed gingersnaps
¼ cup quick-cooking oats, uncooked
1 tablespoon margarine, softened

Combine apple juice, cornstarch, lemon juice, cinnamon, and ginger in a medium saucepan; cook over medium heat, stirring constantly, until mixture is clear and thickened. Stir in plums. Spoon plum mixture into individual dessert dishes; chill thoroughly.
Combine crushed gingersnaps, oats, and margarine; stir until well mixed.

Spread mixture in a baking pan; bake at 350° for 15 minutes or until crumb mixture is browned and crisp, stirring occasionally.
Sprinkle crumb mixture over top of chilled plum mixture, and serve immediately. Yield: 6 servings.

Pass The Butter Sauce

When fresh vegetables are at their flavor peak, our simple Vegetable Butter Sauce is a 5-minute way to dress them up.
The Herb Butter Sauce variation is ideal for mild-flavored vegetables, such as corn, mushrooms, potatoes, or green beans. For stronger flavored vegetables, try the basic butter sauce recipe or the other sauces using sesame seeds, poppy seeds, or almonds.
You can increase the recipe amounts if you serve the sauce to the side.

VEGETABLE BUTTER SAUCE

¼ cup butter
⅛ teaspoon freshly ground pepper

Heat butter in a small skillet over medium heat for 3 to 4 minutes or until butter begins to brown. Stir butter; remove from heat, and stir in pepper. Serve over cooked vegetables. Yield: about ¼ cup.
Herb Butter Sauce: Add 1 tablespoon of one of the following herbs to browned butter: minced fresh basil, marjoram, sage, thyme, parsley, rosemary, or tarragon. Omit pepper. Yield: about ¼ cup.
Almond Butter Sauce: Add ¼ cup slivered almonds to butter before browning. Stir frequently. Omit pepper. Yield: ⅓ cup.
Peanut-Butter Sauce: Add ¼ cup chopped unsalted peanuts to butter before browning. Stir frequently. Omit pepper. Yield: ⅓ cup.
Poppy Seed Butter Sauce: Add 1 teaspoon poppy seeds to butter before browning. Stir frequently. Omit pepper. Yield: about ¼ cup.
Sesame Seed Butter Sauce: Add 1 tablespoon sesame seeds to butter before browning. Stir frequently. Omit pepper. Yield: ¼ cup.
Kathleen Stone,
Houston, Texas.

July

Fruit Syrups Splash On Flavor

Make fruit juices into syrups to flavor wine coolers or breakfast drinks, ices or soups. You can even splash the syrup by itself over ice cream or crushed ice.

When extracting the juice from fresh fruit, you'll need to strain the pulp through a jelly bag—or you can use several thicknesses of cheesecloth.

The fruit syrups will keep up to two weeks in the refrigerator without processing, but for longer storage, process them in standard canning jars as directed in the recipe. You can store canned syrup in a cool, dry place for up to a year. Because citrus juice can be unstable, the orange syrup might discolor after a couple of months, but the flavor should not be affected. After opening canned syrups, you can refrigerate them for two weeks.

FRUIT SYRUP

3⅓ cups prepared fruit juice (see below)
¾ cup sugar
⅓ cup light corn syrup

Combine all ingredients in a large saucepan. Bring to a rolling boil, and boil 1 minute. Remove from heat, and skim off foam. Let cool. Cover and refrigerate up to 2 weeks. For longer storage, pour into hot sterilized jars, leaving ¼-inch headspace. Cover at once with metal lids, and screw on bands. Process in boiling-water bath 10 minutes. Yield: about 2 pints.

Raspberries or blueberries: Start with about 2½ quarts berries. Cook berries in ¼ cup water 3 to 5 minutes or until soft. Strain enough berries through a jelly bag to remove 3⅓ cups juice, discarding pulp.

Strawberries: Wash, cap, and slice about 2½ quarts ripe strawberries. Crush and strain enough strawberries through a jelly bag to remove 3⅓ cups juice, discarding pulp.

Peaches: Peel and slice about 12 large peaches (about 5½ pounds); combine peaches and 1 cup water in a Dutch oven. Cook over medium heat 15 to 20 minutes or until soft. Mash peaches well, and press enough of the peaches through a jelly bag to remove 3⅓ cups juice. Discard remaining pulp.

Oranges: Juice enough oranges (about 7 large, or 4¼ pounds) to measure about 3½ cups juice. Press enough juice through a jelly bag to measure 3⅓ cups, discarding any remaining pulp.

YOGURT FRUIT SOUP

1½ cups vanilla yogurt
¾ cup Fruit Syrup
2 tablespoons milk
Additional Fruit Syrup

Combine yogurt, ¾ cup Fruit Syrup, and milk, blending with a wire whisk; ladle into serving bowls. Pour a small amount of Fruit Syrup in center of each serving, and swirl with a spoon. Yield: 2¼ cups.

FRUITED WINE COOLER

1½ cups dry white wine, chilled
½ cup Fruit Syrup, chilled

Combine wine and Fruit Syrup, stirring well. Serve cooler over ice, if desired. Yield: 2 cups.

BREAKFAST FRUIT JUICY

⅔ cup Fruit Syrup
⅔ cup milk
½ teaspoon vanilla extract
Ice cubes

Combine Fruit Syrup, milk, and vanilla in container of an electric blender. Add enough ice cubes to make mixture measure 2 cups in blender container. Blend until mixture is smooth. Serve immediately. Yield: 2½ cups.

FRUIT ICE

1½ cups water
1 cup Fruit Syrup
2 tablespoons lemon juice

Combine all ingredients; pour mixture into freezer trays. Freeze until almost firm. Spoon mixture into a bowl, and beat at medium speed of an electric mixer until slushy. Return to freezer trays; freeze until mixture is firm. Yield: about 2½ cups.

Tradition Sets A Summer Table

Whether the occasion is a potluck church supper, a family reunion, or a party where the hostess prepares the whole meal, Southern menus for such gatherings are seasoned with tradition.

When you're serving as host or hostess, add some simple touches to give your party a fresh, carefree look.

■ Make the garnishes simple. Tuck fresh mint in the tea pitcher, and arrange a delicate strand of fresh oregano on a platter or atop fresh vegetables in a bowl. Or fill the center of a pound cake with fresh strawberries.

■ Line baskets with colorful fabric for serving fresh fruit or bread.

■ Buy bold-colored paper plates to fit into wicker holders. Spray paint the holders white for vivid color contrast.

■ Wrap eating utensils in bandannas or colorful napkins, and tie with ribbons or flowers. To make inexpensive cloth napkins for a crowd, cut squares of colorful fabric with pinking shears.

■ Perk up the serving table with a pedestal bowl piled high with fresh strawberries. Fill an old crock, jar, pitcher, or freshly carved melon with wildflowers, or place a bowl or basket of fresh vegetables on the table.

DEVILED EGGS

24 hard-cooked eggs
¼ cup mayonnaise
3 tablespoons thousand-island salad dressing
3 tablespoons sweet pickle relish
1 teaspoon dry mustard
¼ teaspoon salt
Gherkin slices

Slice eggs in half lengthwise, and carefully remove yolks. Mash yolks, and stir in mayonnaise. Add dressing, relish, mustard, and salt; stir well. Stuff whites with yolk mixture. Garnish halves with gherkin slices. Yield: 24 servings.

Lana W. Fuller,
Martinsville, Virginia.

Tip: For perfect hard-cooked eggs, place eggs in a saucepan and cover with water; bring to a boil, lower heat to simmer, and cook 14 minutes. Pour off hot water and add cold water; shells will come off easily.

COMPANY BUTTERMILK
FRIED CHICKEN
(pictured on page 168)

2 cups all-purpose flour
1 tablespoon salt
1 teaspoon paprika
½ teaspoon pepper
1 cup buttermilk
1 teaspoon baking powder
3 pounds chicken breasts and legs
Vegetable oil

Combine first 4 ingredients in a plastic or paper bag; shake to mix, and set aside. Combine buttermilk and baking powder in a bowl; mix well.

Dip 2 pieces of chicken in buttermilk mixture; place chicken in bag, and shake to coat. Repeat procedure with remaining chicken. Place chicken in a shallow pan; cover and refrigerate at least 1 hour.

Heat 1 inch of oil in a large skillet to 325°; add chicken, and fry 30 to 35 minutes or until golden brown, turning once. Drain on paper towels. Yield: 8 servings. *Mrs. Roderick W. McGrath,*
Orlando, Florida.

LEMON-STEAMED POTATOES
(pictured on page 168)

16 small new potatoes
½ cup butter or margarine
2 teaspoons grated lemon rind
1 tablespoon lemon juice
⅛ teaspoon salt
⅛ teaspoon pepper
Lemon slices

Peel a ½-inch strip around the center of each potato. Melt butter in a skillet; add lemon rind, lemon juice, and potatoes; stirring gently. Cover and cook over low heat 35 to 40 minutes or until tender, stirring occasionally. Sprinkle with salt and pepper. Transfer to a serving bowl; garnish with lemon. Yield: 6 to 8 servings. *Beth R. McClain,*
Grand Prairie, Texas.

ZUCCHINI AND CORN

½ cup chopped onion
⅓ cup chopped green pepper
¼ cup butter or margarine, melted
4 cups sliced zucchini
1½ cups fresh corn
½ teaspoon salt
¼ teaspoon dried whole oregano
¼ teaspoon dried whole basil

Sauté onion and green pepper in butter until tender. Stir in remaining ingredients; cover and simmer 8 to 10 minutes or until zucchini is crisp-tender. Yield: approximately 6 servings.
Linda Matcek,
Splendora, Texas.

GREEN BEANS
WITH CHERRY TOMATOES
(pictured on page 168)

1½ pounds fresh green beans
1½ cups water
¼ cup butter or margarine
1 tablespoon sugar
¾ teaspoon garlic salt
⅛ teaspoon salt
¼ teaspoon pepper
1½ teaspoons chopped fresh basil or ½
  teaspoon dried whole basil
2 cups halved cherry tomatoes
Fresh basil

Wash beans; trim ends, and remove strings. Cut into 1½-inch pieces. Combine beans and water in a saucepan; bring to a boil. Cover, reduce heat, and simmer for about 20 minutes. Drain.

Melt butter in a skillet; stir in sugar, garlic salt, salt, pepper, and basil. Add tomatoes; stir gently, cooking just until soft. Pour tomatoes and sauce over beans; toss gently.

Transfer vegetable mixture to serving bowl; garnish with fresh basil. Yield: 6 servings. *Katye Hansen,*
Arden, North Carolina.

FRESH CUCUMBER SLICES

7 cups thinly sliced cucumbers
1 large onion, thinly sliced and separated
  into rings
1½ cups water
1½ cups vinegar
1½ cups sugar
¾ teaspoon celery seeds
½ teaspoon garlic salt
½ teaspoon onion salt
½ teaspoon celery salt

Layer sliced cucumbers and onion in a large bowl.

Combine remaining ingredients, and blend thoroughly. Pour marinade over cucumbers. Cover and chill cucumbers at least 2 hours.

Use slotted spoon to serve chilled cucumber slices. Yield: 12 servings.
Glyna Meredith Gallrein,
Anchorage, Kentucky.

CORNMEAL YEAST ROLLS
(pictured on page 168)

¾ cup milk
1¼ cups regular cornmeal
1 cup boiling water
1 package dry yeast
½ cup warm water (105° to 115°)
½ cup butter or margarine, melted
⅓ cup sugar
2 egg yolks, slightly beaten
2 teaspoons salt
4 to 5 cups all-purpose flour

Scald milk; cool to 105° to 115°.

Combine cornmeal and 1 cup boiling water in a large mixing bowl; let stand 10 minutes.

Dissolve yeast in ½ cup warm water in medium mixing bowl; let stand 5 minutes. Add scalded milk, butter, sugar, egg yolks, and salt to yeast mixture; blend well. Gradually add to cornmeal, stirring well. Gradually stir in enough flour to make a soft dough.

Turn dough out onto a lightly floured surface, and knead until smooth and elastic (about 5 minutes). Place dough in a greased bowl, turning to grease top. Cover and let rise in a warm place (85°), free from drafts, 1 hour or until doubled in bulk.

Punch dough down; cover and let rise in a warm place (85°), free from drafts, 1 hour or until doubled in bulk.

Shape into 2½-inch balls; place on greased baking sheets or in greased muffin pans. Let rise in a warm place (85°), free from drafts, 1 hour or until doubled in bulk. Bake at 400° for 18 to 20 minutes or until golden brown. Yield: 4 dozen. *Mrs. Robert Bailey,*
Knoxville, Tennessee.

NO-DOUGH
BLUEBERRY-PEACH COBBLER

½ cup butter or margarine
1 cup all-purpose flour
¾ cup sugar
2 teaspoons baking powder
½ cup milk
2 cups fresh sliced peaches
2 cups fresh blueberries
½ cup sugar

Melt butter in a 2½-quart baking dish. Set aside. Combine flour, ¾ cup sugar, and baking powder; add milk, and stir until blended. Spoon batter over butter in baking dish; do not stir.

Combine peaches, blueberries, and ½ cup sugar; spoon over batter. Do not stir. Bake at 350° for 45 to 55 minutes. Yield: 6 servings. *Barbara Allison,*
Ormond Beach, Florida.

For dessert, bake Chocolate Chip Pound Cake a day ahead. Then serve it to guests at a potluck get-together. It's easy to transport and to serve.

CHOCOLATE CHIP POUND CAKE

1 cup butter or margarine, softened
1 tablespoon shortening
2 cups sugar, divided
6 eggs, separated
3 cups all-purpose flour
½ teaspoon salt
¼ teaspoon baking soda
1 (8-ounce) carton commercial sour cream
1 teaspoon vanilla extract
1 (12-ounce) package semisweet chocolate morsels, divided
1 (4-ounce) package sweet baking chocolate, grated
1 cup sifted powdered sugar
1 to 1½ tablespoons milk

Cream butter and shortening; gradually add 1½ cups sugar, beating until mixture is light and fluffy. Add egg yolks; beat at medium-high speed of an electric mixer for 5 minutes.

Combine flour, salt, and soda; mix well. Add to creamed mixture alternately with sour cream, beginning and ending with flour mixture. Mix just until blended after each addition. Stir in vanilla, 1⅓ cups chocolate morsels, and grated chocolate.

Beat egg whites (at room temperature) until foamy. Gradually add remaining ½ cup sugar, 1 tablespoon at a time, beating until stiff peaks form. Fold egg whites into batter. Spoon batter into a greased and floured 10-inch tube pan. Bake at 325° for 1 hour and

20 to 25 minutes. Cool in pan 10 minutes; invert onto a serving plate.

Combine powdered sugar and 1 tablespoon milk, stirring well. Add more milk if a thinner consistency is desired. Spoon glaze over warm cake. Sprinkle remaining chocolate morsels evenly over glaze. Cool before serving. Yield: one 10-inch cake. *Linda Kay Marris, Ladson, South Carolina.*

A Taste Of Summer

Lush, ripe, juicy melons—there's nothing like them to cool and refresh a menu. Melons are the perfect accompaniment for almost any entrée. Light and nutritious, they add flavor and color without adding a lot of extra calories.

MELON WEDGES WITH BERRY SAUCE

1 cup halved fresh strawberries
1 cup fresh blueberries
½ cup orange juice
¼ cup sugar
1 honeydew melon or cantaloupe, halved and seeded

Combine first 4 ingredients, and mix well. Chill 1 to 2 hours.

Peel melon, and cut into 8 wedges. Spoon chilled berry mixture over wedges. Yield: 8 servings.

Mrs. Bruce Fowler,
Woodruff, South Carolina.

CANTALOUPE-PECAN SALAD

1 (3-ounce) package cream cheese, softened
2 tablespoons mayonnaise
2 tablespoons milk
¼ cup finely chopped celery
2 tablespoons chopped pecans
½ cup frozen whipped topping, thawed
3 cups cantaloupe balls
Lettuce leaves

Combine cream cheese, mayonnaise, and milk; beat at medium speed of electric mixer until smooth. Add celery and pecans, and mix well. Fold in whipped topping; chill.

Spoon cantaloupe balls into lettuce cups formed from outer leaves; top with dressing. Yield: 4 servings.

Peggy Fowler Revels,
Woodruff, South Carolina.

APRICOT DIP

1 cup commercial sour cream
¾ cup apricot preserves
½ cup flaked coconut
⅓ cup finely chopped walnuts
Dash of salt

Combine all ingredients, mixing thoroughly; chill.

Serve with melon balls. Yield: 2 cups. *Azine G. Rush, Monroe, Louisiana.*

FRESH FRUIT COMBO

½ cup honey
2 tablespoons lemon juice
1½ teaspoons ground cinnamon
2½ cups bite-size watermelon pieces
1 orange, sectioned
1 cup sliced strawberries
¾ cup seedless grapes, halved

Combine honey, lemon juice, and cinnamon, mixing well; chill.

Combine fruit, and toss with chilled dressing just before serving. Yield: 6 servings.

Summer Suppers.

It's Summertime— Make The Cooking Easy

Once again it's the time of year to revel in nature's seasonal foods. And whatever you're looking for, without spending a lot of time in the kitchen, you'll find it here in the tenth annual "Summer Suppers" special section.

Come Along to a Fish Fry

The invitation reads "The fish are biting at the Crowns"—words that start mouths watering in anticipation of good food and fun. Bill and Betty Crown of Clearwater, Florida, are quick to say that an informal fish fry is their favorite way to entertain.

If you want to throw a party, consider a fish fry. The Crowns show you how by sharing their time-honored recipes.

Sunshine Sipper Spiced Rum Punch
Dock Dip in Cabbage
Anchovy Mayonnaise
Florida Crackers
Marinated Beer-Battered Fish
Bold-and-Spicy Tartar Sauce
Garlic-Cheese Grits
Green Bean-and-Tomato Salad
Layered Coleslaw
I Remember Pound Cake
With Papaya Topping
Soave White Wine

SUNSHINE SIPPER

1 cup sugar
1 cup water
1⅓ cups fresh lemon juice
Zest of 4 lemons
2 quarts ice water
1½ to 2 cups vodka
Mint sprigs (optional)

Combine sugar and 1 cup water in a small saucepan; cook over medium heat, stirring constantly, until mixture comes to a boil. Reduce heat, and simmer 5 minutes, stirring occasionally. Remove from heat; let cool.

Combine sugar syrup, lemon juice, lemon zest, ice water, and vodka; stir well, and let stand 10 minutes. Remove zest, and serve over crushed ice. Garnish with mint sprigs, if desired. Yield: about 3 quarts.

Note: Zest is gratings of the colored portion of citrus skin.

SPICED RUM PUNCH

4 cups fresh grapefruit juice
2 cups spiced rum
¼ cup sugar
2 tablespoons grenadine
4 cups ginger ale, chilled
Lime wedges (optional)
Maraschino cherries (optional)

Combine grapefruit juice, spiced rum, sugar and grenadine; chill. Add ginger ale, stirring well. Serve over crushed ice, and garnish with lime wedges and cherries, if desired. Yield: 11 cups.

DOCK DIP IN CABBAGE

2 cups mayonnaise
¼ cup chili sauce
¼ cup chopped chives
¼ cup grated onion
1 tablespoon plus 1 teaspoon tarragon vinegar
½ teaspoon curry powder
½ teaspoon salt
¼ teaspoon dried whole thyme
1 medium-size leafy cabbage

Combine mayonnaise, chili sauce, chives, onion, vinegar, curry, salt, and thyme; stir well. Chill 4 hours.

Trim core end of medium-size cabbage to form a flat base. Cut a crosswise slice from top, making it wide enough to remove about a fourth of the head; lift out enough inner leaves from the cabbage to form a shell about 1 inch thick. (Reserve slice and inner leaves of cabbage for other uses.)

Spoon dip into cavity of cabbage; serve with an assortment of fresh vegetables. Yield: 2⅔ cups.

ANCHOVY MAYONNAISE

2 cups mayonnaise
1 (2-ounce) can anchovy fillets, drained and chopped
1 clove garlic, minced
2 hard-cooked egg yolks, finely chopped
¼ cup minced parsley
1½ tablespoons minced capers

Combine all ingredients. Cover and chill 4 hours. Serve with melba toast. Yield: 2 cups.

FLORIDA CRACKERS

15 slices bacon, cut in half
10 rectangular buttery crackers
1 tablespoon plus 2 teaspoons grated Parmesan cheese

Cook bacon until limp; drain well. Break crackers into thirds at perforated lines. Wrap bacon around cracker; place seam side down on a broiler rack. Sprinkle each cracker with cheese. Bake at 350° for 8 to 10 minutes or until bacon is crisp. Yield: 30 appetizers.

MARINATED BEER-BATTERED FISH

3 pounds snook or grouper fillets, cut into fingers
1 (16-ounce) bottle commercial French salad dressing
1½ cups all-purpose flour
4 cups biscuit mix
4 eggs, beaten
2 teaspoons baking powder
2 cups beer
Vegetable oil
Lemon rind curls (optional)
Parsley sprigs (optional)

Place fish fingers in a 13- x 9- x 2-inch baking dish. Pour salad dressing over fish; cover and marinate in refrigerator 6 hours.

Drain fish, and dredge in flour. Set fish aside.

Combine biscuit mix, eggs, baking powder, and beer in a medium-size mixing bowl; stir until smooth.

Dip each fish finger into batter; fry in deep, hot oil (375°) for 1 to 2 minutes on each side or until golden brown and fish flakes easily when tested with a fork. Drain on paper towels.

Garnish fish fingers with lemon rind curls and parsley sprigs, if desired. Yield: 10 servings.

BOLD-AND-SPICY TARTAR SAUCE

2 cups mayonnaise
½ cup diced dill pickles
1 tablespoon spicy brown mustard

Combine all ingredients, stirring well. Chill overnight. Serve with fried fish. Yield: 2½ cups.

Tip: During the week, keep a shopping list handy to write down items as you need them. This will eliminate unnecessary trips to the store. Before your weekly shopping trip, make a complete shopping list. If the list is arranged according to the layout of the store, you will save time and steps.

GARLIC-CHEESE GRITS

7 cups water
1 teaspoon salt
2 cups uncooked regular grits
1 (6-ounce) roll process cheese food with garlic, cubed
6 ounces process cheese food, cubed
1 cup butter or margarine, melted
4 eggs, beaten
½ cup milk
¼ teaspoon pepper
Carrot curls (optional)
Parsley sprigs (optional)

Combine water and salt in a large saucepan; bring to a boil. Gradually add grits, stirring constantly. Return to a boil; cover, reduce heat, and simmer 10 minutes, stirring often. Remove grits from heat. Add garlic cheese, cheese, butter, eggs, milk, and pepper to grits; stir until cheese cubes melt.

Spoon into two lightly greased 8-inch square baking dishes or one 13- x 9- x 2-inch baking dish. Bake at 350° for 45 minutes to 1 hour or until set. Garnish with carrot curls and parsley sprigs, if desired. Yield: 10 servings.

GREEN BEAN-AND-TOMATO SALAD

3 pounds small green beans
1½ pounds tomatoes, cut into wedges
¾ cup olive oil
¼ cup plus 2 tablespoons Worcestershire sauce
¾ teaspoon salt
½ teaspoon pepper
9 green onions, thinly sliced

Wash green beans; trim ends, and remove strings. Cook, covered, in a small amount of boiling water 10 to 12 minutes or until crisp-tender. Drain thoroughly, and cool.

Combine beans and tomatoes in a large shallow container.

Combine olive oil, Worcestershire sauce, salt, and pepper in a jar; cover tightly, and shake vigorously. Pour dressing mixture over bean mixture; cover and chill 2 to 3 hours.

To serve, arrange green beans and tomatoes on serving platter. Garnish with green onions. Yield: 10 servings.

LAYERED COLESLAW

2 large cabbages, coarsely chopped
1½ large green peppers, cut into rings
1½ large red peppers, cut into rings
3 medium onions, sliced and separated into rings
1½ cups sugar
1 tablespoon sugar
2½ teaspoons salt
1½ teaspoons celery seeds
1½ teaspoons dry mustard
1½ cups vinegar
1 cup plus 2 tablespoons vegetable oil
Pitted ripe olives (optional)

Layer half the cabbage, one-third of green and red pepper rings, and half the onion rings in a large salad bowl; repeat layers. Set aside remaining green and red pepper rings for garnish. Sprinkle 1½ cups sugar over top of cabbage mixture; set aside.

Combine 1 tablespoon sugar and next 5 ingredients in a saucepan; stir well. Bring to a boil over medium heat, stirring constantly. Remove from heat; pour over slaw. Cover; chill 4 hours.

Garnish coleslaw with olives, if desired, and remaining pepper rings. Yield: 10 servings.

I REMEMBER POUND CAKE

1 cup butter, softened
3¼ cups sifted powdered sugar
6 eggs
3 cups sifted cake flour
¼ teaspoon salt
⅓ cup milk
1 teaspoon vanilla extract

Cream butter; gradually add sugar, beating at medium speed of an electric mixer until well blended. Add eggs, one at a time, beating after each addition.

Combine flour and salt; add to creamed mixture alternately with milk, beginning and ending with flour mixture. Stir in vanilla. Pour batter into a greased and floured 10-inch tube pan. Bake at 325° for 55 minutes or until a wooden pick inserted in center comes out clean. Cool in pan 10 minutes; remove from pan, and cool completely on a wire rack. Serve with Papaya Topping. Yield: one 10-inch cake.

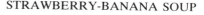

PAPAYA TOPPING

½ cup sugar
½ cup water
3 cups chopped ripe papaya
2 tablespoons lime juice

Combine sugar and water in a heavy saucepan; cook over medium heat 15 minutes, stirring until sugar dissolves and mixture thickens. Add papaya and lime juice; simmer 20 minutes, stirring frequently, until mixture is reduced by half. Serve over pound cake. Yield: about 1½ cups.

Soup—Serve It Cold

Who says that soup has to be hot? Chilled soup, more popular than ever, is just right for warm-weather menus. And it's a great make-ahead recipe.

You'd be surprised how many of your favorite soups taste just as good when chilled. The next time you have hot soup left over, try chilling it. Since chilled food tends to require more seasoning than hot food, you may have to increase the herbs and spices.

VICHYSSOISE

2 bunches green onions, chopped
½ cup chopped onion
2 stalks celery, chopped
½ cup butter or margarine, melted
3 pounds red potatoes, thinly sliced
2 (10¾-ounce) cans chicken broth, diluted
2 cups half-and-half
Pinch of dried whole basil
Salt and pepper to taste

Sauté onions and celery in butter in a large Dutch oven until tender. Add potatoes and broth; cover and cook over medium heat 25 to 30 minutes or until potatoes are tender. Partially mash. (Mixture will be lumpy.) Stir in half-and-half and seasonings. Chill until serving time. Yield: 10½ cups.
Shirley Rogers,
Tiptonville, Tennessee.

FRESH PEA SOUP

1 pound potatoes, peeled and diced (about 3 cups)
4 cups chicken broth, undiluted
2 pounds fresh English peas, shelled, or 2 cups frozen English peas, thawed
1 cup thinly sliced green onions
⅛ teaspoon pepper
1½ cups half-and-half

Combine potatoes and broth in a Dutch oven; bring to a boil. Cover, reduce heat, and simmer 15 minutes or until potatoes are tender. Add peas, and continue cooking 10 minutes or until peas are tender. Remove from heat; stir in green onions and pepper.

Spoon one-third of mixture into container of an electric blender, and blend until smooth. Repeat until all of the mixture is pureed.

Stir in half-and-half. Cover and chill. Yield: 7 cups. *Mrs. Harland J. Stone,*
Ocala, Florida.

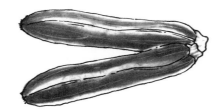

ZUCCHINI SOUP

8 cups sliced zucchini (4 medium zucchini)
½ cup chopped onion
2 cloves garlic, minced
1 cup beef broth
½ teaspoon dried whole basil
½ teaspoon salt
¼ teaspoon pepper
Grated Parmesan cheese
2 slices bacon, cooked and crumbled

Combine zucchini, onion, garlic, broth, basil, salt, and pepper in a Dutch oven; bring to a boil. Cover, reduce heat, and simmer 20 minutes or until zucchini is tender. Cool.

Pour zucchini mixture into container of an electric blender; process until smooth. Chill. To serve, sprinkle each serving with Parmesan cheese and bacon. Yield: 4 cups. *Jane G. Kreer,*
Arlington, Virginia.

STRAWBERRY-BANANA SOUP

2 cups fresh strawberries, sliced
1 small banana, thinly sliced
¼ cup sugar, divided
1 cup commercial sour cream
1 cup whipping cream
¾ cup milk
¼ cup white wine
Fresh strawberry fans

Combine strawberries, banana, and 2 tablespoons sugar; blend well, and set aside. Combine sour cream and remaining 2 tablespoons sugar; add whipping cream, milk, and wine. Whisk until well blended. Fold in strawberries and bananas. Chill 2 hours. Garnish each serving with a strawberry fan. Yield: 4½ cups. *Note:* To make a strawberry fan, spread thin slices of strawberry in a fan shape. *Mrs. Bernie Benigno,*
Gulfport, Mississippi.

Simple But Fabulous Fruit Dishes

To avoid the hustle and bustle of preparing complicated desserts and salads, turn to fresh fruit. It's equally delicious sliced or peeled and prepared in these exceptionally simple recipes.

FRUIT KABOBS

36 mandarin orange slices
24 fresh strawberries
24 green seedless grapes
24 fresh pineapple chunks
½ cup mayonnaise
½ cup marshmallow creme
2 teaspoons grated orange rind
1 teaspoon ground ginger

Thread fruit onto 12 (8-inch) bamboo skewers; chill.

Combine remaining ingredients, mixing well; serve as a dip with fruit kabobs. Yield: 12 kabobs.
Carolyn Epting,
Leesville, South Carolina.

ANYTIME AMBROSIA

1 fresh pineapple
3 large navel oranges, peeled and cut into
    ½-inch slices
¼ cup orange juice
2 tablespoons sifted powdered sugar
⅓ cup flaked coconut
8 maraschino cherries, drained

Peel and trim eyes from pineapple; remove core. Cut pineapple crosswise into 8 slices. Arrange slices on a serving platter. Place an orange slice on top of each pineapple slice. Sprinkle evenly with orange juice, powdered sugar, and coconut. Top with cherries. Yield: 8 servings. *Mildred Bickley, Bristol, Virginia.*

CANTALOUPE SALAD

½ cup mayonnaise
3 tablespoons frozen orange juice
    concentrate, thawed and undiluted
1 medium cantaloupe, chilled
Leaf lettuce
2 cups seedless green grapes

Combine mayonnaise and orange juice concentrate, mixing well; set mixture aside.

Cut cantaloupe into 6 sections; remove seeds, and peel. Place cantaloupe sections on lettuce leaves; spoon ⅓ cup grapes over and around each section. Drizzle with mayonnaise mixture. Yield: 6 servings. *Mary Gilbert, Campton, Kentucky.*

CHILLED POACHED LEMON APPLES

2 cups water
1 cup sugar
1 lemon, thinly sliced
Juice of 1 lemon
8 small cooking apples, peeled and cored

Combine water, sugar, lemon, and lemon juice in a large Dutch oven; bring to a boil. Add apples, and return to boil. Cover, reduce heat, and simmer 12 minutes or until apples are tender, turning once.

Transfer apples to a 2-quart casserole, using a slotted spoon. Bring syrup mixture to a boil; boil 10 minutes or until syrup is reduced to about 1 cup. Pour syrup over apples; cool. Cover and refrigerate. Serve cold. Yield: 8 servings. *Doris T. Ramsey, Martinsville, Virginia.*

GRAPE JUICE-FRUIT REFRESHER

1 quart pineapple or lime sherbet
1⅓ cups sliced fresh strawberries
¼ to ½ cup white grape juice

Spoon sherbet equally into 4 stemmed glasses. Top each with ⅓ cup sliced strawberries. Just before serving, pour 1 to 2 tablespoons grape juice over top. Yield: 4 servings.

Seafood At Its Best

Everyone has a favorite seafood. Whether it's fish, shrimp, or crabmeat, seafood is a great choice for entrées that aren't too filling. Feature it chilled in a salad, or broiled with herbs and spices.

LEMON-GARLIC BROILED SHRIMP

2 cloves garlic, minced
1 cup butter or margarine, melted
¼ cup lemon juice
½ teaspoon salt
¼ teaspoon pepper
2 pounds large fresh shrimp, peeled and
    deveined

Sauté garlic in butter until tender; remove from heat, and stir in lemon juice, salt, and pepper.

Arrange shrimp in a single layer in a shallow baking pan; pour butter sauce over shrimp. Broil 6 inches from heat 5 to 6 minutes or until shrimp are done, basting once with sauce. Yield: 4 to 6 servings. *Sara Arnold, Lewisville, Texas.*

BARBECUED FISH FILLETS

½ cup catsup
½ cup frozen lemonade concentrate,
    thawed and undiluted
1 clove garlic, minced
4 bay leaves
⅛ teaspoon salt
⅛ teaspoon pepper
1 teaspoon prepared mustard
2 large (about 2 pounds) red snapper
    fillets
Vegetable cooking spray

Combine catsup, lemonade, garlic, bay leaves, salt, pepper, and mustard in a large shallow container; stir well. Add fillets; cover and chill 1 hour. Drain fillets, reserving marinade. Place fillets in a fish basket coated with cooking spray.

Grill fish over hot coals 6 to 8 minutes on each side or until fish flakes easily when tested with a fork, basting often with reserved marinade. Remove bay leaves before serving. Yield: 4 servings. *Mrs. John E. Graudin, Summerville, South Carolina.*

SHRIMP-WALNUT SALAD

3 cups water
1 pound unpeeled small fresh shrimp
1 cup diced celery
½ cup chopped walnuts
3 tablespoons commercial French salad
    dressing
Leaf lettuce
4 slices fresh pineapple

Bring water to a boil; add shrimp, and cook 3 to 5 minutes. Drain well; rinse with cold water. Chill. Peel and devein shrimp.

Combine shrimp, celery, walnuts, and salad dressing; stir well. To serve, line salad plates with leaf lettuce, and top each with a pineapple slice; mound shrimp mixture on pineapple slice. Yield: 4 servings.

Mrs. James Strayer, Hilton Head Island, South Carolina.

SEASIDE SALAD

1½ cups water
½ pound unpeeled fresh shrimp
½ pound fresh crabmeat
½ cup cooked regular rice
½ cup diced celery
¼ cup diced pimiento-stuffed olives
¼ cup diced green onions
¼ cup mayonnaise
1½ teaspoons lemon juice
1½ teaspoons grated orange rind
1 teaspoon sugar
½ cup coarsely chopped mandarin orange
    sections
3 ripe avocados, halved and seeded
Additional mandarin orange sections
    (optional)

Bring water to a boil; add shrimp, and cook 3 to 5 minutes. Drain well; rinse with cold water. Chill. Peel and devein shrimp.

Combine shrimp, crabmeat, rice, celery, olives, green onions, mayonnaise, lemon juice, orange rind, and sugar; stir well. Stir in chopped mandarin orange sections. Chill. To serve, fill avocado halves with shrimp mixture. Garnish with additional mandarin orange sections, if desired. Yield: 6 servings.
Gladys Murphy,
Palacios, Texas.

Turn These Beverages Bottoms Up

Fruit flavor or ice cream makes these summertime refreshers just what you need on a hot day. Some are quick drinks that are just right for drop-in guests, and some are even rich enough to serve as dessert drinks.

CRANBERRY SMOOTHIE

2 cups cranberry juice cocktail
1 (8-ounce) carton vanilla yogurt
1 pint fresh strawberries
1 banana, sliced

Combine half of all ingredients in container of an electric blender; process until smooth. Repeat with remaining ingredients; combine mixtures. Pour into individual glasses. Yield: 4¾ cups.
Mrs. Bruce Fowler,
Woodruff, South Carolina.

STRAWBERRY SMOOTHIE

(pictured on page 203)

2 cups vanilla ice cream
1½ cups fresh strawberries
2 tablespoons sugar
2 teaspoons lemon juice
2 cups crushed ice
Additional fresh strawberries

Combine ice cream, 1½ cups strawberries, sugar, lemon juice, and ice in container of an electric blender; process until smooth. Pour into individual glasses, and garnish with additional strawberries. Yield: 4 cups.
T. G. Lovelace,
Roanoke, Virginia.

CHOCOLATE MALT

(pictured on page 203)

1 cup milk
1 tablespoon plus 2 teaspoons chocolate
    malt
1½ tablespoons powdered chocolate
    flavoring for milk
1 quart vanilla ice cream, softened

Combine all ingredients in container of an electric blender; process until smooth. Pour into individual glasses. Yield: 4 cups.
Joyce Petrochko,
St. Albans, West Virginia.

WHISKY SOUR SLUSH

2 (6-ounce) cans frozen lemonade
    concentrate, thawed and undiluted
1 (6-ounce) can frozen orange juice
    concentrate, thawed and undiluted
¾ cup lemon juice
2½ cups bourbon
2 quarts plus 1 cup lemon-lime
    carbonated beverage

Combine all ingredients; mix well. Freeze 8 hours. Remove from freezer 30 minutes before serving. To serve, stir until mixture is slushy and well mixed. Yield: 1 gallon.
Babs Hopping,
Birmingham, Alabama.

RASPBERRY KIR

2⅔ cups Chablis or other dry white wine,
    chilled
1 tablespoon Chambord or other
    raspberry liqueur

Pour ⅔ cup wine in each wine glass. Add ¾ teaspoon Chambord to each one, and stir well. Yield: 4 servings.
Ruth A. Colosimo,
Copperas Cove, Texas.

Easy, Economical Appetizers

When you're entertaining, sometimes the appetizers can be as much trouble to make as the entrée, but not with these recipes. We've carefully selected them because they are all perfect for warm-weather entertaining—they're easy, economical, and appealing.

WATER CHESTNUT DIP

1 (8-ounce) can whole water chestnuts,
    drained and minced
1 (8-ounce) carton commercial sour cream
1 cup mayonnaise
1 clove garlic, minced
¼ cup minced fresh parsley
2 tablespoons minced onion
1 teaspoon soy sauce
½ teaspoon ground ginger

Combine all ingredients; mix well. Chill 4 hours. Serve with fresh vegetables. Yield: 2¼ cups.
Mrs. John H. Walkup, Jr.,
Gravel Switch, Kentucky.

CURRY DIP

¾ cup mayonnaise
1½ tablespoons chili sauce
1½ teaspoons finely chopped onion
1 teaspoon Worcestershire sauce
1¼ teaspoons curry powder
¼ teaspoon garlic salt
Pinch of pepper

Combine all ingredients in a medium mixing bowl; mix well. Serve dip with raw vegetables. Yield: about 1 cup.

Jo Saye,
Birmingham, Alabama.

SWEET 'N' SOUR SPREAD

1 (10-ounce) jar pineapple preserves
1 teaspoon prepared horseradish
1 teaspoon prepared mustard
1 (8-ounce) package cream cheese,
    softened

Combine preserves, horseradish, and mustard; stir well. Cover and refrigerate at least 3 hours.

Spoon pineapple mixture over softened cream cheese, and serve with crackers. Yield: 1 cup.

Kay Castleman Cooper,
Burke, Virginia.

GUACAMOLE MOLD

1 envelope unflavored gelatin
1 cup chicken broth
2 cups mashed avocado
1 cup mayonnaise
1 (8-ounce) carton commercial sour cream
1 (4-ounce) jar diced pimiento, drained
¼ cup finely chopped onion
1 tablespoon lemon juice
½ teaspoon salt
Dash of hot sauce

Sprinkle gelatin over chicken broth in a saucepan; let stand 5 minutes. Place over medium heat, stirring until gelatin dissolves; cool slightly. Add remaining ingredients, stirring well. Pour into a lightly oiled 5-cup mold; chill until firm. Unmold onto serving plate. Serve with crackers. Yield: 5 cups. *Nina Bruner,*
Merritt Island, Florida.

MUSTARD MOUSSE

1 envelope unflavored gelatin
2 tablespoons cold water
½ cup boiling water
1½ teaspoons butter or margarine
½ cup vinegar
2 eggs, beaten
2 tablespoons sugar
1 tablespoon dry mustard
⅛ teaspoon salt
Dash of pepper
Dash of paprika
½ cup whipping cream
Parsley sprigs (optional)
Pimiento-stuffed olive slices (optional)

Soften unflavored gelatin in cold water. Add boiling water; stir until gelatin is dissolved.

Combine butter, vinegar, eggs, sugar, mustard, salt, pepper, and paprika in top of a double boiler; mix well. Place over boiling water and cook, stirring constantly, until thickened. Remove from heat; cool. Chill until consistency of unbeaten egg white. Beat whipping cream until stiff peaks form; fold into mustard mixture.

Pour into a lightly oiled 2-cup mold; chill until firm. Unmold onto serving plate. Garnish with parsley and olive slices, if desired. Serve with assorted crackers. Yield: 2 cups. *Cassie Evans,*
Ewell, Maryland.

Sweet Aroma In The Air, Great Flavor On The Grill

When Southerners cook outdoors, it's usually a family affair. And whether it's meat, fowl, or fish that your family wants, you're sure to find recipes here to interest you.

GRILLED BLACK PEPPER STEAK

1 (1½- to 2-pound) sirloin steak, 1½- to
    2-inches thick
2 large onions, thinly sliced
1 cup red wine vinegar
½ cup vegetable oil
⅓ cup firmly packed brown sugar
1 clove garlic, minced
¼ teaspoon salt
¼ teaspoon dried whole marjoram
¼ teaspoon dried whole rosemary,
    crushed
3 drops of hot sauce
1 tablespoon plus 1 teaspoon coarsely
    ground pepper, divided
Tomato wedges
Fresh parsley sprigs

Place steak in a large shallow dish. Combine onion and next 8 ingredients; pour over steak. Cover and refrigerate 3 hours, turning occasionally.

Remove steak from marinade. Press 2 teaspoons pepper onto each side of steak. Grill over hot coals 15 minutes on each side or to desired degree of doneness.

Place steak on serving platter; garnish with tomato wedges and fresh parsley. To serve, cut into serving pieces. Yield: 3 to 4 servings. *Diane Butts,*
Boone, North Carolina.

TANGY FLANK STEAK

1 (1- to 1½-pound) flank steak
½ cup vegetable oil
3 tablespoons vinegar
3 tablespoons lemon juice
2 tablespoons Worcestershire sauce
2 tablespoons soy sauce
1½ tablespoons chopped fresh parsley
1½ teaspoons salt
2 teaspoons dry mustard
1 teaspoon freshly ground pepper
½ teaspoon garlic salt

Place flank steak in a large shallow container. Combine remaining ingredients; pour over steak. Cover and chill at least 2 hours, turning steak often.

Remove steak from marinade; grill over hot coals 10 to 12 minutes on each side or to desired degree of doneness. Yield: 4 servings. *Trudie Young,*
Johns Island, South Carolina.

TEXAS FLANK STEAK

1 (2-pound) flank steak
½ cup vegetable oil
¼ cup vinegar
½ teaspoon sugar
½ (1.25-ounce) envelope onion soup mix
1 tablespoon Worcestershire sauce

Place flank steak in a shallow dish. Combine remaining ingredients, and pour over steak. Cover and refrigerate 8 hours, turning steak often. Drain steak, reserving the marinade.

Grill steak over hot coals 10 to 12 minutes on each side or to desired degree of doneness, basting occasionally with reserved marinade. Yield: 4 to 6 servings.
James E. Boggess,
Miami, Florida.

GLAZED PORK CHOPS

6 (¾- to 1-inch-thick) pork chops
1 cup firmly packed brown sugar
¼ cup lemon juice
1 teaspoon dry mustard

Place pork chops in a large shallow dish. Combine remaining ingredients, mixing well. Pour over pork chops; cover and marinate in refrigerator 2 hours, turning chops once.

Drain pork chops, reserving marinade. Grill over hot coals 25 minutes on each side or to desired degree of doneness, basting chops often with marinade. Yield: 6 servings.
Sharon McClatchey,
Muskogee, Oklahoma.

HERBED BARBECUED RIBS

3 pounds spareribs
1 (8-ounce) can tomato sauce
1 cup chopped onion
¼ cup firmly packed brown sugar
½ cup water
3 tablespoons catsup
1 tablespoon vegetable oil
½ teaspoon dried whole rosemary, crushed
½ teaspoon dried whole basil, crushed
½ teaspoon pepper

Cut ribs into serving-size pieces, and place in a large shallow dish. Combine remaining ingredients, mixing well. Pour over ribs; cover and marinate in refrigerator 2 hours. Drain, reserving marinade.

Grill ribs over medium-hot coals 30 minutes, turning frequently. Grill an additional 15 to 30 minutes, turning and basting frequently with reserved marinade. Place on serving platter, and serve immediately. Yield: 3 to 4 servings.
Mrs. R. F. Watts,
Glasgow, Kentucky.

GRILLED GROUPER

1 teaspoon Creole seasoning
1 teaspoon dried whole basil
1 teaspoon dried whole oregano
½ teaspoon white pepper
½ teaspoon garlic powder
½ teaspoon Italian seasoning
6 grouper or redfish fillets (about 2 pounds)
½ cup dry white wine
¼ cup olive oil
12 slices bacon, partially cooked
Vegetable cooking spray

Combine Creole seasoning, basil, oregano, white pepper, garlic powder, and Italian seasoning in a small mixing bowl; mix well. Divide mixture in half; set half aside. Sprinkle remaining half on fish fillets. Place fillets in a shallow baking dish, and pour wine over fillets. Cover and marinate in refrigerator 12 hours, turning fillets occasionally.

Drain fish fillets; rub both sides of fillets with olive oil, and sprinkle evenly with reserved seasoning mixture. Wrap 2 slices bacon around each fillet; secure with wooden picks.

Spray a fish basket with cooking spray; place fish in basket. Grill fish over medium-hot coals 7 to 10 minutes on each side or until fish flakes easily when tested with a fork.

Remove fish from grill; remove wooden picks. Place fish on serving platter, and serve immediately. Yield: 6 servings.
Jakk Stovall,
Baton Rouge, Louisiana.

MARINATED CHICKEN IN A SANDWICH

8 chicken breast halves, skinned and boned
1 cup soy sauce
½ cup pineapple juice
¼ cup sherry
¼ cup firmly packed brown sugar
¾ teaspoon minced fresh garlic
8 slices Monterey Jack cheese
8 Kaiser rolls, sliced in half horizontally
Mustard sauce (recipe follows)
Leaf lettuce

Place chicken in a large shallow dish. Combine soy sauce, pineapple juice, sherry, brown sugar, and garlic, mixing well. Pour over chicken, and let marinate for about 30 minutes. Remove from marinade.

Grill chicken breasts over hot coals 25 minutes or until done, turning and basting with marinade approximately every 5 minutes. Place slice of cheese on each chicken breast, and grill an additional 3 minutes or until cheese melts. Remove chicken from grill.

Spread each side of rolls with mustard sauce; place chicken breast on bottom half of each roll; top with lettuce. Cover with roll top, and serve sandwich immediately. Yield: 8 servings.

Mustard Sauce:

½ cup dry mustard
⅔ cup white vinegar
⅔ cup sugar
1 egg

Combine all ingredients in container of an electric blender and blend until smooth. Pour mixture into top of a double boiler; bring water to a boil. Reduce heat to low; cook, stirring constantly, about 7 minutes or until smooth and thickened. Store in an airtight container in refrigerator. Yield: 1⅓ cups.

Tip: To use a griddle or frying pan, preheat to medium or medium-high heat before adding the food. It is properly preheated when a few drops of water spatter when they hit the surface. Add food, and reduce heat to cook without spattering and smoking.

TANGY BARBECUED CHICKEN

1 (2½- to 3-pound) broiler-fryer, cut up
1 egg, beaten
1 cup vinegar
½ cup vegetable oil
2 teaspoons salt
1½ teaspoons poultry seasoning
¼ teaspoon white pepper

Place chicken in a large shallow dish. Combine remaining ingredients, and pour over chicken; then cover and refrigerate 4 hours.

Grill chicken over medium coals 55 to 60 minutes or until done, turning and basting with marinade every 10 minutes. Yield: 4 servings. *Elizabeth W. Dean, Alexandria, Virginia.*

Serve The Salad In A Sandwich

If the kids want a sandwich but you'd prefer a salad, these recipes will solve the summer meal dilemma. You can mound servings of salad onto lettuce leaves, spread it on sandwich buns, or stuff it into pita pockets.

SHRIMP SALAD

3 cups water
1 pound unpeeled fresh shrimp
4 canned artichoke hearts, chopped
⅔ cup chopped celery
½ cup peeled, chopped cucumber
¼ cup chopped green onions
2 tablespoons chopped green pepper
⅓ cup vegetable oil
⅓ cup white wine vinegar
1 tablespoon lemon juice
1 clove garlic, minced
1 teaspoon dried whole basil
1 teaspoon dried whole oregano
¼ teaspoon salt
⅛ teaspoon pepper
2 cups shredded lettuce (optional)
4 pita bread rounds, halved (optional)
1 tablespoon plus 1 teaspoon mayonnaise
   (optional)

Bring water to a boil; add shrimp, and cook 3 to 5 minutes. Drain well; rinse with cold water. Peel and devein shrimp.

Combine shrimp, artichoke hearts, celery, cucumber, green onions, green pepper, oil, vinegar, lemon juice, garlic, basil, oregano, salt, and pepper; toss well. Cover and marinate in refrigerator 3 hours. Drain. Serve over shredded lettuce, or serve in pita halves, if desired.

For pita sandwiches, spread a teaspoon of mayonnaise, if desired, in each bread half. Line each half with ¼ cup lettuce, and fill with about ½ cup shrimp mixture. Serve immediately. Yield: 4 servings. *Delicia Dozier, Birmingham, Alabama.*

SWISS TUNA SALAD

1 (6½-ounce) can white tuna, drained and
   flaked
½ cup chopped celery
½ cup cubed Swiss cheese
¼ cup mayonnaise
½ teaspoon lemon juice
Sesame seed buns or lettuce leaves

Combine first 5 ingredients; mix well. Chill until serving time. Spread on sesame seed buns, or serve on lettuce leaves. Yield: 4 servings.

Note: Sandwiches may be served warm. Wrap individually in aluminum foil; bake at 325° for 15 minutes. *Billie Taylor, Fork Union, Virginia.*

CHEF'S SALAD
(pictured on page 202)

5 cups mixed romaine, leaf, and iceberg
   lettuce, torn
4 (1-ounce) slices Swiss cheese, cut into
   julienne strips
4 (1-ounce) slices ham, cut into julienne
   strips
4 hard-cooked eggs, coarsely chopped
8 cherry tomatoes, halved
¼ cup diced green onions
4 pita bread rounds, halved (optional)
½ cup commercial Ranch-style or
   Thousand Island salad dressing

Combine lettuce, cheese, ham, eggs, tomatoes, and green onions. Serve as is, or spoon the mixture into pita bread halves. Serve salad or sandwiches with salad dressing. Serve immediately. Yield: 4 servings. *Teresa Cox, Caney, Kentucky.*

CHICKEN SALAD WITH ARTICHOKES

4 chicken breast halves, cooked and cubed
1 (14-ounce) can artichoke hearts, drained
   and chopped
¾ cup mayonnaise
¾ cup chopped celery
6 green onions, chopped
1 cup chopped pecans, toasted
¼ teaspoon salt
⅛ teaspoon garlic powder
⅛ teaspoon pepper
Sandwich bread or lettuce leaves

Combine chicken, artichoke hearts, mayonnaise, celery, green onions, pecans, salt, garlic powder, and pepper in a medium bowl; mix well. Refrigerate until serving time. Spread on bread, or serve on lettuce leaves. Yield: 8 to 10 servings. *Sarah J. Jackson, Birmingham, Alabama.*

Fresh Vegetables For Lighter Fare

With nutritionists recommending more complex carbohydrates and dietary fiber, fresh vegetables are important foods.

Cheesy Puff-Top Tomatoes and Stuffed Zucchini are a couple of our favorite vegetable recipes. Tomatoes are an excellent source of vitamin A and vitamin C (ascorbic acid); zucchini contains a fair amount of potassium, vitamin A, and vitamin C.

summer Suppers

Let color be your guide in choosing the most nutritious vegetables. In general, the more intense the color, the higher the nutrients. For example, broccoli is a deeper green than cabbage, and it has a higher vitamin A content.

Careless storage and preparation cause fresh vegetables to lose nutrients. Be sure to cool them immediately after harvest, and keep refrigerated at all times. When buying fresh produce, avoid that which is lying in the sun, or is unrefrigerated, bruised, or damaged. Even if it is a bargain, vitamin A and vitamin C levels will be lower.

To minimize nutrient loss in preparation, reduce the amount of water used to clean and cook vegetables, and reduce cooking time. Trim and peel as little as possible; leave in large pieces, and prepare close to serving time.

CHEESY PUFF-TOP TOMATOES
(pictured on page 203)

1 onion-flavored bouillon cube, crushed
½ cup 1% low-fat cottage cheese
2 tablespoons plus 1 teaspoon grated
   Parmesan cheese
2 egg whites
3 medium tomatoes (about 1½-pounds)

Combine bouillon cube and cottage cheese; let stand 5 minutes. Stir in Parmesan cheese. Beat egg whites until soft peaks form; fold into cottage cheese mixture. Set aside.

Cut tomatoes in half; place cut side up in a 13- x 9- x 2-inch baking pan. Cover and bake at 350° for 5 minutes. Spoon cottage cheese mixture over cut surface of tomatoes. Broil tomatoes 5 inches from heat 3 to 5 minutes. Yield: 6 servings (about 38 calories per tomato half). *Charlotte Ann Pierce, Greensburg, Kentucky.*

STUFFED ZUCCHINI
(pictured on page 203)

2 medium zucchini
Vegetable cooking spray
2 tablespoons water
3 tablespoons chopped onion
½ cup sliced fresh mushrooms
½ cup chopped tomatoes
½ cup chicken broth
½ teaspoon dried whole basil
½ teaspoon dried whole thyme
⅛ teaspoon pepper
1 cup whole wheat bread cubes
2 teaspoons grated Parmesan cheese

Steam whole zucchini 15 minutes or until tender. Slice zucchini lengthwise, and scoop out pulp. Reserve pulp and shells; set aside.

Coat a large skillet with cooking spray; add water, and place over medium heat until hot. Add onion; cook until onion is transparent. Add mushrooms, tomatoes, and reserved zucchini pulp; cook 5 minutes, stirring constantly. Add broth and seasonings; bring to a boil. Remove from heat, and add bread cubes; mix well.

Fill reserved zucchini shells with vegetable mixture. Sprinkle vegetable tops with grated Parmesan cheese. Bake at 350° for 25 minutes or until hot. Yield: 4 servings (about 62 calories per filled zucchini half). *Pati Wilson, Tulsa, Oklahoma.*

ORANGE-GLAZED BEETS

1½ pounds beets
2 tablespoons reduced-calorie margarine
2 teaspoons cornstarch
1 teaspoon sugar
⅛ teaspoon salt
1 teaspoon cider vinegar
1 to 2 teaspoons grated orange rind
½ cup unsweetened orange juice

Leave root and 1 inch of stem on beets; scrub with a vegetable brush. Place beets in a saucepan; cover with water, and bring to a boil. Cover, reduce heat, and simmer 35 to 40 minutes or until tender; drain. Rinse beets with cold water, and drain again. Trim off beet roots and stems, and rub off skins; cut beets into ¼-inch slices.

Melt margarine in a heavy saucepan over low heat; stir in remaining ingredients except beets. Cook over medium heat, stirring constantly, until smooth and thickened. Add beets, stirring gently to coat; cook over low heat 3 to 5 minutes. Yield: 6 servings (about 58 calories per ½-cup serving).
Mrs. B. R. Dasher, Guyton, Georgia.

VEGETABLE SOUP

1 (46-ounce) can no-salt-added tomato
   juice
½ cup water
2 cups shredded cabbage
1 cup chopped yellow squash
1 cup chopped zucchini
1 cup scraped, thinly sliced carrots
1 cup green beans, cut into 1-inch pieces
1 cup sliced fresh mushrooms
½ cup chopped onion
½ cup chopped green pepper
1 bay leaf
1 teaspoon dried whole basil
½ teaspoon salt
⅛ teaspoon pepper

Combine all ingredients in a large Dutch oven; bring to a boil. Cover, reduce heat, and simmer 30 minutes.

Remove bay leaf before serving. Ladle into individual soup bowls or cups, and serve immediately. Yield: 10 cups (about 47 calories per 1-cup serving). *Marilyn Hartman, Chapel Hill, North Carolina.*

Tip: Avoid using two strong-flavored herbs, such as a bay, rosemary, or sage, together as the flavors will fight each other. Instead, use a strong herb in combination with a milder one. The accent herbs are slightly milder than the strong herbs and include basil, tarragon, and oregano. Medium herbs are dill, marjoram, winter savory, fennel, mint, and lemon thyme. Delicate herbs include chervil, chives, parsley, and summer savory.

GARDEN PASTA SALAD

1 cup uncooked shell macaroni
¼ teaspoon salt
1 cup green beans, cut into 1½-inch
  pieces
1 cup cherry tomato halves
¼ cup scored, sliced, and halved
  cucumber
¼ cup commercial Italian reduced-calorie
  salad dressing
¼ cup sliced radishes

Cook macaroni according to package directions, using ¼ teaspoon salt. Drain and set aside.

Place beans in a small amount of boiling water; reduce heat, and cook over medium-high heat 5 minutes or until crisp-tender. Drain and let cool.

Combine pasta, beans, tomatoes, cucumber, and salad dressing; toss gently. Chill. To serve, add radishes, and toss gently. Yield: 4 servings (about 95 calories per 1-cup serving). *Melia Vowels, Vine Grove, Kentucky.*

Desserts To Make Ahead

When you think of summer desserts, fluffy soufflés, creamy mousses, and rich cheesecakes all fit the season. And the best thing about the dessert recipes here is that they're chilled or frozen, so you make them the day before.

Since most of these desserts are pale, add a splash of bold color by garnishing with fresh fruit or chocolate shavings. Or nestle a small spray of colorful flowers next to the serving dish.

AMARETTO MOUSSE

4 egg whites
Dash of salt
¾ cup sugar, divided
2 cups whipping cream
½ cup amaretto
Sliced almonds, toasted

Beat egg whites (at room temperature) and salt until foamy. Add ½ cup sugar, 1 tablespoon at a time, beating until stiff peaks form. Set aside.

Beat whipping cream until foamy; gradually add remaining ¼ cup sugar, beating until soft peaks form. Fold in amaretto. Gently fold whipped cream mixture into egg whites; blend well. Spoon into a bowl. Sprinkle with sliced almonds. Freeze. Yield: 8 to 10 servings. *Pat Boschen, Ashland, Virginia.*

BUTTERSCOTCH CHEESECAKE

1½ cups graham cracker crumbs
⅓ cup firmly packed brown sugar
⅓ cup butter or margarine, melted
1 (14-ounce) can sweetened condensed
  milk
¾ cup water
1 (3⅝-ounce) package butterscotch
  pudding mix
3 (8-ounce) packages cream cheese,
  softened
3 eggs
1 teaspoon vanilla extract
Whipped cream
Crushed butterscotch candies

Combine graham cracker crumbs, brown sugar, and butter; mix well. Firmly press mixture into bottom and up sides of a 9-inch springform pan; set aside.

Combine sweetened condensed milk, water, and pudding mix in a medium saucepan; mixing well. Cook over medium heat, stirring frequently, until thickened and bubbly.

Beat cream cheese with an electric mixer until light and fluffy. Add eggs, one at a time, beating well after each addition. Add pudding mixture and vanilla; beat well. Pour into prepared pan. Bake at 375° for 50 to 55 minutes. Let cool to room temperature on a wire rack; cover and chill 12 hours. To serve; remove sides of pan, and garnish with whipped cream and crushed candy pieces. Yield: one 9-inch cheesecake.
Carol Barclay, Portland, Texas.

GRASSHOPPER SOUFFLÉ
(pictured on page 203)

2 envelopes unflavored gelatin
1 cup water
1 cup sugar, divided
¼ teaspoon salt
6 eggs, separated
½ cup green crème de menthe
½ cup crème de cacao
2 cups whipping cream, whipped
Grated chocolate
Fresh mint leaves

Combine gelatin and water in a small saucepan. Add ½ cup sugar, salt, and egg yolks; mix well. Cook over low heat, stirring constantly, about 10 minutes or until gelatin dissolves and mixture is slightly thickened. Remove from heat; stir in liqueurs. Chill, stirring occasionally, until slightly thickened.

Beat egg whites (at room temperature) until foamy. Gradually add remaining ½ cup sugar, 1 tablespoon at a time, beating until stiff peaks form. Gently fold beaten egg whites and whipped cream into gelatin mixture. Spoon into a 2½-quart soufflé dish. Chill until firm. Garnish with grated chocolate and mint leaves. Yield: 12 to 15 servings. *Sharon W. Wenger, Richmond, Virginia.*

RASPBERRY SOUFFLÉ

1 (10-ounce) package frozen sweetened
  raspberries, partially thawed
2 eggs, separated
½ cup milk
1 envelope unflavored gelatin
2 tablespoons sugar
1 cup whipping cream
1 tablespoon kirsch or other
  cherry-flavored liqueur
Additional whipped cream
Fresh raspberries

Put raspberries through a sieve, and strain. Discard seeds; set puree aside.

Beat egg yolks and milk in a heavy saucepan; stir in gelatin. Cook over medium heat, stirring constantly, about 5 minutes or until thickened and bubbly. Remove from heat; stir in raspberry puree. Chill until consistency of unbeaten egg white.

Beat egg whites (at room temperature) until foamy. Gradually add sugar, 1 tablespoon at a time, beating until stiff peaks form. Beat whipping cream until stiff peaks form. Fold egg whites, whipped cream, and kirsch into raspberry mixture; spoon into a 1-quart soufflé dish. Chill until firm. Garnish with additional whipped cream and fresh raspberries. Yield: 6 servings.

Sophie Lanoix,
Sarasota, Florida.

CHILLED ORANGE SOUFFLÉ

6 eggs, separated
1 tablespoon grated orange rind
1 cup orange juice
½ cup sugar
1 envelope unflavored gelatin
¾ teaspoon cream of tartar
1 (5-ounce) can evaporated milk, chilled
Orange slices, halved (optional)

Cut a piece of aluminum foil or waxed paper long enough to fit around a 1½-quart soufflé dish allowing a 1-inch overlap; fold lengthwise into thirds. Lightly oil one side of foil; wrap around outside of dish, oiled side against dish, extending 3 inches above rim. Secure foil with freezer tape.

Beat egg yolks; combine yolks, orange rind, orange juice, sugar, and gelatin in a large saucepan, stirring well. Cook over medium heat, stirring constantly, until mixture is thickened and bubbly. Remove from heat; cool.

Beat egg whites (at room temperature) and cream of tartar at high speed of an electric mixer until stiff peaks form. Beat evaporated milk at high speed of an electric mixer until stiff peaks form. Fold egg whites and whipped milk into yolk mixture.

Place a ring of orange slice halves in dish standing against sides, if desired. Spoon mixture into dish; cover and chill 8 hours. Remove collar; serve. Yield: 8 servings.

Peggy H. Amos,
Martinsville, Virginia.

Tip: Use a clean toothbrush to remove bits of rind from a grater.

CHOCOLATE RUM MOUSSE

1 (6-ounce) package semisweet chocolate morsels
3 tablespoons water
1 tablespoon rum
5 eggs, separated
½ cup whipping cream
2 tablespoons powdered sugar

Combine chocolate morsels and water in a heavy saucepan; cook over low heat, stirring constantly, until chocolate melts. Remove chocolate from heat; stir in rum. Cool.

Beat egg yolks. Add cooled chocolate mixture; beat until smooth. Beat egg whites (at room temperature) until stiff peaks form; fold into chocolate mixture. Spoon into 8 stemmed glasses or serving dishes; chill 3 to 4 hours.

Beat whipping cream until foamy; gradually add powdered sugar, beating until soft peaks form. Add a dollop to each serving. Yield: 8 servings.

Gwen Louer,
Roswell, Georgia.

Try Using Herbs For Fragrance

Almost everyone has experienced the added zip that herbs give to foods. But have you considered using fresh basil, dill, oregano, or mint to add fragrance to a flower arrangement?

The greatest attraction of most herbs is their foliage and wonderful smell, but some have very showy flowers. Fennel and dill have lacy umbels, or umbrella-shaped blossoms like those of Queen Anne's lace, but they are yellow. Garlic chives bear white blossoms, while chives bloom lavender-pink.

Mint, basil, oregano, lemon verbena, rosemary, and tansy provide interesting background foliage for almost any kind of flower. Their savory scents are released as the leaves are rubbed or crushed. Normal handling in the course of cutting and arranging should be enough to bring out their fragrance.

Tansy provides a mass of fernlike foliage without a strong smell. Mint, verbena, dill, fennel, and oregano have distinct scents yet are not overpowering. Other herbs that work well in arrangements are chives and garlic chives.

You can add color to a vase full of herbs with flowers, such as Transvaal daisies (gerbera), zinnias, lilies, or even mums. Big, bold blossoms are especially nice against the small leaves and fine textures that most herbs offer.

This loose, informal arrangement mixes a variety of summer herbs and flowers. Included are tiger lilies, bee balm, coneflower, Transvaal daisies (gerbera), celosia, dill, garlic chives, Dark Opal basil, lettuce leaf basil, and mint.

Colorful zinnias are combined with the fernlike foliage of tansy for an unusual arrangement. They are held in a shallow vase that sits inside the carved melon.

Gearing Up For A Crowd

Rather than letting your guests juggle plates, silverware, and drinks in their hands or on their laps, why not have seated dining at your next outdoor party? It's not as expensive as you might think.

Tables and Table Covers

Tables are really inexpensive to rent overnight—about $5 to $7 each. Most rental stores carry 48- and 60-inch-diameter folding tables. The 48-inch table seats four people and the larger one will seat six.

The table bases are not very attractive, so you will want some kind of skirt that goes to the floor. Rental stores carry table skirts, but they are more suited to weddings and formal situations. To add a custom look to the tables, you can make your own tablecloths. Most of these tables are standard, so you can make tablecloths to fit a certain size table. Then they'll fit even if you change rental companies.

You'll probably want to top the skirt with an overlay, often called napkin, which protects the skirt from food stains and gives the table a dressier appearance. For the 60-inch tables, you'll need to buy a tablecloth or make the overlay from a sheet because fabric doesn't come that wide. The skirt may be pieced, but the overlay is usually made without any seams, preferably from the width of a sheet.

On the 48-inch round tables you can use most 55- to 60-inch-width fabrics. We've used bright vinyl for the overlays. This vinyl is becoming quite popular to use as tablecloths. It is sold by the yard in 54-inch widths and doesn't have to be hemmed or sewn. A real advantage is that it's reusable and cleans easily. If you can't find it locally, you can probably order the vinyl through a store in a larger city.

Chairs

You can rent chairs, but rental stores don't usually have much variety. Many of them used to carry a white wooden style but have switched to metal and white plastic ones.

Metal folding chairs in colored baked-on enamel finish can be purchased at large discount department stores. If you have some old gray folding chairs, you could liven them up with a bright, new painted finish. To make sure the paint sticks, clean the chairs thoroughly, and sand. Then use a good metal primer and a rust-inhibiting spray paint.

The grid chair is our favorite. For the look and the price, you can't beat it. It's very inexpensive and can be stacked for storage. The metal is coated with a plastic finish that won't scratch as easily as a painted finish.

Setting the Table

You can have a lot of fun finding inexpensive dinnerware, flatware, and glasses. A point you'll want to consider here is whether or not you want to wash and reuse the products.

Paper and plastic party goods are so attractive now that you may not want to bother with anything reusable. However, you can rent glasses, dinnerware, and silver flatware by the dozen at very reasonable prices.

Plates and flatware are good reusable items to purchase. They are easy to wash in the dishwasher and don't take up much storage space. Enameled metal plates or clear glass dinner plates, which are usually sold at import stores, make attractive table settings. Still another idea is to use heavy-duty plastic plates and flatware.

Because you are using multiple tables, you'll probably want simple centerpieces. Painted peach baskets can be filled with small containers of ferns and other greenery. Fresh flowers inserted in the dirt look as if they're growing there. You can use florist picks to keep the flowers fresher for a longer time. Then fill in around the containers with Spanish moss for a finished look.

Helium-filled balloons rising out of baskets or clay pots make exciting centerpieces. Tie the balloons with grosgrain ribbons, and let them float above eye level when guests are seated.

For soft lighting, floating candles make simple and elegant centerpieces. Break off flower blossoms, and float them in the water with the candles. You can also scatter votive candles and blossoms randomly on the tables to complement the attractive centerpieces.

Lending a casual air, inexpensive stainless flatware with plastic handles and plastic glasses and plates mixed with paper ones provide color and make matching table settings an easy task for any hostess.

For shimmering nighttime elegance, a metallic overlay is paired with rented silver. Floating candle centerpieces and plastic dinnerware and glasses are a cut above the average.

From Our Kitchen To Yours

When you eat outdoors, the food just seems to taste better. To make your meal even more enjoyable, here are some suggestions.

—Always keep the weather in mind. With windy conditions, remember to anchor tablecloths and napkins; use napkin rings to keep napkins from blowing away, and set weights on the corners of tablecloths.

When the sun goes down, have plenty of lights scattered about—on tables, throughout the yard, floating in the pool. Candles, torches, and luminaries create a romantic atmosphere.

—Insects are often a problem. Use citronella candles, and keep bug spray close at hand. Position your serving table away from shrubs or flowers.

—It's best to choose foods that will keep well and not be affected by the heat, such as the selections offered in "Tradition Sets a Summer Table" beginning on page 176. Cold foods can be kept chilled by placing the serving bowl in a larger bowl of ice. Keep bottled or canned beverages cold in an ice-filled galvanized washtub, new trash can, or wheelbarrow.

—Just as when entertaining indoors, consider crowd flow outdoors. Set up your beverage table or bar in one area, grill in another, and buffet table in another. To make setting up easier, locate your buffet table close to the kitchen.

Set up the buffet so it's easily reached from both sides. Have foods such as ribs, large cuts of meat, and cakes pre-cut into serving-size pieces. Guests can serve themselves better if they don't have to hold their eating utensils as they are going through the buffet line. To make it easier, preset the tables, or place utensils at the end of the line.

—On the buffet table, try using a grouping of collectibles or a number of candles held by pieces of fresh fruit as a centerpiece. When serving shellfish or barbecued ribs, use vinyl-coated table coverings, and bright-colored terry hand towels can be used as napkins. Group condiments in baskets and bundle silverware in napkins. For a refreshing look, select cool colors for cloths or napkins, serve ice water with a few slices of lime or lemon, and use fruit, herbs, or fresh flowers as table accents.

Fresh Salads For The Season

Salad ingredients offer a pleasing variety of shapes and colors. For example, ruffle-edged leaf lettuce makes an attractive salad bowl liner, while other varieties of lettuce add color contrast.

MAIN-DISH SALAD

5 cups torn lettuce
1 (10-ounce) package frozen English peas, thawed
⅔ cup chopped celery
¼ pound fresh mushrooms, sliced
½ pound cherry tomatoes, halved
2 (1-ounce) slices boiled ham, cut into thin strips
2 (1-ounce) slices Swiss cheese, cut into thin strips
2 hard-cooked eggs, sliced
⅛ teaspoon onion salt
Tangy Red Dressing

Combine all ingredients except Tangy Red Dressing in a large bowl, reserving some of the mushrooms, tomatoes, ham, cheese, and eggs for garnish; toss gently. Arrange reserved ingredients on top of salad. Serve with Tangy Red Dressing. Yield: 3 to 4 servings.

Tangy Red Dressing:

½ cup catsup
2 tablespoons red wine vinegar
2 tablespoons sugar
1 teaspoon celery seeds
1 teaspoon dry mustard
1 teaspoon lemon juice

Combine all ingredients; stir well. Refrigerate. Yield: ⅔ cup.
*Lt. Col. R. G. Sigman,
Fort Walton Beach, Florida.*

GREEN SALAD WITH SOY DRESSING

3 cups iceberg lettuce, torn
3 cups romaine lettuce, torn
1 cup fresh spinach, torn
4 hard-cooked eggs, sliced
1 (1-ounce) slice Swiss cheese, cut in julienne strips
1 (1-ounce) slice Cheddar cheese, cut in julienne strips
¼ cup sunflower kernels, toasted
Soy Dressing

Combine iceburg lettuce, romaine lettuce, and spinach in a large bowl. Top with egg slices, cheese strips, and sunflower kernels. Serve with Soy Dressing. Yield: 10 to 12 servings.

Soy Dressing:

1 stalk celery with leaves
1 small onion, quartered
1 green pepper, quartered
½ cup vegetable oil
Juice and pulp of 1 lemon
2 tablespoons sesame seed butter
2 tablespoons soy sauce

Cut celery into 2-inch pieces. Combine all ingredients in container of an electric blender; process until smooth. Yield: 2 cups.
*Betty Matteson,
Durham, North Carolina.*

PAPRIKA-GREEN BEAN SALAD

1 pound fresh green beans
½ small onion
1 large cucumber, peeled and sliced
Paprika Dressing

Wash beans; trim ends, and remove strings. Cut into 1-inch pieces. Cook beans, covered, in a small amount of boiling water 10 minutes or until crisp-tender; drain well.

Cut onion into thin slices; cut slices in half, and separate layers. Add onion and cucumber to beans. Pour Paprika Dressing over bean mixture, stirring well. Chill at least 2 hours. Use slotted spoon to serve. Yield: 6 servings.

Paprika Dressing:

¼ cup sugar
¼ cup vegetable oil
¼ cup vinegar
½ teaspoon paprika
¼ teaspoon salt
⅛ teaspoon dillseeds
⅛ teaspoon celery seeds

To prepare dressing for salad, combine all ingredients in container of an electric blender; process until smooth. Yield: about ½ cup.
*Mrs. Malcolm Bowles,
Mableton, Georgia.*

CITRUS VINAIGRETTE SALAD

½ cup peanut oil
3 tablespoons orange juice
1 tablespoon lemon juice
¼ teaspoon salt
⅛ teaspoon freshly ground pepper
1 tablespoon chopped parsley
1 pomegranate
1 medium head lettuce, torn
1 orange, peeled and thinly sliced

Combine first 6 ingredients, mixing well. Set aside.

Remove seeds from pomegranate. Combine lettuce, orange slices, and seeds in a large bowl. Toss with dressing. Yield: 4 to 6 servings.

R. A. Colosimo,
Copperas Cove, Texas.

TOSSED SALAD
WITH PARMESAN DRESSING

1 large head lettuce, torn
½ cup cauliflower flowerets
⅓ cup sliced fresh mushrooms
4 radishes, thinly sliced
½ purple onion, sliced and separated into rings
8 slices bacon, cooked and crumbled
Parmesan Dressing

Combine lettuce, cauliflower, mushrooms, and radishes in a large bowl; toss gently. Top with onion and crumbled bacon. Serve salad with Parmesan Dressing. Yield: 8 to 10 servings.

Parmesan Dressing:

1 cup mayonnaise
½ cup grated Parmesan cheese
1 teaspoon sugar
3 to 4 tablespoons milk

Combine all ingredients, mixing well. Yield: about 1¼ cups.

Melinda Dressler,
Birmingham, Alabama.

Can't Wait
For Fresh Corn

Everyone knows the good taste of tender corn on the cob, and our recipes offer ideas for enjoying the succulent grain once it's cut from the cob.

Like other whole grains, corn has a high dietary fiber content. It is also a source of vitamin B-6 and potassium.

You can boost the nutrition of corn even more by combining it with eggs and milk in Corn Pudding. The protein in corn and other grains is improved when combined with high-quality protein from animal products.

Another favorite recipe is Corn Fritters. Just remember to keep the oil hot and the cooking time to a minimum.

Young, freshly harvested corn is sweeter and juicier than corn that has been stored for any length of time. One kernel, gently punctured, can tell the story. If a milky juice flows out, the corn is young and sweet. If the juice is thick and starchy, the corn is older and will be less flavorful.

CORN PUDDING

2 cups corn cut from cob
2 eggs, slightly beaten
¾ cup milk
2 tablespoons sugar
2 tablespoons diced onion
2 tablespoons butter or margarine, melted
1 teaspoon salt
⅛ teaspoon pepper

Combine all ingredients; mix well. Pour into a lightly greased 1-quart baking dish. Bake, uncovered, at 350° for 30 minutes or until firm. Yield: 4 to 6 servings.

Evelyn Milam,
Knoxville, Tennessee.

CORN FRITTERS

2 cups corn cut from cob
¼ cup water
¾ cup all-purpose flour
1 teaspoon baking powder
¾ teaspoon salt
¼ teaspoon pepper
2 eggs, beaten

Combine corn and water in a medium saucepan. Bring to a boil; cover, reduce heat, and simmer 7 to 8 minutes or just until corn is tender. Drain.

Combine flour, baking powder, salt, and pepper in a large mixing bowl; set mixture aside.

Combine eggs and corn; blend corn mixture into flour mixture, stirring just until moistened. Drop by tablespoonfuls into ¾ inch of hot oil (375°). Fry for 45 seconds on each side. Drain well on paper towels. Yield: about 2 dozen.

Mrs. Eugene H. Wayne,
Louisville, Kentucky.

DEVILED CORN

3 cups corn cut from cob
¼ cup plus 2 tablespoons water
3 tablespoons butter or margarine
1 teaspoon prepared mustard
¼ to ½ teaspoon salt
¼ teaspoon pepper
3 drops of hot sauce
¼ cup (1 ounce) shredded Cheddar cheese

Combine corn and water in a medium saucepan. Bring to a boil; cover, reduce heat, and simmer 7 to 8 minutes or just until corn is tender. Drain.

Add butter, mustard, salt, pepper, and hot sauce to corn; blend well. Cook over medium heat until thoroughly heated. Stir in cheese; serve immediately. Yield: 4 servings.

Virginia M. Griffin,
Princeton, Kentucky.

SKILLET CORN MEDLEY

6 ears corn cut from cob
1 large onion, chopped
1 (15-ounce) can whole tomatoes, undrained
1 (0.7-ounce) package Italian salad dressing mix
2 tablespoons bacon drippings
1 teaspoon dried whole basil

Combine all ingredients in a large skillet. Cook, uncovered, over medium heat 30 minutes, stirring frequently. Yield: 8 servings.

Gwyn Prows Groseclose,
Altamonte Springs, Florida.

CURRIED CORN AND CELERY

3 tablespoons butter or margarine, melted
2 cups corn cut from cob
¼ cup diced green pepper
2 tablespoons diced onion
¾ teaspoon curry powder
½ teaspoon salt
¼ teaspoon pepper
1 cup thinly sliced celery
¼ cup commercial sour cream

Combine first 7 ingredients in a skillet over medium heat; stir well. Cover and cook 5 minutes. Stir in celery; cover, and cook an additional 5 minutes or until vegetables are tender. Add sour cream, stirring constantly, just until thoroughly heated. (Do not boil.) Yield: 4 servings.
Dorothy Grant,
Pensacola, Florida.

He Entertains By Cooking

Who makes the best béarnaise sauce in Pine Bluff? Ray Colclasure, of course. Otherwise known as Dr. Béarnaise, this Arkansas dentist can whip out a sauce that's definitely worth talking about.

But this sauce is just one of many culinary delights created in Colclasure's kitchen. Now you too can try some of his special recipes.

BÉARNAISE SAUCE

½ cup white wine
¼ cup tarragon vinegar
1 tablespoon minced shallots
1 tablespoon dried whole tarragon
1 tablespoon dried whole chervil
3 egg yolks
1 tablespoon water
1 cup butter or margarine, softened and divided
Dash of ground red pepper

Combine wine, vinegar, shallots, tarragon, and chervil; cook over medium heat until mixture is reduced to 2 tablespoons. Strain, reserving liquid.

Beat egg yolks and water in top of a double boiler with a wire whisk; gradually add vinegar mixture. Bring water to a boil. Reduce heat to low; add one-third of butter, stirring constantly, until butter melts. Add another one-third butter, stirring until butter melts. Add remaining butter; cook, stirring vigorously, until butter melts and sauce thickens. Remove from heat. Stir in red pepper. Serve over beef, lamb, eggs, or vegetables. Yield: 1 cup.

HERBED VEAL WITH WINE

2 pounds veal cutlets
¼ cup all-purpose flour
¼ cup butter or margarine, melted
2 tablespoons olive oil
¼ teaspoon salt
⅛ teaspoon pepper
2 bunches green onions, chopped
1½ cups chicken broth
1 cup dry white wine
3 cloves garlic, minced
2 tablespoons chopped fresh parsley
1 teaspoon Italian herbs
¼ teaspoon ground cinnamon
Hot cooked rice or noodles

Trim excess fat from veal; cut veal into 1-inch strips, and dredge in flour. Sauté veal in butter and olive oil in a large skillet until lightly browned. Remove veal to a 13- x 9- x 2-inch baking dish; sprinkle with salt and pepper.

Sauté green onions in pan drippings until tender; stir in chicken broth, wine, minced garlic, chopped parsley, Italian herbs, and ground cinnamon. Mix well; pour onion mixture over veal. Bake, uncovered, at 350° for 1 hour.

Serve veal over hot cooked rice or noodles. Yield: 6 to 8 servings.

QUAIL WITH ORANGE SAUCE IN POTATO BASKETS

6 whole quail, dressed
1 teaspoon salt
½ teaspoon pepper
½ cup all-purpose flour
¼ cup vegetable oil
2 tablespoons butter or margarine, melted
1½ cups white wine
2 oranges
1 cup water
Potato Baskets
2 teaspoons cornstarch
½ cup Grand Marnier or other orange-flavored liqueur
½ cup coarsely chopped walnuts

Sprinkle quail with salt and pepper; dredge in flour. Brown in oil and butter in skillet. Remove quail, and set aside.

Add wine to pan drippings; bring to a boil, stirring well. Return quail to skillet; cover, reduce heat to low, and cook 30 minutes, basting occasionally.

Remove rind from oranges. Cut rind into 1½- x ¼-inch strips; place in a small saucepan with 1 cup water. Bring water to a boil; let cook 1 to 2 minutes. Remove rind from water, draining well; set aside. Remove white membrane from oranges; cut each orange into sections. Drain well.

Place each quail in a Potato Basket on serving platter; keep warm. Combine cornstarch and liqueur, stirring well; add to pan drippings in skillet. Bring mixture to a boil; cook 1 minute, stirring constantly. Stir in orange rind, orange sections, and walnuts; heat thoroughly. Spoon sauce over quail to serve. Yield: 6 servings.

Potato Baskets:

5 large baking potatoes, scrubbed and peeled
Vegetable cooking spray
Vegetable oil

Coarsely shred potatoes, dropping pieces into a large bowl of cold water as they are cut; let stand at least 15 minutes. Drain and dry thoroughly on paper towels.

Spray both layers of a "bird's nest" frying basket with vegetable cooking spray. Dip both layers of basket in oil to coat. (This will help prevent potatoes from sticking to basket.) Evenly arrange about ¾ cup of shredded potatoes in the bottom basket, covering completely. Place the smaller basket on top, and secure with clip.

Completely immerse the basket nest in deep hot oil (350°), and fry until golden brown (about 1 to 2 minutes). Remove basket from oil, and unclip; let stand 2 minutes on paper towel. Gently lift out smaller basket; tip larger basket to turn out potato basket. Drain on paper towels.

If potatoes stick to wire basket, tap basket lightly on countertop, and gently pry out with a knife. Repeat procedure with remaining potatoes. Yield: 6 potato baskets.

BACON-STUFFED POTATOES

4 large baking potatoes
Vegetable oil
½ cup chopped shallots
2 tablespoons butter or margarine, melted
1 cup commercial sour cream
¼ cup freshly grated Parmesan cheese
1 teaspoon salt
½ teaspoon pepper
8 slices bacon, cooked and crumbled
Paprika

Wash potatoes, and rub with oil. Bake at 400° for 1 hour or until soft when pierced with a fork. Allow potatoes to cool to touch. Slice away skin from top of each potato; carefully scoop out pulp, leaving shells intact. Mash pulp; set aside.

Sauté shallots in butter until tender. Add shallots and remaining ingredients, except paprika, to potato pulp; stir well. Stuff potato shells with pulp mixture; sprinkle with paprika. Place potatoes in a 9-inch square baking pan; bake at 350° for 15 minutes or until thoroughly heated. Yield: 4 servings.

Tip: Dieters can trim extra calories by substituting yogurt for sour cream in most recipes.

WHITE BEAN POT

2 cups dried Great Northern beans
7 cups water
¾ pound smoked ham, cubed
4 carrots, scraped and diced
1 large tomato, peeled and coarsely
    chopped
1 large onion, chopped
¾ cup chopped fresh parsley
¼ cup chopped celery
1 clove garlic, minced
1 small bay leaf
¾ teaspoon salt
¼ teaspoon pepper
¼ teaspoon paprika
⅛ teaspoon dried whole thyme
⅛ teaspoon dried whole marjoram
Pinch of ground cloves
1 pound knockwurst, cut into ¼-inch
    slices
1 tablespoon butter or margarine, melted

Sort and wash beans; place in a large Dutch oven. Add water, and bring to a boil; cook 2 minutes. Remove beans from heat; cover and let soak 1 hour. Return to heat; bring to a boil, reduce heat, and simmer 1 hour. Add ham, carrots, tomato, onion, parsley, celery, garlic, bay leaf, salt, pepper, paprika, thyme, marjoram, and cloves; stir well. Bring mixture to a boil; cover, reduce heat, and simmer 25 minutes or until vegetables are tender, stirring occasionally. Remove bay leaf.

Brown knockwurst in 1 tablespoon butter in a skillet; stir knockwurst into bean mixture. Yield: about 3½ quarts.

LEMON CHEESECAKE

2 cups graham cracker crumbs
2 tablespoons sugar
¼ cup plus 2 tablespoons butter or
    margarine, melted
3 (8-ounce) packages cream cheese,
    softened
¾ cup sugar
3 eggs
1 tablespoon grated lemon rind
¼ cup lemon juice
2 teaspoons vanilla extract
2 cups commercial sour cream
3 tablespoons sugar
1 teaspoon vanilla extract
Lemon Glaze
Lemon leaves (optional)
Lemon rind twist (optional)

Combine graham cracker crumbs, 2 tablespoons sugar, and butter, mixing well. Press into bottom and up sides of a 9-inch springform pan. Bake at 350° for 5 minutes; let cool.

Beat cream cheese with electric mixer until light and fluffy. Gradually add ¾ cup sugar, mixing well. Add eggs, one at a time, beating well after each addition. Stir in lemon rind, lemon juice, and 2 teaspoons vanilla. Pour into prepared pan. Bake at 350° for 35 minutes.

Combine sour cream, 3 tablespoons sugar, and 1 teaspoon vanilla, mixing well. Spread over cheesecake. Bake at 350° for 10 minutes. Cool cheesecake 30 minutes on a wire rack. Spread Lemon Glaze over cheesecake; cover and refrigerate 8 hours.

Remove sides of springform pan, and garnish cheesecake with lemon leaves and a lemon rind twist, if desired. Yield: 10 to 12 servings.

Lemon Glaze:

½ cup sugar
1½ tablespoons cornstarch
¼ teaspoon salt
¾ cup water
⅓ cup lemon juice
1 egg yolk
1 tablespoon butter or margarine
1½ teaspoons grated lemon rind
2 to 3 drops yellow food coloring
    (optional)

Combine sugar, cornstarch, and salt in a small saucepan. Combine water, lemon juice, and egg yolk, stirring well; add to sugar mixture. Cook over low heat, stirring constantly, until mixture comes to a boil and thickens. Stir in butter, lemon rind, and food coloring, if desired; let cool slightly. Spread over cheesecake. Yield: 1 cup.

MICROWAVE COOKERY

Keep Lunch Simple

If you would like to fix lunch for a few friends, but find you're just too busy, turn to this microwave menu for help. A little time invested now can help you put a complete meal together later in less than 20 minutes.

The key to making this or any other microwave menu quick and fuss-free lies in the order the dishes are assembled and microwaved. It pays to include foods that can be microwaved ahead and then refrigerated and reheated later. Also, try to include foods that have built-in standing times.

With this menu, prepare the Summertime Potatoes several hours before serving time. Cook the apple mixture for

Spicy Apple Ice Cream Sundaes in advance; then refrigerate, and reheat just before serving. About 15 or 20 minutes before mealtime, stir the soup mixture together and make the sandwiches.

Broccoli Soup
Hot Tuna Sandwiches
Summertime Potatoes
Spicy Apple Ice Cream Sundaes

BROCCOLI SOUP

1 cup (½-inch) broccoli flowerets (about ⅓
    pound)
2 tablespoons butter or margarine
1 cup milk
½ cup half-and-half
6 ounces process cheese, cut into ½-inch
    cubes
1 tablespoon cornstarch
1 teaspoon chicken-flavored bouillon
    granules
Dash of ground nutmeg
Dash of ground allspice
2 tablespoons dry white wine

Place broccoli and butter in a 2-quart casserole. Cover with heavy-duty plastic wrap, and microwave at HIGH for 2 minutes or until broccoli is crisp-tender. Stir in milk, half-and-half, cheese, cornstarch, bouillon granules, nutmeg, and allspice. Cover tightly, and microwave at MEDIUM HIGH (70% power) for 3½ minutes, stirring after 2 minutes. Stir in wine. Cover tightly, and microwave on MEDIUM HIGH for 5 to 6 minutes or until thickened, stirring every 2 minutes. Yield: 2½ cups.

HOT TUNA SANDWICHES

2 English muffins, split
1 egg, beaten
1 (6½-ounce) can white tuna, drained and
    flaked
½ cup mayonnaise
¼ cup (1 ounce) shredded Cheddar cheese
2 teaspoons minced green onions
1 teaspoon prepared mustard
Paprika
Cherry tomato halves (optional)
Parsley sprigs (optional)

Toast muffins, and set aside.

Pour beaten egg in a 6-ounce custard cup. Cover with heavy-duty plastic wrap, and microwave at MEDIUM (50% power) for 1 to 1½ minutes or until egg is set. Let stand 3 minutes. Mash egg with a fork until crumbly.

Combine egg, tuna, mayonnaise, cheese, green onions, and mustard, stirring well. Spread over toasted muffins; microwave at HIGH for 1½ to 2 minutes or until heated. Sprinkle with paprika, and garnish with cherry tomato halves and parsley sprigs, if desired. Yield: 4 servings.

SUMMERTIME POTATOES

10 small new potatoes
2 tablespoons water
¼ cup olive oil
3 tablespoons vinegar
2 tablespoons chopped fresh parsley
½ teaspoon garlic salt
½ teaspoon pepper
¼ teaspoon dried whole oregano
Lettuce leaves

Wash potatoes. Prick each potato twice with a fork; place in a 2-quart casserole, and add water. Cover with heavy-duty plastic wrap, and microwave at HIGH for 9 minutes or until tender, stirring after 4 minutes. Let stand 2 minutes. Drain and cool. Cut potatoes into thin slices.

Combine olive oil, vinegar, parsley, garlic salt, pepper, and oregano in a jar. Cover tightly, and shake vigorously; pour over potatoes, and toss gently. Chill thoroughly. Serve over lettuce leaves on individual salad plates. Yield: 4 to 6 servings.

SPICY APPLE
ICE CREAM SUNDAES

2 large cooking apples, peeled and thinly sliced
⅓ cup firmly packed brown sugar
¼ teaspoon ground cinnamon
2 tablespoons water
2 tablespoons butter or margarine
Vanilla ice cream

Combine apples, brown sugar, and cinnamon in a 10- x 6- x 2-inch baking dish. Add water; dot with butter. Cover with heavy-duty plastic wrap, and microwave at HIGH for 6 to 8 minutes or

until apples are tender, stirring every 3 minutes. Let stand, covered, 5 minutes. Serve over ice cream. Yield: 4 servings.

Note: Apples may be cooked ahead, refrigerated, and reheated at HIGH for 1 to 2 minutes, if desired.

Ice Cream Beverages

When the weather gets too hot to bear, cool things down with a refreshing ice cream beverage. Creamy Strawberry Punch contains strawberries, ginger ale, and pineapple sherbet. And for coffee lovers, there's Maple Coffee Floats, with the brew chilled. Nutritious Amazin' Raisin Shake is spicy and different.

CREAMY STRAWBERRY PUNCH

1 (10-ounce) package frozen strawberries, thawed
1 (28-ounce) bottle ginger ale
½ gallon pineapple sherbet, softened
Fresh strawberries (optional)

Place strawberries in container of an electric blender; process until pureed. Pour into punch bowl; add ginger ale and sherbet. Stir until creamy. Serve immediately. Garnish with fresh strawberries, if desired. Yield: about 1 gallon.
Dorothy Burgess,
Huntsville, Texas.

SPARKLING CRANBERRY FLOAT

1 quart cranberry juice cocktail, chilled
1 quart apple juice, chilled
2 (28-ounce) bottles ginger ale, chilled
1 quart pineapple sherbet

Combine cranberry juice, apple juice, and ginger ale in a large bowl. Pour mixture into glasses, and top each serving with a scoop of pineapple sherbet. Yield: 15 cups.
Barbara Hill,
Miami, Florida.

MAPLE-COFFEE FLOATS

4 cups hot, strong coffee
1 teaspoon ground cinnamon
¾ cup maple-flavored syrup
3 cups vanilla ice cream
Ground nutmeg or cinnamon (optional)

Combine coffee and 1 teaspoon cinnamon; add syrup, and chill.

Place ½ cup ice cream in a glass; pour about ¾ cup coffee mixture over ice cream. Repeat procedure for remaining servings. Sprinkle with nutmeg or cinnamon, if desired. Yield: 6 servings.
W. N. Cottrell II,
New Orleans, Louisiana.

AMAZIN' RAISIN SHAKE

1 pint vanilla ice cream
1 cup milk
¼ cup golden raisins
1 teaspoon ground cinnamon
1 teaspoon vanilla extract

Combine ingredients in container of electric blender; process until smooth. Serve immediately. Yield: 3½ cups.
Dan Folta,
Blacksburg, Virginia.

Easy Bar Cookies

It takes only six handy ingredients to mix up a batch of Ranelle Simon's cinnamon-spiced *Janhagel* Cookies. This German cookie recipe depicts Ranelle's German-Polish heritage and came about when hard times pressed cooks to be creative with simple ingredients.

The crispy treats are a tradition of the Simon family of Lafayette, Louisiana. Ranelle's daughter Andrea Ducharme shares the recipe.

JANHAGEL COOKIES

1 cup butter or margarine, melted
1 cup sugar
1 egg, separated
2 cups all-purpose flour
1 teaspoon ground cinnamon
1 cup chopped pecans

Combine butter and sugar; blend well. Add egg yolk; blend well. Stir in flour and cinnamon. Press mixture into a greased waxed paper-lined 15- x 10- x 1-inch jellyroll pan.

Beat egg white until frothy; spread over cookie mixture; sprinkle with pecans. Bake at 350° for 20 minutes or until lightly browned. Let cool 5 minutes before cutting into 3- x 2-inch rectangles. Cool completely in pan; remove waxed paper. Yield: about 2 dozen.

Desserts Easy On The Waistline

Don't deny yourself dessert just because you're concerned about calories. These low-calorie treats start with fruit and only a small amount of added sugar or honey, relying on the natural sugar in fruit or fruit juice for sweetness.

The calories and nutritional value of honey and sugar are similar. When selecting honey for fruit-based desserts, choose one with a mild flavor, such as clover or orange-blossom honey. Buckwheat and tulip poplar honey are stronger and can mask the true flavor of the fruit.

The sweetness of our frozen desserts may surprise you. But that's because desserts taste sweeter when frozen.

BLACKBERRIES AND DUMPLINGS

½ cup all-purpose flour
¼ cup sugar, divided
1 teaspoon baking powder
¼ teaspoon salt
¼ cup skim milk
2 cups fresh blackberries
⅔ cup water
⅛ teaspoon ground nutmeg

Combine flour, 2 tablespoons sugar, baking powder, and salt; stir well. Stir in milk; set aside.

Combine blackberries, remaining 2 tablespoons sugar, and water in a saucepan; stir well. Bring to a boil. Drop about one-fourth of batter at a time into boiling mixture; sprinkle with nutmeg.

Cover and cook over medium heat 10 to 12 minutes or until dumplings are done. Yield: 4 servings (about 144 calories per dumpling and ½ cup blackberry mixture). *Mrs. Quentin Sams, Chuckey, Tennessee.*

MANGO SORBET

2¼ cups chopped ripe mango
½ cup unsweetened orange juice
¼ cup honey
Lime rind curls (optional)
Grated lime rind (optional)

Combine mango, orange juice, and honey in container of an electric blender; process until smooth. Pour mixture into an 8-inch square pan; cover and freeze until firm.

To serve, spoon into individual dessert dishes; garnish with lime curls and lime rind, if desired. Yield: 5 servings (about 111 calories per ½-cup serving). *Cynda A. Spoon, Broken Arrow, Oklahoma.*

MELON-MINT JULEP

1 (20-ounce) can unsweetened pineapple chunks, undrained
½ cup unsweetened orange juice
¼ cup lime juice
2 tablespoons honey
2 tablespoons chopped fresh mint
2 teaspoons grated orange rind
2 teaspoons grated lime rind
3 cups watermelon balls
2 cups honeydew balls
2 cups cantaloupe balls
Mint sprigs (optional)

Drain pineapple, reserving juice; set pineapple aside. Combine pineapple juice, orange juice, lime juice, honey, mint, orange rind, and lime rind in a small bowl; stir well.

Combine reserved pineapple chunks and melon balls in a large bowl. Pour fruit juice mixture over fruit. Cover and chill 2 hours.

To serve, spoon into individual dessert dishes; garnish each with mint sprig, if desired. Yield: 8 servings (about 116 calories per 1-cup serving).

STRAWBERRY-ORANGE ICE

2 cups fresh strawberries
½ cup unsweetened orange juice
¼ cup sugar
2 tablespoons lemon juice
1 tablespoon Grand Marnier or other orange-flavored liqueur
Orange rind curls (optional)
5 small strawberries (optional)

Combine first 5 ingredients in container of an electric blender; process until smooth. Pour mixture into an 8-inch square pan; cover and freeze until slushy. Spoon mixture into container of an electric blender; process until smooth. Pour back into pan; freeze until firm.

To serve, spoon into individual dessert dishes; garnish with orange rind curls and strawberries, if desired. Yield: 5 servings (about 83 calories per ½-cup serving). *Pati Wilson, Tulsa, Oklahoma.*

WATERMELON FROST

3 cups cubed watermelon
¼ cup Triple Sec or other orange-flavored liqueur
3 tablespoons lemon juice
2½ tablespoons sugar
6 watermelon cubes (optional)

Combine watermelon, liqueur, lemon juice, and sugar in container of an electric blender; process until smooth. Pour mixture into an 8-inch square pan; cover and freeze until firm.

To serve, spoon frozen mixture into individual dessert dishes; garnish with watermelon cubes, if desired. Yield: 6 servings (about 80 calories per ½-cup serving). *Christine McQueen, Annville, Kentucky.*

STUFFED PEACH HALVES

4 medium peaches, peeled, halved, and seeded
1 tablespoon lemon juice
2 tablespoons unsweetened flaked coconut, toasted
2 tablespoons raisins
2 tablespoons chopped almonds, toasted
½ teaspoon grated lemon rind
½ teaspoon ground cinnamon
2 tablespoons vanilla low-fat yogurt
2 teaspoons honey
1 teaspoon vanilla extract

Coat peach halves with lemon juice, and set aside.

Combine remaining ingredients; stir well. Spoon about 1 tablespoon mixture into cavity of each peach half; chill. Yield: 8 servings (about 62 calories per filled peach half). *Sheree McIntosh, Flag Pond, Tennessee.*

Stuff Entrées With Flavor

Cornish hens, pork chops, boneless chicken breast halves—and some vegetables—will taste even better when filled with a stuffing. You'll find rice, breadcrumbs, and fruit are just a few of the interesting ingredients that fill the entrées offered here.

To prepare Fruited Stuffed Pork Chops, follow the directions for making pockets in the chops, or have the butcher cut the pockets for you.

One of the best ways to enjoy green peppers is to stuff them with rice, shrimp, and vegetables, as in our Shrimp-Stuffed Peppers. For an attractive and colorful garnish, each serving can be topped with a lemon wedge and additional shrimp.

Sauté onion and celery in ¼ cup butter until tender; remove from heat. Add stuffing mix, mixed dried fruit, and raisins; stir well, and set aside.

Make pockets in pork chops, cutting from rib side just to beginning of fat edge of each chop. Stuff pockets of pork chops with stuffing mixture. Dredge pork chops in flour, and brown in 2 tablespoons butter, turning once. Transfer pork chops to a lightly greased 13- x 9- x 2-inch baking dish; add wine. Cover and bake at 350° for 40 to 45 minutes or until done. Yield: 6 servings.
*Jeannette Safford,
Mobile, Alabama.*

POULET LUZIANNE

10 boneless chicken breast halves, skinned
½ cup chopped pecans
¼ cup chopped onion
1½ tablespoons chopped green onions
¼ cup chopped celery
¼ cup butter or margarine, melted
3 cups French or day-old bread cubes
¾ teaspoon salt
¼ teaspoon dried whole thyme
½ teaspoon pepper
⅛ teaspoon red pepper
1 baking apple, peeled and diced
½ cup finely chopped dried apricots
Apricot glaze (recipe follows)

Place chicken breast halves between two sheets of waxed paper. Flatten to ¼-inch thickness, using a meat mallet or rolling pin; set aside.

Sauté pecans, onion, green onions, and celery in butter until vegetables are tender. Remove from heat; add bread cubes, seasonings, apple, and apricots, stirring well. Spoon about ⅓ cup filling onto each chicken breast; fold sides over, and secure with wooden picks. Place in a lightly greased 13- x 9- x 2-inch baking dish. Cover and bake at 350° for 30 minutes. Baste with apricot glaze; bake, uncovered, an additional 15 minutes, basting every 5 minutes. Broil 6 inches from heat 3 to 5 minutes or until golden. Serve with remaining glaze. Yield: 8 to 10 servings.

Apricot Glaze:

1 cup apricot preserves
¼ cup Triple Sec or other orange-flavored liqueur
2 tablespoons vinegar

Combine all ingredients; stir well. Yield: about 1⅓ cups.
*Joanne C. Champagne,
Covington, Louisiana.*

SHRIMP-STUFFED PEPPERS

4 large or 6 small green peppers
½ cup finely chopped onion
¼ cup chopped celery
2 cloves garlic, minced
¼ cup butter or margarine, melted
1 cup chopped fresh mushrooms
1 pound shrimp, peeled, deveined, and chopped
1½ cups cooked rice
Salt and pepper to taste
4 to 6 cooked whole shrimp (optional)
Lemon wedges (optional)

Cut off tops of green peppers; remove seeds. Cook peppers in boiling water 5 minutes; drain and set aside.

Sauté onion, celery, and garlic in butter in a heavy saucepan until crisp-tender. Add mushrooms, and continue cooking until all vegetables are tender. Stir in chopped shrimp; cook 5 minutes or until done. Add rice, salt, and pepper to shrimp mixture, mixing well.

Stuff peppers with rice mixture. Place peppers in an 8-inch square baking dish; pour ½ cup water into dish. Bake, uncovered, at 350° for 15 minutes. Garnish with cooked shrimp and lemon wedges, if desired. Yield: 4 to 6 servings.
*Sue Helderbrand,
Lafayette, Louisiana.*

FRUITED STUFFED PORK CHOPS

2 tablespoons chopped onion
¼ cup chopped celery
¼ cup butter or margarine, melted
1 cup herb-seasoned stuffing mix
3 (0.9-ounce) packages mixed dried fruit
2 tablespoons raisins
6 (1-inch-thick) center cut pork chops
¼ cup all-purpose flour
2 tablespoons butter or margarine, melted
½ cup dry white wine

CHICKEN CORDON BLEU
IN MUSHROOM SAUCE

4 boneless chicken breast halves, skinned
2 (1-ounce) slices Swiss cheese, halved
2 (1-ounce) slices cooked ham, halved
1 (2¾-ounce) envelope seasoned coating mix for chicken
¼ cup grated Parmesan cheese
1 tablespoon parsley flakes
½ cup all-purpose flour
1 egg, beaten
2 tablespoons milk
2 tablespoons butter or margarine, melted
1 (2½-ounce) jar sliced mushrooms, drained
3 tablespoons Chablis or other dry white wine
Mushroom sauce (recipe follows)

Place chicken breast halves between 2 sheets of waxed paper. Flatten to ¼-inch thickness, using a meat mallet.

Place a piece of Swiss cheese and ham in center of each piece of chicken; roll up lengthwise, tucking edges inside. Secure each roll with a wooden pick.

Combine seasoned coating mix, Parmesan cheese, and parsley flakes; set mixture aside.

Dredge chicken in flour. Combine egg and milk; dip chicken in egg mixture, and roll in coating mixture.

Combine butter and mushrooms in a lightly greased 9-inch baking dish, stirring well. Arrange chicken over mushrooms, and top with mushroom sauce. Bake at 350° for 45 minutes. Remove chicken to serving platter; add wine to mushroom sauce, mixing well. Spoon sauce over chicken. Yield: 4 servings.

Note: Chicken can be frozen after rolling in coating mixture. Remove from freezer; arrange over mushrooms, and add sauce. Bake, unthawed, at 400° for 30 minutes; reduce to 350°, and bake an additional 15 to 30 minutes.

Mushroom Sauce:

1 (10¾-ounce) can cream of mushroom soup, undiluted
⅔ cup milk
¼ teaspoon garlic powder
¼ teaspoon curry powder

Combine all ingredients; mix well. Yield: about 2 cups. *Nelda G. Sawyer, Chouteau, Oklahoma.*

Tip: When a sauce curdles, remove pan from heat and plunge into a pan of cold water to stop cooking process. Beat sauce vigorously or pour into a blender and beat.

TURKEY ROLLUPS

½ cup chopped onion
½ cup sliced celery
⅓ cup butter or margarine, melted
3 cups soft bread cubes
¼ cup chicken bouillon
2 tablespoons chopped fresh parsley
½ teaspoon salt
½ teaspoon rubbed sage
½ teaspoon poultry seasoning
8 (¼-inch-thick) turkey breast slices
⅓ cup all-purpose flour
¼ cup butter or margarine, melted
Paprika
Lemon and lime slices

Sauté onion and celery in ⅓ cup butter until tender; add bread cubes, bouillon, parsley, and seasonings; stirring well. Spoon about ⅓ cup stuffing in center of each piece of turkey; roll up lengthwise, tucking edges inside. Secure each roll with a wooden pick.

Dredge turkey in flour; dip in ¼ cup butter. Place in a lightly greased 9-inch square baking dish; sprinkle with paprika. Cover and bake at 325° for 15 minutes. Uncover and bake an additional 20 minutes or until done. Garnish with lemon and lime slices. Yield: 6 to 8 servings.
Tammy Smith,
Talbott, Tennessee.

TERIYAKI CORNISH HENS

1 (6-ounce) package long grain and wild rice mix
1½ tablespoons cornstarch
¼ cup plus 2 tablespoons water
2 tablespoons butter or margarine
¾ cup teriyaki sauce
Juice of 1 lemon
3 tablespoons sugar
⅛ teaspoon pepper
Pinch of ground ginger
4 (1- to 1½-pound) Cornish hens
½ teaspoon pepper

Prepare rice according to package directions; set aside.

Combine cornstarch and water, stirring well; set aside. Melt butter over medium heat in a heavy saucepan; stir in teriyaki sauce, lemon juice, sugar, ⅛ teaspoon pepper, and ginger. Gradually stir in cornstarch mixture. Cook, stirring constantly, 1 minute or until smooth and bubbly; set aside.

Remove giblets from hens; reserve for another use. Rinse hens with cold water, and pat dry; sprinkle with ½ teaspoon pepper.

Stuff hens with rice, and close cavities. Secure with wooden picks; truss. Place hens, breast side up, in a shallow baking pan.

Bake at 375° for 30 minutes. Baste with teriyaki sauce mixture, and bake an additional 40 minutes, basting every 15 minutes. Yield: 4 servings.
Susan W. Pajcic,
Jacksonville, Florida.

Accent Meals With Kiwifruit

Next time you're shopping the produce section of the grocery store, think twice before you pass up the funny-looking egg-shaped fruit with the fuzzy brown skin. The outside of a kiwifruit may not be very appealing, but inside there's a stunning emerald-green flesh surrounding tiny black edible seeds.

Juicy and tangy-sweet, the flavor of kiwifruit has been compared to a blend of strawberry, pineapple, and lime. The texture is similar to a strawberry or a fresh fig. Besides being delicious, one medium-size kiwifruit contains only about 36 calories, and it is an excellent source of vitamin C (ascorbic acid) and potassium, as well.

The enchanting, nutritious kiwifruit is practically a year-round item. Although harvested when fully mature, the fruit may still need to ripen further once purchased. Choose kiwifruit that is plump and not shriveled. If fruit is hard, let it ripen at room temperature. Once it has ripened, store in the refrigerator up to two weeks.

KIWI-BERRY PIZZA

1 (9-ounce) package golden yellow cake mix
⅔ cup strawberry preserves
1 tablespoon water
1 (1.4-ounce) envelope whipped topping mix
3 to 4 kiwifruit, peeled and thinly sliced
1 pint small strawberries, sliced

Prepare cake mix according to package directions. Pour into a greased and floured 12-inch pizza pan. Bake at 350° for 20 minutes. Let cool in pan 10 minutes; remove to wire rack, and cool completely.

Combine preserves and water in a small saucepan; heat until preserves melt; cool. Set aside.

Prepare whipped topping mix according to package directions. Spread over cake. Top with preserves. Arrange fruit over preserves. Yield: one 12-inch pie.

Kaye Rousseau,
Taylor, Louisiana.

KIWI PARFAIT

1 (3-ounce) package lemon-flavored gelatin
1½ cups boiling water
1 tablespoon grated lemon rind
1 (8-ounce) carton frozen whipped
    topping, thawed
3 kiwifruit, peeled

Dissolve gelatin in boiling water. Stir in lemon rind; chill until consistency of unbeaten egg white. Fold in whipped topping; set aside. Cut 1 kiwifruit into 8 slices; chop remaining 2.

Alternate layers of gelatin mixture and chopped kiwifruit into 8 parfait glasses; chill 1 hour. Garnish with sliced kiwifruit. Yield: 8 servings.

Louise Denmon,
Silsbee, Texas.

Add Shape To Vegetable Salads

Give salads a new look by combining crunchy, colorful vegetables with gelatin. Cheesy-Vegetable Congealed Salad, for example, combines celery and green pepper with tomato soup, cream cheese, and lemon-flavored gelatin. The end result is a firm but creamy salad that can be sliced.

TANGY BEET SALAD

1 (16-ounce) can sliced beets
2 (3-ounce) packages lemon-flavored
    gelatin
½ teaspoon salt
1½ cups chopped celery
1½ tablespoons grated onion
1 tablespoon prepared horseradish

Drain beets, reserving juice; chop beets, and set aside. Add enough water to juice to make 1½ cups; bring beet liquid to a boil. Add gelatin; cook over low heat, stirring until gelatin dissolves. Stir in salt. Chill until the consistency of unbeaten egg white. Fold in chopped beets, celery, onion, and horseradish. Pour into a lightly oiled 4-cup mold; chill until firm. Yield: 8 servings.

Mrs. Loy Cromer,
Anderson, South Carolina.

CHEESY-VEGETABLE CONGEALED SALAD

⅓ cup canned tomato soup, undiluted
1 (8-ounce) package cream cheese, cubed
    and softened
1 cup mayonnaise
1 (6-ounce) package lemon-flavored gelatin
2 cups boiling water
1½ cups finely chopped celery
1 cup chopped pecans
1 green pepper, finely chopped
½ cup finely chopped onion
¼ teaspoon garlic salt
Additional cream cheese (optional)
Cherry tomato wedges (optional)

Heat soup in a heavy saucepan. Add cream cheese; stir until melted. Stir in mayonnaise; cool.

Dissolve gelatin in boiling water; cool. Chill until the consistency of unbeaten egg white. Fold in cream cheese mixture, celery, pecans, green pepper, onion, and garlic salt; pour into a lightly oiled 8-cup mold. Chill until firm. Unmold and garnish with additional cream cheese and cherry tomatoes, if desired. Yield: 12 to 14 servings.

Note: To garnish with tomato flowers, shape cherry tomato wedges in pinwheels around small cream cheese centers.

Mrs. L. R. Givens,
Lubbock, Texas.

ASHEVILLE SALAD

2 envelopes unflavored gelatin
½ cup cold water
1 (10¾-ounce) can tomato soup, undiluted
3 (3-ounce) packages cream cheese,
    softened
1 cup mayonnaise
¾ cup chopped celery
¾ cup chopped green pepper
¼ cup slivered almonds, toasted
3 tablespoons sliced green onions
Lettuce leaves (optional)

Sprinkle unflavored gelatin over cold water; let stand 5 minutes.

Bring tomato soup to a boil. Add gelatin mixture; cook over medium heat until the gelatin dissolves, stirring constantly and scraping sides occasionally. Stir in cream cheese and mayonnaise. Chill until the consistency of unbeaten egg white.

Fold in celery, green pepper, almonds, and green onions; spoon into lightly oiled 4-cup mold. Cover and chill until firm. Unmold on lettuce, if desired. Yield: 6 to 8 servings.

Libby Etherton,
Sylva, North Carolina.

MOLDED GARDEN SALAD

1 (6-ounce) package lemon-flavored gelatin
2 tablespoons lemon juice
½ cup finely chopped cucumber
½ cup thinly sliced radishes
½ cup thinly sliced celery
½ cup thinly sliced cauliflower flowerets
¼ cup finely chopped green onions
Lettuce

Prepare gelatin according to package directions, omitting 1 cup cold water. Add lemon juice, stirring well; chill until the consistency of unbeaten egg white. Fold in cucumber, radishes, celery, cauliflower, and green onions; spoon into a lightly oiled 5-cup mold. Chill until firm. Unmold on lettuce leaves. Yield: 10 servings.

Mrs. James L. Twilley,
Macon, Georgia.

ORANGE-AND-CARROT ASPIC

1 (6-ounce) package orange-flavored
    gelatin
1½ cups boiling water
1 (12-ounce) can carrot juice
3 tablespoons cider vinegar
4 drops of hot sauce
1 (8-ounce) can crushed pineapple,
    drained
½ cup finely chopped celery
2 tablespoons minced onion

Dissolve gelatin in boiling water. Stir in carrot juice, vinegar, and hot sauce; chill until the consistency of unbeaten egg white.

Stir in remaining ingredients. Pour into a lightly oiled 8-inch square dish; chill until firm. Yield: 9 servings.

Mrs. Peter Rosato III,
Memphis, Tennessee.

Vegetables For Dessert? You Bet!

Up until now, you may have planned vegetables as a side dish, a salad ingredient, or perhaps as an appetizer served with a dip. But have you ever put vegetables in a dessert? Beyond the familiar pumpkin pie or sweet potato pie, a number of other vegetables can be made into delightful after-meal treats.

If you're a bit timid, start with Squash Cake. Yellow squash is the vegetable used, but pineapple, orange rind, and spices lend the flavor.

For a more adventurous dessert, try Carrot Ice Cream Pie. It's easy: Mix canned carrots, frozen lemonade concentrate, and sugar; fold into vanilla ice cream, and spread in a commercial graham cracker crust. It's quick to make, but you'll need to allow time for the ice cream to refreeze.

BEET CAKE WITH ALMOND TOPPING

1 cup vegetable oil
2 cups sugar
4 eggs
2 cups all-purpose flour
2 teaspoons baking powder
1½ teaspoons baking soda
1 teaspoon ground cinnamon
3 cups shredded uncooked fresh beets
1 cup chopped walnuts
1 teaspoon vanilla extract
Almond Topping

Combine oil and sugar in a mixing bowl; beat at medium speed of an electric mixer until well blended. Add eggs; beat until well blended.

Combine flour, baking powder, soda, and cinnamon; add to egg mixture, beating until blended. Add beets, walnuts, and vanilla; stir well. Pour into a greased and floured 13- x 9- x 2-inch baking pan; bake at 350° for 45 minutes. Cool completely in pan on a wire rack. Serve with Almond Topping. Yield: one 13- x 9- x 2-inch cake.

Almond Topping:

1 (8-ounce) package cream cheese, softened
½ cup whipping cream
1 teaspoon almond extract

Combine all ingredients; beat with an electric mixer until fluffy. Chill. Yield: 1½ cups. *W. N. Cottrell II, New Orleans, Louisiana.*

SQUASH CAKE

½ pound yellow squash, sliced (about 3 medium-size squash)
1¾ cups sugar
⅔ cup vegetable oil
3 eggs
2 cups all-purpose flour
1 teaspoon baking powder
¾ teaspoon baking soda
½ teaspoon salt
1 teaspoon ground cinnamon
½ teaspoon ground nutmeg
1 teaspoon grated orange rind
1 (8-ounce) can unsweetened crushed pineapple, drained
¾ cup chopped pecans
½ cup shredded coconut
1 teaspoon vanilla extract
Glaze (recipe follows)

Cook squash, covered, in a small amount of boiling water 15 minutes or until tender; drain. Mash and drain again. Set aside 1 cup squash.

Combine sugar and oil in a mixing bowl; beat at medium speed of an electric mixer until well blended. Add eggs; beat until well blended.

Combine flour, baking powder, soda, salt, cinnamon, and nutmeg; blend well. Add to egg mixture. Stir in squash, orange rind, pineapple, pecans, coconut, and vanilla; blend well.

Spoon into a greased and floured 10-inch Bundt pan. Bake at 350° for 55 minutes to 1 hour.

Let cake cool in pan 10 minutes; remove from pan, and let cool completely on a wire rack. Place on serving plate. Spoon glaze over top of cake. Yield: one 10-inch cake.

Glaze:

1 cup sifted powdered sugar
⅛ teaspoon ground cinnamon
1 to 2 tablespoons hot water

Combine powdered sugar and cinnamon. Stir in enough hot water to make mixture drizzling consistency. Yield: enough for one 10-inch cake.
Ruth Stafford, East Bank, West Virginia.

MOCK COCONUT PIE

1 small spaghetti squash
½ cup sugar
½ cup firmly packed brown sugar
2 tablespoons all-purpose flour
1 cup evaporated milk
½ cup water
3 eggs, beaten
3 tablespoons butter or margarine, melted
1 teaspoon coconut extract
1 unbaked (9-inch) pastry shell

Wash squash; cut in half lengthwise, and discard seeds. Place squash, cut side down, in a Dutch oven; add 2 inches water. Bring to a boil; cover, reduce heat, and simmer 20 to 25 minutes or until tender.

Drain squash, and let cool. Using a fork, remove spaghetti-like strands; measure 1½ cups of strands, and set aside. Reserve remainder of squash for other uses.

Combine sugar, flour, evaporated milk, water, eggs, butter, and coconut extract; stir well. Stir in 1½ cups squash strands; pour into pastry shell. Bake at 350° for 50 to 55 minutes or until center is set; cool. Yield: one 9-inch pie.
Betty R. Butts, Kensington, Maryland.

CARROT ICE CREAM PIE

1 (16-ounce) jar sliced carrots, drained
1 (6-ounce) can frozen lemonade concentrate, thawed and undiluted
¼ cup sugar
1 quart vanilla ice cream, softened
1 (9-inch) commercial graham cracker crust

Combine carrots, lemonade concentrate, and sugar in container of an electric blender; process until smooth.

Fold carrot mixture into ice cream. Spoon mixture into graham cracker crust; cover and freeze until pie is firm. Yield: one 9-inch pie. *Libby Winstead, Nashville, Tennessee.*

Right: *For a refreshing summer meal, try Seafood Delight (page 208), which features chilled linguini, shrimp, and vegetables.*

Page 204: *Savor the best of fresh sweet figs in Sliced Fig Snacks, Super Fig Cobbler, and Fig Muffins. (Recipes are on page 206.)*

Above: *Chocolate Malt and Strawberry Smoothie are creamy refreshers. (Recipes are on page 183.)*

Above left: *When there's an abundance of zucchini and tomatoes in your garden, try Stuffed Zucchini and Cheesy Puff-Top Tomatoes. (Recipes are on page 187.)*

Left: *Fresh mint leaves and chocolate shavings give a preview of the liqueurs that flavor Grasshopper Soufflé (page 188).*

Far left: *If salad has become old hat, make a sandwich by stuffing our Chef's Salad (page 186) into pita bread halves.*

August

Figs Are Always A Favorite

Purplish brown, greenish yellow, and deep burgundy. These are the colors that are so characteristic of fresh figs. Once you've tasted their sweet goodness, you will become a fan.

You'll usually find fresh figs available August through early fall. Look for fruit that is soft to the touch; check the aroma for any signs of sourness. Because figs spoil quickly, they should be stored in the refrigerator.

FIG MUFFINS
(pictured on page 204)

½ cup butter or margarine, softened
½ cup sugar
2 eggs
1½ cups all-purpose flour
2 teaspoons baking powder
½ teaspoon ground cinnamon
¼ teaspoon ground cloves
½ cup milk
½ cup fig preserves
½ cup chopped pecans

Cream butter and sugar until light and fluffy. Add eggs, one at a time, beating well after each addition.

Combine flour, baking powder, cinnamon, and cloves; add to creamed mixture alternately with milk, stirring just until moistened. Stir in fig preserves and pecans.

Spoon muffin batter into greased and floured muffin pans, filling three-fourths full. Bake mini-muffins at 350° for 18 minutes and regular muffins for 20 minutes. Serve muffins warm. Yield: 40 mini-muffins or 20 regular muffins.

FIG JAM

6 quarts boiling water
6 quarts fresh figs
Sugar
1 quart water
8 slices lemon

Pour 6 quarts boiling water over figs; let stand 15 minutes. Drain, and thoroughly rinse in cold water. Pat figs dry, and remove stems.

Crush and measure figs; place in a large Dutch oven. Add ½ cup sugar for each cup of crushed figs. Add 1 quart water. Bring to a rapid boil; reduce heat, and simmer, uncovered, 3 hours or until thickened, stirring occasionally.

Ladle jam into hot sterilized jars, leaving ¼-inch headspace; add a slice of lemon to each jar. Cover at once with metal lids, and screw on bands. Process in a boiling-water bath 10 minutes. Yield: 8½ pints.

SLICED FIG SNACKS
(pictured on page 204)

1½ cups dried figs, finely chopped
¾ cup water
½ cup orange juice
⅓ cup sugar
⅓ cup butter or margarine, softened
⅔ cup firmly packed brown sugar
2 eggs
1 teaspoon vanilla extract
2½ cups all-purpose flour
2 teaspoons baking powder
½ teaspoon baking soda

Combine figs, water, juice, and sugar in a medium saucepan. Bring to a boil; reduce heat, and simmer, uncovered, 15 minutes or until thick. Set aside.

Cream butter; add brown sugar, beating well at medium speed of an electric mixer. Add eggs, one at a time, beating well after each addition. Stir in vanilla.

Combine flour, baking powder, and soda. Add flour mixture to creamed mixture, mixing well. Divide dough into thirds. Wrap dough in plastic wrap, and refrigerate 2 to 3 hours.

Roll out one-third of dough on a lightly floured surface into a 16- x 4-inch rectangle. Place on a baking sheet. Spread ½ cup fig mixture, lengthwise, in a 1-inch-wide strip, about ½ inch from edge of dough. Brush water on edges of dough; fold dough over filling, and gently press edges and ends together to seal. Turn roll over so that sealed edge is on bottom. Repeat procedure with remaining dough and filling. Bake at 350° for 17 minutes or until rolls are lightly browned. Let cool. Slice rolls crosswise into ¾-inch slices. Yield: about 4½ dozen.

SUPER FIG COBBLER
(pictured on page 204)

5 cups peeled, halved fresh figs
  (about 2½ pounds)
2 teaspoons lemon juice
¾ cup sugar
3 tablespoons all-purpose flour
½ teaspoon ground cinnamon
½ teaspoon ground nutmeg
1 tablespoon butter or margarine
Cheddar Pastry

Arrange figs evenly in a lightly greased 10- x 6- x 2-inch baking dish; sprinkle with lemon juice. Combine sugar, flour, cinnamon, and nutmeg. Stir well, and sprinkle over figs. Dot with butter.

Roll Cheddar Pastry out to ⅛-inch thickness on a lightly floured surface; cut into 10- x ½-inch strips. Arrange in lattice fashion over figs. Trim edges. Bake at 350° for 40 to 45 minutes. Yield: 6 servings.

Cheddar Pastry:

1 cup all-purpose flour
¼ teaspoon salt
⅓ cup shortening
¼ cup (1 ounce) shredded Cheddar cheese
2 tablespoons cold water

Combine flour and salt; cut in shortening with pastry blender until mixture resembles coarse meal. Stir in cheese. Sprinkle cold water (1 tablespoon at a time) evenly over surface; stir with a fork until dry ingredients are moistened. Shape dough into a ball. Yield: pastry for 1 cobbler.

COOKING LIGHT®

Stay Trim With These Creative Salads

Few foods do as much to perk up languid summer appetites as cool, colorful salads. Our recipes are protein-rich treasures substantial enough for a main dish. Full of flavor and texture variety, their low-calorie components will delight the most weight-conscious gourmet. (Remember that main-dish salads will taste even fresher when served on chilled plates.)

PEPPER STEAK SALAD CUPS

¼ cup commercial reduced-calorie
  Russian salad dressing
1 teaspoon reduced-sodium soy sauce
⅛ teaspoon ground ginger
1 cup cooked roast beef strips
¾ cup sliced fresh mushrooms
½ cup bean sprouts
½ cup small broccoli flowerets
2 medium-size green peppers

Feature Crab-Wild Rice Salad as your dieting entrée. It's only 201 calories per serving.

CRUNCHY CHICKEN SALAD

2½ cups torn fresh spinach
2 cups small broccoli flowerets
1 (8-ounce) can sliced water chestnuts, drained
2 cups chopped cooked chicken breast
1 large tomato, peeled and cut into 12 wedges
1 tablespoon grated Parmesan cheese
2 tablespoons reduced-sodium soy sauce
2 tablespoons red wine vinegar
1 tablespoon vegetable oil
½ teaspoon instant minced onion
¼ teaspoon sugar
⅛ teaspoon pepper
1 teaspoon sesame seeds

Layer spinach, broccoli, water chestnuts, and chicken on a large serving platter; arrange tomato wedges around edge. Sprinkle with Parmesan cheese; cover and chill.

Combine remaining ingredients; stir well. Pour dressing over salad just before serving. Yield: 4 servings (about 262 calories per 2-cup serving).
Mrs. James A. Tuthill,
Virginia Beach, Virginia.

Combine Russian salad dressing, soy sauce, and ginger; stir well. Add beef, mushrooms, sprouts, and broccoli; toss gently. Cover salad, and chill, stirring occasionally.

Cut off tops of peppers; remove seeds. Spoon beef mixture into peppers. Yield: 2 servings (about 309 calories per serving).

Note: Peppers may be blanched, if desired.
Ruth A. Colosimo,
Copperas Cove, Texas.

CRAB-WILD RICE SALAD

½ cup uncooked wild rice
1½ cups water
12 ounces fresh crabmeat, drained and flaked
2 hard-cooked eggs, chopped
1 cup chopped celery
¼ cup plus 2 tablespoons chopped onion
¼ cup plus 2 tablespoons chopped red pepper
¼ cup sweet pickle relish
½ cup plain low-fat yogurt
¼ cup reduced-calorie mayonnaise
1 teaspoon lemon juice
½ pound fresh snow peas

Wash wild rice in 3 changes of hot water; drain. Combine rice with water in a medium saucepan; bring to a boil. Cover, reduce heat to low, and simmer 30 to 45 minutes or until rice is tender.

Combine rice, crabmeat, eggs, celery, onion, red pepper, and relish; stir well.

Combine yogurt, mayonnaise, and lemon juice in a small bowl; stir well. Pour over crab mixture; toss gently to coat. Cover and chill.

Trim ends from snow peas. Place peas in a small amount of boiling water; return to a boil. Cover, reduce heat, and simmer 2 to 3 minutes or until bright green; drain. Rinse with cold water; drain. Chill.

To serve, arrange snow peas on a platter; spoon crab mixture in center of peas. Yield: 6 servings (about 201 calories per 1-cup crab mixture plus 13 snow peas).
Ruth K. Stevens,
Sanford, North Carolina.

Tip: Be sure to save your celery leaves. The outer leaves can serve as seasonings in soups, stuffings, and other cooked dishes. The inner leaves add a nice flavor to tossed salads.

PAELLA SALAD

1½ cups water
½ pound unpeeled fresh medium shrimp
1 (5-ounce) package yellow rice mix
¼ cup tarragon vinegar
2 tablespoons vegetable oil
¼ to ½ teaspoon curry powder
⅛ teaspoon dry mustard
⅛ teaspoon white pepper
2 cups chopped cooked chicken breast
1 medium tomato, peeled and chopped
½ cup frozen English peas, thawed and drained
⅓ cup thinly sliced celery
¼ cup minced onion
1 (2-ounce) jar diced pimiento, drained
Lettuce leaves (optional)
Lemon slices (optional)

Bring water to a boil; add shrimp, and cook 3 to 5 minutes. Drain well; rinse with cold water. Chill. Peel and devein shrimp. Prepare rice according to package directions, omitting butter.

Combine vinegar, oil, curry powder, dry mustard, and pepper; add to rice, stirring well. Add shrimp, chicken, tomato, peas, celery, onion, and pimiento; toss gently. Cover and chill.

Serve on lettuce leaves, and garnish with lemon slices, if desired. Yield: 6 servings (about 230 calories per 1-cup serving).
Kathleen Schoenfelder,
Bradenton, Florida.

CURRIED TUNA SALAD

1 (6½-ounce) can white tuna in water, drained and flaked
½ cup thinly sliced celery
⅓ cup chopped pecans, toasted
1 (8-ounce) can unsweetened pineapple tidbits, drained
3 tablespoons reduced-calorie mayonnaise
¼ teaspoon curry powder
2 cups alfalfa sprouts

Combine tuna, celery, pecans, and pineapple; stir well. Combine mayonnaise and curry powder; stir into tuna mixture. Cover and chill mixture.

To serve, arrange alfalfa sprouts on a serving plate. Spoon tuna in center of sprouts. Yield: 3 servings (about 219 calories per ⅔-cup tuna salad and ⅔-cup sprouts).   *Ann L. Duncan,*
Charlotte, North Carolina.

DILLED MACARONI-CHEESE SALAD

¾ cup uncooked elbow macaroni
1 cup (4 ounces) cubed low-fat Cheddar cheese
⅓ cup thinly sliced celery
⅓ cup chopped green pepper
1 (2-ounce) jar diced pimiento, drained
⅓ cup reduced-calorie mayonnaise
2 teaspoons cider vinegar
¼ teaspoon dried whole dillweed

Cook macaroni according to package directions, omitting salt; drain. Rinse with cold water; drain again.

Combine macaroni, Cheddar cheese, celery, green pepper, and pimiento in a medium bowl. Combine mayonnaise, cider vinegar, and dillweed, and add to macaroni mixture.

Toss mixture lightly to coat. Cover and chill. Yield: 3 servings (about 285 calories per 1-cup serving).
Mrs. Ken Gaddis,
Houston, Texas.

COTTAGE CHEESE SALAD IN TOMATOES

4 medium tomatoes
2¼ cups 1% low-fat cottage cheese
¼ cup chopped green onions
¼ cup chopped green pepper
¼ cup chopped celery
2 tablespoons grated Parmesan cheese
⅛ teaspoon garlic powder

Wash tomatoes. Cut tops from tomatoes; scoop out pulp, leaving shells intact. Chill shells; reserve the pulp for

other uses. Combine remaining ingredients; stir well. Chill.

To serve, stuff tomatoes with cottage cheese mixture. Yield: 4 servings (about 136 calories per stuffed tomato).
Sonja Lovell,
Bryan, Texas.

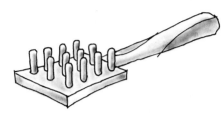

Toss The Pasta, And Serve It Cold

Most of us are used to eating hot spaghetti and macaroni coated in thick sauces. But during the summer, pasta can be served cold, tossed with a variety of fresh ingredients. Combined with favorites, such as shrimp, snow peas, spinach, cheese, and tomatoes, chilled pasta makes a delightfully refreshing main dish or salad.

There are some essential differences between hot and cold pasta dishes. Cold pasta requires the freshest ingredients. For example, canned tomatoes are perfectly acceptable when used in a long-simmering spaghetti sauce, but they just won't do in a cold pasta salad. Also, most of the sauces for cold pasta dishes aren't cooked, or are cooked rather briefly, which means that they are exceptionally easy to prepare.

When cooking pasta, you may wonder how long it should simmer. Some like their pasta al dente, which means it's cooked until it has just a slightly firm texture. Let personal taste be your guide. Frequent tasting during cooking is the best test for desired doneness. But be careful not to overcook it, or the pasta will become too soft.

It's also helpful to know that cold pasta has a tendency to stick together if it's not rinsed after cooking. For this reason, we suggest rinsing cooked pasta with cold water before proceeding with any of the recipes.

Serving long, thin pastas like linguini or fettuccine can be tricky. The best way we've found is to use kitchen tongs or a special wooden pasta fork. This long-handled, oval fork has inch-long dowels sticking out from the flat surface. This allows you to grab the pasta easily and lift it to plates.

CRABMEAT-SHRIMP PASTA SALAD

3 cups water
1 pound unpeeled medium-size fresh shrimp
6 ounces seashell macaroni
1 cup thinly sliced celery
½ medium-size green pepper, finely chopped
½ medium-size red pepper, finely chopped
½ small purple onion, chopped
2 green onions, chopped
1 tablespoon chopped fresh parsley
¼ cup mayonnaise
¼ cup commercial Italian salad dressing
1 tablespoon lemon juice
½ teaspoon dried whole oregano, crushed
¼ teaspoon salt
Dash of pepper
8 ounces lump crabmeat, drained

Bring water to a boil; add shrimp, and cook 3 to 5 minutes. Drain well; rinse with cold water. Chill. Peel and devein shrimp; set aside.

Cook macaroni according to package directions, omitting salt; drain. Rinse with cold water; drain. Add next 6 ingredients; blend. Combine mayonnaise, salad dressing, lemon juice, and seasonings. Add to macaroni mixture. Stir in crabmeat and shrimp. Chill. Yield: 7 servings.   *Janice E. Stephens,*
Richardson, Texas.

SEAFOOD DELIGHT
(pictured on page 201)

4½ cups water
1½ pounds unpeeled medium-size fresh shrimp
1 (16-ounce) package linguini
1 (6-ounce) package frozen snow peas, thawed and drained
6 green onions, chopped
4 medium tomatoes, peeled, chopped, and drained
¾ cup olive oil
¼ cup chopped fresh parsley
⅓ cup wine vinegar
1 teaspoon dried whole oregano
1½ teaspoons dried whole basil
½ teaspoon garlic salt
½ teaspoon coarsely ground black pepper

Bring water to a boil; add shrimp, and cook 3 to 5 minutes. Drain well; rinse with cold water. Chill. Peel and devein shrimp; set aside.

Cook linguini according to package directions, omitting salt; drain. Rinse with cold water, and drain again. Combine shrimp, linguini, and remaining ingredients; toss gently. Cover and chill at least 2 hours. Yield: 10 servings.

MACARONI-VEGETABLE SALAD

1½ cups uncooked corkscrew macaroni
2 medium tomatoes, chopped and drained
1 cup frozen English peas, thawed and drained
8 ounces cooked ham, cut into strips
¾ cup commercial buttermilk-style salad dressing
½ cup chopped green pepper
1 (4-ounce) can sliced mushrooms, drained
Spinach leaves (optional)

Cook macaroni according to package directions; drain. Rinse with cold water, and drain again.

Combine macaroni and remaining ingredients except spinach; gently toss. Cover and chill at least 3 hours. To serve, spoon macaroni mixture into the center of spinach-lined platter, if desired. Yield: 8 servings.

Daisy Cotton,
Karnes City, Texas.

SPINACH-MUSTARD TWIST

1 (16-ounce) package corkscrew macaroni
¼ cup Dijon mustard
2 tablespoons olive oil
1 large clove garlic
½ to ¾ teaspoon salt
¼ teaspoon pepper
1 teaspoon dried whole basil
¼ cup walnuts
1 cup ricotta cheese
1 tablespoon lemon juice
½ pound fresh spinach

Cook macaroni according to package directions, omitting salt; drain. Rinse with cold water, and drain again. Set macaroni aside.

Position knife blade in food processor bowl; add mustard, olive oil, garlic, salt, pepper, basil, and walnuts. Top with cover; process until smooth. Remove cover; add ricotta cheese and lemon juice. Top with cover; process until smooth.

Remove stems from spinach; wash leaves thoroughly. Drain well. Remove cover from processor; add about 1 cup spinach. Top with cover; process 30 seconds or until spinach is minced. Repeat procedure until all spinach is used. Pour sauce over macaroni; toss gently to coat. Cover and chill 2 to 3 hours. Yield: 12 servings.

SEASHELL SALAD

8 ounces seashell macaroni
½ cup mayonnaise
1 tablespoon lemon juice
1 teaspoon salt
1 teaspoon sugar
1 cup diced celery
1 tomato, chopped and drained
1 (2-ounce) jar diced pimiento, drained
2 tablespoons chopped green pepper
¼ teaspoon celery seeds

Cook macaroni according to package directions, omitting salt; drain. Rinse with cold water, and then drain again.

Combine mayonnaise, lemon juice, salt, and sugar; stir into macaroni. Add remaining ingredients; toss well. Cover and chill. Yield: 4 to 6 servings.

Michelle Hilliard,
Rhine, Georgia.

TOMATO-OLIVE PASTA TOSS

4 tomatoes, peeled, seeded, chopped and drained
¼ cup pitted large green olives, sliced
1 clove garlic, minced
½ teaspoon dried whole oregano
1½ tablespoons minced fresh parsley
¼ teaspoon salt
⅛ teaspoon coarsely ground black pepper
¼ cup olive oil
1 tablespoon olive juice
6 ounces fettuccine

Combine tomatoes, olives, garlic, oregano, parsley, salt, and pepper; add oil and olive juice, and mix well. Let stand 2 hours.

Cook fettuccine according to package directions, omitting salt; drain. Rinse with cold water, and drain again. Combine fettuccine and tomato mixture, tossing well. Chill before serving. Yield: 6 servings.

TOMATO-PASTA PRIMAVERA

8 ounces spaghetti
1½ cups quartered mushrooms (about ¼ pound)
1 small green pepper, cut into strips
1 small zucchini, sliced
2 cloves garlic, minced
1 tablespoon vegetable or olive oil
1 (15½-ounce) jar commercial spaghetti sauce
Chopped green onions (optional)

Cook spaghetti according to package directions, omitting salt; drain. Rinse with cold water; drain again. Set aside.

Sauté mushrooms, green pepper, zucchini, and garlic in oil in a large skillet about 10 minutes or until tender. Stir in spaghetti sauce. Spoon over spaghetti; toss gently. Cover and chill.

Garnish with chopped green onions, if desired. Yield: 4 to 6 servings.

Marietta Marx,
Louisville, Kentucky.

PASTA WITH ARTICHOKE HEARTS

1 (16-ounce) can artichoke hearts, drained and quartered
⅔ cup sliced ripe olives
¼ cup olive oil
3 tablespoons lemon juice
2 cloves garlic, minced
3 dashes of hot sauce
½ teaspoon salt
¼ teaspoon coarsely ground black pepper
8 ounces linguini

Combine all ingredients except linguini. Let stand at least 1 hour. Cook linguini according to package directions, omitting salt, and drain.

Rinse linguini with cold water, and drain again. Combine linguini and artichoke mixture. Cover and chill. Toss before serving. Yield: 6 servings.

CRUNCHY ROTELLE SALAD

1 cup uncooked rotelle or wagon wheels
1 cup frozen English peas, thawed and drained
8 ounces cooked ham, cubed
½ cup chopped celery
¼ cup chopped radishes
¼ cup chopped green pepper
¼ cup sweet pickle salad cubes
½ cup mayonnaise
¼ cup sweet pickle juice

Cook rotelle according to package directions; drain. Rinse with cold water, and drain again.

Combine rotelle, English peas, ham, celery, radishes, green pepper, and pickle cubes. Combine mayonnaise and pickle juice; add to rotelle mixture, and toss gently. Cover and chill at least 3 hours. Yield: 4 servings.

Ruth Sherrer,
Fort Worth, Texas.

Best Ever
Baked Beans

One reason baked beans are so popular is that there are so many tasty ways to prepare them. Here are three recipes, each with a different flavor. Yet any of these dishes is bound to be a hit at your next get-together.

THREE-MEAT BAKED BEANS

½ pound Polish sausage, cut into ¼-inch slices
½ pound ground beef
3 tablespoons chopped onion
5 slices bacon, cooked and crumbled
2 (16-ounce) cans pork and beans
⅓ cup catsup
¼ cup firmly packed brown sugar
2 tablespoons molasses
1½ teaspoons Worcestershire sauce
1½ teaspoons prepared mustard

Brown Polish sausage in a skillet; remove from skillet, and discard drippings. Set sausage aside.

Combine ground beef and onion in skillet; cook until meat is browned, stirring to crumble. Drain. Combine ground beef mixture, sausage, and remaining ingredients in a lightly greased 2-quart casserole. Bake, uncovered, at 350° for 30 minutes. Yield: 4 servings.
Carin Usry,
Oklahoma City, Oklahoma.

FAVORITE BAKED BEANS

2 slices bacon
1 small onion, sliced and separated into rings
½ cup chopped green pepper
1 (16-ounce) can baked beans in tomato sauce
2 tablespoons catsup
2 tablespoons brown sugar
1 teaspoon Worcestershire sauce
½ teaspoon prepared mustard

Cook bacon until crisp; drain and crumble, reserving drippings. Set bacon aside. Sauté onion and green pepper in drippings; drain.

Combine onion mixture, crumbled bacon, beans, catsup, brown sugar, Worcestershire sauce, and mustard in a greased 1-quart casserole. Cover and bake at 350° for 45 minutes. Yield: 4 servings.
Patricia Andrews,
McAlester, Oklahoma.

HAWAIIAN-STYLE BAKED BEANS

2 (16-ounce) cans pork and beans
1 (8-ounce) can pineapple chunks, drained
½ cup finely chopped macadamia nuts (optional)
¼ cup chopped green pepper
¼ cup catsup
3 tablespoons brown sugar
2 tablespoons finely chopped onion
1 tablespoon soy sauce
1 tablespoon vinegar

Combine all ingredients; stir well. Spoon into a lightly greased 2-quart casserole; bake at 375° for 45 minutes. Yield: 6 to 8 servings. *Tony Jones,*
Atlanta, Georgia.

Try Catfish Flavored
With Parmesan

Rebecca Thompson of Ashland, Kentucky, tried several versions of her Catfish Parmesan before she arrived at what she believed was a good balance of flavor. "Some of the other ways tasted a little fishy," she says.

Rebecca's recipe features a Parmesan cheese and flour coating, along with a topping of sliced almonds. A delicious entrée, the fish combines perfectly with coleslaw and cornbread or hushpuppies to make a complete meal.

CATFISH PARMESAN

⅔ cup freshly grated Parmesan cheese
¼ cup all-purpose flour
½ teaspoon salt
¼ teaspoon pepper
1 teaspoon paprika
1 egg, beaten
¼ cup milk
5 to 6 small catfish fillets (about 2 pounds)
¼ cup butter or margarine, melted
⅓ cup sliced almonds

Combine cheese, flour, salt, pepper, and paprika; stir well. Combine egg and milk; stir well.

Dip fillets in egg mixture; dredge in flour mixture. Arrange fillets in a lightly greased 13- x 9- x 2-inch baking dish; drizzle with butter. Sprinkle almonds evenly over tops of fillets; bake at 350° for 35 to 40 minutes or until fish flakes easily when tested with a fork. Yield: 6 servings.

Make Gumbo
With A Freezer Mix

Helen McKey of El Toro, Texas, has found an excellent way to use up all her summer okra. She makes her own freezer mix for Okra Gumbo, a savory concoction that also has onion, green pepper, and celery. She adds tomatoes and shrimp when she prepares the dish and serves it over rice.

OKRA GUMBO

1 pint Okra Gumbo Freezer Mix, thawed
2 cups water
1 (16-ounce) can tomatoes, undrained
1 pound medium-size fresh shrimp, peeled and deveined
Salt to taste
Hot cooked rice

Combine mix, water, and tomatoes in a Dutch oven; bring to a boil. Cover and simmer 1 hour. Add shrimp, and simmer 20 minutes; salt to taste. Remove bay leaves. Serve over hot cooked rice. Yield: 6 servings.

Okra Gumbo Freezer Mix:

22 cups sliced okra
6 cups chopped onion (about 6 medium)
2 cups chopped green pepper
1½ cups chopped celery
1 (15-ounce) can tomato sauce
2 tablespoons salt
1 tablespoon cracked black pepper
5 bay leaves

Combine all ingredients in three 13- x 9- x 2-inch baking pans. Cover and bake at 300° for 2 hours or until okra is tender, stirring once after 1 hour. Cool completely. Spoon mixture into 1-pint freezer containers. Label and freeze. Yield: about 6 pints.

Crisp, Fried
Vegetables

Because many people enjoy nibbling on hot, crisp vegetables, every now and then it's fun to fry some. And most of the recipes we offer here can be served either as an appetizer or a side dish.

An old favorite, Fried Tomatoes with Gravy, takes on a sweet taste when brown sugar is added.

FRENCH-FRIED CAULIFLOWER

1 cup plus 2 tablespoons all-purpose
    flour
½ teaspoon salt
1 egg, beaten
1 cup milk
2 tablespoons vegetable oil
1 medium head cauliflower, broken
    into flowerets
Vegetable oil

Combine flour and salt in a medium mixing bowl. Combine egg, milk, and oil in a small mixing bowl. Add egg mixture to flour mixture, stirring just until moistened.

Dip cauliflower into batter; fry in deep hot oil (375°) until golden. Drain on paper towels.

Transfer to a serving platter, and serve immediately. Yield: 6 to 8 servings or about 3½ dozen appetizers.
Cheryl Mays,
Marietta, Georgia.

FRIED OKRA

4 cups sliced okra
½ cup milk
¼ teaspoon salt
¼ teaspoon pepper
¾ cup cornmeal
Vegetable oil

Combine okra, milk, salt, and pepper in a shallow dish; let stand 1 hour or until most of milk is absorbed.

Dredge okra in cornmeal. Fry okra in deep hot oil (375°) until golden brown. Drain on paper towels.

Transfer okra to a serving platter, and serve immediately. Yield: 4 servings.
Mrs. Wesley Ford,
Junction City, Arkansas.

FRIED YELLOW SQUASH

2 medium-size yellow squash, cut into
    ¼-inch slices
¼ cup milk
½ cup self-rising flour
Vegetable oil

Dip squash slices in milk in a small mixing bowl; dredge squash in flour. Fry in ½-inch-deep hot oil (350°) until light golden, turning once. Drain on paper towels.

Transfer squash to a serving platter, and serve immediately. Yield: 2 to 3 servings.
Mary Mertins,
Milton, Florida.

OVEN-FRIED ZUCCHINI

2 medium zucchini
¼ cup Italian-style breadcrumbs
2 tablespoons grated Parmesan cheese
2 tablespoons grated Romano cheese
¼ cup plus 1 tablespoon commercial
    Italian salad dressing

Cut zucchini in half lengthwise; cut each half into eight strips.

Combine breadcrumbs and cheese. Dip zucchini in Italian salad dressing, and roll in breadcrumb mixture. Place zucchini in a single layer on a lightly greased baking sheet. Bake at 475° for 5 minutes. Turn zucchini, and bake an additional 3 to 4 minutes or until golden brown. Serve immediately. Yield: 4 servings.
Mrs. Gene Coleman,
Whispering Pines, North Carolina.

FRIED TOMATOES WITH GRAVY

4 large ripe tomatoes
¼ cup plus 2 tablespoons all-purpose
    flour, divided
¼ cup plus 2 tablespoons butter or
    margarine, divided
¼ teaspoon salt
⅛ teaspoon pepper
1 tablespoon brown sugar
1 cup milk

Cut tomatoes into ½-inch slices; dredge in ¼ cup flour.

Melt ¼ cup butter in a large skillet over medium heat; add tomatoes, and cook until golden brown, turning once. Arrange the tomatoes on a serving platter; sprinkle with salt, pepper, and brown sugar. Keep warm.

Melt remaining 2 tablespoons butter in pan drippings; add remaining 2 tablespoons flour, stirring until smooth. Cook 1 minute, stirring constantly. Gradually add milk; cook over medium heat, stirring constantly, until thickened. Spoon over tomatoes. Serve immediately. Yield: 6 to 8 servings.
Mary Ann Harris,
Franklin, Tennessee.

MICROWAVE COOKERY

Recipes To Make In No Time

Southern Living readers have let us know time and time again what food they like by the recipes they send to us. During the past few years, one of the top interests has been meals that can be prepared quickly. We know this because of the number of microwave recipes we've been receiving. We're pleased to present some of these recipes.

CHICKEN-ASPARAGUS ROLLS

4 chicken breast halves, skinned and
    boned
¼ teaspoon garlic powder
¼ teaspoon dried whole rosemary,
    crushed
¼ teaspoon salt
2 (1-ounce) slices mozzarella cheese,
    halved
1 (10-ounce) package frozen asparagus
    spears, thawed and drained
¼ teaspoon paprika
2 teaspoons grated Parmesan cheese
Parsley sprigs (optional)

Place each chicken breast between two sheets of waxed paper. Flatten to ¼-inch thickness using a meat mallet or rolling pin. Sprinkle with garlic powder, rosemary, and salt.

Place one slice of cheese in center of each piece of chicken. Top with one-fourth of asparagus spears. Roll up lengthwise; secure with wooden picks. Sprinkle each chicken roll with paprika.

Place chicken, seam side down, in a lightly greased 10-inch pieplate; cover with heavy-duty plastic wrap. Microwave at MEDIUM HIGH (70% power) for 3 minutes. Sprinkle chicken rolls with Parmesan. Cover with plastic wrap. Microwave at MEDIUM HIGH for 3 to 5 minutes or until done; give the dish a half-turn at 2-minute intervals. Garnish with parsley, if desired. Yield: 4 servings.
Helen Maurer,
Christmas, Florida.

Tip: Avoid using dishes with sloping sides when cooking casseroles in the microwave. Food on the edges receive the most energy and can overcook.

FISH DELIGHT

2 tablespoons butter or margarine
1 pound fresh spinach
½ cup sliced green onions, divided
4 flounder fillets (about 1½ pounds)
½ teaspoon salt
½ teaspoon pepper
1 tablespoon plus 1 teaspoon barbecue sauce
1 tablespoon plus 1 teaspoon lemon juice
½ cup sliced fresh mushrooms
Paprika

Spread butter on bottom of a 10-inch square baking dish; set aside.

Remove stems from spinach; wash leaves thoroughly. Drain spinach and chop. Place in baking dish over butter; sprinkle with ¼ cup green onions. Layer fish over onions; then sprinkle with salt and pepper.

Combine barbecue sauce and lemon juice; spoon over fish. Top with mushrooms and remaining ¼ cup green onions. Sprinkle with paprika. Cover and microwave at HIGH for 10 minutes or until fish flakes easily when tested with a fork, giving dish a half-turn after 5 minutes. Yield: 4 servings.

Ruth Sherrer,
Fort Worth, Texas.

FRENCH ONION SOUP

2 small onions, thinly sliced
2 tablespoons butter or margarine
2 teaspoons all-purpose flour
2 (14½-ounce) cans beef broth
½ cup water
2 tablespoons Madeira
1 teaspoon Worcestershire sauce
Garlic salt
Grated Parmesan cheese
4 slices French bread, toasted
¼ cup (1 ounce) shredded mozzarella cheese
¼ cup (1 ounce) shredded Swiss cheese

Cut onion slices in half and separate. Combine onion and butter in a 3-quart casserole. Cover and microwave at HIGH for 9 minutes. Stir in flour; cover and microwave at HIGH for 1 minute. Add broth, water, Madeira, and Worcestershire sauce. Cover and microwave at HIGH for 6 to 8 minutes or until mixture boils. Spoon into 4 microwave-safe soup bowls.

Sprinkle desired amount of garlic salt and Parmesan cheese on one side of French bread. Top with remaining cheese. Place on top of each serving of onion soup. Microwave, uncovered, at HIGH for 45 seconds or until cheese melts. Yield: 4 servings.

Helen Boatman,
Chapel Hill, North Carolina.

CARAMEL POPCORN

3 quarts freshly popped popcorn
½ cup butter or margarine
1 cup firmly packed dark brown sugar
¼ cup light corn syrup
½ teaspoon salt
¼ teaspoon baking soda
½ teaspoon vanilla extract

Place popcorn in a lightly greased 4-quart casserole; set aside.

Place butter in a 1½-quart dish. Microwave at HIGH for 1 minute or until melted. Stir in brown sugar, corn syrup, and salt; cover and microwave at HIGH for 4 minutes.

Remove mixture from oven; stir in soda and vanilla. Pour over popcorn; stir until all is coated and no sugar mixture remains in bottom of dish.

Cook popcorn mixture on HIGH for 2½ to 3 minutes, stirring well after each minute.

Remove popcorn from oven; stir well. Spread in a lightly buttered 15- x 10- x 1-inch jellyroll pan; cool thoroughly. Break into pieces, and store in an airtight container. Yield: about 11 cups.

June Ladner,
Gulfport, Mississippi.

Pork Pleasers
For Two

Cooking for two can be a hassle if you have to modify recipes to yield fewer servings. But these recipes make things simple. They feature a variety of pork entrées scaled for two servings.

HAM-AND-BROCCOLI ROLLS

1 (10-ounce) package frozen broccoli spears
1½ teaspoons butter or margarine
1½ teaspoons all-purpose flour
¼ cup milk
⅛ teaspoon salt
1½ teaspoons prepared horseradish
1 teaspoon prepared mustard
¼ teaspoon Worcestershire sauce
¼ teaspoon grated onion
1 egg yolk, beaten
½ cup pineapple juice
6 (6- x 4-inch) slices cooked ham
2 (6- x 4-inch) slices Swiss cheese
2 pineapple slices (optional)
Paprika (optional)

Cook broccoli according to package directions; drain. Set aside.

Melt butter in a heavy saucepan over low heat; add flour, and cook 1 minute, stirring constantly. Gradually add milk; cook over medium heat until thickened. Stir in salt, horseradish, mustard, Worcestershire sauce, and onion. Combine egg yolk and pineapple juice; add to sauce, and stir until thickened.

Divide ham into 2 portions (3 slices each). Top ham with cheese. Arrange half of broccoli on each cheese slice; spoon about 1 tablespoon sauce over broccoli. Roll ham and cheese around broccoli; secure with wooden picks. Place in a 9-inch square baking dish; cover and bake at 350° for 15 to 20 minutes.

To serve, reheat remaining sauce; spoon over ham rolls. Garnish with pineapple slices, and sprinkle with paprika, if desired. Yield: 2 servings.

Brenda Russell,
Signal Mountain, Tennessee.

HAWAIIAN PORK CHOPS

⅓ cup all-purpose flour
½ teaspoon salt
¼ teaspoon pepper
4 (½-inch-thick) center-cut loin pork chops
3 tablespoons vegetable oil
1 (8-ounce) can crushed pineapple, undrained
2 tablespoons brown sugar
¼ teaspoon ground cinnamon
4 green pepper rings

Combine flour, salt, and pepper; dredge pork chops in flour mixture.

Heat oil in a large skillet over medium heat; brown pork chops on both sides. Drain off pan drippings.

Combine pineapple, brown sugar, and cinnamon; spoon evenly onto pork chops. Top each with a green pepper ring. Cover, reduce heat, and simmer 40 minutes or until pork chops are tender. Yield: 2 servings. *Ruth Spitzer, Pinson, Alabama.*

CIDER-SAUCED PORK CHOPS

2 shallots, finely chopped
1 tablespoon plus 1 teaspoon chopped fresh parsley
⅛ teaspoon salt
⅛ teaspoon white pepper
3 (½-inch-thick) pork chops (about 1 pound)
2 tablespoons butter or margarine, melted
½ cup apple cider

Combine shallots, parsley, salt, and pepper; stir well. Pat onto both sides of pork chops, and place chops in a lightly greased 9-inch square baking pan. Drizzle butter over chops; then cover and bake at 325° for 30 minutes.

Remove from oven; uncover and drain drippings. Pour cider over chops; bake, uncovered, an additional 30 minutes or until done. Yield: 2 servings.
Hazel S. Stephenson, Denison, Texas.

STIR-FRY SAUSAGE AND VEGETABLES

6 green onions, chopped
1 cup (about 2 small) cubed yellow squash
2 cloves garlic, minced
2 tablespoons butter or margarine, melted
½ pound smoked sausage, cut into ¼-inch slices
8 cherry tomatoes, halved
2 teaspoons Worcestershire sauce
Chopped parsley (optional)

Sauté onions, squash, and garlic in butter in a heavy skillet for 2 minutes. Add sausage, tomatoes, and Worcestershire sauce; stir-fry until thoroughly heated. Garnish with chopped parsley, if desired. Yield: 2 servings.
Victoria J. Rousuck, Port Aransas, Texas.

Tip: Bent or dented measuring utensils give inaccurate measures. Use only standard measuring cups and spoons that are in good condition.

BACON SPAGHETTI

5 slices bacon, chopped
¼ cup chopped onion
¼ cup chopped green pepper
4 ounces uncooked spaghetti, broken
1 cup boiling water
1 (14½-ounce) can tomatoes, undrained and chopped
1 tablespoon Worcestershire sauce
2 tablespoons grated Parmesan cheese

Combine bacon, onion, and green pepper in a large skillet; sauté 5 minutes. Drain drippings. Add spaghetti, water, and tomatoes.

Cover and simmer 20 minutes or until spaghetti is tender, stirring occasionally. Stir in Worcestershire sauce. To serve, sprinkle each serving with Parmesan cheese. Yield: 2 servings.
Mrs. C. W. Horton, Demopolis, Alabama.

Cheese Breads You're Sure To Love

The aroma of homemade bread fresh from the oven is hard to beat. And when there's cheese added to the bread, you can almost be certain every last crumb will be eaten. Our readers have shared some deliciously different ideas for making cheese breads—so many, in fact, you may have trouble deciding which one to try. Our solution is to try them all.

SAUSAGE-CHEESE MUFFINS

½ pound bulk pork sausage
¼ cup chopped green onions
¼ cup chopped green pepper
¾ cup all-purpose flour
½ cup plain cornmeal
1 teaspoon baking soda
½ teaspoon salt
⅛ teaspoon red pepper
1 egg, beaten
1 cup buttermilk
½ cup (2 ounces) shredded Cheddar cheese

Combine sausage, green onions, and green pepper in a skillet; cook over medium heat until sausage is browned, stirring to crumble. Drain.

Combine flour, cornmeal, soda, salt, and red pepper; stir well. Combine egg

and buttermilk; stir well. Add buttermilk mixture, sausage mixture, and cheese to flour mixture; stir just until moistened. Spoon into greased muffin pans, filling two-thirds full; bake at 400° for 28 to 30 minutes or until golden. Yield: 1 dozen.
Pat Benigno, Gulfport, Mississippi.

HAM-AND-CHEESE BREAD

2 cups biscuit mix
1 cup chopped cooked ham
⅔ cup milk
2 eggs, beaten
3 tablespoons instant minced onion
2 tablespoons vegetable oil
½ teaspoon prepared mustard
1½ cups (6 ounces) shredded Cheddar cheese, divided
3 tablespoons butter or margarine, melted
2 tablespoons sesame seeds

Combine first 7 ingredients and ¾ cup cheese in medium bowl; stir well.

Pour batter into a greased 10-inch piepan; drizzle butter over top. Bake at 375° for 30 minutes. Top with remaining ¾ cup cheese and sesame seeds; bake an additional 5 minutes. Cut into wedges; serve warm. Yield: 6 to 8 servings.
Linda H. Sutton, Winston-Salem, North Carolina.

LITTLE CHEESE LOAVES

1 cup plain cornmeal
1 cup all-purpose flour
¼ cup sugar
1 tablespoon baking powder
2 teaspoons caraway seeds
1 teaspoon seasoned salt
2 eggs, beaten
1⅓ cups milk
1½ cups (6 ounces) shredded sharp Cheddar cheese

Combine cornmeal, flour, sugar, baking powder, caraway seeds, and seasoned salt; stir well. Add remaining ingredients; stir well. Pour into 8 greased and floured 4- x 2- x 2-inch loafpans; bake at 400° for 20 to 25 minutes or until golden brown. Remove immediately from pans. Yield: eight (4- x 2- x 2-inch) loaves.

Note: Bread may be baked in a greased and floured 9-inch square baking pan; bake at 400° for 30 to 35 minutes.
Marie Bowers, Joaquin, Texas.

FRUIT-AND-CHEESE BRAID

1 package dry yeast
½ cup warm water (105° to 115°)
2½ cups biscuit mix
1 egg, beaten
1 tablespoon sugar
1 (8-ounce) package cream cheese, softened
½ cup sugar
1 tablespoon lemon juice
¼ cup peach or strawberry preserves

Dissolve yeast in warm water in a large bowl; let stand 5 minutes. Add biscuit mix, egg, and 1 tablespoon sugar; stir well.

Turn dough out onto a floured surface; knead until smooth (about 1 minute). Place dough on a large greased cookie sheet; roll into a 14- x 9-inch rectangle.

Combine cream cheese, ½ cup sugar, and lemon juice; beat at medium speed of electric mixer until smooth. Spread mixture down center of dough. Make 3-inch cuts toward center at 1-inch intervals on both long sides of dough. Fold strips to center, alternating and overlapping ends; cover and let rise in a warm place (85°), free from drafts, 1 hour or until doubled in bulk. Bake at 350° for 20 minutes. Spoon preserves down center of braid; bake an additional 5 minutes. Cool 10 minutes before serving (may also be served at room temperature). Yield: one 14-inch braid.
Marietta Marx,
Louisville, Kentucky.

Serve A Refreshing Fruit Drink

Fresh fruit is plentiful in the South, so when the weather gets hot, it's natural to turn to fruit and juices for thirst quenchers. In these beverage recipes, our readers use fresh, frozen, or canned fruit and juices for their favorite summer coolers—or year-round drinks.

CHERRY-LEMONADE SYRUP

2 cups sugar
1 cup water
Rind of 3 medium lemons
1¼ cups lemon juice
1 (6-ounce) jar maraschino cherries, undrained

Cinnamon- and clove-spiced fruit juices are mixed with ginger ale for our Spring Cooler. Serve over crushed ice, and add a skewer of fruit to each glass for a summer touch.

Combine sugar, water, and lemon rind in a medium saucepan; bring to a boil. Boil 5 minutes, stirring occasionally. Remove from heat; cool. Stir in lemon juice. Strain syrup through a sieve; press rind, and discard. Add cherries and juice to syrup. Cover and refrigerate. Syrup may be stored in refrigerator for one month.

To make lemonade, combine ¼ cup syrup and 1 cup cold water. Serve over ice. Yield: 2¾ cups.
Mary Helen Hackney,
Greenville, North Carolina.

SPRING COOLER

1½ cups sugar
1½ cups water
4 (3-inch) sticks cinnamon
6 whole cloves
1 (46-ounce) can pineapple juice, chilled
2 cups orange juice
1 cup lemon juice
1 (33.8-ounce) bottle ginger ale, chilled
Orange wedges
Maraschino cherries

Combine sugar, water, cinnamon sticks, and cloves in a saucepan; bring

to a boil. Reduce heat; simmer 30 minutes. Refrigerate 8 hours or overnight; discard spices. Combine sugar syrup and fruit juices; stir well.

To serve, combine juice mixture and ginger ale; stir well. Serve over crushed ice. Place orange wedges and Maraschino cherries on skewers, and place in each glass. Yield: 3½ quarts.
Ferrilyn Welsh,
Warner Robins, Georgia.

SANGRÍA

1 (25.4-ounce) bottle Burgundy or other dry, red wine
1 (10-ounce) package frozen mixed fruit
1 (6-ounce) can frozen lemonade concentrate
¼ cup grenadine syrup
8 ice cubes
1 (32-ounce) bottle club soda, chilled
Orange slice halves (optional)

Combine Burgundy, mixed fruit, lemonade concentrate, grenadine syrup, and ice cubes in a large bowl; let stand 20 minutes. Stir in club soda. Pour into glasses, and top with orange slices, if desired. Yield: 11 cups.
Virginia Stalder,
Nokesville, Virginia.

APPLE JULEP

1 quart unsweetened apple juice, chilled
2 cups unsweetened pineapple juice,
   chilled
1 cup orange juice, chilled
¼ cup lemon juice, chilled
Lemon slices (optional)
Fresh mint sprigs (optional)

Combine first 4 ingredients; mix well. Garnish servings with lemon slices and mint, if desired. Yield: 7¼ cups.

Deborah L. Smith,
Salem, Missouri.

From Our Kitchen To Yours

During the summer, be adventure-some and try some new frozen desserts, such as gelato, granita, and sorbet. Here's some information about the old-time favorites, plus the newer varieties.

Ice cream has milk fat and milk solids as its main ingredients. Depending on state laws, the milk fat content can vary between 10% and 20%; it has to contain a minimum of 10% to be legally labeled an ice cream. The more popular and widely distributed brands contain the highest amount of milk fat. Calorie content of ice cream varies between 125 and 165 per half-cup serving.

Ice milk is prepared from the same ingredients as ice cream but has less milk fat (usually between 2% and 7%). Ice milk often has more sugar than ice cream, and its consistency is usually softer. The calorie content is about 100 per half-cup serving. Most soft-serve frozen dessert is ice milk; it's taken directly from the freezer and not allowed to harden.

Gelato, an Italian ice cream, has a rich color and flavor. The texture is very dense and smooth with little or no air incorporated in the freezing process. Most contain about 12% milk fat, no eggs, and only natural ingredients.

Sherbet is a frozen dessert having only about 1% to 2% milk fat and 2% to 5% milk solids. Typically, it is made up of a dairy ingredient, fruit or fruit juice, water, flavorings, and sweeteners. Sherbet usually has more sugar than ice cream; it's also more sensitive to changes in texture if stored at the wrong temperature and kept too long.

Frozen yogurt is made with yogurt, skimmed milk, fruit or flavorings, and sweetener. Its consistency is similar to soft-serve frozen dessert, and it is low in milk fat. It has less sugar and usually fewer calories than ice milk.

Frozen tofu varies significantly depending on the ingredients. Some frozen tofu is a natural product; it's made with tofu bean curd, soy milk, and a natural sweetener, such as honey. It doesn't contain dairy products, so it has little or no cholesterol. The number of calories will fluctuate according to the ingredients used. Its many flavors include chocolate, pineapple-coconut, amaretto, and maple walnut.

Sorbet is French sherbet. In France, it's often served as a palate refresher or cleanser before the main course in a special meal; in the U.S. it's eaten as a frozen dessert. Sorbet doesn't contain dairy products or egg yolks. It gets its fine texture from adding egg whites and can be made with fruits or vegetables.

Granita, the Italian version of sorbet, also contains no dairy products or egg yolks. It's a frosty combination of fruit, ice, and sweetener, and it has a coarser texture than sorbet (more like that of chipped ice).

Fruit Ice is also nondairy. Made of water, sugar, and fruit juice, it often has a tart fruit flavor.

Magnificent Mangoes

From June through September, you'll find plenty of mangoes in the grocery store. And you're sure to notice them. Ranging in size from a few ounces to several pounds, the oval-shaped fruit has a colorful skin of green or gold with a blush of red or purple.

Inside the mango is a large seed surrounded by a deep yellow flesh. Its flavor has been described as a cross between a peach and a pineapple.

Mangoes, like avocados, are ready to eat when they yield to gentle pressure. Allow the fruit to ripen at room temperature; then refrigerate, uncovered, once it's fully ripe.

Mangoes are versatile and can be used at any stage of maturity. They have a tangy flavor when underripe and can be transformed into a great mock apple pie, dessert sauce, jam, or pickles. When ripe, they go well in fruit or meat salads, baked goods, beverages, jams, and chutneys. Try our Chicken Salad with Mango to discover the refreshing mango flavor.

CHICKEN SALAD WITH MANGO

⅓ cup mayonnaise or salad dressing
2 green onions, chopped
2 teaspoons chives (optional)
2 cups chopped cooked chicken
2 cups chopped ripe mango
1 large tomato, chopped
1 medium-size green pepper, chopped
⅓ cup vegetable oil
1 tablespoon vinegar
1 tablespoon lemon juice
1 teaspoon sugar
Lettuce or spinach leaves

Combine mayonnaise, green onions, and, if desired, chives; chill.

Combine chicken, mango, tomato, and green pepper in a large bowl. Combine oil, vinegar, lemon juice, and sugar in a jar. Cover and shake vigorously. Pour over chicken mixture; chill at least 30 minutes.

Spoon chicken salad mixture onto a lettuce-lined plate. Top with mayonnaise mixture. Yield: 8 servings.

Nita Grochowski,
Bokeelia, Florida.

MANGO-SPICED RUM SAUCE

½ cup water
1 tablespoon butter or margarine
1 tablespoon sugar
1 teaspoon cornstarch
2 tablespoons cold water
1 cup mashed ripe mango
2 to 3 tablespoons spiced rum
Dash of ground nutmeg

Combine ½ cup water, butter, and sugar in a saucepan; bring to a boil.

Dissolve cornstarch in 2 tablespoons cold water; add to sugar mixture, stirring well. Return mixture to a boil; cook 1 minute, stirring frequently. Add mango, rum, and nutmeg; stir well.

To serve warm, spoon sauce over vanilla ice cream. Yield: 1½ cups.

Bette Crown,
Clearwater, Florida.

Tip: Learn to judge food labels carefully and take advantage of products with nutrient information on the label. Nutrition labels indicate the number of calories and the amount of protein, carbohydrates, and fat in a serving of the product. They also give an indication of major vitamins and minerals present in the product.

MANGO ICE CREAM

4 ripe mangoes, peeled and sliced
¼ cup lemon juice
1½ cups sugar
4 egg yolks, beaten
6 cups half-and-half
¼ teaspoon almond extract

Combine mango and lemon juice in container of an electric blender or food processor; process until smooth.

Combine mango puree, sugar, and egg yolks in a bowl; stir well. Add remaining ingredients; stir well. Pour mixture into freezer can of a 1-gallon electric or hand-turned freezer. Freeze according to manufacturer's instructions. Let ice cream ripen 1 hour. Yield: 1 gallon. *Mrs. A. J. Amador, Decatur, Alabama.*

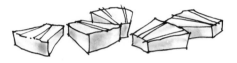

MANGO-PINEAPPLE CRÊPES

1 (20-ounce) can pineapple tidbits, undrained
¼ cup sugar
2½ teaspoons cornstarch
2 teaspoons orange rind
¼ cup orange juice
3 tablespoons butter, softened
1½ cups peeled, chopped ripe mango
Crêpes (recipe follows)
3 tablespoons brandy
Sweetened whipped cream
Additional chopped mango (optional)

Drain pineapple, reserving ½ cup juice; set aside. Combine sugar and cornstarch in a medium saucepan, stirring well; add reserved pineapple juice, orange rind, and orange juice. Cook over medium heat until mixture boils, stirring constantly; boil 1 minute, and remove from heat. Add butter, pineapple, and mango; stir well.

Spoon about ¼ cup mango mixture onto center of each crêpe. Fold edges of crêpe to center, overlapping. Arrange crêpes, seam side up, in a 13- x 9- x 2-inch baking dish. Cover and bake crêpes at 350° for 10 minutes. Remove from oven.

Place brandy in a small, long-handled pan; heat just until warm. (Do not boil.) Remove from heat. Ignite brandy with a long match, and pour over crêpes. Serve crêpes immediately, topped with whipped cream. Garnish with additional chopped mango, if desired. Yield: 5 servings.

Crêpes:

¾ cup milk, divided
½ cup all-purpose flour
1 egg
1 egg yolk
2 tablespoons butter, melted
1½ teaspoons powdered sugar
¼ teaspoon grated orange rind
¼ teaspoon salt

Combine ½ cup milk and next 7 ingredients, beating until smooth. Stir in remaining milk. Refrigerate 2 hours.

Brush the bottom of a 6-inch crêpe pan with vegetable oil. Place over medium heat just until hot, not smoking.

Pour 2 tablespoons batter into pan; quickly tilt pan in all directions so batter covers pan in a thin film. Cook about 30 seconds. Lift edge of crêpe to test for doneness. Crêpe is ready for flipping when it can be shaken loose from pan. Flip the crêpe, and cook about 30 seconds on other side. (This side is usually spotty brown and is the side on which the filling is placed.) Remove crêpe from pan, and repeat procedure until all batter is used.

Place crêpes on a paper towel to cool. Stack between layers of waxed paper. Yield: ten 6-inch crêpes.

*Jenny Peebles,
Miami, Florida.*

MANGO-ORANGE SMOOTHIE

2 cups orange juice
1½ cups pureed ripe mangoes
2 tablespoons sugar

Combine all ingredients; stir well. Chill. Serve mixture over crushed ice. Yield: 4 cups. *Margie Pierce, Miami, Florida.*

MANGO FRAPPÉ

1½ cups chopped ripe mango
1 cup milk
2 tablespoons sugar
1 tablespoon lime juice
¼ teaspoon vanilla extract
4 to 6 ice cubes

Place chopped mango in freezer for 30 minutes. Combine mango, milk, sugar, juice, and vanilla in container of an electric blender; process until smooth. Add ice cubes; process until smooth. Serve immediately. Yield: 3½ cups. *Libby Winstead, Nashville, Tennessee.*

Flavor Bar Cookies With Fruit

Bar cookies are an easy way to make a homemade snack because the entire recipe is baked in one pan. For a different taste, think "fruit" the next time you are ready to mix a batch of bar cookies. Tart lemon, moist apple, zesty apricot, and sweet cherry are fruit flavors that perk up these recipes.

APRICOT-OATMEAL BARS

1¼ cups all-purpose flour
1¼ cups quick-cooking oats, uncooked
½ cup sugar
½ teaspoon baking soda
¼ teaspoon salt
¾ cup butter or margarine, melted
2 teaspoons vanilla extract
1 (10-ounce) jar apricot preserves
½ cup flaked coconut

Combine flour, oats, sugar, soda, and salt in a large bowl; blend well. Add butter and vanilla; mix until crumbly. Reserve 1 cup mixture.

Press remaining crumb mixture into a greased 13- x 9- x 2-inch baking pan. Spread apricot preserves on crust to within ¼ inch from edge of pan. Sprinkle with reserved crumb mixture and coconut. Bake at 350° for 20 to 25 minutes or until lightly browned. Cool and cut into bars. Yield: 2 dozen. *Elizabeth M. Haney, Dublin, Virginia.*

FROSTED APPLE BROWNIES

½ cup shortening
1½ cups sugar
3 eggs
2 cups all-purpose flour
½ teaspoon salt
1 teaspoon baking soda
1 teaspoon ground cinnamon
1 cup finely chopped apple
½ cup chopped pecans
Cream Cheese Frosting

Cream shortening; gradually add sugar, beating well at medium speed of an electric mixer. Add eggs, one at a time, beating after each addition. Combine flour, salt, soda, and cinnamon; gradually add to creamed mixture. Fold in apple and pecans. Pour batter into a greased 15- x 10- x 1-inch jellyroll pan. Bake at 350° for 30 minutes.

Remove from oven, and spread top with Cream Cheese Frosting while slightly warm. Cool completely before cutting into squares. Yield: 4 dozen.

Cream Cheese Frosting:

¼ cup butter or margarine, softened
1 (3-ounce) package cream cheese, softened
1½ cups sifted powdered sugar
1 teaspoon vanilla extract
½ cup chopped pecans

Cream butter and cream cheese; gradually add sugar, beating until light and fluffy. Stir in vanilla and chopped pecans. Yield: about 1¼ cups.

Sally Smith,
Rustburg, Virginia.

TANGY LEMON BARS

⅓ cup butter or margarine
¾ cup all-purpose flour
2 eggs, beaten
1 cup firmly packed brown sugar
¾ cup flaked coconut
½ cup chopped pecans
½ teaspoon vanilla extract
¼ teaspoon baking powder
Lemon Frosting

Cut butter into flour with a pastry blender until mixture resembles coarse meal. Press crumb mixture in an ungreased 11- x 7- x 2-inch baking pan. Bake at 350° for 10 minutes or until lightly browned.

Combine beaten eggs, brown sugar, coconut, chopped pecans, vanilla, and baking powder in a medium mixing bowl; mix well. Pour batter over warm crust. Bake at 350° for 20 minutes.

Remove from oven, and spread top immediately with Lemon Frosting. Cut into bars. Yield: 2 dozen.

Lemon Frosting:

1 cup sifted powdered sugar
1 teaspoon grated lemon rind
2 tablespoons lemon juice

Combine all ingredients in a small bowl; blend well. Yield: about ½ cup.

Dora Farrar,
Gadsden, Alabama.

Tip: When buying fresh citrus, look for fruit that have smooth, blemish-free skins. Indications of high juice content are that fruit feel firm and are heavy for their size.

DELIGHTFUL CHERRY BARS

1 cup all-purpose flour
½ cup butter or margarine, softened
¼ cup sifted powdered sugar
1½ cups firmly packed brown sugar
2 eggs
¼ cup all-purpose flour
½ teaspoon baking powder
½ teaspoon salt
1 cup finely chopped walnuts
½ cup maraschino cherries, drained and chopped
Cherry Frosting

Combine 1 cup flour, butter, and powdered sugar; press in a 13- x 9- x 2-inch baking pan. Bake at 350° for 12 minutes or until lightly browned. Cool.

Combine brown sugar and eggs; beat at medium speed of an electric mixer until fluffy. Combine ¼ cup flour, baking powder, and salt in a bowl; add to egg mixture. Stir in walnuts and cherries. Spread over crust. Bake at 350° for 20 minutes or until set. Cool. Spread with Cherry Frosting. Cut into bars. Yield: 3 dozen.

Cherry Frosting:

2 cups sifted powdered sugar
3 tablespoons butter or margarine, softened
2 to 3 tablespoons milk
1 tablespoon maraschino cherry juice
½ teaspoon almond extract

Combine powdered sugar and butter in a medium bowl; add milk and cherry juice to desired consistency. Stir in almond extract. Yield: 1¼ cups.

Nell H. Amador,
Guntersville, Alabama.

Spice It Up
With Dressing

The next time you pass the salad dressing section in the grocery store, remember that these spicy mixtures can flavor more than just salad greens. They've been used for years as seasonings, as marinades, and as the basis for many flavorful sauces.

Our recipes will encourage you to use salad dressings in new ways, and you can try other easy ideas, as well. For example, anytime you cook fresh vegetables, a splash of salad dressing can add new flavor. And many kinds of meats can benefit from the extra zing of a salad dressing marinade.

SWEET-AND-SOUR CHICKEN

1 (10-ounce) jar peach or apricot preserves
1 (8-ounce) bottle commercial Thousand Island salad dressing
1 (1.75-ounce) envelope onion soup mix
1 (2½- to 3-pound) broiler-fryer, cut up and skinned

Combine first 3 ingredients, stirring well. Dip each piece of chicken in mixture, and place in a lightly greased 13- x 9- x 2-inch baking pan. Cover and bake at 350° for 30 minutes. Remove cover; bake an additional 30 minutes, basting twice with remaining salad dressing mixture. Yield: 4 servings. *Marie Elrod,*
Warner Robins, Georgia.

SAUSAGE-POTATO CASSEROLE

5 cups cubed potatoes, cooked
1 pound smoked sausage, chopped
1½ cups (6 ounces) shredded American cheese, divided
¼ cup sliced green onions
⅛ teaspoon pepper
⅓ cup commercial Italian salad dressing

Combine potatoes, sausage, 1 cup cheese, onions, and pepper; mix well. Pour salad dressing over potato mixture; mix well. Spoon into a lightly greased 8-inch square casserole. Cover and bake at 350° for 15 minutes. Uncover and bake an additional 10 minutes. Sprinkle with remaining ½ cup cheese, and bake an additional 5 minutes or until cheese melts. Yield: 6 servings. *Marcy Hart,*
Killeen, Texas.

EASY MARINATED MUSHROOMS

1 pound small fresh mushrooms
4 cups water
1 teaspoon salt
1 (8-ounce) bottle commercial Italian salad dressing
1 large clove garlic, minced
½ teaspoon dried whole thyme

Clean mushrooms, and trim stem ends. Combine mushrooms, water, and salt in a small saucepan. Bring mixture to a boil; cover, reduce heat, and simmer 2 minutes. Drain mushrooms, and pat dry with a paper towel. Combine mushrooms and remaining ingredients; cover and refrigerate 8 hours. Mushrooms may be stored in refrigerator for 1 week. Yield: 2 cups.

Mildred Bickley,
Bristol, Virginia.

TEXAS CAVIAR

2 (14-ounce) cans black-eyed peas, drained
1 (15½-ounce) can white hominy, drained
2 medium tomatoes, chopped
4 green onions, chopped
2 cloves garlic, minced
1 medium-size green pepper, chopped
1 jalapeño pepper, chopped
½ cup chopped onion
½ cup chopped fresh parsley
1 (8-ounce) bottle commercial Italian salad
  dressing

Combine all ingredients except salad dressing; mix well. Pour salad dressing over black-eyed pea mixture; cover and marinate at least 2 hours in refrigerator. Drain. Serve with tortilla chips. Yield: 7 cups.

Marge Clyde,
San Antonio, Texas.

PARTY BREAD

1 package dry yeast
1 teaspoon sugar
⅓ cup warm water (105° to 115°)
1 cup milk
2 tablespoons butter or margarine
1 (0.6-ounce) envelope Italian salad
  dressing mix
½ teaspoon salt
3 to 3½ cups all-purpose flour

Dissolve yeast and sugar in warm water; let stand 5 minutes. Combine milk and next 3 ingredients in a large mixing bowl; stir in yeast mixture. Gradually stir in enough flour to make a soft dough.

Turn dough out onto a floured surface, and knead until smooth and elastic (about 7 minutes). Place in a well-greased bowl, turning to grease top. Cover and let rise in a warm place (85°), free from drafts, 1 hour or until doubled in bulk.

Punch dough down; shape into a loaf. Place in two well-greased 8½- x 4½- x 3-inch loafpans. Cover and let rise in a warm place (85°), free from drafts, 30 minutes or until doubled in bulk. Bake at 400° for 25 to 30 minutes or until loaf sounds hollow when tapped. Yield: 2 loaves.

Barbara Rogers,
Cleveland, Tennessee.

Last Call For Summer Vegetables

If you're savoring the last of your vegetable garden, these recipes will bring extra flavor to end-of-the-summer meals. And they're easy to prepare—all of them cook in 20 minutes or less.

FRITTER-FRIED OKRA

1 cup all-purpose flour
1 tablespoon baking powder
½ teaspoon salt
2 eggs, beaten
⅓ cup milk
5 cups thinly sliced okra
Vegetable oil

Combine first 3 ingredients in a medium bowl. Combine eggs and milk; add to dry ingredients, and mix until smooth. Stir in sliced okra.

Carefully drop batter by tablespoonfuls into deep hot oil (375°); cook only a few at a time, turning once. Fry 2 to 3 minutes or until fritters are golden brown. Drain well on paper towels. Yield: 3 dozen.

Helen W. Klicker,
Jacksonville, Florida.

MUSHROOM-STUFFED TOMATOES

6 firm tomatoes
½ teaspoon salt
¼ teaspoon pepper
¾ pound fresh mushrooms, sliced
6 green onions, chopped
3 tablespoons butter or margarine, melted
1 tablespoon lemon juice
1 teaspoon Hungarian paprika
3 tablespoons shredded Gruyère cheese
3 tablespoons grated Parmesan cheese

Cut off top of each tomato; scoop out pulp, leaving shells intact. Chop pulp, and drain well. Sprinkle insides of tomato shells with salt and pepper; invert on paper towels to drain.

Sauté mushrooms and green onions in butter. Add tomato pulp, lemon juice, and paprika; reduce heat to medium, and cook 2 minutes. Remove from heat; add Gruyère cheese, stirring until cheese melts. Spoon mixture into tomato shells; place in a 12- x 8- x 2-inch baking dish. Sprinkle with Parmesan cheese. Bake at 350° for 15 to 20 minutes. Yield: 6 servings.

Nancy Reynolds,
Springfield, Virginia.

TOMATO-CUCUMBER SALAD

3 tomatoes, coarsely chopped
1 cucumber, peeled and sliced
1 large green pepper, diced
1 small purple onion, sliced and separated
  into rings
2 tablespoons water
1 tablespoon sugar
1 tablespoon vinegar
½ teaspoon salt
¼ teaspoon celery seeds
¼ teaspoon pepper

Combine vegetables in a large bowl, and set aside.

Combine remaining ingredients in a small saucepan, and heat until sugar dissolves. Pour mixture over vegetables. Cover and chill thoroughly. Use a slotted spoon to serve. Yield: 6 servings.

Mary Jane Wilson,
Bovina, Texas.

ZUCCHINI-CORN COMBO

4 small zucchini, sliced
1 small onion, chopped
1 medium-size green pepper, chopped
2 tablespoons butter or margarine, melted
1½ cups fresh corn
1 large tomato, coarsely chopped
½ teaspoon salt
¼ teaspoon pepper
1 cup (4 ounces) shredded Cheddar cheese

Sauté first 3 ingredients in butter in a skillet. Cover, reduce heat to medium, and cook 3 minutes. Stir in corn and tomato; cover and cook an additional 5 minutes or until vegetables are crisp-tender. Add salt and pepper, tossing gently. Sprinkle with cheese, and serve immediately. Yield: 6 to 8 servings.

Mary Mertins,
Milton, Florida.

SNAP BEANS

1 pound fresh green beans
1 cup water
1 beef-flavored bouillon cube
2 teaspoons chopped fresh oregano

Wash beans; trim ends, and remove strings. Cut into 1-inch pieces. Heat water to boiling in a saucepan; dissolve bouillon cube in water. Add beans to saucepan. Cover, reduce heat, and simmer 12 to 15 minutes or until tender; drain beans, and toss with chopped oregano. Yield: 3 to 4 servings.

Lise Rosenfeld,
Atlanta, Georgia.

September

Chess Pie—
An Oldtime Favorite

Thick and sweet as a Southern drawl, chess pies were born during a time when dessert depended on the creativity of a cook equipped with only farm staples—eggs from the henhouse, cream from the morning milking, home-churned butter kept cool in the spring-house, and sugar. Almost always, a splash of lemon juice or vinegar and a sprinkling of cornmeal and/or flour became characteristic in the lemon-gold layer that was cradled in pastry.

If you've never baked a chess pie, you may notice the filling puffs as it bakes and then slowly begins to fall. It's not unusual for it to crack on top, but to minimize the chances of cracking, let it cool slowly and away from drafts.

COCONUT CHESS PIE

4 eggs, beaten
1½ cups sugar
½ cup butter or margarine, melted
1 tablespoon vinegar
1 teaspoon vanilla extract
½ teaspoon salt
1 cup flaked coconut
1 unbaked 9-inch pastry shell
Toasted flaked coconut (optional)

Combine first 6 ingredients; beat well. Stir in 1 cup coconut; pour into pastry shell. Bake at 325° for 45 to 50 minutes or until set. Cool on a wire rack. Garnish with toasted coconut, if desired. Yield: one 9-inch pie. *Amy Cross, Knoxville, Tennessee.*

BROWN SUGAR CHESS PIE

½ cup sugar
½ cup firmly packed brown sugar
1 tablespoon all-purpose flour
1 tablespoon cornmeal
Pinch of salt
3 eggs
1 teaspoon vinegar
½ teaspoon vanilla extract
¼ cup milk
¼ cup butter or margarine, melted
1 unbaked 8-inch pastry shell

Combine sugar, flour, cornmeal, and salt in a small bowl; mix well. Combine eggs, vinegar, and vanilla in a medium bowl; beat mixture at medium speed of an electric mixer until thoroughly blended. Add dry ingredients, milk, and butter; beat at medium speed of an electric mixer until mixture is smooth. Pour into unbaked pastry shell.

Bake at 350° for 30 minutes or until set. Cool on a wire rack. Yield: one 8-inch pie. *Katherine Wickstrom, Pelham, Alabama.*

APPLE-LEMON CHESS PIE

1 cup sugar
½ teaspoon salt
½ teaspoon grated lemon rind
4 eggs, beaten
3 tablespoons lemon juice
¼ cup butter or margarine, melted
1 cup unsweetened applesauce
1 unbaked 9-inch pastry shell

Combine sugar, salt, and lemon rind; set aside. Combine eggs, lemon juice, butter, and applesauce; add dry ingredients, and beat with an electric mixer until mixture is blended.

Pour into unbaked pastry shell; bake at 450° for 15 minutes. Reduce heat to 350°; bake an additional 15 minutes or until set. Cool on a wire rack. Yield: one 9-inch pie. *Glyna Meredith Gallrein, Anchorage, Kentucky.*

CHOCOLATE CHESS PIE

1½ cups sugar
3½ tablespoons cocoa
Pinch of salt
1 tablespoon all-purpose flour
1 tablespoon cornmeal
½ cup chopped pecans
3 eggs, beaten
½ cup milk
1 tablespoon vanilla extract
1 unbaked 9-inch pastry shell
Sifted powdered sugar (optional)

Combine first 6 ingredients in a medium bowl; mix well. Combine eggs, milk, and vanilla; stir into dry ingredients, mixing well. Pour into pastry shell; bake at 350° for 45 to 50 minutes or until pie is set. Cool on a wire rack. Lightly sift powdered sugar over pie, if desired. Yield: one 9-inch pie. *Maxine Compton, Lampasas, Texas.*

OLD-FASHIONED CHESS PIE

1½ cups sugar
1 tablespoon plus 1 teaspoon cornmeal
½ cup butter, melted
1 tablespoon vinegar
½ teaspoon vanilla extract
3 eggs, beaten
1 unbaked 8-inch pastry shell

Combine first 5 ingredients. Stir in eggs; mix thoroughly. Pour into pastry shell; bake at 350° for 50 to 55 minutes. Yield: one 8-inch pie. *Gwen Templeton, Albertville, Alabama.*

Not Your
Ordinary Rice

Rice is considered a routine side dish in our part of the country, but that doesn't mean it has to look routine. Its texture makes it suitable for molding into a variety of shapes.

Rice is easy to mold, whether it's served plain or combined with other ingredients in an entrée, salad, or side dish. Start with our recipe for Basic Molding Rice. Either mold it as the recipe directs, or use it as a base for the other rice mold recipes that follow.

Rice comes in three varieties: short, medium, and long grain. The shorter the grain, the more moist the end product will be, and the greater the tendency for the rice to cling together. Short-grain rice is more moist than is usually desired. Medium-grain rice produces an end product that adheres well for these recipes. Long-grain rice can be used, but it does not adhere quite as satisfactorily.

For molding, select a rice that is not labeled parboiled or converted. This process gives the grain a desirable texture, but this type of rice does not stick together well in molds.

Almost any type of mold will work for these recipes. Plastic salad molds work fine, as do regular mixing bowls. Just be sure that the mold is ovenproof if the recipe is to be baked. For individual molds, choose brioche pans, small salad molds, custard cups, or empty tuna cans.

For well-shaped molds, press the rice, while hot, into oiled containers unless the recipe directs otherwise. Small molds can be turned out immediately; let larger molds set about 5 minutes.

BASIC MOLDING RICE

2 cups water
½ teaspoon salt
1 cup uncooked regular rice
4 cherry tomato roses (optional)
Fresh watercress or parsley sprigs
  (optional)

Combine water and salt in a heavy saucepan; bring to a boil. Gradually add rice, stirring constantly. Cover, reduce heat, and simmer 15 minutes or until rice is tender and water is absorbed.

Use as directed in recipes, or mold individual servings as follows: Press hot rice into 4 oiled 6-ounce custard cups; immediately invert onto plates. Top each with a tomato rose and watercress or parsley, if desired. Yield: 4 servings.

SAFFRON RICE MOLD

1 recipe Basic Molding Rice
1½ teaspoons chicken-flavored bouillon
  granules
⅛ teaspoon ground saffron
½ cup golden raisins
¼ cup diced onion
2 tablespoons butter or margarine, melted
2 tablespoons slivered almonds, toasted
Spinach leaves
Red pepper strips
Flaked coconut (optional)
Raisins (optional)
Slivered almonds, toasted (optional)
Red pepper cup (optional)

Prepare Basic Molding Rice, omitting salt and adding bouillon granules and saffron. Sauté ½ cup raisins and onion in butter. Combine hot rice, raisin mixture, and 2 tablespoons almonds, stirring well. Spoon into an oiled 4-cup mold; let stand 5 minutes. Invert onto spinach-lined platter, and garnish with red pepper strips.

Serve with coconut, raisins, and almonds, if desired. Place condiments in red pepper cup, if desired. Yield: about 6 servings.

CHILE-RICE MOLD

1 red pepper, cut into 2- x ¼-inch strips
3 tablespoons butter or margarine, melted
½ cup chopped onion
1 recipe Basic Molding Rice
1½ cups commercial sour cream
¼ teaspoon white pepper
2 (4-ounce) cans chopped green chiles,
  drained
1 cup (4 ounces) shredded Monterey Jack
  cheese, divided
Fresh parsley sprigs

Here's a side dish that will probably capture more attention than the entrée. Put Saffron Rice Mold onto leafy spinach; then sprinkle each serving with coconut and raisins. A red pepper cup holds the raisins and adds nice accent color.

Sauté red pepper in butter in a skillet until barely tender. Remove red pepper with a slotted spoon, reserving butter in skillet; set red pepper aside. Sauté onion in remaining butter.

Arrange pepper strips to radiate from bottom center of a greased 1½-quart ovenproof glass bowl. Stir hot Basic Molding Rice, sour cream, and white pepper into onion in skillet. Spoon half the rice mixture into bowl; top with half the chiles and ½ cup cheese. Repeat layers of rice and chiles. Bake at 375° for 15 minutes. Sprinkle top of mold with remaining ½ cup cheese, and bake an additional 5 minutes.

Let cool 5 minutes; invert rice mold onto serving plate, loosening sides gently with a narrow spatula, if necessary. Insert parsley sprigs in center of rice mold. Yield: 6 servings.

MOLDED GAZPACHO-RICE SALAD

1 recipe Basic Molding Rice, chilled
½ cup diced cucumber
1 medium tomato, diced
¼ cup chopped green onions
¼ cup chopped green pepper
1 clove garlic, minced
3 tablespoons olive oil
3 tablespoons tarragon vinegar
⅛ teaspoon white pepper
Lettuce leaves

Combine chilled rice, cucumber, tomato, green onions, green pepper, garlic, olive oil, tarragon vinegar, and white pepper, tossing gently. Spoon into lightly oiled individual ½-cup molds, and chill until ready to serve.

Unmold onto individual lettuce-lined salad plates. Yield: 6 servings.

SHRIMP CREOLE IN A RICE RING

2 medium tomatoes, peeled and chopped
¾ cup chopped onion
¾ cup chopped green pepper
¾ cup chopped celery
3 cloves garlic, minced
¼ cup butter or margarine, melted
¼ cup plus 2 tablespoons water
1 (8-ounce) can tomato sauce
1 (6-ounce) can tomato paste
1½ teaspoons chicken-flavored bouillon
   granules
¾ teaspoon coarsely ground pepper
¾ teaspoon dried whole oregano
¾ teaspoon dried whole basil
¼ teaspoon red pepper
⅛ teaspoon hot sauce
1½ pounds fresh shrimp, peeled
Oregano Rice Ring

Sauté vegetables and garlic in butter in a large skillet. Stir in water, tomato sauce, tomato paste, bouillon granules, pepper, oregano, basil, red pepper, and hot sauce. Bring to a boil. (Mixture will be thick.) Add shrimp; cover, reduce heat, and simmer over medium heat 5 minutes or until shrimp is done. Spoon into and around Oregano Rice Ring. Yield: about 6 servings.

Oregano Rice Ring:

2 recipes Basic Molding Rice
½ teaspoon ground oregano

Prepare Basic Molding Rice according to directions, adding ground oregano with salt. Pack hot cooked rice into an oiled 6-cup ring mold. Let stand 5 minutes. Invert onto large serving plate with sides. Yield: 6 servings.

HAM PILAF MOLD

½ cup chopped onion
½ cup chopped green pepper
2 tablespoons butter or margarine, melted
1 recipe Basic Molding Rice
1½ cups diced cooked ham
½ cup cooked English peas
1 (8-ounce) can crushed unsweetened
   pineapple, well drained
1 tablespoon soy sauce
¼ teaspoon ground allspice
¼ teaspoon pepper
Leaf lettuce

Sauté onion and green pepper in butter until tender. Combine onion mixture, hot rice, and remaining ingredients except lettuce, stirring until blended. Pack into an oiled 5-cup mold; let stand 5 minutes. Invert onto lettuce-lined serving plate. Yield: 6 servings.

COOKING LIGHT®

Fabulous Ways With High-Fiber Foods

When you hear the phrase "high-fiber foods," does wheat bran immediately come to mind? Bran, the outer layer of grains, is a good source of dietary fiber, but don't be shortchanged. A lot of other foods have a high-fiber content, and eating a variety of them makes more sense than ever before.

Fiber isn't a nutrient, but it plays a valuable role in several body functions. And fiber isn't a single substance. The various forms of fiber are similar because they pass through the digestive tract unabsorbed; however, their ability to dissolve in water differs, and this influences how they work in the body.

Insoluble fibers are found in foods such as wheat bran (also known as miller's bran or raw bran), whole grain breads and cereals, vegetables, and fruit and vegetable skins.

Foods that contain soluble fibers include dried beans and legumes, some fruits and vegetables (especially fruits), nuts, brown rice, oats, oat bran, and barley.

Both types of fibers may offer benefits to the weight conscious. The bulkiness of insoluble fibers helps fill you up without a lot of extra calories. Soluble fibers help maintain blood-sugar levels longer, and this helps avoid hunger. And because all high-fiber foods take longer to chew and eat, mealtime is prolonged. This helps promote a feeling of satisfaction and gives the stomach time to signal the brain that you are getting full before you overeat.

Scientists still don't know how much fiber we should eat. Some sources recommend that we consume an amount of 35 to 50 grams a day.

When referring to charts or books for fiber content of specific foods, be sure to use the figures for dietary fiber. Crude fiber values are less accurate, and they underestimate the amount of fiber available for use in the body by two to three times.

Cooking doesn't decrease fiber in most foods, nor does preservation by canning, freezing, or drying. But peeling fruits and vegetables and other methods of processing does. For example, an unpeeled apple has more fiber than applesauce, and apple juice has only a trace of fiber.

ALMOND-VEGETABLE STIR-FRY

1 cup thinly sliced carrots
1 cup (1-inch pieces) fresh green beans
1 tablespoon vegetable oil
1 cup thinly sliced cauliflower
½ cup sliced green onions
1 cup warm water
1 teaspoon chicken-flavored bouillon
   granules
2 teaspoons cornstarch
⅛ teaspoon garlic powder
¼ cup sliced almonds, toasted

Sauté carrots and beans in oil in a skillet for 2 minutes. Add cauliflower and green onions; cook 3 minutes. Combine water, bouillon granules, cornstarch, and garlic powder; mix well. Add liquid to vegetables, and cook about 3 minutes or until thickened. Stir in almonds. Yield: 4 servings (about 106 calories per ¾-cup serving).

Bernadine E. Moore,
Rogers, Arkansas.

VEGETARIAN SUPPER

½ cup chopped onion
2 cloves garlic, minced
1 tablespoon vegetable oil
1½ cups sliced zucchini
1 cup chopped green pepper
½ teaspoon dried whole oregano
¼ teaspoon salt
⅛ teaspoon pepper
2½ cups chopped fresh tomatoes
1 (16-ounce) can kidney beans, drained
2½ cups cooked brown rice (cooked
   without salt or fat)
½ cup (2 ounces) shredded reduced-calorie
   Cheddar cheese

Sauté onion and garlic in oil in a large skillet until onion is tender. Add zucchini, green pepper, oregano, salt, and pepper; cook 5 minutes or until vegetables are tender. Add tomatoes and beans; cover and heat thoroughly. Spoon vegetable mixture over hot rice; sprinkle with cheese. Yield: 5 servings (about 135 calories per 1-cup vegetable mixture plus about 110 calories per ½-cup rice).

Dolly G. Northcutt,
Fairfield, Alabama.

LEAFY BEAN SOUP

½ cup chopped onion
1 clove garlic, minced
1 tablespoon margarine, melted
1 (10¾-ounce) can chicken broth, undiluted
1⅓ cups water
4 cups (about ½ pound) fresh spinach, washed and coarsely chopped
1 (15-ounce) can garbanzo beans, undrained
⅛ teaspoon pepper
1¼ teaspoons grated Parmesan cheese

Sauté onion and garlic in margarine in a Dutch oven until tender. Add broth and water; simmer 10 minutes. Add spinach, beans, and pepper; cover. Simmer 5 minutes. To serve, sprinkle with Parmesan cheese. Yield: 5 cups (about 202 calories per 1-cup serving).

Doris S. Shortt,
Leesburg, Florida.

FRUITY CARROT-AND-SEED SALAD

1 pound carrots, shredded
1 (11-ounce) can mandarin oranges, drained
⅓ cup unsalted sunflower kernels, toasted
½ cup pineapple low-fat yogurt

Combine shredded carrots, oranges, and sunflower kernels in a medium bowl; chill 2 hours.

Stir yogurt into carrot mixture, and serve immediately. Yield: 7 servings (about 95 calories per ½-cup serving).

LEMONY APPLE-BRAN SALAD

2 cups unpeeled, cubed apple
½ cup seedless green grapes, halved
½ cup sliced celery
2 teaspoons finely chopped fresh parsley
½ cup lemon low-fat yogurt
6 lettuce leaves
¼ cup plus 2 tablespoons shreds of wheat bran cereal

Combine apple cubes, grape halves, celery, chopped parsley, and yogurt in a medium mixing bowl; stir well. Cover mixture, and chill 1 to 2 hours.

Place a lettuce leaf on each of 6 individual serving dishes; top with fruit mixture. Sprinkle each serving with 1 tablespoon wheat bran cereal. Yield: 6 servings (about 64 calories per ⅔-cup serving).

Marian J. Brown,
Lynchburg, Virginia.

WHOLE WHEAT CARDAMOM BREAD

2 cups whole wheat flour
1 teaspoon baking powder
½ teaspoon baking soda
½ teaspoon ground cardamom
¼ teaspoon salt
1 egg, beaten
1¼ cups low-fat buttermilk
¼ cup honey
⅓ cup margarine, melted
¼ cup chopped walnuts
¼ cup raisins
Vegetable cooking spray

Combine first 5 ingredients in a mixing bowl, and set aside.

Combine egg, buttermilk, honey, and margarine; mix well. Add buttermilk mixture to dry ingredients, stirring just until dry ingredients are moistened. Stir in chopped walnuts and raisins.

Coat the bottom only of an 8½- x 4½- x 3-inch loafpan with cooking spray. Spoon batter into loafpan; bake at 350° for 50 minutes or until a wooden pick inserted in center comes out clean. Let cool in pan 10 minutes; remove to wire rack, and cool completely. Yield: 16 slices (about 131 calories per ½-inch slice).

Mrs. H. F. Mosher,
Huntsville, Alabama.

PRUNE BAVARIAN

1 (12-ounce) package pitted prunes
2 tablespoons sugar
1 tablespoon unflavored gelatin
¼ cup water
1 cup evaporated skim milk, chilled
1 tablespoon lemon juice
2 tablespoons plus 2 teaspoons frozen whipped topping, thawed
8 lemon twists

Place prunes in a medium saucepan; cover with water. Bring to a boil; reduce heat, and simmer, uncovered, 5 to 10 minutes or until tender. Drain well, and mash. Stir in sugar, and set aside.

Sprinkle gelatin over water in a small saucepan; let stand 1 minute. Place gelatin over medium heat, stirring until gelatin dissolves. Remove from heat, and add to prune mixture.

Combine milk and lemon juice in a chilled bowl; beat at medium speed of an electric mixer until soft peaks form. Fold milk mixture into prune mixture. Spoon into individual serving dishes. Chill until firm. Garnish each serving with 1 teaspoon whipped topping and a lemon twist. Yield: 8 servings (about 149 calories per ½-cup serving).

Bake, Then Stuff The Potatoes

Consider serving stuffed potatoes when you plan meals or parties. Appetizer Caviar Potatoes offer nice variety for a party menu. And stuffed potatoes look pretty on a dinner plate and round out almost any menu. When serving beef, chicken, or seafood, choose one of our baking potatoes teamed with cheese, such as Fluffy Stuffed Potatoes. You'll enjoy our two sweet potatoes with ham or pork recipes.

APPETIZER CAVIAR POTATOES

12 small new potatoes
Vegetable oil
1 to 2 tablespoons butter or margarine, melted
⅓ cup commercial sour cream
Red caviar

Scrub potatoes thoroughly, and rub skins with oil; bake at 400° for 30 minutes or until done. Let potatoes cool to the touch.

Cut each potato in half crosswise, and carefully scoop out pulp, leaving shells intact. Combine potato pulp and melted butter; mash well.

Spoon potato mixture into shells; top potatoes with sour cream and caviar. Yield: 12 appetizer servings.

Brooks Carlson,
Memphis, Tennessee.

FLUFFY STUFFED POTATOES

6 medium baking potatoes
Vegetable oil
1 cup milk
¾ cup (6 ounces) shredded Cheddar cheese
2 tablespoons butter or margarine, melted
1 teaspoon salt
¼ teaspoon dry mustard

Scrub potatoes thoroughly, and rub skins with oil; bake at 400° for 50 to 60 minutes. Let cool to the touch.

Slice skin away from the top of each potato; carefully scoop out pulp, leaving the shells intact. Mash pulp, and stir in milk, cheese, melted butter, salt, and dry mustard.

Spoon potato mixture into shells. Bake potatoes at 400° for 10 minutes or until lightly browned. Yield: 6 servings.

Mrs. Lee Stringfield,
Cottageville, South Carolina.

BACON-STUFFED SWEET POTATOES

8 medium-size sweet potatoes (about 5 pounds)
Vegetable oil
9 slices bacon, cooked and crumbled
½ cup commercial sour cream
2 tablespoons milk
1 egg, beaten
1 teaspoon sugar
1 teaspoon salt
Paprika

Scrub potatoes thoroughly, and rub skins with oil; bake at 400° for 1 hour or until done. Let cool to the touch.

Slice skin away from top of each potato; carefully scoop out pulp, leaving shells intact. Mash pulp; add bacon and next 5 ingredients; mix well.

Spoon into shells; sprinkle with paprika. Bake at 400° for 10 minutes. Yield: 8 servings. *Ethel C. Jernegan, Savannah, Georgia.*

STUFFED SWEET POTATOES

6 medium-size sweet potatoes
Vegetable oil
¼ cup butter or margarine, softened
¼ cup sugar
1 egg
1 teaspoon grated orange rind (optional)
½ teaspoon ground allspice
¼ teaspoon salt
¼ teaspoon ground nutmeg
½ cup miniature marshmallows
⅓ cup chopped pecans

Scrub potatoes thoroughly, and rub skins with oil; bake at 400° for 1 hour or until done. Let cool to the touch.

Slice skin away from top of each potato; carefully scoop out pulp, leaving shells intact. Mash pulp; stir in butter, sugar, egg, orange rind (if desired), and seasonings. Spoon into shells. Top with marshmallows and pecans. Bake at 350° for 15 minutes or until marshmallows are golden brown. Yield: 6 servings. *Rublelene Singleton, Scotts Hill, Tennessee.*

Cook Up Some Fall Vegetables

Now is the best time of year to enjoy rutabagas, parsnips, turnips, kale, and mustard greens. Harvested during the fall and winter months in most of the South, these vegetables make hearty side dishes for cool-weather meals.

When purchasing rutabagas or turnips, look for smooth, round vegetables that are firm to the touch. Their outer skins will need to be peeled before cooking. Parsnips look like a paler version of carrots, and they should be scraped before using.

Kale and mustard greens have a slightly sharper taste than parsnips or rutabagas. Their texture is better if cooked only in the water clinging to their leaves after they are washed.

CANDIED PARSNIPS

2 cups water
2 pounds parsnips, scraped and cut into 2-inch julienne strips
½ teaspoon salt
¼ cup butter or margarine
¼ cup light corn syrup
¼ cup firmly packed brown sugar

Bring water to a boil in a skillet; add parsnips and salt. Cover and simmer 5 to 8 minutes or until the parsnips are crisp-tender. Drain and set aside.

Melt butter in skillet; stir in corn syrup, brown sugar, and parsnips. Cook over medium heat, stirring occasionally, for 5 minutes or until parsnips are glazed. Yield: 6 to 8 servings. *Mrs. R. H. Manderscheid, Houston, Texas.*

CREAMY COOKED TURNIPS

6 medium turnips, peeled and sliced
1 (8-ounce) carton commercial sour cream
1 to 2 tablespoons sugar
½ teaspoon salt
Paprika

Place turnips in a large saucepan; cover with water, and bring to a boil. Cover, reduce heat, and simmer 15 minutes or until turnips are tender. Drain and mash. Add remaining ingredients; mix well. Cook over medium heat just until thoroughly heated. Yield: 6 servings. *Mrs. Melvin Cox, Ash Grove, Missouri.*

BOILED RUTABAGAS

1 large rutabaga, peeled and cut into 1½-inch cubes (5 to 6 cups)
1 teaspoon sugar
1 teaspoon chicken-flavored bouillon granules
1 teaspoon beef-flavored bouillon granules
Dash of pepper

Combine all ingredients in a Dutch oven; add just enough water to cover rutabagas. Bring to a boil; reduce heat to medium high, and cook 10 minutes. Cover, reduce heat, and simmer 15 minutes. Yield: 4 to 6 servings. *Brenda J. Coffell, Huntsville, Alabama.*

MUSTARD GREENS AND POTATOES

¼ pound salt pork
3½ pounds mustard greens
2 cups cubed potatoes
1 cup water

Rinse salt from pork; set aside. Remove stems from mustard greens. Wash leaves thoroughly; tear into bite-size pieces. Place greens in a large Dutch oven (do not add water). Add pork; cover and cook over high heat 10 minutes or until pork is tender. Drain. Add cubed potatoes and 1 cup water; cook over medium heat 20 minutes or until potatoes are tender. Yield: 8 servings. *Mrs. Larry Doskocil, Lott, Texas.*

SCALLOPED KALE

1½ pounds fresh kale
2 tablespoons butter or margarine
2 tablespoons all-purpose flour
1 cup milk
½ teaspoon salt
3 hard-cooked eggs, chopped
1 cup (4 ounces) shredded Cheddar cheese, divided

Remove stems from kale. Wash leaves thoroughly; tear into bite-size pieces. Place kale in a Dutch oven (do not add water); cover and cook over high heat 5 minutes. Drain well.

Melt butter in a large saucepan over low heat; add flour, stirring until smooth. Cook 1 minute, stirring constantly. Gradually add milk, and cook over medium heat, stirring constantly, until thickened and bubbly. Stir in salt, chopped eggs, and kale.

Spoon half of kale mixture into a lightly greased 10- x 6- x 2-inch baking dish; sprinkle with ½ cup cheese. Top with remaining kale mixture. Bake at 400° for 10 minutes. Sprinkle with remaining cheese, and bake an additional 5 minutes. Yield: 6 servings.

Daisy Cotton,
Karnes City, Texas.

What's New With Limas?

Lima beans are especially popular in the South. Often known as butter beans, they may be simply cooked in boiling water with a little salt pork or bacon. Try them marinated, baked, or in a succotash.

Always shell lima beans just before cooking. If you can't find fresh limas, substitute frozen ones.

LIMA BEAN CASSEROLE

2 cups fresh lima beans
½ cup chopped onion
½ cup chopped green pepper
¼ cup butter or margarine, melted
1 (10¾-ounce) can cream of celery soup, undiluted
½ cup (2 ounces) shredded Cheddar cheese
⅓ cup round buttery cracker crumbs

Cook beans in boiling water 15 to 20 minutes or until tender; drain well.

Sauté onion and green pepper in butter in a small skillet until tender. Add soup and onion mixture to beans. Pour into a lightly greased 1-quart baking dish. Bake, uncovered, at 350° for 25 minutes. Combine cheese and cracker crumbs; sprinkle over beans. Bake an additional 5 minutes. Yield: 4 servings.

Libby Winstead,
Nashville, Tennessee.

MARINATED LIMAS

3 cups fresh lima beans
2 tablespoons chopped green onions
2 tablespoons chopped green pepper
⅓ cup vinegar
¼ cup sugar
¼ cup vegetable oil
1 tablespoon prepared horseradish

Cook beans in boiling water 15 to 20 minutes or until tender; drain. Combine beans, onions, and green pepper in a medium bowl.

Combine remaining ingredients in a jar; cover tightly, and shake vigorously. Pour over bean mixture; cover and marinate for several hours before serving. Yield: 6 servings.

Peggy Fowler Revels,
Woodruff, South Carolina.

SPANISH CHEESE LIMAS

2½ cups fresh lima beans
1 cup thinly sliced celery
½ cup finely chopped onion
2 tablespoons vegetable oil
3 tomatoes, peeled and chopped
2 teaspoons Worcestershire sauce
½ teaspoon salt
⅛ teaspoon pepper
Dash of red pepper
1½ cups (6 ounces) shredded American cheese, divided

Cook beans in boiling water 15 to 20 minutes or until tender; drain.

Sauté celery and onion in oil in a large skillet until onion is tender. Add tomatoes; cover, reduce heat, and simmer 10 minutes, stirring frequently. Stir in beans, Worcestershire sauce, salt, and pepper; simmer an additional 10 minutes. Spoon half of bean mixture into a lightly greased 2-quart casserole; sprinkle with half of cheese. Spoon remaining bean mixture over cheese. Bake at 350° for 20 minutes. Sprinkle with remaining cheese; bake an additional 5 minutes or until cheese melts. Yield: 6 servings. *Nancy Tucker,*
Statesville, North Carolina.

No-Fuss Salads For Fall

You don't have to delete salads from the menu just because the summer harvest is over. In fact, fall introduces new crops that provide a number of good ingredients for salads. Fresh broccoli, for instance, is the main ingredient of Curried Broccoli Salad.

Frozen vegetables make the beginning of good salads, too. We used frozen black-eyed peas and a vinegar-and-oil dressing to make Black-Eyed Pea Salad.

CURRIED BROCCOLI SALAD

1½ pounds fresh broccoli
1 cup commercial sour cream
¼ cup milk
½ teaspoon curry powder
¼ teaspoon seasoned salt
¼ teaspoon dry mustard
Dash of pepper

Trim off large leaves of broccoli. Remove tough ends of lower stalks, and wash broccoli thoroughly; cut flowerets and stems into bite-size pieces.

Steam broccoli 8 to 10 minutes or until crisp-tender; cool. Place in a serving dish.

Combine remaining ingredients in a small bowl. Pour over broccoli; toss gently to coat. Cover and chill 2 to 3 hours. Yield: 6 servings.

Cindy Wilkinson,
Sugar Grove, Virginia.

BLACK-EYED PEA SALAD

1 (16-ounce) package frozen black-eyed peas
¼ cup chopped green pepper
¼ cup chopped onion
¼ cup sliced ripe olives
3 tablespoons diced pimiento
¼ cup vegetable oil
¼ cup cider vinegar
2 tablespoons red wine vinegar
2 tablespoons water
¼ teaspoon garlic salt
1 teaspoon pepper
Dash of hot sauce

Cook black-eyed peas according to package directions; drain. Combine peas and green pepper, onion, olives, and pimiento in a medium bowl. Combine oil and remaining ingredients in a jar. Cover tightly; shake vigorously.

Pour dressing over vegetable mixture; toss gently to coat. Cover salad, and chill for 2 to 3 hours. Yield: 6 servings. *Eileen Wehling,*
Austin, Texas.

GRAPE-POPPY SEED SLAW

4 cups coarsely shredded red cabbage
2 cups shredded carrots
2 cups seedless green grapes, halved
¾ cup commercial poppy seed salad dressing

Combine cabbage, carrots, and grapes in a large bowl. Add poppy seed dressing; toss gently to coat. Yield: 8 servings. *Ellice Robinson,*
Birmingham, Alabama.

FRESH SWEET POTATO SALAD

4 cups shredded raw sweet potatoes
  (about 3 medium)
1 medium apple, unpeeled and chopped
½ cup chopped pecans
½ cup commercial sour cream
½ cup mayonnaise
1 teaspoon grated lemon rind
2 tablespoons lemon juice
2 tablespoons honey
¼ teaspoon dried whole tarragon
¼ teaspoon salt
⅛ teaspoon pepper

Combine sweet potatoes, apple, and pecans in a large bowl; stir well.

Combine remaining ingredients in a small bowl; stir well. Pour dressing over sweet potato mixture; stir well. Cover and chill. Yield: 6 to 8 servings.

Pearle E. Evans,
Myrtle Beach, South Carolina.

MICROWAVE COOKERY

Company Coming? Microwave This Menu

When you want to entertain but are on a tight schedule, quick preparation ranks as top priority.

With this in mind, we've designed a microwave menu that's ideal for a dinner party of six. The flavorful meal can be microwaved in minutes. Some of the recipes can even be done ahead.

Start by assembling Southern Praline Ice Cream Sauce the day before. The sauce can be refrigerated overnight and served cold or reheated. Marinated Italian Beans can also be made the day before. In fact, early preparation is best because the beans can marinate.

The next day, microwave Curry-Spiced Rice first. The rice can be reheated later, if needed. Also, it's convenient to peel the shrimp for Garlic-Buttered Shrimp while the rice is cooking. Chill shrimp until you're ready to proceed.

Next, prepare the tomatoes by slicing and adding their topping; then set aside. While the shrimp are cooking, finish any last-minute decorating.

In the remaining minutes, finish microwaving the tomatoes, reheat the rice, and start arranging the food on plates.

Garlic-Buttered Shrimp
Curry-Spiced Rice
Zippy Mustard Tomatoes
Marinated Italian Beans
Southern Praline Ice Cream Sauce

GARLIC-BUTTERED SHRIMP

1 cup butter or margarine
¼ cup chopped green onions
2 teaspoons minced garlic
2½ pounds medium shrimp, peeled
  and deveined
2 teaspoons white wine
1 teaspoon lemon juice
¼ teaspoon salt
⅛ teaspoon coarsely ground black
  pepper
½ teaspoon dried whole dillweed
1 teaspoon chopped fresh parsley

Combine butter, green onions, and garlic in a 2-quart casserole. Microwave at HIGH for 3 to 3½ minutes or until onions are tender. Add shrimp, wine, lemon juice, salt, and pepper, arranging shrimp around outside of dish. Cover with heavy-duty plastic wrap, and microwave at HIGH for 5 to 7½ minutes, stirring twice and rearranging shrimp around outside of dish. Stir in dillweed and parsley. Serve over Curry-Spiced Rice, if desired. Yield: 6 servings.

CURRY-SPICED RICE

¼ cup plus 2 tablespoons chopped
  onion
3 tablespoons butter or margarine
1½ cups uncooked regular rice
2 teaspoons chicken-flavored bouillon
  granules
½ teaspoon ground allspice
½ teaspoon curry powder
¼ teaspoon turmeric
3 cups hot water

Combine onion and butter in a 3-quart casserole. Cover with heavy-duty plastic wrap, and microwave at HIGH for 3 minutes. Stir in remaining ingredients; cover and microwave at HIGH for 5 minutes. Stir well. Cover and microwave at MEDIUM (50% power) for 20 minutes or until liquid is absorbed. Let rice stand 4 to 5 minutes. Yield: 6 servings.

Note: Curry-Spiced Rice can be made earlier in the day and reheated. To reheat, add 1 teaspoon water; cover and microwave at MEDIUM HIGH (70% power) for 3 to 4 minutes.

ZIPPY MUSTARD TOMATOES

3 tablespoons instant minced onion
2 tablespoons butter or margarine
2 tablespoons spicy brown mustard
¾ teaspoon Worcestershire sauce
3 large tomatoes, cored and cut in half
  crosswise
3 tablespoons butter or margarine
¾ cup fine dry breadcrumbs
1 tablespoon chopped fresh parsley
Fresh parsley sprigs (optional)

Combine onion and 2 tablespoons butter in a 1-cup glass measure. Microwave at HIGH for 1 minute. Stir in mustard and Worcestershire sauce. Spread onion mixture over cut surface of each tomato. Place tomatoes in a 12- x 8- x 2-inch baking dish.

Place 3 tablespoons butter in a small bowl. Microwave at HIGH for 50 seconds or until melted. Stir in breadcrumbs and parsley; mix well. Press breadcrumb mixture over onion mixture on each tomato. Cover tomatoes with heavy-duty plastic wrap, and microwave at HIGH for 2½ to 3 minutes or until heated. Garnish with fresh parsley, if desired. Yield: 6 servings.

MARINATED ITALIAN BEANS

1½ pounds fresh green beans
¾ cup water
1½ cups commercial Italian salad dressing
⅓ cup Chablis or other dry white wine
2 tablespoons tarragon vinegar
½ teaspoon dried whole basil
¼ teaspoon pepper
⅛ teaspoon dried whole oregano
2 cloves garlic, crushed
Pimiento strips

Wash beans; trim ends diagonally, and remove strings. Place beans in a 12- x 8- x 2-inch baking dish. Add water; cover with heavy-duty plastic wrap, and microwave at HIGH for 12 to 14 minutes, stirring after 5 minutes, or until crisp-tender. Drain well.

Combine salad dressing, wine, vinegar, basil, pepper, oregano, and garlic, stirring well. Pour marinade over beans; cover and chill 6 to 8 hours or overnight. Remove beans with a slotted spoon. Garnish with pimiento strips. Yield: 6 to 8 servings.

Tip: Add salt to taste after cooking to prevent dark spots from forming on microwaved vegetables.

SOUTHERN PRALINE ICE CREAM SAUCE

1¼ cups coarsely chopped pecans
3 tablespoons butter or margarine
¼ cup butter or margarine
1¼ cups firmly packed brown sugar
3 tablespoons all-purpose flour
¾ cup light corn syrup
1 (5-ounce) can evaporated milk

Spread pecans evenly in a 12- x 8- x 2-inch baking dish; add 3 tablespoons butter. Microwave at HIGH for 8 to 10 minutes, stirring every 4 minutes until toasted; set aside.

Place ¼ cup butter in a large glass bowl. Microwave at HIGH for 55 seconds or until butter melts. Add brown sugar and flour, stirring well. Gradually add corn syrup, stirring well. Microwave at HIGH 3 to 4 minutes, stirring every 2 minutes until mixture comes to a boil. Stir well, and microwave an additional 3 to 4 minutes. Let cool to lukewarm. Gradually stir in milk and pecans. Serve warm or cold over vanilla ice cream. Yield: 3 cups.

Note: Sauce may be refrigerated overnight and reheated the next day. To reheat, microwave at HIGH for 1-minute intervals until sauce reaches desired consistency and temperature.

Five-Minute Croutons

While you're tossing a salad, use leftover French bread to make croutons in the microwave in just 5 minutes. That's what Denise Freibert of Louisville, Kentucky, does when she wants croutons for soups and salads.

Denise simply tosses bread cubes into a mixture of butter and salad seasoning and microwaves for 5 minutes. The preblended salad seasoning mix, which can be found in 3-ounce jars in the spice section of the supermarket, makes the croutons especially easy to do. And since the salad seasoning contains paprika, it turns the croutons a deep golden color.

Whenever she has small pieces of French bread left over, Denise stores them in the freezer until she has enough to make the croutons.

Denise makes a lot of croutons and stores them in an airtight container. When company comes, the croutons are on hand for a quick salad.

MICROWAVE CROUTONS

¼ cup butter or margarine
2 teaspoons salad seasoning
4 cups (¾-inch) French bread cubes

Place butter in a 2-quart shallow baking dish. Microwave at HIGH for 55 seconds or until melted; stir in salad seasoning. Add bread cubes; stir gently to coat. Microwave at HIGH 4½ to 5 minutes, stirring 2 or 3 times; cool. (Croutons will crisp as they cool.) Store croutons in an airtight container. Yield: about 2 cups.

From Our Kitchen To Yours

When choosing microwave cookware, consider the design and the materials.

Materials

Glass is the most popular for microwaving because it doesn't warp, stain, or retain odors. It's so useful that some manufacturers are redesigning their product lines with recessed handles and grips, curved corners, and easy-to-read markings.

When cooking in glass, be sure it's labeled "ovenproof" or "microwave safe" and that the cookware has no metal trim. Do not use fine china and lead crystal in the microwave.

Plastic is one of the best materials for microwave cookware. Most types of plastic can be used, but some are suitable only for heating foods because they'll melt when food they hold reaches higher temperatures. When you're choosing plastic cookware, look for a "safe for microwave cooking" or "microwave safe" label. Usually you can use high-temperature plastics, plastic foam, boil-in-the-bag plastic, and roasting or cooking bags (without wire twists). But you should use only the thermo or high-temperature plastics when cooking foods high in sugar or fat.

Using **metal** in the microwave is one of the most confusing issues to consumers, especially since warnings against using any metal or aluminum foil came with the first microwave ovens. Metal reflects microwave energy away from food and, if used improperly, can cause a sparking, lightning-like effect (called arcing). Small amounts of foil can be used safely in some microwave ovens; check your manual.

Because foil keeps microwaves from penetrating food, using small pieces can help food cook more evenly. It's common to use it for shielding poultry wingtips and leg ends, corners of bar cookies or casseroles in square dishes. To prevent arcing, the amount of food must always be greater than the amount of foil used. Also, be sure that foil or metal is at least 1 inch away from the oven walls. Metal should never be allowed to touch metal during cooking.

Many commercial microwave food products are now being arranged on aluminum foil trays and packed in cardboard cartons. If the directions state that the food can be microcooked, follow this procedure: Remove the foil covering from the top of the tray, and bend down the raised edges. Place the tray back in the carton, and leave one end flap partially open.

Foil trays allow the food to cook only from the top and allow more even heating. Whenever using foil trays in the microwave, be sure that the tray is two-thirds to three-fourths full of food and that it is no more than ¾ inch deep. If the bottom of your microwave is metal, the foil tray should be placed on an inverted pieplate.

Pottery, stoneware, and porcelain can be used in the microwave. If you aren't sure if a dish is microwave proof, use this easy method to check: Fill a heat-resistant glass measuring cup with ½ cup cold water. Put the cup of water in the dish to be tested or on the shelf next to the dish. Microwave at HIGH for 1 minute. If the dish is not too warm to touch, it's microwave proof; if it's too hot to handle, it's not.

Shapes

Ring- or **tube-shaped** dishes are most efficient for the microwave. This shape lets microwaves penetrate food from several different angles to give faster, more even cooking than a square or rectangular dish.

Round or oval shapes do well, too; foods cook more evenly as in the ring-shaped cookware. Whatever shape you choose, keep the depth of the food uniform within a dish by selecting straight-sided containers. Dishes with sloping sides make even cooking difficult.

Depth of the utensil is important; the shallower the dish, the better. A shallow dish exposes more food surface to the microwaves. However, if you're microwaving a sauce, pudding, soup, or cake layer, deeper containers work best. To allow for expansion, use a container that's large enough to hold twice the amount you will be cooking.

Soups And Stews Boost Team Spirit

Spirits will run high when you serve your gang bowls of steaming soup or stew. These soups are ideal to take in a thermos to the game or to offer when everyone is in front of the TV.

CREOLE GUMBO

1 cup vegetable oil
1 cup all-purpose flour
3 large onions, chopped
2 green onions, chopped
2 large green peppers, chopped
2 tablespoons parsley flakes
1 tablespoon minced garlic
2 (14-ounce) cans Italian-style tomatoes, undrained and chopped
2 (10-ounce) packages frozen sliced okra, thawed
1 pound Polish sausage, sliced, cooked, and drained
1 pound crab claws
2 quarts water
4 bay leaves
2 tablespoons lemon juice
2 teaspoons dried whole thyme
1½ teaspoons pepper
1 teaspoon salt
1 teaspoon ground cloves
½ teaspoon dried whole basil
½ teaspoon ground mace
½ teaspoon ground allspice
¼ teaspoon red pepper
2 pounds medium shrimp, peeled and deveined
1 pound fresh crabmeat
1 (12-ounce) container fresh Standard oysters, undrained
Hot cooked rice
Gumbo filé (optional)

Combine oil and flour in a large Dutch oven; cook over low heat 20 to 30 minutes, stirring constantly, until roux is the color of a copper penny. Stir in onions, green peppers, parsley, and garlic; cook 10 minutes, stirring occasionally. Add tomatoes, okra, sausage, crab claws, water, bay leaves, lemon juice, and seasonings; cover, and simmer 1½ hours, stirring occasionally.

Remove and discard crab claws. Stir in shrimp, crabmeat, and oysters; simmer an additional 5 to 10 minutes. Remove and discard bay leaves. Serve gumbo over hot cooked rice, and sprinkle with filé, if desired. Yield: about 6 quarts.
Chér Haile,
Atlanta, Georgia.

SPICY BEEF STEW

1 (8-ounce) can tomato sauce
2 tablespoons vinegar
1 to 2 dried chiles, seeded and chopped
2 bay leaves
2 teaspoons salt
1 teaspoon garlic powder
¼ teaspoon ground cinnamon
¼ teaspoon ground allspice
3 pounds lean beef, cut into 1½-inch cubes
1 tablespoon shortening
2 cups water
5 medium potatoes, peeled and cut into 1½-inch pieces
4 medium carrots, cut into ½-inch slices
¼ cup all-purpose flour
½ cup cold water

Combine first 8 ingredients, mixing well. Pour over beef in a shallow container; cover and marinate 2 hours in the refrigerator.

Heat shortening in a Dutch oven over medium heat. Add beef and marinade; cook, stirring occasionally, until beef is browned. Add 2 cups water, and bring to a boil. Cover, reduce heat, and simmer 1 hour.

Add potatoes and carrots to beef mixture; simmer an additional 30 to 40 minutes or until vegetables are tender. Combine flour and ½ cup water, stirring until smooth. Gently stir flour mixture into beef mixture. Cook until stew is thickened and bubbly. Yield: 11 cups.
Mrs. Herbert W. Rutherford,
Baltimore, Maryland.

FRIDAY NIGHT CHILI

2 pounds ground beef
3 large cloves garlic, minced
2 large onions, chopped
2 (16-ounce) cans kidney beans, undrained
2 cups water
1 (16-ounce) can tomatoes, undrained and chopped
1 (8-ounce) can tomato sauce
2 tablespoons chili powder
2 teaspoons garlic salt
1 teaspoon dried whole oregano
1 teaspoon pepper
1½ teaspoons ground cumin
½ teaspoon red pepper
Hot sauce to taste
Chopped green onions (optional)
Shredded Cheddar cheese (optional)
Corn chips (optional)

Combine ground beef, garlic, and onion in a Dutch oven; cook until beef is browned, stirring to crumble. Drain well. Add beans and next 10 ingredients; reduce heat, and simmer, uncovered, 1 hour, stirring occasionally. Serve with chopped green onions, cheese, or corn chips, if desired. Yield: 2 quarts.
Linda Hawkins,
Bartlesville, Oklahoma.

CLAM BISQUE

½ cup chopped onion
3 tablespoons butter or margarine, melted
2 tablespoons all-purpose flour
3 (6½-ounce) cans minced clams, undrained
1 (8-ounce) bottle clam juice
1 cup evaporated milk
2 tablespoons tomato juice
1 to 2 tablespoons lemon juice
Chopped fresh parsley (optional)

Sauté onion in butter in a heavy saucepan. Add flour, stirring until smooth. Cook 1 minute, stirring constantly. Add clams and clam juice; cook over medium heat, stirring constantly, until mixture is bubbly. Reduce heat, and simmer 5 minutes, stirring constantly. Stir in milk and tomato juice; cook over medium heat, stirring constantly, until mixture is heated. Remove from heat; stir in lemon juice. Garnish servings with parsley, if desired. Yield: 2 quarts.
Mrs. J. L. Stringfield, Sr.,
Cottageville, South Carolina.

These Beverages Score High

Whether you're shouting from excitement or dismay, watching your team play football can certainly make you thirsty. That's why we chose this assortment of beverages to sip on while you enjoy the games this season.

SPICED SPRITZERS

5 cups rosé wine
2 (4-inch) sticks cinnamon
3 whole cloves
2½ cups gingerale, chilled
Lime slices (optional)

Combine wine and spices in a saucepan; cook over medium heat until hot. (Do not boil.) Remove from heat; cool. Cover and chill at least 4 hours.

Remove spices, and stir in gingerale just before serving. Serve over ice, and place a lime slice in each glass, if desired. Yield: 7½ cups.

Cheryl Richardson,
Fairfax Station, Virginia.

CRANBERRY COOLER

4 cups cranberry juice cocktail, chilled
1 cup grapefruit juice, chilled
¾ cup vodka
Lime slices

Mix cranberry juice, grapefruit juice, and vodka in a large pitcher; serve over ice. Garnish with lime slices on rim of glasses. Yield: 5¾ cups.

Marge Killmon,
Annandale, Virginia.

SPICY TOMATO SIPPER

1 (46-ounce) can tomato juice
½ cup water
½ cup vinegar
1 tablespoon prepared horseradish
⅛ teaspoon lemon-pepper seasoning

Combine all ingredients; chill several hours before serving. Yield: 6¾ cups.

Monica C. Foster,
Harmony, North Carolina.

ALMOND-LEMONADE TEA

4 cups strongly brewed tea
3¼ cups water
1 (6-ounce) can frozen lemonade
    concentrate, thawed and undiluted
1 cup sugar
½ to 1 teaspoon almond extract

Combine tea, water, lemonade concentrate, sugar, and almond flavoring in a large pitcher. Stir until sugar dissolves. Serve over ice. Yield: 2 quarts.

Carol Barclay,
Portland, Texas.

JOLLY TODDY

18 whole cloves
6 (4-inch) sticks cinnamon
1 (12-ounce) can frozen grape juice
    concentrate, undiluted
4½ cups water
1 cup sugar
2 teaspoons ground allspice
1 cup lemon juice

Tie cloves and cinnamon sticks in a cheesecloth bag. Combine spice bag, grape juice concentrate, water, sugar, and allspice in a saucepan; bring to a boil. Reduce heat, and simmer, uncovered, 10 minutes.

Remove mixture from heat; stir in lemon juice. Serve hot. Yield: 6½ cups.

Mrs. C. D. Hancock,
LaGrange, Georgia.

MULLED APRICOT NECTAR

1 (46-ounce) can apricot nectar
1 cup orange juice
4 (2-inch) sticks cinnamon
¼ teaspoon whole allspice
¼ teaspoon whole cloves
Cinnamon sticks (optional)
Lemon slices (optional)

Combine apricot nectar and orange juice in a Dutch oven. Tie 4 sticks cinnamon, allspice, and cloves in a cheesecloth bag; add to juice mixture, and bring to a boil. Cover, reduce heat, and simmer 20 to 25 minutes.

Discard spice bag. Serve beverage hot. Garnish each serving with a cinnamon stick and lemon slice, if desired. Yield: 6¾ cups.

Donna York,
Martinez, Georgia.

PEACHES 'N' ALMOND CREAM

2½ cups boiling water
5 almond herbal tea bags
1 (16-ounce) can sliced peaches, drained
2 teaspoons lemon juice
1 quart vanilla ice cream

Pour boiling water over tea bags; cover and let stand 5 minutes. Remove tea bags; chill tea.

Combine half of tea and half each of peaches, lemon juice, and ice cream in container of an electric blender; process until smooth. Repeat procedure with the remaining ingredients. Serve immediately. Yield: 6 cups.

Cathy Darling,
Grafton, West Virginia.

Winning Snacks For The Game

Football Saturday in the South—excitement fills the air. As friends gather at the radio, television, or stadium to boost their favorite team, be prepared with plenty of snacks.

CRACKER SNACKERS

1 (1-ounce) envelope ranch-style salad
    dressing mix
¼ teaspoon dried whole dillweed
¼ teaspoon lemon-pepper seasoning
⅛ teaspoon garlic powder
2 (11-ounce) packages oyster crackers
½ cup vegetable oil

Combine first 4 ingredients in a bowl; add crackers, tossing well. Drizzle oil over cracker mixture; stir well. Place mixture in a large paper bag; fold bag to close, and let stand 2 hours, shaking bag occasionally. Store mixture in an airtight container. Yield: 11½ cups.

Rita W. Cook,
Corpus Christi, Texas.

GRANOLA SNACK MIX

1 (16-ounce) package granola cereal with
    raisins and dates
1 (15-ounce) package hearty granola cereal
1 (8-ounce) package chopped dates
1 cup cashew nuts
1 cup carob-coated raisins
1 cup chocolate-covered peanut butter
    pieces

Combine all ingredients; store in an airtight container. Yield: 12 cups.

Joyce Whitehead,
New Ulm, Texas.

TOASTED PECANS

4 cups pecan halves
¼ cup butter or margarine, melted
1 teaspoon Angostura bitters
1 teaspoon seasoned salt

Spread pecans evenly in a 13- x 9- x 2-inch baking pan. Bake at 300° for 20 minutes.

Combine butter, Angostura bitters, and salt; pour over pecans, stirring well to coat. Bake pecans at 300° an additional 15 minutes, stirring occasionally. Spread on paper towels, and cool completely. Yield: 4 cups.

Mrs. L. D. Howell,
Hendersonville, North Carolina.

MEXICALI SNACK MIX

1½ cups roasted salted peanuts
1½ cups bite-size crispy wheat square
  cereal
1 cup salted sunflower kernels
1 cup Cornnuts
¼ cup butter or margarine, melted
2 teaspoons chili powder
¼ teaspoon ground cumin
¼ teaspoon red pepper
⅛ teaspoon garlic powder

Combine first 4 ingredients in a 15- x 10- x 1-inch jellyroll pan; stir well. Drizzle butter over peanut mixture; stir well. Sprinkle with seasonings; stir well. Bake at 350° for 20 minutes, stirring after 10 minutes. Yield: 5 cups.
Angie White,
Quitman, Texas.

ORANGE POPCORN

3 quarts freshly popped popcorn, unsalted
½ cup butter or margarine
1¼ cups sugar
⅔ cup orange juice
2 tablespoons corn syrup
1 tablespoon plus ½ teaspoon grated
  orange rind
½ teaspoon baking soda
½ teaspoon salt

Place popcorn in a lightly greased roasting pan, and set aside.
Melt butter in a large saucepan; stir in sugar, juice, and syrup. Bring to a boil; boil 5 minutes, stirring constantly. Remove from heat; stir in orange rind, baking soda, and salt.
Quickly pour mixture over popcorn, stirring evenly to coat. Bake at 250° for 1 hour, stirring every 15 minutes. Store in an airtight container. Yield: 2 quarts.

Cookies To Slice And Bake

With these recipes, fresh-baked cookies are as close as your refrigerator. That's because the dough is prepared ahead, shaped into rolls, and chilled. Then when you want crisp, fresh cookies, just slice the dough and bake.
Freezer Peanut Butter-Chocolate Chip Cookies, Orange Refrigerator Cookies, and Crème de Menthe Cookies are some of our choices—all too tempting to resist.

FREEZER PEANUT BUTTER-CHOCOLATE CHIP COOKIES

⅓ cup butter or margarine, softened
½ cup crunchy peanut butter
¾ cup firmly packed dark brown sugar
1 egg
⅓ cup milk
½ teaspoon vanilla extract
2¼ cups all-purpose flour
2 teaspoons baking powder
¼ teaspoon salt
1 cup semisweet chocolate mini-morsels

Cream butter, peanut butter, and sugar at medium speed of an electric mixer until light and fluffy. Add egg, milk, and vanilla, beating well. Combine flour, baking powder, and salt. Add to creamed mixture, mixing well. Stir in chocolate morsels. Shape dough into 2 (8-inch) logs; wrap in waxed paper, and freeze at least 8 hours.
Cut dough into ¼-inch slices; place on ungreased cookie sheets. Bake at 350° for 10 to 12 minutes. Let stand 1 minute; remove cookies to wire racks, and cool completely. Yield: about 4 dozen.
Sue T. Corhern,
Tupelo, Mississippi.

ORANGE REFRIGERATOR COOKIES

½ cup shortening
¾ cup sugar
1 egg
2 tablespoons evaporated milk
1½ tablespoons grated orange rind
1 teaspoon vanilla extract
2 cups all-purpose flour
1½ teaspoons baking powder
½ teaspoon salt
Pecan halves (about ¾ cup)

Cream shortening; gradually add sugar, beating at medium speed of an electric mixer until light and fluffy. Add egg, beating well. Add evaporated milk, orange rind, and vanilla, beating well.
Combine flour, baking powder, and salt; add to creamed mixture, mixing well. Shape dough into two 12- x 2-inch rectangles. Place pecan halves lengthwise down the center of each rectangle; fold sides of dough tightly over pecans,

forming logs. Wrap logs in waxed paper; chill at least 2 hours.
Cut dough into ¼-inch slices; place on ungreased cookie sheets. Bake at 350° for 8 to 10 minutes or until lightly browned. Cool cookies on wire racks. Yield: about 6 dozen.
Marie Harris,
Sevierville, Tennessee.

CRÈME DE MENTHE COOKIES

½ cup butter or margarine, softened
¾ cup sugar
1 egg
2 cups all-purpose flour
½ teaspoon baking soda
½ teaspoon salt
¾ teaspoon vanilla extract
21 crème de menthe wafers, halved
Sifted powdered sugar

Cream butter; gradually add ¾ cup sugar, beating well. Add egg, stirring well. Combine flour, soda, and salt; add to creamed mixture. Stir in vanilla.
Shape dough into two 8- x 1½-inch blocks. Wrap in plastic wrap, and freeze several hours or overnight.
Cut dough into ⅜-inch slices; place a crème de menthe wafer half in center of half the slices. Top with another slice of dough. Gently press edges to seal. Bake at 350° for 10 minutes or until lightly browned. Cool cookies on wire racks. Sprinkle with powdered sugar. Yield: 3½ dozen.
Mrs. Cleo Jackson,
Whispering Pines, North Carolina.

SUGAR PECAN CRISPS

¾ cup butter or margarine, softened
⅔ cup sugar
1 egg
1 teaspoon vanilla extract
¼ teaspoon salt
1¾ cups all-purpose flour
½ cup finely chopped pecans

Cream butter; gradually add sugar, beating at medium speed of an electric mixer until light and fluffy. Add egg, vanilla, and salt, beating well. Stir in flour. Cover and chill 30 minutes.
Shape dough into two 8-inch logs; roll each log in chopped pecans. Wrap logs in waxed paper; chill at least 2 hours.
Cut dough into ¼-inch slices; place on ungreased cookie sheets. Bake at 350° for 10 to 12 minutes or until lightly browned. Cool cookies on wire racks. Yield: about 4 dozen.
Mrs. Mae McClaugherty,
Marble Falls, Texas.

Chicken Is A Sure Bet Every Time

Our readers have always shared ingenious ways to use chicken, and the recipes we offer here are no exception. We think you'll enjoy every one of them. To make sure your chicken preparation is the best it can be, simply remember that you're working with a lean meat. High temperatures or overcooking will make it tough and dry.

TARRAGON CHICKEN

6 chicken breast halves, skinned
½ teaspoon salt
¼ teaspoon pepper
1 tablespoon chopped fresh tarragon or 1 teaspoon dried whole tarragon
½ cup diced onion
1 tablespoon butter or margarine, melted
1½ cups Chablis or other dry white wine
¼ cup water
⅓ cup whipping cream
2 tablespoons butter or margarine
2 tablespoons all-purpose flour
⅛ teaspoon pepper
Hot cooked rice

Place chicken in a lightly greased 12- x 8- x 2-inch baking dish; sprinkle with salt, ¼ teaspoon pepper, tarragon, and onion. Add 1 tablespoon butter, wine, and water; cover and bake at 350° for 1 hour or until chicken is tender. Remove to serving platter, and keep warm.

Pour drippings into a heavy saucepan. Bring to a boil, and cook until drippings are reduced to 1 cup; pour drippings into a small mixing bowl. Add whipping cream; mix well, and set aside.

Melt 2 tablespoons butter in a saucepan over low heat; add flour, stirring until smooth. Cook 1 minute, stirring constantly. Gradually add whipping cream mixture; cook over medium heat, stirring constantly, until the mixture is thickened and bubbly. Stir in ⅛ teaspoon pepper. Serve chicken and gravy over rice. Yield: 6 servings.
Susan Kamer Shinaberry,
Charleston, West Virginia.

Tip: When grilling chicken, place bony or rib-cage side of chicken down next to heat first. The bones act as an insulator and keep chicken from browning too fast.

CHICKEN CREOLE

¼ cup vegetable oil
¼ cup all-purpose flour
1 green pepper, chopped
1 medium onion, chopped
2 cups coarsely chopped cooked chicken
1 (28-ounce) can tomatoes, undrained and chopped
1 (2-ounce) can sliced mushrooms, drained
2 tablespoons chopped fresh parsley
2 teaspoons Worcestershire sauce
2 to 3 cloves garlic, minced
1 teaspoon soy sauce
1 teaspoon sugar
½ teaspoon pepper
¼ teaspoon salt
3 dashes of hot sauce
Hot cooked rice
Filé powder (optional)

Heat vegetable oil in a heavy skillet over high heat; stir in ¼ cup flour. Cook, stirring constantly, about 5 minutes or until mixture is the color of a copper penny.

Reduce heat; add green pepper and onion, and cook 10 to 15 minutes or until tender, stirring occasionally. Add chicken, tomatoes, mushrooms, parsley, Worcestershire sauce, garlic, soy sauce, sugar, pepper, salt, and hot sauce; cover and simmer 20 minutes. Serve creole over hot cooked rice; sprinkle with filé powder, if desired. Yield: 4 servings.
Jan Wilson Lewis,
Simpsonville, South Carolina.

CREAMED CHICKEN OVER CORNBREAD

2 tablespoons butter or margarine
2 tablespoons all-purpose flour
1½ cups milk
3 cups cubed cooked chicken
1 (10¾-ounce) can cream of mushroom soup, undiluted
1 (2-ounce) jar diced pimiento, drained
Cornbread (recipe follows)
Shredded Cheddar cheese
Chopped green onions

Melt butter in a heavy saucepan over low heat; add flour, stirring until smooth. Cook 1 minute, stirring constantly. Gradually add milk; cook over medium heat, stirring constantly, until mixture is thickened and bubbly. Stir in chicken, mushroom soup, and pimiento; cook, stirring constantly, just until thoroughly heated.

To serve, slice cornbread rectangles in half horizontally; spoon on chicken mixture, and sprinkle with cheese and green onions. Yield: 6 servings.

Cornbread:

1 cup yellow cornmeal
¾ cup all-purpose flour
2 teaspoons baking powder
1 teaspoon salt
1 cup milk
1 egg, beaten
¼ cup vegetable oil

Combine first 4 ingredients in a bowl. Combine milk, egg, and oil; add to cornmeal mixture. Stir just until dry ingredients are moistened. Spoon batter into a greased 8-inch square pan. Bake at 425° for 20 minutes or until lightly browned. Cut into 6 rectangles. Yield: 6 servings.
Mrs. Ansel L. Todd,
Royston, Georgia.

EASY CHICKEN ENCHILADAS

2 cups chopped cooked chicken
2 cups commercial sour cream
1 (10¾-ounce) can cream of chicken soup, undiluted
2 cups (8 ounces) shredded Monterey Jack cheese
2 cups (8 ounces) shredded longhorn cheese
1 (4-ounce) can chopped green chiles, drained
2 tablespoons chopped onion
⅛ teaspoon salt
¼ teaspoon pepper
10 (10-inch) flour tortillas
Vegetable oil
1 cup (4 ounces) shredded longhorn cheese

Combine first 9 ingredients; mix well. Fry tortillas, one at a time, in 2 tablespoons oil in a medium skillet 5 seconds on each side or just until tortillas are softened; add additional oil, if necessary. Drain on paper towels.

Place a heaping ½ cup of chicken mixture on each tortilla; roll up each tortilla, and place seam side down in a 13- x 9- x 2-inch baking dish.

Cover and bake at 350° for 20 minutes. Sprinkle tortillas with 1 cup longhorn cheese, and bake, uncovered, an additional 5 minutes. Serve enchiladas immediately. Yield: 5 servings.
Paula Lattimore,
Port Arthur, Texas.

CHICKEN SALAD IN CREAM PUFF BOWL

½ cup water
¼ cup butter or margarine
½ cup all-purpose flour
¼ teaspoon celery seeds
Dash of salt
2 eggs
1 cup shredded lettuce
Chicken salad (recipe follows)
Cherry tomatoes (optional)
Parsley sprig (optional)

Combine water and butter in a medium saucepan; bring to a boil. Combine flour, celery seeds, and salt; add to butter mixture, stirring vigorously over medium-high heat until mixture leaves sides of pan and forms a smooth ball. Remove pan from heat, and let mixture cool 4 to 5 minutes.

Add eggs, one at a time, beating thoroughly with a wooden spoon after each addition; then beat until dough is smooth. Spread dough evenly in a greased 9-inch pieplate, covering bottom and sides. Bake at 425° for 15 minutes; reduce heat to 325°, and bake an additional 25 minutes. Cool on a wire rack away from drafts. Carefully remove puff bowl from pieplate, and place on a serving platter, if desired.

Arrange lettuce around inside edge of puff bowl. Fill with chicken salad; garnish with cherry tomatoes and parsley, if desired. Yield: 6 servings.

Chicken Salad:

3 cups chopped cooked chicken
1 hard-cooked egg, chopped
1 cup diced celery
¼ cup sweet pickle relish
¼ cup chopped onion
1 tablespoon lemon juice
½ teaspoon seasoned salt
Dash of pepper
½ cup mayonnaise

Combine all ingredients except mayonnaise in a bowl; mix well. Stir in mayonnaise. Yield: about 4 cups.
Mrs. Kenneth B. Waldron,
Mountain Rest, South Carolina.

Tip: Fresh meat, poultry, and fish should be loosely wrapped and refrigerated; use in a few days. Loosely wrap fresh ground meat, liver, and kidneys; use in one or two days. Wieners, bacon, and sliced sandwich meats can be stored in original wrappings in the refrigerator. Store all meat in the coldest part of the refrigerator.

He's An Indoor, Outdoor Cook

In El Dorado, Arkansas, Ray Black bends over a billowing charcoal grill and slaps his special sauce on a rack of pork ribs. "I've cooked in a barrel, on a pit in the ground, on a campsite stove, a gas grill, and the very best thing for ribs is smoking them over charcoal."

Ray has been cooking outdoors for a long time, but in recent years, he has moved indoors and started cooking Chinese style, as well. One of his favorite Oriental dishes is his own version of Egg Foo Yong with shrimp.

We think you'll enjoy trying Ray's recipes, along with specialties from other Southern men who love to cook.

BARBECUED SPARERIBS

5 cloves garlic, crushed
½ cup chopped onion
½ cup butter or margarine, melted
1 (8-ounce) can tomato sauce
2 tablespoons lemon juice
1 tablespoon Pickapeppa sauce
⅛ teaspoon red pepper
3½ pounds spareribs

Cook garlic and chopped onion in butter 15 minutes. Stir in remaining ingredients except spareribs; cook 15 minutes, stirring occasionally.

Place ribs over medium coals; grill, covered, 60 to 75 minutes, basting frequently with sauce. Cut into serving-size pieces (3 to 4 ribs per person). Yield: 3 to 4 servings.
Ray Black,
El Dorado, Arkansas.

EGG FOO YONG

½ cup water
10 medium unpeeled shrimp
4 eggs, beaten
¼ cup water
Pinch of salt
1 tablespoon vegetable oil, divided
1 slice gingerroot
¼ cup plus 2 tablespoons bean sprouts, divided
¼ cup plus 2 tablespoons chopped green onions, divided
Egg Foo Yong Sauce

Bring ½ cup water to a boil; add shrimp, and cook 3 to 5 minutes. Drain well; rinse with cold water. Peel and chop shrimp.

Combine eggs, ¼ cup water, and salt. Heat 1 teaspoon oil in a large skillet. Add gingerroot; stir-fry 1 to 2 minutes. Remove gingerroot from skillet; set aside. Add 2 tablespoons bean sprouts and 2 tablespoons green onions; stir-fry 1 minute. Add 2 tablespoons shrimp to mixture; stir-fry 1 minute. Spoon ¼ cup egg mixture into skillet, shaping mixture into a 3-inch circle with a spatula. Cook until browned on one side; turn and brown other side.

Repeat procedure using reserved gingerroot and remaining bean sprouts, onions, shrimp, and egg mixture. Serve with Egg Foo Yong Sauce. Yield: 3 servings.

Egg Foo Yong Sauce:

2½ teaspoons arrowroot
2 tablespoons water
1 cup chicken broth
1 teaspoon soy sauce
1 teaspoon chopped green onions

Dissolve arrowroot in water. Combine broth and soy sauce in a saucepan. Heat until warmed; stir in arrowroot mixture. Cook over low heat until thickened, stirring constantly. Add onions, and cook until onions are heated. Yield: 1 cup.
Ray Black,
El Dorado, Arkansas.

SAUSAGE-BEEF CHILI

3 pounds ground chuck
1 pound bulk Italian sausage
1¾ cups chopped onion
1 cup chopped green pepper
¾ cup chopped celery
2 cloves garlic, minced
4 (15½-ounce) cans ranch-style beans, undrained
2 (14½-ounce) cans stewed tomatoes
1 (29-ounce) can tomato sauce
1 (12-ounce) can beer
1 (6-ounce) can tomato paste
½ cup plus 2 tablespoons chili powder
2 tablespoons taco salsa
1 hot green pepper
¼ teaspoon dried whole oregano

Combine ground chuck, sausage, onion, green pepper, celery, and garlic in a large Dutch oven; cook until beef and sausage are browned, stirring to crumble. Drain.

Add remaining ingredients to ground chuck mixture. Cover; cook over medium-low heat 1½ hours, stirring frequently. Remove hot pepper before serving. Yield: 4½ quarts. *Rod Kinney,*
Birmingham, Alabama.

BLUE CHEESE DRESSING

4 ounces blue cheese, crumbled
1 cup mayonnaise
½ cup milk
½ cup minced onion
1 teaspoon celery seeds

Combine all ingredients in a jar. Cover tightly, and shake vigorously. Chill. Shake dressing before serving. Yield: 2 cups.   *Ray M. Jackson,*
Birmingham, Alabama.

FRENCH-FRIED MUSHROOMS WITH TARTAR SAUCE

½ cup all-purpose flour
⅛ teaspoon salt
⅛ teaspoon pepper
3 eggs, beaten
1½ teaspoons vegetable oil
1½ teaspoons water
32 large fresh mushrooms
1½ cups fine dry breadcrumbs
Vegetable oil
Tartar sauce (recipe follows)

Combine flour, salt, and pepper.
Combine eggs, oil, and water, mixing well. Clean mushrooms with damp paper towels. Dredge mushrooms in flour mixture, and dip in egg mixture; roll in breadcrumbs. Refrigerate at least 1½ hours.

Deep fry mushrooms in hot oil (375°) until golden brown. Drain on paper towels. Serve mushrooms with tartar sauce. Yield: 32.

Tartar Sauce:

1½ cups mayonnaise
8 anchovy fillets, finely chopped
1 hard-cooked egg, finely chopped
2 tablespoons minced fresh parsley
2 tablespoons capers
2 teaspoons lemon juice
1 teaspoon chopped chives
1 teaspoon Dijon mustard
½ teaspoon dried whole tarragon, crushed

Combine all ingredients, stirring well. Store in refrigerator. Yield: 2 cups.
Frank A. Gault,
Whiteville, North Carolina.

Bread For Outdoor Meals

September's here, but it's still warm enough to migrate to picnic tables, quilts on the lawn, or screened-in porches. The menu is usually casual— and the bread recipes we offer are ideal for those informal settings.

OVERNIGHT ROLLS

1 package dry yeast
¼ cup warm water (105° to 115°)
2 cups water
½ cup plus 2 tablespoons sugar
½ cup shortening
2 eggs, beaten
1 tablespoon salt
6½ cups all-purpose flour, divided

Dissolve yeast in ¼ cup warm water; let stand 5 minutes.

Heat 2 cups water, sugar, and shortening in a saucepan until shortening melts. Cool to 105° to 115°. Add yeast mixture, eggs, salt, and 1 cup flour, mixing well. Gradually stir in remaining flour. (Dough will be soft.)

Place dough in a well-greased bowl, turning to grease top. Cover and let rise in a warm place (85°), free from drafts, 1 hour or until doubled in bulk.

Punch dough down. Cover and let rise in a warm place (85°), free from drafts, 1 hour or until doubled in bulk. Punch dough down; cover and refrigerate overnight.

Divide dough into fourths; divide each fourth into 9 equal pieces. Roll each piece of dough into a ball, and place balls about 2 inches apart on greased baking sheets.

Cover and let rise in a warm place (85°), free from drafts, 1½ hours or until doubled in bulk. Bake at 375° for 10 to 12 minutes or until golden brown. Yield: 3 dozen rolls.   *Meryl Warren,*
Tallahassee, Florida.

CRUSTY CHEESE BREAD

1 package dry yeast
1 tablespoon honey
½ cup warm water (105° to 115°), divided
2½ cups all-purpose flour
⅓ cup instant nonfat dry milk powder
2 tablespoons butter or margarine, melted
1 teaspoon salt
2 eggs, beaten separately
Cheese Topping

Combine yeast and honey in ¼ cup warm water, stirring well. Set aside.

Position knife blade in food processor bowl; add flour, dry milk powder, butter, and salt. Top with cover and process until well blended. Add yeast mixture and 1 egg to flour mixture; process until well blended. With the processor running, pour remaining ¼ cup warm water through the food chute in a slow, steady stream. Process until well blended. Let dough stand 1½ minutes. Place dough in a well-greased bowl, turning to grease top. Cover and let rise in a warm place (85°), free from drafts, 1 hour or until doubled in bulk.

Divide dough into 2 equal portions. Pat each portion evenly into a greased 8-inch round cakepan. Beat remaining egg; brush tops of dough with beaten egg, and sprinkle with Cheese Topping. Let rise in a warm place (85°), free from drafts, 1 hour. Bake at 375° for 18 to 20 minutes.

Remove bread from pans; let cool on wire racks. To serve, cut bread into wedges. Yield: 2 loaves.

Cheese Topping:

2 tablespoons grated Parmesan cheese
2 tablespoons finely chopped pecans
1 tablespoon sesame seeds, toasted
⅛ teaspoon ground ginger

Combine all ingredients; mix well.
Alice McNamara,
Eucha, Oklahoma.

FIERY BEER HUSH PUPPIES

1 cup regular yellow cornmeal
1 cup all-purpose flour
1 teaspoon baking powder
1 tablespoon sugar
1 teaspoon salt
2 eggs, beaten
1 cup beer
¾ cup finely chopped onion
1 to 2 tablespoons finely chopped jalapeño pepper
Vegetable oil

Combine cornmeal, flour, baking powder, sugar, and salt in a medium mixing bowl; stir well. Add eggs, beer, onion, and jalapeño pepper; stir well.

Carefully drop batter by rounded teaspoonfuls into 1-inch-deep hot oil (365°); cook only a few at a time, turning once. Fry 1 to 2 minutes or until hush puppies are golden brown. Serve immediately. Yield: 4 dozen.
Mrs. N. L. Coppedge,
Shreveport, Louisiana.

EASY GARLIC ROLLS

1 (1-pound) loaf frozen commercial bread
  dough, thawed
¼ cup unsalted butter, melted
1 egg, beaten
½ teaspoon garlic salt
1 tablespoon chopped fresh parsley

Divide dough into 20 portions; shape into balls. Combine remaining ingredients; stir well. Dip dough balls into butter mixture, and place in a lightly greased 9-inch round cakepan. Cover and let rise in a warm place (85°), free from drafts, 1 hour or until doubled in bulk. Bake at 350° for 25 to 30 minutes or until golden brown. Yield: 20 rolls.
Mrs. R. D. Walker,
Garland, Texas.

Count On Flounder Fillets

When a recipe calls for fish fillets, flounder is a good choice. This white-fleshed fish is lean (less than 5% fat), with a mild flavor that blends well with a variety of foods and seasonings.

There are a few points to look for in fresh-cut fillets to determine quality. The fish should smell fresh, with a mild seaweed scent and have firm, elastic, moist flesh. Ragged edges, white cottony patches, soft flesh, and brown spots are signs of poor quality.

SEAFOOD WITH DILL MAYONNAISE

4 flounder fillets (about 1 pound)
½ pound fresh shrimp, peeled and
  deveined
½ cup mayonnaise
½ teaspoon dried whole dillweed
¼ teaspoon salt
¼ teaspoon pepper
Juice of ½ lemon
1 teaspoon chopped fresh parsley

Arrange fillets in a greased 13- x 9- x 2-inch baking dish; top with shrimp.
Combine mayonnaise, dillweed, salt, pepper, and lemon juice; spoon over fillets. Bake at 350° for 15 minutes or until fish flakes easily when tested with a fork. Sprinkle with parsley. Yield: 3 to 4 servings. *Jennifer B. Lewis,*
Columbia, South Carolina.

STUFFED FLOUNDER FILLETS

⅓ cup chopped celery
2 tablespoons chopped onion
⅓ cup butter, melted
1 cup herb-seasoned stuffing mix
1 tablespoon chopped fresh parsley
1 teaspoon grated lemon rind
1 tablespoon lemon juice
¼ teaspoon salt
¼ teaspoon pepper
4 flounder fillets (about 1 pound)
3 tablespoons butter, melted
¾ teaspoon chopped fresh dillweed or ¼
  teaspoon dried whole dillweed
Paprika
4 lemon slices
Fresh dillweed

Sauté celery and onion in ⅓ cup melted butter in a medium-size skillet until tender. Remove from heat; stir in stuffing mix, parsley, lemon rind, lemon juice, salt, and pepper; set aside.
Cut each fillet in half. Arrange 4 halves in a lightly greased 9-inch square baking pan. Spoon one-fourth of stuffing mixture on each. Top with a fillet half. Combine 3 tablespoons butter and ¾ cup fresh dillweed; drizzle over stuffed fillets. Sprinkle with paprika. Place a lemon slice on each; bake at 350° for 25 to 30 minutes or until fish flakes easily when tested with a fork. Garnish with fresh dillweed. Yield: 4 servings. *Mrs. Joe D. Wilson,*
Pulaski, Virginia.

BAKED FLOUNDER AU FROMAGE

4 flounder fillets (about 1 pound)
4 (1-ounce) slices Muenster cheese
2 teaspoons breadcrumbs
¼ teaspoon paprika

Arrange fillets in a lightly greased 13- x 9- x 2-inch baking dish. Place a cheese slice on top of each fillet. Combine breadcrumbs and paprika; sprinkle fillets evenly with breadcrumb mixture. Bake fish at 425° for 15 minutes or until fish flakes easily when tested with a fork. Yield: 3 to 4 servings.
Florence A. Roux,
Greensboro, North Carolina.

FLOUNDER WITH HOLLANDAISE-SHRIMP SAUCE

8 flounder fillets (about 2½ pounds)
2 tablespoons lemon juice
½ teaspoon salt
¼ teaspoon white pepper
1 (⅞-ounce) package hollandaise sauce mix
1 (8-ounce) package frozen cooked small
  shrimp, thawed and drained

Arrange fillets in a lightly greased 15- x 10- x 1-inch jellyroll pan; sprinkle with lemon juice, salt, and pepper. Set fillets aside.
Prepare hollandaise sauce according to package directions. Add shrimp.
Bake fillets, uncovered, at 375° for 10 minutes. Drain off liquid. Pour hollandaise sauce over fillets, and bake an additional 5 minutes or until fish flakes easily when tested with a fork. Yield: 8 servings. *Helen S. Englander,*
Kansas City, Missouri.

FLOUNDER AMBASSADOR

4 flounder fillets (about 1 pound)
⅛ teaspoon salt
⅛ teaspoon pepper
½ cup chopped fresh parsley
2 tablespoons butter, melted
2 tablespoons lemon juice
¼ pound fresh mushrooms, sliced
1 tablespoon all-purpose flour
½ cup whipping cream
¼ cup milk
1 tablespoon Dijon mustard
2 tablespoons Parmesan cheese
1 tablespoon fine dry breadcrumbs
¼ teaspoon paprika

Arrange fillets in a lightly greased 12- x 8- x 2-inch baking dish. Sprinkle with salt, pepper, and parsley; set aside.
Combine butter and lemon juice in a skillet; add mushrooms, and sauté 2 to 3 minutes. Add flour, stirring until smooth. Gradually add whipping cream and milk; cook over medium heat, stirring constantly, until mixture is thickened and bubbly. Stir in mustard; spread sauce over fillets. Sprinkle with cheese, breadcrumbs, and paprika. Bake at 350° for 25 to 30 minutes or until fish flakes easily when tested with a fork. Yield: 4 servings.
Mary B. Quesenberry,
Dugspur, Virginia.

Tip: Rub hands with fresh parsley to remove any unpleasant odors.

Different Flours For Baking

Strolling down the grocery store aisle, you may notice different flours on the shelf. If you hesitate to try one because you're not sure how to use it, read on. The recipes we offer for bread and cake use a variety of flours.

Flours differ in their ability to yield gluten—which is produced when liquid acts on two specific proteins as a batter is mixed or a dough is kneaded. Gluten gives baked goods a porous structure and makes them lighter in texture. Wheat flours are the only ones to contain both these proteins in just the right amounts.

Cake flour, a type of wheat flour that is low in protein and gluten content, forms the soft, white, fine-textured crumb that is desirable in cakes.

All-purpose flour is usually made from a blend of hard and soft wheat. A softer blend is heavily marketed in the South because quick breads are so popular. But harder blends are generally better for yeast breads because they let breads rise more and keep them from being dense. Hard wheat absorbs more liquid than soft wheat, so that a range of flour may be called for in a bread recipe to get the right consistency in the dough.

Whole wheat flour is bulkier than all-purpose flour because the entire wheat kernel is milled. The quality and amount of gluten it yields is less than all-purpose flour. Bread made with whole wheat flour alone is coarser and more compact than bread made with a combination of whole wheat flour and all-purpose flour or bread flour. Whole wheat flour should be stored in an air-tight container in the freezer to prevent rancidity.

Rye flour used alone results in a compact, dense, but moist product. It has a distinct flavor and works well in steamed bread and sour rye bread. Because this flour yields little gluten, it performs best when combined with all-purpose flour or bread flour.

Soy flour is made from soybeans and is highly flavored. It has a high protein content, but lacks gluten-forming properties. It, too, is best used in combination with all-purpose or bread flour.

Bread flour, a wheat flour, has a high amount of gluten-yielding protein (more than all-purpose flour), which makes it great for yeast breads. It gives them a better volume, a tender quality, and a finer grain. With this type of flour, a longer kneading period may be necessary to help develop the gluten.

Unbleached flour, another type of wheat flour, is slightly higher in protein than all-purpose flour, but it doesn't give the same quality baked product. Bleaching helps the flour mature and improves dough-making properties by giving a better gluten structure. Unbleached flour used alone gives bread a relatively low volume and a fairly coarse-grained texture. It does work well in French bread. Simply storing unbleached flour for several months before using it will help it mature and improve its baking performance.

BUTTER-NUT POUND CAKE

1½ cups butter-flavored vegetable shortening
2 cups sugar
4 eggs
2½ cups sifted cake flour
½ cup self-rising flour
½ teaspoon salt
1 cup milk
1 teaspoon vanilla butter-and-nut flavoring or butter flavoring

Cream shortening; gradually add sugar, beating at medium speed of an electric mixer until light and fluffy. Add eggs, one at a time, beating after each addition.

Combine flour and salt; add to creamed mixture alternately with milk, beginning and ending with flour. Stir in flavoring.

Pour batter into a greased and floured 10-inch tube pan. Bake at 325° for 1½ hours or until a wooden pick inserted in center comes out clean. Cool in pan 10 minutes; remove from pan, and cool completely on a wire rack. Yield: one 10-inch cake.

Shirley R. Turner,
Douglasville, Georgia.

BUTTERMILK WHITE CAKE

6 egg whites
1 teaspoon cream of tartar
1 cup shortening
2 cups sugar
2¾ cups sifted cake flour
1 teaspoon baking soda
¾ teaspoon salt
1 cup buttermilk
½ teaspoon vanilla extract
½ teaspoon lemon extract
Lemon Filling
Fluffy Frosting
Lemon slices (optional)

Combine egg whites (at room temperature) and cream of tartar in a large bowl. Beat egg whites at high speed of electric mixer until stiff peaks form; set egg whites aside.

Cream shortening; gradually add sugar, beating at medium speed of an electric mixer until well blended.

Combine cake flour, soda, and salt; add to creamed mixture alternately with buttermilk, beginning and ending with flour mixture. Stir in flavorings. Fold in one-fourth of beaten egg whites; blend well. Fold in remaining egg whites.

Pour batter into 3 greased and floured 9-inch round cakepans. Bake at 350° for 25 minutes or until a wooden pick inserted in center comes out clean. Cool cake layers in pans 10 minutes; remove from pans, and cool completely on wire racks.

Spread Lemon Filling between layers; spread top and sides with Fluffy Frosting. Garnish with lemon slices, if desired. Yield: one 3-layer cake.

Lemon Filling:

1 cup water
¾ cup sugar
3 tablespoons cornstarch
Grated rind and juice of 2 lemons
2 tablespoons butter or margarine
4 egg yolks, slightly beaten

Combine all ingredients except egg yolks in a heavy saucepan; cook over medium heat, stirring constantly, until mixture comes to a boil. Boil 1 minute; remove from heat.

Stir about one-fourth of hot mixture into egg yolks; add to remaining hot mixture, stirring constantly. Return to heat and cook, stirring constantly, 1 minute. Remove from heat; let cool. Yield: 1¾ cups.

Fluffy Frosting:

2 egg whites
1 cup sugar
2 tablespoons light corn syrup
2 tablespoons cold water
Dash of salt
½ teaspoon vanilla extract
½ teaspoon lemon extract

Combine all ingredients in top of a large double boiler; beat at low speed of an electric mixer 30 seconds or just until mixture is blended.

Place over boiling water, and beat constantly at high speed about 7 minutes or until stiff peaks form; remove from heat. If necessary, beat an additional 2 minutes or until frosting is thick enough to spread. Yield: enough for one 3-layer cake. *Mrs. L. E. Pyatt, Amarillo, Texas.*

WHOLE WHEAT BUNS

½ cup golden raisins
1 cup milk, scalded
¼ cup honey
¼ cup vegetable oil
1 teaspoon salt
1 egg yolk, beaten
1 package dry yeast
1½ cups whole wheat flour
1 cup unbleached flour
1 teaspoon ground cinnamon
¼ cup salted sunflower kernels

Place raisins in a small bowl; cover with hot water, and set aside.

Combine milk, honey, oil, salt, and egg yolk in a bowl; cool to lukewarm (105° to 115°). Add yeast, and stir until dissolved.

Combine flour and cinnamon; stir well. Add to milk mixture; stir well. Place dough in a well-greased bowl, turning to grease top. Cover and let rise in a warm place (85°), free from drafts, 1½ hours or until doubled in bulk.

Drain raisins well; press dry with paper towels. Turn dough out onto a lightly floured surface; knead in raisins and sunflower kernels. Shape dough into 20 small balls; place on a greased baking sheet, and let rise in a warm place (85°), free from drafts, 45 minutes or until doubled in bulk. Bake at 400° for 8 to 10 minutes. Remove buns from pan; cool on wire racks. Yield: 20 buns.

Ella C. Stivers,
Houston, Texas.

Multi-Grain Bread is a good example of how a variety of flours work well together. Oats, cornmeal, wheat germ, and raw bran add extra nutrition to the bread.

(85°), free from drafts, 1 hour or until doubled in bulk.

Punch dough down, and divide in half; shape each half into a loaf. Place in 2 greased 8½- x 4½- x 3-inch loafpans. Cover and let rise in a warm place (85°), free from drafts, 45 minutes or until doubled in bulk. Bake at 350° for 25 minutes or until loaves sound hollow when tapped. Remove from pans, and cool on wire racks. Yield: 2 loaves.

Marilyn Westemeir,
Beggs, Oklahoma.

BUTTERMILK WHEAT BREAD

1 package dry yeast
2 tablespoons sugar
½ cup warm water (105° to 115°)
1 cup buttermilk
¼ cup vegetable oil
2 tablespoons honey
1 egg, beaten
1¾ cups whole wheat flour
1 teaspoon salt
⅛ teaspoon baking powder
2¼ to 2¾ cups bread flour

Combine yeast, sugar, and water in a large bowl; let stand 5 minutes. Add buttermilk, oil, honey, and egg; stir well. Stir whole wheat flour, salt, and baking powder into yeast mixture. Gradually stir in enough bread flour to make a soft dough.

Turn dough out onto a floured surface, and knead until smooth and elastic (about 8 to 10 minutes). Place in a well-greased bowl, turning to grease top. Cover and let rise in a warm place

MULTI-GRAIN BREAD

1 package dry yeast
2 cups warm water (105° to 115°)
½ cup all-purpose flour
¼ cup firmly packed brown sugar
2 eggs
¼ cup honey
½ cup quick-cooking oats, uncooked
½ cup plain cornmeal
¼ cup medium rye flour
¼ cup whole wheat flour
¼ cup wheat germ
2 tablespoons soy flour
2 tablespoons raw bran
1½ teaspoons salt
4 to 4½ cups all-purpose flour

Combine first 4 ingredients in a large mixing bowl, stirring well. Add eggs and honey; beat at medium speed of an electric mixer until blended.

Combine oats, cornmeal, rye flour, wheat flour, wheat germ, soy flour, raw

bran, and salt; stir well. Stir into yeast mixture. Gradually stir in enough all-purpose flour to make a soft dough. Turn dough out onto a well-floured surface, and knead until smooth and elastic (about 8 to 10 minutes). Place in a well-greased bowl, turning to grease top. Cover and let rise in a warm place (85°), free from drafts, 1 hour or until doubled in bulk.

Punch dough down; cover and let rise in a warm place (85°), free from drafts, 1 hour or until doubled in bulk. Punch dough down, and divide in half; shape each half into a loaf. Place in two well-greased 9- x 5- x 3-inch loafpans. Cover and let rise in a warm place (85°), free from drafts, 40 minutes or until doubled in bulk.

Bake at 350° for 25 minutes or until loaves sound hollow when tapped. Remove loaves from pans, and cool on wire racks. Yield: 2 loaves.

Carolyn Beyer,
Fredericksburg, Texas.

Right: *Country hams provide Southerners with good eating. This versatile meat can be used in a multitude of ways—sliced and served as an entrée, teamed with homemade biscuits, or cooked in a variety of recipes. (Information and recipes begin on page 252.)*

Page 238: *Egg-Stra Special Chicken Pie, Biscuit-Topped Chicken Pie, and Turkey Pot Pie offer three versions of an old favorite. (Recipes begin on page 264.)*

Use Cake Mixes For Convenience

Make no apologies that these cakes are made from a mix. The many choices among cake mixes now at the grocery store open up a world of opportunity for imaginative cooks. Our readers know the convenience of mixes, and they've created some delicious treats.

CHOCOLATE-CHERRY CAKE

1 (18.25-ounce) package fudge cake mix without pudding
1 (21-ounce) can cherry pie filling
2 eggs, beaten
1 teaspoon almond extract
Chocolate frosting (recipe follows)

Combine first 4 ingredients in a large bowl; stir until well blended. Pour into a greased and floured 13- x 9- x 2-inch baking pan. Bake at 350° for 40 minutes or until a wooden pick inserted in center comes out clean. Spread with frosting. Yield: one 13- x 9- x 2-inch cake.

Chocolate Frosting:

1 cup sugar
¼ cup plus 1 tablespoon butter or margarine
¼ cup milk
1 cup semisweet chocolate morsels

Combine sugar, butter, and milk in a saucepan. Bring to a boil, and cook 2 minutes, stirring constantly. Remove from heat; add chocolate morsels. Stir until mixture is smooth. Yield: frosting for 13- x 9- x 2-inch cake.

Mrs. Donald Heun,
Louisville, Kentucky.

CHOCOLATE CAKE ROYAL

3 tablespoons instant coffee powder
½ cup boiling water
1 (18.25-ounce) package devil's food cake mix without pudding
1 cup water
2 eggs
Brandy Cream Frosting

Dissolve coffee powder in ½ cup boiling water. Combine coffee, cake mix, 1 cup water, and eggs. Mix according to package directions. Pour batter into a greased and floured 13- x 9- x 2-inch baking pan. Bake at 350° for 40 minutes or until a wooden pick inserted in center comes out clean. Cool in pan 10 minutes; remove from pan to wire rack, and let cool completely.

Spread with Brandy Cream Frosting. Yield: one 13- x 9- x 2-inch cake.

Brandy Cream Frosting:

½ cup butter or margarine, softened
1 (16-ounce) package powdered sugar, sifted and divided
3 tablespoons brandy, divided
1 to 2 tablespoons whipping cream

Combine butter and 2 cups powdered sugar; add 2 tablespoons brandy, and blend well. Add remaining powdered sugar and brandy. Add whipping cream until desired consistency is reached. Yield: enough frosting for one 13- x 9- x 2-inch cake.
Cheryl Richardson,
Fairfax Station, Virginia.

STACKED PINEAPPLE UPSIDE-DOWN CAKE

¼ cup butter or margarine, melted
⅔ cup firmly packed brown sugar
1 (20-ounce) can sliced pineapple, drained
⅔ cup maraschino cherries, halved
½ cup chopped pecans
1 (18.25-ounce) package yellow cake mix without pudding
Caramel frosting (recipe follows)

Combine butter and brown sugar; spread evenly into 2 greased 9-inch round cakepans. Arrange pineapple slices, cherries, and pecans on top.

Prepare cake mix according to directions. Pour batter into pans; bake at 350° for 30 to 40 minutes or until wooden pick inserted in center comes out clean.

Remove immediately from pans, and cool completely on wire racks.

Stack layers, pineapple side up, on serving plate. Spread warm caramel frosting on sides of cake. Yield: one 2-layer cake.

Caramel Frosting:

½ cup butter or margarine
1 cup firmly packed brown sugar
3 tablespoons milk
2 cups sifted powdered sugar

Combine butter and brown sugar in a medium saucepan. Bring to a boil, stirring constantly; cook 2 minutes. Add milk; return to a boil. Remove from heat; let stand 5 minutes.

Add powdered sugar to mixture, beating until smooth. Yield: enough to frost sides of one 2-layer cake.
Mary Jo Angelo,
Birmingham, Alabama.

LEMON-PINEAPPLE CAKE

1 (18.25-ounce) package lemon or orange supreme cake mix without pudding
1 (3½-ounce) package instant coconut cream pudding mix
¾ cup vegetable oil
4 eggs
1 (12-ounce) can lemon-lime carbonated beverage
Pineapple Topping

Combine cake mix, pudding mix, and oil; beat at medium speed of an electric mixer until well blended. Add eggs, one at a time, beating after each addition. Add lemon-lime beverage; mix well. Pour batter into three greased and floured 9-inch cakepans. Bake at 350° for 35 minutes or until a wooden pick inserted in center comes out clean.

Let cake layers cool in pans 10 minutes; remove from pans, and let cool completely. Spread Pineapple Topping between layers and on top of cake. Yield: one 9-inch cake.

Note: Cake may also be baked in a greased and floured 13- x 9- x 2-inch baking pan. Bake for the same amount of time as layers for layer cake; let cool in pan completely. Spread Pineapple Topping on top of cake.

Pineapple Topping:

1 (20-ounce) can crushed pineapple, undrained
1 cup sugar
3 tablespoons cornstarch
¼ cup butter or margarine
1 (3½-ounce) can flaked coconut

Combine pineapple, sugar, and cornstarch in a small saucepan; stir well. Bring to a boil; reduce heat, and cook 1 minute, stirring frequently. Stir in butter and coconut. Yield: 3½ cups.
Gwendolyn Loveless,
Haleyville, Alabama.

STRAWBERRY MERINGUE CAKE

1 (18.25-ounce) package chocolate cake
    mix without pudding
4 egg whites
¼ teaspoon cream of tartar
1 cup sugar
1 pint fresh strawberries, sliced and
    divided
2 tablespoons sugar
1 cup whipping cream

Prepare cake mix according to package directions. Pour batter into 2 greased and floured 9-inch round cakepans. Beat egg whites (at room temperature) and cream of tartar until soft peaks form. Gradually add sugar, 1 tablespoon at a time, beating until stiff peaks form. Spread meringue over batter. Bake at 350° for 35 minutes. Cool in pans 10 minutes. Remove and cool, meringue side up, on wire racks.

Combine ½ cup strawberries and 2 tablespoons sugar in a mixing bowl; mash well. Add whipping cream; beat until soft peaks form. Place one cake layer on a serving plate; spread half of whipped cream mixture over cake layer. Arrange half of remaining sliced strawberries on top, and top with second cake layer. Repeat layer of whipped cream mixture and strawberries. Cover and chill. Yield: one 9-inch cake.
Mrs. P. J. Davis,
Drexel, North Carolina.

Light The Rum For Peaches Foster

Jerry Hadder of Knoxville made a simple substitution and came up with a great dessert idea. He used peaches instead of bananas in a favorite Bananas Foster recipe to create Peaches Foster.

PEACHES FOSTER

2 tablespoons butter or margarine
¼ cup firmly packed brown sugar
4 medium peaches, peeled and sliced
Dash of ground cinnamon
2 tablespoons rum
Vanilla ice cream

Melt butter in a medium skillet; add sugar, and cook over medium heat until bubbly. Add sliced peaches; heat 3 to 4 minutes, basting constantly with syrup. Stir in cinnamon.

Place rum in a small, long-handled pan; heat just until warm. Ignite with a long match, and pour over peaches. Serve sauce immediately over vanilla ice cream. Yield: 6 servings.

Make It Sweet And Sour

When you think of a sweet-and-sour dish, what comes to mind? If your answer is pork, chicken, or meatballs, we've got you covered in these recipes.

Sweet-and-Sour Pork makes enough to serve a crowd. A combination of water chestnuts, bean sprouts, and pineapple adds texture to the entrée.

Sweet-and-Sour Meatballs is a bit different from most recipes. Our version puts frozen brussels sprouts in the spotlight, with coriander for flavor.

SWEET-AND-SOUR CHICKEN

1 (20-ounce) can pineapple chunks,
    undrained
¼ cup vinegar
3 tablespoons soy sauce
3 tablespoons dry sherry
1 tablespoon sugar
1 tablespoon cornstarch
½ teaspoon salt
1 egg, beaten
⅓ cup water
½ cup all-purpose flour
1 pound boneless chicken breasts, cut into
    1-inch pieces
¾ cup peanut oil
1 sweet red pepper, cut into strips
1 green pepper, cut into strips
1 small onion, sliced and separated into
    rings
Hot cooked rice

Drain pineapple, reserving juice; set pineapple aside. Combine juice, vinegar, soy sauce, sherry, sugar, cornstarch, and salt, stirring until cornstarch dissolves; set aside.

Combine egg, water, and flour in a small mixing bowl; stir until smooth. Add chicken pieces to batter, stirring until well coated. Heat oil in a wok to 375°; cook half the chicken in oil until lightly browned. Drain on paper towels; set aside. Repeat with remaining chicken. Set aside.

Drain oil from wok, reserving 2 tablespoons in wok. Heat wok to 350°. Add red pepper, green pepper, and onion; stir-fry 1 to 2 minutes or until crisptender. Remove from wok; set aside.

Stir cornstarch mixture, and add to wok. Cook, stirring constantly, until smooth and thickened. Add reserved chicken, vegetables, and pineapple; stir gently, and cook until thoroughly heated. Serve over rice. Yield: 4 servings. *Teresa Garrison Sands,*
Irmo, South Carolina.

SWEET-AND-SOUR MEATBALLS

1 pound lean ground beef
1 cup soft breadcrumbs
1 egg, beaten
¼ teaspoon ground coriander
¼ teaspoon salt
¼ cup vegetable oil
1 (10-ounce) package frozen brussels
    sprouts
¼ cup chopped onion
1 tablespoon vegetable oil
1 (15½-ounce) can pineapple chunks,
    undrained
1 (8½-ounce) can sliced water chestnuts,
    drained
Sweet-and-Sour Sauce
Hot cooked rice

Combine beef, breadcrumbs, egg, coriander, and salt; stir well. Shape into 1-inch balls. Heat ¼ cup oil in wok. Fry meatballs in hot oil (325°) 10 minutes or until done. Remove from wok; drain on paper towels. Wipe wok clean.

Cook brussels sprouts according to package directions; set aside. Sauté onion in 1 tablespoon oil in wok until tender. Drain pineapple chunks, reserving ½ cup juice. Reduce heat in wok; add meatballs, brussels sprouts, water chestnuts, pineapple, and Sweet-and-Sour Sauce; stir well. Cook until thoroughly heated. Serve over rice. Yield: 4 to 6 servings.

Sweet-and-Sour Sauce:

⅓ cup sugar
⅓ cup cider vinegar
¼ cup catsup
2 tablespoons soy sauce
2 tablespoons dry sherry
2 tablespoons cornstarch
½ cup reserved pineapple juice

Combine sugar, vinegar, catsup, soy sauce, and sherry in a small saucepan. Dissolve cornstarch in reserved pineapple juice; add to sugar mixture. Bring mixture to a boil; cook 1 minute or until thickened, stirring constantly. Yield: 1¼ cups.
Mrs. James F. Crowell,
Princeton, Kentucky.

SWEET-AND-SOUR PORK

1 (3¾-pound) pork shoulder
¾ cup all-purpose flour, divided
1 tablespoon plus 1 teaspoon ground
  ginger
½ cup vegetable oil
2 (15¼-ounce) cans pineapple chunks,
  undrained
½ cup vinegar
½ cup soy sauce
½ cup sugar
1 tablespoon Worcestershire sauce
1 tablespoon salt
¾ teaspoon pepper
2 small green peppers, cut into strips
1 (16-ounce) can bean sprouts, drained
1 (8-ounce) can sliced water chestnuts,
  drained
2 tablespoons chili sauce
Hot cooked rice

Trim fat from pork, and cut meat into 1-inch cubes.

Combine ¼ cup flour and ginger; dredge pork in flour mixture. Heat oil in a large Dutch oven over medium heat; add pork, and cook until browned. Remove pork, and drain on paper towels.

Drain pineapple, reserving juice; set pineapple aside. Add enough water to pineapple juice to make 2¾ cups; gradually stir into remaining ½ cup flour. Add to Dutch oven; stir well. Add pork, vinegar, soy sauce, Worcestershire sauce, salt, and pepper. Cover, reduce heat, and simmer 1 hour or until pork is tender, stirring occasionally.

Add pineapple, green pepper, bean sprouts, water chestnuts, and chili sauce; cook 5 minutes. Serve over rice. Yield: 8 to 10 servings.

Mike Singleton,
Scotts Hill, Tennessee.

Pralines With A New Flavor Twist

Pralines may seem unique to the South, but this sinfully sweet confection originally came from France. The melted sugar-and-nut mixture first consisted of a single almond with a caramelized sugar coating. Today, pecans are the nut of choice, and the size is like that of a cookie.

In making pralines, there are two secrets to success: Use an accurate candy thermometer, and work rapidly.

PLANTATION COFFEE PRALINES

2 cups sugar
1 cup buttermilk
¼ cup water
1 tablespoon instant coffee powder
1 teaspoon baking soda
⅛ teaspoon salt
2 cups chopped pecans
2 tablespoons butter or margarine,
  softened
2 teaspoons vanilla extract

Combine first 6 ingredients in a large Dutch oven; bring to a boil, stirring constantly. Cook over medium heat, stirring constantly, until mixture reaches soft ball stage (236°). Remove from heat, and stir in remaining ingredients. Beat vigorously with a wooden spoon until mixture just begins to thicken. Working rapidly, drop by rounded tablespoonfuls onto greased waxed paper; let cool. Yield: 2 dozen.

Wake Up To A Different Breakfast

Pancakes, eggs, and grits are always good for breakfast. But with the help of our recipes, you can give these favorites new interest. You may even want to serve them for supper.

BREAKFAST WAKE-UPS

2 large ripe tomatoes
4 eggs
¼ cup (1 ounce) shredded Cheddar cheese
¼ cup soft breadcrumbs
¼ teaspoon salt
⅛ teaspoon pepper
¼ teaspoon parsley flakes
2 tablespoons butter or margarine, melted

Cut tomatoes in half, crosswise; scoop out pulp, leaving shells intact; invert to drain. Place tomatoes in an 8-inch square baking dish. Break an egg into each tomato half. Bake, uncovered, at 400° for 15 to 20 minutes or to desired degree of doneness. Combine remaining ingredients, stirring well. Spoon breadcrumb mixture evenly over top of eggs. Bake an additional 5 minutes; let stand 5 minutes before serving. Yield: 4 servings.

Sharlyn Davis,
Norfolk, Virginia.

SCRAMBLED EGG CASSEROLE

1 (6-ounce) package Canadian bacon,
  chopped
¼ cup chopped onion
¼ cup plus 2 tablespoons butter or
  margarine, melted and divided
1 dozen eggs, beaten
Cheese sauce (recipe follows)
1 (4-ounce) can sliced mushrooms, drained
1½ cups soft breadcrumbs
Paprika

Sauté Canadian bacon and onion in 3 tablespoons butter in a large skillet until onion is tender. Add eggs; cook over medium heat, stirring constantly, until set. Remove from heat; stir in cheese sauce and mushrooms. Spoon into a lightly greased 12- x 8- x 2-inch baking dish. Combine breadcrumbs and remaining 3 tablespoons butter; mix well, and sprinkle over egg mixture. Sprinkle crumbs lightly with paprika; cover and chill for at least 8 hours or overnight.

Remove from refrigerator; let stand 30 minutes. Bake, uncovered, at 350° for 30 minutes. Yield: 6 servings.

Cheese Sauce:

2 tablespoons butter or margarine
2½ tablespoons all-purpose flour
2 cups milk
1 cup (4 ounces) shredded Cheddar cheese
½ teaspoon salt
¼ teaspoon pepper

Melt butter in a heavy saucepan over low heat; add flour, stirring until smooth. Cook 1 minute, stirring constantly. Gradually add milk; cook over medium heat, stirring constantly, until thickened and bubbly. Add last 3 ingredients; stir until cheese melts. Yield: about 3 cups.

Mary Andrew,
Winston-Salem, North Carolina.

GRITS-SAUSAGE CASSEROLE

1½ cups quick-cooking grits
1 pound bulk pork sausage
1½ cups (6 ounces) shredded sharp
  Cheddar cheese
1 egg, beaten
1 to 2 tablespoons picante sauce
1 tablespoon minced dehydrated onion

Cook grits according to package directions; set aside.

Cook sausage over medium heat until browned, stirring to crumble. Drain. Combine grits, sausage, and remaining ingredients; spoon into a greased shallow 2-quart baking dish. Bake, uncovered, at 350° for 30 minutes. Yield: 8 servings.

Ava C. Tussell,
Panama City, Florida.

CHEESE GRITS

4 cups water
½ teaspoon salt
1 cup quick-cooking grits
2 cups (8 ounces) shredded Cheddar
  cheese
½ cup butter or margarine
½ cup milk
2 eggs, beaten

Bring water and salt to a boil; stir in grits. Cook grits according to package directions. Remove from heat; add cheese and butter, stirring until melted. Stir in milk.

Add a small amount of hot grits to eggs, stirring well; stir egg mixture into remaining grits. Pour grits into a lightly greased 2½-quart casserole. Bake at 350° for 40 minutes or until set. Yield: 6 to 8 servings.   *Lona B. Shealy,*
Leesville, South Carolina.

WHEAT GERM PANCAKES

1 cup all-purpose flour
½ cup sweetened wheat germ
1 tablespoon sugar
2½ teaspoons baking powder
½ teaspoon salt
1¼ cups skim milk
2 tablespoons vegetable oil
½ cup small-curd cottage cheese

Combine first 5 ingredients. Combine milk and oil; add to dry ingredients, stirring just until moistened. Stir in cottage cheese. For each pancake, pour about ¼ cup batter onto a preheated, lightly oiled griddle or skillet. Turn pancakes over when tops are covered with bubbles and edges appear slightly dry. Yield: 10 (4-inch) pancakes.
Kathy Hunt,
Dallas, Texas.

SUPPER PANCAKE

2 tablespoons butter or margarine
2 eggs, beaten
½ cup milk
½ cup all-purpose flour
½ cup (2 ounces) shredded Cheddar
  cheese
½ cup cubed cooked ham
½ cup frozen chopped broccoli, partially
  thawed

Melt butter in a 9-inch pieplate, tilting to coat. Combine eggs, milk, and flour; beat at medium speed of an electric mixer until smooth. Stir in cheese, ham, and broccoli. Pour mixture into prepared pieplate. Bake at 400° for 15 minutes. Serve immediately. Yield: 6 servings.   *Wilma H. Ferguson,*
Clinton, Mississippi.

BREAKFAST PIE

½ pound bulk pork sausage, cooked and
  drained
1 (12-ounce) carton creamed cottage
  cheese
1 cup (4 ounces) shredded Cheddar cheese
1 (3-ounce) package cream cheese,
  softened
2 eggs
1 cup biscuit mix
¼ cup chopped green onions
2 eggs, beaten
¼ cup milk
1 tablespoon sesame seeds, toasted

Combine first 5 ingredients; set aside.
Combine biscuit mix and onions in a small bowl. Combine 2 beaten eggs and milk; pour into biscuit mix. Stir only until mixture is moistened.
Spoon half of batter into a greased 9-inch pieplate. Spoon on cheese mixture. Top with remaining batter.
Sprinkle with toasted sesame seeds. Bake at 375° for 30 to 35 minutes or until knife inserted in center comes out clean. Let stand 5 minutes before cutting. Yield: 6 servings.   *Mary Pappas,*
Richmond, Virginia.

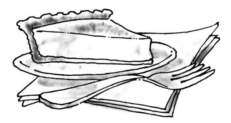

MUSHROOM-QUICHE LORRAINE

1 cup sliced fresh mushrooms
½ cup chopped onion
2 tablespoons butter or margarine, melted
4 ounces sliced Swiss cheese, cut into
  strips
Pastry (recipe follows)
4 slices bacon, cooked and crumbled
3 eggs, beaten
1 egg yolk
⅛ teaspoon pepper
1½ cups half-and-half

Sauté mushrooms and onion in butter until just tender; drain, and set aside.
Place half of cheese in partially baked pastry shell. Top with mushroom mixture and bacon; sprinkle with remaining cheese. Combine eggs, egg yolk, pepper, and half-and-half, mixing well; pour over layered ingredients. Bake at 350° for 40 minutes or until filling is set. Remove from oven, and let stand 10 minutes before serving. Yield: one 9-inch quiche.

Pastry:

1½ cups all-purpose flour
½ teaspoon salt
½ cup plus 1 tablespoon shortening
3 to 4 tablespoons cold water
1 egg white

Combine flour and salt; cut in shortening with a pastry blender until mixture resembles coarse meal. With a fork, stir in enough cold water (1 tablespoon at a time) to moisten dry ingredients. Shape dough into a ball.
Roll dough to ⅛-inch thickness on a lightly floured surface. Place in a 9-inch pieplate; trim off excess pastry around edges. Fold edges under and flute; brush with egg white. Prick bottom and sides of pastry with a fork.
Bake at 400° for 3 minutes; remove from oven, and gently prick with a fork. Bake an additional 5 minutes. Yield: one 9-inch pastry shell.
Mary Helen Hackney,
Greenville, North Carolina.

Whip Up Frozen Apricot Fluff

Frozen Apricot Fluff takes just a few minutes to mix up. It's also stored in the freezer, so that you can make it several days ahead and serve it at a moment's notice.

FROZEN APRICOT FLUFF

1 cup crisp, coarse macaroon crumbs
1 (16-ounce) can apricot halves, drained
  and chopped
1 cup sugar
1 tablespoon lemon juice
1 cup whipping cream
Sweetened whipped cream (optional)
Lemon slices (optional)
Fresh mint sprigs (optional)

Place half of macaroon crumbs in an 8-inch square baking pan; set aside.
Combine apricots, sugar, and lemon juice; mix well. Beat whipping cream until stiff peaks form; fold into apricot mixture. Pour into pan, spreading evenly; top with reserved crumbs. Cover and freeze at least 6 hours. Cut into squares to serve. Garnish each serving with a dollop of whipped cream, lemon slice, and mint sprig, if desired. Yield: 9 servings.   *Marge Killmon,*
Annandale, Virginia.

October

Feast On New Fondue

Tabletop cooking is popular because it requires just a little advance preparation, and the host can escape from the kitchen and join the party. Each person can leisurely cook his own selections.

When cooking fondue, you'll need at least one pot for every four people. The pot should be deep and made of heavy metal. It should be narrower at the top to avoid spatters when frying.

You'll need a cooker that uses canned heat or has a burner for denatured alcohol. Both fuels are available in hardware stores or drugstores. An electric fondue pot will work with this menu if the manufacturer says it's acceptable for heating oil.

Make sure the stand for the cooker is stable, because the oil you'll be cooking with will be very hot. Place a tray under the cooker to catch hot drippings. To speed the process, you might want to heat the pot of oil on the kitchen cook surface first and then transfer it to the fondue cooker.

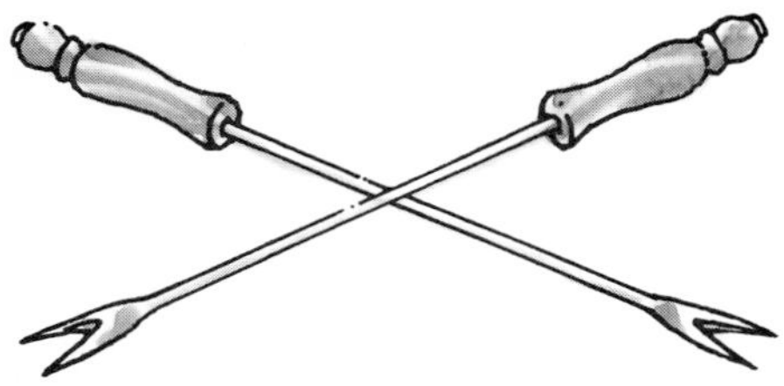

SHRIMP FONDUE
(pictured on page i)

1½ to 2 pounds large fresh shrimp
Peanut or vegetable oil

Peel shrimp, leaving tails on. Fry in hot oil (375°) for 1 minute or until done. Serve with assorted sauces. Yield: 6 to 8 servings.

WALNUT-FRIED BRIE
(pictured on page i)

1 cup walnuts, toasted and ground
½ cup dry breadcrumbs
1 egg, beaten
3 tablespoons milk
2 (8-ounce) rounds Brie cheese, chilled
⅓ cup all-purpose flour
Peanut or vegetable oil

Combine walnuts and breadcrumbs. Combine egg and milk. Slice each round of Brie into 6 or 8 wedges. Dip each wedge of cheese in egg mixture; dredge in flour. Dip wedges again in egg mixture; dredge in walnut mixture, coating cheese completely. Place on waxed paper-lined plate; chill at least 30 minutes. Fry cheese in hot oil (375°) for 1 to 2 minutes or until golden brown. Serve warm with assorted sauces. Yield: 6 to 8 servings.

BROWNED NEW POTATOES
(pictured on page i)

12 to 16 small new potatoes
Peanut or vegetable oil

Scrub potatoes; peel a strip around center of each potato. Place in a baking pan, and bake at 400° for 25 minutes or until almost done. Fry in hot oil (375°) until browned and tender. Serve with assorted sauces. Yield: 6 to 8 servings.

CLASSIC BÉARNAISE SAUCE
(pictured on page i)

4 egg yolks
1½ tablespoons lemon juice
1½ tablespoons tarragon vinegar
¼ teaspoon dried whole tarragon
⅛ teaspoon salt
⅛ teaspoon white pepper
¾ cup butter or margarine, melted
Carved red cabbage (optional)

Combine first 6 ingredients in container of an electric blender; blend until lemon colored. Add butter in a slow, steady stream, continuing to blend until thick. Pour into serving dish; cover with plastic wrap, letting wrap touch the sauce. Chill until ready to serve. Serve at room temperature. Serve in a carved red cabbage, if desired. Yield: 1⅓ cups.

HORSERADISH SOUR CREAM
(pictured on page i)

1 (8-ounce) carton commercial sour cream
¼ cup mayonnaise
2 to 2½ tablespoons prepared horseradish
⅛ teaspoon salt
¼ teaspoon white pepper
Carved red pepper (optional)
Chopped fresh parsley

Combine first 5 ingredients, stirring well. Cover and chill. Serve in a carved red pepper, if desired. Sprinkle with parsley. Yield: 1¼ cups.

HERBED GREEN SAUCE
(pictured on page i)

1 (10-ounce) package frozen spinach, thawed
½ cup coarsely chopped fresh parsley
½ teaspoon dried whole dillweed
1 clove garlic, cut in half
2 green onions, cut in 1-inch pieces
⅛ teaspoon pepper
1 cup mayonnaise
Carved acorn squash (optional)

Press spinach between paper towels to remove as much liquid as possible.

Insert metal chopping blade in food processor bowl. Combine spinach and next 5 ingredients in bowl, and process 1 minute, scraping sides of bowl occasionally. Stir mixture into mayonnaise. Serve at room temperature in a carved acorn squash, if desired. Yield: 2 cups.

Chocolate Cookies Everyone Will Love

If you have a cookie jar, fill it with these chocolate delights.

To help you make perfect chocolate cookies every time, here are some tips. First, chocolate burns easily and should never be melted over high heat. It's safer to melt chocolate in the top of a double boiler or in a heavy saucepan. To use the microwave oven, just put ½ to 1 cup semisweet chocolate morsels in a microwave-safe container, and microwave at MEDIUM (50% power) for 2½ to 3 minutes. Chocolate squares can also be melted in the microwave on MEDIUM power; they require about 1 minute per square.

Second, be careful not to drop water in melting chocolate or expose it to steam. Chocolate becomes thick and grainy when even a small amount of liquid is added during melting. (For more on chocolate, turn to page 246.)

Before baking your cookies, check to see whether the cookie sheets should be greased or ungreased. We found it's best to use shiny cookie sheets; dark sheets absorb heat, causing cookies to burn on the bottom. Arrange the cookies about 2 inches apart on the sheets unless the recipe specifies otherwise.

When making bar cookies, be sure to use the pan size called for in the recipes. If the pan is too small, the cookies may not bake through properly. If the pan is too large, they may be too dry.

BROWNIE WAFFLE COOKIES

⅓ cup shortening
1 (1-ounce) square unsweetened chocolate
1 egg, beaten
½ cup sugar
2 tablespoons milk
½ teaspoon vanilla extract
¾ cup all-purpose flour
½ teaspoon baking powder
¼ teaspoon salt
1 cup finely chopped pecans, divided

Combine shortening and chocolate in a heavy saucepan. Place over low heat, stirring constantly, until melted; cool. Combine egg, sugar, milk, and vanilla in a bowl. Stir in chocolate mixture.

Combine flour, baking powder, and salt; add to chocolate mixture. Stir in ⅔ cup pecans.

Preheat waffle iron at medium heat. Drop batter by level tablespoonfuls onto iron, spacing about 2 inches apart. Sprinkle with reserved pecans. Close iron, and bake about 3 minutes or until done. Remove cookies to wire racks to cool. Yield: 2 dozen cookies.

Madeline Gibbon,
Little Rock, Arkansas.

CHOCOLATE-MINT CHIP COOKIES

2 (1-ounce) squares unsweetened chocolate
½ cup butter or margarine, softened
1 cup sugar
2 eggs
½ teaspoon vanilla extract
2 cups all-purpose flour
1 teaspoon baking powder
⅛ teaspoon salt
6 ounces mint chips, cut into small pieces

Place chocolate in top of a double boiler; bring water to a boil. Reduce heat to low; cook until chocolate melts. Set aside to cool slightly.

Cream butter; gradually add sugar, beating at medium speed of an electric mixer. Add eggs, one at a time; beat after each addition. Stir in vanilla.

Combine flour, baking powder, and salt; add to mixture, beating well. Stir in melted chocolate; mix well. Stir in mint chips.

Drop dough by rounded teaspoonfuls onto lightly greased cookie sheets. Bake at 350° for 8 to 10 minutes. Cool slightly on cookie sheets; remove to wire racks to cool completely. Yield: 5 dozen.

Caren Bezanson,
Westminster, Maryland.

CHOCOLATE PINWHEEL COOKIES

1 (1-ounce) square unsweetened chocolate
½ cup butter or margarine, softened
¾ cup sugar
1 egg
1 teaspoon vanilla extract
1¼ cups all-purpose flour
¼ teaspoon baking powder
¼ teaspoon salt

Place chocolate in top of a double boiler; bring water to a boil. Reduce heat to low; cook until chocolate melts. Set aside to cool slightly.

Cream butter; gradually add sugar, beating at medium speed of an electric mixer until light and fluffy. Add egg and vanilla, beating well. Combine flour, baking powder, and salt; gradually add to creamed mixture, mixing well. Halve dough; stir melted chocolate into one portion. Cover and chill dough 2 hours.

Roll each portion of dough out to a 12- x 10-inch rectangle on lightly floured plastic wrap. (Dough will be soft.) Invert chocolate dough onto plain dough; peel off plastic wrap. Press chocolate dough firmly with a rolling pin; roll up jellyroll fashion starting with long side; cover. Chill 8 hours.

Cut dough with an electric knife into ¼-inch-thick slices; place on lightly greased cookie sheets. Bake at 350° for 12 to 14 minutes. Remove cookies to wire racks to cool. Yield: about 4 dozen.

Mrs. Earl L. Faulkenberry,
Lancaster, South Carolina.

CHOCOLATE CHIP COOKIES

1 cup butter or margarine, softened
⅔ cup sugar
1 cup firmly packed brown sugar
2 eggs
1 tablespoon plus 2 teaspoons water
1 teaspoon vanilla extract
2⅔ cups all-purpose flour
1½ teaspoons baking soda
1½ cups semisweet chocolate morsels
1⅓ cups chopped pecans

Cream butter; gradually add sugar, beating well at medium speed of an electric mixer. Add eggs to mixture, beating well after each addition; mix in water and vanilla.

Combine flour and soda; add to creamed mixture, mixing well. Stir in chocolate morsels and pecans. Drop dough by teaspoonfuls onto lightly greased cookie sheets. Bake at 375° for 8 to 10 minutes. Remove cookies to wire racks to cool. Yield: 8 dozen.

Zelda M. Beall,
Pineville, Louisiana.

CHOCOLATE-CRÈME DE MENTHE BARS

4 (1-ounce) squares unsweetened chocolate
1 cup butter or margarine
4 eggs
2 cups sugar
1 cup all-purpose flour
½ teaspoon salt
1 teaspoon vanilla extract
Crème de Menthe Frosting
½ cup semisweet chocolate morsels

Combine chocolate and butter in a saucepan; place over low heat, and stir until melted. Let stand 10 minutes.

Beat eggs until thick and lemon colored; gradually add sugar, beating well at medium speed of an electric mixer. Add flour, salt, and vanilla; beat at low speed of mixer 1 minute. Add chocolate mixture, and blend. Pour into a lightly greased and floured 13- x 9- x 2-inch baking pan. Bake at 350° for 25 to 30 minutes or until a wooden pick inserted in center comes out clean. Cool 10 minutes; spread Crème de Menthe Frosting on top. Chill 4 hours.

Place chocolate morsels in a small, heavy saucepan; cook over low heat, stirring constantly, until melted. Drizzle over frosting. Cut into bars immediately. Chill at least 1 hour. Store in airtight container in refrigerator. Yield: 4 dozen bars.

Crème de Menthe Frosting:

4 cups sifted powdered sugar
½ cup butter or margarine, softened
¼ cup half-and-half
¼ cup green Crème de Menthe
1 cup chopped walnuts

Combine all ingredients except walnuts in a bowl; beat at high speed of an electric mixer until smooth. Stir in nuts. Yield: frosting for 4 dozen bars.

Mary Miller,
Jackson, Mississippi.

AMARETTO BROWNIES

1 cup shortening
4 (1-ounce) squares unsweetened chocolate
2 cups sugar
4 eggs, beaten
2 tablespoons amaretto or other
   almond-flavored liqueur
1½ cups all-purpose flour
½ teaspoon salt
Amaretto Frosting
3 to 4 tablespoons sliced almonds

Combine shortening and chocolate in a heavy saucepan; place over low heat, stirring constantly, until melted. Add sugar, stirring until combined. Remove from heat, and cool. Stir in eggs and amaretto.

Combine flour and salt; add to creamed mixture, stirring well. Pour batter into a lightly greased 13- x 9- x 2-inch baking pan. Bake at 400° for 20 minutes; cool. Frost with Amaretto Frosting. Sprinkle with sliced almonds, and cut into squares. Yield: 2½ dozen.

Amaretto Frosting:

¼ cup butter or margarine
1 (1-ounce) square unsweetened chocolate
2 tablespoons half-and-half
2½ cups sifted powdered sugar
Dash of salt
2 tablespoons amaretto

Combine butter and chocolate in a heavy saucepan; place over low heat, stirring constantly, until melted. Stir in half-and-half. Add powdered sugar, salt, and amaretto, stirring until smooth. Yield: enough frosting for 2½ dozen brownies. *Gayle Nicholas Scott,*
Chesapeake, Virginia.

WHOOPIE PIES

½ cup shortening
1 cup sugar
1 egg, beaten
1 egg yolk
1 teaspoon baking soda
½ cup hot water
½ cup buttermilk
2¼ cups all-purpose flour
½ cup cocoa
½ teaspoon baking soda
¼ teaspoon salt
Fluffy Filling

Cream shortening; gradually add sugar, beating at medium speed of an electric mixer. Add beaten egg and egg yolk, beating well.

Dissolve 1 teaspoon soda in hot water; add buttermilk, and set aside. Combine flour, cocoa, ½ teaspoon soda, and salt; add to creamed mixture alternately with buttermilk mixture, beginning and ending with flour mixture. Mix until all ingredients are moistened.

Drop dough by rounded teaspoonfuls onto lightly greased cookie sheets; bake at 400° for 8 minutes. Cool slightly on cookie sheets; remove to wire racks to cool. Spread flat side of half the cookies with Fluffy Filling; top with remaining cookies, flat side down. Yield: 3 dozen.

Fluffy Filling:

1 egg white
2½ cups sifted powdered sugar
½ cup shortening
2 tablespoons all-purpose flour
1 tablespoon milk
1 teaspoon vanilla extract

Beat egg white (at room temperature) until stiff peaks form. Add remaining ingredients; beat at medium speed of electric mixer until mixture is blended. Yield: enough filling for 3 dozen pies.
Debbie C. Fadeley,
Toms Brook, Virginia.

From Our Kitchen To Yours

What tastier treats can you prepare for family or friends than chocolate desserts? Adding the finishing touch to any meal, they are rich in flavor and guaranteed to tempt.

Kinds of Chocolate

Chocolate is sold in many varieties. Our featured cookie recipes on this page and page 245 use three of the more common types—unsweetened, cocoa, and semisweet.

Unsweetened chocolate is pure chocolate liquor, the base of all chocolate, that has been cooled and molded into 1-ounce blocks. This bitter chocolate is used primarily for cooking.

Cocoa, or unsweetened chocolate powder, a highly concentrated form of chocolate, is made by removing most of the cocoa butter from the chocolate liquor. The remaining liquor is then ground into cocoa's familiar powdered form. Cocoa has the lowest fat content of chocolate products because most of the cocoa butter has been removed.

Semisweet and sweet baking chocolates are made by blending unsweetened chocolate with varying amounts of sweeteners and cocoa butter. Semisweet chocolate comes in 1-ounce squares or morsels, which are chips specially formulated to hold their shape softly when baked. Morsels labeled "chocolate-flavored" are chocolate substitutes. They are made from processed cocoa and vegetable oil rather than from unsweetened chocolate and cocoa butter.

Another type of chocolate is called **milk chocolate.** The familiar candy bar form is made by blending cocoa butter, sweeteners, milk, and flavorings with unsweetened chocolate.

What About White Chocolate?

White chocolate contains no cocoa solids; therefore, it cannot technically be called chocolate. It is a blend of vegetable fat, sugar, dry milk solids, vanilla, and cocoa butter. The small amount of cocoa butter creates a hint of chocolate fragrance, while milk and vanilla provide most of the flavor.

Storing Chocolate

The solid forms of chocolate generally stay fresh for over a year when stored in a cool, dry place at about 65° to 70°. Refrigerator temperatures are too low for the delicate product. High temperatures and moisture cause the chocolate surface to "bloom," or turn a misty-gray color.

This discoloration begins when moisture dissolves the sugar or when a temperature above 78° melts the chocolate, causing the cocoa butter to rise to the surface. Quality and flavor are not affected; only the rich brown color is dulled. Chocolate regains its original color when melted.

Cocoa is less sensitive to storage temperature and humidity. To prevent lumping and loss of color, however, store cocoa in a tightly sealed container at moderate temperature and humidity.

Chocolate Substitutions

Our recipes specify the type of chocolate we use for testing. If you need to make substitutions, here is a guide.
—For each 1-ounce square unsweetened chocolate, substitute 3 tablespoons cocoa plus 1 tablespoon shortening.
—For 1 cup (6 ounces) semisweet chocolate morsels or for 6 ounces semisweet chocolate squares, substitute 2 ounces unsweetened chocolate, ¼ cup plus 3 tablespoons sugar, and 2 tablespoons of shortening.
—For 1 (4-ounce) bar sweet baking chocolate, substitute ¼ cup cocoa, ¼ cup plus 2 teaspoons sugar, and 2 tablespoons plus 2 teaspoons shortening.

Garnishing With Chocolate

Chocolate can be grated, curled, or made into leaves that add flair to all types of desserts. When making garnishes, use dry utensils, handle the chocolate as little as possible, and refrigerate the garnishes if you do not use them immediately.

When grating chocolate, briefly chill both the grater and chocolate. Wipe the surface with a dry cloth frequently to prevent clogging. You can use any solid form of chocolate for grating.

For curls, spread melted semisweet chocolate into a 3-inch-wide strip on waxed paper; chill until chocolate feels slightly tacky. Pull a vegetable peeler slowly across length of chocolate, letting chocolate curl up on top of peeler. Chill until firm.

For leaves, spread a ⅛-inch-thick layer of melted semisweet chocolate on the underside of each leaf; chill. When firm, grasp leaf at stem end, and carefully peel it from chocolate. (For instructions and how-to photographs for making hearts, see page 26.)

Carry These Cakes Anywhere

If you plan to bake a cake for an upcoming cake walk, Halloween party, or other fall festivity, be sure to take a look at our recipes especially suited for such casual celebrations. These cakes are tasty, quick to make, and easy to transport. And because we included only lightly frosted tube and one-layer cakes, party guests can eat them from a napkin or paper plate.

GERMAN CHOCOLATE CHIP CAKE

1 (18.25-ounce) package German chocolate cake mix without pudding
1 (9.9-ounce) package coconut-pecan frosting mix
1 cup water
½ cup vegetable oil
4 eggs
1 (6-ounce) package semisweet chocolate mini-morsels
Sifted powdered sugar (optional)

Combine first 5 ingredients in a large mixing bowl; beat at low speed of an electric mixer 4 minutes. Stir in chocolate morsels; spoon into a greased and floured 10-inch Bundt pan. Bake at 350° for 1 hour and 5 to 10 minutes or until a wooden pick inserted in center comes out clean.

Cool in pan 10 minutes; remove from pan, and let cool completely on a wire rack. Sprinkle with powdered sugar, if desired. Yield: one 10-inch cake.

Linda Keith,
Dallas, Texas.

PEAR CAKE WITH CARAMEL DRIZZLE

3 eggs, beaten
1¾ cups sugar
1 cup vegetable oil
1 tablespoon vanilla extract
1½ cups all-purpose flour
1 cup whole wheat flour
2 teaspoons baking powder
1 teaspoon baking soda
1 teaspoon ground allspice
3 cups peeled, chopped pears (about 4 medium)
1 cup chopped pecans
Caramel Drizzle

Combine eggs, sugar, and oil in a large bowl; beat at medium speed of an electric mixer. Add vanilla.

Combine flour, baking powder, soda, and allspice; add to sugar mixture alternately with pears. Stir in pecans. Spoon into a well-greased and floured Bundt pan. Bake at 375° for 55 minutes or until a wooden pick inserted in center comes out clean.

Cool cake in pan 10 minutes; remove from pan, and let cool completely on a wire rack.

Spoon Caramel Drizzle over cake. Yield: one 10-inch cake.

Caramel Drizzle:

¼ cup butter
¼ cup firmly packed dark brown sugar
2 tablespoons milk
1 cup sifted powdered sugar
½ teaspoon vanilla extract
Pinch of salt

Melt butter, and cook over medium heat until light brown, stirring constantly. Add brown sugar, and cook until sugar melts. Remove from heat; add milk, stirring constantly. Slowly add powdered sugar, vanilla, and salt, beating at medium speed of an electric mixer. Beat until mixture reaches glaze consistency. Yield: about 1⅓ cups.

Gloria Pedersen,
Brandon, Mississippi.

BANANA-BLUEBERRY CAKE

3 cups all-purpose flour
2½ cups sugar
1 teaspoon baking soda
¼ teaspoon salt
3 eggs, beaten
1 cup vegetable oil
½ cup buttermilk
1½ teaspoons vanilla extract
2 cups mashed banana
1 cup chopped pecans
1 cup canned blueberries, drained

Combine first 4 ingredients in a large bowl. Combine eggs, oil, and buttermilk in a small bowl; add to dry ingredients, stirring until dry ingredients are moistened. Do not beat. Add vanilla, banana, and pecans; stir well. Gently stir in blueberries.

Spoon batter into a greased and floured 10-inch tube pan. Bake at 350° for 1 hour and 30 to 35 minutes or until a wooden pick inserted in center comes out clean. Cool in pan 10 minutes; remove cake from pan, and cool completely. Yield: one 10-inch cake.

Mrs. Joe M. Campbell,
Spartanburg, South Carolina.

COFFEE SNACK CAKE

¼ cup butter or margarine, softened
1 cup firmly packed brown sugar
1 egg
1½ cups all-purpose flour
½ teaspoon baking soda
1½ teaspoons baking powder
½ teaspoon ground cinnamon
1 cup hot strong coffee
½ cup raisins
1 cup sifted powdered sugar
1 tablespoon hot strong coffee
1 teaspoon vanilla extract

Cream butter; gradually add brown sugar, beating at medium speed of an electric mixer until light and fluffy. Add egg, beating well.

Combine flour, soda, baking powder, and cinnamon; add to creamed mixture alternately with 1 cup coffee, beginning and ending with flour mixture. Mix well after each addition; stir in raisins.

Pour batter into a greased and floured 13- x 9- x 2-inch baking pan. Bake at 350° for 20 to 25 minutes or until a wooden pick inserted in center comes out clean.

Combine powdered sugar, 1 tablespoon coffee, and vanilla; mix well. Drizzle over warm cake; cool before cutting. Yield: 15 servings.

Jodie McCoy,
Tulsa, Oklahoma.

APPLESAUCE-SPICE SQUARES

¼ cup butter or margarine, softened
⅔ cup firmly packed brown sugar
1 egg
1 cup all-purpose flour
1 teaspoon baking soda
½ teaspoon salt
1 teaspoon pumpkin pie spice
1 cup applesauce
½ cup raisins
Browned Butter Frosting

Cream butter; gradually add sugar, beating at medium speed of an electric mixer. Add egg, beating well.

Combine flour, soda, salt, and pumpkin pie spice; add to creamed mixture alternately with applesauce, beginning and ending with flour mixture. Mix just until blended after each addition. Stir in raisins.

Spoon batter into a greased and floured 8-inch square pan; bake at 350° for 25 minutes or until a wooden pick inserted in center comes out clean. Remove from oven; cool. Spread with Browned Butter Frosting. Cut in squares to serve. Yield: 9 servings.

Browned Butter Frosting:

3 tablespoons butter or margarine
1½ cups sifted powdered sugar
1 to 2 tablespoons milk
1 teaspoon vanilla extract

Melt butter in a saucepan over medium heat; cook, stirring constantly, until golden brown. Remove from heat; transfer to bowl. Add remaining ingredients; beat until smooth. Yield: enough for one 8-inch cake layer.

Shari Murphy,
Herndon, Virginia.

New Flavor Toppings

After you've tried the variety of syrups and sauces available at the grocery store, treat yourself to flavor changes. These two recipes will give new flavor to your breakfasts.

ANISE SUGAR SYRUP

2 cups firmly packed dark brown sugar
1 cup water
¼ cup dry sherry
2 tablespoons corn syrup
1 teaspoon anise seeds

Combine all ingredients in a heavy saucepan; bring to a boil. Cook, uncovered, 10 minutes. Strain. Serve at room temperature over waffles or pancakes. Yield: 2 cups.   *Mrs. Bruce Fowler,*
Woodruff, South Carolina.

BLUEBERRY SAUCE

1 (16-ounce) package frozen blueberries, thawed
½ cup water
1 tablespoon plus 1 teaspoon cornstarch
3 tablespoons sugar
1 tablespoon lemon juice

Drain blueberries; reserving juice. Combine juice, water, cornstarch, and sugar in a medium saucepan. Cook about 5 minutes over low heat, stirring occasionally, until thick and bubbly. Add blueberries; cover and cook 5 minutes. Stir in lemon juice. Serve over pancakes, waffles, or French toast. Yield: 2½ cups.   *Beth R. McClain,*
Grand Prairie, Texas.

COOKING LIGHT®

Poultry Fits Any Diet

The days when poultry was reserved for the Sunday dinner table are past. Now an abundant supply of this high-protein, low-fat, and low-cholesterol food makes it a mainstay for many people, especially those concerned about their weight and health.

Much of the fat in poultry is concentrated in or right under the skin. Calories in a chicken breast are cut by 26% and in a drumstick by 31% when the skin is removed. A sharp pair of kitchen or poultry shears makes the task easy.

Fresh poultry in the grocery store has passed rigorous food safety inspections, so take the proper precautions to keep it safe at home. Use fresh poultry within two days after purchase, or freeze it. To freeze, remove the poultry from its original packaging, and wrap it in a moisture/vapor-proof material. Frozen poultry will keep its quality for up to one year. For safety's sake, it is always best to thaw frozen poultry in the refrigerator. Allow 1 to 1½ days for a 4-pound bird to thaw in the refrigerator.

CHICKEN LA FRANCE

4 chicken breast halves (about 2 pounds), skinned and boned
1 tablespoon vegetable oil
2¼ cups fresh sliced mushrooms
⅓ cup chopped shallots
2 tablespoons capers, drained
2 tablespoons chopped fresh parsley
¼ to ½ teaspoon dried whole tarragon
½ cup Chablis or other dry white wine
2 tablespoons no-salt-added Dijon mustard
⅛ teaspoon pepper

Place each piece of chicken between 2 sheets of plastic wrap, and flatten to ¼-inch thickness using a meat mallet or rolling pin. Set aside.

Heat oil in a large skillet; sauté mushrooms and shallots in oil 3 to 4 minutes. Add capers, parsley, and tarragon, stirring well. Add chicken to mixture, and cook over medium heat 1 to 2 minutes on each side.

Combine wine, mustard, and pepper, stirring well; pour over chicken. Simmer, uncovered, 5 to 6 minutes, turning chicken once. Yield: 4 servings (about 229 calories per chicken breast half with vegetables).   *Dian L. Andree,*
Jacksonville, Alabama.

SPINACH-STUFFED CHICKEN ROLLS

6 chicken breast halves, skinned and boned
⅓ cup uncooked brown rice
1 (10-ounce) package frozen chopped spinach
Vegetable cooking spray
⅓ cup diced onion
1 teaspoon Worcestershire sauce
¼ teaspoon salt
¼ teaspoon pepper
¼ teaspoon dried whole rosemary, crushed
¼ teaspoon dried whole marjoram
2 tablespoons grated Parmesan cheese
Lemon-Chive Sauce
Steamed shredded carrots (optional)

Place each piece of chicken between 2 sheets of plastic wrap, and flatten to

¼-inch thickness, using a meat mallet or rolling pin; set aside.

Cook rice according to package directions, omitting salt and fat; set aside.

Cook spinach according to package directions, omitting salt. Drain well, pressing between layers of paper towels; set aside.

Coat a skillet with cooking spray; place over medium-high heat until hot. Add onion, and sauté until tender. Remove from heat; stir in rice, spinach, Worcestershire sauce, salt, pepper, rosemary, marjoram, and cheese.

Spread about one-third cup mixture over each chicken breast; roll up, starting with short side. Place seam side down in a 12- x 8- x 2-inch baking dish; cover and bake at 350° for 15 minutes. Uncover and bake an additional 15 to 20 minutes, basting occasionally with Lemon-Chive Sauce.

To serve, slice chicken rolls crosswise, and drizzle with remaining Lemon-Chive Sauce. Garnish with steamed shredded carrots, if desired. Yield: 6 servings (about 209 calories per chicken roll with sauce).

Lemon-Chive Sauce:

1⅓ cups canned chicken broth
1½ tablespoons cornstarch
⅛ teaspoon pepper
2 to 3 tablespoons lemon juice
2 tablespoons chopped chives

Combine chicken broth and cornstarch in a small saucepan; stir well. Cook over medium heat, stirring constantly, until smooth and thickened. Remove from heat; stir in pepper, lemon juice, and chives. Yield: 1¼ cups.

STIR-FRY CHICKEN AND VEGETABLES

1 egg white
1 tablespoon Chablis or other dry white wine
1 tablespoon cornstarch
¼ teaspoon salt
1 pound boneless chicken breasts, skinned and cut into bite-size pieces
¼ cup vegetable oil
¼ cup reduced-sodium soy sauce
1 cup thinly sliced carrots
½ cup sliced green onions
1 clove garlic, crushed
1 small green pepper, thinly sliced
1 cup thinly sliced zucchini
1 cup thinly sliced mushrooms
⅓ cup slivered almonds, toasted
2½ cups hot cooked brown rice (cooked without salt or fat)

Combine first 4 ingredients; stir well. Add chicken pieces, tossing gently to coat; let stand 1 hour.

Heat oil in a large skillet. Remove chicken from marinade; sauté chicken in oil until lightly browned. Add soy sauce and carrots, stirring well. Cook an additional 2 minutes. Add green onions, garlic, and green pepper; stir-fry an additional 2 to 3 minutes. Add zucchini, mushrooms, and almonds; cook 2 to 3 minutes. Serve over hot rice. Yield: 5 servings (about 299 calories per 1¼ cups chicken mixture plus 110 calories per ½ cup rice).
Priscilla Evans,
Albertville, Alabama.

HERB-BAKED CHICKEN FINGERS

1½ teaspoons chicken-flavored bouillon granules
½ teaspoon dry mustard
½ cup boiling water
1 clove garlic, minced
2 teaspoons Worcestershire sauce
1 teaspoon dried whole oregano
½ teaspoon paprika
2 or 3 dashes of hot sauce
2 pounds boneless chicken breasts, skinned and cut into 30 strips
Paprika (optional)

Dissolve chicken bouillon granules and mustard in boiling water; add garlic and next 4 ingredients, and stir well.

Place chicken strips in a 1½-quart casserole. Pour herb mixture over chicken. Bake, uncovered, at 350° for 30 to 35 minutes or until chicken is tender; drain. Sprinkle with additional paprika, if desired. Yield: 5 servings (about 214 calories per 6 chicken fingers).
Bunnie George,
Birmingham, Alabama.

CHUTNEY CHICKEN

1 (3½-pound) broiler-fryer, cut up and skinned
3 medium-size red apples, unpeeled
1 medium onion, thinly sliced
1½ cups unsweetened apple juice
3 tablespoons lemon juice
1 tablespoon apple pie spice
1 teaspoon white pepper
2 tablespoons chopped crystallized ginger
¼ cup dry-roasted salted peanuts
⅓ cup raisins
1 tablespoon reduced-calorie margarine
3 (3-inch) sticks cinnamon
1 tablespoon cornstarch
Apple-Cinnamon Rice
Parsley (optional)

Place chicken in an ungreased 13- x 9- x 2-inch baking dish. Core apples, and cut into ½-inch slices. Arrange apple and onion slices over chicken.

Combine apple juice and lemon juice; pour over chicken. Sprinkle with spices, peanuts, and raisins; dot with margarine, and top with cinnamon sticks. Cover and bake at 350° for 1 hour or until done, basting occasionally with cooking juices.

Skim fat from cooking juices, using a basting bulb; reserve 1 cup cooking juices. Cool slightly, and place in a small saucepan; stir in cornstarch. Bring to a boil over medium heat, stirring constantly. Cook 1 minute.

To serve, place Apple-Cinnamon Rice in middle of serving platter; arrange chicken around ring, top with sauce, and garnish with parsley, if desired. Yield: 6 servings (about 157 calories per 1/6 of chicken mixture with sauce plus 127 calories per ½ cup rice).

Apple-Cinnamon Rice:

¾ cup unsweetened apple juice
¾ cup water
1 cup uncooked long-grain regular rice
1 (3-inch) stick cinnamon

Combine apple juice and water in a medium saucepan; bring to a boil. Add rice and cinnamon stick. Cover, reduce heat, and simmer 20 minutes or until liquid is absorbed. Yield: 3 cups.
Elizabeth M. Haney,
Dublin, Virginia.

SKILLET CHICKEN DINNER

Vegetable cooking spray
8 chicken drumsticks, skinned
1 pound sweet potatoes, peeled and cut into ¾-inch slices
8 pearl onions
⅓ cup chopped celery leaves
1 bay leaf
1 cup unsweetened pineapple juice
1 medium-size green pepper, cut into strips
2 cups frozen English peas

Coat a large skillet with cooking spray; place over medium heat until hot. Brown chicken on all sides. Add sweet potatoes and next 4 ingredients; bring to a boil. Cover, reduce heat, and simmer 20 minutes. Add green pepper and English peas; cover and cook 8 minutes or until crisp-tender. Remove bay leaf. Yield: 4 servings (about 358 calories per 2 drumsticks and 1 cup vegetables).
Janice Denning,
Garland, Texas.

ORANGE-GLAZED GRILLED CORNISH HENS

2 (1¼-pound) Cornish hens
½ cup reduced-sugar orange marmalade
1 tablespoon bold and spicy mustard
¼ teaspoon ground ginger
1 tablespoon salt-free herb-and-spice steak sauce

Rinse hens with cold water; remove skin and fat, and split hens lengthwise, using poultry shears.

Combine remaining ingredients in a small saucepan; cook over low heat until thoroughly heated.

Cook hens, bone side up, 6 inches from hot coals on covered grill 20 minutes. Baste hens with warm glaze, and turn over. Grill an additional 15 minutes or until done, basting occasionally. Yield: 4 servings (about 183 calories per ½ hen).

Add Fruit To Coleslaw

The coming of fall means a new crop of cabbage, and there's no better way to serve it than in coleslaw. But why not try a new recipe for coleslaw? Our recipes take a different twist because they all contain fruit.

PARTY PEACH SLAW

8 cups coarsely shredded cabbage
1 (29-ounce) can peach slices, drained
½ cup diced onion
1 tablespoon sugar
2 teaspoons prepared mustard
½ teaspoon salt
½ cup vegetable oil, divided
¼ cup vinegar
1 tablespoon chopped fresh parsley
1 teaspoon celery seeds

Combine cabbage, peaches, and onion in a large bowl; cover and chill.

Combine sugar, mustard, and salt in a small bowl. Add ¼ cup oil; beat at medium speed of an electric mixer until blended. Add vinegar alternately with remaining ¼ cup oil; beat well. Stir in parsley and celery seeds. Chill 1 hour.

Pour dressing over cabbage mixture, tossing gently to coat. Yield: 10 servings. *Sara A. McCullough, Broaddus, Texas.*

THREE-FRUIT COLESLAW

1 small cabbage, shredded
1 small carrot, shredded
1 (8-ounce) can pineapple tidbits, drained
¼ cup raisins
¼ cup flaked coconut
⅓ to ½ cup mayonnaise

Combine first 5 ingredients in a large bowl; cover and chill.

Stir in mayonnaise just before serving. Yield: 6 to 8 servings.
Janet Tuohy, Stuart, Florida.

COLORFUL PINEAPPLE SLAW

4 cups shredded cabbage
1 (8-ounce) can pineapple tidbits, drained
1 cup (4 ounces) shredded Cheddar cheese
½ cup sliced pimiento-stuffed olives
⅓ cup diced pimiento, drained
¼ cup diced onion
¼ cup mayonnaise
1 tablespoon lemon juice
⅛ teaspoon pepper
¼ cup whipping cream, whipped

Combine first 6 ingredients in a large mixing bowl; chill at least 1 hour.

Just before serving, combine mayonnaise, lemon juice, and pepper; stir well. Fold in whipped cream. Pour over slaw; toss gently to coat. Yield: 6 to 8 servings. *Cyndi Copenhauer, Virginia Beach, Virginia.*

PEANUTTY-PEAR SLAW

2 cups shredded cabbage
1 (8-ounce) can pear halves, drained and diced
3 tablespoons salted peanuts
¼ teaspoon celery salt
2 tablespoons vinegar
⅓ cup commercial sour cream

Combine first 5 ingredients in a medium bowl. Stir in sour cream; mix well. Cover and chill 1 hour. Yield: 3 to 4 servings. *Dora S. Hancock, Pottsboro, Texas.*

BANANA-NUT SLAW

4 cups finely shredded cabbage
¼ cup shredded carrots
½ cup mayonnaise
1 teaspoon sugar
¼ teaspoon celery salt
⅛ teaspoon ground white pepper
1½ teaspoons milk
1 tablespoon vinegar
3 tablespoons salted peanuts
1 medium banana, sliced

Combine cabbage and carrots in a medium bowl; stir well. Combine mayonnaise and next 5 ingredients in a small bowl; add to cabbage mixture, stirring well. Cover and chill 2 hours.

Add peanuts and banana; toss gently to mix. Serve immediately. Yield: 6 servings. *Jean Voan, Shepherd, Texas.*

MICROWAVE COOKERY

Here's A Shortcut To Toasting Nuts

Toasting pecans, peanuts, walnuts, and almonds until lightly browned gives a robust flavor to recipes. If you're used to following the oven method, you'll notice that microwave-toasted nuts don't brown as much as those prepared conventionally. Use your nose rather than your eyes as a guide to toasting nuts. The nuts will give off a toasted aroma. You'll know they're ready then.

Remember to stir every couple of minutes, and let stand for a few minutes after microwaving. The nuts will actually cook further while standing. Taste a sample after the nuts stand, and microwave 1 or 2 additional minutes if you desire a more toasted flavor.

When the recipe calls for chopped nuts, for best results, chop them before microwaving. Also combine nuts and butter before microwaving to give them a deeper golden color, a little more flavor, and a crisp texture. All of the nuts we mention here can be toasted without butter, but you may want to add it.

Although times for toasting will vary with microwave wattages, use the following methods for peanuts, pecans, walnuts, and almonds.

■ **Peanuts:** Spread 2 cups peanuts on a glass pizza plate or pieplate. Dot with butter or margarine. Microwave at

HIGH for 7 minutes for a light roast or 8 minutes for a regular roast, stirring every 2 minutes. Let peanuts stand 3 to 5 minutes.

■ **Pecans and Walnuts:** Spread 1½ cups nuts on a glass pizza plate or pieplate. Microwave at HIGH for 5 to 6 minutes, stirring at 2-minute intervals.

■ **Almonds:** Spread ¼ cup almonds on a glass pieplate. Microwave at HIGH for 3 minutes, stirring once.

VEGETABLE-FILLED FISH ROLLS

¼ cup sliced almonds
3 tablespoons butter or margarine, divided
¾ cup frozen English peas, thawed
¼ cup chopped fresh mushrooms
2 tablespoons chopped onion
1 pound flounder fillets
½ teaspoon salt
½ teaspoon dried whole tarragon, crushed
2 teaspoons cornstarch
½ teaspoon chicken-flavored bouillon granules
½ cup milk
1 teaspoon chopped fresh parsley

Combine almonds and 2 tablespoons butter in a glass pieplate. Microwave at HIGH for 3 to 3½ minutes or until lightly toasted, stirring once. Drain and set aside.

Combine English peas, mushrooms, onion, and remaining 1 tablespoon butter in a microwave-safe bowl. Microwave at HIGH for 2 to 2½ minutes or until onion is tender. Stir in 2 tablespoons reserved almonds.

Cut fish lengthwise into 2-inch-wide strips. Sprinkle one side of each strip with salt and tarragon. Curl each piece loosely with seasoned side inward, leaving a 1½-inch hole in center of each fish roll; secure with wooden picks.

Arrange fish rolls around outside edge of an 8-inch glass pieplate; spoon vegetable-almond mixture into center of fish rolls. Cover dish with waxed paper; microwave at HIGH for 4 to 4½ minutes or until fish flakes easily when tested with a fork, giving dish a half-turn after 2 minutes.

Carefully remove wooden picks, and transfer fish to serving platter.

Combine cornstarch, bouillon granules, and milk in a 4-cup glass measure; microwave at HIGH for 2½ minutes or until mixture thickens, stirring once. Stir in parsley and remaining 2 tablespoons almonds and spoon over fish rolls. Yield: 4 servings.

JULIENNE VEGETABLES WITH WALNUTS

1 (3-ounce) package walnuts, coarsely chopped
½ pound carrots, cut into 3-inch julienne strips
¼ cup water
⅛ teaspoon salt
2 medium zucchini, cut into 3-inch julienne strips
1½ tablespoons butter or margarine
2 teaspoons chopped fresh parsley
¼ teaspoon ground nutmeg

Spread walnuts in a glass pieplate. Microwave at HIGH for 4 to 5 minutes or until toasted, stirring every 2 minutes. Set walnuts aside.

Combine carrots, water, and salt in a 2-quart casserole. Cover tightly with heavy-duty plastic wrap. Microwave at HIGH for 4 minutes. Add zucchini, mixing well. Cover and microwave at HIGH for 3 to 4 minutes. Let stand, covered, for 3 minutes.

Place butter in a 1-cup glass measure; microwave at HIGH for 40 seconds or until butter is melted. Stir in parsley and nutmeg.

Drain vegetables; pour butter mixture over vegetables, tossing to coat. Stir in walnuts. Yield: 4 to 6 servings.

PECAN-COCONUT CLUSTERS

1½ cups pecan pieces
8 ounces dark almond bark
1 cup flaked coconut

Spread pecans on a large glass pizza plate or pieplate. Microwave at HIGH for 5 to 6 minutes or until lightly toasted, stirring at 2-minute intervals. Set aside.

Place almond bark in a 2-quart microwave-safe bowl. Microwave at MEDIUM (50% power) for 3 to 4 minutes or until melted. Stir until smooth. Cool 2 minutes.

Stir in coconut and reserved pecans. Drop by rounded teaspoonfuls onto waxed paper. Let cool completely. Yield: about 4 dozen.

PEANUT DESSERT SAUCE

1 cup coarsely chopped raw peanuts
¼ cup butter or margarine
1¼ cups firmly packed light brown sugar
¾ cup light corn syrup
3 tablespoons all-purpose flour
1 (5-ounce) can evaporated milk

Spread peanuts on a large glass pizza plate or pieplate. Microwave at HIGH for 7 minutes or until nuts are lightly toasted, stirring at 2-minute intervals. Let stand 5 minutes, stirring every minute. Set aside.

Place butter in a 1-quart microwave-safe glass dish. Microwave at HIGH for 55 seconds or until melted. Add sugar, corn syrup, and flour; stirring well. Microwave at HIGH for 3 to 4 minutes or until mixture is very hot, stirring after 2 minutes. Gradually stir in milk; add reserved peanuts; mix well. Serve warm over ice cream. Yield: about 2¼ cups.

Reach For Convenience In A Can

There's a lot to be said for canned vegetables. Not only are they handy to keep on the pantry shelf, but they also allow you to enjoy a wider variety of vegetables year-round. And regardless of what you may have heard, canned vegetables are nutritious, too.

The canning process does account for some vitamin and mineral loss. But some of these water-soluble nutrients are recovered when the canning liquid is used in the recipe.

DRESSED-UP PICKLED BEANS

1 (16-ounce) can whole green beans, drained
½ cup olive oil
3 tablespoons garlic-flavored vinegar
1 tablespoon diced pimiento, drained
1 tablespoon pickle relish
1 tablespoon capers, drained
1 tablespoon chopped chives
¼ teaspoon freshly ground pepper
Pinch of salt
Pinch of sugar
Pinch of paprika
Pinch of crushed red pepper

Place beans in a small shallow dish, and set aside.

Combine remaining ingredients in a jar; cover tightly, and shake vigorously. Pour over beans; cover and chill 8 hours. Yield: 4 to 6 servings.

Daisy Cook,
Tyler, Texas.

BARBECUED GREEN BEANS

5 slices bacon
⅓ cup chopped onion
2 (15-ounce) cans cut green beans, drained
⅓ cup commercial barbecue sauce
3 tablespoons catsup
1 small clove garlic, minced
Pinch of pepper

Cook bacon in a large skillet until crisp; remove bacon, reserving 1 tablespoon drippings in skillet. Crumble bacon, and set aside. Sauté onion in drippings until tender. Stir in bacon and remaining ingredients; cook over medium heat until thoroughly heated. Yield: 6 servings.   *Janet Queen, Arlington, Texas.*

DEVILED BEETS

1 (16-ounce) can whole beets, undrained and diced
2 tablespoons butter or margarine
2 tablespoons prepared mustard
2 tablespoons honey
1 teaspoon Worcestershire sauce

Heat beets and beet liquid in a saucepan over low heat; drain well. Add remaining ingredients; cook over low heat, stirring until thoroughly heated. Yield: 4 servings.   *Kitty Cromer, Anderson, South Carolina.*

ASPARAGUS MOUSSE SALAD

1 (15-ounce) can green asparagus, undrained
1 envelope unflavored gelatin
½ cup mayonnaise
½ teaspoon seasoned salt
¼ cup lemon juice
¼ cup slivered almonds
½ cup whipping cream, whipped
Lettuce leaves (optional)

Drain asparagus; set asparagus aside. Heat liquid in a small saucepan; add gelatin, stirring to dissolve. Let mixture cool. Cut asparagus into ¼-inch pieces, and set aside.

Combine mayonnaise and next 3 ingredients; stir well. Add asparagus, and fold into whipped cream.

Spoon into lightly oiled individual molds; chill until firm. Unmold salad onto lettuce leaves, if desired. Yield: 6 to 8 servings.   *Mrs. Farmer L. Burns, New Orleans, Louisiana.*

CREOLE BLACK-EYED PEAS

4 slices bacon
1 cup chopped onion
1 cup chopped green pepper
1 cup chopped celery
1 (14½-ounce) can tomatoes, drained and chopped
1 (16-ounce) can black-eyed peas, drained
2 to 3 teaspoons sugar
1 bay leaf

Cook bacon in a large skillet until crisp; remove bacon, reserving drippings in skillet. Crumble bacon, and set aside.

Sauté onion, green pepper, and celery in drippings until tender. Stir in remaining ingredients, and cook over low heat 10 to 15 minutes, stirring occasionally. Remove bay leaf, and sprinkle peas with crumbled bacon. Yield: 6 servings.   *Thelma Jordan, Port Arthur, Texas.*

Cookin' Country Ham

Country ham (pictured on page 237) has long been a favorite food in the South. Fortunately, there are a number of commercial producers, with Smithfield, Virginia, the most famous.

Buying a Country Ham

Most producers sell whole cooked country hams as well as the uncooked version. In grocery stores almost everywhere you can purchase vacuum-packed slices ready for frying.

But if you still want to prepare the ham from start to finish, here are a few guidelines. First, decide on the size ham you need. Count on 64 slices from a 10-pound ham, and 10 slices for every additional pound. The 64 slices will make 25 servings if the ham is the only meat, 38 servings if you serve an additional entrée, or about 250 ham biscuits. The cost is about $30 to $50 a ham.

Preparing Country Ham

Many are coated with mold. Scrub or cut off the mold as soon as the ham is received. Rinse ham with a mixture of equal parts of vinegar and water. Hang it in a cool place to store; if mold reoccurs, repeat process. The ham will continue to age; the cooler the storage place, the less it will age.

Country hams will always taste salty. Soaking in water for 24 hours will remove some salt and add moisture back to the cured ham. Salt-conscious people should soak hams up to 72 hours, changing the water daily.

To carve, start from the shank end, and cut a V-shaped chunk a few inches from the end. Use a sharp knife to shave thin slices at a 45-degree angle.

Storing Cooked Country Ham

Once country ham is cooked, it should be wrapped tightly in brown paper or aluminum foil and refrigerated. Never use plastic wrap because it holds in moisture and speeds spoilage. Even uncooked slices should be refrigerated. Cooked cured ham will keep in the refrigerator up to six weeks.

Country ham can be frozen, although the flavor is not as good afterward. It should be frozen no longer than three months. To freeze, package slices of ham together, and wrap in freezer paper or heavy-duty foil.

Using the Leftovers

Every part of a ham serves a purpose. (See sketch below.) The skin, fat, and shank and butt ends are seasonings for turnip and mustard greens. The bone is used to make broth.

Even small bits of ham can be used. Vonnie Edwards, of Surry, Virginia, suggests stirring them into scrambled eggs, omelets, quiches, rice, potato salad, macaroni, cheese balls, and tossed salad. For appetizers, she wraps small leftover slices around bite-size pieces of cheese, fresh fruit, or fruit pickles.

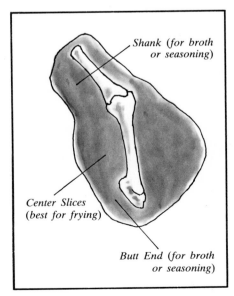

Shank (for broth or seasoning)

Center Slices (best for frying)

Butt End (for broth or seasoning)

■ Wallace Edwards, ham producer in Surry, Virginia, says his family developed this method of cooking country ham with an oven-cooking bag for moister results. In another recipe, members of the Edwards family use leftover ham in their favorite oyster-and-ham combo.

EDWARDS' ROASTED COUNTRY HAM

1 (10- to 14-pound) uncooked country ham
1 tablespoon all-purpose flour
1 quart water
Whole cloves
1 cup soft breadcrumbs
1 cup firmly packed brown sugar

Place ham in a large container, cover with water, and let soak 24 hours. Pour off water. Scrub ham with a stiff brush, and rinse well.

Place flour in a large oven-cooking bag; shake vigorously to dust inside of bag. Place bag on a 15- x 10- x 1-inch jellyroll pan. Place ham in bag; add water. Close bag with ovenproof bag tie. Make six ½-inch slits in top of bag. Insert meat thermometer through bag into ham, making sure it does not touch bone. Bake at 325° for 2½ to 3½ hours or until meat thermometer registers 142° (about 15 minutes per pound).

Remove ham from oven; slit bag down center, and remove ham. Discard bag and drippings; return ham to pan. Trim skin from ham, leaving an even layer of fat. Score fat in a diamond pattern, and stud with cloves. Combine breadcrumbs and brown sugar in a small bowl; stir well.

Press brown sugar mixture firmly over ham; bake at 425° for 10 to 15 minutes or until lightly browned and crusty. Yield: 25 to 35 servings.

EDWARDS' OYSTERS AND HAM

1 (10-ounce) package frozen patty shells
1 teaspoon chicken-flavored bouillon granules
½ cup boiling water
1 (12.5-ounce) container fresh oysters, undrained
3 tablespoons butter or margarine
3 tablespoons all-purpose flour
1 cup whipping cream
½ teaspoon lemon juice
¼ teaspoon Worcestershire sauce
⅛ teaspoon onion salt
⅛ teaspoon dry mustard
2 tablespoons butter or margarine
⅔ cup diced cooked country ham
Coarsely ground pepper
Chopped parsley

Bake patty shells according to package directions; remove centers, and discard. Set shells aside.

Dissolve bouillon granules in boiling water; set aside. Drain oysters, reserving liquid; set aside.

Melt 3 tablespoons butter in a heavy saucepan over low heat; add flour, stirring until smooth. Cook about 1 minute, stirring constantly.

Gradually add bouillon, oyster liquid, and whipping cream; cook over medium heat, stirring constantly, until mixture is thickened and bubbly. Stir in lemon juice, Worcestershire sauce, onion salt, and dry mustard. Remove mixture from heat; cover and set aside.

Melt 2 tablespoons butter in a heavy skillet; add oysters. Cook over medium heat, stirring constantly, until edges begin to curl; drain.

Add oysters and ham to sauce; cook over medium heat, stirring constantly, just until thoroughly heated. Spoon over patty shells. Sprinkle with ground pepper and parsley. Yield: 6 servings.

■ A brown sugar-crusted Smithfield ham is standard fare in many Virginia homes for Thanksgiving and Christmas dinners. But tradition calls for serving the ham with another meat, such as turkey, according to Jim Groves of V. W. Joyner's, the oldest commercial ham company in Smithfield, Virginia. Jim shares his ham recipe below.

SMITHFIELD HAM WITH BROWN SUGAR GLAZE

1 (12- to 14-pound) uncooked Smithfield ham
Whole cloves
2 cups firmly packed brown sugar

Place ham in a large container, cover with water, and let soak 24 hours. Pour off water. Scrub ham in warm water with a stiff brush, and rinse well.

Drain ham; place in a large cooking container, and cover with water. Bring to a boil; cover, reduce heat, and simmer 3 to 4 hours or until meat thermometer registers 142° (about 15 minutes per pound). Bone will become very loose when ham is done. Drain ham, and let cool.

Trim skin from ham. Place ham, fat side up, on a rack in a shallow roasting pan. Cover and chill.

Score fat in a diamond pattern, and stud with cloves; pat brown sugar on ham. Place roaster on lowest rack in oven. Broil 5 inches from heat 4 to 5 minutes or until sugar caramelizes. Yield: 30 to 35 servings.

■ Jim Groves's mother, Jeanne, also of Smithfield, Virginia, came up with this creative use for leftover ham.

VEAL-AND-SMITHFIELD HAM SWIRLS

½ cup chopped green onions
½ cup unsalted butter, melted
2 cups soft breadcrumbs
2 cloves garlic, minced
1 cup chopped fresh parsley
1 egg, beaten
2 tablespoons chicken broth
4 (½-inch-thick) boneless veal steaks (about 1¾ pounds)
2 teaspoons Dijon mustard
½ pound thinly sliced cooked Smithfield ham
1 tablespoon unsalted butter, melted
½ cup white wine
Onion Butter

Sauté green onions in ½ cup butter in a large skillet until tender. Remove from heat; add breadcrumbs and next 4 ingredients. Stir well, and set aside.

Flatten veal steaks to ¼-inch thickness, using a meat mallet or rolling pin. Spread mustard evenly over veal; top each steak with a ham slice. Pat ¼ cup onion mixture evenly over ham slices; roll up jellyroll fashion, and secure with a wooden pick. Place veal rolls, seam side down, on a rack in a shallow pan. Brush with 1 tablespoon melted butter. Bake at 325° for 30 to 35 minutes or until tender. Remove veal from pan to serving platter; remove toothpicks, and cut into ½-inch slices.

Add white wine to pan; bring to a boil, stirring to loosen pan drippings. Pour over veal steaks; top with Onion Butter. Yield: 6 to 8 servings.

Onion Butter:

1 cup chopped purple shallots
1 cup red wine
½ cup unsalted butter, softened

Combine purple shallots and wine in a saucepan; cook over medium heat about 5 minutes or until wine evaporates. Cool. Combine shallot mixture and butter. Place butter mixture onto waxed paper, and shape into a log 2 inches in diameter. Chill well. Cut into ½-inch slices to serve. Yield: ½ cup.

■ Nationally acclaimed for his new American cuisine, Chef Marcel Desaulniers of The Trellis in Colonial Williamsburg, Virginia, has made a hit with customers by serving Crab With Chile Cornbread.

CRAB WITH CHILE CORNBREAD

½ cup unsalted butter
2 pounds lump crabmeat
White pepper
Chile Cornbread
32 thin slices cooked country ham
  (about 3 pounds)
Lemon slices
Fresh watercress

Melt butter in a nonstick skillet; add crabmeat. Cook over medium heat, stirring gently, until thoroughly heated. Add pepper to taste, and remove from heat; keep warm.

Slice Chile Cornbread into 16 (½-inch-thick) slices. Place 2 slices country ham on each cornbread slice, and top with about ⅓ cup crabmeat. Garnish with lemon slices and fresh watercress. Yield: 8 servings.

Chile Cornbread:

1 sweet red pepper, finely chopped
1 green pepper, finely chopped
1 jalapeño pepper, broiled, peeled, seeded, and chopped
1 medium onion, finely chopped
1 clove garlic, minced
1 tablespoon butter, melted
⅛ teaspoon pepper
1 dash of hot sauce
½ cup whole kernel corn, drained
1 package dry yeast
1 tablespoon sugar
½ cup warm water (105° to 115°)
2 cups all-purpose flour
½ cup masa harina
¼ cup yellow cornmeal
1 tablespoon salt
2 eggs
¼ cup plus 2 tablespoons unsalted butter, softened
¾ to 1 cup all-purpose flour
1 egg yolk, beaten
1 tablespoon water

Sauté peppers, onion, and garlic in 1 tablespoon butter until tender. Stir in pepper, hot sauce, and corn; cook until thoroughly heated. Remove from heat; let cool.

Dissolve yeast and sugar in warm water in a large mixing bowl; let stand 5 minutes. Combine 2 cups flour, masa harina, cornmeal, and salt; mix well.

Gradually stir into yeast mixture; add eggs, one at a time, mixing with hands until smooth. Turn out onto a lightly floured surface; knead in softened butter, 1 tablespoon at a time, until dough is smooth and elastic.

Place dough in a well-greased bowl, turning to grease top. Cover and let rise in a warm place (85°), free from drafts, 1 hour or until doubled in bulk.

Punch dough down. Turn out onto a floured surface; gradually add corn mixture and remaining ¾ to 1 cup flour, kneading until no longer sticky. Shape into a loaf; place in a well-greased 9- x 5- x 3-inch loafpan.

Cover and let rise in a warm place (85°), free from drafts, 30 minutes or until doubled in bulk. Combine egg yolk and 1 tablespoon water, and brush dough lightly with mixture; bake at 350° for 50 to 55 minutes or until loaf sounds hollow when tapped. Yield: 1 loaf.

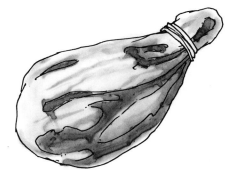

■ Chef John Torentinos re-creates his state's versions of the famous Kentucky Hot Brown and Kentucky Jack at Kenlake State Resort Park in Hardin. His recipe for fried country ham is as downhome as recipes come. But for a twist on the traditional redeye gravy, he adds a pinch of paprika for flavor and some flour for thickening.

KENTUCKY HOT BROWN

1 tablespoon butter or margarine
2 tablespoons all-purpose flour
1 cup milk
⅛ teaspoon chicken-flavored bouillon granules
2 tablespoons shredded Cheddar cheese
3 ounces thinly sliced cooked turkey breast
3 ounces thinly sliced cooked country ham
2 slices bread, toasted
2 slices bacon, cooked
1 slice tomato
1 teaspoon grated Parmesan cheese
Paprika
Fresh parsley

Melt butter in a heavy saucepan over low heat; add flour and cook 1 minute, stirring constantly. Gradually add milk and bouillon granules; cook over medium heat, stirring constantly, until thickened. Add Cheddar cheese; stir until cheese melts. Set aside.

Warm turkey and ham in skillet. Place 1 piece of toast in the center of an ovenproof plate. Cut remaining piece of toast in half, and place one half on each side of the plate. Cover toast with turkey and ham. Spoon cheese sauce over meat, and bake at 300° for 10 minutes. Top with bacon and tomato; bake an additional 5 minutes. Sprinkle with Parmesan cheese and paprika. Garnish with parsley. Yield: 2 servings.

KENTUCKY JACK

2 (¼-inch-thick) slices uncooked country ham
2 tablespoons water
4 slices tomato
2 English muffins, halved and toasted
4 (1-ounce) slices Cheddar cheese
4 (1-ounce) slices Swiss cheese

Place ham in a large skillet over medium heat. Add water, and fry 4 to 5 minutes on each side. Remove ham slices from skillet; add tomatoes to skillet, and grill lightly.

Place equal amounts of ham over each muffin half. Top each with a slice of tomato, Cheddar cheese, and Swiss cheese. Place on a baking sheet, and broil 1 to 2 minutes or until cheese melts. Yield: 4 servings.

COUNTRY HAM
WITH REDEYE GRAVY

2 (¼-inch-thick) slices uncooked country ham
2 tablespoons vegetable oil
1 cup strong black coffee
2 tablespoons all-purpose flour
½ teaspoon paprika

Cut gashes in fat to keep ham from curling. Sauté ham in oil in a heavy skillet over low heat 3 to 4 minutes on each side. Remove the ham from skillet, and keep warm.

Combine coffee and flour; add to pan drippings, stirring constantly, until thickened. Add paprika. Serve with ham. Yield: 2 servings.

■ Savor leftover country ham in bread or quiches. Or grind the last bit of ham for a favorite entrée of Smith Broadbent III and his brother Bob, third-generation ham producers in Cadiz, Kentucky.

COUNTRY HAM LOAVES

1½ cups ground cooked country ham
½ cup mayonnaise
6 slices day-old bread
1½ cups (6 ounces) shredded sharp
   Cheddar cheese
½ cup plus 2 tablespoons butter or
   margarine, softened

Combine ham and mayonnaise; mix well. Spread ham mixture over 4 slices of bread; stack 2 spread slices on top of each other. Top each sandwich with remaining slice of bread; cut each sandwich in half.

Combine cheese and butter; mix until well blended. Frost top and sides of each sandwich with cheese mixture; refrigerate several hours.

Place a wire rack on a baking sheet; place ham loaves on rack. Bake at 450° for 2 minutes or until cheese melts. Yield: 4 servings.

COUNTRY HAM BREAD WITH HERB BUTTER

1 package dry yeast
½ cup warm water (105° to 115°)
3 tablespoons butter or margarine,
   melted
3 tablespoons sugar
2 cups buttermilk
1 egg, beaten
1 cup cornmeal
2 teaspoons pepper
½ teaspoon red pepper
5½ to 6 cups all-purpose flour
2½ cups cooked, ground country
   ham
Cornmeal
Herb Butter

Sprinkle yeast over warm water in a large bowl; let stand 5 minutes. Add butter, sugar, buttermilk, egg, cornmeal, pepper, and red pepper; stir well. Gradually stir in enough flour to make a stiff dough. Turn dough out onto a lightly floured surface. Knead in ham, kneading until dough is elastic. Place in a greased bowl, turning to grease top. Cover and let rise in a warm place (85°), free from drafts, 2 hours or until doubled in bulk. Grease two 9-inch cakepans; sprinkle with cornmeal.

Punch dough down; divide in half, and shape each half into a round loaf.

Place in cakepans; brush with water. Cover and let rise in a warm place (85°), free from drafts, 30 to 40 minutes or until doubled.

Bake at 375° for 30 to 40 minutes or until loaves sound hollow when tapped. Remove from pan, and cool. Serve with Herb Butter. Yield: 2 loaves.

Herb Butter:

½ cup butter or margarine
½ cup chopped fresh chives
¼ cup minced fresh parsley
1 tablespoon lemon juice
Dash of pepper

Combine all ingredients; mix well. Chill thoroughly. Serve butter with warm bread. Yield: ½ cup.

Please Pass The Hominy

Hominy may be one of the South's best kept secrets. These small kernels of hulled, dried corn are eaten more often here than in other regions of the country, and they are virtually unknown in many parts of the world.

Hominy works well alone as an entrée or as a side dish; it's often substituted for rice or potatoes. The kernels add a nice texture, much like that of potatoes, to soup. It also graces many breakfast tables disguised in its ground form—grits.

HOMINY-CHILI CASSEROLE

1 (15-ounce) can chili with beans
1 (2.2-ounce) can sliced ripe olives,
   divided
1 small onion, finely chopped
1 (15½-ounce) can golden hominy,
   drained
1 cup (4 ounces) shredded sharp
   Cheddar cheese

Combine chili and half of olives; spoon into a lightly greased 1½-quart casserole dish. Top with onion and hominy; bake at 350° for 25 minutes. Sprinkle with cheese and remaining olives; bake 5 minutes. Yield: 4 servings.
   Elsie Mankin Jeris,
Pensacola, Florida.

SOUTHWEST SOUP

⅓ cup chopped green pepper
¼ cup chopped onion
1 tablespoon vegetable oil
1 (10¾-ounce) can tomato soup, undiluted
1 (10¾-ounce) can chicken broth,
   undiluted
1⅓ cups water
1 (4-ounce) can chopped green chiles,
   drained
1 (14½-ounce) can golden hominy, drained

Sauté green pepper and onion in oil in a Dutch oven until tender. Add remaining ingredients. Cook, stirring occasionally, until soup is thoroughly heated. Yield: 4 servings.
   Peggy Fowler Revels,
Woodruff, South Carolina.

MEXICAN HOMINY

2 onions, chopped
2 cloves garlic, minced
2 tablespoons vegetable oil
1 quart chicken broth
1 pound lean boneless pork, cut into
   ½-inch pieces
3 dried red chiles, washed, stemmed,
   seeded, and finely chopped
1 teaspoon dried whole oregano
½ teaspoon coarsely ground black pepper
¼ pound hot Italian sausage, sliced
1 (15-ounce) can white hominy, drained

Sauté onion and garlic in oil in a large Dutch oven until tender. Add chicken broth, pork, chiles, oregano, and pepper; bring to a boil. Cover, reduce heat, and simmer 2 hours.

Cook sausage in a small skillet until browned; drain well. Add sausage and hominy to pork mixture. Simmer 15 to 20 minutes. Yield: 6 servings.

Tip: Crush dried herbs gently with a mortar and pestle to enhance their flavor. Slightly bruising fresh plants will increase their effectiveness.

Entrées From The Sea

When you need a main dish in 30 minutes or less, seafood can't be beat for versatility, flavor, and ease of preparation. Shrimp, oysters, and fish fillets or steaks add variety to menus.

GLAZED SALMON STEAKS

¼ cup firmly packed dark brown sugar
¼ cup butter or margarine, melted
2 tablespoons soy sauce
2 tablespoons dry sherry
4 (1- to 1¼-inch-thick) salmon steaks
Fresh watercress

Combine sugar, butter, soy sauce, and sherry, stirring until sugar dissolves. Place salmon steaks in an aluminum foil-lined baking pan; brush with half of sugar mixture. Let sit 15 minutes. Broil 5 minutes or until fish flakes easily when tested with a fork.

Remove fish from oven, and brush with remaining mixture. Transfer to a serving platter. Garnish with watercress. Yield: 4 servings. *Eileen Wehling, Austin, Texas.*

SKEWERED SWORDFISH

¼ cup lemon juice
2 tablespoons vegetable oil
1 tablespoon minced parsley
½ teaspoon salt
¼ teaspoon pepper
2 pounds (½-inch-thick) swordfish steaks, cut into 1-inch cubes
Bay leaves
Vegetable oil
3 tablespoons vegetable oil
3 tablespoons lemon juice
1 tablespoon minced parsley
¼ teaspoon salt
¼ teaspoon pepper

Combine ¼ cup lemon juice, 2 tablespoons oil, 1 tablespoon parsley, ½ teaspoon salt, and ¼ teaspoon pepper; add fish, gently tossing to coat. Cover and marinate 1 hour in the refrigerator.

Remove fish from marinade. Alternate fish and bay leaves on 4 skewers. Brush fish with oil. Grill over medium-hot coals 4 to 5 minutes on each side or until done.

Combine 3 tablespoons oil and remaining ingredients; brush over fish. Remove from skewers; discard bay leaves. Yield: 4 servings. *Doris Garton, Shenandoah, Virginia.*

SHRIMP CREOLE

½ cup chopped onion
½ cup chopped green pepper
¼ cup butter or margarine, melted
3 tablespoons all-purpose flour
1 cup water
1 (8-ounce) can tomato sauce
2 bay leaves
½ teaspoon salt
¼ teaspoon hot sauce
1 pound medium shrimp, peeled and deveined
Hot cooked rice

Sauté onion and green pepper in butter in a large skillet until tender. Stir in flour; cook 1 minute, stirring constantly. Gradually add water and tomato sauce; cook over medium heat, stirring constantly, until mixture is thickened and bubbly. Stir in bay leaves, salt, and hot sauce. Cover, reduce heat, and simmer 20 minutes. Add shrimp; cover and simmer 5 to 8 minutes or until shrimp are done, stirring occasionally. Serve over rice. Yield: 4 servings. *Jane Moss, Victoria, Texas.*

WILD RICE-OYSTER CASSEROLE

1 (12-ounce) container Standard oysters, undrained
1 (6-ounce) package long-grain and wild rice mix
1 cup sliced fresh mushrooms
½ cup sliced celery
2 tablespoons butter or margarine, melted
3 tablespoons all-purpose flour
¼ cup half-and-half
¼ cup chopped fresh parsley
2 tablespoons sherry
2 tablespoons fine dry breadcrumbs

Drain oysters, reserving ¼ cup oyster liquid; set oysters and reserved oyster liquid aside.

Cook rice according to package directions; set aside.

Sauté mushrooms and celery in butter in a large skillet 5 minutes. Add oysters, and cook an additional 5 minutes or until oyster edges curl. Add flour, stirring until smooth. Cook 1 minute, stirring constantly. Gradually add reserved oyster liquid and half-and-half; cook over medium heat, stirring constantly, until mixture is thickened and bubbly.

Stir in rice, parsley, and sherry. Spoon mixture into a lightly greased 1-quart baking dish; sprinkle with breadcrumbs. Bake at 350° for 20 minutes or until thoroughly heated. Yield: 6 servings. *Virginia B. Stalder, Nokesville, Virginia.*

Meatballs Spice Up The Menu

Whether you need an appetizer or an entrée, you just can't go wrong with meatballs. These hearty little bites quickly disappear from appetizer buffets, and they're a meal in themselves teamed with rice or pasta and served with a salad.

SWEDISH MEATBALLS

1 pound ground beef
1 egg, beaten
½ cup fine dry breadcrumbs
2 tablespoons finely chopped onion
¾ teaspoon salt
¼ teaspoon ground nutmeg
2 tablespoons vegetable oil
2 (3-ounce) packages cream cheese, cubed
¾ cup milk
½ cup water
2 tablespoons chopped fresh parsley
⅛ teaspoon salt
⅛ teaspoon dried whole thyme
Hot cooked noodles (optional)

Combine beef, egg, breadcrumbs, onion, ¾ teaspoon salt, and nutmeg in a large mixing bowl; mix well. Shape into 1-inch meatballs. Heat oil in a large heavy skillet; add meatballs, and brown on all sides. Remove meatballs from pan; set aside. Drain drippings, reserving 2 tablespoons in skillet.

Stir cream cheese, milk, water, parsley, ⅛ teaspoon salt, and thyme into drippings; cook over medium heat, stirring constantly, until smooth and thickened. Return meatballs to skillet. Serve over noodles, if desired. Yield: 4 servings. *Suzanne B. McDonald, Monroeville, Alabama.*

HAM BALLS

1½ pounds cooked ham, ground
½ pound ground fresh pork
2 eggs
1 cup milk
1¾ cups corn flake crumbs
1½ cups firmly packed brown sugar
½ cup vinegar
½ cup water
1 teaspoon dry mustard

Combine ham, pork, eggs, milk, and corn flake crumbs; mix well. Shape into 1-inch meatballs, and place in a 13- x 9- x 2-inch baking pan.

Combine brown sugar, vinegar, water, and dry mustard, and mix well. Pour mixture over ham balls, and bake at 350° for 45 to 50 minutes, basting ham balls occasionally.

Remove ham balls from oven, and serve warm with wooden picks. Yield: 5 dozen.
Violet Nelson, Columbia, South Carolina.

SAUERKRAUT MEATBALLS

¼ **pound bulk pork sausage**
¼ **pound cooked ham, ground**
¼ **pound cooked corned beef, ground**
¼ **cup finely chopped onion**
⅛ **teaspoon parsley flakes**
1 **cup all-purpose flour**
½ **teaspoon salt**
½ **teaspoon dry mustard**
1 **cup milk**
1 **(32-ounce) jar chopped sauerkraut, well drained**
2 **eggs, beaten**
⅔ **cup water**
½ **teaspoon salt**
1 **cup all-purpose flour**
3 **cups soft breadcrumbs**
Vegetable oil
Creamy Mustard Sauce

Cook sausage in a large skillet over medium heat, stirring to crumble; drain. Add ham, corned beef, onion, and parsley flakes; cook, stirring frequently, until thoroughly heated. Add 1 cup flour, ½ teaspoon salt, and mustard; stir well. Gradually add milk, stirring constantly; cook until thickened. Stir in sauerkraut. Let cool; cover and refrigerate 1 to 2 hours.

Shape mixture into ¾-inch balls, and set aside.

Combine eggs, water, and ½ teaspoon salt; mix well. Dredge meatballs lightly in 1 cup flour, dip in egg mixture, and coat with breadcrumbs. Cook in 2 inches hot oil (360°) for 1 to 1½ minutes or until browned; drain on paper towels. Serve with Creamy Mustard Sauce. Yield: about 6½ dozen.

Creamy Mustard Sauce:

1 **cup sugar**
2 **tablespoons dry mustard**
2½ **teaspoons cornstarch**
2 **egg yolks, beaten**
1 **cup half-and-half**
1½ **tablespoons cider vinegar**
Fresh parsley sprigs

Combine first 3 ingredients in a heavy saucepan; mix well. Combine egg yolks and half-and-half; stir well. Gradually stir egg mixture into dry ingredients;

cook over medium heat, stirring constantly, until smooth and thickened. Stir in vinegar. Let cool.

Pour sauce into serving dish; garnish with fresh parsley sprigs. Yield: about 1¾ cups.
Julia Garmon, Alexandria, Virginia.

A Hot Pasta Side Dish

Lots of flavor and fresh ingredients are the key to some of today's most popular restaurant selections. And that's just what you'll find when you sample this recipe from Mary Pappas of Richmond, Virginia.

Mary tosses steamed zucchini, squash, broccoli, onion, and mushrooms with spaghetti. Butter, whipping cream, cheese, and fresh cracked pepper give the spaghetti a rich taste.

This recipe is an excellent choice for serving instead of a baked potato with grilled fish or even a steak dinner. Or make it your entrée. Mary suggests fixing a quick meal consisting of the pasta, a green salad, and hot bread.

Prepare rich-flavored Fresh Vegetables With Spaghetti in just a matter of minutes.

FRESH VEGETABLES WITH SPAGHETTI

2 **medium zucchini, sliced**
2 **medium-size yellow squash, sliced**
1 **cup fresh broccoli flowerets**
½ **cup sliced onion**
1 **cup sliced mushrooms**
1 **(12-ounce) package spaghetti, broken in half**
½ **cup butter or margarine, melted**
½ **cup whipping cream**
¾ **cup grated Parmesan cheese**
Freshly ground pepper

Arrange zucchini, squash, broccoli, and onion in a steamer rack. Place rack over boiling water; cover and steam 5 to 7 minutes or until almost crisp-tender. Add mushrooms; cover and steam an additional minute.

Cook spaghetti according to package directions; drain. Add butter, whipping cream, cheese, and pepper; toss well. Add vegetables to spaghetti; toss gently. Serve warm. Yield: 8 to 10 servings.

Tip: Plan your menus for the week, but stay flexible enough to substitute good buys when you spot them. By planning ahead, you can use leftovers in another day's meal.

Mushrooms To Stuff And Serve

When it comes to stuffed mushrooms, you'll find these recipes offer some of the tastiest ideas yet. The results are hearty enough to serve at a supper buffet party but elegant enough for a formal occasion, too.

Medium to large mushrooms work best for stuffing. Remember that mushrooms will shrink more than half the original size during cooking.

When preparing mushrooms, clean them with a damp towel or a soft vegetable brush; never soak them. To remove the stems easily, use the tip of a knife or a spoon; or simply twist the stem, and pull it out.

CRAWFISH-STUFFED MUSHROOMS

½ cup chopped onion
¼ cup chopped celery
¼ cup chopped green pepper
1 tablespoon chopped fresh parsley
¼ cup butter or margarine, melted
½ teaspoon dried ground thyme
½ teaspoon salt
¼ teaspoon pepper
5 drops of hot sauce
1 pound crawfish tails, cooked, peeled, and chopped
1 cup herb-seasoned breadcrumbs
18 large fresh mushrooms
Paprika
¼ cup butter or margarine, melted

Sauté onion, celery, green pepper, and parsley in ¼ cup butter. Add thyme, salt, pepper, hot sauce, crawfish, and breadcrumbs, stirring well.

Clean mushrooms with damp paper towels. Remove mushroom stems, and reserve for other uses.

Spoon crawfish mixture into mushroom caps; sprinkle with paprika, and drizzle with remaining ¼ cup butter. Bake, uncovered, at 350° for 10 to 15 minutes. Yield: 18 stuffed mushrooms.

Mae Bowman,
Baton Rouge, Louisiana.

MUSHROOMS WITH STEMS

24 medium-size fresh mushrooms
1 (14-ounce) can hearts of palm, drained
Lettuce
⅓ cup commercial Italian salad dressing

Clean mushrooms with damp paper towels. Remove mushroom stems, and reserve for other uses. Cut each heart of palm into thirds. Place a piece of heart of palm in each mushroom cap, to look like the original mushroom stem. Arrange the mushrooms on a large lettuce-lined serving plate with "stems" up. Drizzle salad dressing over each mushroom. Cover and chill 10 minutes or until ready to serve. Yield: 24 stuffed mushrooms.

Barbara Fowler,
Montgomery, Alabama.

BLACK OLIVE-STUFFED MUSHROOMS

14 medium to large fresh mushrooms
½ cup grated Parmesan cheese
¼ cup black olives, sliced
1 tablespoon Worcestershire sauce
6 slices bacon, cooked and crumbled

Clean mushrooms with damp paper towels. Remove mushroom stems, and reserve for other uses; set caps aside.

Combine cheese, olives, and Worcestershire sauce, mixing well. Spoon mixture into mushroom caps; sprinkle with bacon. Bake, uncovered, at 350° for 10 to 15 minutes. Yield: 14 stuffed mushrooms.

Janie Daniels,
Charleston, South Carolina.

CHEESE 'N' BACON-STUFFED MUSHROOMS

20 large fresh mushrooms
1 (8-ounce) package cream cheese, softened
2 tablespoons commercial sour cream
4 slices bacon, cooked and crumbled
1 clove garlic, minced
1 tablespoon minced onion
½ teaspoon dillseeds
Pinch of dried whole dillweed
Additional dried whole dillweed

Clean mushrooms with damp paper towels. Remove mushroom stems, and reserve for other uses; set caps aside.

Combine cream cheese and sour cream in a small bowl; beat at medium speed of an electric mixer until smooth. Add bacon, garlic, onion, dillseeds, and pinch of dillweed; blend well. Spoon mixture into mushroom caps. Sprinkle with additional dillweed.

Place mushroom caps in a lightly greased 12- x 8- x 2-inch casserole. Bake at 350° for 15 minutes or until lightly browned. Yield: 20 stuffed mushrooms.

Leslie Bailey Heaton,
Raleigh, North Carolina.

Canned Soups As Starters

The most time-consuming part of making soup is preparing the tasty broth or creamy sauce, which is the base. To prepare quickly, start with a can of soup. Add the selected ingredients and seasonings to complement the canned soup. The result? Homemade soup.

APPETIZER TOMATO SOUP

1 (10¾-ounce) can tomato soup, undiluted
1 (8-ounce) carton plain yogurt
1¾ cups milk
1 teaspoon Worcestershire sauce
¼ teaspoon celery salt
⅛ teaspoon onion powder
Additional plain yogurt (optional)

Combine first 6 ingredients; stir well. Cover; chill completely. Ladle into bowls, and top with additional yogurt, if desired. Yield: 4 cups.

M. B. Quesenberry,
Dugspur, Virginia.

CREAMY TOMATO SOUP

1 (10¾-ounce) can tomato soup, undiluted
1 (12-ounce) can evaporated milk
1 (14½-ounce) can stewed tomatoes, undrained and chopped
½ cup (2 ounces) shredded Cheddar cheese
6 slices bacon, cooked and crumbled

Combine soup and milk in a medium saucepan, stirring with a wire whisk. Add tomatoes and cheese; cook over low heat until cheese melts and soup is hot. Ladle into bowls, and sprinkle with bacon. Yield: 4⅔ cups.

Tony Jones,
Atlanta, Georgia.

CHEESY-BROCCOLI SOUP

1 (10-ounce) package frozen chopped broccoli
½ cup chopped onion
¼ cup chopped green pepper
2 tablespoons butter or margarine, melted
1 (10¾-ounce) can cream of chicken soup, undiluted
1½ cups milk
1 cup water
¾ pound process American cheese, cubed

Cook broccoli according to package directions, omitting salt; drain well.

Sauté onion and green pepper in butter in a medium saucepan.

Add broccoli and remaining ingredients to saucepan; cook over medium heat until cheese melts, stirring often. Serve immediately. Yield: 5½ cups.

Carol Barclay,
Portland, Texas.

CREAM OF BROCCOLI SOUP

2 (10-ounce) packages frozen chopped broccoli
1 (10¾-ounce) can cream of chicken soup, undiluted
1 (10¾-ounce) can cream of celery soup, undiluted
1 cup half-and-half
1 teaspoon garlic powder
½ teaspoon pepper
⅛ teaspoon curry powder

Cook broccoli according to package directions, omitting salt. (Do not drain.) Add remaining ingredients, stirring well. Reduce heat, and simmer 1 hour. Serve hot. Yield: 7½ cups.

Laurie McKernan,
Maitland, Florida.

POT-OF-GOLD SOUP

1 (14½-ounce) can chicken broth, undiluted
2 cups water
¾ teaspoon salt
1 (1¼-pound) cauliflower, broken into flowerets
4 medium carrots, sliced ½ inch thick
1 onion, quartered
½ cup milk
1½ teaspoons butter or margarine
½ teaspoon ground curry powder
⅛ teaspoon pepper

Combine broth, water, and salt in a heavy saucepan; bring to a boil. Add cauliflower, carrots, and onion; cover and simmer 15 minutes or until vegetables are tender.

Place 1 cup vegetables and liquid into container of an electric blender; cover and process until smooth. Pour mixture into another saucepan.

Repeat procedure until all vegetables are smooth. Add milk and remaining ingredients; stir until butter melts. Serve soup hot. Yield: 8 cups.

Ursula Hennessy,
Springfield, Virginia.

Nuts Add Crunch To Pies

One of the sure signs of fall and winter is the appearance of fresh unshelled nuts in the grocery store. And what better way to make use of them than in a homemade pie.

CHOCOLATE-PRALINE PIE

2 eggs
½ cup sugar
½ cup butter or margarine, melted
2 tablespoons praline liqueur
1 (6-ounce) package semisweet chocolate morsels
1 cup chopped pecans
1 unbaked 9-inch pastry shell
Vanilla ice cream (optional)

Combine first 4 ingredients; beat at medium speed of an electric mixer until well blended. Stir in chocolate morsels and pecans. Pour mixture into pastry shell; bake at 350° for 30 minutes. Serve with ice cream, if desired. Yield: one 9-inch pie.

Bernice Williams,
Halifax, Virginia.

MOLASSES-PECAN PIE

3 eggs
½ cup sugar
1 cup light molasses
1 tablespoon cornmeal
1 teaspoon vinegar
¼ cup butter or margarine, melted
1 cup chopped pecans
Pastry (recipe follows)
Whipped cream (optional)
Pecan half (optional)

Beat eggs at medium speed of an electric mixer until thick and lemon colored. Add sugar and next 4 ingredients; beat until blended. Stir in chopped

pecans. Pour mixture into pastry shell. Bake at 350° for 35 to 40 minutes. Let cool completely.

Garnish each serving with a dollop of whipped cream and a pecan half, if desired. Yield: one 9-inch pie.

Pastry:

1 cup all-purpose flour
½ teaspoon salt
⅓ cup shortening
3 tablespoons cold water

Combine flour and salt; cut in shortening with pastry blender until mixture resembles coarse meal. Sprinkle cold water evenly over surface; stir with a fork until dry ingredients are moistened. Shape into a ball.

Roll dough to ⅛-inch thickness on a lightly floured surface. Place in a 9-inch pieplate; trim off excess pastry along edges. Fold edges under, and flute. Yield: one 9-inch pastry shell.

Marcia Hunt,
Gulfport, Mississippi.

CARAMEL-PEANUT PIE

2 cups sugar, divided
1 cup boiling water
2 tablespoons all-purpose flour
5 eggs, separated
2 cups milk
1 cup chopped peanuts
1 teaspoon vanilla extract
2 baked 9-inch pastry shells
¼ cup sugar

Place 1 cup sugar in a heavy skillet; cook over medium-high heat, stirring constantly, until sugar melts and forms a light brown syrup. Reduce heat to low; gradually add boiling water in a slow stream, stirring constantly with a wire whisk. Remove from heat.

Combine 1 cup sugar and flour in a heavy saucepan; stir well. Add egg yolks, milk, and caramelized sugar mixture; stir well. Cook over low heat, stirring constantly, until mixture thickens.

Stir chopped peanuts and vanilla into mixture. Pour into pastry shells.

Beat egg whites (at room temperature) until foamy. Gradually add ¼ cup sugar, 1 tablespoon at a time, beating until stiff peaks form.

Spread meringue over hot filling, sealing to edge of pastry. Bake at 350° for 12 to 15 minutes or until golden brown. Let pies cool to room temperature. Yield: two 9-inch pies.

Mrs. J. W. Hopkins,
Abilene, Texas.

EASY CRANBERRY COBBLER

3 cups cranberries
¾ cup chopped walnuts
¾ cup sugar, divided
1 egg
½ cup all-purpose flour
⅓ cup butter or margarine,
    melted
Vanilla ice cream

Place cranberries in a lightly greased 8-inch square baking dish; sprinkle with walnuts and ½ cup sugar. Set aside.

Combine egg and remaining ¼ cup sugar; beat at high speed of an electric mixer until smooth and slightly thickened. Add flour and butter; beat at low speed of an electric mixer until smooth. Spoon batter over berry mixture; bake at 325° for 45 to 50 minutes or until lightly browned.

Serve cobbler warm; top each serving with a scoop of ice cream. Yield: 6 servings.   *Edith Askins,*
Greenville, Texas.

SOUR CREAM PIE

2 eggs, beaten
1½ cups commercial sour cream
1 cup sugar
2 tablespoons all-purpose flour
1 teaspoon vanilla extract
½ cup golden raisins
½ cup chopped Brazil nuts
1 unbaked 9-inch pastry shell

Combine eggs, sour cream, sugar, flour, and vanilla; beat at medium speed of an electric mixer until blended. Stir in raisins and Brazil nuts. Pour mixture into pastry shell. Bake at 400° for 10 minutes; reduce heat to 350°, and bake an additional 30 minutes or until set. Yield: one 9-inch pie.   *Daisy Cook,*
Tyler, Texas.

You'll Love
These Crêpes

Gloria Different is a good cook, and the people in her hometown of Harvey, Louisiana, know it. Several years ago, she won first place in the dessert category of a newspaper's cooking contest. Her prize-winning recipe for Amaretto-and-Orange Crêpes is one you'll be proud to serve.

AMARETTO-AND-ORANGE CRÊPES

1 (3-ounce) package cream cheese,
    softened
1 tablespoon amaretto liqueur
1 (11-ounce) can mandarin oranges,
    drained and divided
Dessert Crêpes
½ cup butter or margarine, melted
½ cup sugar
1 teaspoon cornstarch
½ cup orange juice
1 teaspoon grated orange rind
1 tablespoon brandy
2 tablespoons amaretto liqueur
¼ cup sliced almonds, toasted

Combine the softened cream cheese, 1 tablespoon amaretto liqueur, and 12 mandarin orange segments; stir well.

Spread cream cheese mixture evenly over each crêpe. Fold crêpe in half, and then into quarters. Place in a 13- x 9- x 2-inch baking dish.

Combine butter and next 3 ingredients in a saucepan. Cook over low heat, stirring constantly, until thickened. Add remaining oranges, rind, brandy, and 2 tablespoons amaretto.

Spoon sauce over crêpes; keep warm. To serve, sprinkle with toasted almonds. Yield: 6 filled crêpes.

Dessert Crêpes:

¼ cup all-purpose flour
½ teaspoon sugar
⅛ teaspoon salt
½ cup milk
2 eggs
1½ tablespoons butter or margarine,
    melted
Vegetable oil

Combine flour, sugar, salt, and milk, beating until smooth. Add eggs, and stir well; stir in butter. Refrigerate batter at least 2 hours. (This allows flour particles to swell and soften so the crêpes will be light in texture.)

Brush the bottom of a 10-inch crêpe pan or heavy skillet with oil; place over medium heat just until hot, not smoking. Pour 3 tablespoons batter into pan; quickly tilt pan in all directions so that batter covers pan in a thin film. Cook batter 1 minute.

Lift edge of crêpe to test for doneness. Crêpe is ready for flipping when it can be shaken loose from pan. Flip crêpe, and cook about 30 seconds on other side. (This side is usually spotty brown and is the side on which the filling is placed.)

Place crêpes on a towel to cool. Stack between layers of waxed paper to prevent sticking. Repeat until all batter is used. Yield: 6 crêpes.

Make Baked Goods
Light And Airy

Have you ever been curious why yeast breads rise, popovers puff, and muffins expand during baking? Leavening agents are the answer. The three most common types of leavening include steam formed in baking, air beaten into egg whites, and carbon dioxide gas formed when certain ingredients are combined. For instance, the gas forms when yeast and sugar are combined, when baking soda is mixed with buttermilk and molasses, or when baking powder is added to batter.

CHEESY CREAM PUFFS
WITH CHICKEN SALAD

1 cup water
½ cup butter or margarine
1 cup all-purpose flour
¼ teaspoon salt
4 eggs
¼ cup grated Parmesan cheese
Chicken salad (recipe follows)
Sliced pimiento-stuffed olives (optional)

Combine water and butter in a medium saucepan; bring to a boil. Add flour and salt, all at once, stirring vigorously over medium-high heat until mixture leaves sides of pan and forms a smooth ball. Remove from heat, and cool 5 minutes.

Add eggs, one at a time, beating thoroughly with a wooden spoon after each addition. Add cheese; beat until dough is smooth. Drop by rounded teaspoonfuls onto lightly greased baking sheets or pipe a 2-inch rosette using a 6-B star tip. Bake at 400° for 20 minutes or until puffed and golden. Let cool away from drafts.

Just before serving, cut top third off cream puffs; pull out and discard soft dough inside. Spoon chicken salad into cream puffs; replace tops. Garnish with olives, if desired. Yield: 3 dozen.

Chicken Salad:

**3 cups chopped cooked chicken (about 4
  breast halves)**
1 cup diced celery
2 hard-cooked eggs, chopped
⅔ cup mayonnaise
¼ cup pimiento-stuffed olives, chopped
2 tablespoons minced onion
½ teaspoon lemon juice
¼ teaspoon Italian seasoning
¼ teaspoon salt

Combine all ingredients, stirring well;
cover and chill. Yield: 4 cups.

Sally Pressley,
Birmingham, Alabama.

CHEESE SPOON BREAD

2 cups milk
1 cup cornmeal
¼ cup butter or margarine, softened
**½ cup (2 ounces) shredded mild Cheddar
  cheese**
4 eggs, separated
1 teaspoon salt

Place milk in top of a double boiler
over boiling water; cook until hot. Stir
in cornmeal; cook, stirring until thickened. Remove from heat; stir in butter,
cheese, egg yolks, and salt. Stir mixture
until cheese melts.

Beat egg whites (at room temperature) until stiff peaks form; fold into
cornmeal mixture. Pour into a greased
2-quart casserole; bake at 350° for 30 to
35 minutes or until puffed and browned.
Serve immediately. Yield: 8 servings.

Betty Burnside,
Newport, North Carolina.

BUTTERFLAKE HERB LOAF

4½ to 5½ cups all-purpose flour, divided
¼ cup sugar
1 tablespoon salt
1 package dry yeast
1½ cups milk
⅓ cup shortening
2 eggs
Herb Butter

Combine 2 cups flour, sugar, salt, and
yeast in a large mixing bowl. Heat milk
and shortening in a small saucepan to
120° to 130°. Gradually add hot mixture
to flour mixture; add eggs. Beat 3 minutes at low speed of an electric mixer.
Gradually stir in enough of remaining
flour to make a soft dough.

Turn dough out onto a lightly floured
surface, and knead 5 minutes until
smooth and elastic. Shape into a ball,
and place in a greased bowl, turning to
grease top. Cover and let rise in a warm
place (85°), free from drafts, 1 hour or
until doubled in bulk.

Punch dough down, and divide in
half; roll each half into a 15- x 9-inch
rectangle; spread rectangle with half of
Herb Butter. Roll up jellyroll fashion
starting at long side; seal ends. Place
seam side down in a greased 9- x 5- x
3-inch loaf pan. Repeat procedure with
remaining dough and Herb Butter.
Cover and let rise in a warm place
(85°), free from drafts, 40 minutes or
until doubled in bulk.

Bake at 350° for 25 to 30 minutes or
until loaves sound hollow when tapped.
Yield: 2 loaves.

Herb Butter:

½ cup butter or margarine, softened
½ teaspoon caraway seeds
½ teaspoon dried whole basil
½ teaspoon grated onion
¼ teaspoon dried whole oregano
¼ teaspoon garlic powder
⅛ teaspoon red pepper

Combine all ingredients in a small
bowl, stirring well. Yield: ½ cup.

Sue-Sue Hartstern,
Louisville, Kentucky.

WHEAT GERM BISCUITS

1½ cups all-purpose flour
½ cup wheat germ
1 tablespoon baking powder
½ teaspoon salt
¼ cup shortening
¾ cup milk

Combine flour, wheat germ, baking
powder, and salt in a medium bowl; cut
in shortening with a pastry blender until
mixture resembles coarse meal. Add
milk; stir until dry ingredients are
moistened.

Turn dough out onto a well floured
surface, and knead 5 to 6 times. Roll
dough to ½-inch thickness; cut with a
2-inch biscuit cutter. Place on a lightly
greased baking sheet. Bake at 450° for
10 to 12 minutes or until biscuits are
lightly browned. Yield: about 1 dozen.

Dottie Cycotte,
Norwood, North Carolina.

STEAMED BUTTERMILK
BROWN BREAD

½ cup cornmeal
½ cup all-purpose flour
½ cup whole wheat flour
2 tablespoons sugar
¾ teaspoon baking soda
Dash of salt
½ cup raisins
1 cup buttermilk
¼ cup molasses

Combine first 6 ingredients in a medium mixing bowl; stir in raisins.

Combine buttermilk and molasses in
a small mixing bowl; add to dry ingredients, stirring well. Spoon mixture into
a well-greased 4-cup mold; cover tightly
with aluminum foil.

Place mold on a shallow rack in a
large deep kettle with enough boiling
water to come halfway up sides of
mold. Cover kettle. Steam bread 2
hours in continuously boiling water.
(Add water as needed.)

Unmold bread onto wire rack to cool.
Yield: one 6-inch round loaf.

Norma Zeigler,
Huntsville, Alabama.

VERY MOIST GINGERBREAD

1 cup butter or margarine, softened
1 cup sugar
2 eggs, beaten
¾ cup molasses
½ cup buttermilk
3 cups all-purpose flour
2 teaspoons ground ginger
1 teaspoon ground cinnamon
½ teaspoon ground cloves
¼ teaspoon salt
2 teaspoons baking soda
¾ cup boiling water

Cream butter; gradually add sugar,
beating at medium speed of an electric
mixer until light and fluffy. Beat in
eggs, molasses, and buttermilk.

Combine flour, ginger, cinnamon,
cloves, and salt in a small bowl.

Dissolve soda in boiling water. Add
flour mixture to creamed mixture alternately with soda water, beginning and
ending with flour mixture. Beat well.

Pour batter into a greased and
floured 13- x 9- x 2-inch baking pan.
Bake at 350° for 40 minutes or until a
wooden pick inserted in center comes
out clean.

Cut into squares; serve warm or at
room temperature. Yield: 12 servings.

Stella Trevathan,
Cleveland, Texas.

CARROT-DATE-NUT MUFFINS

½ cup butter or margarine, softened
½ cup firmly packed brown sugar
2 eggs
½ cup quick-cooking oats, uncooked
½ cup chopped dates
½ cup chopped walnuts
1 cup finely shredded carrots
1½ cups all-purpose flour
1 tablespoon baking powder
1 teaspoon salt
¼ cup milk

Combine butter and sugar; stir well. Add eggs, one at a time, stirring after each addition. Add oats, dates, walnuts, and carrots; stir well. Combine flour, baking powder, and salt; add to oat mixture alternately with milk, beginning and ending with the flour mixture.

Spoon into greased and floured muffin pans, filling three-fourths full. Bake at 350° for 25 minutes or until a wooden pick inserted in center comes out clean. Remove muffins from pans, and let cool on wire racks. Yield: 12 muffins.

Faye Creech,
Moore, Oklahoma.

Appetizers To Freeze Or Serve Now

Get a headstart on the season by stocking your freezer with these easy appetizers. When friends stop by or your family gathers, you'll be ready to entertain. With most of the preparation out of the way, you can spend more time having fun.

CHEESY CRAB CANAPÉS

1 (8-ounce) jar process cheese spread
1 (6-ounce) can crabmeat, drained
¼ cup butter or margarine, softened
1 tablespoon mayonnaise
½ teaspoon seasoned salt
¼ teaspoon garlic salt
10 English muffins, halved
Pimiento strips (optional)

Combine first 6 ingredients; blend well. Spread about 2 tablespoons cheese mixture on each muffin half. Cut each half into quarters. Garnish quarters with pimiento strips, if desired. Place on baking sheets, and broil 5 minutes or until crisp.

To freeze, place unbaked canapés on baking sheets, and place uncovered in freezer until frozen. Remove from baking sheets, and store in an airtight container in freezer. To serve, remove canapés from freezer; place on ungreased baking sheets. Broil, unthawed, 5 to 7 minutes. Yield: 6½ dozen.

Mrs. Delbert Snyder,
Williamsburg, Virginia.

SALMON BALL

1 (15½-ounce) can salmon, drained and flaked
1 (8-ounce) package cream cheese, softened
½ cup chopped pecans
2 tablespoons grated onion
1 tablespoon lemon juice
1 tablespoon prepared horseradish
¼ teaspoon salt
¼ cup chopped fresh parsley
Lemon slices (optional)

Combine first 7 ingredients; stir well. Chill thoroughly. Shape into a ball, and roll in chopped parsley. Serve with assorted crackers, and garnish with lemon slices, if desired.

To freeze, place salmon ball in an airtight container in freezer. To serve, remove from freezer; let thaw completely. Yield: one 6-inch ball.

Lucille Greenfield,
Batesville, Arkansas.

PARTY RYE APPETIZERS

1 pound bulk pork sausage
1 pound process cheese, cut into 1-inch cubes
2 tablespoons catsup
1 teaspoon Worcestershire sauce
½ teaspoon dried whole oregano
⅛ teaspoon garlic powder
2 (8-ounce) loaves party rye bread

Brown sausage in a heavy skillet; drain well.

Place cheese in a heavy saucepan over low heat; stir frequently until cheese melts. Add sausage, catsup, Worcestershire sauce, oregano, and garlic powder; mix well. Spread about 2 teaspoons of sausage mixture on each bread slice. Bake on an ungreased baking sheet at 375° for 10 minutes.

To freeze, place unbaked slices on baking sheets, and place uncovered in freezer until frozen. Remove from baking sheets, and store in an airtight container in freezer. To serve, place on ungreased baking sheets. Bake, unthawed, at 375° for 10 minutes. Yield: approximately 5 dozen appetizers.

Mrs. Charles Hellem,
Columbia, Missouri.

PIZZA PARTY SNACKS

1 (2-ounce) can sliced mushrooms, drained
½ cup (2 ounces) shredded sharp Cheddar cheese
½ cup (2 ounces) shredded Swiss cheese
⅓ cup chopped pepperoni
⅓ cup mayonnaise
¼ cup chopped onion
3 tablespoons chopped ripe olives
6 English muffins, halved

Combine all ingredients except muffins; blend well. Spread mixture on muffin halves. Bake at 450° for 8 minutes or until cheese is bubbly. Serve warm.

To freeze, place unbaked muffin halves on baking sheets, and place uncovered in freezer until frozen. Remove from baking sheets, and store in airtight container in freezer. To serve, remove from freezer; place on ungreased baking sheets. Bake, unthawed, at 350° for 15 minutes. Yield: 1 dozen.

Thomas C. Stinnett,
Little Rock, Arkansas.

CHEESE ROUNDS

1 (1½-pound) loaf day-old sliced sandwich bread
2 (5-ounce) jars sharp process cheese spread
½ cup butter or margarine, softened
1 egg, beaten
¼ teaspoon red pepper

Cut bread with a 1½-inch round cutter making 84 circles. Set aside.

Combine remaining ingredients in a small bowl; blend well. Spread cheese mixture on one bread circle; top with another piece of bread. Spread cheese mixture on sides and top. Place rounds on an ungreased baking sheet, and bake at 400° for 12 minutes.

To freeze, place unbaked cheese rounds on baking sheets, and place uncovered in freezer until frozen. Remove from baking sheets, and store in an airtight container in freezer. To serve, remove from freezer; place on ungreased baking sheet. Bake, unthawed, at 400° for 12 to 14 minutes. Yield: 3½ dozen.

Pat Scott,
Birmingham, Alabama.

November

Delicious Down-Home Pot Pies

Centuries ago, the first pot pies were made in deep dishes and sealed on top with a thick pastry crust. Southerners still love this traditional favorite and have since found tasty variations for the top crust and the meaty filling, as you'll see in our recipes here. In some versions, the recipes have been adjusted to fit busy life-styles by using convenience products. Chicken or turkey is featured in these pot pies, but one can easily be substituted for the other.

If you're really in a hurry, a mixture of breadcrumbs, parsley, and herbs makes a quick-and-easy topping. You can even spread cooked mashed potatoes over the meat filling for creating an old-fashioned "shepherd's pie."

You'll find that some of our recipes call for using whole broiler-fryers for the most economical chicken pot pies. Turkey, canned chicken, or chicken parts may be substituted; just be sure to have canned or frozen broth on hand, if necessary. To substitute turkey or leftover chicken for these recipes, just remember that one 3-pound whole broiler-fryer equals about 3 cups chopped cooked chicken.

EGG-STRA SPECIAL CHICKEN PIE
(pictured on page 238)

6 chicken breast halves
5 cups water
3 tablespoons butter or margarine
¼ cup all-purpose flour
1 cup commercial sour cream
½ cup half-and-half
½ teaspoon salt
¼ teaspoon pepper
2½ cups all-purpose flour
1¼ teaspoons salt
¾ cup plus 1 tablespoon butter-flavored
  shortening
6 to 8 tablespoons cold water
3 hard-cooked eggs, sliced
2 tablespoons chopped fresh parsley

Combine chicken and 5 cups water in a Dutch oven; bring to a boil. Cover, reduce heat, and simmer 40 minutes or until tender. Drain, reserving 1½ cups broth. Skin, bone, and cut chicken into bite-size pieces.

Melt butter in a heavy saucepan over low heat; add ¼ cup flour, stirring until smooth. Cook 1 minute, stirring constantly. Gradually add reserved chicken broth; cook over medium heat, stirring constantly, until mixture is thickened and bubbly. Add sour cream, half-and-half, ½ teaspoon salt, and pepper; stir until smooth. Stir in chicken; set aside.

Combine 2½ cups flour and 1¼ teaspoons salt; cut in shortening with a pastry blender until mixture resembles coarse meal. Sprinkle cold water (1 tablespoon at a time) evenly over surface, stirring with a fork until dry ingredients are moistened.

Roll two-thirds of dough into a 17- x 13-inch rectangle. Place in a 12- x 8- x 2-inch baking dish; trim off excess pastry. Fill pastry with chicken mixture; arrange eggs on top. Sprinkle with parsley. Roll remaining one-third pastry to ⅛-inch thickness; cut into strips. Arrange strips lattice style over parsley, sealing edges to sides of dish. Bake at 400° for 35 minutes; let stand 10 minutes before serving. Yield: 6 servings.

Barbara Coleman,
Marshall, Texas.

CHICKEN POT PIE WITH CHEESE CRUST

2 (2½-pound) broiler-fryers, cut up
2 quarts water
2 chicken-flavored bouillon cubes
1 medium tomato, peeled and quartered
½ cup chopped celery
1 cup chopped onion, divided
½ cup chopped fresh parsley, divided
1 cup sliced mushrooms
½ cup butter or margarine, melted
½ cup all-purpose flour
1½ teaspoons salt
⅛ teaspoon pepper
Cheese Crust

Combine chicken pieces, water, bouillon cubes, tomato, celery, ½ cup onion, and ¼ cup parsley in a large Dutch oven. Bring to a boil; cover, reduce heat, and simmer 40 minutes. Remove chicken from Dutch oven, reserving 3 cups broth. Cool chicken.

Remove chicken from bone; chop meat. Place in a lightly greased 12- x 8- x 2-inch baking dish.

Sauté mushrooms and remaining ½ cup onion in butter until tender. Add flour and cook, stirring constantly, 1 minute. Add reserved chicken broth; cook over medium heat, stirring constantly, until thickened and bubbly. Stir in salt, pepper, and remaining ¼ cup chopped parsley. Pour sauce over chopped chicken.

Prepare Cheese Crust; roll to a 15- x 11-inch rectangle. Place pastry over chicken; trim off excess pastry along edges. Fold edges under and flute, sealing to edges of casserole. Make slits in pastry to allow steam to escape.

Roll out dough scraps, and cut into desired shapes. Dampen with water, and arrange shapes over pastry, if desired. Bake pie at 400° for 30 to 35 minutes. Yield: 6 servings.

Cheese Crust:

1¼ cups all-purpose flour
¼ teaspoon salt
⅓ cup vegetable shortening
¾ cup (3 ounces) shredded medium
  Cheddar cheese
3 tablespoons cold water

Combine flour and salt; cut in shortening with pastry blender until mixture resembles coarse meal. Stir in Cheddar cheese. Sprinkle cold water (1 tablespoon at a time) evenly over surface; stir with a fork until all ingredients are moistened. Shape into a ball. Yield: enough pastry for one 12- x 8-inch crust.

Claire E. Sirmons,
Tifton, Georgia.

BISCUIT-TOPPED CHICKEN PIE
(pictured on page 238)

1 (3-pound) broiler-fryer, cut up
1½ teaspoons salt, divided
1 cup chopped carrots
1 cup frozen English peas
2½ cups diced potatoes
¼ cup chopped celery
½ teaspoon white pepper
1 teaspoon onion powder
¾ teaspoon poultry seasoning
3 tablespoons all-purpose flour
1 (5-ounce) can evaporated milk
1 cup chopped fresh mushrooms
Biscuit Topping
Butter or margarine, melted (optional)

Place chicken in a Dutch oven; cover with water and 1 teaspoon salt. Bring to a boil. Cover, reduce heat, and simmer 45 minutes or until tender. Drain chicken, reserving 2¾ cups broth. Set chicken aside.

Add remaining ½ teaspoon salt and next 7 ingredients to broth, and cook 20 minutes or until vegetables are tender. Combine flour and milk. Add to vegetable mixture, stirring constantly, until mixture is thickened.

Remove chicken from bone, and cut into bite-size pieces. Add chicken and mushrooms to vegetable mixture; mix well. Spoon into a lightly greased 13- x 9- x 2-inch baking dish. Arrange Biscuit Topping rounds over top of chicken mixture; bake at 400° for 25 minutes or until biscuits are golden. Brush tops of biscuits with butter, if desired. Yield: 6 to 8 servings.

Biscuit Topping:
½ **cup shortening**
2 **cups self-rising flour**
⅔ **cup milk**

Cut shortening into flour with a pastry blender until mixture resembles coarse meal. Add milk, and mix well.

Turn dough out onto a lightly floured surface. Roll dough to ⅓-inch thickness; cut rounds with a 2¾-inch biscuit cutter. Yield: 15 biscuit rounds.

Effie White,
Weaver, Alabama.

POTATO-TOPPED TURKEY PIE

4 **carrots, thinly sliced**
2 **stalks celery, chopped**
2 **small onions, minced**
1 **small green pepper, minced**
1 **cup sliced fresh mushrooms**
3 **tablespoons butter or margarine, melted**
2 **cups cooked English peas**
4 **cups cubed cooked turkey**
1 **teaspoon dried whole thyme**
1 **teaspoon dried whole basil**
½ **teaspoon rubbed sage**
¼ **cup butter or margarine**
¼ **cup whole wheat flour**
2 **cups turkey or chicken broth**
½ **cup half-and-half**
¼ **teaspoon ground nutmeg**
Pinch of red pepper
7 **cups peeled, cubed potatoes (about 6)**
½ **to ¾ cup milk**
¼ **cup grated Parmesan cheese, divided**
1½ **teaspoons salt**
2 **tablespoons butter or margarine**

Sauté first 5 ingredients in 3 tablespoons butter in a large Dutch oven until tender. Add English peas, turkey, thyme, basil, and sage; mix well. Set aside.

Melt ¼ cup butter in a heavy saucepan over low heat; add flour, stirring until smooth. Cook 1 minute, stirring constantly. Gradually add turkey broth and half-and-half; cook over medium heat, stirring constantly, until mixture is thickened and bubbly. Stir in nutmeg and red pepper. Add sauce to vegetable mixture; mix well. Pour into a greased 13- x 9- x 2-inch casserole.

Cook potatoes in water to cover until tender; drain well, and mash. Combine potatoes, ½ cup milk, 2 tablespoons Parmesan cheese, salt, and 2 tablespoons butter, mixing well. Add enough milk for spreading consistency. Spoon potatoes over vegetable mixture, and spread evenly, sealing edges. Sprinkle with remaining 2 tablespoons Parmesan cheese. Bake at 350° for 1 hour or until lightly browned. Yield: 8 servings.

Sara A. McCullough,
Broaddus, Texas.

CRUMB-CRUST CURRIED TURKEY PIE

¼ **cup golden raisins**
½ **cup boiling water**
1½ **cups herb-seasoned stuffing mix**
¼ **cup butter or margarine, melted**
2 **tablespoons water**
1 **(10-ounce) can cream of celery soup, undiluted**
1 **cup milk**
1½ **cups cubed cooked turkey**
1 **cup cooked English peas**
1 **(4-ounce) can sliced mushrooms, drained**
1 **tablespoon chopped onion**
¾ **teaspoon curry powder**
⅛ **teaspoon salt**
⅛ **teaspoon pepper**

Combine raisins and boiling water in a small bowl; let stand 5 minutes. Drain, and set aside.

Combine stuffing mix, butter, and water; mix well. Set aside ¼ cup stuffing mixture. Press remaining mixture in bottom and 1 inch up sides of four 10-ounce custard cups or ramekins.

Combine soup and milk; add raisins, turkey, and remaining ingredients, blending well. Pour mixture evenly into prepared dishes. Sprinkle each serving with 1 tablespoon reserved stuffing mixture. Bake pies, uncovered, at 375° for 20 minutes or until bubbly. Yield: 4 servings.

Note: This recipe can be made a day ahead. Do not sprinkle with crumb mixture. Cover individual dishes; refrigerate overnight. To bake, remove from refrigerator and uncover. Sprinkle with crumb mixture, and bake at 375° for 25 to 30 minutes or until bubbly.

Rublelene Singleton,
Scotts Hill, Tennessee.

TURKEY POT PIE
(pictured on page 238)

2 **(10¾-ounce) cans chicken broth, diluted**
1 **bay leaf**
½ **teaspoon white pepper**
2 **cups cubed potatoes**
1 **(16-ounce) package frozen mixed vegetables**
1 **stalk celery, chopped**
3 **tablespoons butter or margarine**
3 **tablespoons all-purpose flour**
3 **cups cubed cooked turkey**
4 **hard-cooked eggs, sliced**
Pastry for 9-inch pie

Combine broth, bay leaf, and pepper in a large Dutch oven; bring to a boil. Add potatoes; cover, reduce heat to medium, and cook 5 minutes. Add frozen vegetables and celery; return to a boil. Cover, reduce heat, and simmer 8 to 12 minutes. Remove bay leaf. Drain and set aside, reserving broth.

Melt butter in a Dutch oven over medium heat; add flour, stirring until smooth. Cook 1 minute, stirring constantly. Gradually add reserved broth; cook, stirring constantly, until mixture is thickened and bubbly. Stir in vegetables, turkey, and eggs; spoon mixture into a 2½-quart casserole. Place pastry over turkey mixture. Trim edges, seal, and flute. Roll out dough scraps, and cut into desired shapes. Dampen with water, and arrange over pastry, if desired. Cut slits in top of pastry to allow steam to escape. Bake at 400° for 20 minutes or until golden brown. Yield: 6 to 8 servings.

Betty Tucker,
Birmingham, Alabama.

For an extra-special touch, use leftover pastry cut into various shapes to decorate the top of Turkey Pot Pie before baking. Be sure to cut slits in the pastry to allow steam to escape while the pie bakes.

Headstart On The Holidays

Santa couldn't have planned it better himself. Our collection of holiday food gifts—fruitcakes, cookies, liqueurs, and more—is made to order for the busiest of holiday seasons.

The key is to begin preparation early to allow time for subtle flavors to blend and develop. Each recipe will stay fresh for up to four weeks after it's been prepared, so you can fill lots of Christmas orders, even in November.

And wrapping and packaging your gifts can be as rewarding as the preparation, especially when you use bright ribbons, tins, greenery, tissue, and wrapping paper. Or you can place your gifts in unique serving utensils.

Desserts such as Kentucky Fruitcake are always welcome. Glyna Meredith Gallrein shares her secret to success. The cake is wrapped in cheesecloth that's soaked in bourbon, making the cake's flavor "just right."

Mrs. Bill Anthony of Poteau, Oklahoma, uses cookie crumbs to give Crème de Cacao Balls their surprising, almost amaretto-like flavor. She serves them with eggnog ice cream or on a tray of sweets.

Coffee-Flavored Liqueur makes a distinctive gift as well. Scout out your favorite antique roost for a bottle the recipient will treasure long after the holidays are over.

KENTUCKY FRUITCAKE

1 (15-ounce) package golden raisins
1½ cups water
1½ cups sugar
¼ cup butter or margarine
1½ cups chopped pecans
½ pound candied green cherries, chopped
½ pound candied red cherries, chopped
1 pound candied pineapple, chopped
2½ cups all-purpose flour, divided
3 eggs, beaten
1 teaspoon baking powder
1 teaspoon baking soda
½ teaspoon salt
1 teaspoon ground cinnamon
½ teaspoon ground cloves
½ teaspoon ground allspice
½ cup bourbon (optional)
Candied red cherries, sliced (optional)
Sliced almonds (optional)

Combine first 3 ingredients in a saucepan; bring to a boil. Reduce heat, and simmer 5 minutes. Add butter, and remove from heat. Cool and drain, reserving liquid in a large mixing bowl. Set liquid and raisins aside.

Combine pecans and candied fruit; dredge in ½ cup flour, stirring to coat evenly. Set aside.

Add eggs to reserved liquid; mix well. Combine remaining 2 cups flour, baking powder, soda, salt, and spices; mix well. Add to egg mixture. Stir in raisins and fruit mixture; blend well. Spoon batter into a greased, floured brown paper-lined 10-inch tube pan. Bake at 275° for 2 to 2½ hours or until a wooden pick inserted in center comes out clean. Cool completely in pan. Remove cake, and take off paper.

Moisten several layers of cheesecloth with ½ cup bourbon, if desired; wrap cake in cheesecloth. Wrap with aluminum foil; store in a cool place at least 1 week, remoistening cheesecloth as needed. Garnish with sliced cherries and almonds, if desired. Yield: one 10-inch cake. *Glyna Meredith Gallrein, Anchorage, Kentucky.*

CRÈME DE CACAO BALLS

2½ cups crushed cream-filled chocolate sandwich cookies (about 30)
1 cup finely chopped pecans
1 cup sifted powdered sugar
⅓ cup crème de cacao
2 tablespoons dark corn syrup
Sifted powdered sugar

Combine first 5 ingredients in a medium bowl; mix well. Shape into 1-inch balls; roll balls in powdered sugar. Store in an airtight container in refrigerator. Before serving, roll again in powdered sugar. Yield: about 4 dozen.
Mrs. Bill Anthony, Poteau, Oklahoma.

FUDGE

4½ cups sugar
1 (12-ounce) can evaporated milk
2 tablespoons butter or margarine
Pinch of salt
3 (4-ounce) bars sweet baking chocolate, broken into pieces
1 (12-ounce) package semisweet chocolate morsels
2 cups coarsely chopped pecans
1 (8-ounce) jar marshmallow cream

Combine first 4 ingredients in a heavy saucepan; bring mixture to a boil, and cook 6 minutes, stirring constantly. Add remaining ingredients; stir until blended. Pour into a buttered 13- x 9- x 2-inch pan. Chill until set. Cut into 1-inch pieces. Store in an airtight container in refrigerator. Yield: 6 pounds.
Lorraine G. Bennett, Virginia Beach, Virginia.

ORANGE-CRANBERRY CHUTNEY

6 medium oranges
1 (12-ounce) package cranberries
¾ cup raisins
2 cups sugar
¼ cup finely chopped crystallized ginger
1 (2-inch) stick cinnamon
1 small clove garlic
½ teaspoon ground curry

Peel 2 oranges; slice peels into julienne strips to yield ¼ cup. Squeeze peeled oranges to yield ½ cup juice. Peel remaining 4 oranges, and remove orange sections.

Combine all ingredients except orange sections in a Dutch oven. Cook over medium heat, stirring constantly, until sugar dissolves and cranberry skins pop. Remove mixture from heat. Take out cinnamon stick and garlic; discard. Stir in orange sections.

Quickly spoon into hot sterilized jars, leaving ¼ inch headspace. Cover at once with metal lids, and screw on bands. Process in boiling-water bath 10 minutes. Yield: 5 half pints.

COFFEE-FLAVORED LIQUEUR

5 cups sugar
1 (2-ounce) jar instant coffee powder
4 cups boiling water
1 quart vodka
1 vanilla bean

Combine sugar and coffee; pour boiling water over mixture; stir occasionally, and let cool. Stir in vodka. Pour mixture evenly into 3 quart-size bottles or jars. Cut vanilla bean in 3 parts; place 1 piece in each jar. Cover and let stand 12 days. Transfer to decorative bottles. Yield: 9 cups. *Millie Givens, Savannah, Georgia.*

Start With Holiday Spirit

Start with lots of festive spirit. Mix in Southern hospitality. Add tasty food, and you have the perfect combination for holiday entertaining.

We are pleased to share our ninth annual special section on holiday dinners. We hope you gain a wealth of recipes and food ideas that will make this the most delicious season ever.

For those who like to do it up big, we begin our section in Pine Bluff, Arkansas, at the home of Lydia and Roderick Reed. "We've added to our home over the years to make it convenient for entertaining," Lydia tells us. "As you can see, we like parties." And so it is—Lydia adds an inviting touch to each room with flowers, a warm fire, or something to nibble. "I enjoy serving meals made up of heavy appetizers. That way everyone can just snack or eat a full dinner," says Lydia.

Because she's active in The Junior League of Pine Bluff, it's only natural that whenever Lydia plans a party like this, she includes recipes from *Southern Accent,* the League's cookbook. "The book has been around for 10 years, so some of us feel the recipes are practically part of our families," she claims.

Pine Bluff is duck country, so it comes as no surprise that Buffet Wild Duck heads the table. It's followed by Wild Rice and Sausage, Elegant Scalloped Corn, Wilted Lettuce, and Hot Biscuits. A silver antique supper set offers Country-Style Pea Soup, Shrimp Manale, Brandied Cranberries, and Pimiento Broccoli.

Guests choose from three pies for dessert—Grandmother's Pecan Pie, Sweet Potato Pie, and Apricot Fried Pies. Jefferson County Punch, a heady combination, is the perfect accompaniment for this fine holiday meal.

The hostess at this party likes meals that are made up of appetizer-size servings, so she offers a large number of recipes for guests to sample.

JEFFERSON COUNTY PUNCH

1½ cups sugar
2½ cups water
2½ cups lemon juice
1 (25.6-ounce) bottle dark rum
2 (25.6-ounce) bottles sauterne, chilled
½ cup applejack brandy
1 (25.4-ounce) bottle champagne, chilled
1 (33.8-ounce) bottle club soda, chilled

Combine sugar and water in a small saucepan. Bring to a boil; cover, reduce heat, and simmer 5 minutes. Chill.

Add lemon juice, rum, sauterne, and brandy to sugar mixture. Chill until ready to serve.

Pour punch into a chilled punch bowl. Add champagne and club soda; serve immediately (may be served over ice, if desired). Yield: 5½ quarts.

COUNTRY-STYLE PEA SOUP

1 (1-pound) package dried split peas
10 cups water
2 pounds ham hocks
1 medium onion, chopped
1 stalk celery, chopped
1 clove garlic, minced
⅛ teaspoon pepper
Salt to taste (optional)
Parsley sprigs (optional)

Combine first 7 ingredients in a Dutch oven. Bring to a boil; reduce heat, and simmer, uncovered, 1 hour or until peas are soft. Remove ham hock. Put the pea mixture through a food mill or sieve. Cook over low heat until thoroughly heated. Add salt to taste, and garnish with parsley sprigs, if desired. Yield: 6 cups.

SHRIMP MANALE

3 quarts water
4 pounds unpeeled large shrimp
2 cups unsalted butter
2 cups olive or vegetable oil
2 (6-ounce) bottles hot sauce
8 bay leaves
6 cloves garlic, crushed
Juice of 4 lemons
2 tablespoons plus 2 teaspoons fines
    herbes
2 tablespoons Worcestershire sauce
1 to 2 teaspoons freshly ground black
    pepper
Lettuce leaves (optional)
Lemon twists (optional)

Bring 3 quarts water to a boil in a large Dutch oven. Add shrimp, and cook 3 to 5 minutes. Drain well; rinse thoroughly with cold water. Peel and devein shrimp.

Melt butter in a heavy saucepan; add next 8 ingredients. Bring to a boil; reduce heat, and simmer, uncovered, 5 minutes.

Add shrimp to sauce mixture, and marinate in refrigerator 1 hour. Spoon into a serving dish, using a slotted spoon. Garnish shrimp with lettuce leaves and lemon twists, if desired. Yield: 20 appetizer servings.

BUFFET WILD DUCK

2 to 3 large cooking apples, cored and cut
    into wedges
10 (1½- to 2-pound) wild ducks, dressed
2 cups Burgundy wine
1 cup water
1 teaspoon salt
½ teaspoon pepper
Butter Sauce
Orange twists (optional)
Fresh rosemary leaves (optional)

Place apple wedges in cavities of ducks. Arrange ducks in a single or double layer in an extra-large roaster or two large Dutch ovens; pour Burgundy and water over ducks. Cover and bake at 350° for 3 hours or until ducks are very tender, basting occasionally.

Remove ducks from roaster, discarding apple wedges and pan drippings; let ducks chill thoroughly.

Bone ducks, and cut meat into bite-size pieces; return to roaster. Sprinkle meat with salt and pepper. Drizzle Butter Sauce over meat; toss gently. Cover and bake at 350° for an additional 30 minutes or until thoroughly heated. Transfer meat to serving platter, and garnish with orange twists and rosemary, if desired. Yield: 20 servings.

Butter Sauce:

1 cup butter, melted
⅓ cup lemon juice
¼ cup chopped fresh parsley
¼ cup sliced green onions
1 tablespoon Worcestershire sauce
1½ teaspoons prepared mustard

Combine all ingredients in a saucepan; heat thoroughly. Yield: 1⅔ cups.

WILD RICE AND SAUSAGE

1 pound bulk pork sausage
1 cup chopped celery
1 large onion, chopped
1 medium-size green pepper, chopped
1 clove garlic, minced
3 cups chicken broth
1 (10¾-ounce) can cream of mushroom
    soup, undiluted
1 (10¾-ounce) can cream of chicken soup,
    undiluted
1 (8-ounce) can sliced water chestnuts,
    drained
2 (4-ounce) cans sliced mushrooms,
    drained
1 (6-ounce) package long-grain and wild
    rice mix
Dash of dried whole thyme
1 (2-ounce) package sliced almonds
Parsley sprigs (optional)

Combine sausage, celery, onion, green pepper, and garlic in a large skillet; cook over medium heat until sausage is browned and vegetables are tender, stirring to crumble meat. Drain. Stir in remaining ingredients except almonds and parsley; mix well. Spoon into a lightly greased 3-quart casserole, and sprinkle with almonds. Bake at 350° for 1½ hours. Garnish with parsley, if desired. Yield: 12 servings.

Note: Prepare recipe again to serve a larger crowd.

ELEGANT SCALLOPED CORN

¾ cup (3 ounces) Cheddar cheese, cubed
1 (17-ounce) can cream-style corn
1 cup cracker crumbs
½ cup chopped celery
½ cup chopped onion
2 eggs, well beaten
1 cup milk
2 tablespoons butter or margarine, melted
Paprika
Parsley
Sweet red pepper rings

Combine cheese, corn, cracker crumbs, celery, and onion; stir in eggs, milk, and butter, mixing well. Pour into a greased 2-quart casserole. Bake, uncovered, at 350° for 50 minutes. Sprinkle with paprika; garnish with parsley and pepper rings. Yield: 8 servings.

Note: Prepare recipe again to serve a larger crowd.

PIMIENTO BROCCOLI

3 pounds fresh broccoli
1 cup chopped green onions
½ cup butter or margarine, melted
¾ cup pimiento, coarsely chopped
1½ tablespoons grated lemon rind
½ cup lemon juice
½ teaspoon salt
¼ teaspoon pepper

Trim off large leaves of broccoli; wash thoroughly, and cut stalks about one inch from flowerets. Steam flowerets in a small amount of boiling water 10 to 15 minutes or until crisp-tender.

Sauté green onions in butter in a saucepan until tender. Stir in remaining ingredients; reduce heat, and simmer 5 minutes. Place broccoli in a large serving dish; spoon sauce over broccoli, and toss gently. Yield: 12 servings.

WILTED LETTUCE

8 cups torn leaf lettuce
6 to 8 small green onions, chopped
8 slices bacon
½ cup vinegar
2 tablespoons plus 2 teaspoons brown sugar
Cherry tomatoes (optional)

Combine lettuce and green onions in a large bowl; set aside. Cook bacon in a skillet until crisp; remove bacon, reserving drippings in skillet. Crumble bacon, and sprinkle over lettuce.

Add vinegar and brown sugar to bacon drippings; bring to a boil, stirring constantly, until sugar dissolves. Pour over lettuce; toss gently. Garnish with cherry tomatoes, if desired. Serve immediately. Yield: 8 servings.

BRANDIED CRANBERRIES

4 cups fresh cranberries
2 cups sugar
¼ cup brandy
¼ cup sugar

Place cranberries in a shallow baking pan; sprinkle with 2 cups sugar. Bake at 350° for 30 minutes, stirring occasionally. Remove from oven; stir in brandy and ¼ cup sugar. Chill. Yield: 2 cups.

HOT BISCUITS

2½ cups all-purpose flour
2 teaspoons baking powder
½ teaspoon baking soda
½ teaspoon salt
¼ cup plus 2 tablespoons shortening
1 cup milk
1½ teaspoons lemon juice

Combine flour, baking powder, soda, and salt; mix well. Cut in shortening with a pastry blender until mixture resembles coarse meal.

Combine milk and lemon juice; add to flour mixture, stirring just until dry ingredients are moistened. Turn dough out onto a floured surface, and knead 3 or 4 times.

Roll dough to a 16- x 12-inch rectangle; carefully fold in half lengthwise. Roll up jellyroll fashion, starting with folded edge. Cut roll into ¾-inch slices. Place slices cut side down on a greased baking sheet. Bake at 425° for 10 minutes or until tops are golden. Yield: about 20 biscuits.

SWEET POTATO PIE

2 cups mashed cooked sweet potatoes
½ cup butter or margarine, softened
2 eggs, separated
1 cup firmly packed brown sugar
¼ teaspoon salt
½ teaspoon ground cinnamon
½ teaspoon ground nutmeg
½ teaspoon ground ginger
½ cup milk
¼ cup sugar
1 unbaked (9-inch) pastry shell

Combine sweet potatoes, butter, egg yolks, brown sugar, salt, and spices. Stir in milk, and mix well. Beat egg whites (at room temperature) at high speed of an electric mixer 1 minute. Gradually add ¼ cup sugar, 1 tablespoon at a time, beating until stiff peaks form.

Fold egg whites into sweet potato mixture. Spoon mixture into unbaked pastry shell. Bake at 400° for 10 minutes; reduce heat to 350°, and bake an additional 45 minutes or until set. Yield: one 9-inch pie.

APRICOT FRIED PIES

1 (6-ounce) package dried apricots
⅓ cup sugar
4 cups all-purpose flour
½ teaspoon salt
1 cup shortening
1 cup cold water
Vegetable oil
Sifted powdered sugar
Additional dried apricots (optional)

Place a 6-ounce package apricots in a medium saucepan; add water to cover. Cover pan and cook over low heat 15 minutes or until apricots are tender. Mash apricots, and add sugar; set aside.

Combine flour and salt; cut in shortening with pastry blender until mixture resembles coarse meal. Sprinkle cold water (1 tablespoon at a time) evenly over surface; stir with a fork until dry ingredients are moistened. Shape into a ball, and chill.

Divide dough in half. Roll one portion to ⅛-inch thickness on a lightly floured surface; cut into 3½-inch circles. Spoon about 1 teaspoon apricot filling on half of each pastry circle; moisten edges of circles with water. Fold circles in half; press edges together with a fork dipped in flour. Repeat procedure with the remaining dough.

Heat ½ inch oil to 375° in a large skillet. Cook pies until golden brown, turning once; drain well on paper towels. Sprinkle with powdered sugar. Garnish with additional dried apricots, if desired. Yield: about 3 dozen.

GRANDMOTHER'S PECAN PIE

1 cup sugar
1 cup dark corn syrup
3 eggs
2 tablespoons butter or margarine, melted
1 teaspoon vanilla extract
1 cup coarsely chopped pecans
1 unbaked (9-inch) pastry shell
Whipped cream (optional)

Combine sugar and corn syrup in a small saucepan; bring to a boil. Beat eggs at medium speed of an electric mixer until blended. Gradually add hot sugar mixture to eggs, beating constantly. Stir in butter, vanilla, and pecans. Pour mixture into pastry shell; bake at 350° for 40 minutes. Serve with whipped cream, if desired. Yield: one 9-inch pie.

Beverages For That Holiday Spirit

Whether you're serving drinks to guests at a big holiday bash or to drop-in visitors, you want the beverage to be special. Take your pick of spiked, spiced, hot, or cold concoctions with these recipes.

S. Jones Price, Jr., of Birmingham, says he stores the citrus syrup for his Old-Fashioneds in the refrigerator ready to pour over crushed ice. The fruit-flavored mixture sparked with Canadian whiskey can be made ahead and chilled.

For teetotalers' parties, Cranberry-Cinnamon Punch will be a hit. The cinnamon flavor and Christmas-red color come from melted red candies.

Hot beverages are in demand on extra-chilly days. For those times, keep a pot of Bourbon Wassail or Hot Apple Juice simmering on the stove.

BOURBON WASSAIL

2 tablespoons grated orange rind
2 tablespoons whole cloves
2 tablespoons whole allspice
2 (2-inch) sticks cinnamon
1 gallon apple cider or apple juice
1 cup orange juice
1 cup bourbon

Combine orange rind and spices in a cheesecloth bag; set aside.

Combine apple cider and orange juice in a large Dutch oven; add spice bag. Bring mixture to a boil. Cover, reduce heat, and simmer 15 minutes. Discard spice bag. Add bourbon to cider mixture. Serve hot. Yield: 1 gallon.
Paulette E. Paolozzi,
Annapolis, Maryland.

Tip: Serving a large amount of steaming hot beverage at a party? Then set up a table by an electrical outlet so that you can serve the hot drink from an electric slow cooker. Mix up the beverage in the cooker. Once the drink is hot, the lowest setting will keep it brewing throughout the evening.

OLD-FASHIONEDS

2 cups Sweet Citrus Syrup
6 cups lemon-lime carbonated beverage
3 cups Canadian whiskey
½ teaspoon aromatic bitters
Crushed ice
Orange, lemon, and lime slices
Maraschino cherries

Combine first 4 ingredients, and mix well. Fill glasses with crushed ice; pour mixture over ice. Garnish with fruit. Yield: 16 servings.

Sweet Citrus Syrup:
1 (12-ounce) can frozen concentrate five-fruit citrus beverage
½ cup grenadine syrup or maraschino cherry juice
1 tablespoon sugar

Combine all ingredients in a saucepan; bring to a boil. Remove from heat, and let cool. Pour into a container; cover and refrigerate up to two weeks. Yield: 2 cups.

Note: For each individual serving, place 2 tablespoons Sweet Citrus Syrup, ¼ cup plus 1 tablespoon lemon-lime carbonated beverage, 3 tablespoons whiskey, and a dash of aromatic bitters in a glass. Mix well. Add enough finely crushed ice to fill glass; stir gently. Garnish with citrus slices and a cherry.
S. Jones Price, Jr.,
Birmingham, Alabama.

MOCHA PUNCH

7 cups brewed coffee, chilled
½ gallon chocolate ice cream, softened and divided
2½ cups whipping cream, whipped and divided
¼ cup rum
Grated semisweet chocolate

Combine coffee, half of ice cream, and 4 cups whipped cream in a large mixing bowl or punch bowl; stir gently with a wire whisk until almost smooth. Add rum; stir gently. Fold in remainder of ice cream. Garnish each serving with a dollop of remaining whipped cream and a sprinkle of grated chocolate. Yield: 1 gallon.   *Mrs. John A. Wyatt,*
Palmyra, Tennessee.

CRANBERRY-CINNAMON PUNCH

¼ cup red cinnamon candies
1 quart water
2 quarts cranberry juice cocktail, chilled
1 (6-ounce) can frozen limeade concentrate, thawed and undiluted
1 (6-ounce) can frozen orange juice concentrate, thawed and undiluted

Combine candies and water in a small saucepan; cook over medium heat, stirring constantly, until candy melts. Remove from heat; cool. Cover and chill. Add the remaining ingredients; stir well. Yield: 3 quarts.   *Amy Cross,*
Knoxville, Tennessee.

HOT APPLE JUICE

2 quarts apple juice
½ cup firmly packed brown sugar
1 (3-inch) stick cinnamon
6 whole cloves
4 (3- x ½-inch) strips orange rind
Ground nutmeg

Mix all ingredients except nutmeg in a Dutch oven; simmer 20 minutes. Remove and discard spices.

To serve, pour into individual mugs, and sprinkle each serving with nutmeg. Yield: 2 quarts.   *Mrs. Paul Raper,*
Burgaw, North Carolina.

Right: *Sausage Dressing (page 280) is seasoned just right so that it doesn't overpower the mild taste of turkey.*

Page 274: *A fruity topping gives Cranberry-Pineapple Rolls (page 275) a festive look.*

Above: *Set out dessert in the den or library (from front) Christmas Coeur á la Crème with apple wedges, Spirited Chocolates, and Peppermint Patties. (Recipes begin on page 278.)*

Left: *Give Cream Cheese Pound Cake (page 287) a festive touch with commercial strawberry topping.*

Far left: *Serve Turkey-Rice Pilaf (page 284) hot or cold; it's good either way.*

Fruit Makes It Special

Fruit—it's a symbol of the season, so why not stir it into your favorite recipes? Fruit goes well with so many other foods that you'll find tasty ways to add it to appetizers, breads, sauces, meat, vegetables, and desserts.

CRANBERRY-PINEAPPLE ROLLS
(pictured on page 274)

1 package dry yeast
¼ cup warm water (105° to 115°)
½ cup milk, scalded
¼ cup butter or margarine
1½ tablespoons sugar
½ teaspoon salt
1 egg, beaten
2½ to 3 cups all-purpose flour
¾ cup whole-berry cranberry sauce
¼ cup drained crushed pineapple
½ teaspoon grated orange rind

Dissolve yeast in warm water in a large bowl; let stand 5 minutes. Combine milk, butter, sugar, and salt; mix well. Cool to lukewarm (105° to 115°). Add to yeast mixture, mixing well. Add egg. Gradually stir in enough flour to make a soft dough.

Turn dough out onto a floured surface, and knead until smooth and elastic (about 8 to 10 minutes). Place in a well-greased bowl, turning to grease top. Cover and let rise in a warm place (85°), free from drafts, 1 hour or until doubled in bulk.

Roll dough out to ¼-inch thickness; cut with a 1¼-inch cutter into 90 circles. Arrange 5 circles around side of each of 15 greased muffin cups, and place 1 circle in center. Cover; let rise in a warm place, free from drafts, 30 minutes or until doubled in bulk.

Punch down center of rolls. Combine cranberry sauce, pineapple, and orange rind. Spoon about 2 teaspoons mixture into the center of each roll. Bake at 400° for 12 minutes or until lightly browned. Yield: 15 rolls.

Mary M. Hoppe,
Kitty Hawk, North Carolina.

APRICOT BRIE SPREAD

½ cup water
3 tablespoons chopped dried apricots
1½ teaspoons brandy
2 tablespoons ground pecans
1 (4½-ounce) can Brie cheese
1 sheet frozen phyllo pastry, thawed
2 teaspoons butter or margarine, melted
Seedless green grape clusters

Combine water, apricots, and brandy in a small saucepan; bring mixture to a boil and cook, stirring constantly, 10 minutes or until soft. Stir in pecans.

Slice casing from top of Brie, cutting to within ¼ inch of edge. Slice Brie in half horizontally. Shape a shallow aluminum foil cup larger than cheese; place bottom half of cheese in foil. Spread with apricot mixture; top with remaining cheese.

Cut phyllo sheet into two 4½-inch circles. Brush each phyllo circle with butter, and place on top of Brie, pressing edges down. Place on a baking sheet; broil 8 inches from heat 3 to 4 minutes or until golden brown. Place Brie spread on serving plate, and garnish with grapes. Serve with assorted crackers. Yield: 8 servings.

CRANBERRY-NUT RELISH

1 small thin-skin orange, quartered
2 cups fresh cranberries
1 medium apple, quartered and seeded
2 cups pecan halves
¾ cup sugar

Position knife blade in food processor bowl; add orange. Cover with top; process 3 minutes or until orange peel is finely chopped. Add cranberries, apple, and pecans; pulse 4 times, scraping sides of processor bowl between each pulse. Remove cranberry mixture from processor bowl, and add sugar, stirring well. Cover and chill. Yield: 3 cups.

Beverly Hyde,
Talladega, Alabama.

TROPICAL CRÊPES

2 (8-ounce) cans pineapple tidbits, undrained
1 tablespoon plus 1 teaspoon cornstarch
1 teaspoon rum flavoring
1 cup whipping cream
⅓ cup cream of coconut
12 Basic Dessert Crêpes
¼ cup flaked coconut

Combine pineapple and cornstarch in a small saucepan; mix well. Cook over medium heat, stirring constantly, until thickened. Stir in rum flavoring. Remove from heat; cool.

Beat whipping cream until stiff peaks form. Fold cream of coconut into whipped cream; spread down center of each crêpe. Fold sides over, and place seam side down on serving dishes. Spoon pineapple sauce over crêpes; sprinkle with coconut. Yield: 12 crêpes.

Basic Dessert Crêpes:

1½ cups all-purpose flour
1 tablespoon sugar
¼ teaspoon salt
2 cups milk
1 teaspoon vanilla extract
3 eggs
2 tablespoons butter or margarine, melted
Vegetable oil

Combine flour, sugar, salt, milk, and vanilla, beating until smooth. Add eggs, and beat well; stir in butter. Refrigerate batter at least 2 hours. (This allows flour particles to swell and soften so that crêpes are light in texture.)

Brush bottom of a 6-inch crêpe pan or heavy skillet with oil; place over medium heat until just hot, not smoking.

Pour 2 tablespoons batter into pan; quickly tilt pan in all directions so batter covers pan in a thin film. Cook 1 minute or until lightly browned.

Lift edge of crêpe to test for doneness. Crêpe is ready for flipping when it can be shaken loose from pan. Flip crêpe, and cook about 30 seconds on other side. (This side is usually spotty brown and is the side on which the filling is placed.)

Place crêpes on a towel to cool. Stack between layers of waxed paper to prevent sticking. Repeat until all batter is used. Yield: 2 dozen (6-inch) crêpes.

SWEET POTATO-BANANA CASSEROLE

6 medium-size sweet potatoes, peeled and
  quartered
1 medium banana, mashed
¼ cup pineapple juice
¼ cup sugar
2 tablespoons half-and-half
¼ teaspoon almond extract
⅛ teaspoon salt
1½ cups miniature marshmallows

Cook sweet potatoes in boiling water to cover for 20 minutes or until tender. Mash potatoes; set aside.

Combine mashed banana and pineapple juice; mix well. Add potatoes, sugar, half-and-half, almond flavoring, and salt; mix well. Spoon into a greased 8-inch square casserole.

Cover and bake at 350° for 30 minutes or until thoroughly heated. Uncover. Top with marshmallows, and bake an additional 7 minutes or until golden brown. Yield: 6 to 8 servings.
*Bernice T. Bates,
Jackson, Mississippi.*

Plan A Party Like The Pros

Sometime during the holidays, why not open your house to family and friends with an elaborate appetizer and dessert buffet? Sound like a job for a professional caterer? Not necessarily. We've put together a party plan that lets you be in charge, but it's also sophisticated enough that guests will think professionals are in the kitchen.

A successful party is one where presentation and service appear effortless and the hostess has more time with her guests. That means she has to work hard beforehand. We planned this menu so that all the recipes can be prepared ahead of time and chilled or frozen until ready to serve. Then the only thing you have to do on the day of the party is to arrange the food on serving trays and garnish it.

For your convenience, our menu also makes use of commercially prepared items, such as party rolls for the smoked turkey and frozen puff pastry for the Ham-and-Cheese Puffs. And you can buy the smoked turkey on our menu from a restaurant instead of smoking it yourself.

In this season of hustle and bustle, you'll want guests to remember the easygoing hospitality of your home. So follow these hints for a party that you'll enjoy, too.

Gearing Up For the Party

Get your invitations in the mail at least three weeks ahead of time—earlier if you think others are planning events around the same time. Don't hesitate to put an RSVP on the invitation, and include a date by which you'd like your friends to respond.

If your house is small and your guest list is large, consider staggering the hours on the invitations. That way everyone won't be there at the same time.

You'll want to plan your menu and make out a timetable of things to do at least two weeks ahead. Once you decide on the menu, make out a grocery list in two parts: things that can be bought and prepared ahead of time and stored, and perishables that need to be purchased a day or two before the party.

Plan two different work schedules, too. The first should include anything that can be done early, such as preparing some food, checking linens, polishing silver, or ordering items that need to be rented. The second schedule should organize all the things you'll need to do the day of the party. Allow extra time to relax and get yourself ready for the party so you can greet early arrivals.

The Menu Is Most Important

When planning your menu, stay away from recipes that involve much last-minute cooking, and make use of commercial foods when you can. Don't be afraid to pick up items from the bakery. Your guests probably won't know unless you tell them.

Concentrate on dishes that guests can easily serve themselves. If you don't

have room to seat everyone, it's probably best to offer all finger foods. Our menu requires no forks.

Take Stock of Equipment

As you put each recipe on the menu, determine the equipment it will require. Do you have the right size muffin pans or enough refrigerator and oven space?

Portable toaster ovens can expand your oven space, and insulated ice chests come in handy for keeping beverages and other items cold. You might even be able to borrow a little space in a neighbor's refrigerator as you prepare recipes in advance.

If you don't own enough of one china, crystal, or silver pattern to serve everyone at a large party, you're in the majority. There's nothing wrong with mixing and matching the different patterns you have. You can help unify them with the color of linens or accessories you use.

Keep the Crowd Moving

When you give a party, folks always congregate around the food; scatter the food, and you'll scatter the crowd. They'll visit with more people if you subtly motivate them to move from room to room.

If you're setting up one large buffet table, the way you arrange the food can help guests serve themselves quickly and easily. Place the food on the table in a logical serving order so guests won't need to backtrack. For example, plates are always placed where the line begins. Put napkins and silverware where the line ends, so that guests won't have to hold on to them as they serve themselves. If any food needs to be kept in electric warmers, make sure outlets are nearby.

Setting the Mood

Many hostesses no longer routinely telephone the florist to order a formal flower arrangement when they entertain. Flowers or greenery arrangements may often be from their own yard or more casually arranged florist varieties.

Today's informal entertaining provides a wonderful opportunity for displaying originality by using whatever is on hand. Many hostesses have favorite decorative pieces—such as figurines, bowls, and carvings—that work well as table displays. Shells, rocks, driftwood, and plants all make creative accessories. Cut greenery and plaid ribbon will also brighten the holiday setting and require little time or special skill to arrange. Just remember that for a table center-piece, the arrangement should not be above eye level.

Candles can also set a festive mood. You can scatter them as singles or ar-range in groups throughout the house, dimming supplemental lighting as the evening progresses.

Tackling Our Menu

These recipes, which will serve about 25 people, were grouped so that you can spread out food preparation over the week before the event. The Ham-and-Cheese Puffs can be made and fro-zen up to a month ahead of time.

The Horseradish-Chive Butter, Little Feta Cheesecakes, Peppermint Patties, and Spirited Chocolates can be made three or four days in advance. Store the Peppermint Patties in an airtight con-tainer at room temperature; store the remaining items covered in the refriger-ator. You can smoke the turkey (or purchase it) up to two days ahead. Re-frigerate it until ready to serve.

The Eggplant Spread, Sour Cream Dip, and Christmas Cœur à la Crème will be best when made the day before the party. Let the Eggplant Spread come to room temperature before serv-ing, but keep the others refrigerated until ready to serve.

OPEN-HOUSE MENU
Ham-and-Cheese Puffs
Smoked Turkey
Horseradish-Chive Butter
Rolls
Little Feta Cheesecakes
Eggplant Spread
Sour Cream Dip   Fresh Vegetables
Christmas Cœur à la Crème
Peppermint Patties
Spirited Chocolates
White Wine

HAM-AND-CHEESE PUFFS

1½ (1-pound) packages frozen puff pastry, thawed
⅓ cup peach preserves
⅓ cup spicy prepared mustard
23 (1-ounce) slices cooked ham
12 (¾-ounce) slices Swiss cheese
2 egg yolks, beaten

Working with one portion at a time, roll each of the 3 portions of puff pastry into an 18- x 9-inch rectangle on a lightly floured surface. Cut 15 (3-inch) squares from each portion of rolled dough. Cut 15 (¾-inch) rounds from each dough portion.

Combine peach preserves and mus-tard; stir well. Spread about ½ teaspoon on each square of dough, leaving a ¾-inch margin around edges. Cut each ham square and each cheese square into 4 (1½-inch) squares. Layer a ham square, a cheese square, and another ham square diagonally on one pastry square. Brush yolk over edges of square. Fold all corners to the middle; pinch edges to seal. Brush one side of a small round of dough with yolk; place on top of ham-and-cheese bundle, egg side down. Press slightly in center. Re-peat procedure to use remaining ingre-dients. Place on ungreased baking sheets, and freeze at least 15 minutes. Bake at 425° for 15 to 17 minutes or until puffed and lightly browned. Yield: 45 appetizers.

Note: Pastries may be frozen before baking. Freeze on baking sheets; when frozen, place in airtight container, and freeze up to one month. To bake, place pastries on baking sheets, and bake as directed above.

HORSERADISH-CHIVE BUTTER

1 cup butter, softened
¼ cup chopped fresh or frozen chives
2 tablespoons prepared horseradish

Combine all ingredients. Spoon into butter molds, if desired. Chill until ready to serve. Invert molds and press gently to remove butter. Serve butter at room temperature with smoked turkey. Yield: 1 cup.

LITTLE FETA CHEESECAKES

½ cup fine dry breadcrumbs
½ cup ground pecans
¼ cup butter or margarine
1 (8-ounce) package cream cheese, softened
4 ounces feta cheese, crumbled
1 egg
2 tablespoons milk
⅛ teaspoon hot sauce
Herbed Tomato Sauce
Sliced ripe olives
Fresh parsley sprigs

Combine first 3 ingredients; stir well. Line 1¾-inch muffin pans with minia-ture paper liners. Spoon and press about 1 teaspoon mixture into bottom of each liner.

Beat cream cheese at medium speed of an electric mixer until light and fluffy; add feta cheese and egg, beating well. Stir in milk and hot sauce. Spoon mixture evenly into paper liners. Bake at 350° for 10 to 12 minutes. Let cool; cover and chill.

Remove paper liners. Spoon about ½ teaspoon Herbed Tomato Sauce over each cheesecake. Garnish with a slice of olive and a parsley sprig. Cover and chill cheesecakes until ready to serve. Yield: about 4 dozen.

Herbed Tomato Sauce:

½ cup tomato sauce
2 tablespoons tomato paste
1 tablespoon minced onion
1 small clove garlic, minced
¼ teaspoon dried whole basil
¼ teaspoon dried whole oregano
⅛ teaspoon pepper

Combine all ingredients in a sauce-pan; stir until blended. Cook over me-dium heat 5 minutes or until thickened. Yield: ⅔ cup.

Tip: Most cheeses should be wrapped in moisture-proof airtight wrappers. One exception is "moldy" cheeses, such as blue cheese, which needs to breathe and should be kept in covered contain-ers with the tops loosened a bit. All cheese keeps best on the bottom shelf of the refrigerator.

EGGPLANT SPREAD

1 medium eggplant
1 tomato, peeled and finely chopped
1 small onion, finely chopped
½ cup finely chopped red pepper
1 clove garlic, minced
3 tablespoons olive oil
2 tablespoons red wine vinegar
½ teaspoon salt
¼ teaspoon pepper
Lettuce leaves
Bagel Crisps

Cook unpeeled eggplant in boiling water to cover for 10 to 15 minutes or until tender. Drain and cool. Peel and finely chop the eggplant.

Combine eggplant, tomato, onion, red pepper, garlic, olive oil, vinegar, salt, and pepper, stirring gently. Cover and chill at least 8 hours, stirring occasionally.

To serve, spoon spread into lettuce-lined bowl. Serve at room temperature with Bagel Crisps. Yield: 3¾ cups.

Bagel Crisps:

6 bagels
⅓ cup butter or margarine, softened
Sesame seeds (optional)

Cut bagels into ¼-inch slices using a serrated knife; place on baking sheet. Spread butter on bagels; sprinkle with sesame seeds, if desired. Bake at 300° for 20 minutes or until bagels are lightly browned and crisp. Remove bagels to a wire rack to cool. Store in an airtight container at room temperature. Yield: about 2½ dozen.

SOUR CREAM DIP

1 (16-ounce) carton commercial sour cream
½ cup chili sauce
¼ cup plus 2 tablespoons chopped fresh parsley
2 cloves garlic, minced
½ teaspoon white pepper
Chopped fresh parsley

Combine first 5 ingredients, mixing well. Chill thoroughly.

To serve, sprinkle dip with parsley. Serve with assorted fresh vegetables. Yield: 2½ cups.

CHRISTMAS CŒUR À LA CRÈME
(pictured on page 273)

1 cup whipping cream
1 tablespoon buttermilk
1½ cups small curd cottage cheese
1 (8-ounce) package cream cheese, softened
3 tablespoons powdered sugar
⅓ cup whipping cream, whipped
Cranberry Sauce
Fresh cranberries (optional)
Green apple wedges

Combine 1 cup whipping cream and buttermilk in a small mixing bowl; stir well. Cover and let stand at room temperature 20 to 24 hours or until thickened (about the consistency of sour cream). If necessary, chill mixture overnight before completing recipe. (If chilled, let mixture return almost to room temperature before proceeding.)

Combine cottage cheese, cream cheese, and powdered sugar in a mixing bowl; beat at medium speed of an electric mixer until smooth. Gradually add thickened cream mixture, beating until smooth. Fold in whipped cream.

Line a 4-cup mold with cheesecloth, letting cloth hang over edges. Spoon cheese mixture into prepared pan. Fold cheesecloth over top; cover and chill mold overnight.

To serve, unfold cheesecloth, and unmold cheese mold onto serving plate that has a rim around edges to hold sauce. Remove cheesecloth, and spoon Cranberry Sauce around base of mold. Drizzle small amount of Cranberry Sauce on top of cheese mold. Garnish mold with fresh cranberries, if desired, and serve with green apple wedges. Yield: one 4-cup mold.

Cranberry Sauce:

1 cup cranberry juice cocktail
1 tablespoon cornstarch
⅓ cup sugar
3 tablespoons brandy or rum

Combine cranberry juice cocktail and cornstarch in a small saucepan, stirring until cornstarch is blended. Stir in sugar; cook over medium heat until sugar dissolves and mixture thickens. Stir in brandy, and let mixture cool before serving. Yield: 1¼ cups.

PEPPERMINT PATTIES
(pictured on page 273)

1 cup butter or margarine, softened
1½ cups sugar
1 egg
1 to 1½ teaspoons peppermint extract
2½ cups all-purpose flour
1½ teaspoons baking powder
¼ teaspoon salt
Red food coloring

Cream butter; gradually add sugar, beating until light and fluffy. Add egg and peppermint extract; beat well. Combine next 3 ingredients; add to mixture, beating just until blended.

Divide dough in half; add a few drops red food coloring to one half, and knead until color is distributed. Cover and refrigerate both halves until firm.

Divide each portion of dough into 2 equal portions. On floured waxed paper, roll one white portion and one red portion into an 8-inch square. Invert white dough onto red dough; peel waxed paper from white dough. Tightly roll dough jellyroll fashion, peeling waxed paper from red dough as you roll. Repeat with remaining dough. Cover with waxed paper, and chill.

Cut dough into ¼-inch slices; place on ungreased baking sheets. Bake at 350° for 10 minutes. Remove to wire racks to cool. Yield: 4 dozen.

SPIRITED CHOCOLATES
(pictured on page 273)

2 tablespoons butter or margarine, softened
2 tablespoons plus 1 teaspoon Kirsch or Chambord
2½ to 3 cups sifted powdered sugar
2 (12-ounce) packages semisweet chocolate morsels

Combine butter and liqueur; blend well. Stir in enough powdered sugar to make mixture the consistency of craft dough, kneading as necessary. Shape mixture into 4 dozen balls; chill.

Place chocolate in top of a double boiler; bring water to a boil. Reduce heat to low; cook until chocolate melts. Let chocolate stand over hot water as you mold chocolates.

Spoon about ½ teaspoon melted chocolate into each plastic mold intended for chocolate-covered cherries. Spread chocolate to cover sides of mold using the back of a small spoon. Freeze about 10 minutes or until firm. Place one fondant ball in each mold; spoon in additional chocolate to fill molds. Chill until firm.

Invert plastic molds, and gently tap to release candy. Store in the refrigerator. Yield: 4 dozen.

Note: Candy mixture may also be dipped in melted chocolate if chocolate-covered cherry molds are unavailable.

Vegetables For Special Dinners

Family members expect their favorite vegetable recipes—the ones savored for special occasions—to accompany the traditional turkey and dressing. Casseroles seem to be favored because many of them can be assembled in advance and baked just before dinner.

ASPARAGUS-ARTICHOKE CASSEROLE

½ cup chopped green pepper
1 tablespoon butter or margarine, melted
2 (8-ounce) packages frozen chopped asparagus
1 (10¾-ounce) can cream of mushroom soup, undiluted
1 cup chopped artichoke hearts
1 (3-ounce) can sliced ripe olives, drained
1½ cups mushrooms, sliced
3 hard-cooked eggs, sliced
1¼ cups (5 ounces) shredded Cheddar cheese

Sauté green pepper in butter in a skillet 5 minutes; set aside.

Cook asparagus according to package directions; drain, reserving ¼ cup liquid. Combine liquid and soup; mix well.

Layer half each of asparagus, green pepper, artichokes, olives, mushrooms, eggs, and soup mixture in a greased 2-quart casserole. Repeat layers. Bake, uncovered, at 350° for 30 minutes. Sprinkle with cheese, and bake an additional 5 minutes. Yield: 8 servings.

*Tony Jones,
Atlanta, Georgia.*

CARROT CASSEROLE

5½ cups sliced peeled carrots (about 2½ pounds)
1½ cups water
1 chicken-flavored bouillon cube
1 bunch green onions, chopped
2 tablespoons butter or margarine, melted
8 ounces process American cheese spread, cubed
1 (8-ounce) carton commercial sour cream
¼ cup milk
1 tablespoon seasoned dry breadcrumbs
1 tablespoon chopped fresh parsley

Combine first 3 ingredients in a medium saucepan; cover, bring to a boil, and cook 15 to 20 minutes or until carrots are crisp-tender. Drain.

Sauté green onions in butter in a skillet; remove from heat. Add cheese spread, sour cream, and milk; blend well. Stir in sliced carrots. Spoon into a greased 2-quart casserole. Sprinkle with breadcrumbs and parsley. Bake at 350° for 20 minutes or until hot. Yield: 8 servings.

*Betty Willis,
Nashville, Tennessee.*

CAULIFLOWER CASSEROLE

1 large head cauliflower, cut into flowerets
1 (10¾-ounce) can cream of shrimp soup, undiluted
1 (8-ounce) carton commercial sour cream
2 tablespoons butter or margarine, melted and divided
¼ teaspoon pepper
¼ cup dry breadcrumbs

Cook cauliflower in a small amount of boiling water 6 to 8 minutes or until crisp-tender. Drain well; place flowerets in a buttered 2-quart shallow casserole. Set aside.

Combine soup, sour cream, 1 tablespoon butter, and pepper; stir well. Pour over cauliflower. Combine breadcrumbs and remaining 1 tablespoon butter; stir well. Sprinkle over soup mixture; bake at 350° for 20 to 25 minutes or until bubbly. Yield: 6 servings.

*Ann Elsie Schmetzer,
Madisonville, Kentucky.*

ORANGE SWEET POTATOES

8 medium-size sweet potatoes
1 cup firmly packed light brown sugar
2 tablespoons cornstarch
½ teaspoon salt
2 teaspoons grated orange rind
2 cups orange juice
⅓ cup sherry
¼ cup plus 2 tablespoons butter or margarine

Cook sweet potatoes in boiling water 20 minutes or until almost tender. Drain and cool. Peel potatoes, and slice crosswise into ½-inch slices. Arrange slices overlapping in a 13- x 9- x 2-inch greased baking dish.

Combine brown sugar, cornstarch, and salt in a heavy saucepan; add orange rind and juice. Cook over medium heat, stirring constantly, until thickened. Remove from heat, and stir in sherry and butter; pour over potatoes. Bake, uncovered, at 350° for 15 minutes or until tender. Yield: 8 servings.

*Gladys L. Cloninger,
Atlanta, Georgia.*

PEAR-SWEET POTATO CASSEROLE

1 (16-ounce) can pear halves, undrained
3 cups mashed cooked sweet potatoes
   (about 4 medium)
¼ cup butter or margarine, melted and
   divided
3 tablespoons brown sugar
¼ teaspoon salt
¼ teaspoon ground nutmeg
2 tablespoons honey
1 teaspoon grated orange rind
1 (16-ounce) can whole-berry cranberry
   sauce

Drain pear halves, reserving syrup;
set pear halves aside.

Combine 2 tablespoons pear syrup,
sweet potatoes, 3 tablespoons butter,
brown sugar, salt, and nutmeg; beat at
medium speed of an electric mixer until
light. Spoon into a greased, shallow 1½-
quart casserole. Arrange pear halves,
cut side up, over potatoes.

Combine honey, remaining 1 tablespoon butter, and orange rind in a small
saucepan; bring to a boil and drizzle
half of honey mixture over pears. Bake,
uncovered, at 350° for 30 minutes. Drizzle remaining half of honey mixture
over pears, and bake casserole an additional 15 minutes.

Before serving, fill each pear half
with cranberry sauce. Yield: 6
servings.   *Mrs. Lauren D. Martin,*
Knoxville, Tennessee.

DEVILED PEAS IN TOAST CUPS

½ cup chopped onion
¼ cup chopped green pepper
2 tablespoons butter or margarine, melted
½ cup cream of mushroom soup,
   undiluted
1 cup frozen English peas, thawed
1 (4-ounce) jar diced pimiento, drained
8 slices bread
Pimiento pieces (optional)

Sauté onion and green pepper in butter until tender; remove from heat. Stir
in soup, peas, and diced pimiento;
spoon into a greased 1-quart baking
dish. Bake at 350° for 25 minutes.

Remove crusts from bread; press each
slice into a 6-ounce custard cup. Bake
at 350° for 20 minutes or until lightly
browned; remove from oven.

Remove toast cups from custard cups;
fill each with English pea mixture. Garnish with pimiento pieces, if desired.
Yield: 8 servings.   *Katherine Mabry,*
Athens, Alabama.

Dressing With A Difference

Turkey may taste the same regardless
of the cook, but you can always count
on a variety of dressings. To some
cooks, the perfect dressing recipe calls
for cornbread and sausage; for others,
it's white bread and raisins.

Sausage Dressing combines white
bread and cornbread for a better texture. Using broth instead of milk helps
keep the mixture moist during baking.

SAUSAGE DRESSING
(pictured on page 271)

1 pound bulk pork sausage
2 medium onions, diced
4 stalks celery, diced
5 cups cornbread crumbs
3 cups white bread cubes, toasted
2 teaspoons rubbed sage
¼ teaspoon pepper
3 to 3½ cups chicken or turkey broth
2 eggs, beaten
Celery leaves (optional)

Cook sausage, onions, and diced celery in a skillet over medium heat until
sausage is browned and onion and celery are tender. Drain. Place in a large
bowl; add remaining ingredients, except
celery leaves, stirring well.

Spoon into a greased 13- x 9- x 2-inch
baking dish. Bake at 350° for 30 minutes or until thoroughly heated. Garnish
with celery leaves, if desired. Yield: 8
to 10 servings.   *Mrs. John Rucker,*
Louisville, Kentucky.

PRETZEL DRESSING

3 cups chopped celery
2 large onions, chopped
½ pound fresh mushrooms, sliced
1 clove garlic, minced
1 cup butter or margarine, melted
9 cups (three 9½-ounce bags) coarsely
   chopped pretzels
½ cup chopped fresh parsley
3 (10½-ounce) cans low-sodium chicken
   broth
2 eggs, beaten

Sauté celery, onions, mushrooms, and
garlic in butter in a large skillet until
vegetables are tender; set aside.

Combine pretzel crumbs and parsley;
add chicken broth and eggs; stir well.
Let stand until moisture is absorbed
(about 15 minutes). Add vegetables to
pretzel mixture; stir well.

Spoon into a greased 13- x 9- x 2-inch
baking dish. Bake at 350° for 40 minutes or until browned. Yield: 8 to 10
servings.   *W. N. Cottrell II,*
New Orleans, Louisiana.

SQUASH DRESSING

2 cups sliced yellow squash
1 medium onion, chopped
1 cup water
2 cups cornbread crumbs
1 (10¾-ounce) can cream of chicken soup,
   undiluted
¼ cup butter or margarine, melted
¼ teaspoon pepper

Combine squash, onion, and water in
a medium saucepan; bring to a boil.
Cover, reduce heat, and simmer 10 minutes or until squash and onion are
tender. Drain well; mash.

Combine squash mixture with remaining ingredients, stirring well. Spoon into
a greased 1½-quart casserole. Bake at
350° for 25 minutes or until thoroughly
heated. Yield: 4 to 6 servings.
Doris F. Ward,
Starkville, Mississippi.

*Tip: Keep all dry foods in their origi-
nal containers or airtight ones.*

KENTUCKY CORNBREAD DRESSING

3 cups crumbled cornbread
2 cups soft white breadcrumbs
1½ cups milk
⅓ cup bacon drippings
1 egg
1 cup chopped onion
¾ to 1 cup raisins
1 teaspoon rubbed sage
½ teaspoon salt
Additional milk (optional)

Combine first 9 ingredients in a large mixing bowl; stir well. Add additional milk, if desired, for a moister consistency. Pour into a greased 8-inch square baking dish. Bake, uncovered, at 350° for 30 to 40 minutes or until lightly browned. Yield: 6 to 8 servings.
Mrs. Robert Collins,
Fairfax, Missouri.

Use Dairy Eggnog In These Dishes

Commercial dairy eggnog predictably appears in the grocery store right before Thanksgiving and Christmas and seems to disappear much too quickly. So take advantage of the tasty foods you can prepare using the rich mixture.

EGGNOG CHRISTMAS SALAD

2 (3-ounce) packages raspberry-flavored gelatin
3 cups boiling water
1 (14-ounce) jar orange-cranberry relish
1 (20-ounce) can unsweetened crushed pineapple, undrained
2 envelopes unflavored gelatin
3 tablespoons lime juice
1½ cups commercial dairy eggnog
¾ cup diced celery
Lettuce leaves (optional)

Dissolve raspberry-flavored gelatin in boiling water; stir in orange-cranberry relish. Pour mixture into a lightly oiled 8-cup mold. Chill until partially set.

Drain pineapple, reserving juice; set pineapple aside. Soften unflavored gelatin in pineapple juice, and let stand 5 minutes. Cook gelatin mixture over low heat until the gelatin dissolves; add lime juice and eggnog.

Chill until the consistency of unbeaten egg white. Fold in pineapple and celery. Pour over cranberry layer. Chill until set. Unmold onto lettuce leaves, if desired. Yield: 14 servings.
Henrietta McGrew,
Prospect, Kentucky.

EGGNOG CHIFFON PIE

1 envelope unflavored gelatin
¼ cup milk
1½ cups commercial dairy eggnog
3 eggs, separated
½ cup sugar, divided
3 tablespoons brandy
½ teaspoon vanilla extract
1 baked 9-inch pastry shell
½ cup whipping cream
1 tablespoon sugar
Chocolate curls (optional)

Combine gelatin and milk in a small bowl; let stand 5 to 10 minutes.

Heat eggnog in top of a double boiler over boiling water. Beat egg yolks and ¼ cup sugar until thick. Gradually stir about ½ cup hot eggnog into yolk mixture; add to remaining eggnog, stirring constantly. Cook over simmering water, stirring frequently, 10 to 12 minutes or until mixture thickens and coats a metal spoon. Remove from heat, and add gelatin mixture; stir until dissolved. Stir in brandy and vanilla. Chill mixture until the consistency of unbeaten egg white.

Beat egg whites (at room temperature) until foamy. Add ¼ cup sugar, 1 tablespoon at a time, beating until soft peaks form. Fold egg whites into eggnog mixture; pour into cooled pastry shell. Refrigerate until set.

Beat whipping cream and 1 tablespoon sugar until stiff peaks form. Garnish pie with whipped cream and, if desired, chocolate curls. Yield: one 9-inch pie.
Mrs. Robert H. Kirk,
Winchester, Virginia.

COFFEE-EGGNOG PUNCH

2 (1-quart) cartons commercial dairy eggnog
¼ cup firmly packed brown sugar
2 tablespoons instant coffee powder
¼ teaspoon ground cinnamon
1 cup brandy
¼ cup Kahlúa or other coffee-flavored liqueur
1 cup whipping cream
¼ cup sifted powdered sugar
1 teaspoon vanilla extract
Ground cinnamon

Combine first 4 ingredients in a large mixing bowl; beat at low speed of an electric mixer until smooth. Stir in brandy and Kahlúa; chill 1 to 2 hours. Pour into punch bowl; set aside.

Combine whipping cream, powdered sugar, and vanilla; beat until stiff peaks form. Spoon onto eggnog; sprinkle lightly with cinnamon. Yield: 9½ cups.
Mildred Bickley,
Bristol, Virginia.

HOLIDAY EGGNOG PUNCH

4 cups commercial dairy eggnog
2 (10-ounce) bottles ginger ale, chilled
1 (6-ounce) can frozen orange juice concentrate, thawed and undiluted

Combine eggnog, ginger ale, and orange juice concentrate in a large bowl; stir well. Serve punch immediately. Yield: 7½ cups.
Nocua Doss Whittington,
Van Buren, Arkansas.

COOKING LIGHT®

A Holiday Meal Without All The Calories

The holidays signal a time for overindulgence in beverages, food, and fun. But careful planning can help you ward off an unwelcome reminder—unwanted pounds.

It takes only 500 calories a day for one week to add a pound to your weight, and extra calories add up fast during this time. For example, the traditional holiday meal contains over 2,000 calories. The basic foods of a turkey dinner with all the trimmings are actually low in calories and very nutritious. It's the extras, such as butter, gravies, sauces, and sugary confections and pastries, that send calories soaring.

We've scaled down the traditional feast to 532 calories for the entire meal. All you sacrifice is calories, not flavor. And if there isn't room for dessert, you'll save an additional 133 calories.

**Roast Turkey Breast
With Special Gravy
Zucchini Dressing or
Sweet Potato-Apple Bake
Glorified Brussels Sprouts
Cranberry Relish
Garden-Patch Salad Molds
Pumpkin Chiffon**

ROAST TURKEY BREAST WITH SPECIAL GRAVY

1 cup apple cider
1 cup chicken broth
¼ cup salt-free herb-and-spice steak sauce
2 tablespoons reduced-sodium soy sauce
¼ teaspoon pepper
1 (3- to 4-pound) turkey breast, skinned
1½ tablespoons cornstarch

Combine cider, broth, steak sauce, soy sauce, and pepper. Reserve 1½ cups mixture in a small saucepan for gravy; set aside. Use remaining cider mixture for basting turkey breast; set aside.

Place turkey breast on a rack in a roasting pan; insert meat thermometer into meaty portion so that it does not touch bone. Baste with cider mixture. Cover and bake at 325° about 1 to 2 hours or until meat thermometer registers 170°, basting frequently with cider mixture. Let cool 10 to 15 minutes before slicing.

Combine cornstarch with reserved 1½ cups cider mixture in saucepan. Bring to a boil, and cook 1 minute, stirring constantly, until thickened. Serve with sliced turkey breast. Yield: 8 to 10 servings (about 166 calories per 3 ounces turkey breast plus 9 calories per tablespoon gravy).

ZUCCHINI DRESSING

4¾ cups chopped zucchini
½ cup plus 2 tablespoons chopped onion
½ cup plus 2 tablespoons diced celery
1 cup boiling water
1 cup unsalted chicken broth
2 eggs, slightly beaten
1 (8-ounce) package herb-seasoned stuffing
1 teaspoon poultry seasoning
½ teaspoon butter flavoring
¼ teaspoon rubbed sage
⅛ teaspoon pepper
Vegetable cooking spray

Cook zucchini, onion, and celery in 1 cup boiling water 15 minutes; drain well. Mash. Add chicken broth, eggs, stuffing mix, poultry seasoning, flavoring, sage, and pepper; stir well. Spoon mixture into a shallow 2-quart baking dish coated with cooking spray. Bake, uncovered, at 350° for 25 minutes or until heated. Yield: 8 servings (about 149 calories per 1-cup serving).

SWEET POTATO-APPLE BAKE

1 large cooking apple, peeled and quartered
2 cups mashed sweet potatoes
2 eggs, separated
½ teaspoon vanilla extract
Vegetable cooking spray
1½ teaspoons reduced-calorie margarine
Apple slices (optional)
Lemon juice (optional)

Place apple quarters in a saucepan; cover with water, and bring to a boil. Reduce heat, and simmer 5 to 8 minutes or until apples are tender. Drain.

Position knife blade in food processor bowl; add apples. Top with cover, and process until smooth. Combine apples, sweet potatoes, egg yolks, and vanilla; stir well, and set aside.

Beat egg whites (at room temperature) until peaks are stiff but not dry. Fold into sweet potato mixture. Pour mixture into a 1-quart casserole coated with cooking spray; dot with margarine. Bake at 350° for 40 to 45 minutes or until browned. Garnish with apple slices dipped in lemon juice, if desired. Yield: 8 servings (about 121 calories per ½-cup serving).
*Mrs. A. K. Wyborny,
Mabank, Texas.*

GLORIFIED BRUSSELS SPROUTS

1 (11-ounce) can mandarin oranges, undrained
2 pounds fresh brussels sprouts
1½ cups water
¼ teaspoon salt
¼ teaspoon white pepper
2 tablespoons lemon juice
2 teaspoons cornstarch
½ teaspoon dried whole basil
1 (8-ounce) can sliced water chestnuts, drained

Drain oranges, reserving liquid; set both aside.

Wash brussels sprouts, and remove discolored leaves. Cut off stem ends, and slash bottom of each sprout with a shallow X. Combine brussels sprouts, water, salt, and pepper in a saucepan; bring to a boil. Cover, reduce heat, and simmer 10 minutes or until tender; drain well.

Combine reserved liquid from oranges, lemon juice, cornstarch, and basil in a small saucepan, stirring until cornstarch dissolves. Bring mixture to a boil; boil 1 minute, stirring constantly. Pour orange sauce over brussels sprouts. Add reserved oranges and water chestnuts; toss. Yield: 8 servings (about 70 calories per 1-cup serving).

CRANBERRY RELISH

½ thin-skinned orange, seeded and chopped
1½ cups fresh cranberries
1 medium apple, unpeeled and chopped
1 (8-ounce) can unsweetened pineapple tidbits, drained

Position knife blade in food processor bowl; add orange. Cover with top; process 3 minutes or until orange peel is finely chopped. Add remaining ingredients, and pulse 4 times, scraping sides of processor bowl between each pulse. Cover and chill. Yield: 2½ cups (about 14 calories per 2 tablespoons).

Joanne Nanney,
Shelby, North Carolina.

GARDEN-PATCH SALAD MOLDS

2 envelopes unflavored gelatin
2⅔ cups water, divided
2 tablespoons sugar
¼ teaspoon salt
½ cup vinegar
1 tablespoon lemon juice
1¼ cups thinly sliced cucumbers, unpeeled and cut into fourths
1 cup thinly sliced radishes
¼ cup chopped celery
Vegetable cooking spray
Cucumber slices (optional)

Sprinkle gelatin over ⅔ cup water in a saucepan; let stand 1 minute. Add sugar and salt; cook over medium heat, stirring constantly, until gelatin dissolves. Stir in remaining 2 cups water, vinegar, and lemon juice. Chill until

consistency of unbeaten egg white; fold in vegetables. Pour into eight ½-cup molds coated with cooking spray; chill. Unmold onto cucumber slices, if desired. Yield: 8 servings (about 26 calories per ½-cup serving).

PUMPKIN CHIFFON

1 envelope unflavored gelatin
¼ cup water
¼ cup plus 2 tablespoons sugar, divided
3 tablespoons cornstarch
⅛ teaspoon salt
1¼ teaspoons ground cinnamon
¼ teaspoon ground nutmeg
¼ teaspoon ground ginger
1 cup canned pumpkin
¾ cup evaporated skim milk
2 tablespoons reduced-calorie margarine
5 egg whites
⅓ cup frozen whipped topping, thawed
2 tablespoons plus 2 teaspoons chopped pecans, toasted

Soften gelatin in water; let stand 1 minute.

Combine 3 tablespoons sugar, cornstarch, salt, and spices in a medium saucepan; stir well. Stir in pumpkin and milk. Cook over medium heat, stirring constantly, until smooth and thickened. Add gelatin mixture and margarine; stir until margarine melts. Let cool, stirring occasionally.

Beat egg whites (at room temperature) at high speed of an electric mixer 1 minute. Gradually add remaining 3 tablespoons sugar, one at a time, beating until stiff peaks form and sugar dissolves (2 to 4 minutes). Fold into pumpkin mixture; spoon into serving dishes. Cover and chill. Garnish each serving with 2 teaspoons whipped topping and 1 teaspoon pecans. Yield: 8 servings (about 133 calories per ½-cup serving).
Irene F. Pankey,
Richmond, Virginia.

Tip: To maintain high quality in eggs, always store eggs large end up in their original container.

Winning Ways With Turkey Leftovers

After the big turkey feast, the question always seems to remain—what can be done with the leftovers? If turkey sandwiches seem too boring, why not try some of these suggestions?

TURKEY-CARROT SALAD

1¾ cups chopped cooked turkey
⅔ cup chopped celery
1 medium carrot, scraped and grated
3 tablespoons chopped onion
¼ cup mayonnaise
1 tablespoon prepared mustard
1½ teaspoons sugar

Combine all ingredients in a medium bowl; toss gently. Chill at least 1 hour. Yield: 3 to 4 servings.

Rubie Mae Walker,
Lynchburg, Virginia.

TURKEY-SWISS CASSEROLE

1 (10-ounce) package frozen green beans
2 cups chopped cooked turkey
1 cup (4 ounces) shredded Swiss cheese
1 (10¾-ounce) can cream of chicken soup
⅛ teaspoon ground nutmeg
1 cup biscuit mix
1 egg, beaten
¼ cup butter or margarine, melted
2 tablespoons milk
1 tablespoon chopped fresh parsley

Cook green beans according to package directions, omitting seasonings. Drain. Add turkey, cheese, soup, and nutmeg; stir well. Spoon mixture into a greased 1½-quart casserole.

Place biscuit mix in a medium bowl. Combine egg, butter, and milk; add to biscuit mix, stirring just until blended. Spoon biscuit mixture around edge of casserole, leaving center open. Sprinkle parsley in center of casserole. Bake at 350° for 25 to 30 minutes. Yield: 4 servings.

Elaine Jamerson,
Selmer, Tennessee.

Plenty of vegetables and herbs grace this bowl of steaming Turkey Carcass Soup.

Prepare rice mix according to package directions; set aside. Cook peas according to package directions; drain well, and set aside. Combine rice, peas, and remaining ingredients except cabbage; toss. Serve hot or cold on cabbage leaves, if desired. Yield: 6 servings.

Mrs. C. D. Marshall,
Culpeper, Virginia.

ORIENTAL TURKEY-ORANGE SKILLET

⅓ cup halved fresh mushrooms
⅓ cup diced green pepper
1 green onion, diced
1 small jalapeño pepper, diced
1 clove garlic, crushed
2 tablespoons orange juice
2 tablespoons soy sauce
1 teaspoon butter or margarine
2 cups chopped cooked turkey
2 cups cooked rice
2 oranges, peeled and sectioned

Combine mushrooms, green pepper, onion, jalapeño pepper, garlic, juice, soy sauce, and butter in a skillet. Cover and cook over medium heat 5 minutes, stirring occasionally. Stir in remaining ingredients; cover and cook 5 minutes or until thoroughly heated, stirring occasionally. Yield: 4 to 6 servings.

Mrs. Derrick A. Luttrell,
Jackson, Mississippi.

TURKEY CARCASS SOUP

1 turkey carcass
4 quarts water
6 small potatoes, diced
4 large carrots, diced
2 stalks celery, diced
1 large onion, chopped
1½ cups shredded cabbage
1 (7½-ounce) can tomatoes, drained and chopped
½ cup uncooked barley
1 tablespoon Worcestershire sauce
1½ teaspoons salt
1 teaspoon dried parsley flakes
1 teaspoon dried whole basil
1 bay leaf
¼ teaspoon pepper
¼ teaspoon paprika
¼ teaspoon poultry seasoning
Pinch of dried whole thyme

Place turkey carcass and water in a large Dutch oven; bring to a boil. Cover, reduce heat, and simmer 2 hours. Remove carcass from broth, and pick all meat from bones.

Return meat to broth, and add remaining ingredients. Simmer 1 hour or until vegetables are tender. Remove bay leaf. Yield: 5 quarts.

Mrs. Carl M. Day, Jr.,
Laurens, South Carolina.

TURKEY-RICE PILAF
(pictured on page 272)

1 (6-ounce) package long-grain and wild rice mix
1 (10-ounce) package frozen English peas
3 cups chopped cooked turkey
½ cup toasted pine nuts
2 tablespoons dry sherry
2 tablespoons white wine vinegar
¼ cup chicken broth
¼ teaspoon salt
¼ teaspoon pepper
Cabbage leaves (optional)

TURKEY-ASPARAGUS CASSEROLE

2½ cups chopped cooked turkey
1 (10¾-ounce) can cream of mushroom soup, undiluted
1 (10¾-ounce) can cream of celery soup, undiluted
¼ cup plus 2 tablespoons slivered almonds, toasted
1 (10-ounce) package frozen asparagus, thawed, drained, and cut into 1-inch pieces
¼ cup chopped pimiento, drained
1 (2.8-ounce) can French-fried onion rings

Combine first 4 ingredients in a bowl; stir well. Spoon half of mixture into a greased 8-inch square baking dish.

Combine asparagus and pimiento; stir gently. Sprinkle over mixture in baking dish. Spoon remaining turkey mixture on top. Cover and bake at 350° for 35 minutes; uncover. Sprinkle with onion rings, and bake, uncovered, an additional 10 minutes. Yield: 4 servings.

Helen Goggans,
Kingsland, Arkansas.

His Fruitcake Is A Tradition

It's a safe bet to say that you can find dozens of fruitcakes stashed around the Fort Worth, Texas, home of Marty Aronowitz by December. He has made these cakes every holiday season for the past 34 years.

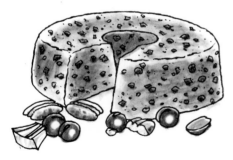

ARONOWITZ FRUITCAKE

1 pound pitted dates, chopped
1 pound pecans, chopped
¼ pound red candied cherries, chopped
¼ pound green candied cherries, chopped
½ pound candied sliced pineapple, chopped
1 cup sugar
1 cup all-purpose flour
2 teaspoons baking powder
1 teaspoon ground nutmeg
½ teaspoon salt
4 eggs, beaten
1 teaspoon vanilla extract

Combine dates, pecans, cherries, and pineapple in a large mixing bowl; set

aside. Combine dry ingredients; add to fruit mixture, stirring well. Stir in eggs and vanilla.

Spoon batter into a greased and brown paper-lined 10-inch tube pan. Bake at 250° for 2 hours or until a wooden pick inserted in center comes out clean. Cool cake completely in pan. Remove from pan, and remove brown paper. Yield: one 10-inch cake.

Note: Cake may be baked in 2 greased and brown paper-lined 8-inch loafpans at 250° for 1 hour and 20 minutes or until wooden pick inserted comes out clean.

Here's A Time-Saving Menu

If you'd rather be greeting guests than cooking in the kitchen on Thanksgiving Day, you'll welcome this make-ahead menu. All of the recipes can be prepared at least partially the day before, which leaves only a few details to attend to the day you serve the menu.

The secret is to plan ahead. Be sure to make note of which recipes require the same temperature and can be baked together, how much refrigerator space you have, and which baking containers you will need.

To make this menu work best, use the following time and preparation suggestions. Start a week ahead of time; make Easy Whole Wheat Rolls, and freeze them. You can even make the cornbread portion of our Cornbread Dressing recipe; then crumble, and freeze. Two days before, bake the Cream Cheese Pound Cake.

The day before serving, bake the turkey breast, and reserve the remaining herb-butter sauce. Prepare Raspberry Salad and Marinated Vegetables, both of which can be served from the refrigerator. Put together Cornbread Dressing and Sweet Potatoes With Sherry and Walnuts; cover and store in the refrigerator without baking.

On the day your guests arrive, put the dressing and sweet potato casserole in the oven to bake. (Place the sweet potatoes in the oven after the dressing has baked 15 minutes so that they will be ready at the same time.) Meanwhile, slice the turkey, and reheat the butter sauce to serve with it. Once the dressing and sweet potatoes are ready, set the oven at 375°. Thawed whole wheat rolls will bake in 5 minutes.

Herb Butter-Basted Turkey Breast
Cornbread Dressing
Marinated Vegetables
Sweet Potatoes
With Sherry and Walnuts
Raspberry Salad
Easy Whole Wheat Rolls
Cream Cheese Pound Cake
Wine   Coffee

HERB BUTTER-BASTED TURKEY BREAST

½ cup butter or margarine, melted
¼ cup lemon juice
2 tablespoons soy sauce
2 tablespoons minced green onions
1 teaspoon dried whole sage, crushed
1 teaspoon dried whole thyme
1 teaspoon dried whole marjoram
½ teaspoon salt
¼ teaspoon pepper
1 (5- to 5½-pound) turkey breast
Red and green grapes (optional)

Combine first 9 ingredients in a saucepan; bring to a boil. Remove from heat; set aside.

Place turkey breast in a lightly oiled 13- x 9- x 2-inch baking pan; baste with butter mixture. Cover pan with foil. Insert meat thermometer through foil into thickest portion of breast, making an opening so that thermometer does not touch foil. Bake at 325° for 2 hours or until thermometer registers 170°, basting often with butter mixture. Transfer turkey to serving platter. Garnish with grapes, if desired. Yield: 10 to 12 servings.

Shirley Shepherd,
San Antonio, Texas.

CORNBREAD DRESSING

2 cups cornmeal
1 tablespoon sugar
1 tablespoon baking powder
1 teaspoon salt
2 eggs, beaten
1 (12-ounce) can evaporated milk
¼ cup vegetable oil
2 cups chopped fresh mushrooms
1 cup chopped celery
½ cup chopped green onions
3 tablespoons butter or margarine, melted
3 eggs, beaten
2 (14½-ounce) cans chicken broth
1 (10¾-ounce) can cream of chicken soup, undiluted
¾ cup sliced almonds
1 teaspoon poultry seasoning
¼ teaspoon pepper
Dash of parsley flakes
Fluted mushroom
Fresh parsley

Combine first 4 ingredients; add 2 eggs, milk, and oil, mixing well.

Place a well-greased 10-inch cast-iron skillet in a preheated 350° oven for 5 minutes or until skillet is hot. Remove from oven; spoon batter into skillet. Bake at 350° for 35 to 40 minutes or until lightly browned; cool. Crumble cornbread into a large bowl.

Sauté mushrooms, celery, and green onions in 3 tablespoons butter until tender. Combine cornbread, sautéed vegetables, 3 eggs, broth, soup, almonds, poultry seasoning, pepper, and parsley flakes, mixing well. Spoon into a greased 13- x 9- x 2-inch baking dish. Bake at 350° for 45 minutes. Garnish dressing with mushroom and parsley. Yield: 12 servings.

Note: To make recipe a day ahead, prepare dressing, cover, and refrigerate overnight before baking. To bake, remove from refrigerator, and let stand 30 minutes. Bake at 350° for 55 minutes.

Mrs. Clifford C. Beasley, Sr.,
Gainesville, Florida.

Tip: Wash or chop vegetables and open cans before you begin preparing any recipe. It is also a good idea to have most ingredients measured before beginning to cook.

MARINATED VEGETABLES

1½ cups vegetable oil
1 cup cider vinegar
1 tablespoon sugar
2 to 3 teaspoons dried whole dillweed
1 teaspoon salt
1 teaspoon garlic salt
1 teaspoon pepper
1 pound fresh broccoli
1 head cauliflower, broken into flowerets
5 yellow squash, thinly sliced
5 medium carrots, diagonally sliced
6 medium-size fresh mushrooms, sliced

Combine oil, vinegar, sugar, dillweed, salt, garlic salt, and pepper in a jar. Cover tightly, and shake vigorously.

Trim large leaves from broccoli. Wash broccoli, and break off flowerets; reserve stalks for another use.

Combine the broccoli flowerets and remaining vegetables in a large bowl. Pour the dressing over vegetables; toss gently. Cover and refrigerate 24 hours. Yield: 10 to 12 servings.

Jamie Del Sole,
Winston-Salem, North Carolina.

SWEET POTATOES WITH SHERRY AND WALNUTS

8 cups mashed cooked sweet potatoes (about 6 medium)
4 eggs, beaten
1 cup firmly packed brown sugar
½ cup sherry
½ teaspoon salt
Chopped walnuts

Combine sweet potatoes, eggs, brown sugar, sherry, and salt; blend well. Spoon into a greased 2½-quart casserole. Sprinkle chopped walnuts around outside edges of casserole. Cover and refrigerate overnight.

Remove from refrigerator; let stand 30 minutes. Bake, uncovered, at 350° for 40 minutes or until thoroughly heated. Yield: 10 to 12 servings.

Mary Pappas,
Richmond, Virginia.

RASPBERRY SALAD

1 (6-ounce) package raspberry-flavored gelatin
1 (3-ounce) package raspberry-flavored gelatin
2¼ cups boiling water
1 (25-ounce) jar applesauce
1 cup cranberry juice cocktail
3 tablespoons lemon juice
Lettuce leaves
Fresh cranberries

Dissolve gelatin in boiling water in a large bowl; stir in applesauce, cranberry juice cocktail, and lemon juice. Pour into an oiled 8-cup mold; chill until firm. Unmold onto a lettuce-lined serving platter. Garnish with cranberries. Yield: 10 to 12 servings.

Bobbie Collins,
Shelbyville, Tennessee.

EASY WHOLE WHEAT ROLLS

2 packages dry yeast
2¼ cups warm water (105° to 115°)
¼ cup shortening
2 eggs, beaten
½ cup plus 1 tablespoon sugar
2 teaspoons salt
3 to 3½ cups whole wheat flour
3 to 3½ cups all-purpose flour
About ¼ cup butter or margarine, melted

Dissolve yeast in warm water in a large bowl; let stand 5 minutes. Add shortening, eggs, sugar, and salt; beat at medium speed of an electric mixer until well blended. Gradually stir in enough of each flour to make a soft dough.

Turn dough out onto a well-floured surface, and knead until smooth and elastic (about 5 minutes). Place in a well-greased bowl, turning to grease top. Cover and let rise in a warm place (85°), free from drafts, 1 hour or until doubled in bulk.

Punch dough down, and divide into fourths; shape each portion into about 13 (1½-inch) balls. Place 2 inches apart on greased baking sheets.

Cover and let rise in a warm place, free from drafts, 30 minutes or until doubled in bulk. Bake at 375° for 15 minutes; brush with melted butter. Yield: 4 dozen.

Note: Rolls can be prepared ahead of time and frozen. Bake 10 minutes; let cool, and freeze. Let rolls thaw, and bake at 375° for 5 minutes.

Juliette Raban,
Uriah, Alabama.

CREAM CHEESE POUND CAKE
(pictured on page 273)

1 cup butter, softened
½ cup shortening
1 (3-ounce) package cream cheese, softened
2½ cups sugar
5 eggs
3 cups sifted cake flour
1 teaspoon baking powder
½ teaspoon salt
1 cup buttermilk
1 teaspoon vanilla extract
1 teaspoon lemon extract
Commercial strawberry topping
Fresh strawberries (optional)

Cream butter, shortening, and cream cheese; gradually add sugar, beating at medium speed of an electric mixer until light and fluffy. Add eggs, one at a time, beating after each addition.

Combine flour, baking powder, and salt; add to creamed mixture alternately with buttermilk, stirring just until blended. Stir in flavorings.

Spoon batter into a greased and floured 10-inch tube pan; bake at 325° for 1½ hours or until a wooden pick inserted in center comes out clean.

Let cake cool in pan 10 to 15 minutes; remove from pan, and cool completely. Serve cake with strawberry topping. Garnish each serving of cake with fresh strawberries, if desired. Yield: one 10-inch cake.

Mattie Parker,
Columbus, Georgia.

A Personal Touch for Your Table

Fabric runners bring tabletops to life. They can provide color for holiday gatherings, as well as throughout the year. By using a runner, you don't need a centerpiece that is overly dramatic or overly large because a runner takes the focus of the centerpiece and spreads it out. A fabric runner can be placed over a tablecloth or can dress the table by itself, lending color or emphasizing a theme for holiday dinners.

Runners can be purchased, but they're so easy to sew that you may want to make your own. Most are from 12 to 15 inches wide, and they can be as long as you want. If they hang over the edge of the table, it's best to allow about 12 inches on each side to keep them from looking skimpy.

Table runners use such small amounts of material that you can afford to make them in rich fabrics, if desired. Many types and weights of fabric are suitable, as long as they can be cleaned. For instance, it's simple to make a runner from upholstery fabric. Cut a single thickness, hem along the sides, and finish on the ends with trim.

The festive holiday runners used on the round table (below) are made with a thin fabric that's lined with an iron-on interfacing to give it body. They were made like long tubes, with the seam going up the center of the back. One end is stitched closed; then the tube is turned right side out, and the other end of the tube is topstitched.

The lace runner (below, left) is the easiest to make. This was 12-inch-wide lace found in the bridal section of a fabric store. The sides are already finished, and the cut ends are trimmed along the pattern of the lace. No sewing is needed if you carefully select the lace. Just make sure you find a lace that is the same along both sides, keeping in mind that some patterns do have distinct top and bottom edges.

A no-sew runner can be made from 12-inch-wide lace that's purchased by the yard. If the ends are trimmed along the pattern, it won't ravel.

A pair of runners on a round table combines with a matching overlay on the buffet. Because a small amount of fabric is used, the bold print isn't overpowering.

Treat Friends To Tasty Gifts

This year's selection of gifts can be easy and fun when you prepare them in your microwave oven. A gift that's good to eat is always appreciated, and making it yourself allows you to add a personal touch. For something unusual, you'll delight in sharing a jar of Vinaigrette Dressing and Croutons or Coarse-and-Sweet Mustard.

VINAIGRETTE DRESSING AND CROUTONS

½ cup water
¼ cup plus 2 tablespoons vinegar
¼ cup plus 2 tablespoons sugar
1 tablespoon all-purpose flour
1 teaspoon dry mustard
1 teaspoon salt
⅛ teaspoon coarsely ground pepper
¼ cup chopped onion
1¼ cups vegetable oil
Croutons (recipe follows)

Combine first 4 ingredients in a 1-quart glass measure. Microwave at HIGH, uncovered, 4 to 5 minutes or until mixture boils and thickens, stirring once. Cool slightly. Pour into container of electric blender; add mustard, salt, pepper, and onion; process 30 seconds. With blender running, slowly add oil. Pour into desired containers. Serve dressing with croutons over salad greens. Yield: 2½ cups.

Croutons:

4 cups bread cubes, cut into ½-inch pieces
¼ cup butter or margarine
1 clove garlic, minced
1 teaspoon minced fresh parsley
2 tablespoons grated Parmesan cheese

Place bread cubes in a 9-inch glass pieplate; set aside. Place butter and garlic in a 1-cup glass measure; microwave at HIGH for 45 seconds to 1 minute or until butter melts. Drizzle over bread cubes, tossing to coat. Sprinkle with parsley and cheese. Microwave at HIGH, uncovered, 5 to 6 minutes or until lightly toasted, stirring 2 or 3 times. Let cool. Store in airtight container. Yield: 2 cups.

COARSE-AND-SWEET MUSTARD

⅓ cup mustard seeds
⅓ cup water
2 tablespoons dry mustard
⅔ cup cider vinegar
1 small onion, chopped
2 tablespoons brown sugar
2 cloves garlic, minced
1 teaspoon salt
½ teaspoon ground cinnamon
½ teaspoon ground allspice
2 tablespoons honey

Combine mustard seeds, water, and dry mustard in a small bowl; let stand at room temperature at least 3 hours.
Combine vinegar, onion, brown sugar, garlic, salt, cinnamon, and allspice in a 2-cup glass measure.
Microwave brown sugar mixture at HIGH, uncovered, 6 to 7 minutes. Strain into container of electric blender. Add mustard mixture, and process 15 to 20 seconds or until mixture reaches desired texture. Stir in honey.
Spoon mustard into containers, and chill at least 3 days before using. Yield: about 1 cup.

TOASTED PECAN CHEESE LOG

½ cup chopped pecans
2 tablespoons diced green pepper
2 tablespoons diced onion
½ teaspoon butter or margarine
1 (8-ounce) package cream cheese
2 cups (8 ounces) shredded Cheddar cheese
½ (0.6-ounce) envelope Italian salad-dressing mix
1 tablespoon diced pimiento, drained
½ teaspoon Worcestershire sauce
Dash of red pepper

Spread pecans in a single layer in a 9-inch square baking dish. Microwave at HIGH, uncovered, 5 to 6 minutes or until toasted. Set aside.
Combine green pepper, onion, and butter in a microwave-safe bowl; cover with heavy-duty plastic wrap. Microwave at HIGH 45 seconds or until vegetables are crisp-tender, stirring once. Drain, and set aside.
Place cream cheese in a microwave-safe bowl. Microwave at MEDIUM LOW (30% power) 1½ to 2 minutes or until cream cheese is softened. Combine cream cheese, cooked vegetables, and remaining ingredients; mix well. Shape mixture into an 11- x 2-inch log; roll in toasted pecans. Cover and chill. Serve with assorted crackers. Yield: one 11- x 2-inch cheese log.

CHRISTMAS FREEZER JELLY

2 cups cranapple juice
1 (1¾-ounce) package powdered pectin, divided
4½ cups sugar, divided
2 cups apple juice
4 drops green food coloring (optional)

Combine cranapple juice and 2 tablespoons (½ package) pectin in a 2-quart glass measure. Microwave at HIGH, uncovered, 7 to 10 minutes or until mixture boils, stirring once. Stir in 2 cups sugar. Microwave at HIGH 5 to 7 minutes or until mixture boils hard for 1 full minute. Skim off any foam with a metal spoon.
Pour into hot sterilized glasses or jars, filling each half full. Set aside until jelly is partially set.
Combine apple juice, food coloring, if desired, and remaining 2 tablespoons pectin in a 2-quart glass measure. Microwave at HIGH, uncovered, 7 to 8 minutes or until mixture boils, stirring once. Stir in remaining 2½ cups sugar. Microwave at HIGH for 5 to 7 minutes or until mixture boils hard for 1 full minute. Skim off any foam with a metal spoon.
Carefully spoon mixture into jars over first layer of jelly, leaving ¼ inch headspace. Cover with lids, and let stand at room temperature 24 hours. Store in freezer. To serve, remove from freezer, and allow to come to room temperature. Yield: 7 half pints.

PRALINES

2 cups sugar
2 cups pecan halves
¾ cup buttermilk
2 tablespoons butter or margarine
⅛ teaspoon salt
1 teaspoon baking soda

Combine sugar, pecan halves, buttermilk, butter, and salt in a 4-quart casserole, stirring well. Microwave at HIGH 12 to 13 minutes, stirring every 4 minutes. Stir in soda until foamy. Microwave at HIGH 1 to 1½ minutes. Beat mixture with a wooden spoon until mixture just begins to thicken.
Working rapidly, drop by tablespoonfuls onto greased waxed paper; let pralines stand until firm. Yield: about 2 dozen.
Bunnie George, Birmingham, Alabama.

Tip: Avoid doubling a candy recipe. It is better to make a second batch.

SHERRY-ORANGE NUTS

2 cups walnut halves
2 cups pecan halves
1 cup orange juice
⅓ cup dry sherry
2¾ cups sifted powdered sugar

Combine walnuts, pecans, orange juice, and sherry in a large bowl. Cover and let stand 4 hours. Drain nuts, and place in a 2-quart casserole. Add powdered sugar, stirring well.

Microwave at HIGH, uncovered, 10 to 11 minutes or until mixture becomes partially dry, stirring every 3 minutes. Spread nuts on greased baking sheets to cool. Store in covered container. Yield: 4 cups.

From Our Kitchen To Yours

Fragrant aromas from Mother's kitchen are treasured childhood memories, especially during the holidays. Distinctive spice scents floating through the house meant Christmas was near and homemade delicacies were being prepared. Sharing these freshly baked goods with family, friends, and neighbors continues the Southern tradition of an old-fashioned Christmas.

Begin preparing for the holidays with a large assortment of goodies that have been tested by our foods staff. Recipes for gift-giving can be found in "Headstart on the Holidays" on page 266, "Treat Friends to Tasty Gifts" on facing page, and "Easy-to-Bake Breakfast Breads" on page 290. Some of these recipes can be made ahead—as much as a month early.

With just a little imagination and inspiration, you can make gifts from the kitchen your specialty. Creative packaging need not be elaborate or expensive—a little leftover lace and a lot of personal touch can make your gifts unique.

Packaging should not compete with the appeal of the food but should display it attractively. Simple supplies often found at home can make your gift decorative.

Wrappings and Trimmings

To wrap breads and cakes, such as Stollen (page 291) or Kentucky Fruitcake (page 266), choose from plastic wrap, colored foil paper, bright tissue paper, or aluminum foil teamed with colorful trimmings. Doilies, cloth or paper napkins, dish towels, and scraps of fabric, such as calico, gingham, or felt, also work well.

Finish off your gifts with ribbon, braid, yarn, lace, or fabric strips. Holly sprigs, small pine cones, kitchen magnets, ornaments, and perky labels add extra charm.

Include the recipe and information on storing and serving the gift. Also note how long the food will keep.

Choosing Your Containers

An endless choice of containers is available. Many small items, such as cookies, candies, and nuts, work well in clear plastic bags; you can also place the filled bags in foil boxes, decorative tins, tote bags, or baskets lined with any of the wrapping suggestions previously given. Package jellies, spreads, sauces, liqueurs, and salad dressings in jars, crocks, cocktail tumblers, mugs, or decorative bottles.

Mailing Tips

If you want to send some goodies across the country instead of next door, follow these tips.

—Cookies are the easiest baked goods to mail. Crisp cookies that are high in sugar and shortening are the best choice for mailing. Soft, moist cookies travel well and are suitable for many areas, but they mold quickly in humid climates. On the other hand, fragile, lacy-textured cookies tend to shatter easily. Frosted cookies are also not recommended for mailing.

—Cool cookies and other baked goods completely before packaging.

—Coffee or shortening cans, snack food cans, shoe boxes, and heavy plastic boxes make practical containers for shipping baked goods.

—Wrap two cookies back-to-back or individually with aluminum foil or plastic wrap. Cushion bottom and sides of container with crumpled foil, plastic wrap, or paper towels. Pack the cookies, as tightly as possible, without crushing. Fill spaces with foil or plastic wrap, and seal the lid with tape.

—Place filled containers inside a fiberboard packing box. Fill spaces with crumpled newspaper, shredded paper, or plastic foam. Seal the box with filament tape.

—Bear in mind that address labels should be readable from 30 inches. Use ink that will not wash off or smear easily. Label the package "Perishable Food." And be sure to include a return address inside the package.

Make A Spice Mix

Mulling spices are popular during the holidays and are generally used to season warm beverages. Carol Barclay of Portland, Texas, makes a big batch of Barclay House Mulling Spices. You can package the mix in little bundles to give as gifts, or place in a bowl for festive potpourri.

BARCLAY HOUSE MULLING SPICES

8 oranges
8 lemons
8 ounces stick cinnamon
8 ounces whole cloves
8 ounces whole allspice
2 tablespoons whole coriander
2 tablespoons orange oil
1½ teaspoons cinnamon oil

Peel colored rind from oranges and lemons, cutting into white membrane as little as possible. Cut rind into ¼-inch-wide strips. Place strips on a wire rack on a baking sheet. Let stand in a warm, dry place 24 hours or until rind is dry.

Combine orange and lemon rind with remaining ingredients in a large airtight container; mix well. Store 7 days to allow flavors to mix. Stir occasionally.

If desired, place 2 ounces (about ½ cup) spices in a 9-inch square cheesecloth; tie securely. Repeat with remaining mixture. Yield: 2 pounds or 16 (2-ounce) packages.

Hot Mulled Juice: Place ½ cup Barclay House Mulling Spices in a 9-inch square cheesecloth; tie securely. Bring ½ gallon apple or cranapple juice to a boil in a Dutch oven. Turn heat off; add spices to mixture. Let steep, covered, 15 to 30 minutes. Discard spices. Yield: 10 to 12 servings.

Hot Mulled Wine: Place ½ cup Barclay House Mulling Spices in a 9-inch square cheesecloth; tie securely. Combine ½ gallon Burgundy, 2 cups pineapple juice, and ½ cup sugar in a Dutch oven; bring to a boil. Turn heat off; add spices to mixture. Let steep, covered, 15 to 30 minutes. Discard spices. Yield: 12 to 14 servings.

Easy-To-Bake Breakfast Breads

The aroma of freshly baked bread conjures up memories of home and the holidays. But there's so little time for baking from scratch. With this in mind, we've selected breakfast bread recipes using convenience products.

SWEET RAISIN ROLLUPS

¾ cup raisins
⅓ cup chopped pecans
¼ cup commercial sour cream
2 tablespoons honey
2 tablespoons butter or margarine, softened
1 teaspoon grated lemon rind
1 teaspoon ground cinnamon
1 (10-ounce) can refrigerated flaky biscuits
1 tablespoon butter or margarine, melted
¾ cup sifted powdered sugar
1 teaspoon butter or margarine, melted
1 to 1½ tablespoons milk
½ teaspoon vanilla extract

Combine raisins, pecans, sour cream, honey, 2 tablespoons butter, lemon rind, and cinnamon; mix well.

Separate biscuit dough; roll out each biscuit on a lightly floured surface to a 7- x 4-inch oval. Spread 1 rounded tablespoonful filling on each. Roll dough, starting at narrow end, and place seam side down on an ungreased baking sheet. Brush the 10 rolls with 1 tablespoon melted butter. Bake at 375° for 12 to 15 minutes or until golden brown.

Combine last 4 ingredients; stir until smooth. Drizzle over warm rollups. Yield: 10 rolls. *Sandra Russell, Gainesville, Florida.*

MAPLE-NUT COFFEE TWIST
(pictured on back cover)

1 (16-ounce) package hot roll mix
¾ cup warm water (105° to 115°)
1 egg
3 tablespoons sugar
1 teaspoon maple flavoring
½ cup sugar
1 teaspoon ground cinnamon
⅓ cup chopped pecans
1 teaspoon maple flavoring
¼ cup plus 2 tablespoons butter or margarine, melted
1½ cups sifted powdered sugar
¼ teaspoon maple flavoring
2 to 3 tablespoons milk

Dissolve yeast from hot roll mix in warm water in a large mixing bowl; let stand 5 minutes. Stir in egg, 3 tablespoons sugar, and 1 teaspoon maple flavoring. Gradually stir in hot roll flour mixture to make a stiff dough.

Turn dough out onto a floured surface, and knead until smooth and elastic (about 2 to 3 minutes). Place in a well-greased bowl, turning to grease top. Cover and let rise in a warm place (85°), free from drafts, 40 to 45 minutes or until doubled in bulk.

Combine ½ cup sugar, cinnamon, pecans, and 1 teaspoon maple flavoring.

Punch dough down, and divide into thirds. Roll each portion out on a floured surface to a 12-inch circle. Place one circle on a greased 12-inch pizza pan. Brush with 2 tablespoons melted butter; sprinkle with one-third of cinnamon mixture. Repeat procedure with remaining 2 dough circles, stacking last 2 circles on circle in pizza pan.

Place a 2-inch biscuit cutter in the center of top circle (do not cut through dough). Cut dough into 16 wedges, cutting from biscuit cutter to outside edge of dough. Gently lift each wedge, and twist 5 times to form a spiral pattern. Remove cutter. Cover and let rise in a warm place (85°), free from drafts, until doubled in bulk.

Bake at 375° for 15 to 20 minutes or until golden brown. Let cool 10 minutes. Combine powdered sugar, ¼ teaspoon maple flavoring, and milk; stir until smooth. Drizzle over coffee cake. Yield: 1 (12-inch) coffee cake.

Ruby Berger, Cushing, Oklahoma.

CREAM CHEESE COFFEE CAKE

½ cup sugar
1 teaspoon ground cinnamon
2 (10-ounce) cans refrigerated flaky biscuits
1 (3-ounce) package cream cheese, cut into 20 pieces
¼ cup butter or margarine, melted
⅓ cup chopped pecans
1 cup sifted powdered sugar
1 to 1½ tablespoons hot water
½ teaspoon vanilla extract

Combine ½ cup sugar and cinnamon; set aside.

Separate biscuit dough; roll out each on a lightly floured surface to a 3-inch circle. Place one piece of cream cheese in center of circle; sprinkle with 1 teaspoon sugar-cinnamon mixture. Pinch edges together to seal, and form a ball;

set aside. Repeat procedure with remaining biscuits, cream cheese, and sugar-cinnamon mixture.

Place butter in bottom of a 10-inch Bundt pan; sprinkle remaining sugar-cinnamon mixture and pecans over butter. Layer balls of dough over pecans, seam side up. Bake at 350° for 35 minutes or until golden. Invert onto a serving plate.

Combine 1 cup powdered sugar, water, and vanilla; stir until smooth. Drizzle over cake. Yield: one 10-inch coffee cake. *Barbara Brannum, Birmingham, Alabama.*

NUTTY BUNS

1 (10-ounce) can refrigerated flaky biscuits
2 tablespoons mayonnaise
¼ cup sugar
1 teaspoon ground cinnamon
½ cup finely chopped pecans
½ cup sifted powdered sugar
1 tablespoon hot water or orange juice

Separate biscuits; cut each in half. Brush with mayonnaise. Combine ¼ cup sugar, cinnamon, and pecans; roll biscuits in mixture. Place 2 pieces in each greased muffin cup. Bake at 400° for 10 to 12 minutes or until golden. Combine ½ cup powdered sugar and water; drizzle over each biscuit. Yield: 10 biscuits. *Marie Bordelon, Moreauville, Louisiana.*

GLAZED LEMON KNOTS

1 (3-ounce) package cream cheese, softened
¼ cup sugar
½ teaspoon grated lemon peel
2 teaspoons lemon juice
2 (8-ounce) cans refrigerated crescent dinner rolls
½ cup sifted powdered sugar
1 tablespoon lemon juice

Combine first 4 ingredients in a small bowl; mix well. Set aside.

Separate roll dough into 8 rectangles; press perforations to seal. Spread about 2 teaspoons of cheese mixture over each rectangle. Roll dough jellyroll fashion, starting at long side. Stretch dough slightly; tie in a loose knot. Place on an ungreased baking sheet. Bake at 375° for 15 to 20 minutes or until golden brown. Combine ½ cup powdered sugar and 1 tablespoon lemon juice; drizzle glaze over warm rolls, and serve. Yield: 8 rolls. *Jill Rorex, Dallas, Texas.*

BUTTERED RUM-NUT ROLLS

1 cup firmly packed brown sugar, divided
¼ cup plus 2 tablespoons butter or
    margarine, melted
1 tablespoon milk
2 teaspoons all-purpose flour
½ teaspoon rum extract
¼ cup chopped pecans
1 (16-ounce) loaf frozen bread dough,
    thawed
½ teaspoon rum extract

Combine ½ cup brown sugar, ¼ cup butter, milk, flour, and ½ teaspoon rum extract; cook over low heat until mixture boils. Pour into a lightly greased 10- x 7- x 1½-inch baking pan. Sprinkle pecans over sugar mixture.

Roll dough on a lightly floured surface to measure a 14- x 12-inch rectangle. Brush dough with 1 tablespoon melted butter. Mix remaining ½ cup brown sugar and ½ teaspoon rum extract; sprinkle over dough. Roll dough tightly jellyroll fashion, beginning at long side, being careful to keep it 14 inches in length. Cut roll into 12 slices; place in prepared pan. Brush top with remaining butter.

Cover and let rise in a warm place (85°), free from drafts, 45 minutes or until doubled in bulk. Bake at 350° for 25 to 30 minutes. Turn rolls onto serving tray immediately. Yield: 12 rolls.

Mrs. Farmer L. Burns,
New Orleans, Louisiana.

STOLLEN

½ cup raisins
½ cup chopped pecans
2 tablespoons chopped candied red
    cherries
2 tablespoons chopped candied green
    cherries
1½ teaspoons brandy or rum
1 (16-ounce) loaf frozen bread dough,
    thawed
1 tablespoon butter or margarine, melted
Powdered Sugar-Brandy Glaze

Combine raisins, pecans, cherries, and brandy; mix well. Set aside.

Place bread dough on a lightly floured surface; flatten dough with rolling pin to 1-inch thickness. Spoon fruit mixture in center of dough, and knead dough until fruit is evenly distributed.

Roll dough to an oval shape, ½ inch thick. Fold in half, short sides overlapping; seal edges. Place dough on a well-greased baking sheet; brush with melted butter. Cover and let rise in a warm place (85°), free from drafts, 40 minutes or until doubled in bulk.

Bake at 350° for 25 to 30 minutes or until loaf sounds hollow when tapped. Cool 10 minutes on wire rack; drizzle while warm with the Powdered Sugar-Brandy Glaze. Yield: 1 loaf.

Powdered Sugar-Brandy Glaze:
1½ cups sifted powdered sugar
1 tablespoon plus 2 teaspoons brandy or
    rum
1 tablespoon fresh lime juice

Combine all ingredients, mixing well. Yield: about ¾ cup.

Helen Oberhofer,
Bradenton, Florida.

Pumpkin, Glorious Pumpkin!

Our array of pumpkin favorites will garnish a festive table and please your family and guests.

These recipes can be made with either fresh or canned pumpkin, so you can pull a can from the shelf or use a pumpkin from your garden.

One 5-pound pumpkin yields 4½ cups mashed cooked pulp, and one 16-ounce can of pumpkin can be substituted for 2 cups of mashed fresh pumpkin. Fresh pumpkin has a lighter color and more water than canned pumpkin, so you may notice a difference as you make substitutions. The texture should be similar to that of canned pumpkin.

If you use fresh pumpkin, wash the pumpkin well and cut it crosswise. Place halves, cut side down, on a 15- x 10- x 1-inch jellyroll pan. Bake at 325° for 45 minutes or until fork-tender; cool 10 minutes. Peel pumpkin; discard seeds. Puree the pulp in a food processor, or mash thoroughly.

PUMPKIN-TOMATO SOUP

¾ cup finely chopped green pepper
¼ cup chopped green onions
¼ cup minced fresh parsley
2 tablespoons butter or margarine, melted
1 (16-ounce) can pumpkin or 2 cups
    mashed cooked pumpkin
1 (14-ounce) can plum tomatoes,
    undrained and chopped
2 cups chicken broth
¼ teaspoon salt
¼ teaspoon pepper
Commercial sour cream (optional)

Sauté green pepper, green onions, and parsley in butter in a Dutch oven about 5 minutes or until tender. Add remaining ingredients except sour cream; bring to a boil. Cover, reduce heat, and simmer about 15 minutes. Serve soup hot with a dollop of sour cream, if desired. Yield: 7 cups.

Sandra Russell,
Gainesville, Florida.

NUTTY PUMPKIN MUFFINS

¾ cup firmly packed brown sugar
2 eggs
¼ cup butter or margarine, melted
1 cup canned or mashed cooked pumpkin
½ cup buttermilk
2 cups all-purpose flour
2 teaspoons baking powder
1 teaspoon ground cinnamon
1 teaspoon ground allspice
½ teaspoon salt
¼ teaspoon ground cloves
½ cup chopped walnuts or pecans
½ cup raisins

Combine sugar, eggs, and butter in a large mixing bowl; beat until sugar dissolves. Add pumpkin and buttermilk; beat until smooth.

Combine remaining ingredients; add to pumpkin mixture, stirring just to moisten dry ingredients. Spoon into greased muffin pans, filling two-thirds full. Bake at 400° for 20 to 25 minutes. Yield: 1½ dozen.

Betty R. Butts,
Kensington, Maryland.

NO-BAKE PUMPKIN TARTS

1 (16-ounce) can pumpkin or 2 cups
    mashed cooked pumpkin
1 (12-ounce) can evaporated milk
1 (3-ounce) package egg custard mix
2 egg yolks
¼ cup firmly packed brown sugar
1¼ teaspoons pumpkin pie spice
12 (3-inch) commercial graham cracker
    crumb tart shells
Whipped cream (optional)
Pecan halves (optional)

Combine first 6 ingredients in a saucepan; mix well. Cook over medium-high heat, stirring constantly, until mixture boils. Remove from heat; cover with waxed paper, and cool slightly.

Spoon into tart shells. Chill until set. Garnish with whipped cream and pecan halves, if desired. Yield: 12 servings.

Carolyn Look,
El Paso, Texas.

RICH PUMPKIN PIE

Pastry for 9-inch pie
3 eggs, slightly beaten
1 cup canned or mashed cooked pumpkin
½ cup firmly packed brown sugar
1 cup half-and-half
2 tablespoons plus 2 teaspoons apricot
   brandy
¼ teaspoon salt
½ teaspoon ground cinnamon
¼ teaspoon ground mace
¼ teaspoon ground cloves
2 tablespoons finely chopped candied
   ginger
Whipped cream (optional)

Roll pastry to ⅛-inch thickness on a lightly floured surface. Place in a 9-inch pieplate; trim off excess pastry along edges. Fold edges under, and flute. Prick bottom and sides of pastry with a fork. Bake at 400° for 3 minutes; remove from oven, and gently prick with a fork. Bake an additional 5 minutes. Set aside to cool.

Combine eggs and next 8 ingredients; blend well. Pour into cooled pastry shell. Sprinkle top with candied ginger. Bake at 375° for 30 to 35 minutes. Garnish pie with whipped cream, if desired. Yield: one 9-inch pie.

Erma Morris,
Lubbock, Texas.

PUMPKIN KAHLÚA CAKE

1 (18.5-ounce) package spice cake mix
   without pudding
1 (16-ounce) can pumpkin or 2 cups
   mashed cooked pumpkin
4 eggs
¼ cup water
1 (1.4-ounce) envelope whipped topping
   mix
Kahlúa Glaze

Combine cake mix and pumpkin in a mixing bowl; beat at low speed of an electric mixer until cake mix is moistened. Increase electric mixer speed to medium, and add the eggs, one at a time, beating well after each addition. Add water and whipped topping mix; beat batter 2 minutes.

Pour batter into a greased and floured 13- x 9- x 2-inch baking pan. Bake at 350° for 45 minutes or until a wooden pick inserted in center comes out clean. Cool in pan 10 minutes. Remove cake from pan, and place on a serving tray. Allow cake to cool slightly. Drizzle cake with Kahlúa Glaze. Yield: one 13- x 9- x 2-inch cake.

Kahlúa Glaze:

1½ cups sifted powdered sugar
¼ cup butter or margarine, melted
2 tablespoons Kahlúa

Combine powdered sugar, butter, and Kahlúa in a small bowl; stir until mixture is smooth. Yield: about ⅔ cup.

Ella Gaquin,
Palm Bay, Florida.

Cook Chestnuts For Eating Pleasure

When you begin to peel and eat roasted chestnuts, don't be surprised if you start to sing or hum a familiar tune. These rich, brown nuggets are known for putting people in a festive mood. You may never have tried it, but cooking chestnuts—whether you actually roast or boil them—is easier than you might think.

To roast chestnuts on an open fire, cut an X in the flat side of each chestnut shell, using a sharp paring knife. Place chestnuts in a long-handled wire popcorn popper or chestnut roaster. Cook over medium heat for 15 to 20 minutes or until tender, shaking pan often to distribute heat evenly and to keep the nuts from burning. Let cool to touch, and peel with a sharp paring knife while chestnuts are warm.

Oven-roasted chestnuts are prepared in a similar way. Cut an X in the flat side of each shell. Place chestnuts in a shallow pan. Bake at 400° for 15 minutes, shaking pan occasionally. Let cool to touch, and peel with a sharp paring knife while chestnuts are warm.

The method for **boiling chestnuts** is somewhat different. Cut an X in the flat side of each shell. Place chestnuts in a saucepan; cover with water, and bring to a boil. Boil 5 minutes; drain. Pour lukewarm water over chestnuts in saucepan. Remove from water, one at a time, and peel with a sharp paring knife while chestnuts are warm.

Raw chestnuts have a high-moisture content. They keep best when stored at a low temperature and high humidity. Fresh raw chestnuts stored in the refrigerator will keep up to 6 months. And, of course, they can be stored even longer if they're frozen. When placed in a moisture-vapor-proof bag, fresh raw chestnuts will keep in the freezer until the next harvest.

Fast-And-Flavorful Chicken For Four

Because chicken is a favorite of many families, a new and easy recipe is always welcomed, especially if it's brimming with flavor. The ingredients in these recipes may seem numerous, but the actual cooking is easy. Because the dishes are baked or simmered, you'll have time to prepare the rest of the meal while the chicken is cooking.

TANGY CHICKEN

4 chicken breasts, skinned
½ teaspoon salt
½ teaspoon pepper
½ teaspoon ground thyme
½ teaspoon minced garlic
1 medium onion, finely chopped
¼ cup lemon juice
¼ cup vinegar
¼ cup butter or margarine, melted

Place chicken in an 8-inch square baking dish. Combine remaining ingredients, and pour over chicken. Cover and bake at 350° for 30 minutes. Uncover and bake an additional 30 minutes or until chicken is done. Yield: 4 servings.

Hazel Sellers,
Albany, Georgia.

COUNTRY POULET

2 tablespoons butter or margarine
3¼ pounds chicken breasts, thighs, and
   legs, skinned
¾ cup chicken broth
¾ cup dry white wine
1 clove garlic, minced
1 bay leaf
½ teaspoon dried whole thyme
¼ teaspoon dried whole marjoram
¼ teaspoon salt
2 cups frozen baby carrots
2 cups frozen small whole onions
1 tablespoon cornstarch
2 tablespoons water

Melt butter in a large skillet; add chicken, and brown on all sides. Add chicken broth, wine, and seasonings; cover, reduce heat, and simmer 35 minutes. Add carrots and onions; cover and cook 10 to 15 minutes or until tender. Discard bay leaf; remove chicken and vegetables to a serving platter.

Dissolve cornstarch in water; stir into broth mixture. Bring to a boil over medium heat, stirring constantly; cook 1 minute, or until thickened and bubbly. Pour over chicken. Yield: 4 servings.
Carol S. Noble,
Burgaw, North Carolina.

MUSTARD CHICKEN

¾ cup vinegar
¾ cup prepared mustard
½ cup vegetable oil
¾ cup beer
¾ teaspoon seasoned salt
½ teaspoon salt
½ teaspoon garlic salt
½ teaspoon onion salt
½ teaspoon ground red pepper
¼ teaspoon pepper
1 (2½- to 3-pound) broiler-fryer, cut up and skinned

Combine all ingredients except chicken; stir well. Dip chicken pieces in mustard sauce, and place in a lightly greased 13- x 9- x 2-inch baking dish. Bake at 375° for 45 to 50 minutes or until done. Yield: 4 servings.
Patty Braud,
Hattiesburg, Mississippi.

CHICKEN CHARLEMAGNE

1 (3- to 3½-pound) broiler-fryer, cut up and skinned
Salt and pepper
¼ cup butter or margarine
8 green onions, sliced
½ cup sliced celery
1 carrot, scraped and cut diagonally into ½-inch slices
1 cup light beer
1 (14½-ounce) can stewed tomatoes, undrained
¼ teaspoon dried whole thyme
1 bay leaf
2 tablespoons all-purpose flour
¼ cup water
Hot cooked rice

Sprinkle chicken with salt and pepper. Melt butter in a large skillet; add

chicken, and cook until browned on all sides. Remove chicken, reserving drippings in skillet.

Add green onions, celery, and carrots to drippings; sauté 2 to 3 minutes. Add beer, tomatoes, thyme, and bay leaf; bring to a boil. Return chicken to skillet. Cover, reduce heat, and simmer 40 to 45 minutes or until chicken is done. Place chicken on serving platter.

Dissolve flour in water; gradually stir flour mixture into liquid in skillet. Cook over medium heat, stirring constantly, until thickened and bubbly. Remove bay leaf, and pour flour mixture over chicken. Serve over rice. Yield: 4 servings. *Mrs. Farmer L. Burns,*
New Orleans, Louisiana.

Casual Entrées For A Group

Try these casual entrées before an evening of cards with friends. They're just right for teens or adults, and each recipe makes enough to feed a group.

CHAMPION SEAFOOD GUMBO

1 quart water
1 teaspoon dried whole thyme
1 teaspoon chopped fresh parsley
1 teaspoon salt
2 bay leaves
1 dried hot pepper
2 pounds medium shrimp
½ pound Polish sausage, sliced
1 large onion, chopped
1 teaspoon dried whole thyme
2 tablespoons chopped fresh parsley
2 tablespoons all-purpose flour
1 teaspoon chicken-flavored bouillon granules
1 (10¾-ounce) can cream of chicken soup, undiluted
1 (11-ounce) can crab soup, undiluted
2 cups tomato juice
⅛ teaspoon hot sauce
¼ teaspoon pepper
1 pound lump crabmeat
Hot cooked rice
Filé powder (optional)

Combine first 6 ingredients in a Dutch oven; bring to a boil. Add shrimp, and cook 3 to 5 minutes. Drain well, reserving 3 cups liquid; discard bay leaves and hot pepper. Rinse

shrimp with cold water. Chill. Peel and devein shrimp; set aside.

Combine sausage and next 3 ingredients in a large Dutch oven; sauté until sausage is browned. Drain, if necessary. Stir in flour and bouillon granules. Add reserved shrimp liquid, cream of chicken soup, and next 4 ingredients, mixing well. Bring to a boil; cover, reduce heat, and simmer 20 minutes. Add crabmeat; simmer 5 minutes. Serve over rice; sprinkle with filé powder, if desired. Yield: about 3 quarts.
Allyson Davis,
Cedar Rapids, Iowa.

BEEF TIPS AND NOODLES

4 pounds boneless sirloin, cut into ½-inch cubes
½ cup all-purpose flour
½ cup vegetable oil
2 cloves garlic, minced
1 (28-ounce) can tomatoes, undrained and chopped
1 large onion, chopped
½ cup chopped green pepper
2 teaspoons ground cumin
½ teaspoon salt
½ teaspoon pepper
Hot cooked noodles

Dredge beef in flour; brown in hot oil in a large Dutch oven, stirring occasionally. Add remaining ingredients except noodles; cover and bring to a boil. Reduce heat, and simmer 1 hour or until meat is tender. Serve over noodles. Yield: 12 to 14 servings. *Marge Clyde,*
San Antonio, Texas.

FAVORITE CHILI CON CARNE

1 cup coarsely chopped onion
3 cloves garlic, minced
½ cup chopped green pepper
2 tablespoons vegetable oil
2 pounds lean ground beef
4 large tomatoes, peeled and quartered
4 cups cooked kidney beans, drained
1 teaspoon salt
¼ cup chili powder

Sauté onion, garlic, and green pepper in hot oil in a Dutch oven. Add ground beef; cook over medium heat until browned, stirring to crumble beef. Drain well.

Add remaining ingredients; bring to a boil. Cover, reduce heat, and simmer 1 hour, stirring occasionally. Yield: 2 quarts.
Mrs. Ben Killion,
Fayetteville, Arkansas.

BAKED HAM
WITH ORANGE SAUCE

1 (15-pound) fully cooked sugar-cured
    ham
3 tablespoons spicy brown mustard
1½ tablespoons peanut butter
2 tablespoons whole cloves
¾ cup firmly packed brown sugar
Orange slices (optional)
Parsley sprigs (optional)
Orange Sauce

Remove hard outer crust of ham.
Place ham on a rack in roasting pan;
insert meat thermometer, making sure it
does not touch fat or bone. Bake, uncovered, at 325° for 3 hours. Cool ham;
cover and refrigerate 8 hours.

Score outside of ham in a diamond
pattern. Combine mustard and peanut
butter, stirring until smooth; spread
mixture over surface of ham. Insert
cloves in ham at 1-inch intervals. Pat
brown sugar over mustard mixture.
Bake ham at 325° for 1 hour or until
thermometer registers 140°. Slice and
arrange on platter; garnish with orange
slices and parsley, if desired. Serve with
Orange Sauce. Yield: 30 servings.

Orange Sauce:

2 cups orange juice
2 tablespoons cornstarch
⅓ cup orange marmalade
1¼ teaspoons spicy brown mustard

Combine orange juice and cornstarch
in a saucepan; stir until cornstarch dissolves. Bring mixture to a boil; cook 1
minute, stirring constantly. Add marmalade and mustard; stir until smooth.
Yield: 2½ cups.   *Jenny Peebles,*
                        Miami Shores, Florida.

PORK SLOPPY JOES

4 pounds ground lean pork
1½ cups finely chopped celery
2 (10¾-ounce) cans tomato soup,
    undiluted
1 (18-ounce) jar barbecue sauce
2 tablespoons instant minced onion
Hamburger buns

Cook pork and chopped celery in a
large Dutch oven until browned, stirring
to crumble pork. Drain well.

Combine pork mixture, soup, barbecue sauce, and onion. Bring mixture to
a boil over medium heat; reduce heat to
low, and simmer 20 minutes. Serve on
hamburger buns. Yield: 16 servings.
                        Aimee Goodman,
                        Knoxville, Tennessee.

VENISON STEW

2 pounds boneless venison, cut into
    ½-inch cubes
½ cup all-purpose flour
¼ cup bacon drippings
4 carrots, cut into ½-inch slices
2 (10½-ounce) cans beef broth, undiluted
2 cups red wine
2 bay leaves
1 (10½-ounce) can French onion soup,
    undiluted
1 large onion, coarsely chopped
1 large green pepper, coarsely chopped
¼ teaspoon salt
¼ teaspoon pepper
Hot cooked rice or biscuits (optional)

Dredge venison in flour; brown in hot
bacon drippings in a large Dutch oven.
Add remaining ingredients except rice;
cover, reduce heat, and simmer 2 hours.
Remove bay leaves before serving.
Serve over rice or biscuits, if desired.
Yield: 2½ quarts.   *Robert M. Turner,*
                        Ocala, Florida.

COOKING LIGHT®

Good News About Winter Vegetables

The pleasure of eating fresh vegetables isn't reserved strictly for summertime. Colder temperatures bring an
abundance of certain produce to the
grocery store. Look for plenty of cruciferous vegetables (those of the cabbage
family), including brussels sprouts, broccoli, cauliflower, rutabagas, cabbage,
and turnips. A variety of vitamin A-
and vitamin C-rich vegetables, such as
carrots, spinach, broccoli, winter
squash, cabbage, brussels sprouts, and
green leafy vegetables, also grace the
produce bins. These colorful vegetables
are not only full of vitamins and minerals but are also high in dietary fiber
content. And their healthful benefits
don't stop there.

Recent studies suggest that these
foods and some of their nutrients may
help protect against particular types of
cancer. Specifically, foods high in beta-
carotene or pro-vitamin A (the plant
form of the vitamin that can be converted to vitamin A in the body) may
help protect against cancer of the
esophagus, larynx, lung, and bladder.
Vitamin C-rich foods may offer some

protection against esophagus and stomach cancer, and the cruciferous vegetables may help deter colon cancer.

The food you eat is just one of many
factors that may influence your risks of
getting cancer. Certainly more research
is needed to better understand the role
foods and certain nutrients play. But
choosing cruciferous vitamin A- and
vitamin C-rich vegetables more often
still adds up to a healthy way of eating.

BROCCOLI TOSS

2 cups broccoli flowerets
1½ cups cauliflower flowerets
1 cup cherry tomato halves
2 tablespoons minced onion
¼ cup red wine vinegar
1 tablespoon olive oil
1 clove garlic, minced
1 teaspoon Dijon mustard
½ teaspoon dried parsley flakes
Dash of pepper

Cook broccoli and cauliflower, covered, in a small amount of boiling water
3 minutes. Drain well; place in a shallow 1-quart dish. Add cherry tomatoes
and onion; set aside.

Combine vinegar and remaining ingredients in a jar. Cover tightly, and
shake vigorously.

Pour dressing over vegetables, tossing
gently to coat. Cover and chill 2 hours,
stirring occasionally. Yield: 4 servings
(about 73 calories per 1-cup serving).
                        Tammy Randermann,
                        Brenham, Texas.

CASSEROLE
OF BRUSSELS SPROUTS

1 pound fresh brussels sprouts
1 cup water
¼ cup chopped onion
2 teaspoons reduced-calorie margarine,
    melted
1 (16-ounce) can tomatoes, undrained
    and chopped
1 tablespoon cornstarch
1 teaspoon dried whole basil
½ teaspoon dry mustard
Pepper to taste

Wash brussels sprouts thoroughly,
and remove discolored leaves. Cut off
stem ends, and slash bottom of each
sprout with a shallow X. Place sprouts
in a large saucepan; add water, and
bring to a boil. Cover, reduce heat, and

simmer 5 minutes or until tender; drain. Place sprouts in a 1-quart casserole.

Sauté onion in margarine in a heavy skillet until tender. Add remaining ingredients to skillet, stirring well. Cook over medium heat, stirring constantly, until mixture is thickened and bubbly.

Pour sauce over brussels sprouts. Cover and bake at 350° for 25 to 30 minutes. Yield: 4 servings (about 76 calories per 1-cup serving).

Joan McDonald,
Weirton, West Virginia.

TURNIPS AND CARROTS JULIENNE

2 cups 1½-inch julienne-cut carrots
2 cups 1½-inch julienne-cut turnips
½ cup skim milk
1½ teaspoons cornstarch
1 teaspoon chopped chives
½ teaspoon chicken-flavored bouillon granules
⅛ teaspoon white pepper

Cook carrots, covered, in a small amount of boiling water 1 minute; add turnips, and cook an additional 4 minutes or until crisp-tender. Drain well.

Combine milk and remaining ingredients in a small saucepan; blend well. Cook, stirring constantly, until thickened and bubbly. Pour over vegetables; toss to coat. Yield: 5 servings (about 46 calories per ½-cup serving).

SWEET-AND-SOUR CABBAGE

2 tablespoons white wine vinegar
1 tablespoon sugar
¼ teaspoon salt
4 whole cloves
4 peppercorns
2 bay leaves
Dash of ground coriander
Dash of freshly ground pepper
4 cups shredded cabbage
½ cup chopped onion
1 tablespoon reduced-calorie margarine, melted
2 small red apples, unpeeled and cut into wedges

Combine vinegar, sugar, salt, cloves, peppercorns, bay leaves, coriander, and pepper in a large mixing bowl; stir well. Add the shredded cabbage; toss gently to coat. Cover cabbage and marinade, and let stand 1 hour.

Sauté onion in margarine in a large skillet until tender. Add cabbage and marinade; bring to a boil. Cover, reduce heat, and simmer 8 to 10 minutes,

stirring occasionally. Stir in apples; cover and simmer an additional 8 minutes. Remove bay leaves, cloves, and peppercorns before serving. Yield: 6 servings (about 51 calories per ⅔-cup serving).

Frances Spedaliere,
Virginia Beach, Virginia.

CRUNCHY COLESLAW

4 cups shredded cabbage
1 cup shredded carrots
⅓ cup chopped onion
1 (6-ounce) can frozen unsweetened apple juice concentrate, thawed and undiluted
¼ cup cider vinegar
1 tablespoon vegetable oil
½ teaspoon celery seeds
½ teaspoon prepared mustard

Combine cabbage, carrots, and onion in a large bowl; set aside. Combine remaining ingredients in a jar; cover tightly, and shake vigorously. Pour over cabbage mixture; toss gently to coat. Cover and chill 8 hours. Yield: 6 servings (about 80 calories per ¾-cup serving).

Dolly G. Northcutt,
Fairfield, Alabama.

BUTTERNUT-ORANGE BAKE

1 (2-pound) butternut squash
1 (11-ounce) can mandarin oranges, drained
2 teaspoons reduced-calorie margarine, melted
½ teaspoon maple flavoring
¼ teaspoon ground cinnamon
2 eggs, separated
2 tablespoons chopped pecans, toasted

Cut squash in half lengthwise, and remove seeds. Place cut side down in a shallow baking dish; add hot water to depth of ½ inch in dish. Cover and bake at 375° for 35 minutes or until tender. Let cool; carefully scoop out pulp. Mash pulp with potato masher.

Combine 2 cups squash and next 4 ingredients, stirring well. Beat egg yolks until thick and lemon colored; stir into the squash mixture.

Beat egg whites (at room temperature) until stiff but not dry. Gently fold into squash mixture. Spoon mixture into 6 ungreased individual 6-ounce soufflé dishes.

Bake at 375° for 20 minutes or until puffed and lightly browned. Garnish tops with pecans; serve immediately. Yield: 6 servings (about 96 calories per ½-cup serving).

MASHED RUTABAGAS

2¼ pounds rutabagas
3 cups water
1 teaspoon chicken-flavored bouillon granules
1 tablespoon honey
¼ teaspoon ground allspice
¼ teaspoon ground nutmeg
Dash of red pepper

Peel and cut rutabagas into ¼- to ½-inch slices; boil in unsalted water 30 to 40 minutes or until tender. Drain, reserving ½ cup liquid. Dissolve bouillon granules in liquid. Mash rutabagas with a potato masher.

Combine 4 cups mashed rutabagas, bouillon mixture, honey, allspice, nutmeg, and red pepper; stir well. Yield: 8 servings (about 51 calories per ½-cup serving).

Stir Up A Bowl Of Pimiento Cheese

Ask a dozen people to tell you about their favorite pimiento cheese spread, and you'll probably get a dozen different descriptions. Creamy, chunky, slightly sweet, and with a hint of garlic are several of the textures and flavors you'll hear about. Some even say it's a special combination of specific cheeses that makes the difference.

CHUNKY PIMIENTO CHEESE

2 cups (8 ounces) shredded sharp Cheddar cheese
2 cups (8 ounces) shredded medium Cheddar cheese
1 (4-ounce) jar diced pimiento, drained
1 tablespoon vinegar
1 teaspoon sugar
¾ to 1 cup salad dressing or mayonnaise

Combine all ingredients; stir well. Cover and chill. Yield: 2¾ cups.

Vida Duke,
Paris, Texas.

CREAMY PIMIENTO CHEESE

1 (8-ounce) package cream cheese,
    softened
2 cups (8 ounces) shredded sharp Cheddar
    cheese, softened
¼ cup plus 2 tablespoons mayonnaise
Dash of garlic powder
1 (4-ounce) jar diced pimiento, drained

Combine cheeses in a large mixing
bowl; beat at medium speed of an electric mixer until light and fluffy. Add
mayonnaise and garlic powder; mix
well. Stir in pimiento. For best consistency, serve at room temperature. To
store, cover and chill. Yield: 4½ cups.
Patricia Flint,
Staunton, Virginia.

PIMIENTO AND THREE CHEESES

2 cups (8 ounces) shredded Cheddar
    cheese
1 cup (4 ounces) shredded process cheese
1 cup (4 ounces) shredded process
    American cheese
1 (4-ounce) jar diced pimiento, drained
1 (2-ounce) jar diced pimiento, drained
⅓ cup mayonnaise
2 tablespoons milk
1 teaspoon lemon juice

Combine all ingredients; stir well.
Cover and chill. Yield: 3 cups.
Eos Steele,
Athens, Alabama.

Green Chiles Make The Difference

If you like the flavor of Southwest
cuisine, these recipes are for you. Each
calls for green chiles, an important ingredient in Southwestern cookery.
We've used canned as well as fresh
green chiles in these recipes. If you
have trouble finding the fresh ones,
check your local specialty food store or
gourmet market.

When shopping, choose fresh green
chiles that are thick walled and firm,
with a glossy appearance. Generally,
the more red shading on the pepper,
the hotter it will be.

When handling green chiles, be sure
to wear rubber gloves and keep your
hands away from your eyes. Chemicals
in the peppers can cause a burning sen-
sation to bare skin.

CHILES RELLENOS EGG ROLLS

12 fresh green chiles
1 pound ground beef
1 medium onion, chopped
1 clove garlic, minced
2 cups (8 ounces) shredded Cheddar
    cheese
½ teaspoon salt
½ teaspoon ground cumin
¼ teaspoon dried whole oregano
12 egg roll wrappers
Vegetable oil
Picante sauce (optional)

Place chiles on a baking sheet; broil 3
to 4 inches from heat, turning often
with tongs, until chiles are blistered on
all sides. Immediately place chiles in a
plastic bag; fasten securely, and let
steam 10 to 15 minutes. Remove peel
from chiles.

Slit each chile lengthwise, and rinse
under cold water to remove seeds. (If
you have sensitive skin, wear rubber or
plastic gloves when rinsing and cutting
chiles.) Remove stems from chiles; set
chiles aside.

Cook beef, onion, and garlic in a skillet until meat is browned; drain. Add
cheese and seasonings, stirring well.

Place 2 tablespoons beef mixture on
each chile; roll up jellyroll fashion.
Place chiles diagonally off center on
each egg roll wrapper; fold corner over
chile. Fold sides over; brush edges of
egg roll wrapper lightly with water. Roll
up, and press edges together to seal.

Heat vegetable oil to depth of 4 to 5
inches to 375° in a large saucepan. Place
2 or 3 filled egg rolls in hot oil, and fry
30 seconds on each side or until golden
brown; drain on paper towels. Repeat
with the remaining egg rolls. Serve with
picante sauce, if desired. Yield: 1
dozen.
Carol Barclay,
Portland, Texas.

MEXICAN STEW OLÉ

1½ pounds stew beef, cut into 1-inch
    cubes
¼ cup all-purpose flour
¼ cup vegetable oil
1 large onion, chopped
1 clove garlic, minced
4 (4-ounce) cans chopped green chiles,
    drained
½ teaspoon salt
1 to 1½ teaspoons coarsely ground
    pepper
2 tablespoons red wine vinegar
1 cup Burgundy or other dry red wine
1 (15-ounce) can tomato sauce

Dredge meat in flour; cook in hot oil
in a Dutch oven until meat is browned.
Add remaining ingredients; stir well.
Cover, reduce heat, and simmer 2½
hours, stirring meat occasionally. Yield:
5½ cups.
Stephen H. Badgett,
Memphis, Tennessee.

CHICKEN ENCHILADAS

4 chicken breast halves
1 cup chopped onion
1 clove garlic, minced
2 tablespoons olive oil
2 (16-ounce) cans tomatoes, undrained
1 (15-ounce) can tomato sauce
2 (4-ounce) cans chopped green chiles,
    undrained
1 teaspoon sugar
1 teaspoon ground cumin
½ teaspoon dried whole oregano
½ teaspoon dried whole basil
½ teaspoon dried whole cilantro
¼ teaspoon salt
¾ cup commercial sour cream
2 cups (8 ounces) shredded Cheddar
    cheese, divided
12 (6-inch) flour tortillas
Commercial sour cream (optional)

Place chicken in a Dutch oven; cover
with water, and bring to a boil. Cover,
reduce heat, and simmer 45 minutes or
until chicken is tender. Remove chicken
from broth, and let cool; reserve broth
for other uses. Remove chicken from
bone, and chop; set aside.

Sauté onion and garlic in hot oil until
tender; set aside. Place tomatoes in container of an electric blender; process
until pureed; add to onion mixture.
Add tomato sauce, green chiles, sugar,
and seasonings; stir well. Bring to a
boil; cover, reduce heat, and simmer 1
hour. Stir in ¾ cup sour cream.

Spoon 2 heaping tablespoonfuls each
of chicken and cheese on tortilla; roll
tortilla up tightly, and place seam side
down in lightly greased 13- x 9- x 2-inch
baking dish.

Pour tomato mixture over enchiladas.
Bake, uncovered, at 350° for 40 minutes. Remove from oven; add the remaining cheese, and bake an additional
5 minutes. Serve with additional sour
cream, if desired. Yield: 6 servings.
Sheree Garvin,
Wilkesboro, North Carolina.

CHILE-SAUSAGE SQUARES

1 cup biscuit mix
⅓ cup milk
¼ cup mayonnaise, divided
1 pound bulk pork sausage
½ cup chopped onion
1 egg, beaten
2 cups (8 ounces) shredded sharp Cheddar
   cheese
2 (4-ounce) cans chopped green chiles,
   drained

Combine biscuit mix, milk, and 2 tablespoons mayonnaise; stir well. Spread mixture in a greased 13- x 9- x 2-inch baking dish; set aside.

Cook sausage and onion in a skillet until meat is browned, stirring to crumble meat. Drain well between paper towels. Layer sausage mixture over biscuit mixture.

Combine egg, cheese, and chiles; spread over sausage mixture. Bake at 350° for 30 minutes. Let stand 5 minutes before serving. Yield: 8 servings or about 40 appetizer servings.

Mary Jane Wilson,
Bovina, Texas.

CHILE-CHEESE SPREAD

¼ cup milk
2 cups (8 ounces) shredded sharp Cheddar
   cheese
1 (4-ounce) can chopped green chiles,
   drained
2 tablespoons butter or margarine,
   softened
⅛ teaspoon garlic powder

Scald milk; pour over cheese. Beat at medium speed of an electric mixer until mixture is almost smooth. Add remaining ingredients, and beat 1 minute. Serve spread with assorted crackers. Yield: 1⅔ cups. *Phyllis Rodesney,*
Midwest City, Oklahoma.

TEX-MEX TORTILLA APPETIZERS

1 (8-ounce) package cream cheese,
   softened
1 (4-ounce) can chopped green chiles,
   drained
2 green onions, minced
¼ teaspoon garlic salt
12 (6-inch) flour tortillas
Picante sauce

Combine cream cheese, green chiles, green onions, and garlic salt in a small bowl. Spread 1 heaping tablespoonful of

cream cheese mixture on each tortilla. Roll up jellyroll fashion. Place seam side down on baking sheet; cover and chill 2 hours. Slice each tortilla roll into 4 pieces. Serve with picante sauce. Yield: 4 dozen.

Note: Appetizers may be frozen. To freeze, place uncut tortilla rolls on baking sheet; cover and place in freezer until frozen. Remove from baking sheet, and store in an airtight container in freezer. To serve, remove from freezer and thaw. Slice each tortilla roll into 4 pieces. *Mrs. J. C. Hohf,*
Victoria, Texas.

Try Hot Salads For A Change

If winter menus have become routine, you might try fixing a hot salad. These salads use familiar ingredients in creative, tasty ways.

BAKED CHICKEN SALAD

2 cups diced cooked chicken
2 cups chopped celery
½ cup sliced water chestnuts
¼ cup plus 2 tablespoons lemon juice
3 tablespoons diced pimiento, drained
2 hard-cooked eggs, chopped
1 (10¾-ounce) can cream of chicken soup,
   undiluted
½ cup mayonnaise
1 cup herb-seasoned stuffing mix
¼ cup butter or margarine, melted

Combine chicken, celery, water chestnuts, lemon juice, pimiento, eggs, soup, and mayonnaise; mix well. Spoon chicken mixture into a lightly greased shallow 2-quart casserole.

Combine stuffing mix and butter; mix well. Sprinkle over casserole. Bake at 350° for 30 minutes. Yield: 6 servings.

Mrs. Nels E. Johnson,
McLean, Virginia.

HOT TURKEY SALAD

2 cups chopped cooked turkey
2 cups chopped celery
½ cup mayonnaise
½ cup chopped almonds, toasted
2 teaspoons minced onion
½ cup (2 ounces) shredded Cheddar
   cheese
½ cup crushed potato chips

Combine turkey, celery, mayonnaise, almonds, and onion in a large mixing bowl; mix well. Spoon into a greased shallow 1-quart casserole. Cover and bake at 350° for 15 minutes. Sprinkle with cheese and potato chips; bake an additional 5 minutes. Yield: 4 servings.

Jenny Peebles,
Miami Shores, Florida.

HOT DUTCH POTATO SALAD

10 slices bacon (about ½ pound)
2 tablespoons all-purpose flour
2 tablespoons sugar
1 teaspoon dry mustard
⅔ cup vinegar
⅔ cup water
1 teaspoon salt
¼ teaspoon pepper
3 large potatoes, cooked, peeled, and
   sliced
½ cup chopped celery
⅓ cup chopped green onions

Cook bacon in a large skillet until crisp; remove bacon, reserving 2 tablespoons drippings in skillet. Crumble bacon, and set aside.

Combine flour, sugar, and dry mustard; mix well. Add to drippings, stirring until smooth. Cook 1 minute, stirring constantly. Gradually add vinegar and water; cook over medium heat, stirring constantly, until mixture is thickened and bubbly. Stir in salt and pepper; remove mixture from heat, and set aside.

Layer half each of the potatoes, celery, green onions, and bacon in a lightly greased 12- x 8- x 2-inch baking dish. Pour half the sauce over bacon. Repeat layers with the remaining ingredients. Cover and bake at 350° for 20 minutes. Uncover and bake an additional 10 minutes. Yield: 8 servings.

Carol Barclay,
Portland, Texas.

Tip: Keep potatoes and onions in a cool, dark place with plenty of air circulation to prevent sprouting.

HOT GREEN BEAN SALAD

2 (16-ounce) cans French-cut green beans,
   drained
½ cup sugar
½ cup vinegar
½ cup vegetable oil
1 medium purple onion, thinly sliced
½ cup water chestnuts, sliced
1 (4-ounce) jar sliced pimiento, drained
4 slices bacon, cooked and crumbled
Lettuce leaves

Place beans in a shallow dish. Combine sugar, vinegar, and oil in a small mixing bowl, and pour over green beans. Cover and chill 1 hour.

Drain beans. Add onion, water chestnuts, and sliced pimiento; toss gently. Spoon into a lightly greased 2-quart casserole, and sprinkle bacon over top. Bake at 350° for 30 minutes. Serve hot over lettuce leaves. Yield: 6 servings.

Dorsella Utter,
Louisville, Kentucky.

Yeast Breads To Fix And Freeze

Has the push of the holidays ruled out possibilities for homemade bread? Think again—these make-ahead yeast breads fit in the freezer and debut during the holidays.

Homemade breads say you care. Take our Old-Fashioned Cinnamon Rolls to a neighbor who has lots of company, or top off your own brimming table with Luscious Orange Rolls. In fact, you can't go wrong when you bake any of the other rolls and breads from these recipes, all traditional favorites.

Ensure your bread's perfect quality by following proper techniques. Remember, liquid ingredients that are too hot or too cold will kill the yeast. And kneading is important to develop gluten, the protein that gives bread its shape. Follow the recipe closely, letting the dough rise by the methods suggested. Once the dough has risen, lightly press two fingertips into it. If an indentation remains, the dough is ready to be punched down.

Each recipe has its own distinctive flavor and directions for shaping. Freeze the bread in an airtight container or wrapped in aluminum foil. Some will come out of the freezer ready to serve after thawing; others will need extra baking time.

OLD-FASHIONED CINNAMON ROLLS

1 package dry yeast
½ cup warm water (105° to 115°)
½ cup boiling water
¼ cup shortening
¼ cup butter or margarine
⅓ cup sugar
1 egg
1 egg yolk
1½ teaspoons salt
3½ to 4 cups bread flour, divided
¼ cup butter or margarine,
   melted
⅔ cup chopped pecans
½ cup raisins
¼ cup sugar
2 teaspoons ground cinnamon
Glaze (recipe follows)

Dissolve yeast in ½ cup warm water.

Combine ½ cup boiling water, ¼ cup shortening, ¼ cup butter, and ⅓ cup sugar; stir until shortening melts. Cool to 105° to 115°. Add yeast mixture, egg, egg yolk, and salt; mix well. Gradually add 2 cups flour, beating at medium speed of an electric mixer until smooth. Stir in enough remaining flour to form a soft dough.

Turn dough out onto a lightly floured surface, and knead until smooth and elastic (about 5 to 7 minutes). Place dough in a greased bowl, turning to grease top. Cover and let rise in a warm place (85°), free from drafts, 1 hour or until doubled.

Punch dough down, and divide in half; roll each half into a 15- x 9-inch rectangle. Spread each with 2 tablespoons butter, ⅓ cup pecans, and ¼ cup raisins. Combine ¼ cup sugar and the cinnamon; sprinkle half over each rectangle. Starting at long end, roll up jellyroll fashion. Cut each roll into 9 (1½-inch) slices; place slightly apart in two greased 9-inch square pans. Cover and let rise in a warm place (85°), free from drafts, 1 hour.

Bake at 350° for 20 to 25 minutes or until golden brown. Drizzle with glaze while warm. Yield: 1½ dozen.

Glaze:

1½ cups sifted powdered sugar
3 to 4 tablespoons milk
½ teaspoon vanilla extract

Combine all ingredients; mix well. Yield: ½ cup.

To freeze, bake rolls at 350° for 15 minutes; cool. Wrap in aluminum foil; freeze. To serve, let rolls thaw. Bake at 350° for 5 to 10 minutes or until golden brown; glaze while warm.

Dee Buchfink,
Oologah, Oklahoma.

LUSCIOUS ORANGE ROLLS

1 envelope dry yeast
¼ cup warm water (105° to 115°)
½ cup commercial sour cream
¾ cup sugar, divided
1 teaspoon salt
¼ cup plus 2 tablespoons butter or
   margarine, melted
2 eggs, beaten
3 to 3½ cups all-purpose flour,
   divided
3 tablespoons grated orange rind
2 tablespoons butter or margarine,
   softened
Orange Glaze

Dissolve yeast in warm water; let stand 5 minutes. Combine sour cream, ¼ cup sugar, and salt in a small mixing bowl; mix well. Add ¼ cup plus 2 tablespoons melted butter, eggs, 2 cups flour, and yeast mixture; mix well. Gradually add enough remaining flour to make a soft dough.

Turn dough out on a floured surface, and knead until smooth and elastic (about 5 minutes). Place in a well-greased bowl, turning to grease top. Cover and let rise in a warm place (85°), free from drafts, 1½ to 2 hours or until doubled in bulk.

Punch dough down, and divide in half. Roll each half into a 12-inch circle on a floured surface. Combine remaining ½ cup sugar and orange rind in a small mixing bowl.

Spread each circle with 1 tablespoon butter; sprinkle with half of orange-sugar mixture. Cut each circle into 12 wedges. Roll up each wedge tightly; place point side down on greased baking sheets. Cover and let rise in a warm place, free from drafts, 1 hour or until almost doubled in bulk. Bake at 350° for 18 to 20 minutes or until golden. Drizzle Orange Glaze over hot rolls; remove immediately from baking sheets. Yield: 2 dozen.

Orange Glaze:

¼ cup sugar
¼ cup commercial sour cream
2 tablespoons butter or margarine
1 tablespoon orange juice

Combine all ingredients in a small saucepan; mix well. Bring to a boil, and cook 3 minutes, stirring constantly. Yield: ½ cup.

To freeze, bake rolls at 350° for 15 minutes; cool. Omit glaze. Wrap in aluminum foil; freeze. To serve, place rolls on lightly greased baking sheets, and thaw. Bake at 350° for 8 to 10 minutes or until golden; glaze as above.

Pankey Kite,
Macon, Georgia.

GOLDEN YAM ROLLS

1 package dry yeast
¼ cup warm water (105° to 115°)
¼ cup butter-flavored shortening
½ cup milk, scalded
¼ cup sugar
1 teaspoon salt
¼ to ½ teaspoon ground nutmeg
¼ teaspoon ground cinnamon
¾ cup mashed cooked yams
1 egg, beaten
3 to 3½ cups all-purpose flour
¼ cup butter or margarine, melted

Dissolve yeast in warm water; let stand 5 minutes. Combine shortening, milk, sugar, salt, nutmeg, and cinnamon in a large mixing bowl; stir until shortening melts. Cool to 105° to 115°. Add yams, egg, and yeast mixture, mixing well. Gradually stir in enough flour to make a soft dough.

Turn dough out onto a floured surface, and knead until smooth and elastic (about 8 minutes). Place in a well-greased bowl, turning to grease top. Cover and let rise in a warm place (85°), free from drafts, 1 hour or until doubled in bulk.

Punch dough down. Roll out to ¾-inch thickness on a lightly floured surface. Cut with a 2-inch biscuit cutter, and place in a greased 13- x 9- x 2-inch pan. Brush with melted butter. Cover and let rise in a warm place, free from drafts, 30 minutes or until doubled in bulk. Bake at 375° for 20 to 25 minutes or until browned. Yield: 15 rolls.

To freeze, prepare and bake rolls as directed; cool. Wrap in aluminum foil. To serve, let thaw; reheat in foil at 350° for 15 to 20 minutes. *Hazel Slucher, Taylorsville, Kentucky.*

SOUTHERN POTATO ROLLS

2 packages dry yeast
1½ cups warm water (105° to 115°)
⅓ cup sugar
1 tablespoon salt
2 eggs
½ cup butter or margarine, softened
½ cup unseasoned mashed cooked potatoes
5½ to 6 cups bread flour, divided
1 egg, beaten
1 tablespoon water
Sesame seeds or poppy seeds

Dissolve yeast in 1½ cups warm water in a large bowl; stir in sugar and salt. Let stand 5 minutes. Add 2 eggs, butter, mashed potatoes, and 3 cups flour; beat at medium speed of an electric mixer about 2 minutes or until smooth.

Stir in enough remaining flour to make a stiff dough.

Turn dough out onto a floured surface, and knead until smooth and elastic (about 4 to 5 minutes). Place in a well-greased bowl, turning to grease top. Cover and chill 2 hours or until doubled in bulk.

Punch dough down, and separate into thirds. Work with one-third of dough at a time; leave remaining dough in refrigerator. Divide each third into 12 portions. Roll each portion into a 12-inch rope. Moisten ends with water, and press together to make a circle; twist each circle forming a figure eight. Place on greased baking sheets. Or coil the rope starting at one end, and wrap around, forming a wider circle each time. Tuck loose end under. Repeat procedure with remaining dough.

Combine 1 egg and 1 tablespoon water. Brush each roll with egg mixture; sprinkle with sesame seeds. Bake at 400° for 10 to 12 minutes or until golden. Yield: 3 dozen.

To freeze, prepare and bake rolls as directed; let cool. Place in an airtight container, and freeze. To serve, let thaw. Wrap in aluminum foil; reheat at 350° for 15 to 20 minutes.

Marilyn Tesoros, Houston, Texas.

FANCY DINNER ROLLS

2 packages dry yeast
⅔ cup warm milk (105° to 115°)
4 eggs
4 egg yolks
¼ cup sugar
2 teaspoons salt
About 3 cups bread flour, divided
1 cup butter or margarine, softened
About 3 cups all-purpose flour
1 egg yolk
1 teaspoon water

Dissolve yeast in warm milk; let stand 5 minutes. Combine eggs, 4 egg yolks, sugar, and salt in a large bowl; mix well. Add 1½ cups bread flour; beat until smooth. Add butter, beating until smooth. Add remaining bread and all-purpose flours to make a stiff dough; beat well.

Turn dough out onto a floured surface, and knead until smooth and elastic (3 minutes). Place in a well-greased bowl, turning to grease top. Cover and let rise in a warm place (85°), free from drafts, 1 hour or until doubled in bulk. Punch dough down. Divide dough into 4 portions; cover 1 portion, and set

aside. Cut each of the 3 portions in half. Shape each half into 4 balls; yielding a total of 24 balls. Place in greased muffin pans. Cut reserved dough into 4 portions; divide each into 6 pieces. Shape into 24 small balls. Make an indentation in each large ball. Brush holes with water; press small balls into indentations. Cover and let rise in a warm place, free from drafts, 1 hour or until doubled in bulk.

Combine remaining egg yolk and 1 teaspoon water; brush tops of rolls. Bake at 375° for 10 to 12 minutes or until golden. Yield: 2 dozen.

To freeze, bake rolls at 375° for 5 to 7 minutes; cool. Wrap in aluminum foil; freeze. To serve, let thaw; bake in foil at 375° for 5 to 6 minutes or until golden. *Jonnie Carroll, Duck Hill, Mississippi.*

HOSPITALITY LOAF BREAD

1 package dry yeast
½ teaspoon sugar
½ cup warm water (105° to 115°)
1 cup milk, scalded
⅓ cup shortening, melted
¼ cup plus 2 tablespoons sugar
2 teaspoons salt
2 egg whites
5 to 5½ cups all-purpose flour

Dissolve yeast and ½ teaspoon sugar in warm water; let stand 5 minutes. Combine next 4 ingredients in a bowl; mix well. Cool to 105° to 115°. Add egg whites and yeast mixture, mixing well. Gradually stir in enough flour to make a soft dough.

Turn dough out onto a floured surface, and knead until smooth and elastic. Place in a well-greased bowl, turning to grease top. Cover and refrigerate 8 hours.

Punch dough down, and divide in half; shape each into a loaf. Place in two well-greased 8¼- x 4½- x 3-inch loafpans. Cover and let rise in a warm place (85°), free from drafts, 1½ hours or until doubled in bulk. Bake at 350° for 25 minutes or until loaves sound hollow when tapped. Yield: 2 loaves.

To freeze, bake loaf as directed; let cool. Wrap in foil, and freeze. To serve, let thaw or reheat in foil at 250° for 10 to 15 minutes. *Mary Belle Purvis, Greeneville, Tennessee.*

Favorite Family Desserts

Family style is the only way to go with these basic, down-home desserts. Tailored to fit a busy schedule, each recipe uses tasty, easy-to-find ingredients in a variety of ways.

PLUM PUDDING-GELATIN MOLD

1 (3-ounce) package raspberry gelatin
1½ cups boiling water
½ cup golden raisins
¼ cup currants
½ teaspoon ground cinnamon
¼ teaspoon ground cloves
⅛ teaspoon ground ginger
⅛ teaspoon salt
1 (8-ounce) can crushed pineapple, drained
1 cup chopped pecans
¼ cup chopped mixed candied fruit
¼ cup chopped dates

Dissolve gelatin in boiling water; stir in raisins, currants, cinnamon, cloves, ginger, and salt. Chill until consistency of unbeaten egg white.

Fold remaining ingredients into gelatin mixture. Spoon into a lightly oiled 6-cup mold or 10 to 12 individual molds. Chill until firm. Unmold to serve. Yield: 10 to 12 servings.
Martha Short,
Jackson, Missouri.

APPLE-CRANBERRY CRUNCH

3 cups diced peeled apple
2 cups cranberries
½ cup sugar
¼ cup orange juice
¼ cup butter or margarine, melted
1 cup regular oats
½ cup firmly packed brown sugar
⅓ cup all-purpose flour
½ cup chopped pecans
Vanilla ice cream or whipped cream

Combine apple, cranberries, ½ cup sugar, and orange juice in medium bowl; mix well. Spoon into a lightly greased 10- x 6- x 2-inch baking dish. Combine butter, oats, brown sugar, flour, and pecans; mix well. Spoon evenly over apple-cranberry mixture; bake, uncovered, at 350° for 40 to 45 minutes. Serve warm or cool with vanilla ice cream. Yield: 6 to 8 servings.
Lil Summerville,
Gastonia, North Carolina.

PEACH-CARAMEL COBBLER

1 (29-ounce) can sliced peaches
¼ cup all-purpose flour
¼ teaspoon salt
1 (11-ounce) package refrigerated
   caramel-Danish rolls with nuts
½ teaspoon grated lemon rind (optional)
¾ cup ginger ale
1 tablespoon butter or margarine

Drain peaches, reserving 1 cup syrup; set aside.

Combine flour, salt, commercial sugar-nut mixture from refrigerated rolls, and lemon rind, if desired, in a heavy saucepan. Stir in ginger ale and reserved peach syrup. Cook over medium heat, stirring constantly, until smooth and thickened. Stir in butter and peaches; bring to a boil. Pour hot peach mixture into a lightly greased 8-inch square baking dish. Separate caramel rolls, and arrange on top of mixture. Bake at 375° for 18 to 23 minutes or until rolls are golden brown. Yield: 8 servings.
Mrs. P. J. Davis,
Drexel, North Carolina.

CRUNCHY ICE CREAM TREATS

2¼ cups corn square cereal, crushed
1 tablespoon butter or margarine
¼ cup crunchy peanut butter
1½ tablespoons brown sugar
1 quart vanilla ice cream, softened
¼ cup hot fudge topping or fruit
   preserves

Place crushed cereal in an 8-inch square pan; bake at 325° for 10 minutes or until toasted. Place 10 (5-ounce) paper cups in a 12-cup muffin pan for easy handling.

Combine crushed cereal, butter, peanut butter, and brown sugar; press 1 tablespoon mixture into the bottom and slightly up sides of each cup. Freeze 10 minutes. Spoon enough ice cream into cup to cover crumbs. Spoon a heaping teaspoon of fudge topping in each cup. Layer remaining ice cream into cups. Cover cups with one large piece of aluminum foil. Insert a popsicle stick into each cup through foil. Freeze 8 hours or until firm. Peel off cups to serve. Yield: 10 servings.
Helen H. Maurer,
Christmas, Florida.

CHOCO-MAPLE FROZEN DESSERT

1⅔ cups vanilla wafer crumbs
¼ cup butter or margarine, melted
½ cup butter or margarine, softened
1 cup sifted powdered sugar
3 eggs
3 (1-ounce) squares unsweetened chocolate,
   melted
¾ cup whipping cream
2 tablespoons maple syrup
1 cup miniature marshmallows
½ cup chopped pecans, divided

Combine vanilla wafer crumbs and ¼ cup melted butter. Press into a lightly greased 8-inch square dish.

Cream ½ cup softened butter and powdered sugar, beating well. Gradually add eggs and chocolate, beating well after each addition. Spread mixture evenly over crumbs; place in freezer.

Combine whipping cream and maple syrup; beat until stiff peaks form. Fold in marshmallows and ¼ cup pecans. Spread evenly over chocolate layer. Sprinkle with remaining pecans. Freeze 8 hours. Cut into squares to serve. Yield: 9 servings.
Daisy Cotton,
Karnes City, Texas.

Applaud The Versatile Apple

Fresh apples are an important part of autumn. To help you enjoy this year's crop, we've come up with choices including entrées, salads, and desserts.

When buying apples, choose varieties that are suitable for your purposes. Stayman, York Imperial, and Rome Beauty are good choices for cooking. Red or Golden Delicious or Jonathan apples are best for dishes that will not be cooked.

GLAZED APPLE PORK CHOPS

4 (¾-inch-thick) center cut pork chops
Salt
¾ cup all-purpose flour
3 tablespoons vegetable oil
4 cups (½-inch-thick) peeled, sliced
   cooking apples
½ cup firmly packed brown sugar
3 tablespoons maple-flavored syrup

Sprinkle pork chops lightly with salt; dredge in flour.

Heat oil in a heavy skillet; brown chops on both sides. Remove chops from skillet; drain off drippings, reserving 1 tablespoon in skillet. Return chops to skillet, and top with apples, brown sugar, and syrup. Cover and simmer 35 to 40 minutes. Yield: 4 servings.

Thelma Brooks,
Winter Haven, Florida.

CHEESY APPLE SALAD

3 medium apples, unpeeled and cut into thin wedges
2 cups sliced celery
1 (20-ounce) can pineapple chunks, drained
1 (8-ounce) package sharp Cheddar cheese, cubed
¾ cup slivered almonds, toasted
½ cup commercial sour cream
½ cup mayonnaise
Leaf lettuce (optional)

Combine first 5 ingredients in a mixing bowl; set aside.

Combine sour cream and mayonnaise; mix well. Pour over apple mixture; toss gently to mix. Chill 1 to 2 hours; serve on lettuce-lined plates, if desired. Yield: 10 servings.

Bertha Fowler,
Woodruff, South Carolina.

BRANDY-APPLE PIE

10 cups peeled and thinly sliced cooking apples (about 3 pounds), divided
2 tablespoons lemon juice
¾ cup apricot preserves, divided
⅓ cup sugar
¼ cup golden raisins
¼ cup brandy
3 tablespoons butter or margarine, softened
1 tablespoon grated lemon rind
¼ teaspoon ground nutmeg
¼ teaspoon ground cinnamon
1 unbaked (9-inch) pastry shell
3 tablespoons sugar
2 tablespoons sugar
Whipped cream or vanilla ice cream (optional)

Combine 2 cups apples and lemon juice; toss gently. Set aside.

Combine remaining 8 cups apples, ¼ cup apricot preserves, ⅓ cup sugar, raisins, brandy, butter, lemon rind, and spices in a large saucepan; mix well. Bring to a boil; reduce heat and simmer, uncovered, 25 to 30 minutes or until apples are soft and liquid is absorbed. Remove mixture from heat; cool 30 minutes.

Pour cooked apple mixture into pastry shell. Drain lemon juice from reserved apple slices; arrange slices on top of cooked mixture. Sprinkle with 3 tablespoons sugar; bake at 375° for 25 to 30 minutes or until apples are tender. Remove from oven; set aside.

Combine remaining ½ cup preserves and 2 tablespoons sugar in a small saucepan; cook over medium heat, stirring constantly, until sugar and preserves dissolve. Spread over pie. Serve warm or cool with whipped cream or vanilla ice cream, if desired. Yield: one 9-inch pie.

Carolyn Brandtley,
Greenville, Mississippi.

GOLDEN APPLE-OATMEAL CAKE

1 cup regular oats, uncooked
1 cup all-purpose flour
¾ teaspoon baking soda
½ teaspoon salt
½ teaspoon ground allspice
1 cup sugar
½ cup vegetable oil
1 egg
1 teaspoon vanilla extract
1 cup peeled, diced cooking apples
⅓ cup chopped walnuts
Vanilla ice cream (optional)

Combine first 5 ingredients in a large bowl; set aside.

Combine sugar, oil, egg, and vanilla; add to dry mixture, stirring well. Stir in apples and walnuts. Spread batter in a greased and floured 8-inch square baking pan. Bake at 350° for 45 minutes or until a wooden pick inserted in center comes out clean. Serve warm or cool with ice cream, if desired. Yield: 9 servings.

Mrs. W. J. Scherffius,
Mountain Home, Arkansas.

APPLE PIE CAKE

¼ cup butter or margarine, softened
1 cup sugar
1 egg
1 cup all-purpose flour
1 teaspoon salt
1 teaspoon ground cinnamon
2 tablespoons hot water
1 teaspoon vanilla extract
3 cups peeled, diced cooking apples
½ cup chopped pecans
Rum Butter Sauce
Whipped cream (optional)

Cream butter; gradually add sugar, beating at medium speed of an electric mixer. Add egg; beat until blended.

Combine flour, salt, and cinnamon;

mix well. Add to creamed mixture; beat on low speed of an electric mixer until smooth. Stir in water and vanilla. Fold in apples and pecans; spoon into a greased and floured 9-inch pieplate. Bake at 350° for 45 minutes or until a wooden pick inserted in center comes out clean. Serve warm or cold with Rum-Butter Sauce and whipped cream, if desired. Yield: one 9-inch pie.

Rum-Butter Sauce:

½ cup firmly packed brown sugar
½ cup sugar
¼ cup butter or margarine, softened
½ cup whipping cream
1 tablespoon rum

Combine first 4 ingredients in a small saucepan; mix well. Bring to a boil, and cook 1 minute. Stir in rum. Yield: about 1¼ cups.

Elyce Waddington,
Crystal River, Florida.

Make Muffins For A Change

Muffins make a great breakfast food, snack item, or mealtime bread alternative. And Rose Alleman of St. Amant, Louisiana, offers a tasty variation.

PEACHY-ALMOND MUFFINS

1 (16-ounce) can sliced peaches, drained
1½ cups all-purpose flour
½ teaspoon salt
½ teaspoon baking soda
⅔ cup sugar
2 eggs, beaten
½ cup vegetable oil
½ teaspoon vanilla extract
¼ teaspoon almond extract
½ cup sliced almonds, toasted

Chop peaches; drain, and set aside. Combine flour, salt, soda, and sugar in a mixing bowl; make a well in center of dry ingredients. Add eggs and oil; stir until dry ingredients are moistened. Add peaches and remaining ingredients; stir until blended.

Spoon batter evenly into greased or paper-lined muffin pans, filling two-thirds full. Bake at 350° for 35 minutes for 6 jumbo muffins, 20 to 25 minutes for 12 regular-size muffins, or 18 minutes for 36 miniature muffins. Yield: 6 jumbo muffins, or 12 regular-size muffins, or 36 miniature muffins.

Fancy A Soup Or Salad

Hot and brimming with flavor, soups add a warm note to meals. On the other hand, crisp salads are cool and relaxing. The good news is they can be served together so both can be enjoyed in the same meal or served separately as a first course or accompaniment.

MACARONI-CHICKEN SALAD

2 cups uncooked seashell macaroni
2 cups sliced celery
1½ cups diced cooked chicken
½ cup minced onion
½ cup chopped green pepper
½ cup sweet pickle cubes
½ cup sliced pimiento-stuffed olives
1 cup mayonnaise
2 teaspoons prepared mustard

Cook macaroni according to package directions; drain. Rinse and drain again.
Combine macaroni, celery, chicken, onion, green pepper, pickles, and olives. Combine mayonnaise and mustard. Spoon over salad; toss gently. Cover and chill. Yield: 6 servings.
Connie Burgess,
Knoxville, Tennessee.

QUICK BEEF STEW

1 tablespoon vegetable oil
1 pound ground chuck
1 cup chopped onion
1 cup chopped celery
1 (16-ounce) can whole tomatoes, undrained and chopped
2 cups water
2 cups cubed potatoes
1 cup sliced carrots
1 (10-ounce) package frozen mixed vegetables
1 teaspoon salt
½ teaspoon coarsely ground black pepper

Combine oil, ground chuck, onion, and celery in a large Dutch oven. Cook over high heat until beef is browned, stirring to crumble beef. Cover, reduce heat to low, and cook 15 minutes, stirring occasionally. Drain well. Add remaining ingredients. Bring to a boil; cover, reduce heat, and simmer 20 minutes or until vegetables are tender. Yield: 9 cups.
Audrey Donahew,
Garland, Texas.

GOLDEN CREAM OF POTATO SOUP

6 cups cubed, peeled, red potatoes
2 cups water
1 cup sliced celery
1 cup scraped and thinly sliced carrot
½ cup finely chopped onion
2 teaspoons dried parsley flakes
2 chicken-flavored bouillon cubes
1 teaspoon salt
⅛ teaspoon pepper
3 cups milk, divided
¼ cup all-purpose flour
¾ pound process cheese, cubed

Combine first 9 ingredients in a Dutch oven; bring to a boil. Cover, reduce heat, and simmer 7 to 8 minutes or until vegetables are tender.
Gradually stir ¼ cup milk into flour making a smooth paste. Stir into soup. Add remaining 2¾ cups milk and cheese; cook over medium heat until soup is thickened. Yield: 9 cups.
Mary Pappas,
Richmond, Virginia.

HOT TOMATO JUICE SOUP

¾ cup chopped onion
2 stalks celery, chopped
2 tablespoons butter or margarine, melted
2 quarts tomato juice
2 teaspoons low-sodium beef-flavored bouillon granules
2 teaspoons Worcestershire sauce
2 teaspoons Dijon mustard
¼ teaspoon hot sauce
Lemon slices (optional)
Celery leaves (optional)

Sauté onion and celery in butter in a Dutch oven until transparent. Add tomato juice and next 4 ingredients. Bring to a boil; reduce heat, and simmer 10 minutes. To serve, garnish with lemon slices and celery leaves, if desired. Yield: 10 cups.
Gloria Pedersen,
Brandon, Mississippi.

MUSTARD POTATO SALAD

½ cup milk
3 tablespoons mayonnaise
1 tablespoon prepared mustard
1½ teaspoons celery seeds
½ teaspoon salt
¼ teaspoon white pepper
4 cups cubed cooked potatoes
5 hard-cooked eggs, diced
¼ cup chopped onion
Radicchio or lettuce leaves (optional)

Combine first 6 ingredients; mix well. Combine potatoes, eggs, onion, and mayonnaise mixture; toss gently. Chill. Garnish with radicchio or lettuce leaves, if desired. Yield: 6 servings.
Mrs. R. L. Lyerly,
Mocksville, North Carolina.

SPINACH SALAD

½ cup vegetable oil
¼ cup sugar
¼ cup chili sauce
1 small onion, minced
2 tablespoons red wine vinegar
½ teaspoon salt
½ teaspoon dry mustard
½ teaspoon Worcestershire sauce
¼ teaspoon red pepper
1 pound spinach, torn
⅔ cup torn Bibb lettuce
1 hard-cooked egg, grated
¾ cup cooked and crumbled bacon

Combine first 9 ingredients in a jar. Cover tightly, and shake vigorously. Chill several hours.
Combine spinach and lettuce in a salad bowl; sprinkle with egg and bacon. Serve with dressing. Yield: 4 to 6 servings.
Mrs. Joseph Laux,
Toney, Alabama.

Fry A Batch Of Pies

If the thought of a sweet fried pie makes your mouth water, then get out the skillet. In no time, you can prepare these fruit-filled favorites. Each pie contains dried apples or peaches covered with pastry.

FRIED APPLE PIES

1 (8-ounce) package dried apples
1 quart water
½ cup plus 2 tablespoons sugar
1 to 1½ teaspoons ground cinnamon
Pastry (recipe follows)
Vegetable oil
Sugar

Combine apples and water in a Dutch oven; bring to a boil. Reduce heat, and cook, uncovered, until mixture thickens. Stir in ½ cup plus 2 tablespoons sugar and cinnamon. Refrigerate overnight.

Each of our Little Peach Pies gives you a taste of sweet fruit and flaky pastry.

Roll pastry onto a lightly floured surface to ¼-inch thickness. Cut into 4-inch circles. Place about 1 tablespoon apple mixture on half of each circle; fold pastry in half. Moisten edges with water; press edges together with a fork dipped in flour.

Heat ½ inch oil in a large skillet. Cook pies until golden, turning once. Drain on paper towels. Sprinkle with sugar. Yield: about 3 dozen.

Pastry:

**4 cups self-rising flour
1 cup butter or margarine, softened
¾ cup water**

Combine all ingredients, mixing well. Refrigerate overnight. Yield: enough for about 3 dozen 4-inch pies.

Note: Uncooked pies may be frozen, then thawed and fried. *Robbie King,*
Macon, Georgia.

Tip: To freshen air throughout the house, boil 1 tablespoon of whole cloves in a pan of water.

LITTLE PEACH PIES

**1 (8-ounce) package dried peaches, chopped
3 cups water
½ cup sugar
¼ cup golden raisins
2 teaspoons butter or margarine
¼ teaspoon ground nutmeg
Pastry (recipe follows)
Vegetable oil
Sugar**

Combine peaches and water in a saucepan; bring to a boil. Reduce heat, and simmer, uncovered, 40 minutes or until peaches are tender, adding more water, if necessary. Drain well. Stir in ½ cup sugar, raisins, butter, and nutmeg, mixing well.

Divide pastry evenly into 8 portions; roll each portion into a 6-inch circle. Place about 3 tablespoons fruit mixture on half of each circle. Moisten edges of circles with water. Fold circles in half; press edges together with a fork dipped in flour.

Heat ¾ inch oil to 375° in a large skillet. Cook pies until golden, turning once. Drain on paper towels. Sprinkle with sugar. Yield: 8 pies.

Pastry:

**2 cups all-purpose flour
½ teaspoon baking soda
½ teaspoon salt
½ teaspoon ground nutmeg
⅓ cup shortening
¼ cup plus 3 tablespoons cold water
1 teaspoon vinegar**

Combine flour, soda, salt, and nutmeg; cut in shortening with pastry blender until mixture resembles coarse meal. Sprinkle water and vinegar evenly over surface; stir with a fork until all ingredients are moistened. Shape dough into a ball. Yield: enough for eight 6-inch pies.
Geneva Welch,
Frankston, Texas.

Cornish Hens For Two

The season's choice for two is Cranberry Cornish Hens, a recipe from Shirley Hilliker of Merritt Island, Florida.

Shirley bastes the hens with a tangy mixture of lemon juice, wine, and cranberry sauce, evenly covering every part exposed to direct heat. You may need to shield the legs of the hen if they become too brown. If so, simply wrap aluminum foil around the overcooked areas of the hen.

CRANBERRY CORNISH HENS

**1 cup jellied cranberry sauce
½ cup dry white wine
1 tablespoon plus 1 teaspoon lemon juice
2 (22-ounce) Cornish hens
Salt**

Combine cranberry sauce, wine, and lemon juice in a heavy saucepan. Cook over medium heat, stirring constantly, until cranberry sauce melts and mixture is smooth; keep warm.

Remove giblets from hens; reserve for another use. Rinse hens with cold water, and pat dry; sprinkle cavities with salt. Close cavities, and secure with wooden picks; truss. Brush hens with cranberry mixture, coating all sides. Place hens, breast side up, in a lightly greased shallow baking pan. Bake at 350° for 1¼ to 1½ hours, basting frequently with remaining cranberry mixture. Yield: 2 servings.

Soup's On

There is no better welcome during cold weather than the aroma of simmering soup. Gather in the kitchen, and help yourself. Even for company, serving soup straight from the kettle is very appropriate for casual fare. Keep the soup hot and serving simple. Everyone will feel at home. With these recipes, you can be assured they'll want to help themselves to seconds.

Soup brimming with meat and vegetables can be a heart-warming and substantial entrée. We've selected thick, chunky, meaty homemade soups to serve as a main course. Add a side dish of onions to munch and cornbread to dip. To complete the meal, serve tossed salad or cole slaw.

Charles Betts of Little Rock suggests allowing Hearty Bean-and-Barley Soup to mellow for a day to obtain the greatest flavor potential. This is a good idea for most soups, making them convenient for weekend cooking.

HEARTY BEAN-AND-BARLEY SOUP

2 pounds dried Great Northern beans
2 quarts water
1 cup fine barley
1 ham hock
2 cups coarsely chopped ham
1 pound ground beef, cooked and drained
1 large onion, chopped
8 cloves garlic, chopped
6 carrots, sliced
4 (10½-ounce) cans consommé
1 to 1½ teaspoons salt
1 teaspoon pepper
¼ cup Worcestershire sauce
½ teaspoon hot sauce
2 fresh jalapeño peppers, split and seeded

Sort and wash beans; place in a large Dutch oven. Cover with water 2 inches above beans; let soak overnight. Drain. Add 2 quarts water; bring to a boil.

Add remaining ingredients; cover, reduce heat, and simmer 2½ hours, stirring occasionally. Yield: 5½ quarts.

Note: Add water, if desired, for a thinner consistency. Soup may be frozen, if desired. *Charles Betts, Little Rock, Arkansas.*

LEEK-VEGETABLE SOUP

2 pounds beef shank
¼ cup vegetable oil
4 small leeks, split and cut into 1-inch pieces
2 large onions, sliced and separated into rings
2 (16-ounce) cans tomatoes, chopped and undrained
2 cups water
½ to 1 teaspoon salt
½ to 1 teaspoon pepper
4 stalks celery, cut into pieces
4 carrots, sliced

Brown beef in hot oil in a Dutch oven. Add leeks, onion, tomatoes, water, salt, and pepper; bring to a boil. Cover, reduce heat, and simmer 1 hour. Add celery and carrots; cover and simmer 30 minutes or until tender. Remove beef shank from soup; remove meat from bone, and shred; add meat to soup. Yield: 7 cups. *Ruth Sherrer, Fort Worth, Texas.*

OLD-FASHIONED VEGETABLE SOUP

1½ pounds beef or ham bones with meat
8 cups water
3 stalks celery, chopped
3 large carrots, chopped
2 medium onions, chopped
1 (28-ounce) can tomatoes, undrained and chopped
1 bay leaf
1½ teaspoons salt
½ teaspoon pepper
½ teaspoon dried whole basil
½ teaspoon dried whole thyme
½ teaspoon dried whole marjoram
2 cups frozen green lima beans
1 cup frozen corn
1 cup frozen green peas
½ cup macaroni

Combine first 12 ingredients in a large Dutch oven. Bring to a boil; cover, reduce heat, and simmer 1 hour. Add lima beans, corn, and peas. Return to a boil; reduce heat and simmer, uncovered, 15 minutes. Stir in macaroni, and continue to cook for 10 to 12 minutes. Remove bay leaf. Yield: 3½ quarts.

LENTIL SOUP

¾ pound dried lentil beans
2 carrots, sliced
2 onions, chopped
2 stalks celery, chopped
1 tablespoon butter or margarine, melted
1 (¾-pound) Polish sausage, sliced, browned, and drained
½ pound cooked ham, chopped
1 bay leaf
1 teaspoon ground thyme
2 whole cloves
1 teaspoon sugar
1 teaspoon vinegar
1 teaspoon tomato paste
1 (¾-ounce) envelope brown gravy mix
4 cups water
2 medium potatoes, peeled and cubed

Sort and wash beans. Place beans in a large Dutch oven. Cover with water 2 inches above beans; let soak overnight. Sauté carrots, onion, and celery in butter in a large Dutch oven. Add remaining ingredients except potatoes. Drain beans; add to vegetable mixture. Cover and simmer 25 minutes. Add potatoes and cook an additional 20 minutes. Add water for a thinner consistency, if desired. Remove bay leaf. Yield: 3 quarts. *Birgit Castagneto, Enterprise, Alabama.*

Quick Dressings And Sauces

Make plain food fancy with a special dressing or sauce. The food processor helps make preparation faster and easier because for most of these recipes, all the ingredients are mixed together and processed in a matter of minutes.

To make oil-based sauces and dressings add vegetable oil through the food chute while the machine is running. The fast mixing action of the processor knife blade blends the mixture so well that it is less likely to separate quickly as a dressing mixed by hand.

SEAFOOD SAUCE

4 hot peppers, seeded
2 cups catsup
¼ cup tomato sauce
2 tablespoons plus 2 teaspoons lemon juice
1 (5-ounce) jar prepared horseradish

Position knife blade in food processor bowl; add peppers, and top with cover;

process about 30 seconds or until peppers are finely chopped. Add remaining ingredients, and process 1 minute, scraping sides of bowl twice. Chill. Serve with shrimp or other seafood. Yield: 3 cups.   *Suzanne Thomas, Trafford, Alabama.*

PEANUT HOT SAUCE

4 small cloves garlic
1 (½-inch-thick) sliced gingerroot, peeled and quartered
1 small onion, quartered
1 cup salted, dry roasted peanuts
1½ cups water, divided
2 teaspoons cornstarch
1½ teaspoons crushed red pepper flakes
1 teaspoon ground coriander
2 tablespoons brown sugar
2 tablespoons soy sauce
2 teaspoons lemon juice
¾ teaspoon coconut extract

Position knife blade in food processor bowl; top with cover. Drop garlic and gingerroot through food chute with processor running; process about 10 seconds or until garlic and gingerroot are minced. Add onion, and process 10 seconds. Remove processor cover; add peanuts to processor bowl, replace cover, and pulse 3 or 4 times.

Combine ½ cup water and cornstarch; set aside. Combine peanut mixture, red pepper flakes, remaining 1 cup water, and remaining ingredients in a saucepan; cook over medium heat 5 minutes. Add cornstarch mixture and cook, stirring constantly, 2 to 3 minutes or until sauce thickens. Serve with beef, poultry, or pork. Yield: 2 cups.

Alice McNamara, Eucha, Oklahoma.

POPPY SEED DRESSING

1½ cups sugar
⅔ cup cider vinegar
3 tablespoons onion juice
2 teaspoons dry mustard
1 teaspoon salt
2 cups vegetable oil
3 tablespoons poppy seeds

Position knife blade in food processor bowl; add first 5 ingredients. Top with cover, and pulse 2 or 3 times. Gradually pour oil through food chute with processor running. Add poppy seeds; pulse 2 or 3 times. Serve over fruit salad. Yield: 2⅔ cups.

Glynda Corley, Pearland, Texas.

RUSSIAN-STYLE SALAD DRESSING

2 sprigs parsley
1 clove garlic
1 green onion, cut into thirds
¼ cup wine vinegar
¼ cup catsup
1 teaspoon dried whole basil
1 teaspoon dried whole oregano
1 teaspoon dry mustard
⅛ teaspoon salt
⅛ teaspoon pepper
¾ cup olive oil

Position knife blade in food processor bowl; add all ingredients except olive oil. Top with cover, and process 15 seconds. Gradually pour oil through food chute with processor running; process 30 seconds. Chill. Serve over salad greens. Yield: 1 cup.

Mrs. F. C. Baldwin, Jr., Richmond, Virginia.

A Fresh Look At Frozen Vegetables

There's a knack to making frozen vegetables flavorful, and we think we've found it—cook 'em with pizzazz. You'll understand what we mean when you sit down to these vegetable side dishes.

STIR-FRIED GREEN BEANS

1 (16-ounce) package frozen green beans
2 tablespoons vegetable oil
1½ tablespoons butter or margarine
1 tablespoon soy sauce
1 tablespoon dry sherry
1 teaspoon sugar
½ teaspoon chicken-flavored bouillon granules
2 cloves garlic, crushed
2 green onions, sliced

Thaw and drain green beans; set aside. Combine remaining ingredients in a large heavy skillet. Cook over medium heat 2 minutes. Add green beans; stir-fry until crisp-tender. Yield: 6 servings.   *J. C. Haynes, South Ponte Vedra Beach, Florida.*

CHINESE-STYLE BAKED PEAS

½ cup thinly sliced onion
1 (6-ounce) can sliced mushrooms, drained
¼ cup butter or margarine, melted
1 (10-ounce) package frozen peas, thawed and drained
1 (14-ounce) can bean sprouts, drained
1 (8-ounce) can sliced water chestnuts, drained
1 (10¾-ounce) can cream of mushroom soup, undiluted
⅓ cup milk
½ teaspoon salt
Dash of pepper
1 cup chow mein noodles

Sauté onion and mushrooms in butter in a large skillet until tender. Add peas, bean sprouts, and water chestnuts. Spoon mixture into a shallow, lightly greased 2-quart casserole.

Combine soup, milk, salt, and pepper, mixing well; stir into pea mixture. Sprinkle chow mein noodles around edge of casserole. Bake, uncovered, at 350° for 30 minutes. Yield: 6 servings.

Jerri Roach, La Follette, Tennessee.

ASPARAGUS-AND-EGG SALAD

1 (10-ounce) package frozen asparagus spears
½ cup commercial onion dip with chives
1½ tablespoons lemon juice
1 teaspoon vinegar
¼ teaspoon paprika
Lettuce leaves
2 hard-cooked eggs, sliced
6 pimiento-stuffed olives, sliced

Cook asparagus according to package directions, omitting salt; drain and chill.

Combine dip and next 3 ingredients. Chill. Place asparagus on lettuce. Top with dressing, eggs, and olives. Yield: 4 servings.   *Janie L. Budd, Winston-Salem, North Carolina.*

Tip: When boiling eggs, add 1 teaspoon salt to the water. This prevents a cracked egg from draining.

Classic Rolls Fit Any Menu

One whiff of yeast rolls baking and folks will come running. Hot and buttery, crisp and golden, Hard Rolls were favorites in our test kitchens.

Butter-and-Herb Rolls are downright delicious. A creamy mixture of butter, caraway seeds, basil, garlic, and onion is spread between two rounds to make a unique bread appropriate for luncheons or dinner.

Three-Day Refrigerator Rolls are good for someone on a busy schedule. The dough for these rolls will keep for up to three days after the first rising, so that you can shape and bake the rolls whenever you have the time.

THREE-DAY REFRIGERATOR ROLLS

1 package dry yeast
2 tablespoons warm water (105° to 115°)
2 cups milk
½ cup sugar
½ cup shortening
5 to 5½ cups all-purpose flour, divided
½ to ¾ teaspoon salt

Dissolve yeast in warm water in a large bowl; let stand 5 minutes. Combine milk, sugar, and shortening in a saucepan; cook over low heat until shortening melts. Cool to 105° to 115°. Stir into yeast mixture; add 2½ cups flour and salt, mixing at low speed of an electric mixer until well blended. Stir in enough remaining flour to make a soft dough.

Turn dough out onto a floured surface, and knead until smooth and elastic (8 to 10 minutes). Place in a well-greased bowl, turning to grease top. Cover tightly, and refrigerate 8 hours or up to 3 days before shaping.

Remove desired amount of dough from refrigerator, shape into 1½-inch balls. Place in greased pans. Cover and let rise in a warm place (85°), free from drafts, 1 hour or until doubled in bulk. Bake at 375° for 20 minutes or until golden. Yield: 3 dozen.

*Stella Trevathan,
Cleveland, Texas.*

Tip: To thaw frozen bread or rolls, wrap in aluminum foil and heat at 325° for 5 minutes.

BUTTER-AND-HERB ROLLS

2 packages dry yeast
¼ cup warm water (105° to 115°)
1 cup milk, scalded
¼ cup sugar
⅓ cup shortening
1 tablespoon salt
2 eggs
4½ to 5 cups all-purpose flour, divided
Herb Butter

Dissolve yeast in warm water in a large bowl; let stand 5 minutes. Combine milk, sugar, shortening, and salt in a saucepan; place over low heat, stirring until shortening melts. Cool to 105° to 115°. Stir into yeast mixture; add eggs and 1 cup flour, beating well at medium speed of an electric mixer. Gradually stir in enough remaining flour to make a soft dough.

Turn dough out onto a floured surface, and knead until smooth and elastic (about 2 to 3 minutes). Place in a well-greased bowl, turning to grease top. Cover and let rise in a warm place (85°), free from drafts, 1½ hours or until doubled in bulk.

Punch dough down, and divide in half; roll each half to ¼-inch thickness. Cut into rounds with a 2½-inch cutter, brush with Herb Butter and place another round on top of butter. Place in a lightly greased 13- x 9- x 2-inch pan. Brush tops of rolls with Herb Butter; cover and let rise in a warm place, free from drafts, 1 hour and 30 minutes or until doubled in bulk. Bake at 375° for 15 minutes or until golden. Serve with Herb Butter. Yield: 2 dozen.

Herb Butter:

½ cup butter, softened
½ teaspoon caraway seeds
½ teaspoon dried whole basil
¼ teaspoon garlic powder
½ teaspoon grated onion

Combine all ingredients; mix well. Yield: ½ cup. *Patricia H. Smith,
Gore, Virginia.*

HARD ROLLS

2 packages dry yeast
2 cups warm water (105° to 115°)
2 teaspoons sugar
1 teaspoon salt
4½ to 4¾ cups all-purpose flour
¼ cup butter or margarine, melted and divided

Brush these classic Hard Rolls with butter right after baking.

Dissolve yeast in warm water in a large mixing bowl; let mixture stand 5 minutes. Add sugar and salt; mix well. Gradually stir in enough flour to make a soft dough.

Turn dough out onto a floured surface, and knead until smooth and elastic (about 8 to 10 minutes). Place in a well-greased bowl, turning to grease top. Cover and let rise in a warm place (85°), free from drafts, 45 minutes or until doubled in bulk.

Punch dough down, and divide in half; shape into 18 (3½- x 1½-inch) loaf-shaped rolls. Place on greased baking sheets. Score tops of rolls with scissors, making ¼-inch-deep slashes; brush with 2 tablespoons butter. Cover and let rise in a warm place, free from drafts, 30 minutes or until doubled in bulk. Bake at 400° for 25 to 30 minutes or until golden. Brush with remaining butter. Yield: 1½ dozen. *Joan Grimmett,
Ravenswood, West Virginia.*

Right: For a holiday treat, add a splash of spirits to Sherried Ambrosia (page 317), a traditional Southern dessert.

Page 310: Chocoholics will savor these desserts: (from front) Sweetheart Fudge Pie, Chocolate-Glazed Triple-Layer Cheesecake, and Brown Sugar Fudge Cake. (Recipes begin on page 315.)

Above: *Here are flavorful variations on two classic holiday dishes. Layered Cranberry Salad (page 325) has a lemon layer that tastes like eggnog. Hot Fruit Compote (page 324) is flavored with coconut macaroons and brandy.*

Right: *Dazzle your guests with this spectacular entrée. Stuffed Crown Roast of Pork (page 323) is filled with a sausage-apple mixture, ringed with apple wedges, and topped with gold frills.*

December

Food Traditions Make The Holidays

A holiday recipe is often one that brings warm memories of a friend or loved one. In fact, many recipes hold a link to generations long since gone. Descendants carry on a family tradition that began years ago by preparing handed-down favorites each year.

Some recipes are "always" given by friends to frien~ ~ach Christmas. Others are ~ ~h, ~d for specific times d~ ~, holidays—Christmas ~orning ~ea~ ~t, Christmas dinner, or ~n annual party. Sharing such traditions and good times with family and friends makes the holidays memorable.

ROAST DUCKLINGS WITH CHERRY SAUCE
(pictured on page iv)

2 (3½- to 4½-pound) dressed ducklings
1 teaspoon salt
2 (6-ounce) packages long grain and wild rice
½ cup orange juice
2 teaspoons grated orange rind
1 (16-ounce) can pitted dark sweet cherries, undrained
1 tablespoon sugar
1 tablespoon cornstarch
¼ cup port wine
1 tablespoon lemon juice
Orange slices (optional)
Seedless green grapes (optional)
Parsley sprigs (optional)

Remove giblets and neck from ducklings; reserve for other uses, if desired. Cut ducklings in half. Sprinkle with salt; place on a rack in a shallow roasting pan. Bake at 325° for 1½ hours or until meat thermometer registers 190°.

Cook rice according to package directions, omitting ½ cup water; add orange juice. Add orange rind to cooked rice; spoon onto a large serving platter. Place ducklings on rice; keep warm.

Drain cherries, reserving ¾ cup juice; set cherries aside. Combine cherry juice, sugar, and cornstarch in a small saucepan; blend well. Add wine and lemon juice; bring to a boil, and cook 1 minute until thickened. Stir in cherries, and heat thoroughly. Serve cherry sauce with ducklings and rice. Garnish ducklings with orange slices, grapes, and parsley, if desired. Yield: 4 servings.
Virginia B. Stalder, Nokesville, Virginia.

SWEET POTATO BALLS
(pictured on page iv)

4 large sweet potatoes
⅔ cup firmly packed brown sugar
1 teaspoon grated orange rind
4 to 6 tablespoons orange juice
8 large marshmallows
2 cups flaked coconut, toasted

Wash sweet potatoes; place in a large Dutch oven, and cover with water. Simmer 25 to 30 minutes or until tender. Let cool to the touch; peel, mash, and measure 4 cups potatoes. Stir in brown sugar, orange rind, and orange juice, mixing well.

Shape ½ cup potato mixture around each marshmallow; roll in coconut. Place potato balls in a 13- x 9- x 2-inch baking dish and bake at 350° for 15 to 20 minutes. Yield: 8 servings.
Note: Potato balls may be frozen unbaked, if desired. Thaw before baking.
Melanie Smith, Molena, Georgia.

GLAZED CINNAMON ROLLS

1 cup milk
1 cup water
½ cup butter or margarine
6 to 6½ cups all-purpose flour, divided
½ cup sugar
3 packages dry yeast
2 teaspoons salt
1 egg, beaten
¼ cup butter or margarine, melted, and divided
⅔ cup firmly packed brown sugar, divided
1 tablespoon ground cinnamon, divided
1 cup sifted powdered sugar
2 tablespoons milk
½ teaspoon vanilla extract
Green and red candied cherries

Combine first 3 ingredients in a small saucepan; heat until very warm (120°). Set aside.

Combine 2 cups flour, ½ cup sugar, yeast, and salt in a large bowl; stir well. Gradually add milk mixture to flour mixture, stirring well; add egg. Beat at medium speed of an electric mixer until smooth. Gradually stir in enough remaining flour to make a slightly stiff dough.

Turn dough out onto a well-floured surface, and knead until smooth and elastic (10 minutes). Place in a greased bowl, turning to grease top. Cover and let rise in a warm place (85°), free from drafts, 1 hour or until doubled in bulk.

Punch dough down; cover, and let rest 15 minutes. Set half of dough aside.

Turn remaining half of dough out onto a lightly floured surface; roll to a 20- x 12-inch rectangle; brush 2 tablespoons melted butter over dough, leaving a ½-inch border. Combine ⅓ cup brown sugar and 1½ teaspoons cinnamon; sprinkle mixture over rectangle. Beginning at long side, roll up jellyroll fashion; press edges and ends together securely. Cut into 1-inch slices; place cut side down in a greased 13- x 9- x 2-inch pan. Cover pan with greased plastic wrap; refrigerate 8 hours. Repeat with remaining dough and filling ingredients.

Before baking, cover and let rise in a warm place (85°), free from drafts, 1 hour or until doubled in bulk. Bake at 375° for 20 minutes.

Combine powdered sugar, 2 tablespoons milk, and vanilla; drizzle over warm rolls. Garnish with candied cherry pieces. Yield: 40 rolls.

For Caramel-Nut Rolls:

Prepare dough and filling as for Glazed Cinnamon Rolls. Cut filled dough rolls into 1-inch slices.

Combine 1 cup brown sugar, 1 cup melted butter, and ¼ cup corn syrup; mix well. Spread mixture evenly in two greased 13- x 9- x 2-inch pans. Sprinkle ½ cup chopped pecans in each pan. Place roll slices, cut side down, on pecan topping. Cover pan with greased plastic wrap; refrigerate 8 hours.

Before baking, cover and let rise in a warm place (85°), free from drafts, 1 hour or until doubled in bulk.

Bake at 375° for 20 minutes. Invert rolls onto serving trays to serve. Yield: 40 rolls.
Mrs. R. D. Walker, Garland, Texas.

Tip: Sifting flour, with the exception of cake flour, is no longer necessary. Simply stir the flour, gently spoon it onto a dry measure, and level the top. Powdered sugar, however, should be sifted to remove the lumps.

DARK PRALINE CLUSTERS
(pictured on cover)

2 cups firmly packed dark brown sugar
1 cup whipping cream
¼ cup water
2 tablespoons butter or margarine
1 teaspoon vanilla extract
Dash of salt
2 cups coarsely chopped pecans

Combine sugar, whipping cream, and water in a heavy saucepan; bring to a boil, stirring constantly. Reduce heat to medium and cook, stirring occasionally, until mixture reaches soft ball stage (236°). Remove from heat; stir in butter, vanilla, and salt. Beat with a wooden spoon until mixture is creamy and begins to thicken. Quickly stir in pecans. Working rapidly, drop by tablespoonfuls onto greased waxed paper; let cool. Yield: about 2 dozen.

Paula Watson,
Tomball, Texas.

AMBROSIA COOKIES
(pictured on cover)

1 cup butter or margarine, softened
1 cup firmly packed dark brown sugar
1 cup sugar
2 eggs
2 cups all-purpose flour
1½ cups uncooked regular oats
2 teaspoons baking powder
½ teaspoon baking soda
½ teaspoon salt
1 cup chopped dates
1 cup golden raisins
1 cup flaked coconut
1 cup chopped pecans
1 teaspoon grated orange rind
1 teaspoon grated lemon rind
1 teaspoon vanilla extract
½ teaspoon almond extract
½ teaspoon orange extract
About 4 dozen candied cherries, halved

Cream butter; gradually add sugar, beating at medium speed of an electric mixer. Add eggs, one at a time, beating well after each addition.

Combine flour and next 4 ingredients; stir well. Add flour mixture and remaining ingredients, except candied cherries, to creamed mixture; stir well. Drop by rounded teaspoonfuls 2 inches apart onto lightly greased cookie sheets; lightly press a cherry half into each cookie. Bake at 350° for 14 to 16 minutes; cool on cookie sheets 10 minutes. Transfer to cooling racks (cookies firm as they cool). Yield: about 8 dozen.

Cynthia J. Perry,
Paris, Tennessee.

Your friends will love homemade gifts of Old-Fashioned Sugar Cookies, Dark Praline Clusters, and Ambrosia Cookies, also pictured in color on the cover.

OLD-FASHIONED SUGAR COOKIES
(pictured on cover)

1 cup butter, softened
1 cup sugar
1 egg
3½ cups all-purpose flour
1¼ teaspoons baking powder
⅛ teaspoon baking soda
½ teaspoon ground cinnamon
½ teaspoon ground nutmeg
Red or green food coloring (optional)
Additional sugar
Colored sugar sprinkles (optional)

Cream butter; gradually add 1 cup sugar, beating until light and fluffy. Add egg; beat well. Combine flour, baking powder, soda, cinnamon, and nutmeg; add to creamed mixture, mixing until blended. Tint with food coloring, if desired. Cover and chill dough.

Work with one-fourth of dough at a time; store remainder in refrigerator. Place dough on a lightly greased cookie sheet; roll out to ¼-inch thickness. Cut dough with floured cookie cutter, leaving 1 to 2 inches between each cookie. Remove excess dough from cookie sheet; combine with remaining dough in refrigerator. Repeat procedure with remaining dough. Sprinkle cookies with additional sugar before baking.

Decorate cookies with colored sugar sprinkles, if desired. Bake at 350° for 10 to 12 minutes or until cookies are lightly browned.

Cool on cookie sheets 3 to 5 minutes; remove from cookie sheets, and cool completely on wire racks. Repeat procedure with remaining dough. Yield: about 6½ dozen 2½- to 3½-inch cookies.

Gladys Stout,
Elizabethton, Tennessee.

DATE-FILLED
OATMEAL COOKIES

1 cup shortening
½ cup sugar
½ cup firmly packed brown sugar
2½ cups self-rising flour
½ cup buttermilk
2 cups quick-cooking oats, uncooked
1 teaspoon vanilla extract
Date Filling
½ teaspoon ground cinnamon
1 tablespoon sugar

Cream shortening; gradually add sugar, beating at medium speed of an electric mixer until light and fluffy. Add flour alternately with buttermilk, beginning and ending with flour. Stir in oats and vanilla; mixing well.

Roll cookie dough to ⅛-inch thickness on a lightly floured surface. Cut with a 2-inch round cutter, and place half of cookies on a greased cookie sheet. Place about 1 teaspoon Date Filling on each cookie on the cookie sheet; top with another cookie. Press edges together with a fork. Combine cinnamon and 1 tablespoon sugar; sprinkle on top of cookies. Bake at 350° for 12 to 14 minutes. Cool on wire racks. Yield: 4 dozen.

Date Filling:

1 cup chopped dates
½ cup firmly packed brown sugar
½ cup water

Combine all ingredients; cook over medium heat about 10 minutes, stirring until thickened. Cool slightly before filling cookies. Yield: 1 cup.

Arlene Grimm,
Huntsville, Alabama.

APPLE HOLIDAY FRITTERS

1 cup all-purpose flour
1 teaspoon salt
1 teaspoon baking powder
1 teaspoon sugar
2 eggs, slightly beaten
½ cup milk
1 teaspoon vegetable oil
1 teaspoon vanilla extract
4 medium cooking apples
Vegetable oil
Glaze (recipe follows)

Combine first 4 ingredients in a medium mixing bowl. Combine eggs, milk, oil, and vanilla; add to dry ingredients, stirring well.

Peel, core, and slice each apple into 8 wedges. Dip into batter, and fry in deep, hot oil (375°) 2 to 3 minutes or until golden brown. Drain fritters on paper towels, and serve immediately with glaze for dipping fritters. Yield: 6 to 8 servings.

Glaze:

1½ cups sifted powdered sugar
⅛ teaspoon salt
3 to 3½ tablespoons milk
½ teaspoon vanilla extract
1 tablespoon butter or margarine, melted

Combine all ingredients, mixing well. Yield: ¾ cup.
Note: For fritter variation, chop apples, and stir into batter. Drop by tablespoonfuls into hot oil, and fry.

Pamela Clayton,
Ferriday, Louisiana.

CHOCOLATE CAKE
WITH DOUBLE FROSTING
(pictured on cover)

¾ cup plus 2 tablespoons cocoa
1 cup boiling water
2 tablespoons butter or margarine, softened
2 cups sugar
2 cups sifted cake flour
1 teaspoon baking soda
½ teaspoon baking powder
1 teaspoon salt
½ cup shortening
½ cup buttermilk
2 eggs
1 teaspoon vanilla extract
Never Fail Frosting
Chocolate Frosting
Chocolate curls (optional)

Combine cocoa, boiling water, and butter, stirring until mixture is smooth; set aside to cool.
Combine sugar and next 4 ingredients in a mixing bowl; add cocoa mixture and shortening, beating at medium speed of an electric mixer until blended. Add buttermilk, eggs, and vanilla; beat 2 minutes or until blended.
Pour batter into 3 waxed paper-lined and greased 8-inch round cakepans. Bake at 350° for 25 to 30 minutes or until a wooden pick inserted in center comes out clean. Cool in pans 10 minutes; remove layers from pans, and let cool completely on wire racks.
Spread Never Fail Frosting between layers and on top of cake. Spread Chocolate Frosting over top and sides of cake. Garnish with chocolate curls, if desired. Yield: one 3-layer cake.

Never Fail Frosting:

1 cup sugar
⅓ cup water
2 tablespoons light corn syrup
2 egg whites
¼ cup sifted powdered sugar
1 teaspoon vanilla extract
1/2 cup chopped pecans

Combine 1 cup sugar, water, and corn syrup in a heavy saucepan. Cook over medium heat, stirring constantly, until clear. Cook without stirring until candy thermometer registers 232°.
Beat egg whites (at room temperature) until soft peaks form; continue to beat, slowly adding syrup mixture. Add ¼ cup powdered sugar and vanilla; continue beating until stiff peaks form and frosting is thick enough to spread. Stir in pecans. Yield: 3 cups.

Chocolate Frosting:

2 (1-ounce) squares unsweetened chocolate
½ cup butter or margarine, softened
1 (16-ounce) package powdered sugar, sifted
1 egg
1 tablespoon whipping cream or half-and-half
2 teaspoons vanilla extract
1½ teaspoons lemon juice

Place chocolate in top of a double boiler; bring water to a boil. Reduce heat to low; cook until chocolate melts. Set aside to cool slightly.
Cream butter with electric mixer; add melted chocolate and remaining ingredients, beating until mixture is smooth. Yield: 2¾ cups.

Katherine Holland Mabry,
Athens, Alabama.

CHRISTMAS EVE PUNCH
(pictured on cover)

1 (32-ounce) bottle cranberry juice cocktail
1 (46-ounce) can unsweetened pineapple juice
2 cups orange juice
⅔ cups lemon juice
½ cup sugar
2 teaspoons almond extract
1 (33.8-ounce) bottle ginger ale, chilled

Combine first 6 ingredients; chill. To serve, add ginger ale, stirring well. Yield: about 4½ quarts.

Marcia Branan,
Savannah, Georgia.

Holiday Desserts

Bring On Dessert!

Southern expectations require that desserts this time of year be something extra special whether they are steeped in tradition or new, fresh, and creative. Whatever your pleasure, you'll find sweets in this fourth edition of "Holiday Desserts" to dazzle your family and friends all through the season.

Chocolate—A Grand Finale

Southerners often reach for chocolate first, so it seems natural that these sensational chocolate desserts should lead a special section devoted to desserts. You'll find a variety of choices, too, so select the one that best fits your needs.

Chocolate-Glazed Triple-Layer Cheesecake is a make-ahead dessert guaranteed to give you rave reviews. Three layers of flavored filling are capped with a glossy chocolate glaze. Chilling the glaze may tend to dull the sheen, so make the cake ahead of time, and chill. Then add the glaze, and garnish before serving. Just be sure to allow enough time for the glaze to set.

To garnish the cheesecake, use chocolate curls or leaves for the elegance of chocolate-on-chocolate. If you've never made chocolate leaves, it's simpler than you might think. First, select fresh mint or other nonpoisonous plant leaves. Use a paintbrush to brush a heavy coat of melted semisweet morsels onto the back or ribbed side of each leaf. Chill until firm. Paint another coat of chocolate over the first one, and chill again. Once the chocolate is firm, gently and quickly pull the leaves away from the chocolate. The chocolate will melt easily from the heat of your hands, so handle it as little as possible. Chocolate leaves will keep their shape at room temperature. For a unique touch of class, you might even try making some white-chocolate leaves to mix with the dark ones. For the most elegant chocolate dessert, remember to keep the garnish very simple.

CHOCOLATE-GLAZED TRIPLE LAYER CHEESECAKE
(pictured on page 310)

1 (8½-ounce) package chocolate wafer cookies, crushed (about 2 cups)
¾ cup sugar, divided
¼ cup plus 1 tablespoon butter or margarine, melted
2 (8-ounce) packages cream cheese, softened and divided
3 eggs, divided
1 teaspoon vanilla extract, divided
2 (1-ounce) squares semisweet chocolate, melted
1⅓ cups commercial sour cream, divided
⅓ cup firmly packed dark brown sugar
1 tablespoon all-purpose flour
¼ cup chopped pecans
5 ounces cream cheese, softened
¼ teaspoon almond extract
Chocolate glaze (recipe follows)
Chocolate leaves (optional)

Combine cookie crumbs, ¼ cup sugar, and butter in a medium bowl; blend well. Press into the bottom and 2 inches up sides of a 9-inch springform pan. Set aside.

Combine 1 (8-ounce) package cream cheese and ¼ cup sugar; beat until fluffy. Add 1 egg and ¼ teaspoon vanilla; blend well. Stir in melted chocolate and ⅓ cup sour cream. Spoon over chocolate crust.

Combine remaining (8-ounce) package cream cheese, brown sugar, and flour; beat until mixture is fluffy. Add 1 egg and ½ teaspoon vanilla; blend well. Stir in pecans. Spoon gently over chocolate layer.

Combine 5 ounces cream cheese and remaining ¼ cup sugar; beat until fluffy. Add egg; blend well. Stir in remaining 1 cup sour cream, ¼ teaspoon vanilla, and almond extract. Spoon gently over praline layer.

Bake at 325° for 1 hour; turn off oven, and leave cheesecake in oven for 30 minutes; open door of oven, and leave cheesecake in oven an additional 30 minutes. Cool. Chill 8 hours. Remove from pan. Spread warm chocolate glaze over cheesecake. Garnish with chocolate leaves, if desired. Yield: 10 to 12 servings.

Chocolate Glaze:

6 (1-ounce) squares semisweet chocolate
¼ cup butter or margarine
¾ cup sifted powdered sugar
2 tablespoons water
1 teaspoon vanilla extract

Combine chocolate and butter in top of a double boiler; cook until melted. Remove from heat; stir in remaining ingredients. Stir until smooth. Spread over cheesecake while glaze is warm. Yield: enough for one 9-inch cheesecake. *Mrs. Randy Bryant, Franklin, Virginia.*

ALMOND ICE CREAM BALLS

1 pint vanilla or chocolate ice cream
1 (2-ounce) package slivered almonds, chopped and toasted
½ cup commercial fudge sauce
1 teaspoon amaretto or 1 teaspoon almond extract

Scoop ice cream into 4 large balls, and place on a baking sheet; freeze at least 1 hour or until firm. Quickly coat sides with almonds; freeze balls until serving time.

Combine fudge sauce and liqueur. To serve, place ice cream ball in a dessert bowl; top with sauce. Serve immediately. Yield: 4 servings.
Sandra Lester Purcell, University, Alabama.

BROWN SUGAR FUDGE CAKE

(pictured on page 310)

½ cup shortening
2 cups firmly packed brown sugar
3 eggs
2 (1-ounce) squares unsweetened chocolate, melted
2¼ cups sifted cake flour
1 teaspoon baking soda
½ teaspoon salt
1 cup buttermilk
1 teaspoon vanilla extract
Creamy Chocolate Frosting
Grated semisweet chocolate

Cream shortening; gradually add sugar, beating at medium speed of an electric mixer. Add eggs, one at a time, beating well after each addition. Add chocolate; beat well.

Combine flour, soda, and salt; add to creamed mixture alternately with buttermilk, beginning and ending with flour mixture. Mix just until blended after each addition. Stir in vanilla.

Pour batter into 3 greased and floured 8-inch round cakepans. Bake at 350° for 25 to 30 minutes or until a wooden pick inserted in center comes out clean. Cool in pans 10 minutes; remove from pans, and let cool completely on wire racks. Spread Creamy Chocolate Frosting between layers and on top and sides of cake. Yield: one 3-layer cake.

Creamy Chocolate Frosting:

¾ cup butter or margarine
¾ cup cocoa
½ cup milk
¼ teaspoon salt
2¼ teaspoons vanilla extract
6¾ cups sifted powdered sugar

Combine first 3 ingredients in a small saucepan; cook over low heat, stirring constantly, until butter melts. Remove from heat; add salt, vanilla, and sugar. Beat on high speed of an electric mixer until spreading consistency, adding additional milk, if necessary. Yield: enough for one 3-layer cake.   *Agnes Shelton, Gretna, Virginia.*

Tip: Store food in coolest area of kitchen, away from oven and range.

SWEETHEART FUDGE PIE

(pictured on page 310)

½ cup butter or margarine, softened
¾ cup firmly packed brown sugar
3 eggs
1 (12-ounce) package semisweet chocolate morsels, melted
2 teaspoons instant coffee powder
1 teaspoon rum extract
½ cup all-purpose flour
1 cup coarsely chopped walnuts
1 unbaked 9-inch pastry shell
½ cup whipping cream, whipped
Maraschino cherries with stems (optional)

Cream butter; gradually add brown sugar, beating at medium speed of an electric mixer until light and fluffy. Add eggs, one at a time, beating well after each addition. Add melted chocolate, coffee powder, and rum extract, mixing well. Stir in flour and walnuts. Pour mixture into prepared 9-inch pastry shell. Bake at 375° for 25 minutes; cool completely on a wire rack. Chill.

Before serving, pipe whipped cream on top of pie. Garnish pie with maraschino cherries, if desired. Yield: one 9-inch pie.   *Peggy H. Amos, Martinsville, Virginia.*

CHOCOLATE VELVET TORTE

8 (1-ounce) squares sweet baking chocolate
¾ cup butter or margarine
¼ cup plus 2 tablespoons all-purpose flour
6 eggs, separated
½ cup sugar
⅔ cup raspberry preserves
Chocolate glaze (recipe follows)

Combine chocolate squares and butter in a heavy saucepan; cook over low heat until melted, stirring often. Remove from heat, and stir in flour. Add egg yolks, one at a time, stirring well after each addition; set aside.

Beat egg whites (at room temperature) until foamy; gradually add sugar, 1 tablespoon at a time, beating until stiff peaks form and sugar dissolves.

Fold egg whites into chocolate mixture. Pour into 3 greased and floured 8-inch round cakepans; bake at 350° for 20 to 25 minutes or until a wooden pick inserted in center comes out clean. Cool

in pans 10 minutes (layers settle as they cool). Remove layers from pans; cool on wire racks.

Spread ⅓ cup raspberry preserves between each layer; drizzle chocolate glaze on top. Yield: one 3-layer torte.

Chocolate Glaze:

4 (1-ounce) squares sweet baking chocolate
2 tablespoons water
3 tablespoons butter or margarine

Combine chocolate squares and water in a heavy saucepan; cook over low heat until melted, stirring often. Remove from heat; stir in butter. Cool until desired consistency, stirring occasionally. Yield: enough for one 8-inch torte.   *Heather Riggins, Nashville, Tennessee.*

A Splash Of Spirits Makes The Dessert

The flavors of rum, brandy, bourbon, and other liquors add a spirited flavor to an assortment of desserts. Some are baked, some are chilled, and some are simply whirled in the blender and served in frosted glasses. Whatever the process, the results are spirited desserts.

BANANA KABANA

2 medium-size ripe bananas, cut into 1-inch slices
¾ cup Kahlúa or other coffee-flavored liqueur
½ cup plus 2 tablespoons cream of coconut
½ cup half-and-half
5 cups crushed ice

Combine all ingredients except ice in container of an electric blender; process until smooth. Gradually add crushed ice, processing until mixture reaches desired consistency. Serve immediately. Yield: 4 cups.   *Terri Cohen, Germantown, Maryland.*

SHERRIED AMBROSIA
(pictured on page 307)

7 navel oranges
¼ to ½ cup sugar
½ cup flaked coconut
½ cup dry sherry
½ cup maraschino cherries

Peel oranges, and cut into ½-inch slices; cut slices into quarters. Alternate layers of oranges, sugar, and coconut until all ingredients are used. Pour sherry over fruit. Add cherries; cover and chill until serving time. Yield: 6 to 8 servings.
Margaret L. Hunter,
Princeton, Kentucky.

EGGNOG PIE

1 envelope unflavored gelatin
3 tablespoons brandy
1 cup milk
3 eggs, separated
¼ cup sugar
¼ cup bourbon or dark rum
1½ teaspoons vanilla extract
¼ teaspoon ground nutmeg
Pinch of salt
3 tablespoons sugar
1 cup whipping cream, divided
1 tablespoon powdered sugar
Ground nutmeg
Pecan Crust

Dissolve gelatin in brandy; set aside. Scald milk in top of a double boiler. Beat egg yolks and ¼ cup sugar at medium speed of an electric mixer. Gradually stir about one-fourth of hot milk into yolk mixture; add to remaining hot milk, stirring constantly. Cook over simmering water, stirring until mixture is thick and coats a spoon, about 3 to 5 minutes. Remove from heat, stir in softened gelatin, bourbon, vanilla, and ¼ teaspoon nutmeg. Chill, stirring occasionally, until mixture mounds when dropped from a spoon.

Beat egg whites (at room temperature) and salt until foamy; add 3 tablespoons sugar, and beat until stiff. Fold into custard. Beat ½ cup whipping cream until soft peaks form; fold into custard. Pour filling into prepared Pecan Crust; chill 3 hours or until set.

Beat remaining ½ cup whipping cream until foamy; add 1 tablespoon powdered sugar, and beat until soft peaks form. Garnish pie with whipped cream and sprinkle with nutmeg. Yield: one 10-inch pie.

Pecan Crust:

1 cup pecans, toasted
22 vanilla wafers
¼ cup sugar
¼ cup butter or margarine, melted

Position knife blade in food processor bowl; add pecans and vanilla wafers. Top with cover; process until finely ground. Add sugar and butter through food chute; pulse 3 or 4 times or until well mixed. Press mixture firmly into a lightly greased 10-inch pieplate. Bake at 325° for 5 minutes. Let cool on wire rack. Yield: 1 (10-inch) pie crust.
Marcia Loomis,
St. Louis, Missouri.

WHISPERS

1 quart coffee ice cream, softened
¼ cup cognac
¼ cup white crème de cacao
¼ cup Kahlúa or other coffee-flavored liqueur

Chill stemmed glasses 30 minutes.
Combine all ingredients in container of an electric blender; process until smooth. Pour mixture into glasses; serve immediately. Yield: about 3 cups.
Curt Treloar,
Largo, Florida.

COOKING LIGHT®

Sweet Desserts Without Much Sugar

Most desserts rely on sugar to make them sweet, but our selections reduce the sugar to a very small amount. Instead, we use a variety of sweet spices, unsweetened fruit juice, or a splash of spirits to enhance the sweet flavor without excessive calories. Sweet spices such as allspice, anise, cardamom, cinnamon, ginger, nutmeg, mace, and cloves or blends, such as apple pie spice and pumpkin pie spice, aren't really sweet. But their addition to desserts makes the food seem sweeter.

CHERRIES JUBILITE

1 (16-ounce) package frozen unsweetened dark cherries, thawed and undrained
1 teaspoon cornstarch
¼ cup brandy
3 cups vanilla ice milk

Combine cherries and cornstarch in a medium saucepan. Bring to a boil; cook over medium heat 1 minute or until thickened. Remove from heat.

Place brandy in a small, long-handled saucepan; heat just until warm (do not boil). Remove from heat. Ignite brandy, and pour over cherries; stir until flames die down. Serve immediately over ½-cup servings of ice milk. Yield: 6 servings (about 158 calories per serving).
Lyn Renwick,
Charlotte, North Carolina.

TART CRANBERRY-ORANGE ICE

2 (12-ounce) packages fresh cranberries
1 quart unsweetened orange juice, divided
1 teaspoon lemon juice
1 cup sugar
⅛ teaspoon ground cardamom

Wash cranberries; combine with 2 cups orange juice, lemon juice, and sugar in a large saucepan. Cook 7 to 10 minutes, stirring occasionally, or until cranberries pop; put through a food mill. Add remaining orange juice and cardamom to cranberry mixture; stir well. Pour into a 9-inch square pan. Place in freezer 3 to 4 hours or until almost frozen.

Place mixture in a mixing bowl; beat at medium speed of an electric mixer until fluffy. Return to pan. Freeze 8 hours. Yield: 16 servings (about 97 calories per ½-cup serving.)

GLAZED ORANGES AND PINEAPPLE

1 (8-ounce) can unsweetened pineapple slices, undrained
2 large oranges, peeled and sliced crosswise
½ cup plus 2 tablespoons unsweetened orange juice
1 tablespoon sugar
2 tablespoons brandy
2 teaspoons cornstarch
¼ teaspoon ground cinnamon

Drain pineapple, reserving juice. Combine pineapple and orange slices in a shallow container; set aside.

Combine reserved pineapple juice and remaining ingredients in a small saucepan; bring to a boil, stirring constantly. Boil mixture 1 minute; remove from heat, and pour over pineapple and oranges. Chill thoroughly. Yield: 4 servings (about 112 calories per serving).

LIGHT PLUM PUDDING

1 cup plain low-fat yogurt
1⅔ cups raisins (½ pound)
1½ cups currants (½ pound)
¼ teaspoon salt
½ cup all-purpose flour
1½ cups dry breadcrumbs
¼ cup honey
1 teaspoon ground allspice
1 teaspoon ground cinnamon
1 teaspoon ground mace
1 egg yolk, beaten
¼ cup brandy
2 tablespoons frozen orange juice concentrate, thawed and undiluted
3 tablespoons vegetable oil
3 egg whites
Vegetable cooking spray
Special Hard Sauce
Strip of orange rind (optional)

Combine first 10 ingredients in a large bowl; stir well. Combine egg yolk, brandy, orange juice concentrate, and oil; stir into fruit mixture.

Beat egg whites (at room temperature) until stiff peaks form; fold into fruit mixture. Spoon into an 8-cup mold coated with cooking spray. Cover mold tightly with aluminum foil.

Light Plum Pudding lives up to its name, offering a light alternative to the traditionally rich Christmas dessert.

Place mold on a shallow rack in a large deep kettle with enough boiling water to come halfway up sides of mold. Cover kettle; steam pudding 3 hours in continuously boiling water (add additional water as needed). Unmold and serve warm with Special Hard Sauce. Garnish with orange rind, if desired. Yield: 16 servings (about 194 calories per slice plus 21 calories per 2 teaspoons Hard Sauce).

Note: To store, cover and chill. Serve at room temperature.

Special Hard Sauce:

4 ounces Neufchâtel cheese, softened
3 tablespoons sifted powdered sugar
1 teaspoon brandy

Combine first 2 ingredients, beating at medium speed of an electric mixer until smooth. Add brandy; beat until fluffy. Chill. Yield: ¾ cup.

Virginia Bennack,
San Antonio, Texas.

DIETER'S APPLE CHEESECAKE

2 envelopes unflavored gelatin
⅓ cup water
1¾ cups unsweetened apple juice
2 eggs, separated
¼ cup sugar
3 cups part-skim ricotta cheese
1 teaspoon ground cinnamon
½ teaspoon ground nutmeg
2 tablespoons reduced-calorie margarine
1 tablespoon brown sugar
1 teaspoon brandy
2 medium-size cooking apples, unpeeled and thinly sliced

Sprinkle gelatin over water in a medium saucepan; let stand 5 minutes.

Combine apple juice, egg yolks, and sugar; stir well. Add to gelatin; cook over medium heat 3 to 4 minutes, stirring constantly. Set aside.

Combine ricotta, ⅓ cup gelatin mixture, cinnamon, and nutmeg; beat at medium speed of an electric mixer until smooth. Stir in remaining gelatin mixture; chill until consistency of unbeaten egg white.

Beat egg whites (at room temperature) until soft peaks form; fold into gelatin mixture. Pour into an 8-inch springform pan. Chill until firm.

Melt margarine in a skillet; add brown sugar and brandy, stirring well. Add apples and sauté until tender. Cool and arrange on top of dessert. Yield: 8 servings (about 240 calories per 1-inch slice).
Billie Jean Reynolds,
Coral Springs, Florida.

COFFEE-NUT MOUSSE

¼ cup walnuts
1 envelope unflavored gelatin
1½ tablespoons instant coffee granules
1½ cups skim milk
2 egg whites
2 tablespoons sugar
1¼ cups frozen whipped topping, thawed and divided
1 tablespoon chopped walnuts

Grind ¼ cup walnuts in blender or food processor; set aside.

Combine gelatin and coffee granules in a medium saucepan. Add milk, and let stand 1 minute. Cook over low heat, stirring constantly, until smooth and thickened. Remove from heat; stir in walnuts. Chill until consistency of unbeaten egg white.

Beat egg whites (at room temperature) until foamy; gradually add sugar, 1 tablespoon at a time, beating until stiff peaks form. Fold egg whites and 1 cup whipped topping into chilled coffee mixture.

Spoon into individual parfait glasses, and garnish with remaining ¼ cup whipped topping and 1 tablespoon walnuts. Yield: 6 servings (about 133 calories per ½-cup serving).
Mary Frances Donnelly,
Roanoke, Virginia.

Tip: For a great dessert, pour cream sherry over chilled grapefruit.

Sweets For Sharing

Making gifts in the kitchen for friends and neighbors is a holiday tradition in many families. Although it's a small gesture money-wise, it's a special way of saying you care during the season of love and goodwill. Everyone likes the personal touch, and it's especially appreciated in a food gift.

ALMOND HOLLY LEAVES

1 pound butter, softened
1 cup sifted powdered sugar
2 eggs, beaten
4 cups all-purpose flour
1 cup almonds, toasted and finely chopped

Cream butter; gradually add powdered sugar, beating well. Add eggs, and beat well. Stir in flour and almonds.

Roll dough to ¼-inch thickness on a floured surface with a floured rolling pin; cut into holly leaf shapes with a 1½-inch cookie cutter. Place cookies on ungreased cookie sheets, and bake at 350° for 10 minutes or until edges are golden. Cool on wire racks. Yield: about 12 dozen.
Note: Cookies cut into larger sizes may be fragile.
Mrs. Howard E. Erdman,
Denton, Texas.

AMARETTO DESSERT TRUFFLES

12 (1-ounce) squares semisweet chocolate
½ cup butter or margarine
2 egg yolks
½ cup whipping cream
¼ cup amaretto
Finely chopped almonds or cocoa

Melt chocolate in top of a double boiler. Remove from heat, and add butter, stirring in 1 tablespoon at a time.

Beat egg yolks until thick and lemon colored. Gradually stir about one-fourth of hot mixture into yolks; add to remaining hot mixture, stirring constantly. Stir in whipping cream and amaretto.

Return to heat, and cook 1 minute or until mixture is thickened and smooth, stirring constantly.

Cover and refrigerate overnight or until firm enough to roll into balls. Roll truffles in chopped almonds or cocoa. Store in refrigerator. Yield: 14 (2½-inch) balls or 42 (1-inch) balls.

BRANDY BALLS

1¼ cups butter or margarine, softened
½ cup sugar
1 egg yolk
3 cups all-purpose flour
¼ teaspoon salt
¼ cup plus 2 tablespoons brandy
1 cup pecans, finely chopped
About 1 cup sifted powdered sugar

Cream butter and ½ cup sugar in a large mixing bowl. Add egg yolk, and mix well. Combine flour and salt. Gradually add flour mixture to butter mixture alternately with brandy, beginning and ending with flour mixture. Stir in pecans. Chill dough 1 hour.

Roll dough into 1-inch balls, and place on a greased cookie sheet. Bake at 350° for 10 minutes or until lightly browned. Let cool slightly, and roll in powdered sugar. Yield: 5 dozen.
Cathie Way,
Shallowater, Texas.

SUGAR-AND-HONEY PECANS

1½ cups sugar
½ cup water
¼ cup honey
¼ teaspoon salt
½ teaspoon vanilla extract
3 cups pecan halves

Combine first 4 ingredients in a saucepan; mix well. Cook mixture over medium heat, stirring constantly, until sugar dissolves. Continue cooking, without stirring, until mixture reaches soft ball stage (240°). Remove from heat; stir in vanilla. Beat with a wooden spoon until mixture begins to thicken. Stir in pecan halves. Working rapidly, pour mixture onto waxed paper, and separate pecans with a fork. Let cool. Yield: 4 cups.
Gladys Cloninger,
Atlanta, Georgia.

MERINGUE SURPRISE COOKIES

3 egg whites
¼ teaspoon cream of tartar
1 teaspoon vanilla extract
¼ teaspoon peppermint extract
Dash of salt
1 cup sugar
36 milk chocolate kisses

Combine egg whites (at room temperature), cream of tartar, flavorings, and salt in a small bowl; beat at high speed of an electric mixer until soft peaks form. Gradually add sugar, 1 tablespoon at a time, beating until stiff peaks form and sugar dissolves.

Drop by scant tablespoonfuls onto a lightly greased cookie sheet. Press a chocolate kiss into center of each cookie; spoon meringue around kiss, and swirl top.

Bake at 275° for 30 minutes or until set. Immediately remove cookies to wire rack, and cool. Store in an airtight container. Yield: 3 dozen.
Madeline Gibbons,
Little Rock, Arkansas.

FRUITCAKE COOKIES

1½ cups all-purpose flour
½ teaspoon ground cloves
½ teaspoon ground cinnamon
½ teaspoon ground nutmeg
¼ teaspoon baking soda
¼ teaspoon salt
3 cups chopped pecans
½ pound candied pineapple, chopped
½ pound chopped dates
¼ pound candied red cherries, chopped
¼ pound candied green cherries, chopped
½ cup butter or margarine, softened
1 cup firmly packed brown sugar
2 eggs
⅓ cup white wine
1½ tablespoons milk

Combine first 6 ingredients in a small bowl. Set aside ½ cup of mixture for dredging fruit.

Combine pecans, pineapple, dates, and cherries in a large bowl; mix well. Dredge fruit mixture in ½ cup reserved flour mixture.

Cream butter in a large mixing bowl; gradually add sugar, beating until fluffy.

Add eggs, one at a time, beating at medium speed of an electric mixer. Add dry ingredients alternately with wine and milk, beginning and ending with flour mixture. Stir in fruit mixture.

Drop dough by level teaspoons onto greased cookie sheets. Bake at 325° for 15 minutes or until golden. Cool on wire rack. Yield: 4 dozen.
Mrs. Hugh Teague,
Plainview, Texas.

ROCKY ROAD BROWNIES

½ cup butter or margarine, softened
1 cup sugar
1 (1-ounce) square unsweetened chocolate, melted
2 eggs, beaten
½ cup chopped pecans
½ cup all-purpose flour
2 (3-ounce) packages cream cheese, softened
¼ cup butter or margarine, softened
¼ cup sugar
1 egg, beaten
¼ cup chopped pecans
1 tablespoon all-purpose flour
¼ teaspoon vanilla extract
½ cup semisweet chocolate mini-morsels
2 cups miniature marshmallows
2 (1-ounce) squares unsweetened chocolate
½ cup milk
½ cup butter or margarine
¼ teaspoon vanilla extract
4 cups sifted powdered sugar

Cream ½ cup butter and 1 cup sugar. Add next 4 ingredients, and mix well. Spoon into a greased and floured 13- x 9- x 2-inch pan. Set aside.

Combine cream cheese, ¼ cup butter, and ¼ cup sugar. Add 1 egg, ¼ cup pecans, 1 tablespoon flour, and ¼ teaspoon vanilla; mix well. Spoon carefully over chocolate layer in pan. (Do not mix layers together.) Sprinkle chocolate morsels over cream cheese layer. Bake at 350° for 35 to 45 minutes. Remove from oven, and cool slightly. Top with marshmallows.

Combine 2 squares chocolate, milk, and ½ cup butter in top of a double boiler; bring water to a boil. Reduce heat to low; cook until chocolate melts, stirring occasionally. Remove from heat, and stir in ¼ teaspoon vanilla and 4 cups powdered sugar. Spread frosting over brownies; cool.

Cut cooled brownies into squares. Serve immediately, or store in refrigerator. Yield: 3½ dozen. *Clodette Maner,*
Lubbock, Texas.

Plan Ahead For Desserts

Stock your refrigerator and freezer with scrumptious desserts, and you'll be all set for any event that pops up over the holidays. It also leaves you time to enjoy the season's festivities without cooking until the last minute.

SOUR CREAM CHEESECAKE

1 cup graham cracker crumbs
¼ cup finely chopped pecans
1 tablespoon brown sugar
3 tablespoons butter or margarine, melted
3 (8-ounce) packages cream cheese, softened
1 cup sugar
4 eggs
2 teaspoons vanilla extract
1 (16-ounce) carton commercial sour cream
¾ cup red currant or raspberry jelly
1 quart strawberries, sliced

Combine first 4 ingredients, mixing well; firmly press into bottom of a 9-inch springform pan. Chill.

Beat cream cheese with an electric mixer until light and fluffy; gradually add 1 cup sugar, mixing well. Add eggs, one at a time, beating well after each addition; stir in vanilla. Fold sour cream into cream cheese mixture, and pour into prepared pan. Bake at 500° for 8 minutes. Reduce heat to 225°, and bake 50 minutes. Turn off oven; open oven door slightly, and let cheesecake stand in oven 20 minutes. Remove from oven;

let cool to room temperature on a wire rack. Chill 8 hours or overnight.

Heat currant jelly in a medium saucepan over low heat; cool. Arrange sliced strawberries on top of cheesecake. Spoon melted jelly evenly over strawberries. Yield: 10 to 12 servings.

Vivienne Grossman,
Boca Raton, Florida.

ICE CREAM CAKE

1 (18.5-ounce) package chocolate cake mix without pudding
½ gallon chocolate chip ice cream
1 (6-ounce) package semisweet chocolate morsels
3 tablespoons butter or margarine
1 (1-pound) package sifted powdered sugar
¼ cup plus 2 tablespoons evaporated milk
1 teaspoon vanilla extract
Red and green candied cherries

Prepare cake mix according to package directions; pour batter into 2 greased and floured 9-inch round cakepans. Bake according to package directions. Cool in pans 10 minutes; remove layers from pans, and cool completely.

Split layers horizontally. Place one layer on a serving plate. Remove ice cream from container; slice off ½-inch layer of ice cream, and place it on cake layer. Place small chunks of ice cream on exposed areas of cake, if necessary, to cover entire surface. Repeat procedure with remaining cake layers and ice cream, leaving top layer of cake uncovered. Cover ice cream cake, and freeze until firm.

Place chocolate morsels and butter in top of a double boiler; bring water to a boil. Reduce heat to low, and cook until chocolate and butter melt, stirring well. Pour chocolate mixture into a mixing bowl. Add powdered sugar, milk, and vanilla; beat with an electric mixer until smooth. Spread on top and sides

of cake while frosting is still slightly warm. Garnish with candied cherries. Serve cake immediately, or freeze several hours or overnight. Yield: one 4-layer cake.

Denise Petter,
Gulfport, Mississippi.

PUMPKIN-ORANGE DELIGHT

1½ cups all-purpose flour
1½ cups chopped pecans
¾ cup butter or margarine, softened
1 (8-ounce) package cream cheese, softened
1 cup sifted powdered sugar
1 cup whipped topping
½ cup sugar
1 envelope unflavored gelatin
½ teaspoon ground ginger
½ teaspoon ground cinnamon
½ teaspoon ground nutmeg
3 eggs, separated
½ cup milk
1¼ cups canned pumpkin
1 teaspoon orange rind
¼ cup orange juice
½ cup sugar
2 cups whipped topping
Orange rind

Combine first 3 ingredients, mixing well. Press flour mixture into a 13- x 9- x 2-inch baking pan. Bake at 350° for 30 to 35 minutes; cool completely.

Combine cream cheese and powdered sugar, beating until fluffy; fold in 1 cup whipped topping. Spread over crust.

Combine ½ cup sugar, gelatin, ginger, cinnamon, and nutmeg in a large saucepan. Combine egg yolks and milk; add to saucepan, and cook over medium heat, stirring constantly, until mixture boils. Stir in pumpkin, 1 teaspoon orange rind, and orange juice. Chill mixture until partially set.

Beat egg whites (at room temperature) and ½ cup sugar until stiff peaks form; fold into pumpkin mixture. Spread over cream cheese layer. Spread 2 cups whipped topping over pumpkin layer. Chill thoroughly. Garnish with orange rind. Yield: 15 servings.

Kathryn Smith,
Sebring, Florida.

HOLIDAY PETITE CHEESECAKES

2 (8-ounce) packages cream cheese, softened
¾ cup sugar
2 eggs
1 tablespoon lemon juice
1 teaspoon vanilla extract
1½ teaspoons Grand Marnier or other orange-flavored liqueur
¼ cup semisweet chocolate mini-morsels
18 vanilla wafers
1 (16-ounce) carton commercial sour cream
3 tablespoons sugar
½ teaspoon vanilla extract
Mandarin orange slices
Green and red maraschino cherries
Semisweet chocolate mini-morsels
Milk chocolate kisses

Beat cream cheese in a mixing bowl until light and fluffy. Gradually add ¾ cup sugar, beating well. Add eggs, one at a time, beating well after each addition. Stir in lemon juice and 1 teaspoon vanilla. Divide mixture into 3 portions. Add Grand Marnier to first portion, mixing well. Add ¼ cup chocolate mini-morsels to second portion, mixing well. Keep third portion plain.

Place a vanilla wafer in each paper-lined muffin cup; spoon cream cheese mixture over wafers, filling cups three-fourths full. (Keep flavors separate.) Bake at 375° for 20 minutes.

Combine sour cream, 3 tablespoons sugar, ½ teaspoon vanilla; mix well. Place a heaping tablespoon of sour cream mixture over cheesecakes as soon as they are removed from oven. Spread mixture to edges. Bake at 375° for an additional 5 to 7 minutes or until topping is set. Leave in muffin pans, and refrigerate overnight. Garnish with orange slices, cherries, and chocolate mini-morsels and kisses, if desired. Yield: 18 servings.

Mary Jo Angelo,
Birmingham, Alabama.

Tip: Use a timer when cooking. Set the timer so it will ring at various intervals, and check the progress of the dish. However, try to avoid opening the oven door unless necessary.

HOT FUDGE SUNDAE DESSERT

1 (12-ounce) package vanilla wafers,
   crushed
½ cup finely chopped pecans
¾ cup butter or margarine, melted
½ gallon vanilla ice cream, softened
Chocolate sauce (recipe follows)

Combine vanilla wafer crumbs, pecans, and butter, mixing well. Press half of crumb mixture into a 13- x 9- x 2-inch dish. Spread ice cream evenly over crust. Press remaining crumb mixture over ice cream. Cover and freeze until firm. To serve, cut into squares, and top each serving with chocolate sauce. Yield: 15 servings.

Chocolate Sauce:

1 cup sugar
3 tablespoons all-purpose flour
¼ cup plus 1 tablespoon cocoa
1 cup milk
2 tablespoons butter or margarine
1 teaspoon vanilla extract

Combine first 4 ingredients in a medium saucepan. Cook over medium heat until slightly thickened, stirring constantly. Remove from heat, and stir in butter and vanilla. Yield: about 2 cups.
Dana L. Bryant,
Shreveport, Louisiana.

RUM TRIFLE

½ cup rum
¾ cup slivered almonds, toasted
¾ cup golden raisins
1 (3-ounce) package vanilla pudding mix
½ cup whipping cream, whipped
1 (10-ounce) loaf angel food cake, cut into
   ½-inch cubes
½ cup whipping cream
Slivered almonds, toasted (optional)
Whole fresh strawberries (optional)

Combine first 3 ingredients in a small bowl; let stand 1 hour.

Prepare pudding mix according to package directions using 2½ cups milk; cool. Fold whipped cream into pudding.

Layer one-third each of cake, raisin mixture, and pudding in a 3½-quart glass bowl; repeat layers twice, ending with pudding. Cover and chill at least 3 hours. Before serving, beat ½ cup whipping cream until soft peaks form; spread over trifle. Garnish with almonds and strawberries, if desired. Yield: 8 to 10 servings.
Virginia B. Stalder,
Nokesville, Virginia.

Paint Your Christmas Cookies

If you like to bake and decorate Christmas cookies, let the artist in you come out this year. Our Painted Cookies might be just the novel recipe you look for during the holidays. And while the cookies look difficult to make, they're actually so easy that children could make them if they had help with the rolling and cutting.

The "paint" is a simple mixture of egg yolk, water, and food coloring. Once the cookies are rolled and cut, just paint on some playful designs, and bake the cookies as usual. You can paint the designs by freehand, or press the cookies with smaller, shaped cutters to imprint a design to paint.

To make the paint, use one egg yolk for every two colors desired. Add ¼ teaspoon water, and beat mixture with a fork until smooth. Divide the yolk mixture into two custard cups. Stir in enough food coloring (paste or liquid type) to make the desired colors. The paint dries out quickly, so keep it covered when not in use. Stir in a few drops of water, if necessary, to keep paint a workable consistency.

Painting the cookies is so much fun that you might like to make the process a family tradition. You can make the cookies to give as gifts or even to use as ornaments. If you wish to make ornaments, cut a small hole in the top of the cookie before baking, using a plastic drinking straw; then bake as usual. Thread colorful cord or ribbon through the hole after the cookies cool.

PAINTED COOKIES

1 cup butter or margarine, softened
1 cup sugar
2 eggs
¼ cup milk
2 teaspoons vanilla extract
4 cups all-purpose flour
1 teaspoon baking powder
¾ teaspoon baking soda
Egg Yolk Paint

Cream butter at medium speed of an electric mixer; gradually add sugar, beating until mixture is light and fluffy. Add eggs, one at a time, beating after each addition. Add milk and vanilla, and mix well. Combine flour, baking powder, and soda; add flour mixture to creamed mixture, stirring until blended. (Dough will be soft.)

Shape dough into 2 balls; wrap each ball in waxed paper, and allow balls to chill at least 4 hours.

Work with half of dough at a time; store remainder in refrigerator. Roll dough to ⅛-inch thickness on floured waxed paper; cut with 2½- to 3-inch cookie cutters, and transfer dough shapes to lightly greased cookie sheets.

Paint assorted designs on cookies using a small art brush and Egg Yolk Paint. Bake at 375° for 6 to 8 minutes; cool on wire racks. Yield: 5 dozen.

Egg Yolk Paint:

1 egg yolk, beaten
¼ teaspoon water
Paste or liquid food coloring

Combine egg yolk and water; stir well. Divide mixture evenly into 2 custard cups; tint as desired with food coloring. Keep paint covered until ready to use. If paint thickens, add a few drops of water, and stir mixture well. Yield: 1½ tablespoons.

Note: Prepare 1 recipe Egg Yolk Paint for every 2 colors of paint desired.

Extraordinary Holiday Entrées

At Christmastime, friends and family gather from far and near, and traditions abound. For many, turkey with dressing is the expected fare. But surprises can be fun. Let your guests anticipate Christmas dinner as much as they look forward to opening their gifts.

These recipes will entice you to try something different—one might even become a holiday tradition. And you'll bask in the raves you'll receive for preparing such a spectacular entrée.

CORNISH HENS IN PORT AND SOUR CREAM

6 (1- to 1½-pound) Cornish hens
1½ teaspoons lemon-pepper seasoning
1 teaspoon poultry seasoning
¾ teaspoon salt
2 cooking apples, sliced
1 clove garlic
½ cup butter or margarine
1 (10¾-ounce) can consommé
1¼ cups water
½ cup port wine
¾ pound fresh mushrooms, sliced
¼ cup butter or margarine, melted
1 teaspoon browning and seasoning sauce
2 tablespoons cornstarch
¼ cup water
½ cup commercial sour cream

Remove giblets from hens; reserve for another use. Rinse hens with cold water, and pat dry. Sprinkle cavities with lemon-pepper seasoning, poultry seasoning, and salt; place apple slices in cavities. Close cavities; secure with wooden picks, and truss. Rub outside of hens with garlic.

Melt ½ cup butter in a skillet; brown hens in butter on all sides. Place hens in a 15- x 10- x 3-inch roasting pan.

Combine consommé, water, and wine; pour mixture over hens. Bake at 350° for 1 hour, basting frequently with pan drippings.

Place hens on a serving platter; keep warm. Reserve 2 cups pan drippings. Sauté mushrooms in ¼ cup butter. Add reserved pan drippings and browning sauce. Dissolve cornstarch in ¼ cup water; stir into mushroom mixture. Cook, stirring constantly, until thickened. Whisk in sour cream. Do not boil. Serve with Cornish hens. Yield: 6 servings.

Martha Bearden,
Amarillo, Texas.

STUFFED CROWN ROAST OF PORK
(pictured on page 309)

1 (16-rib) crown roast of pork (about 8 pounds)
½ teaspoon salt
⅛ teaspoon pepper
1 pound bulk pork sausage
1 (20-ounce) can apple slices, undrained and chopped
9 slices dry raisin bread, cut into ½-inch cubes
¼ cup apple juice
¾ teaspoon salt
1 teaspoon ground cinnamon
½ teaspoon ground cardamom
¼ teaspoon ground allspice
Apple wedges (optional)
Watercress (optional)

Sprinkle roast on all sides with ½ teaspoon salt and ⅛ teaspoon pepper; place roast, bone ends up, in a shallow roasting pan.

Cook sausage in a skillet until browned, stirring to crumble; drain well. Combine sausage and next 7 ingredients; stir to moisten bread.

Fill center of roast with sausage mixture; cover with aluminum foil. Punch a hole in foil; insert meat thermometer into roast, making sure it does not touch foil, bone, or fat. Bake at 325° for 3 to 3½ hours or until meat thermometer registers 160°. Garnish with apple wedges and watercress, if desired. Yield: 8 servings.

Kathy Hunt,
Dallas, Texas.

STUFFED HAM

1 (15- to 18-pound) fully cooked ham
2 (1-pound) loaves white bread, toasted and crumbled
24 saltine crackers, crushed
3 (10-ounce) jars sweet pickle relish
10 hard-cooked eggs, grated
1 cup butter or margarine, melted
¾ cup firmly packed brown sugar
¼ cup prepared mustard
1 cup peach pickle juice
3 eggs, beaten
3 tablespoons ground turmeric
¼ teaspoon salt
¼ teaspoon pepper
¼ teaspoon red pepper

Insert meat thermometer into ham, making sure it does not touch bone. Bake, uncovered, at 325° for 3¾ to 5½ hours (15 to 18 minutes per pound) or until meat thermometer registers 140°. Remove ham from oven, reserving drippings. Let cool to touch. Cut through one side of ham; remove bone.

Combine remaining ingredients; mix well. Fill cavity of ham with about one-third of dressing mixture. Bring cut edges of ham over stuffing, and tie securely with string. Press remaining dressing on ham, covering completely. Lightly brush with reserved drippings. Bake at 325° for 30 minutes. Cool to room temperature; cover and chill before serving. Yield: 25 to 30 servings.

Jane Adams,
Decatur, Alabama.

STUFFED TENDERLOIN

2 cups herb-seasoned stuffing mix
1 (1-pound) slice smoked ham, diced
1 cup finely chopped onion
1 (3½-ounce) package sliced pepperoni, minced
2 eggs, beaten
⅓ cup water
½ teaspoon garlic powder
¼ teaspoon pepper
1 (7- to 7½-pound) beef tenderloin
Paprika
6 slices bacon
1 cup water
1 bay leaf
4 whole cloves
1½ tablespoons cornstarch
⅛ teaspoon pepper

Combine first 8 ingredients; mix well, and set aside.

Trim excess fat from beef tenderloin. Remove 3 to 4 inches of small end; reserve for other uses. Cut tenderloin lengthwise to within ¼ inch of other edge, leaving one long side connected. Spoon stuffing mixture into opening of tenderloin. Fold top side over stuffing. Tie tenderloin securely with heavy string at 2- to 3-inch intervals. Sprinkle paprika over all sides, and place on a rack in a shallow roasting pan. Arrange bacon over top.

Place 1 cup water, bay leaf, and cloves in roasting pan. Bake at 350° for 60 to 70 minutes or until a meat thermometer registers 140° (rare) or 160° (medium).

Transfer tenderloin from rack to serving platter, reserving ¼ cup drippings; keep tenderloin warm. Remove bay leaf and cloves. Add water to reserved drippings to make 1½ cups. Combine dripping mixture and cornstarch in a medium saucepan; stir well. Cook over medium heat, stirring constantly, until thickened and bubbly. Stir in pepper. Serve with tenderloin. Yield: 14 to 16 servings.

Glenda Rumsey,
Sylacauga, Alabama.

Make These Dishes The Day Before

December's merry days are here, and suddenly ovens heat up, friends start calling, the greenery comes out, and the table is decorated. It's time for holiday sharing! And one of the best ways is to invite family and friends to dinner.

Our collection of holiday make-ahead dishes is colorful and festive, offering a variety of foods to complete your menus with flair.

These dishes can be made the night before or early in the day to free your time. Be sure to cover the dishes with plastic or aluminum foil to seal in freshness. Double-check cooking times and temperatures for your entire menu so that dishes may be served hot with your bread and entrée. And because all of the baked recipes in this article go into a 350° oven, they may be cooked at the same time.

STUFFED CELERY

1 (8-ounce) package cream cheese, softened
¼ cup mayonnaise
1 cup chopped pecans
1 clove garlic, crushed
¾ to 1 teaspoon Beau Monde seasoning
¼ cup chopped fresh parsley
10 stalks celery, cut into 3-inch pieces
Paprika

Combine first 6 ingredients; mix well. Spoon into celery pieces; sprinkle with paprika. Cover and chill 8 hours or overnight. Yield: 2½ dozen.
Mrs. Richard J. Rudolph,
Houston, Texas.

STUFFED CARROTS

12 medium carrots, scraped
½ cup cooked regular rice
½ cup dry breadcrumbs
⅓ cup (1½ ounces) shredded Cheddar cheese
½ teaspoon salt
⅛ teaspoon pepper
1 teaspoon finely chopped onion
1 teaspoon finely chopped green pepper
2 tablespoons butter or margarine, melted
Fresh chopped parsley
Carrot curl (optional)
Parsley sprigs (optional)

Cut carrots 3 inches from top, reserving smaller end for another use. Cook carrots in a small amount of water 20 minutes or until tender, but firm. Let cool completely. Scoop out the center of each carrot.

Combine rice and next 7 ingredients; toss to mix. Stuff carrots with mixture; place in a 13- x 9- x 2-inch baking dish. Cover and chill up to 24 hours. Remove from refrigerator; let stand 30 minutes. Bake, uncovered, at 350° for 15 minutes or until carrots are hot. Sprinkle with chopped parsley. Garnish with a carrot curl and parsley sprigs, if desired. Yield: 6 servings. *Virginia M. Griffin,*
Princeton, Kentucky.

BROCCOLI-AND-EGG CASSEROLE

1 (10-ounce) package frozen chopped broccoli
½ cup chopped onion
1 tablespoon butter or margarine, melted
1 (10-ounce) can cream of mushroom soup, undiluted
1 cup (4 ounces) shredded Cheddar cheese
½ teaspoon dry mustard
4 hard-cooked eggs, chopped
1 (2.8-ounce) can French-fried onion rings

Cook broccoli according to package directions, omitting salt. Drain and set aside. Sauté onion in butter in a saucepan until tender. Add soup, cheese, and mustard; heat until bubbly.

Layer half of broccoli and half of eggs in a greased 1½-quart casserole; pour half of soup mixture over eggs. Repeat layers. Cover and refrigerate 8 hours or overnight. Remove from refrigerator; let stand 30 minutes. Bake, uncovered, at 350° for 25 minutes. Add onion rings, and bake an additional 5 minutes. Yield: 4 to 6 servings.
Maude Crenshaw,
Jacksonville, North Carolina.

ASPARAGUS-AND-ENGLISH PEA CASSEROLE

2 (10-ounce) packages frozen asparagus
1 (10-ounce) package frozen English peas
1 (6-ounce) jar sliced mushrooms, drained
1 (2-ounce) jar diced pimiento, drained
3 tablespoons butter or margarine
3 tablespoons all-purpose flour
¾ cup milk
1 (5-ounce) jar sharp process cheese spread
¼ teaspoon salt
⅛ teaspoon pepper
½ cup fine dry breadcrumbs
3 tablespoons butter or margarine, melted

Cook asparagus according to package directions, omitting salt. Drain asparagus, reserving ¾ cup cooking liquid. Set liquid aside. Cut asparagus into 2-inch pieces. Place asparagus in a lightly greased 12- x 8- x 2-inch casserole.

Cook peas according to package directions, omitting salt. Drain well. Place peas over asparagus. Layer mushrooms and pimiento over peas; set aside.

Melt 3 tablespoons butter in a heavy saucepan over low heat; add flour, stirring until smooth. Cook 1 minute. Combine reserved ¾ cup asparagus liquid and milk. Gradually add to flour mixture; cook over medium heat, stirring constantly, until mixture is thickened and bubbly. Stir in cheese spread, salt, and pepper. Pour over vegetables in casserole.

Combine breadcrumbs and 3 tablespoons melted butter; sprinkle over sauce. Cover and refrigerate 8 hours or overnight. Remove from refrigerator; let stand 30 minutes. Bake, uncovered, at 350° for 40 minutes or until thoroughly heated. Yield: 8 servings.
Marie W. Harris,
Sevierville, Tennessee.

BOURBON SWEET POTATOES

2 (29-ounce) cans sweet potatoes, drained and mashed
¾ cup firmly packed brown sugar
½ cup butter or margarine, melted
¼ to ⅓ cup bourbon
½ teaspoon vanilla extract
2 cups miniature marshmallows

Combine first 5 ingredients, mixing well. Spoon mixture into a lightly greased 1½-quart casserole. Cover and refrigerate 8 hours or overnight.

Remove from refrigerator; let stand 30 minutes. Bake, uncovered, at 350° for 25 minutes. Remove from oven; top with marshmallows. Bake an additional 7 minutes or until marshmallows are golden. Yield: 6 to 8 servings.
Rose Alleman,
Prairieville, Louisiana.

HOT FRUIT COMPOTE
(pictured on page 308)

8 soft coconut macaroons
1 (16½-ounce) can pitted dark sweet cherries, drained
1 (16-ounce) can sliced peaches, drained
1 (15¼-ounce) can pineapple chunks, drained
1 (17-ounce) can apricot halves, drained
1 (16-ounce) can pear halves, drained
1 (21-ounce) can cherry pie filling
½ cup brandy

Crumble macaroons in a shallow pan. Bake at 400° for 3 to 4 minutes or until lightly toasted, stirring occasionally; cool. Sprinkle half of macaroons in a 2½-quart casserole. Layer remaining ingredients in order given. Sprinkle on remaining macaroons; cover and refrigerate 8 hours or overnight.

Remove fruit from refrigerator; let stand 30 minutes. Bake, uncovered, at 350° for 35 to 40 minutes or until bubbly. Yield: 8 to 10 servings.

Diane Koser,
Herndon, Virginia.

LAYERED CRANBERRY SALAD

(pictured on page 308)

1 (3-ounce) package vanilla pudding mix
1 (3-ounce) package lemon-flavored gelatin
2 cups water
2 tablespoons lemon juice
1 (3-ounce) package raspberry-flavored gelatin
1 cup boiling water
1 (16-ounce) can whole cranberry sauce
½ cup chopped celery
¼ cup chopped pecans
1 (1.4-ounce) package whipped topping mix
½ teaspoon ground nutmeg
Lettuce leaves

Combine first 3 ingredients in a saucepan; cook over medium heat, stirring constantly, until gelatin dissolves. Stir in lemon juice. Chill until consistency of unbeaten egg white.

Dissolve raspberry gelatin in 1 cup boiling water. Stir in cranberry sauce; blend well. Stir in celery and pecans. Chill until partially set.

Prepare whipped topping mix according to package directions, adding nutmeg. Fold into lemon gelatin mixture. Spoon 1½ cups mixture into a lightly oiled 7-cup mold. Chill until set.

Spoon raspberry gelatin mixture over lemon mixture; chill until set. Spoon remaining lemon mixture over raspberry layer. Chill until firm. Unmold on lettuce leaves. Yield: 12 to 14 servings.

Mrs. Charles Hellem,
Columbia, Missouri.

Tip: When squeezing fresh lemons or oranges for juice, first grate the rind by rubbing the washed fruit against surface of grater, taking care to remove only the outer colored portion of the rind. Wrap in plastic in teaspoon portions and freeze for future use.

Food Gifts For The Diet Conscious

A homemade delicacy is a gift from the heart, and it's a modern way to put a personal touch back into gift giving without breaking your budget. Recipe ideas for sugary-sweet confections and high-sodium, high-fat snacks abound this time of year, but they don't help much if you're trying to select a food gift for a calorie-conscious friend. That's how our recipes differ. Each recipe trims away unnecessary ingredients and unwanted calories to focus on a healthier way of eating.

HERB PRETZELS WITH LOWER SODIUM HORSERADISH MUSTARD

1 package dry yeast
½ teaspoon sugar
1½ cups warm water (105° to 115°)
2 cups all-purpose flour
2½ cups whole wheat flour
¼ teaspoon salt
½ teaspoon onion powder
½ teaspoon garlic powder
1 teaspoon Italian seasoning
Vegetable cooking spray
1 egg white, beaten
2 teaspoons water
3 tablespoons grated Parmesan cheese
Lower Sodium Horseradish Mustard

Dissolve yeast and sugar in warm water in a large mixing bowl. Add flour, salt, and seasonings; mix until blended. (Dough will be very stiff.)

Turn dough out onto a lightly floured surface, and knead until smooth and elastic (about 8 to 10 minutes). Place dough in a bowl coated with cooking spray, turning to grease top. Cover and let rise in a warm place (85°), free from drafts, 1 hour or until doubled in bulk.

Using kitchen shears dipped in flour, cut dough into 24 pieces; roll each piece into a ball. With floured hands, roll each ball to form a rope 14 inches long. Twist each ball into a pretzel shape. Place pretzels 1½ inches apart on aluminum foil-lined baking sheets coated with cooking spray.

Combine egg white and 2 teaspoons water; stir well. Brush each pretzel with egg white mixture; sprinkle with Parmesan cheese. Bake at 475° for 12 to 15 minutes or until golden. Remove pretzels to a wire rack to cool. Serve warm with Lower Sodium Horseradish Mustard. Yield: 2 dozen (about 82 calories per pretzel plus 5 calories per teaspoon mustard).

Lower Sodium Horseradish Mustard:

1 tablespoon cornstarch
¼ teaspoon salt
2 teaspoons dry mustard
¼ cup cider vinegar
2 teaspoons prepared horseradish
¾ cup hot water
2 teaspoons honey
1 egg yolk

Combine first 3 ingredients in a small saucepan; stir in vinegar and horseradish. Slowly stir in hot water and honey. Cook over low heat, stirring constantly, until thickened and bubbly.

Beat egg yolk. Gradually stir about one-fourth of hot mixture into yolk; add to remaining hot mixture, stirring constantly. Cook, stirring constantly, 1 minute. Cover and chill mixture 2 to 3 hours. Yield: ¾ cup.

CARROT-CHEESE BALL

2 cups shredded carrots
1 (8-ounce) package Neufchâtel cheese, softened
1 cup (4 ounces) shredded low-calorie process Cheddar cheese
1 clove garlic, minced
¼ cup nutlike cereal nuggets
1 tablespoon chopped fresh parsley

Press carrots between paper towels to remove excess moisture; set aside.

Combine Neufchâtel cheese and Cheddar cheese in a medium bowl; stir well. Add carrots and garlic; stir well. Cover and chill 1 hour.

Combine cereal nuggets and parsley; stir well. Shape cheese mixture into a ball; roll in cereal mixture. Wrap in waxed paper, and chill at least 1 hour. Yield: 1 ball (about 32 calories per tablespoon).

Marie A. Davis,
Drexel, North Carolina.

CURRIED POPCORN MIX

2 tablespoons plus 2 teaspoons
    reduced-calorie margarine
1 teaspoon Worcestershire sauce
½ to ¾ teaspoon curry powder
⅛ to ¼ teaspoon garlic powder
2 cups crispy corn cereal squares
4 cups popped corn (popped without salt
    or fat)
½ cup chopped dried apricots
⅓ cup raisins
3 tablespoons flaked coconut

Melt margarine in a nonstick skillet; remove from heat. Add Worcestershire sauce, curry powder, and garlic powder; stir well. Add cereal; stir to coat.

Combine remaining ingredients in a large bowl. Add cereal mixture; toss gently. Yield: 7 cups (about 110 calories per 1-cup serving).
Jan Lovell,
Pine Bluff, Arkansas.

FRUITED CURRY-RICE MIX

2 cups uncooked brown rice
1 tablespoon dried orange rind
2 teaspoons dried green onion flakes
3½ teaspoons chicken-flavored bouillon
    granules
½ teaspoon curry powder
1 tablespoon dried parsley flakes
½ cup chopped unsalted peanuts
½ cup raisins

Combine all ingredients; stir well. Store in an airtight container. Yield: 3 cups mix.

When ready to use, bring 2 cups water to a boil in a medium saucepan; add 1 cup rice mix. Cover, reduce heat, and simmer 45 to 50 minutes or until liquid is absorbed. Yield: 2½ cups (about 134 calories per ½-cup serving).

DRIED FRUIT NUGGETS

1 (8-ounce) package whole pitted dates
1 (5-ounce) package dried apricots
⅓ cup raisins
⅓ cup flaked coconut
¼ cup sesame seeds, toasted

Combine all ingredients except sesame seeds in container of food processor. Process until pureed. Shape into balls, using 1½ teaspoons mixture per ball. Roll in sesame seeds. Store in airtight container in refrigerator up to 2 weeks. Yield: 3½ dozen (about 19 calories per ball).
Mrs. Gilbert Cyrus,
La Grange, Georgia.

PEACHY-RAISIN SPREAD

3 cups unsweetened apple juice
2 (8-ounce) packages dried peach halves
1½ cups golden raisins
1 (3-inch) stick cinnamon, broken
4 whole cloves

Combine first 3 ingredients in a saucepan. Tie cinnamon and cloves in a cheesecloth bag; add to peach mixture.

Bring mixture to a boil; reduce heat, and simmer 15 minutes, stirring occasionally. Remove spice bag.

Place mixture in container of an electric blender; process until pureed. Spoon into half-pint jars. Store in refrigerator. Yield: 4 cups (about 11 calories per teaspoon).
Laura C. Lawrence,
Hagerstown, Maryland.

Savory Appetizers

Planned parties or impromptu gatherings call for tasty little treats to enjoy with a drink. It's nice to have the ingredients on hand for a quick appetizer when friends drop in for a visit. It's even nicer to have an appetizer stashed in the freezer to warm and serve at a moment's notice.

MEAT TURNOVERS

¼ pound ground beef
1 green onion, minced
¼ cup chopped green pepper
2 tablespoons chopped red pepper
1 teaspoon all-purpose flour
¼ teaspoon salt
¼ teaspoon pepper
Dash of chili powder
Dash of garlic powder
Pastry (recipe follows)
1 egg yolk
1 tablespoon water
Commercial sour cream

Combine ground beef, green onion, and chopped green and red pepper in a heavy skillet. Cook until meat is browned; drain. Stir in flour, salt, pepper, chili powder, and garlic powder; cook 1 minute, stirring constantly. Set aside. Cool to room temperature.

Roll pastry to ⅛-inch thickness on a lightly floured surface. Cut into 3-inch rounds. Place 1 teaspoon meat mixture in center. Combine egg yolk and water; brush edges of pastry with yolk mixture, and fold in half. Seal edges. Place on lightly greased baking sheets, and brush tops with egg yolk mixture. Bake at 375° for 15 to 20 minutes or until puffed and lightly browned. Serve with sour cream. Yield: about 2 dozen.

Pastry:

2 cups all-purpose flour
½ teaspoon salt
½ teaspoon baking powder
¼ cup butter or margarine
1 egg, beaten
½ cup commercial sour cream

Combine flour, salt, and baking powder; cut in butter with pastry blender until mixture resembles coarse meal. Stir in egg and sour cream. Shape into a ball; chill 1 hour. Yield: enough pastry for 2 dozen turnovers.

Note: These turnovers may be baked and frozen. Reheat to serve.
Carol Kaiser,
Yoakum, Texas.

SHRIMP-IN-A-PICKLE

7½ cups water
2½ pounds unpeeled fresh shrimp
3 medium onions, sliced
2½ tablespoons capers with juice
1 cup vegetable oil
½ cup red wine vinegar
½ cup tarragon vinegar
Juice of ½ lemon
2 tablespoons sugar
½ teaspoon salt
1 tablespoon Worcestershire sauce
8 bay leaves, broken
½ to 1 teaspoon hot sauce

Bring water to a boil; add shrimp, and cook 3 to 5 minutes. Drain well; rinse with cold water. Peel and devein shrimp. Layer shrimp and onion in an airtight container. Combine remaining ingredients, mixing well. Pour over shrimp and onion. Cover and chill 24 hours, stirring occasionally. Yield: 10 appetizer servings.
Mary Larsh,
Franklin, Virginia.

FLAKY SCALLOP APPETIZERS

¾ pound scallops
1 (10-ounce) package frozen chopped
  spinach, thawed
1 clove garlic, minced
2 tablespoons butter or margarine, melted
½ cup chopped walnuts, toasted
1½ cups (6 ounces) shredded Swiss cheese
¼ cup grated Parmesan cheese
1 egg, beaten
¼ teaspoon pepper
⅛ teaspoon ground nutmeg
20 sheets frozen phyllo pastry, thawed
½ cup butter or margarine, melted

Place scallops in a skillet, and add water to cover. Bring to a boil; reduce heat, and simmer 3 to 5 minutes. Drain and finely chop scallops. Set aside.

Place spinach on paper towels, and squeeze until barely moist. Set aside.

Sauté garlic in 2 tablespoons butter in a large skillet; remove from heat. Add scallops, spinach, walnuts, cheeses, egg, and seasonings; stir well.

Cut sheets of phyllo in half crosswise. Working with one at a time, fold each half lengthwise into thirds; brush with melted butter. Place 1 tablespoon spinach mixture at base of phyllo strip, folding the right bottom corner over to opposite edge, forming a triangle. Continue folding back and forth into a triangle to end of strip. Repeat process with remaining phyllo.

Place triangles, seam side down, on baking sheets. Brush tops with ½ cup melted butter; bake at 375° for 12 to 15 minutes or until lightly browned. Yield: 40 appetizers.   *Ginny Munsterman,*
Garland, Texas.

MARINATED HERB MUSHROOMS

1 pound small fresh mushrooms
⅓ cup cider vinegar
2 tablespoons vegetable oil
1½ teaspoons fines herbes
1½ teaspoons sugar
½ teaspoon salt
1 (4-ounce) jar diced pimiento, drained

Clean mushrooms with damp paper towels; trim ends from stems.

Combine remaining ingredients in a bowl. Add mushrooms, tossing gently to coat. Cover and chill 8 hours, stirring occasionally. Yield: 12 to 15 appetizer servings.   *Mrs. Robert W. Meyer,*
Seminole, Florida.

ANTIPASTO RELISH

1 (14-ounce) can artichoke hearts, drained
2 (4-ounce) cans mushroom stems and
  pieces, drained
1 (4-ounce) jar diced pimiento, drained
½ cup finely chopped celery
¼ cup finely chopped green pepper
⅓ cup white vinegar
⅓ cup olive oil
¼ cup instant minced onion
1 teaspoon sugar
¼ to ½ teaspoon garlic powder
1 teaspoon seasoned salt
2½ teaspoons Italian seasoning
½ teaspoon seasoned pepper

Chop artichoke hearts and mushrooms; place in a bowl. Add pimiento, celery, and green pepper, mixing well. Combine vinegar and remaining ingredients in a saucepan. Bring to a boil; remove from heat, and cool. Pour over vegetables, and mix well. Serve relish with crackers. Yield: 4¼ cups.
Jan Hobson,
Tampa, Florida.

Vegetables For Festive Menus

While it may take hours to prepare the turkey or ham and the dessert for your holiday meal, vegetables are usually best if they're cooked quickly, which helps save time. These recipes will make tasty additions to any of your holiday favorites.

VEGETABLE MEDLEY

2 tablespoons vegetable oil
3 medium carrots, scraped and cut into
  thin diagonal slices
2 stalks celery, cut into thin diagonal
  slices
1 green pepper, cut into 1-inch pieces
1 small onion, thinly sliced
1 tablespoon soy sauce
1 tablespoon catsup
1 tablespoon water

Heat oil in a large skillet; add vegetables, and sauté 4 minutes. Stir in remaining ingredients; cover, reduce heat to low, and cook 4 to 5 minutes or until vegetables are crisp-tender. Yield: 4 servings.   *Susan McLemore,*
Knoxville, Tennessee.

BRAISED CARROTS AND CELERY

2 tablespoons butter or margarine
6 medium carrots, cut into julienne strips
4 stalks celery, cut into julienne strips
1 medium onion, chopped
⅓ cup white wine or vermouth
½ teaspoon salt
⅛ teaspoon pepper
Sliced toasted almonds (optional)

Melt butter in a heavy saucepan. Add vegetables, wine, salt, and pepper; cover and cook over low heat 10 to 15 minutes or until crisp-tender. Garnish with almonds, if desired. Yield: 6 servings.   *Lilyan Oulehla,*
Bayonet Point, Florida.

MIXED VEGETABLE CASSEROLE

1 (10-ounce) package frozen broccoli
1 (8-ounce) package frozen brussels
  sprouts
1 (10-ounce) package frozen cauliflower
1 cup chopped celery
1 (10¾-ounce) can cream of mushroom
  soup, undiluted
1 (8-ounce) jar processed cheese spread

Cook broccoli, brussels sprouts, and cauliflower according to package directions; drain. Layer in a greased 8-inch square baking dish; top with celery. Combine soup and cheese spread; mix well. Spoon over vegetables.

Bake, uncovered, at 350° for 30 minutes or until thoroughly heated. Yield: 6 to 8 servings.   *Mrs. Harold Kling,*
Blackwell, Oklahoma.

BRUSSELS SPROUTS IN WINE BUTTER

1 cup chicken broth
2 (10-ounce) packages frozen brussels
  sprouts
⅓ cup dry white wine
1½ tablespoons butter or margarine
⅛ teaspoon white pepper

Bring chicken broth to a boil in a saucepan. Reduce heat, and add brussels sprouts; simmer 10 minutes. Stir in wine, butter, and pepper; simmer 5 minutes. Drain well. Yield: 6 servings.
Mary Lou Vaughn,
Dallas, Texas.

Tip: Always turn saucepan and skillet handles toward the back of the range to prevent accidents.

HOLIDAY PEAS AND RICE

¼ cup butter or margarine
1 cup uncooked regular rice
¼ teaspoon rubbed sage
2 (10¾-ounce) cans chicken broth, undiluted
1 cup water
1 (10-ounce) package frozen English peas
¼ cup diced pimiento

Melt butter in a saucepan; add rice and sage, and cook until golden brown, stirring occasionally. Add broth and water; bring to a boil. Cover, reduce heat, and simmer 15 minutes. Add peas; simmer 10 minutes. Stir in pimiento. Yield: 6 servings.

Mrs. Clayton Turner,
De Funiak Springs, Florida.

MICROWAVE COOKERY

Entrées Feature Convenience And Ease

When it comes to planning a menu, the entrée is usually the toughest decision. Preparation time required and the type of kitchen cookware needed often narrow your choices. But if you own a microwave oven, you may be surprised to learn how it can increase your entrée options. For example, for stir-fry recipes you can use the browning skillet in the microwave if you don't have a wok.

ORIENTAL BEEF WITH PEA PODS

1 pound boneless top round steak
1 clove garlic, minced
1 tablespoon cornstarch
2 tablespoons soy sauce
2 tablespoons dry sherry
1 teaspoon brown sugar
⅛ teaspoon ground ginger
2 tablespoons water
2 tablespoons vegetable oil
1 (6-ounce) package frozen pea pods
1 sweet red pepper, cut into strips
¼ pound fresh mushrooms, sliced

Partially freeze steak; slice diagonally across grain into 2½- x ½-inch strips. Combine garlic, cornstarch, soy sauce, and next 4 ingredients; add beef, toss well, and refrigerate 15 minutes.

Preheat an uncovered browning skillet in microwave oven at HIGH for 6 minutes. Add oil to hot skillet, tilting to coat surface. Drain beef, reserving marinade; add beef to preheated skillet, stirring well. Microwave at HIGH for 3 to 4 minutes or until beef is no longer pink, stirring well after 2 minutes. Set beef aside.

Place reserved marinade in a 1-quart casserole. Microwave, uncovered, at HIGH for 1½ to 2 minutes or until mixture boils and thickens, stirring twice. Stir in meat; set aside.

Place package of frozen pea pods in microwave oven; microwave at HIGH for 1½ to 2 minutes or until partially thawed. Stir pea pods, red pepper strips, and mushrooms into meat mixture. Microwave, uncovered, at HIGH 2 to 3 minutes or until vegetables are crisp-tender and mixture is hot, stirring twice. Yield: 4 servings.

SAUCY HAM LOAF

1 (8-ounce) can crushed pineapple, undrained
½ cup firmly packed brown sugar
1 tablespoon lemon juice
1½ teaspoons cornstarch
1 teaspoon dry mustard
1 pound ground cooked ham (about 4 cups)
½ pound ground pork (about 2 cups)
2 slices bread, cubed
⅓ cup chopped onion
2 eggs, beaten
¼ cup milk
1 teaspoon prepared horseradish

Drain pineapple, reserving ½ cup pineapple juice. Set pineapple aside. Combine reserved juice, brown sugar, lemon juice, cornstarch, and dry mustard in a 4-cup glass measure. Microwave at HIGH, uncovered, 3 to 4 minutes or until mixture is thickened and bubbly. Stir in ¼ cup pineapple; set sauce aside.

Combine remaining ¼ cup pineapple and remaining ingredients; mix well. Press ham mixture into an ungreased 9- x 5-inch microwave-safe loafpan. Cover with waxed paper, and microwave at HIGH for 7 minutes, rotating once. Insert temperature probe through waxed paper into center of loaf; set temperature probe at 155°. Microwave at HIGH until temperature reaches 155° (8 to 9 minutes). Drain off drippings. Cover loaf, and let stand 5 minutes or until temperature reaches 160°.

Slice loaf, and spoon reserved sauce over slices. Yield: 6 servings.

PINEAPPLE-CHICKEN KABOBS

4 chicken breast halves, skinned and boned
½ cup vegetable oil
¼ cup soy sauce
¼ cup dry white wine
1 tablespoon sesame seeds
2 tablespoons lemon juice
½ teaspoon garlic powder
½ teaspoon freshly ground ginger
8 fresh mushrooms
3 small zucchini, cut into 1-inch pieces
1 large red pepper, cut into 1-inch pieces
8 pearl onions
3 tablespoons water
1 (8-ounce) can pineapple chunks, drained

Cut chicken into 1-inch pieces. Combine next 7 ingredients in a large bowl; mix well. Add chicken; cover and marinate at least 8 hours.

Combine mushrooms, zucchini, red pepper, onions, and water in a microwave-safe bowl; cover and microwave at HIGH for 3 to 4 minutes. Drain vegetables, and set aside.

Drain chicken, reserving marinade. Alternate chicken, pineapple, and vegetables on 12-inch wooden skewers, packing loosely. Place kabobs on a microwave-safe roasting rack or in a shallow, microwave-safe baking dish. Cover with waxed paper, and microwave at HIGH for 6 to 8½ minutes, rearranging kabobs and basting with marinade at 2-minute intervals. Yield: 4 servings.

Beverages To Warm You

For some interesting hot beverages, these concoctions of coffee, tea, and milk are heated, spiked, and spiced. All are perfect as cool-weather bracers.

FRENCH HOT CHOCOLATE

4 (1-ounce) squares unsweetened chocolate
¼ cup water
4 cups milk
½ cup half-and-half
½ cup sugar
¼ teaspoon salt
¼ teaspoon ground mace
⅛ teaspoon ground allspice
1 teaspoon vanilla extract
½ teaspoon almond extract
⅛ teaspoon ground nutmeg
½ cup whipping cream, whipped

Combine chocolate and water in a heavy saucepan; stir over low heat until chocolate melts. Gradually add milk, half-and-half, sugar, salt, mace, and allspice. Cook over medium heat, stirring with a wire whisk, until mixture is hot. Stir in vanilla and almond flavorings. Pour into cups. Fold nutmeg into whipped cream. Top each cup with whipped cream. Yield: 5 cups.

D. Scott Irving,
Gainesville, Florida.

HOT PEPPERMINT FLIP

1 egg
⅔ cup whipping cream
1 tablespoon sugar
½ cup peppermint schnapps
½ cup brandy
3 cups hot strong coffee
Whipped cream (optional)
Peppermint sticks (optional)

Combine first 5 ingredients in container of an electric blender; blend at high speed for 30 seconds. Pour half of brandy mixture into a bowl; set aside. Gradually add half of coffee to blender; blend until frothy. Pour into individual cups; repeat procedure with reserved mixture and coffee. Garnish each serving with whipped cream and a peppermint stick, if desired. Yield: 5 cups.

Joanne W. Gross,
Lufkin, Texas.

ALMOND TEA

4 cups water
¾ to 1 cup sugar
¼ cup lemon juice
1½ cups hot strong tea
2⅔ cups pineapple juice
¼ cup instant orange breakfast drink mix
¾ teaspoon almond extract
¾ teaspoon vanilla extract

Combine water, sugar, and lemon juice in a Dutch oven; simmer 5 minutes. Add remaining ingredients; cook until thoroughly heated. Yield: 2 quarts.

Carol Barclay,
Portland, Texas.

HOT MOLASSES-MILK PUNCH

2 tablespoons molasses
2 tablespoons sugar
2 tablespoons water
½ teaspoon ground ginger
4 cups milk
½ cup dark rum
Freshly grated nutmeg

Combine first 4 ingredients in a 2-quart saucepan; cook over low heat, stirring until sugar dissolves. Gradually add milk; cook over low heat until thoroughly heated, stirring occasionally (do not boil). Remove from heat; stir in rum. Serve hot; sprinkle with nutmeg. Yield: 5 cups.

Carrie B. Bartlett,
Gallatin, Tennessee.

BRANDIED COFFEE NOG

2 egg yolks, slightly beaten
1½ cups milk
1 cup half-and-half
2 tablespoons light corn syrup
1 tablespoon plus 1 teaspoon instant coffee powder
⅓ cup brandy
¼ cup light corn syrup
¼ cup water
2 egg whites

Combine the first 5 ingredients in a large saucepan. Cook over medium heat, stirring constantly, until mixture thickens. Remove from heat; stir in brandy. Set aside.

Combine ¼ cup corn syrup and water in a small saucepan. Cook, uncovered, over high heat until boiling. Reduce heat, and simmer 2 minutes.

Beat egg whites (at room temperature) until soft peaks form. Gradually add the hot syrup to egg whites, beating until stiff peaks form. Whisk egg whites into coffee mixture. Serve immediately. Yield: 6 cups.

Patricia Andrews,
McAlester, Oklahoma.

Breakfast For Christmas Morning

Christmas morning is most meaningful when family traditions are observed. Some families say a special blessing. Others remember seasons past or significant events of the year. Some toast the holiday with champagne or sparkling cider. Your family may have a Christmas tradition all its own. Whatever it is, bring out the crystal, spread the table with food—and celebrate!

ORANGE FRENCH TOAST

2 eggs, beaten
1 cup orange juice
10 slices commercial raisin bread
1½ cups vanilla wafer crumbs (about 33 wafers)
2 to 3 tablespoons butter or margarine, divided
Additional butter (optional)
Maple syrup (optional)

Combine eggs and orange juice; beat well with a whisk. Quickly dip each slice of raisin bread into egg mixture, and coat bread on all sides with vanilla wafer crumbs.

Melt 1 tablespoon butter in a large skillet; arrange 3 or 4 slices bread in a single layer in skillet, and cook over medium heat 1 to 2 minutes on each side or until browned. Repeat with remaining bread slices, adding more butter as needed. Serve with butter and warm maple syrup, if desired. Yield: 5 servings.

Mrs. Harland J. Stone,
Ocala, Florida.

BRUNCH EGG CASSEROLE

¼ cup butter or margarine
¼ cup all-purpose flour
1 cup milk
1 cup half-and-half
4 cups (16 ounces) shredded sharp Cheddar cheese
¼ teaspoon dried whole thyme
¼ teaspoon dried whole marjoram
¼ teaspoon dried whole basil
18 hard-cooked eggs, sliced
¼ cup minced fresh parsley
1 pound bacon, cooked and crumbled
1½ cups breadcrumbs
2 tablespoons butter or margarine, melted

Melt ¼ cup butter in a heavy saucepan over low heat; add flour, stirring until smooth. Cook 1 minute, stirring constantly. Gradually add milk and half-and-half; cook over medium heat, stirring constantly, until mixture is thickened and bubbly. Add cheese and herbs, stirring until cheese melts.

Layer half each of egg slices, parsley, bacon, and cheese sauce in a lightly greased 13- x 9- x 2-inch baking dish. Repeat layers of ingredients.

Combine breadcrumbs and 2 tablespoons butter; sprinkle over casserole. Cover and refrigerate casserole 8 hours or overnight.

Remove from refrigerator; let stand 30 minutes. Bake, uncovered, at 350° for 30 minutes. Yield: 8 to 10 servings.

Thelma Peedin,
Newport News, Virginia.

COUNTRY EGGS

¼ cup finely chopped onion
¼ cup finely chopped green pepper
1 tablespoon butter or margarine, melted
6 eggs
¼ cup milk
¼ teaspoon salt
¼ teaspoon pepper
½ cup (2 ounces) shredded Cheddar
  cheese

Sauté onion and green pepper in butter in a large skillet until tender. Combine eggs, milk, salt, and pepper; mix well. Pour egg mixture into hot skillet, and cook slowly, stirring frequently. Remove from heat. Sprinkle with cheese; cover and let stand about 1 minute before serving. Yield: 4 servings.

Patricia Hill,
Roan Mountain, Tennessee.

APPLE PULL-APART BREAD

3 to 3½ cups all-purpose flour, divided
2 tablespoons sugar
1 package dry yeast
1 teaspoon salt
1 cup milk
½ cup butter or margarine, melted and
  divided
1 egg, beaten
1 large cooking apple, peeled and chopped
⅔ cup sugar
½ cup finely chopped pecans
½ teaspoon ground cinnamon
1 cup sifted powdered sugar
1 to 1½ tablespoons hot water
½ teaspoon vanilla extract

Combine 1 cup flour, 2 tablespoons sugar, yeast, and salt in a large bowl; blend well. Heat milk and 2 tablespoons butter to 120°; add egg. Blend well. Add milk mixture to flour mixture; beat at medium speed of an electric mixer until smooth. Stir in enough remaining flour to make a stiff dough.

Turn dough out onto a lightly floured surface, and knead 4 or 5 times or until smooth and elastic. Cover and let rest 20 minutes.

Combine apple, ⅔ cup sugar, pecans, and cinnamon; set aside.

Divide dough in half; cut each half into 16 equal pieces. Shape each piece into a ball, and roll out on a lightly floured surface to a 2½-inch circle. Place 1 teaspoon apple mixture in center of circle. Pinch edges together to seal and form a ball. Dip each ball into remaining melted butter.

Place 16 balls in a greased 10-inch tube pan. Sprinkle with ¼ cup apple mixture. Repeat procedure with remaining dough, apple mixture, and butter. Place remaining 16 balls over first layer of balls, and sprinkle evenly with remaining apple mixture.

Bake at 350° on lowest rack in oven for 40 minutes or until golden. Let cool 10 minutes; invert onto a serving plate.

Combine 1 cup powdered sugar, water, and vanilla, stirring until smooth. Drizzle over bread. Yield: one 10-inch coffee cake.

Mrs. Paul Raper,
Burgaw, North Carolina.

FRUIT COMPOTE

1 (16-ounce) can pear halves, undrained
  and chopped
1 (15¼-ounce) can pineapple chunks,
  undrained
1 (10-ounce) package frozen strawberries,
  thawed and undrained
1 (8¾-ounce) can fruit cocktail, undrained
2 bananas, sliced
2 apples, cored and cubed
½ cup maraschino cherries
1 (3½-ounce) package instant vanilla
  pudding mix

Combine fruit; blend. Stir in pudding mix. Cover; refrigerate 8 hours or overnight. Serve with a slotted spoon. Yield: 8 servings.

Pauline Lester,
Saluda, South Carolina.

From Our Kitchen To Yours

Cooks—both novice and experienced—are planning their holiday menus. To help in the preparation, we are answering our readers' most frequently asked questions. The home economists in our test kitchens hope these solutions will help you relax and enjoy your sensational dinner.

What is the safest way to thaw a turkey? The refrigerator is the safest method. Leave the turkey in its original wrapper, place in a pan, and refrigerate. A 4- to 12-pound turkey takes one to two days; a 12- to 20-pound turkey takes two to three days; and a 20- to 24-pound turkey takes three to four days to thaw.

How do you roast a turkey? First, rinse the turkey thoroughly, and pat dry. Sprinkle the cavity lightly with salt and pepper. Place turkey on a rack in a shallow roasting pan, and insert a meat thermometer into the thickest part of the thigh or breast, making sure thermometer does not touch the bone. Bake, uncovered, at 325°, without adding any water to the pan. Baste occasionally with pan drippings or melted butter. The turkey is done when the thermometer registers 180° to 185°; cooking time depends on weight.

How can I be sure my gravy won't lump? Follow our procedure. Place flour and water in a jar; shake until the flour is thoroughly dissolved. Slowly pour this mixture into the pan juices, and cook over medium heat until thickened, stirring constantly.

What is the easiest method for unmolding a gelatin salad? First, run a spatula around the edges to let air underneath. Then wet a dish towel with hot water, and wring out the excess moisture. Wrap the towel around the bottom and sides of the mold, and let it stand one or two minutes until the salad loosens slightly from the sides. Invert a serving plate over the salad; then carefully flip the mold and plate over. Lift the mold off. Repeat the procedure, if necessary, until the mold releases. Don't use the towel too long or the salad will begin to melt.

How can "skin" be prevented from forming on cooked puddings and pie fillings? Covering the surface with waxed paper or plastic wrap after removing from the heat will prevent the skinlike film from forming.

What can I do to keep my pie crust from becoming soggy? We suggest prebaking the pastry at 425° for five minutes before filling shell, or lightly brushing the pastry with a beaten egg white before baking.

Can marshmallows be substituted for marshmallow creme? Substituting these two different products is not recommended. They have different chemical properties and do not react the same in most recipes.

How can I make whipped cream garnishes ahead and prolong the fluffy texture? Using a large decorating tip, pipe the whipped cream onto a waxed paper-lined baking sheet, and place in the freezer. About 20 minutes before serving, remove the garnishes from freezer, and place on the dessert.

How do you make dipping chocolate used to coat bonbons, chocolate-covered cherries, and peanut butter balls? We use two methods in our kitchens. Melt semisweet chocolate and a small amount of shortening in the top of a double boiler. (Use 2 teaspoons shortening for every 6 ounces of chocolate morsels.) Dip the candies into the melted chocolate, and place on waxed paper. Confections coated using this method must be stored in the refrigerator.

For a chocolate coating that does not need refrigeration, melt chocolate almond bark in the top of a double boiler; dip candies, and place on waxed paper until firm. Store these confections in an airtight container.

My party punch needs a festive ice mold; how do I make one? For added flair in your punch bowl, use any metal mold, and arrange slices of citrus fruits and maraschino cherries on the bottom. Fill the mold one-third full with fruit juice or water, and freeze (this prevents the fruit from floating to the top). Gently fill mold with additional juice or water, and freeze until ready to use.

How can I make colored sugar to decorate cookies? Drop one to three drops of food coloring into a small jar; swirl the jar to coat the sides. Add ¼ to ⅓ cup granulated sugar, and shake vigorously until sugar is evenly coated.

How do I prevent fruitcake from drying out? Wrap the cake in a linen towel or cheesecloth dampened with brandy, bourbon, or your favorite spirits. Either place the wrapped cake in a cake tin or carefully enclose in aluminum foil; then refrigerate.

If your cake has already dried out, turn it upside down, and punch holes all over the bottom with a wooden pick. Drop small amounts of frozen orange juice concentrate over cake. After concentrate has melted, turn cake right side up; wrap and store as directed above.

Salad Savvy For Winter Meals

Don't settle for ordinary salads. With just a little savvy, you'll be mixing, molding, and garnishing congealed salads like a gourmet chef.

There are numerous types of garnishes to dress up salads. Of course, a crisp Bibb lettuce works well when used sparingly. Bright maraschino cherries, frosted grapes, or ingredients in the salad make excellent garnishes. Cut fans of apple slices, or try curling lemon or orange rinds and carrot strips in cold water. You can tie greenery with the rinds or simply use them alone atop a dollop of mayonnaise or sour cream.

If unmolding the salad is ever a problem, review your techniques. Make sure you dissolve the gelatin in a bowl other than the mold. When the salad has congealed and is ready for serving, wrap a hot towel around bottom and sides of mold; let stand one or two minutes, and invert the mold onto a serving platter. Lift mold off. See "From Our Kitchen to Yours," page 330.

CREAMY CARROT-NUT SALAD

1 (6-ounce) package orange-flavored gelatin
2 cups boiling water
1 (8-ounce) carton commercial sour cream
1 (15¼-ounce) can crushed pineapple in juice, undrained
2 cups finely shredded carrots
½ cup chopped pecans
Dash of salt
Mint or lettuce leaves (optional)
Carrot curl or orange rind (optional)
Mayonnaise (optional)

Dissolve gelatin in boiling water; add sour cream, and stir until well blended. Stir in pineapple, carrots, pecans, and salt. Spoon into a lightly oiled 6-cup mold or individual molds. Cover and chill until firm. Garnish with remaining ingredients, if desired. Yield: 9 servings.
Lauren Salter,
Marietta, Georgia.

SANGRÍA SALAD

2 envelopes unflavored gelatin
1½ cups water
½ cup sugar
1½ cups rosé
1 cup orange juice
2 tablespoons lemon juice
3 oranges, peeled and sectioned
1 large apple, cored and chopped
1 cup seedless red grapes, halved
Lettuce leaves
Additional red grapes (optional)

Sprinkle gelatin over water in a saucepan; let stand 5 minutes. Add sugar; place over medium heat, stirring until dissolved. Remove from heat. Add rosé, orange juice, and lemon juice, stirring well; chill until the consistency of unbeaten egg white. Fold in fruit; spoon into a lightly oiled 6-cup mold. Chill until firm. Unmold onto lettuce-lined plate to serve. Garnish with additional grapes, if desired. Yield: 12 servings.
Mrs. John R. Allen,
Dallas, Texas.

SPARKLING CITRUS MOLD

2 envelopes unflavored gelatin
1 (12-ounce) can lemon-lime carbonated beverage
1 (15¼-ounce) can crushed pineapple, undrained
¾ cup orange sections, chopped and undrained
Lettuce leaves
Sour Cream Dressing
Chopped pecans

Sprinkle gelatin over lemon-lime beverage in a saucepan; let stand 1 minute. Cook over low heat, stirring constantly, until gelatin dissolves. Stir in pineapple and orange sections; pour into an oiled 5-cup mold. Chill until firm. Unmold salad on lettuce leaves; serve with Sour Cream Dressing and chopped pecans. Yield: 10 servings.

Sour Cream Dressing:

1 (8-ounce) carton commercial sour cream
¼ cup honey
1 teaspoon ground cinnamon

Combine all ingredients; mix well. Yield: 1 cup. *Frances Pearson Bowles,*
Mableton, Georgia.

APPLE CRUNCH SALAD

1 (6-ounce) package lemon-flavored gelatin
2 cups boiling water
½ cup cold water
¼ cup plus 2 tablespoons lemon juice
¼ teaspoon salt
1 cup diced celery
1 cup diced red Delicious apple, unpeeled
½ cup golden raisins
½ cup (2 ounces) shredded American cheese

Dissolve gelatin in boiling water; add cold water, lemon juice, and salt. Chill until the consistency of unbeaten egg white. Stir in remaining ingredients. Pour into a lightly oiled 8-inch square dish. Cover and chill until firm. Yield: 9 servings.
Louise Denmon,
Silsbee, Texas.

Fresh Ideas For Leftover Ham Or Turkey

If you find yourself stuck with leftover ham or turkey, don't despair. Instead, take a look at all the tasty ways our readers serve them.

For starters, try using leftover ham to make Easy Ham Stir-Fry. This tasty recipe is a winner that teams ham with onion, green pepper, celery, and rice for a filling main dish that your family will love.

If you're looking for a fresh way to use leftover turkey, make Layered Turkey Salad. You start with a base of lettuce and add peas, water chestnuts, crunchy celery, and green pepper. After the turkey is sprinkled on, it's covered with mayonnaise, cheese, and bacon.

EASY HAM STIR-FRY

2 tablespoons vegetable oil
1 cup diagonally sliced celery
½ cup chopped onion
½ cup chopped green pepper
2 cups cubed cooked ham
Dash of garlic powder
Freshly ground pepper to taste
2 cups cooked rice
2 slices bacon, cooked and crumbled
2 tablespoons soy sauce

Pour oil around top of preheated wok, coating sides; allow to heat at medium high (325°) for 1 minute. Add celery, onion, and green pepper; stir-fry 2 minutes or until vegetables are crisp-tender. Add ham, garlic powder, and pepper to vegetables; stir-fry 3 to 4 minutes. Add rice, and stir-fry 2 to 3 minutes. Stir in bacon and soy sauce. Yield: 4 to 6 servings.

Patsy M. Smith,
Lampasas, Texas.

TOP-OF-STOVE SUPPER

1 tablespoon butter or margarine
2 potatoes, thinly sliced
½ teaspoon salt
¼ teaspoon pepper
1 tablespoon diced onion
1 tablespoon diced green pepper
1 cup diced cooked ham
2 eggs, slightly beaten
¼ cup (1 ounce) shredded Cheddar cheese

Melt butter in a large heavy skillet. Layer next 6 ingredients in skillet. Cover and cook over low heat 30 minutes. Pour eggs over mixture; cook an additional 15 minutes. Top with cheese; cover and cook 5 minutes or until cheese melts. Yield: 3 to 4 servings.

Mrs. Jack Fuqua,
Roanoke, Virginia.

LAYERED TURKEY SALAD

4 cups torn iceberg lettuce
1 (10-ounce) package frozen peas, thawed and drained
1 (8-ounce) can sliced water chestnuts, drained
1 large stalk celery, sliced
½ cup chopped onion
½ cup chopped green pepper
2 cups coarsely chopped cooked turkey
1½ cups mayonnaise
1 tablespoon sugar
1½ cups (6 ounces) shredded Swiss cheese
8 slices bacon, cooked and crumbled

Layer first 7 ingredients in a 13- x 9- x 2-inch dish. Combine mayonnaise and sugar; spread over turkey. Top with cheese and bacon. Cover; chill. Yield: 8 servings.

Mrs. James S. Stanton,
Richmond, Virginia.

CURRIED TURKEY SOUP

¼ cup chopped onion
¼ cup butter or margarine, melted
1 teaspoon curry powder
2 cups chicken broth
1½ cups water
1 cup diced potatoes
½ cup diced carrots
½ cup diagonally sliced celery
¼ teaspoon pepper
1½ cups diced cooked turkey
½ (10-ounce) package frozen French-style green beans
1 tablespoon chopped fresh parsley
½ teaspoon dried whole oregano
3 tablespoons all-purpose flour
⅔ cup half-and-half

Sauté onion in butter in a Dutch oven until transparent. Stir in curry powder; cook 2 minutes. Add broth and next 5 ingredients; bring to a boil. Reduce heat; simmer 15 minutes. Stir in turkey, beans, parsley, and oregano. Continue cooking 15 minutes or until tender.

Combine flour and half-and-half; stir until smooth. Add to soup mixture, and cook until thickened. Yield: 6 servings.

Jamie Freeman,
Orlando, Florida.

TURKEY-AND-BROCCOLI CASSEROLE

1 medium onion, chopped
1 medium-size green pepper, chopped
2 stalks celery, chopped
3 tablespoons butter or margarine, melted
1 (10-ounce) package frozen broccoli spears
1½ cups coarsely chopped cooked turkey
1 cup cooked rice
1 (10¾-ounce) can cream of mushroom soup, undiluted
1 (8-ounce) can sliced water chestnuts, drained
1 cup (4 ounces) shredded Cheddar cheese
½ cup (2 ounces) shredded jalapeño cheese
½ teaspoon salt
¼ teaspoon pepper

Sauté onion, green pepper, and celery in butter in a large skillet until vegetables are tender; set aside.

Cook broccoli according to package directions; drain. Cut broccoli spears in half; arrange in a greased shallow 2-quart casserole.

Combine sautéed vegetables and remaining ingredients; spoon over broccoli. Bake, uncovered, at 375° for 30 minutes or until heated. Yield: 4 to 6 servings.

Mrs. L. C. Morton,
Gallion, Alabama.

Hot Cocoa, Instantly

When the weather's cool enough to cozy up to a crackling fire, it's nice to have a cup of steaming cocoa between your palms. That's especially true if you can keep a quick mix, such as Instant Cocoa Mix, on hand. When you serve this cocoa, try adding a cinnamon-stick stirrer to each cup to give it a slightly spicy taste.

INSTANT COCOA MIX

2¾ cups instant nonfat dry milk powder
1½ cups instant cocoa mix for milk
½ cup nondairy coffee creamer
½ cup powdered sugar
1 cup miniature marshmallows

Combine ingredients in a large bowl, and mix well. Store cocoa mix in an airtight container.

To serve, place ⅓ cup mix in a cup. Add 1 cup boiling water, and stir well. Yield: 5 cups mix.

Libby Dillon,
Boone, North Carolina.

Garnished with parsley and a pretty red bow, Festive Sandwich Wreath is an eye-catching party food that actually offers two kinds of party sandwiches.

He Adds Flair To Home Cooking

If you drop in on junior high music teacher Charles Humpston in Jonesborough, Tennessee, you'll find him spooning into a tall glass of buttermilk and cornbread just as often as you'll find him whipping up one of the artfully prepared meals he's famous for.

To Charles, being "fancy" means coming up with his own recipes, garnishing them as an artist would paint a canvas, and presenting them to his family and friends to enjoy. The recipes below are some of his favorites. See if they don't become yours, as well.

Festive Sandwich Wreath

Festive Sandwich Wreath is always a favorite at parties hosted by Virginia Gentry and husband, Mack, of Hospitality Farms in Sutherlin, Virginia.

This is Virginia's original recipe. An accomplished cook, she recognized a good idea when she saw a sandwich wreath using white bread. Virginia then put her food know-how to work and came up with this attractive party rye-and-pumpernickel version.

FESTIVE SANDWICH WREATH

1 (4½-ounce) can deviled ham
¼ cup finely chopped celery
1½ teaspoons Worcestershire sauce
1 (4¾-ounce) can chicken spread
¼ cup finely chopped apple
1 tablespoon commercial sour cream
Butter or margarine, softened
20 slices party rye bread
20 slices party pumpernickel bread
Parsley

Combine first 3 ingredients in a small bowl; mix well. Chill 1 hour. Combine chicken spread, apple, and sour cream; mix well. Chill 1 hour.

Spread butter on one side of each bread slice. Spread 10 slices of rye bread with ham mixture; top with pumpernickel bread slice.

Spread 10 slices of pumpernickel bread with chicken mixture; top with rye bread slice.

Arrange sandwiches vertically around rim of a 9-inch plate, alternating breads and fillings. Garnish with parsley. A red bow may be added, if desired. Yield: 20 appetizer servings.

Tip: Make certain your refrigerator or freezer is cold enough. Refrigerator temperature should be maintained at 34°F to 40°F, and freezer temperature at 0°F or lower. To allow the cold air to circulate freely, make sure that foods are not overcrowded.

FETTUCCINE SUPREME

1½ cups water
½ pound small unpeeled fresh shrimp
½ cup shredded carrots
6 ounces uncooked fettuccine
½ cup butter or margarine
1 (8-ounce) carton commercial
   sour cream
Freshly ground pepper

Bring water to a boil; add shrimp, and cook 3 to 5 minutes. Drain well; rinse with cold water. Chill. Peel and devein shrimp; set aside.

Steam carrots over boiling water 5 minutes; set aside.

Cook fettuccine according to package directions; drain. Add butter, stirring until melted. Stir in sour cream, carrots, and shrimp; spoon into serving dish. Sprinkle with pepper; serve immediately. Yield: 6 servings.

ARTICHOKE SALAD

1 head iceberg lettuce, shredded
1 (14-ounce) can artichoke hearts, drained
   and quartered
1 (14-ounce) can hearts of palm, drained
   and sliced
1 small purple onion, sliced and separated
   into rings
1 (2-ounce) jar diced pimiento, drained
¼ cup freshly grated Parmesan cheese
Commercial Italian salad dressing

Line a large platter or individual salad plates with lettuce. Arrange artichoke hearts, hearts of palm, onion, and pimiento over lettuce. Sprinkle with cheese. Serve with salad dressing. Yield: 8 servings.

CUSTARD-FILLED
ACORN SQUASH

3 small acorn squash
1 (3-ounce) package cream cheese,
    softened
¼ cup firmly packed brown sugar
3 eggs
2 tablespoons milk
2 tablespoons amaretto
½ teaspoon vanilla extract
¼ cup sliced almonds
Fresh parsley sprigs (optional)
Green grapes (optional)

Cut squash in half lengthwise; remove seeds. Place cut side down in a shallow baking pan, and add boiling water to a depth of ½ inch. Cover and bake at 325° for 25 minutes.

Combine cream cheese, brown sugar, eggs, milk, amaretto, and vanilla; beat at medium speed of an electric mixer until smooth. Uncover squash; fill squash halves evenly with cream cheese mixture. Sprinkle with almonds. Bake, uncovered, 20 minutes or until custard is set. Remove to serving platter; garnish with parsley and grapes, if desired. Yield: 6 servings.

MILE-HIGH CHEESECAKE

1¼ cups graham cracker crumbs
⅓ cup butter or margarine, melted
4 (8-ounce) packages cream cheese,
    softened
1¼ cups sugar
2 teaspoons all-purpose flour
4 eggs
2 teaspoons milk
1 teaspoon grated orange rind
1 teaspoon grated lemon rind
Dash of salt
Whipped cream
Chocolate shavings
Mint leaves (optional)
Orange wedges (optional)

Combine graham cracker crumbs and butter, mixing well. Press into bottom and up sides of a buttered 8-inch springform pan; set aside.

Beat cream cheese at medium speed of an electric mixer until light and fluffy. Gradually add sugar and flour, mixing well. Add eggs, one at a time, beating well after each addition. Add

milk, orange and lemon rind, and salt; mix well. Spoon into prepared pan; bake at 375° for 15 minutes. Reduce oven temperature to 300°; bake 1 hour.

Turn off oven; allow cheesecake to cool in oven 30 minutes. Let cool to room temperature; refrigerate 8 hours. Carefully remove sides of springform pan; spread top with whipped cream, and sprinkle with chocolate shavings. Garnish serving plate with mint leaves and orange wedges, if desired. Yield: 10 to 12 servings.

FREEZER FRUIT SHERBET

4 medium-size bananas
1 (20-ounce) can crushed pineapple,
    undrained
1 (16-ounce) bottle maraschino cherries,
    undrained
1 (6-ounce) can frozen orange juice
    concentrate, undiluted
1 cup milk
¼ cup lemon juice
½ cup sugar

Combine first 3 ingredients in container of an electric blender; blend until smooth. Pour mixture into large mixing bowl. Combine remaining ingredients in container of electric blender.

Blend until smooth, and add to blended fruit. Mix all ingredients well; cover and freeze until firm. Yield: about 2 quarts.

AMARETTO RICE PUDDING

3 eggs, beaten
⅔ cup sugar
¼ teaspoon salt
2 cups milk, scalded
1½ cups cooked rice
¼ teaspoon ground cinnamon
¼ cup amaretto
1 teaspoon vanilla extract
¼ teaspoon ground nutmeg

Combine first 3 ingredients in a medium mixing bowl. Slowly add scalded milk, stirring constantly. Stir in rice, cinnamon, amaretto, and vanilla.

Spoon mixture into a buttered 1½-quart baking dish. Place dish in a larger shallow pan; add 1 inch of water to pan. Bake at 325° for 1 hour.

Stir pudding mixture; sprinkle evenly with nutmeg, and bake an additional 30 minutes. Remove dish from pan; let cool. Yield: 6 servings.

Cookies
With Spirits

Friends of Mrs. Jim Shipp in Memphis, Tennessee, have looked forward to her Christmas gift of Bourbon Fruit Cookies for 30 years. The cookies are ideal for gift-giving because they pack well and stay fresh for a long time.

In fact, if you like to do your holiday baking early, Mrs. Shipp's cookies can help you get ahead. It's the bourbon in them that keeps the cookies fresh and moist tasting, she says. "I really think that they taste better after they've aged awhile."

BOURBON FRUIT COOKIES

1 pound red candied cherries, chopped
1 pound green candied pineapple, chopped
1 pound pecan halves, chopped
1 (15-ounce) package golden raisins
3 cups all-purpose flour, divided
1 teaspoon baking soda
1 teaspoon ground cinnamon
1 teaspoon ground nutmeg
1 teaspoon ground cloves
½ cup butter or margarine, softened
½ cup firmly packed brown sugar
4 eggs
½ cup bourbon
3 tablespoons milk

Combine cherries, pineapple, pecans, raisins, and ½ cup flour; toss well to coat. Set aside.

Combine remaining flour, soda, and spices; set aside.

Cream butter; gradually add sugar, beating until light and fluffy. Add eggs, and beat well. Add dry ingredients, bourbon, and milk; mix well. Stir in fruit mixture.

Drop dough by teaspoonfuls onto lightly greased cookie sheets. Bake at 300° for 20 minutes. Yield: 9 dozen.

Cooked Candies
Feature Pecans

If pecan candies are a tradition at your home this time of year, you'll want to try New Orleans-Style Pralines and bite-size slices of Chocolate-Nut Log Candy to celebrate the season.

To cook these candies, you may want to use a candy thermometer to get the most accurate temperature reading. For these recipes, cook the mixture to the soft ball stage—between 234° and 240°.

The temperature we've listed for each recipe is the one that gave us the best results. Be sure to watch the temperature of the mixture carefully while it's cooking. If it gets too hot, the candy will be dry and crumbly. If it isn't cooked long enough, the finished product will be runny and sticky.

CHOCOLATE-NUT LOG CANDY

1⅓ cups sugar
¼ teaspoon salt
2 tablespoons cocoa
¾ cup milk
1 tablespoon light corn syrup
2 tablespoons butter or margarine
1 teaspoon vanilla extract
½ cup finely chopped pecans

Combine sugar, salt, and cocoa in a heavy saucepan; mix well. Gradually stir in milk and syrup. Cook over medium heat, stirring occasionally, until soft ball stage (236°). Remove from heat; stir in butter and vanilla. Pour onto a buttered 15- x 10- x 1-inch jellyroll pan; let cool 10 minutes.

With buttered hands, knead candy occasionally for 10 to 15 minutes or until cool enough to hold its form. Shape into a 12- x 1¼-inch rope; roll in pecans. Wrap in buttered plastic wrap. Let candy stand at room temperature for 1 hour or until completely cooled. Cut into ½-inch slices. Yield: 2 dozen.
Mrs. Ben Killion,
Fayetteville, Arkansas.

NEW ORLEANS-STYLE PRALINES

1½ cups sugar
1½ cups firmly packed brown sugar
1 cup evaporated milk
¼ cup butter or margarine
2 cups pecan halves
1 teaspoon vanilla extract

Combine sugar and milk in a Dutch oven; bring to a boil, stirring occasionally. Cook over medium heat, stirring frequently, until mixture reaches 228°. Add butter and pecans, and continue cooking, stirring constantly, until mixture reaches soft ball stage (236°). Remove from heat, and stir in vanilla. Beat vigorously with a wooden spoon until mixture just begins to thicken. Working rapidly, drop by rounded tablespoonfuls onto greased waxed paper; let stand until firm. Yield: 3 dozen.
Rose Alleman,
Prairieville, Louisiana.

Oranges Add Tangy Flavor

From entrées to desserts, oranges make a tasty contribution. The juice, pulp, and orange rind all add to the refreshing flavors of these recipes.

When only the juice or pulp is used, grate the colored rind before cutting the orange, and freeze it for later use. Avoid using the white portion of the rind because it is bitter. Orange rind adds zest to baked items, sauces, meats, and soups. But use it sparingly; a teaspoon goes a long way.

After juicing an orange, freeze the hollow shell. It can be used as a container for sauces. After collecting several shells, use them to serve ice cream, mashed sweet potatoes, or salads.

Some recipes use oranges sliced to include the membrane that separates the sections. This membrane contains nutrients that are saved by slicing the fruit rather than sectioning it.

ORANGE-CRANBERRY PORK CHOPS

6 (¾-inch-thick) pork chops
1 tablespoon vegetable shortening, melted
2 tablespoons water
1 teaspoon salt
¼ cup sugar
¼ cup light corn syrup
2 tablespoons grated orange rind
2 cups orange sections, including juice
2 cups fresh cranberries
Hot cooked rice

Trim fat from pork chops; brown chops in shortening in a large skillet. Drain, if necessary. Add water and salt; cover and cook over medium heat 45 to 50 minutes or until chops are done. Add sugar and next 4 ingredients, and cook an additional 5 minutes. Serve over rice. Yield: 6 servings.
Nancy Swinney,
Tallahassee, Florida.

SWEET POTATO DELIGHT

8 medium-size sweet potatoes (about 4½ pounds)
3 oranges
¼ cup plus 1 tablespoon butter or margarine, melted
¾ cup firmly packed brown sugar
3 tablespoons cornstarch
½ teaspoon salt
2 cups orange juice
½ cup chopped pecans

Place sweet potatoes in a Dutch oven; cover with water. Bring to a boil over medium heat; cover, reduce heat, and simmer 10 to 12 minutes or until fork tender. Drain potatoes and let cool. Peel potatoes, and cut into ½-inch slices; set aside.

Grate 2 tablespoons rind from oranges; set rind aside. Peel oranges, and cut into ½-inch slices. Layer half each of sweet potato slices and orange slices in a lightly greased 13- x 9- x 2-inch baking dish. Repeat layers.

Combine butter, brown sugar, cornstarch, and salt in a heavy saucepan; blend well. Gradually add orange juice; cook over medium heat, stirring constantly, until mixture is thickened and bubbly. Stir in orange rind; pour over sweet potatoes and oranges. Sprinkle with pecans. Bake at 350° for 30 minutes. Yield: 8 to 10 servings.
Rublelene Singleton,
Scotts Hill, Tennessee.

CITRUS SALAD BOWL

2 oranges
1 grapefruit, peeled and sectioned
1 (20-ounce) can pineapple chunks, undrained
½ cup commercial sour cream
1 tablespoon brown sugar
¼ teaspoon ground ginger
Dash of ground nutmeg
Lettuce leaves
1 large avocado, peeled and thinly sliced
¼ cup chopped pecans, toasted

Grate 1 teaspoon rind from oranges; set rind aside. Peel oranges, and cut into ½-inch slices; quarter each slice. Combine orange slices, grapefruit, and pineapple in a medium bowl; cover and chill fruit.

Combine sour cream, brown sugar, 1 teaspoon reserved orange rind, ginger, and nutmeg; set aside.

To serve, arrange lettuce leaves on individual salad plates. Place avocado slices on lettuce. Drain fruit mixture; spoon fruit over avocado slices. Top with dressing, and sprinkle with pecans. Yield: 4 to 6 servings.
Sara A. McCullough,
Broaddus, Texas.

ORANGE MERINGUE CAKE

2¼ cups sifted cake flour
1½ cups sugar
1 tablespoon baking powder
1 teaspoon salt
5 egg yolks
1 tablespoon grated orange
    rind
¾ cup orange juice
½ cup vegetable oil
7 egg whites
½ teaspoon cream of tartar
Orange Filling
Meringue Frosting

Combine first 4 ingredients in a large bowl. Combine egg yolks, orange rind, orange juice, and oil; add to dry ingredients, and beat at medium speed of an electric mixer until smooth.

Beat egg whites (at room temperature) until foamy; add cream of tartar, and beat until stiff. Fold egg yolk mixture gently into egg whites; blend well. Spoon batter into an ungreased 10-inch tube pan. Bake at 325° for 1 hour or until cake springs back when lightly touched with fingers. Invert cake; cool 1 hour or until completely cooled.

Remove cake from pan, and slice into 5 equal layers. Place bottom layer of cake on an ovenproof platter or wooden board; spread with one-fourth of Orange Filling. Repeat with remaining layers and filling, ending with cake on top. Spread top and sides with Meringue Frosting. Bake at 400° for 5 minutes or until lightly browned. Yield: one 10-inch tube cake.

Orange Filling:

1 cup sugar
½ cup cornstarch
1 teaspoon salt
3 cups orange juice
¼ cup lime juice
6 egg yolks, beaten
1 tablespoon grated orange
    rind

Combine sugar, cornstarch, and salt in a medium saucepan; gradually stir in orange juice and lime juice. Cook over medium heat, stirring constantly, until mixture thickens and boils.

Slowly stir a small amount of hot mixture into egg yolks; add to remaining hot mixture, stirring constantly. Boil 1 minute longer, stirring constantly.

Remove saucepan from heat, and stir in grated orange rind; let cool completely. Yield: 3½ cups.

Meringue Frosting:

5 egg whites
1 teaspoon cream of tartar
¾ cup sugar

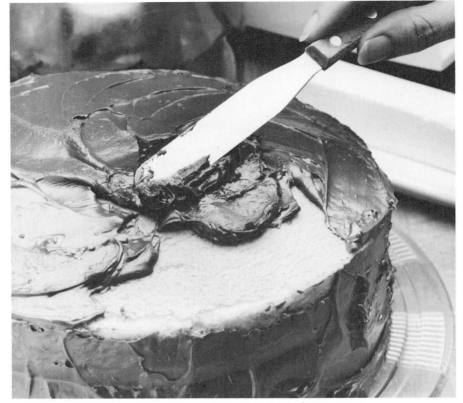

Spread Fluffy Chocolate Frosting onto any two-layer cake. Cocoa gives it a rich chocolate flavor and eliminates the extra trouble of melting chocolate.

Beat egg whites (at room temperature) and cream of tartar until foamy. Gradually add sugar, 1 tablespoon at a time, beating until stiff peaks form. Yield: enough for one 10-inch cake.

Sandra Russell,
Gainesville, Florida.

Processor-Quick Frostings And Toppings

If a fine cloud of powdered sugar coats your kitchen when you mix up a frosting, then you'll welcome the food processor versions here. Powdered sugar is easily mixed with other ingredients all at once in the food processor for our cream cheese and chocolate frostings, simplifying one of the steps in making frostings.

And because sweet sauces are increasingly popular with unfrosted cakes, we've included some dessert toppings that are just suited for slices of pound cake, angel food cake, or even fresh fruit. The processor gives toppings a creamy texture in a matter of seconds.

As with most processor recipes, there's no need to soften cream cheese for frosting and dessert-topping recipes; cut it into small chunks right from the refrigerator. For the smoothest consistency, it will help to soften butter before mixing.

FLUFFY CHOCOLATE FROSTING

½ cup butter, softened
4 cups sifted powdered sugar
¾ cup cocoa
½ cup evaporated milk
1 teaspoon Grand Marnier or other
    orange-flavored liqueur

Position knife blade in food processor bowl; add all ingredients in order listed. Top with cover; pulse 2 or 3 times. Process about 1 minute, scraping sides of processor bowl occasionally. Yield: 2 cups or enough for one 2-layer cake.

Joanie Meyer,
Okarche, Oklahoma.

ORANGE DESSERT SAUCE

1 (3-ounce) package cream cheese, cubed
2 tablespoons sugar
¼ cup commercial sour cream
1 (11-ounce) can mandarin oranges,
    drained and divided
Mint leaves (optional)

Position knife blade in food processor bowl. Combine first 3 ingredients in processor bowl; process 1 minute, scraping sides of processor bowl occasionally. Add ¼ cup mandarin oranges, and pulse 3 times; chill. Arrange remaining mandarin oranges over slices of cake; spoon sauce over oranges. Garnish with mint leaves, if desired. Yield: ¾ cup.
Mrs. Bruce Fowler,
Woodruff, South Carolina.

CREAM CHEESE FROSTING

1 (8-ounce) package cream cheese, cubed
1 tablespoon butter or margarine
1 (16-ounce) package powdered sugar,
    sifted
½ teaspoon vanilla extract

Position knife blade in food processor bowl; add all ingredients. Top with cover, and process 15 seconds or until well creamed, scraping sides of processor bowl occasionally. Yield: 1¾ cups or enough frosting for one 13- x 9- x 2-inch cake.
Katy Holt,
Arkadelphia, Arkansas.

PROCESSOR
DEVONSHIRE SAUCE

2 lemons
1 (3⅜-ounce) package vanilla instant
    pudding mix, divided
2 (3-ounce) packages cream cheese, cubed
2 cups milk

Cut four 4-inch strips from lemons. Extract juice from lemons; set aside. Position knife blade in food processor bowl; add lemon strips. Top with cover, and process 1 minute. Add 1 teaspoon instant pudding mix to processor bowl; process 1 minute or until lemon rind is finely chopped. Add cream cheese and process until smooth. Gradually pour milk and reserved lemon juice through food chute with processor running. Add remaining pudding mix, and process 1 minute. Chill sauce. Serve over fresh fruit. Yield: 3 cups.
Margaret L. Hunter,
Princeton, Kentucky.

One Of The Season's Best

We can think of no better way to celebrate the Christmas season than with Elegant Amaretto-Chocolate Mousse. Full of rich chocolate and almond flavor, it's simply impossible to resist. It's so elegant that it just may be the hit of the holiday season.

ELEGANT
AMARETTO-CHOCOLATE
MOUSSE

1 (6-ounce) package semisweet chocolate
    morsels
18 whole blanched almonds
½ cup amaretto
2 envelopes unflavored gelatin
¼ cup water
4 eggs, separated
⅓ cup sugar
2 cups milk
2 cups whipping cream, whipped and
    divided
2 (3-ounce) packages ladyfingers, split

Place chocolate in top of a double boiler; bring water to a boil. Reduce heat to low; cook until chocolate melts. Dip larger end of each almond into chocolate, and place on a waxed paper-lined cookie sheet. Chill until chocolate is firm.
Gradually stir amaretto into remaining melted chocolate; set aside.
Combine gelatin and water in a medium saucepan. Beat egg yolks slightly;

This rich chocolate mousse is irresistible.

stir into gelatin mixture. Add sugar and milk, mixing well. Cook over low heat, stirring until slightly thickened. Remove from heat, and stir in chocolate mixture. Chill until consistency of unbeaten egg white.
Beat egg whites (at room temperature) until stiff peaks form. Set aside 1 cup whipped cream for garnish. Fold egg whites and remaining 3 cups whipped cream into chocolate mixture.
Line bottom and sides of a 9-inch springform pan with ladyfingers. Spoon chocolate mixture into pan. Cover and chill until firm.
Place dessert on a serving platter, and remove rim from pan. Garnish with remaining cup of whipped cream and chocolate-dipped almonds. Yield: 14 to 16 servings.

Serve Chicken Nuggets

Our recipe for Lemon-Chicken Nuggets makes fried chicken, a Southern favorite, even more versatile as an appetizer. Although you can buy bite-size fried chicken pieces almost everywhere now, you'll want to try this version for the tangy lemon flavor it offers.

LEMON-CHICKEN NUGGETS

1 cup milk
¼ cup lemon juice
½ teaspoon salt
½ teaspoon paprika
¼ teaspoon pepper
4 chicken breast halves, skinned and
    boned
1 cup all-purpose flour
Vegetable oil
Honey (optional)
Barbecue sauce (optional)

Combine milk, lemon juice, salt, paprika, and pepper in a mixing bowl, mixing well. Cut chicken into 1-inch pieces; marinate in milk mixture 8 hours. Remove chicken from marinade, and dredge in flour.
Heat 1½ inches oil in a large heavy skillet to 350°. Fry 1 minute on each side or until golden brown. Drain on paper towels. Serve with honey or barbecue sauce, if desired. Yield: 8 appetizer servings.
Lockie Burge,
Sulphur Rock, Arkansas.

Appendices

EQUIVALENT WEIGHTS AND MEASURES

Food	Weight or Count	Measure or Yield
Apples	1 pound (3 medium)	3 cups sliced
Bacon	8 slices cooked	½ cup crumbled
Bananas	1 pound (3 medium)	2½ cups sliced, or about 2 cups mashed
Bread	1 pound	12 to 16 slices
	About 1½ slices	1 cup soft crumbs
Butter or margarine	1 pound	2 cups
	¼ -pound stick	½ cup
Cabbage	1 pound head	4½ cups shredded
Candied fruit or peels	½ pound	1¼ cups chopped
Carrots	1 pound	3 cups shredded
Cheese, American or Cheddar	1 pound	About 4 cups shredded
cottage	1 pound	2 cups
cream	3 - ounce package	6 tablespoons
Chocolate morsels	6 - ounce package	1 cup
Cocoa	1 pound	4 cups
Coconut, flaked or shredded	1 pound	5 cups
Coffee	1 pound	80 tablespoons (40 cups perked)
Corn	2 medium ears	1 cup kernels
Cornmeal	1 pound	3 cups
Crab, in shell	1 pound	¾ to 1 cup flaked
Crackers, chocolate wafers	19 wafers	1 cup crumbs
graham crackers	14 squares	1 cup fine crumbs
saltine crackers	28 crackers	1 cup finely crushed
vanilla wafers	22 wafers	1 cup finely crushed
Cream, whipping	1 cup (½ pint)	2 cups whipped
Dates, pitted	1 pound	3 cups chopped
	8 - ounce package	1½ cups chopped
Eggs	5 large	1 cup
whites	8 to 11	1 cup
yolks	12 to 14	1 cup
Flour, all-purpose	1 pound	3½ cups
cake	1 pound	4¾ to 5 cups sifted
whole wheat	1 pound	3½ cups unsifted
Green pepper	1 large	1 cup diced
Lemon	1 medium	2 to 3 tablespoons juice; 2 teaspoons grated rind
Lettuce	1 pound head	6¼ cups torn
Lime	1 medium	1½ to 2 tablespoons juice; 1½ teaspoons grated rind
Macaroni	4 ounces (1 cup)	2¼ cups cooked
Marshmallows	11 large	1 cup
	10 miniature	1 large marshmallow
Marshmallows, miniature	½ pound	4½ cups
Milk, evaporated	5.33 - ounce can	⅔ cup
evaporated	13 - ounce can	1⅝ cups
sweetened condensed	14 - ounce can	1¼ cups
Mushrooms	3 cups raw (8 ounces)	1 cup sliced cooked
Nuts, almonds	1 pound	1 to 1¾ cups nutmeats
	1 pound shelled	3½ cups nutmeats
peanuts	1 pound	2¼ cups nutmeats
	1 pound shelled	3 cups
pecans	1 pound	2¼ cups nutmeats
	1 pound shelled	4 cups
walnuts	1 pound	1⅔ cups nutmeats
	1 pound shelled	4 cups

Food	Weight or Count	Measure or Yield
Oats, quick-cooking	1 cup	1¾ cups cooked
Onion	1 medium	½ cup chopped
Orange	1 medium	⅓ cup juice; 2 tablespoons grated rind
Peaches	2 medium	1 cup sliced
Pears	2 medium	1 cup sliced
Potatoes, white	3 medium	2 cups cubed cooked or 1¾ cups mashed
sweet	3 medium	3 cups sliced
Raisins, seedless	1 pound	3 cups
Rice, long-grain	1 cup	3 to 4 cups cooked
pre-cooked	1 cup	2 cups cooked
Shrimp, raw in shell	1½ pounds	2 cups (¾ pound) cleaned, cooked
Spaghetti	7 ounces	About 4 cups cooked
Strawberries	1 quart	4 cups sliced
Sugar, brown	1 pound	2⅓ cups firmly packed
powdered	1 pound	3½ cups unsifted
granulated	1 pound	2 cups

EQUIVALENT MEASUREMENTS

3 teaspoons	1 tablespoon		2 cups	1 pint (16 fluid ounces)
4 tablespoons.............	¼ cup		4 cups	1 quart
5⅓ tablespoons............	⅓ cup		4 quarts	1 gallon
8 tablespoons.............	½ cup		⅛ cup	2 tablespoons
16 tablespoons............	1 cup		⅓ cup.....................	5 tablespoons plus 1 teaspoon
2 tablespoons (liquid)...	1 ounce		⅔ cup.....................	10 tablespoons plus 2 teaspoons
1 cup......................	8 fluid ounces		¾ cup.....................	12 tablespoons

HANDY SUBSTITUTIONS

Ingredient Called For	Substitution
1 cup self-rising flour	1 cup all-purpose flour plus 1 teaspoon baking powder and ½ teaspoon salt
1 cup cake flour	1 cup sifted all-purpose flour minus 2 tablespoons
1 cup all-purpose flour	1 cup cake flour plus 2 tablespoons
1 teaspoon baking powder	½ teaspoon cream of tartar plus ¼ teaspoon soda
1 tablespoon cornstarch or arrowroot	2 tablespoons all-purpose flour
1 tablespoon tapioca	1½ tablespoons all-purpose flour
2 large eggs	3 small eggs
1 egg	2 egg yolks (for custard)
1 egg	2 egg yolks plus 1 tablespoon water (for cookies)
1 (8-ounce) carton commercial sour cream	1 tablespoon lemon juice plus evaporated milk to equal 1 cup; or 3 tablespoons butter plus ⅞ cup sour milk
1 cup yogurt	1 cup buttermilk or sour milk
1 cup sour milk or buttermilk	1 tablespoon vinegar or lemon juice plus sweet milk to equal 1 cup
1 cup fresh milk	½ cup evaporated milk plus ½ cup water
1 cup fresh milk	3 to 5 tablespoons nonfat dry milk solids in 1 cup water
1 cup honey	1¼ cups sugar plus ¼ cup water
1 (1-ounce) square unsweetened chocolate	3 tablespoons cocoa plus 1 tablespoon butter or margarine
1 tablespoon fresh herbs	1 teaspoon dried herbs or ¼ teaspoon powdered herbs
¼ cup chopped fresh parsley	1 tablespoon dried parsley flakes
1 teaspoon dry mustard	1 tablespoon prepared mustard
1 pound fresh mushrooms	6 ounces canned mushrooms

Recipe Title Index

An alphabetical listing of every recipe by exact title
All microwave recipe page numbers are preceded by an "M"

Pepper Steak Salad Cups, 206
Peppy Skillet Potatoes, 110
Pesto Broiled Flounder, 150
Pesto Salad Dressing, 150
Pesto-Stuffed Mushrooms, 150
Pico de Gallo, 19
Pimiento and Three Cheeses, 296
Pimiento Broccoli, 268
Pimiento-Cheese Bread, 166
Pimiento Cheese Spread, 127
Piña Colada Chicken, 21
Pineapple-Baked Ham, 48
Pineapple-Cheese Spread, 126
Pineapple-Chicken Kabobs, M328
Pineapple Dessert Chimichangas, 4
Pineapple-Ginger Dip, 104
Pineapple-Honey Pears, 94
Pineapple Jam, 116
Pineapple-Orange Sauce Flambé, 116
Pineapple Pickles, 116
Pineapple Spritz, 94
Pineapple Topping, 239
Pink Divinity, 49
Pinto Salad, 169
Piquant Chicken, 76
Pistachio-Pasta Salad, 141
Pistachio-Stuffed Mushrooms, 141
Pizza Crust, 77
Pizza Party Snacks, 262
Pizza Quiche, 53
Plantation Coffee Pralines, 241
Plum Pudding-Gelatin Mold, 300
Poppy Seed Dressing, 123, 305
Pork Chops Fiesta, 118
Pork Sloppy Joes, 294
Pork Tenderloin Picatta, 76
Pork Tenderloin Towers, 75
Pork Tenderloin with Blue Cheese, 76
Port Wine-Cherry Salad, 11
Potato Baskets, 193
Potato Chip Cookies, 93
Potatoes in Cream-Wine Sauce, 18
Potato Loaves, 162
Potato-Snow Pea Stir-Fry, 173
Potato-Tomato Bake, 17
Potato-Topped Turkey Pie, 265
Pot-of-Gold Soup, 259
Poulet Luzianne, 197
Powdered Sugar-Brandy Glaze, 291
Pralines, M288
Pretzel Dressing, 280
Princess Chicken, 122
Processor Devonshire Sauce, 337
Processor Potato Casserole, 159
Prune Bavarian, 223
Pull-Apart Maple Wheat Bread, 166
Pumpkin Chiffon, 283
Pumpkin Kahlúa Cake, 292
Pumpkin-Nut Waffles, 96
Pumpkin-Orange Delight, 321
Pumpkin-Tomato Soup, 291

Quail with Currant Jelly Sauce, 94
Quail with Orange Sauce in Potato
  Baskets, 193
Quick-and-Easy Broccoli, 55
Quick-and-Easy Broiled Zucchini, 169
Quick-and-Easy Chili con Carne, 2
Quick Beef Stew, 302
Quick Bran Muffins, 85
Quick Bread Mix, 8
Quick Chicken Soup, M72
Quick Chocolate Mint Sauce, M58

Quick Curried Rice, 81
Quick Mix Waffles, 9
Quick Pan Pizza, 160
Quick Peanut Butter Cookies, 109
Quick Pear Sundaes, 71
Quick Shrimp Gumbo, 71

Raspberry Kir, 183
Raspberry Salad, 286
Raspberry Soufflé, 188
Ratatouille-Bran Stuffed Eggplant, 44
Ratatouille Supreme, 172
Rémoulade Dressing, 123
Rhubarb Congealed Salad, 140
Rhubarb-Peach Pie, 140
Rhubarb-Strawberry Bavarian, 140
Rice-and-Vegetable Salad, 42
Rice au Gratin Supreme, 78
Rice Chantilly, 82
Rice Pilaf, 82
Rich Chocolate-Nut Cake, 8
Rich Pumpkin Pie, 292
Roast Cornish Hens, 89
Roast Ducklings with Cherry Sauce, 312
Roasted Rosemary Lamb, 89
Roast Turkey, 47
Roast Turkey Breast with Special
  Gravy, 282
Rocky Road Brownies, 320
Rolled Tortilla Dippers, 4
Rosy Pickled Eggs, 68
Royal Cherry Sauce, 83
Rum-Butter Sauce, 301
Rum Trifle, 322
Russian-Style Salad Dressing, 305

Saffron Rice Mold, 221
Salad Dressing for Fruit, 40
Salad Niçoise, 35
Salmon Ball, 262
Salmon Loaf with Cucumber-Dill Sauce, 5
Salmon-Stuffed Avocados, 74
Salt-Free Raisin Batter Bread, 33
Sangría, 214
Sangría Salad, 331
Saucy Ham Loaf, M328
Saucy Pork Chop, M140
Sauerkraut Meatballs, 257
Sausage-Bean Supper, 52
Sausage-Beef Chili, 232
Sausage-Cheese Muffins, 213
Sausage Dressing, 280
Sausage-Egg Casserole, M12
Sausage Grits, 92
Sausage-Mushroom Breakfast Casserole, 95
Sausage-Potato Casserole, 217
Sautéed Oysters, 132
Savory Barbecue Sauce, 153
Scallop Appetizer, 155
Scalloped Corn, 111
Scalloped Kale, 224
Scalloped Oysters, 132
Scrambled Egg Casserole, 241
Scrambled Egg Tostadas, 95
Seafood Bisque, 66
Seafood Delight, 208
Seafood Sauce, 304
Seafood Spread, M58
Seafood with Dill Mayonnaise, 234
Seashell Salad, 209
Seaside Salad, 183
Seasoned Popovers, 86
Seasoned Stuffed Burgers, 136

Sesame Brussels Sprouts, 55
Sesame-Cheese Muffins, 16
Sesame Chicken, 122
Sesame-Citrus Green Salad, 33
Sherried Ambrosia, 317
Sherry-Orange Nuts, M289
Shrimp Creole, 256
Shrimp Creole in a Rice Ring, 222
Shrimp Dip, 84
Shrimp Fondue, 244
Shrimp-in-a-Pickle, 326
Shrimp Manale, 268
Shrimp Salad, 186
Shrimp Salad in Pastry, 105
Shrimp Salad on the Half Shell, 73
Shrimp-Stuffed Peppers, 131, 197
Shrimp Toast, 91
Shrimp-Walnut Salad, 182
Shrimp with Asparagus en Papillote, 145
Simple Cucumber Cooler, 147
Skewered Swordfish, 256
Skillet Chicken Dinner, 249
Skillet Corn Medley, 192
Slender French Toast, 103
Sliced Fig Snacks, 206
Smithfield Ham with Brown Sugar
  Glaze, 253
Smoked Cornish Hens, 142, 154
Smoked Ham, 92
Smoked Sausage, 154
Snap Beans, 218
Soft-as-a-Cloud Sour Cream Biscuits, 138
Sour Cream Cheesecake, 320
Sour Cream Dip, 278
Sour Cream Dressing, 331
Sour Cream Pie, 260
Sour Cream Topping, 120
Southern Oven-Fried Chicken, 37
Southern Potato Rolls, 299
Southern Praline Ice Cream Sauce, M227
South-of-the-Border Black-Eyed Peas, 7
South-of-the-Border Stuffed Potatoes, 54
Southwest Soup, 255
Soy-Chicken Kabobs, 156
Soy Dressing, 191
Soy Fish Steaks, M112
Spaghetti with Herbal Dressing, 158
Spanakópita, 58
Spanish Cheese Limas, 225
Spanish Sprout Salad, 22
Spanish-Style Fillets, M112
Sparkling Citrus Mold, 331
Sparkling Cranberry Float, 195
Special Hard Sauce, 318
Special White Bread, 57
Spiced Rum Punch, 179
Spiced Spritzers, 229
Spiced Tea Mix, 32
Spiced Zucchini Bread, 162
Spicy Apple Ice Cream Sundaes, M195
Spicy Apple-Oat Muffins, 45
Spicy Baked Peaches, 39
Spicy Beef Stew, 228
Spicy Chili Salad, 71
Spicy French Dressing, 123
Spicy Plum Sauce, 11
Spicy Pumpkin Bisque, 67
Spicy Tomato Sipper, 229
Spiked Tea Punch, 101
Spinach-and-Ham Rollups, 84
Spinach-and-Orange Salad, 15
Spinach Dip, 159
Spinach-Mustard Twist, 209

Month-by-Month Index

An alphabetical listing within the month of every food article and accompanying recipes
All microwave recipe page numbers are preceded by an "M"

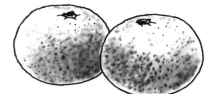

General Recipe Index

A listing of every recipe by food category and/or major ingredient
All microwave recipe page numbers are preceded by an "M"

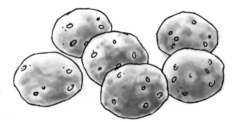

Garlic-Buttered Shrimp, M226
Gumbo, Quick Shrimp, 71
Manale, Shrimp, 268
Peppers, Shrimp-Stuffed, 131, 197
Pickle, Shrimp-in-a-, 326
Salad, Crabmeat-Shrimp Pasta, 208
Salad, Fruited Shrimp, 156
Salad in Pastry, Shrimp, 105
Salad on the Half Shell, Shrimp, 73
Salad, Shrimp, 186
Salad, Shrimp-Walnut, 182
Sauce, Flounder with
    Hollandaise-Shrimp, 234
Spread, Chunky Shrimp, 18
Szechuan Shrimp, 173
Toast, Shrimp, 91
Soufflés
Grasshopper Soufflé, 188
Orange Soufflé, Chilled, 189
Potato Soufflé, Sweet, 121
Raspberry Soufflé, 188
Spinach Soufflé, 108
Soups. *See also* Chili, Chowders, Gumbos,
    Stews.
Bean-and-Barley Soup, Hearty, 304
Bean Pot, White, 194
Bean Soup, Leafy, 223
Bisque, Clam, 228
Bisque, Seafood, 66
Bisque, Spicy Pumpkin, 67
Bisque, Spinach-Potato, 66
Bisque, Tomato-Shrimp, 66
Broccoli Soup, 161, M194
Broccoli Soup, Cheesy-, 258
Broccoli Soup, Cream of, 259
Broccoli-Swiss Soup, 6
Carrot-Leek Soup, 34
Chicken Enchilada Soup, 22
Chicken Soup, Curried, 34
Chicken Soup, Quick, M72
Cucumber Soup, Cold Minted, 34
Egg Drop Soup, 16
Lentil Soup, 304
Minestrone Soup, 144
Mushroom Soup, M73
Onion Soup, French, M212
Pea Soup, Country-Style, 267
Pea Soup, Fresh, 181
Potato Soup, Golden Cream of, 302
Potato Soup, Three-, 16
Pot-of-Gold Soup, 259
Pumpkin-Tomato Soup, 291
Southwest Soup, 255
Strawberry-Banana Soup, 181
Tomato Juice Soup, Hot, 302
Tomato Soup, Appetizer, 258
Tomato Soup, Creamy, 258
Tomato Soup with Parmesan Cheese,
    Cream of, 161
Tomato-Vegetable Soup, 9
Turkey Carcass Soup, 284
Turkey Soup, Curried, 332
Vegetable Soup, 187
Vegetable Soup, Garden, 160
Vegetable Soup, Leek-, 304
Vegetable Soup, Old-Fashioned, 304
Vichyssoise, 181
Watercress-and-Leek Soup, 161
Yogurt Fruit Soup, 176
Zucchini Soup, 181
Spaghetti
Bacon Spaghetti, 213
Herbal Dressing, Spaghetti with, 158

Tetrazzini, Herbed Turkey, 47
Vegetables with Spaghetti, Fresh, 257
Spinach
Bisque, Spinach-Potato, 66
Casserole, Creamy Spinach, 111
Chicken Rolls, Spinach-Stuffed, 248
Creamed Spinach, 110
Dip, Spinach, 159
Florentine, Baked Eggs, M12
Florentine, Fish, 35
Mushrooms, Spinach-Stuffed, 81
Quiche, Greek Spinach, 10
Quiches, Individual Spinach, 38
Rollups, Spinach-and-Ham, 84
Salads
    Combination Spinach Salad, 22
    Fresh Spinach Salad, 130
    Orange Salad, Spinach-and-, 15
    Spinach Salad, 302
    Twist, Spinach-Mustard, 209
Sauce, Herbed Green, 244
Soufflé, Spinach, 108
Spanakópita, 58
Tomatoes, Spinach-Stuffed Baked, 14
Spreads. *See also* Appetizers/Spreads.
Apricot Brie Spread, 275
Cheese Spread, 135
Cheese Spread, Chile-, 297
Cheese Spread, Pimiento, 127
Eggplant Spread, 278
Egg Salad Spread, 127
Garden Spread, 135
Ham Spread, 126
Mustard Spread, 105
Pineapple-Cheese Spread, 126
Raisin Spread, Peachy-, 326
Seafood Spread, M58
Sweet 'n' Sour Spread, 184
Sprouts
Beans with Sprouts, Sweet-and-Sour, 32
Salad, Spanish Sprout, 22
Squash. *See also* Zucchini.
Acorn
    Custard-Filled Acorn Squash, 334
Butternut
    Bake, Butternut-Orange, 295
Pie, Mock Coconut, 200
Stir-Fry, Two-Squash, 174
Tomato Squash, 111
Yellow
    Cake, Squash, 200
    Dressing, Squash, 280
    Fried Yellow Squash, 211
    Marinated Cucumbers and
        Squash, 146
    Stuffed Yellow Squash, Italian, 111
Stews. *See also* Chili, Gumbos, Soups.
Bean Pot, White, 194
Beef Stew, 51
Beef Stew, Quick, 302
Beef Stew, Spicy, 228
Mexican Stew Olé, 296
Oyster Stew, Golden, 132
Venison Stew, 294
Strawberries
Bavarian, Rhubarb-Strawberry, 140
Cake, Strawberry Cream, 61
Cake, Strawberry Meringue, 240
Cheesecake, Almost Strawberry, 32
Dessert, Strawberry-Lemon, 162
Ice, Strawberry-Orange, 196
Melon, Berry-Filled, 93
Parfait, Surprise Strawberry, 151

Pie, Strawberry-Yogurt, 124
Pizza, Kiwi-Berry, 198
Punch, Creamy Strawberry, 195
Ring, Strawberry-Cheese, 14
Sauce, Melon Wedges with Berry, 178
Shortcake Squares, Strawberry, 124
Smoothie, Strawberry, 183
Soup, Strawberry-Banana, 181
Stuffed Strawberries with Walnuts, 124
Topping, Strawberry, 32
Stroganoff
Beef Stroganoff, Light, 36
Stuffings and Dressings
Cornbread Dressing, 286
Cornbread Dressing, Kentucky, 281
Pretzel Dressing, 280
Sausage Dressing, 280
Squash Dressing, 280
Zucchini Dressing, 282

Sweet-and-Sour
Beans with Sprouts, Sweet-and-Sour, 32
Cabbage, Sweet-and-Sour, 295
Chicken, Sweet-and-Sour, 217, 240
Marinade, Sweet-and-Sour, 113
Meatballs, Sweet-and-Sour, 240
Pork, Sweet-and-Sour, 241
Salad, Sweet-and-Sour Bean, 147
Sauce, Sweet-and-Sour, 240
Spread, Sweet 'n' Sour, 184
Syrups
Anise Sugar Syrup, 248
Cherry-Lemonade Syrup, 214
Citrus Syrup, Sweet, 270
Fruit Syrup, 176

Tacos
al Carbón, Tacos, 19
Tea
Almond-Lemonade Tea, 229
Almond Tea, 329
Minted Tea, 101
Mix, Spiced Tea, 32
Punch, Spiked Tea, 101
Tofu
Dip, Tofu, 109
Sandwiches, Open-Face Tofu-Veggie, 5
Tomatoes
Aspic, Tomato-Artichoke, 92
Baked Tomatoes, Spinach-Stuffed, 14
Bake, Potato-Tomato, 17
Biscuits, Tomato, 72
Bisque, Tomato-Shrimp, 66
Butter, Tomato, 128
Cabbage and Tomatoes, Tasty, 72
Cacciatore, Chicken, 42
Cheese Herbed-Topped Tomatoes, 108
Cheesy Puff-Top Tomatoes, 187
Cherry Tomatoes, Green Beans with, 177

Tomatoes *(continued)*

Fried Tomatoes with Gravy, 211
Mustard Tomatoes, Zippy, M226
Okra, Tomatoes and, 170
Pasta Toss, Tomato-Olive, 209
Pesto, Tomatoes, 150
Primavera, Tomato-Pasta, 209
Ratatouille-Bran Stuffed Eggplant, 44
Salad in Tomatoes, Cottage Cheese, 208
Salad, Tomato-Avocado, 74
Salad, Tomato-Cucumber, 218
Salsa, Chunky, 130
Sauce, Linguine with Tomato-Cream, 158
Skillet, Cabbage-and-Tomato, 110
Soup, Appetizer Tomato, 258
Soup, Creamy Tomato, 258
Soup, Hot Tomato Juice, 302
Soup, Pumpkin-Tomato, 291
Soup, Tomato-Vegetable, 9
Soup with Parmesan Cheese, Cream of
Tomato, 161
Spicy Tomato Sipper, 229
Squash, Tomato, 111
Stuffed Tomatoes, Mushroom-, 218

Tortillas. *See also* Burritos, Enchiladas,
Tacos.

Appetizers, Tex-Mex Tortilla, 297
Buñuelos, King-Size, 5
Chicken-Tortilla Stack, Cheesy, 3
Chimichangas, 114
Chimichangas, Pineapple Dessert, 4
Dippers, Rolled Tortilla, 4
Fajitas, Favorite, 114
Salad in a Shell, Mexican, 4
Sandwich, Tex-Mex Ham-and-Cheese, 4

Tuna

Croquettes with Parsley Sauce,
Tuna, 108
Salad, Curried Tuna, 208
Salad, Swiss Tuna, 186
Salad, Tuna-and-Cannellini Bean, 143
Sandwiches, Hot Tuna, M194

Turkey

Breast, Herb Butter-Basted Turkey, 285
Casserole, Turkey-and-Broccoli, 332
Casserole, Turkey-Asparagus, 284
Casserole, Turkey-Swiss, 283
Lasagna, Lean, 37
Loaf, Cranberry-Glazed Turkey, 171
Loaf, Ground Turkey, 171
Patties, Stuffed Ground Turkey, 171
Pie, Crumb-Crust Curried Turkey, 265
Pie, Potato-Topped Turkey, 265
Pie, Turkey Pot, 265
Pilaf, Turkey-Rice, 284
Roast Turkey, 47
Roast Turkey Breast with Special
Gravy, 282
Rollups, Turkey, 198
Salad, Hot Turkey, 10, 297
Salad, Layered Turkey, 332
Salad, Meal-in-One, 43
Salad, Turkey-Carrot, 283
Salad with Sautéed Walnuts, Turkey, 117
Skillet, Oriental Turkey-Orange, 284
Soup, Curried Turkey, 332
Soup, Turkey Carcass, 284
Tetrazzini, Herbed Turkey, 47

Turnips

Cooked Turnips, Creamy, 224
Julienne, Turnips and Carrots, 295

Vanilla

Ice Cream, Vanilla, 129

Veal

Amelio, Veal, 142
Herbed Veal with Wine, 193
Lemon Veal Piccata, 118
New Orleans Veal with Crabmeat, 94
Swirls, Veal-and-Smithfield Ham, 253
Wine Sauce, Veal and Carrots in, M139

Vegetables. *See also* specific types.

Casserole, Mixed Vegetable, 327
Chicken and Vegetables, Almond, 21
Combo, Garden, 172
Crêpes, Vegetable-Filled Bran, 44
Egg Rolls, Vegetarian, 148
en Papillote, Chicken and
Vegetables, 145
Fish Rolls, Vegetable-Filled, M251
Julienne Vegetables with Walnuts, M251
Marinated Vegetables, 286
Medley, Spring Vegetable, 115
Medley, Steamed Vegetable, 50
Medley, Vegetable, 327
Pasta Primavera, Almost, 38
Pâté, Vegetable-Chicken, 66
Ratatouille-Bran Stuffed Eggplant, 44
Ratatouille Supreme, 172
Salads
Congealed Salad,
Cheesy-Vegetable, 199
Greek Salad, Garden, 173
Macaroni-Vegetable Salad, 209
Marinated Vegetable Salad,
Fresh, 173
Mixed Vegetable Salad, 136
Rice-and-Vegetable Salad, 42
Vinaigrette Salad,
Vegetable-Chicken, 135
Walnuts, Vegetable Salad with, 118
Winter Vegetable Salad, 42
Sandwiches, Open-Face Tofu-Veggie, 5
Sauce, Vegetable Butter, 174
Skillet, Vegetable-Beef, 172
Soups
Garden Vegetable Soup, 160
Leek-Vegetable Soup, 304
Old-Fashioned Vegetable Soup, 304
Tomato-Vegetable Soup, 9
Vegetable Soup, 187
Spaghetti, Fresh Vegetables with, 257
Spread, Garden, 135
Stir-Fry, Almond-Vegetable, 222
Stir-Fry Chicken and Vegetables, 249
Stir-Fry Chicken-and-Vegetables, 68
Stir-Fry Sausage and Vegetables, 213
Stir-Fry, Three-Vegetable, 174
Succotash, Summer, 170
Supper, Vegetarian, 222
Topper, Vegetable-Cheese Potato, 6
Turnovers, Vegetable, 24

Venison

Chili, Venison, 3
Stew, Venison, 294

Waffles

Banana-Ginger Waffles, 96
French Waffles, 138
Pumpkin-Nut Waffles, 96
Quick Mix Waffles, 9

Walnuts

Brie, Walnut-Fried, 244
Frosting, Nutty Coconut, 8
Mousse, Coffee-Nut, 319
Muffins, Carrot-Date-Nut, 262
Muffins, Nutty Pumpkin, 291
Salad, Shrimp-Walnut, 182
Salad with Walnuts, Vegetable, 118
Sautéed Walnuts,
Turkey Salad with, 117
Sherry-Orange Nuts, M289
Strawberries with Walnuts, Stuffed, 124
Sweet Potatoes with Sherry and
Walnuts, 286
Topping, Nutty, 16
Vegetables with Walnuts, Julienne, M251

Watermelon. *See* Melons.

Wheat Germ

Biscuits, Wheat Germ, 261
Pancakes, Wheat Germ, 242

Wild Rice. *See* Rice/Wild Rice.

Wok Cooking

Beef Stew, 51
Chicken and Vegetables, Almond, 21
Chicken-and-Vegetables, Stir-Fry, 68
Chicken, Braised Bourbon, 51
Chicken, Lemon, 173
Chicken, Princess, 122
Chicken, Sweet-and-Sour, 240
Chicken with Pineapple, Oriental, 42
Egg Rolls, 81
Egg Rolls, Vegetarian, 148
Ham Stir-Fry, Easy, 332
Meatballs, Sweet-and-Sour, 240
Pear Fritters, Ol' Timey, 51
Pork Tenderloin, Curried, 76
Potato Pudding, Sweet, 52
Potato-Snow Pea Stir-Fry, 173
Shrimp, Szechuan, 173
Squash Stir-Fry, Two-, 174
Vegetable Stir-Fry, Three-, 174

Yogurt

Dressing, Sweet-Hot Yogurt, 40
Pie, Strawberry-Yogurt, 124
Soup, Yogurt Fruit, 176

Zucchini

Bake, Zucchini-Beef, 146
Bread, Spiced Zucchini, 162
Bread, Zucchini, 93
Broiled Zucchini, Quick-and-Easy, 169
Combo, Zucchini-Corn, 218
Corn, Zucchini and, 177
Dressing, Zucchini, 282
Fried Zucchini, Oven-, 211
Fried Zucchini with Cocktail Sauce,
French, 146
Frittata, Zucchini, 103
Muffins, Zucchini, 146
Provençal, Zucchini, 146
Soup, Zucchini, 181
Stuffed Zucchini, 54, 187
Stuffed Zucchini, Beef-, M139

Favorite Recipes

Record your favorite recipes below for quick and handy reference

Recipe	Source/Page	Remarks